THREE ROADS TO
Magdalena

Published in cooperation with the
William P. Clements Center for Southwest Studies,
Southern Methodist University

THREE ROADS TO
Magdalena

Coming of Age in a
Southwest Borderland,
1890–1990

DAVID WALLACE ADAMS

UNIVERSITY PRESS OF KANSAS

© 2016 by the University Press of Kansas
All rights reserved

Published by the University Press of Kansas (Lawrence, Kansas 66045), which was organized by the Kansas Board of Regents and is operated and funded by Emporia State University, Fort Hays State University, Kansas State University, Pittsburg State University, the University of Kansas, and Wichita State University

Library of Congress Cataloging-in-Publication Data
Names: Adams, David Wallace.
Title: Three roads to Magdalena : coming of age in a Southwest borderland, 1890–1990 / David Wallace Adams.
Description: Lawrence, Kansas : University Press of Kansas, 2016. | Includes bibliographical references and index.
Identifiers: LCCN 2016000655| ISBN 9780700622542 (hardback) | ISBN 9780700622559 (ebook)
Subjects: LCSH: Magdalena (NM)—Ethnic relations—History. | Cultural pluralism—New Mexico—Magdalena—History. | Hispanic Americans—New Mexico—Magdalena—Social life and customs. | Whites—New Mexico—Magdalena—Social life and customs. | Navajo Indians—New Mexico—Magdalena—Social life and customs. | School children—New Mexico—Magdalena—History. | Coming of age—New Mexico—Magdalena—History. | Intercultural communication—New Mexico—Magdalena—History. | Magdalena (N.M.)—Biography. | Interviews—New Mexico—Magdalena. | BISAC: HISTORY / United States / State & Local / Southwest (AZ, NM, OK, TX). | SOCIAL SCIENCE / Children's Studies. | SOCIAL SCIENCE / Ethnic Studies / Hispanic American Studies.
Classification: LCC F804.M34 A33 2016 | DDC 305.8009789/62—dc23
LC record available at http://lccn.loc.gov/2016000655.

British Library Cataloguing-in-Publication Data is available.

Printed in the United States of America

10 9 8 7 6 5 4 3 2 1

The paper used in this publication is recycled and contains 30 percent postconsumer waste. It is acid free and meets the minimum requirements of the American National Standard for Permanence of Paper for Printed Library Materials Z39.48-1992.

For Vicki and our family—
Jason, Nathaniel, Amanda, Ryan, and Sam

CONTENTS

Preface ix

Introduction 1

PART ONE   **Cultures and Their Scripts**

1. Family and Religion 21
2. Work and Play 63
3. Pleasures and Transitions 107

PART TWO   **Boundaries and Border Crossings**

4. Points of Contact 145
5. Anglos and Hispanics at School 176
6. The Alamo Navajos at School 222

PART THREE   **Pasts and Promises**

7. Together and Apart 265
8. Legacies and Departures 299

Afterword 338

Acknowledgments 341

List of Abbreviations 345

Notes 347

Selected Bibliography 401

Index 415

PREFACE

Even when it stands vacant the past is never empty.
—Ivan Doig

The first time I saw Magdalena, New Mexico, was in the fall of 1981. I was on sabbatical from my university and had taken a positon as curriculum director of a new school on the Alamo Navajo Indian reservation, located some 30 miles northwest of the town of Magdalena. My reason for taking this position was simple enough: I was in the midst of writing a book on the late-nineteenth-century federal Indian boarding school system and wanted to see Native American education up close in the new era of self-determination.

The Alamo school was two years into its existence, and I thought I might be able to assist the community in its struggle to move forward. As a native Californian I had driven across the Southwest countless times, but west-central New Mexico was new to me. Thus in 1981 I found myself driving 75 miles south out of Albuquerque along the Rio Grande Valley to Socorro, where I turned west on Highway 60 for the 30-mile climb into the high desert country of Magdalena. In its heyday, I was soon to learn, Magdalena was a genuine western boomtown, built on the twin economies of mining and livestock. In 1981, the boom years were long over, but unlike the nearby mining settlement of Kelly, now a ghost town, Magdalena had somehow managed to hold on.

After settling my family, including the dog, in town and acquainting myself with my responsibilities at Alamo, I began asking locals where I might read about the history of the area. Time and again I was referred to *No Life for a Lady* by Agnes Morley Cleaveland, a classic memoir by a spirited Anglo woman who grew up on the New Mexico frontier. A wonderful book, I concluded, but hardly one that did justice to the larger story of how the three groups in the region—Navajo, Hispanic, and Anglo—had negotiated the complex ethnocultural borderland they inhabited. I decided to write this history, focusing on what it had been like for locals to grow up in the region. I purchased a tape recorder and began interviewing the oldest people who would talk to me, a few born in the 1890s. By year's end I had amassed a large collection of oral histories, and after two subsequent sabbaticals, the number of interviewees grew even larger. During this stretch of years, I was working on other projects, including the boarding school book, so I simply shelved the untranscribed recordings, knowing I would return to the Magdalena project at a later date. When I did, I found I had more than 3,000 pages of material.

But beyond the vague theme of coming of age, what was this book to be really about? Eventually, I settled on four questions. First, what has it meant culturally to grow up Navajo, Hispanic, Anglo, and combinations thereof in a region characterized by ongoing and shifting patterns of intergroup contact? Second, how did power relations among the three groups affect the coming-of-age experience? Third, in what ways has the relative influence of identity-shaping institutions and domains of experience shifted over time? Finally, what role did children play in a region marked by both boundary maintenance and border crossings? This book, then, is written at the intersection of borderland and childhood history.

As Jeremy Adelman and Stephen Aron have pointed out, the word "frontier" has suffered much of late in the hands of scholars writing histories of the West. Closely identified with Frederick Jackson Turner, the term has come to denote a "triumphalist and Anglocentric narrative of continental conquest."[1] Because of these associations, historians in search of a more inclusive story have either broadened the term's meaning or, more generally, migrated to borderland history as a more fitting lens for explaining what happens when nations or peoples meet in contested landscapes and negotiate each other's "otherness." As Brian DeLay observes, borderland history is necessarily about "multi-vocality."[2] The Southwest is an ideal region for such studies.

As noted above, my study fuses childhood (broadly defined) with borderland history. Although the subject of "growing up" is a prominent theme in both fiction and autobiography, it has received little systematic attention from historians. When they have done so the focus has mostly been on the subject of schooling, and then the narratives have been largely divorced from the larger contextual canvas of children's lives. An important exception is Steven Mintz's masterful *Huck's Raft: A History of American Childhood*.[3] As a regional study, Elliot West's *Growing Up with the Country: Childhood on the Far Western Frontier* is another standout example and has contributed immensely to the shape of this study.[4] I offer my own study as a contribution in the following respects: it is focused on a particular area of the West, it is multicultural in focus, and it is largely based on oral history.

Few subjects in historiography have of late provoked more discussion and debate than the relationship of memory to history. Kerwin Lee Klein writes:

> We sometimes use *memory* as a synonym for *history* to soften our prose, to humanize it, and make it more accessible. *Memory* simply sounds less distant, and perhaps for that reason, it often serves to help draw readers into a sense of the relevance of history for their own lives. Memory appeals to us partly because it projects an immediacy we feel has been lost from history.... In contrast with history, memory fairly vibrates with the fullness of Being.[5]

But as Klein and others point out, memory cannot be synonymous with history, and indeed, often the two are at odds. Memory is unstable, selective, contingent, self-serving, and even self-deceiving. Even more problematic for the historian, memory is frequently beyond interrogation. As Richard White writes, "We turn our lives into stories, and, in doing so, we can stop them where we choose. Our stories do in a small way what memoirs and autobiographies do on a grander scale: they allow a self-fashioning that gives remembered lives a coherence that the day-to-day lives of actual experience lack. History, of course, also imposes coherence, but the historian works with less malleable stuff than memory."[6]

Still, few would deny that memory offers an invaluable window into the past, especially for cultural historians writing the histories of groups for whom traditional written sources are all too rare. But how to protect against the triumph of memory (or inaccurate memory) over history? In this study I have relied upon several strategies. First, multiple interviews were conducted in each group, male and female, allowing for a considerable range of intragroup accounts on the same or related subjects. This cross-checking was not fool-proof for the simple reason that inaccurate memory can be collective as well as individual, and never more so than in conflict-ridden landscapes. A second evidentiary screen in this undertaking is its multicultural focus, that is to say, its multivocality across groups—in this case three groups. (I remember all too well the look of concern on an interviewee's face when he realized I was writing a history not just of *his* group but *their* groups as well.) Borderland history allows for—indeed calls out for—conflicting group perspectives on encounters with the "other." (In that regard, it might be argued that borderland history is ethnohistory writ large.) Third, I have scrutinized the individual interviews for internal consistency. Again, the consistency test is not a guarantee against conscious or unconscious recalibrations of memory, but it still offers another means of ferreting out imagined or exaggerated moments in a personal narrative. Finally, as the endnotes will show, the personal narratives I collected have been supplemented by an extensive investigation of available primary and secondary sources relevant to the project. Census data, newspapers, marriage records, state and federal documents, school records, and memoirs have all been invaluable.

Along the way in this venture I have encountered a number of challenges. The first was convincing individuals that their stories, that is to say their lives, were of historic importance. Time and again, I heard them protest, "Why do you want to talk to me? I'm a nobody." After I explained what I was up to, they almost always relented. Second, I realized early on that many of those I interviewed did not want to be identified by name. The reason was clear enough. Like any borderland region, west-central New Mexico has had its share of intergroup conflict, and many were hesitant to see their names attached to a particular event on which differing points of view or lingering resentments still exist. In response to this reluctance I struck the following bargain: I would not connect the speaker's name to any given story but acknowledge his or her contribution by listing their names in a separate section of the book. Thus, unless permission was granted, I have employed any number of pseudonyms throughout the text. In the case of the Alamo Navajos I have scrambled existing surnames (because the distinctiveness of the Alamo surnames is a significant part of this group's history) and have fashioned pseudo–personal names, again, unless permission was acquired. Third, I soon learned that as a non-Navajo-speaking Anglo male, I needed help interviewing older Navajos. For female Navajos the issue was particularly important—sharing personal stories across gender lines with a *biligáana* was, culturally speaking, a nonstarter. Thankfully, local interviewers and transcribers stepped forward to aid me in this area.

The preeminent challenge, however, was actually constructing the narrative. Two aspects of this endeavor were particularly difficult. The first was architectural. Historians often struggle with the process of weaving myriad facts, events, and personal accounts into a coherent narrative. Doing borderland history presents its own sort of problems but especially when three groups, not two, are central to the story. The challenge was when to keep the three groups apart and when to pull them together, and in the process, never lose sight of the larger drama unfolding in this regional "meeting ground." As Patricia Nelson Limerick writes, in the history of the West,

> everyone became an actor in everyone else's play; understanding any part of the play now requires us to take account of the whole. It is perfectly possible to watch a play and keep track of, even identify with, several characters at once, even when those characters are in direct conflict with each other and within themselves. The ethnic diversity of Western history asks only that: pay attention to the parts, and pay attention to the whole.[7]

Whether the narrative I have constructed measures up to this standard, only the reader can judge. The second issue involves voice. Because this history ends in 1990, I was an observer of some of the events I describe in the last chapter. The reader should be forewarned of a shift from past to present tense and a more subjective tone at this point in the narrative.

A few words on terminology and editing are also in order. Anyone writing New Mexico history is faced with the problem of choosing between referents for a group variously identified as Hispanics, Hispanos, and Spanish Americans. After going back and forth on the issue, I have finally landed on Hispanics as a catchall designation. (As the reader will discover, how this group has come to name itself is a complicated story of its own.) On the matter of editing, the reader will note that many of the quotations from "informants" contain all manner of grammatical errors, and in some cases, missing words as well. I have done very little editing of these "raw" passages in the interest of capturing the speakers' voices. That is to say, I have rarely employed the bracketed corrections that often speckle narratives of this sort. The only exception to the general rule of not tinkering with quoted matter is when I have patched together, without ellipses, different sections from the same interview on a subject addressed multiple times.

In the midst of one of my several interviews with Candelaria García, she said to me, "Someday you will get all the stories." Of course, I did not get all of them, but I got a lot of them. Now it is time to share them.

Welcome to west-central New Mexico.

THREE ROADS TO
Magdalena

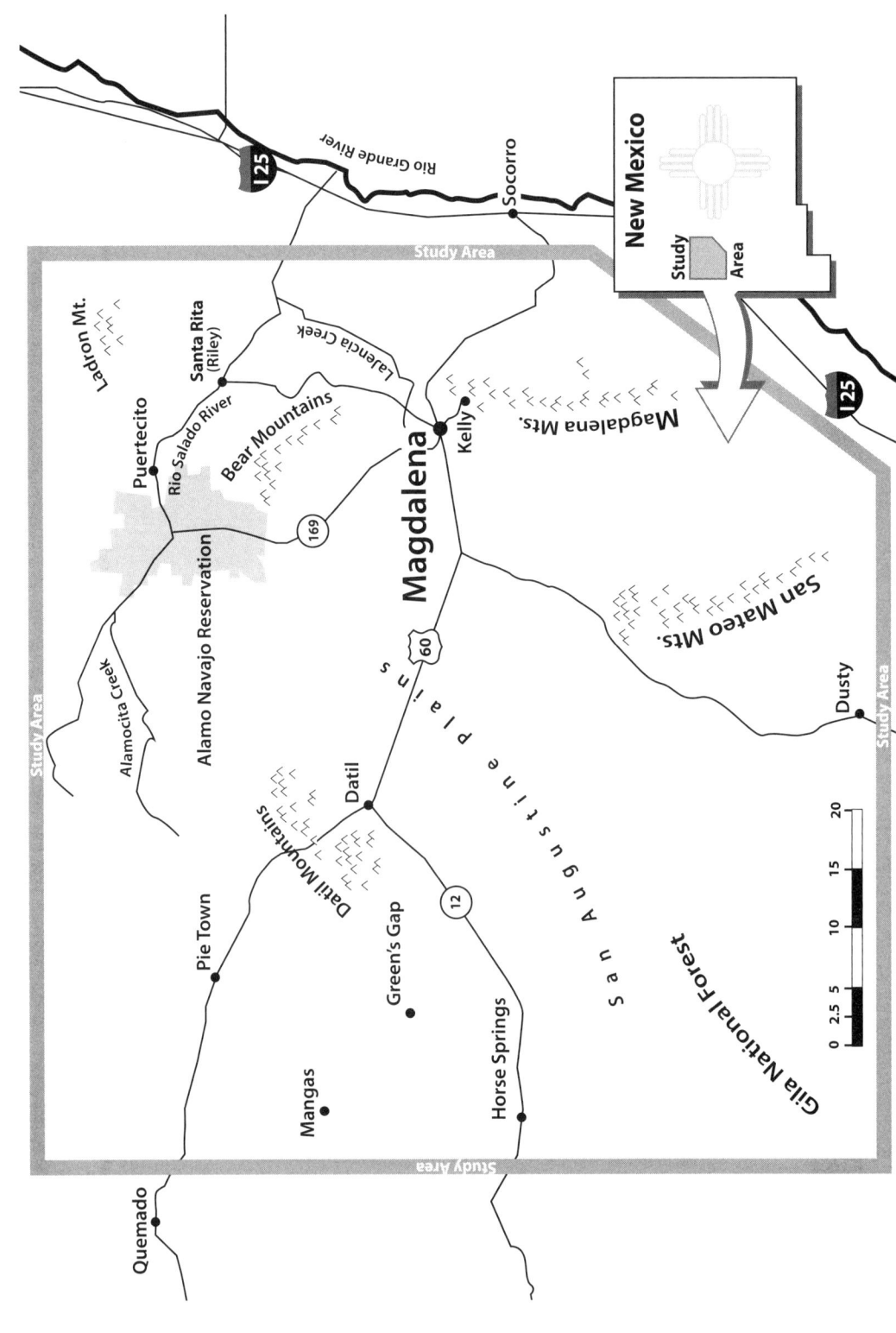

INTRODUCTION

There are various versions of the legend, but on the essentials there is general agreement. Sometime in the sixteenth century, during one of the Spanish *entradas* into present-day New Mexico, a few mounted soldiers and a priest left the main body of the expedition to explore the high mountain country west of the Rio Grande. After arriving in the high country, the Spaniards were attacked by a party of Apaches, whereupon the soldiers retreated to some nearby mountains to make an effective defense. Arriving at their destination, they immediately noticed the Apaches withdrawing from their pursuit. The reason was soon clear enough. Unknowingly, the Spaniards had chosen for their retreat a location held in awe by the region's *Indios*. For as the soldiers now observed, on the mountain above them appeared a natural formation of stone and shrubbery in the shape of a woman's face—the apparent reason for the Apaches' retreat. Realizing their good fortune, the priest contemplated the image and was reminded of a legend in his native Spain, the story of how St. Mary Magdalene, upon the death of the Lord Jesus, had followed St. James to Spain, where she spent her remaining years devoted to prayer in the mountains. Upon her death, it was said, Mary's face miraculously appeared on a nearby mountain. How fitting, the soldiers agreed, to christen this mountain before them La Sierra de María Magdalena.[1]

So we begin at the outskirts of the Spanish empire, when a band of soldiers gave a holy name to a mountain, and unknowingly, to a town as well, a town that would not spring forth for some 300 years. Meanwhile, three peoples, two of them riding the tides of conquest and empire, would settle the mountains and plains of New Mexico.[2] To understand this story—or rather stories—of coming of age, one must begin with how each of the three peoples came to know the territory.

Hispanics

In the summer of 1540, under the command of Francisco Vázquez de Coronado, the Spanish made their first *entrada* into the region of New Mexico. The motives underlying the expedition were multiple.[3] Over the next two

Mary Magdalene on the mountain, Magdalena, New Mexico. (Photo by Hoss Fosso. Courtesy of Magdalena, New Mexico, Public Library.)

years Coronado and his forces wrought all manner of cruelties upon the Native Americans they encountered, but before withdrawing they had learned something of the territory and peoples who inhabited it—namely that the center of the region, indeed its very lifeblood, was a 200-mile stretch of the Rio Grande River along which more than 60,000 Indians, grouped into four linguistic divisions, lived in some 100 villages—so-called Pueblos. Over the course of the sixteenth century other *entradas* would follow. The culmination of these occurred in 1598 when Conquistador Juan de Oñate entered New Mexico with a colonizing force of more than 600, including women and children, with the objective of planting a permanent settlement in the north. Because the southernmost division of the Pueblos, the Piros, appear to have suffered least from earlier incursions—and no doubt for pragmatic reasons as well—when Oñate passed through their country the natives offered up baskets of maize, prompting the conquistador to name one of the larger villages Socorro, or Succor.[4] But the Piros would not escape Spanish colonizing designs. By 1626 Fray Alonso de Benavides had established several missions in the region, announcing at one point that the Pueblo peoples were all baptized, and in what was clearly an exaggeration, that they had forsaken their pagan beliefs for Christianity. The Spanish cultural threat aside, the Piros were headed for trouble. By the end of the century, draught, famine, epidemics, and periodic Apache raids had devastatingly reduced their numbers to a fraction of their former levels.[5]

Meanwhile the more concentrated presence of the Spanish in the north had not gone well for the Pueblos, and by the 1670s most were united in bitter determination to expel their colonizers. The failure of the Spaniards to protect them against nomadic raiders, the continued extortion of labor and food (made all the worse by a spell of draught and famine), the soldiers' sexual assaults on Pueblo women, the harsh punishments for resistance, and the unrelenting war on their religious rituals—all converged to produce the so-called Great Pueblo Rebellion of 1680. When it was all over, the Spanish were driven out of New Mexico, leaving behind a death toll that included 21 of the province's 33 priests and some 400 settlers. As the Spanish limped south, the vulnerable Piros either joined the refugees in their march to El Paso or melted into Pueblo villages in the north.[6]

But Spanish visions of conquest and colonization were not to be denied. Thirteen years later Diego de Vargas marched north and finally established Spanish suzerainty over the upper Rio Grande. The Spanish were soon making two broad distinctions regarding the region: *Rio Arriba* in the north, which spanned the area between Taos and Bernalillo, and *Rio Abajo,* which extended south to Socorro. Because Rio Arriba possessed the most arable land, was home to most of the Pueblos, and served as a gateway to the Plains Indian trade, Spanish interest and settlement remained concentrated in this northern zone, and here the shape of Hispanic culture assumed its most pronounced form.[7]

Recolonization in the Socorro region progressed more slowly. In 1771 the governor of New Mexico proclaimed plans to resettle the old Pueblo of Socorro.[8] The announcement failed to entice many Spanish, but the prospect of attaining land was attractive to numbers of Hispanicized Indians, many of them perhaps of Piro lineage. Three years later, Fray Miguel de Menchero reported that some sixty Indian families, six Spanish families, and one priest occupied the village.[9] Still, because the settlement was an easy mark for Indian raiders in search of livestock and captives, life on this stretch of the Rio Grande remained a precarious quest for survival. As farmers tilled their fields and herders grazed their sheep, they cocked an eye to the horizon for Apache raiding parties.

Three features of Spanish colonial life merit special attention: religion, race, and social status. Regarding the first, the Holy Catholic Church shaped much of settlers' everyday outlook and existence. The seven sacraments marked the days and years of their existence. The priest baptized their children, sanctified their marriages, and sent the dead on their way to a greater glory. As Catholics they believed that the church signified the mystical body of Christ, and throughout the year they ritualistically marked the life, death, and resurrection of the Lord Jesus, born to the Virgin Mary. There were saints to be venerated, fields to be blessed, churches to be plastered, and cemetery crosses to be straightened. To know the catechism, pray the rosary, light candles in darkened chapels, confess one's sins in the expectation of the Father's forgiveness, enter into communion with Christ—all these gave shape and meaning to Hispanic communities living on the rim of Christendom.[10]

On the matter of race, New Mexico society was a complex outgrowth of Iberian conceptions and new world conditions. On the Spanish frontier race and blood lineage served as primary markers in the social hierarchy. At the top of the racial pyramid were those true *españoles* who prided themselves in their *limpieza de sangre,* or blood purity, which signified that its possessor was a person of honor, a *gente de razón,* and defender of the one true faith. Next were the *mestizos,* a designation that over time became a catchall descriptor for those of mixed Spanish-Indian ancestry. Further down the social scale were Hispanicized Indians, and at the bottom of the racial hierarchy were those *indios bárbaros,* mostly Apaches, Navajos, and Comanches still outside the bounds of Spanish "civilizing" influence.[11]

Social status, or *calidad,* constituted a third defining feature of New Mexico life. During the early colonial period social relations on the frontier were heavily influenced by the Spanish "feudal patriarchal ideology," which, as Ramón Gutiérrez has argued, was constructed around the masculine ideals of conquest, domination, and protection. These ideals, in turn, reinforced notions of honor and virtue. According to Gutiérrez, "A person without honor was worse than dead in colonial New Mexico." Moreover, because race, honor, and virtue were interconnected, it followed that the latter two qualities were possessed in declining proportion as one descended the racial hierarchy. Thus, the "most vice-ridden aristocrat always enjoyed more honor-status than the most virtuous peasant."[12] At the same time, the requirements for honor and status were gender specific. Whereas male status was generally enhanced by success in the game of sexual conquest, female virtue (and ultimately family honor) revolved around a pubescent female's possession of virginal purity when taken to the marriage bed, that she be *sin vergüenza,* or without sin.[13]

But the Spanish colonial frontier was hardly a static one. Changes in both social and political realms were in the making. In the first instance, the early and elaborate racial demarcations and correspondence to degrees of *calidad* were difficult to sustain on the outskirts of the frontier where race mixing was common. On the New Mexico frontier, bloodlines melted and melted again, and by the late eighteenth century were mostly blurred, enabling enterprising *mestizos* to take advantage of new opportunities to "whiten" their status. As David Weber observes, "Whitening occurred throughout Spain's empire, for a person's social status, or *calidad*, was never fixed solely by race, but rather defined by occupation and wealth as well as parentage and skin color."[14]

In the political realm, the twin events of Mexican independence in 1821, followed twenty-five years later by a disastrous war with its northern neighbor, were monumental developments, the latter ending with Mexico's cession of one-third of its territory to the United States. However much *nuevomexicanos* were reluctant to embrace their new status as Americans, as historian Andrés Reséndez notes, the New Mexican northern frontier was a "world of exceedingly fluid identities." Indeed, for some Hispanics the territory's remoteness, the perpetual political factionalism in Mexico City, the inability of the Mexican military to protect northern settlements against Indian raids, and finally, the region's growing trade ties with its northern neighbor, all made hitching the region's future to the United States a welcome development. The last factor was central. The north-south exchange across the Santa Fe Trail both economically tethered New Mexico to the United States and contributed to concentration of wealth in a few New Mexican families. For this small but influential elite, the future lay with the United States, not the failing Mexican state. Hence, Howard Lamar's observation that the bloodless 1846 invasion of New Mexico was a "conquest of merchants."[15]

So it was that without resistance General Stephen Watts Kearney marched into the plaza of Las Vegas, New Mexico, on August 15, 1846, and proclaimed that the Americans had come as friends, not enemies, as protectors, not conquerors. Those who remained "peaceably at home, attending to their crops and their herds" had nothing to fear from the invading army. As for rumors that the Americans posed a threat to their religious faith, Kearney announced, "I am not Catholic myself—I was not brought up in that faith; but at least one-third of my army are Catholics, and I respect a good Catholic as much as a good Protestant." Only good things would flow from the US Army's arrival, Kearney assured the crowd. "From the Mexican government you have never received protection. The Apaches and the Navajhoes [sic] come down from the mountains and carry off your sheep, and even your women, whenever they please. My government will correct all this. It will keep off the Indians, protect you in your persons and property; and, I repeat again, will protect you in your religion." In any event, *nuevomexicanos* should understand that this new turn in the fortunes of empire could not be reversed. Those who chose the path of resistance would be hanged. "There goes my army—you see but a small portion of it; there are many more behind—resistance is useless."[16]

Anglos

Like the Spanish before them, Anglo Americans were a people bent on empire. Since Jefferson's time, those who contemplated the nation's future concluded that time and providence had truly smiled on the young republic. Just as assuredly as the sun rose and set, so the US "empire of liberty" appeared destined to extend all the way to the Pacific. Whether Americans viewed themselves as a chosen people with a providential destiny or secular-minded believers in agrarian idealism, both concurred that the West was a blank slate upon which to write their system. The pioneer settlers would lead the way. Settler colonialism was on the march.[17]

Pioneer settlers were bearers of a uniquely American civilization rooted in the ideological pillars of republicanism, Protestantism, and capitalism.[18] From pulpits, the halls of Congress, newspapers, and schoolbooks, these beliefs provided a coherent definition of what it meant to be an American. From these beliefs flowed a host of ideas about freedom, democracy, individualism, property, and virtue that, bundled together, provided a compelling rationale for the republic's sweep across time and space. "We will measure our strength by the grandeur of our object," Horace Bushnell proclaimed in the midst of the war with Mexico. "The wilderness shall bud and blossom as the rose before us; and we shall not cease, till a Christian nation throws up its temples of worship on every hill and plain; till knowledge, virtue, and religion, blending their dignity and their healthful power, have filled our great country with a manly and happy race of people, and the bands of a complete Christian commonwealth are seen to span the continent."[19]

By the standards of republicanism, Protestantism, and capitalism, supporters of the Mexican war judged both the Spanish legacy and the Mexican regime fundamentally deficient. More than a mere war over territorial aggrandizement, a US victory over Mexico symbolized the triumph of republicanism over autocratic despotism, Protestantism over Catholicism, and capitalism over feudalism. Thus, in the middle of the war the *New York Sun* offered that Mexicans were "perfectly accustomed to being conquered, and the only new lesson we shall teach is that our victories will give liberty, safety, and prosperity to the vanquished, if they know enough to profit by the appearance of our stars. To *liberate* and *ennoble*—not to *enslave* and *debase*—is our mission."[20]

The problem with such beneficent professions is that they frequently masked deeper racial justifications for the war. For embedded in references to the nation's supposed destiny was the lurking assertion that Anglo Americans, by virtue of their racial heritage, were a people apart, biologically and culturally superior to those who stood in the path of westward expansion—namely, Indians and Mexicans. Even before the 1840s many Americans were convinced that Indians, unable to make the transition from "savagism" to "civilization," were headed for extinction. Savagism might just be in the blood.[21] American colonizers were quick to project assumptions about racial inferiority onto Mexicans as well. Because Mexicans were largely a *mestizo,* or "mongrel," people, might they also be incapable of becoming fully civilized and embracing republican institutions?[22]

American observers on the scene did little to disabuse skeptics' suspicions on the question. Josiah Gregg's account of the Santa Fe trade, published in 1844 under the title *Commerce of the Prairies,* presented a mixed but largely negative picture of the Mexicans he encountered in his travels. A little over a decade later, William Watts Hart Davis, who served as US attorney in New Mexico, published his now classic *El Gringo,* in which he offered an equally uncomplimentary assessment of New Mexicans. Except for a few *ricos* (rich people), who took great pride in their fairness of skin, most of the population was "dark and swarthy" owing to the frequent intermarriage between members of the upper and lower classes, leading to the constant addition of a "new stream of dark blood" into the former's racial makeup. The purported result: "They possess the cunning and deceit of the Indian, the politeness and spirit of revenge of the Spaniard, and the imaginative temperament and fiery impulse of the Moor." According to him, although displaying "smartness and quickness of perception," they lacked the "stability of character and soundness of intellect that give such vast superiority to the Anglo-Saxon race over every other people." Still, he regarded the prospects for the population's long-term political integration bright. In fact, the vices of Mexicans were "more the result of habit, example, and education" than of any natural depravity. In time, they would make good Americans. "We claim that our free institutions make men better, wiser, and happier; then let us endeavor, through their agency, to work out the regeneration of the people of New Mexico, morally, socially, and religiously."[23]

Before the assimilation of Mexicans could be accomplished, the US military needed to pacify and subjugate the Indians—mainly Navajos and Apaches—who swept down into settlements in search of livestock and captives. General Kearney all but acknowledged the army's limitations in solving the problem when he issued a proclamation near Socorro granting locals permission to march into "the Country of their enemies, the Navajoes, to recover their Property, to make reprisals and obtain redress for the many insults received from them." The only restraint: "The Old, the Women and the Children of the Navajoes, must not be injured." Because Hispanics had a long tradition of conducting raids, Kearney's restrictions were no doubt dismissed out of hand.[24] By the 1880s, the Apache and Navajo threat to settlers west of Socorro was all but eliminated.

Miners were the first to penetrate the high country. In 1866, Civil War veteran J. S. Hutchason staked claims on three mines—the Graphic, the Juanita, and the Kelly—the latter giving the town its name. Located in the Magdalena Mountains, Kelly commanded a sweeping view of the future town of Magdalena, just 3 miles and 1,000 feet below. By 1881 other miners were sinking shafts in mines with names such as Alhambra, Ambrosia, Hardscrabble, Cimarron, Iron Mask, Legal Tender, and Waldo. In the coming years, the mines of Kelly turned out a little gold and modest quantities of silver and copper. The rich veins of lead and zinc ore, however, drew more highly capitalized mining companies into the area and spawned the town's real growth. From 1866 to 1904, the Kelly mines produced $8,700,000 in wealth; from 1904 to 1928 the figure rose to nearly $22,000,000. During these years Kelly was a bona fide boomtown. By 1910 it claimed a population of 2,600 with two hotels, several stores, a number of saloons, two dance halls, a schoolhouse, a Catholic church, and a cemetery. But like so many mining towns, Kelly eventually went bust. Following World War II production fell off sharply, and the mountainside town, mostly populated by Hispanics who had moved into the area to work the mines, limped into oblivion.[25]

Livestock growers and homesteaders shaped the region most profoundly. By the 1880s both Hispanics and Anglos grazed thousands of cattle and sheep across the high desert country. Grass and water were the two priorities. As for the former, there was lots of it: on the high tablelands, on the San Augustine Plains, in mountain pastures, and on secluded canyon floors. At the same time, cattle ranchers were soon cognizant of two stark realities: first, 160 acres (the amount of acreage allowed under the terms of the Homestead Act of 1862) were insufficient to support a family, let alone a thriving stock-raising enterprise; and second, land was worthless without access to water, which in arid New Mexico was scarce. Those who underestimated these realities were in for difficult times. Thus, in the days of the open range, ranchers filed on homesteads with water and then proceeded to graze their livestock over a far greater expanse of land than they actually owned. By 1890, 241,000 cattle were grazing in Socorro County, a good percentage of this number in the western high country.[26]

Whereas the first settlers mainly consisted of stock companies and ranchers, two pieces of federal legislation sparked an altogether different sort of settlement. The Enlarged Homestead Act of 1909 provided for 350-acre grants of land without water, minerals, and timber. The Stock Raising Homestead Act of 1916 expanded the acreage to 640. Both bills drew settlers into the arid land, many intoxicated with a utopian faith in the possibilities of dry farming. Although the large ranches would be the long-term beneficiaries of this migration (buying up the acreage of dirt-broke homesteaders), for the moment the possibility of acquiring free land, with the only stipulation that it be "proved up," was an infectious dream. Thus, until the early 1930s a slow but constant trickle of wagons and trucks passed through Magdalena headed for a dry-farming community situated almost atop the Continental Divide—a settlement called Pie Town. By the mid-1930s, Pie Town and the surrounding region were home to some 250 settlers. Others moved still further west toward the small and largely Hispanic settlements of Mangas and Quemado.[27]

Although some homesteaders raised a few cows, most scratched out a living by farming pinto beans, planting a family garden, harvesting piñon nuts, and supplementing their income by working for local ranchers or a lumber mill. Agnes Morley Cleaveland later recalled having sympathy for the wave of homesteaders passing through Datil in search of their 640 acres. "I watched the homesteaders as they trekked by. They came in family groups, in any sort of conveyance that would roll, their household furnishings piled high and the overflow—washtubs, baby buggies, chicken coops—wired to any anchorage that would hold." She also recalls the reaction of Ray Morley, her brother and a major rancher in the area, a man who knew something about stock raising in the high desert. When she expressed sympathy for the newcomers, he shot back:

Cowboys and cow pens, photo taken from the rear of a railroad car, Magdalena, New Mexico, 1900. (Rio Grande Historical Collections, New Mexico State University Library, no. RG94-46.)

Use your bean. Take this ranch country as it is and not as it ought to be. It's arid. Rainfall, including snow, averages about thirteen inches a year, and the moisture and the heat don't come together. When it's hot, it's dry; when it's wet, it's cold. We're lucky if we get two months' growing weather a year. The forage which nature has finally adapted to these conditions will support one cow on fifty acres of land, one sheep on five. It's not a country for the small farmer. Even if a homesteader with his six hundred and forty acres of dry land can get water at three or four hundred feet depth, he can't stand the expense of maintaining a deep well.... But suppose he does keep his well up. His six hundred and forty acres will not support over sixteen head of cattle. How many people will sixteen head of cattle support? It just naturally can't be done.[28]

He was right. The Pie Town settlement held on until the 1940s, when the pull of defense jobs and the push of hardscrabble existence led to a steady abandonment of the dry-farming dream.

Largely against the backdrop of livestock and mining economies the town of Magdalena sprang to life. After 1884, the year the Atchison, Topeka, and Santa Fe Railroad ran a 30-mile spur up from Socorro (followed by an extension up to Kelly), Magdalena soon became a vast funnel for shipping cattle, sheep, wool, and mineral ore. Within a few years it possessed all the earmarks of a bustling frontier town: stockyards, two general stores, two livery stables, two lumberyards, two banks, three or four hotels, several saloons, four brothels, four churches, and a schoolhouse. With a population of 600 in 1893, Magdalena soon acquired the reputation of being the largest shipping point in New Mexico and, some claimed, the entire West. Cattle towns such as Dodge City and Wichita had had their day in the sun. Now the promise of the frontier resided in Magdalena, New Mexico, where a collection of frontier types—cowboys, sheepherders, miners, homesteaders, gamblers, wagon freighters, merchants, pious women, prostitutes, and schoolchildren—joined the boom.[29] "Please give us a room that is not directly over the barroom," Agnes recalls her mother saying to the hotel clerk in 1886, when they passed through Magdalena: "I'm afraid those bullets will come up through the floor." The Morleys survived the night and struck out the next day across the San Augustine Plains for their new home in the Datil Mountains.[30]

Alamo Navajos

As Hispanics and Anglos moved into the country northwest of Magdalena they could not help but notice a small band of Navajos living in the area. The Navajos call themselves the *Diné* (meaning "The People"). In 1890 the population of this group was probably no more than 150. (By 1990, the number would reach nearly 1,300.) Early in the 1900s, when the federal government first took notice of the Navajos, it called them the Puertocito Navajos, after a small Hispanic settlement on the Rio Salado, a mostly dry-bed river that fed into the Rio Grande.[31] Later, they would officially be known as the Alamo Navajos. In some respects, the occasional reference to the group as the "Lost Band of the Navajos" is the most fitting one. For if the Alamo Navajos were not lost to themselves, their early history is largely absent from the written record.

There are two theories as to this group's origins. The first traces their origins to the 1860s when some 8,000 Navajos in the north were rounded up and marched south on the infamous "Long Walk" to Fort Sumner, New Mexico, where they were imprisoned for four years alongside a number of Mescalero Apaches. According to this interpretation the Alamo band began as an "escapee" settlement of Navajos and Apaches who either avoided capture or slipped away from the army after incarceration.[32] But other evidence suggests that the settlement predated the 1860s.[33] Historian Albert

Schroeder, for instance, has argued that as early as the eighteenth century some Navajos moved south into central New Mexico, bringing them into greater contact with Apaches in the area. This contact, according to Schroeder, "inaugurated an era of confused relations between Navajos and Apaches—war alternating with peace in bewildering succession." By the early nineteenth century, Schroeder maintains, Navajos, sometimes in concert with Apaches, were raiding along the Rio Grande for livestock and probably captives as well, fueling the ongoing cycle of Hispanic-Indian conflict. One Alamo elder, in fact, contends that prior to the Long Walk the band lived along the Rio Salado much closer to Socorro until the "Spanish people came and kill some men and took the women and children for slaves. The people who got away moved up the Salado River all the way up to Alamo." Growing up in the 1870s, Casamira Baca always remembered the stories he heard as a child of the period before the Long Walk, when the Alamos were continually threatened by Apache and Mexican raiding. "There was no safe place; the people were continually on the run. They would move about, searching for hiding places, carrying what little possessions they had, including their children. It was a time of fear and unrest."[34]

Whatever their origins—and both theories might be correct—it is clear that by the 1860s a small band of mostly Navajos was living in the Rio Salado region. In 1863, General Thomas Carlton informed Colonel Edwin Rigg at Fort Craig that some 15 miles west of Lemitar, the "Navajos drive their stolen cattle and 'jerk' the flesh at their leisure. Cannot you make arrangements for a party of resolute men from your command to be stationed there, for, say, thirty days, and kill every Navajo and Apache they can find?" The plan apparently came to naught, and the Alamo Navajos held on through the course of the Fort Sumner internment. After the US government removal of the Apaches from the region in the 1880s, the Alamo band settled into a pattern of farming, raising sheep, and living off the land. As William Quinn, who conducted an investigation of the group's history for the Bureau of Indian Affairs, says of this period, "The sight of a small band of Navajos in an extremely remote, isolated area—assuming they were sighted at all by anyone—would have been as ordinary as the sunrise." As we shall see, this would all change shortly.[35]

To the outside world, including the "Big Navajos" up north, the Alamo band has always been something of a mystery. One area of confusion has been the assumption that the band was an offshoot of the *Diné Anaa'í*, or Enemy Navajos, a band of mixed Navajo-Spanish lineage that over the course of the eighteenth and early nineteenth centuries enriched itself by collaborating with Hispanic aggressors.[36] Because the Enemy Navajos have historically always been associated with the Cañoncito area of the Navajo reservation, and because the Alamos, like the Cañoncito Navajos, are geographically cut off from the main reservation, many northern Navajos easily assumed that the two groups were one and the same. But the Alamos have never acknowledged the connection. One-time headman Martíniano Apachito recalls, "This is why I almost got into a fight with Al or Hal Gorman. They were calling us the enemy outsiders."[37]

Another source of confusion concerning the Alamo band's cultural and historical identity stems from its admixture of Apache bloodlines. The extent of Apache infusion is evident in two respects: clan affiliations and Alamo surnames. A 1949 study, for instance, found that a little over a third of the band identified its primary clan affiliation as *Tsisi,* an Apache clan and the single largest clan at Alamo. At the same time, two of the prominent surnames are "Apachito" and "Apache."[38] A third factor calling into question the band's cultural credentials was the large number of Spanish surnames—such as Ganadonegro, Secatero, Herrera, Vicente, and Monte—names largely absent among the "Big Navajos." From oral accounts it is clear that the Alamo acquired these surnames around 1900 from local ranchers, or in at least one instance, a Catholic priest, displacing traditional names that translated into the likes of Blue Boy, Curly Hair, Yellow Man, Thin Man, Skinny Lady, Light-Skinned Woman, and Run-Around Shoe.[39] This prevalence of Spanish names lent support to the perception that the Alamo Navajos, if they were not Apaches, surely must be "Mexicans turned into Navajos."[40] Finally, the distinctiveness of the Alamo Navajos is revealed by the nickname they acquired from other natives in the region—namely, that they were the *Tsé deałíí,* or "Rock-Chewer," Navajos. When the short-tempered Alamo men were aroused to anger, it was said, they would literally chew rocks. Like so much of the early history of the band, oral accounts differ as to the origins of the sobriquet. Some attribute it to the Mescalero Apaches, others to the Zunis. Whatever the origins of the rock-chewing image, older Alamos can recall numerous instances when they were stung by the term.[41]

Several aspects of the Alamo band's past—its geographical separateness from the Big Navajos, the mystery surrounding its origins, the Apache admixture, the unusual surnames—all speak to the group's distinctiveness. Yet this point cannot be emphasized enough: the Alamo Navajos were essentially Navajo in their cultural makeup. Turning the clock back to 1900, one would have found a small band of Indians speaking Navajo, living in hogans clustered in largely matrilocal "outfits" (residence groups generally composed of the bride's parents, her maternal grandparents, and her sisters' families), identifying with mainly Navajo clans, subscribing to long-standing Navajo taboos, and conducting their social relations much like the Navajos in the north. Through ceremonies, prayers, and storytelling, Alamo elders were transmitting to youth the essential elements of the Navajo cosmological and spiritual worldview—how the *Diné* lived in several worlds below the earth's surface before their emergence; how First Man and First Woman gave birth to Changing Woman; how Changing Woman created the main clans from parts of her body; how She, impregnated by the Sun, gave birth to the Hero Twins; how the Twins journeyed to the Sun and slew the four monsters who threatened the existence of the *Diné*; how the trickster Coyote was both holy yet untrustworthy; and how one's well-being depended on both correct behavior and the avoidance of dangerous and evil forces.[42] At the core of this outlook was the ideal of *hózhó*, variously translated by scholars as order, harmony, balance, peacefulness, but most often beauty. "In beauty may we dwell, in beauty may we walk," the traditional Navajo prayer begins.[43] The older Alamos remember this world, and a few still subscribe to it. "I think about it lots of times," one old man reflects.[44]

But *hózhó* did not solve the everyday challenge of subsistence. Before 1900, and for many years thereafter, the band's subsistence economy revolved around farming, livestock raising, hunting, and gathering. Corn, several squashes, and beans were the main crops cultivated but also smaller quantities melons, beets, and chilies were grown. Most families had a few sheep, goats, and horses, although the latter only figured into their diet in times of severe crises. The number of sheep and goats per outfit varied greatly, so in some quarters the decision to butcher an animal was not taken lightly. (A 1948 government study showed that one-third of Alamo families possessed no sheep whatsoever.) Knowledgeable gatherers also searched the banks of the Rio Salado, nearby mountains, and remote canyons for wild potatoes, spinach, celery, berries, cactus fruit, and piñon (nuts). Finally, Navajo hunters periodically relied on wild game—principally deer—to get them through the winter, although turn-of-the-century game laws raised the stakes for excessive hunting. But other game also found its way into Alamo skillets and boiling pots.[45] "We used to eat prairie dog, rabbit," recalls an old man who came of age in the 1920s. "We used to kill porcupine. Porcupine is good to eat. They don't eat nothing but trees and weeds. I eat bobcat too. Bobcat don't eat nothin' bad." By tradition and circumstance, waste was held to a minimum. When killing a deer, "we eat everything. Sheep too. We don't waste nothin'. We eat head and the brain, tongue, the feet and everything."[46]

As the world closed in around them, the Alamo Navajos were gradually drawn into a wider circle of economic relationships. During the wet years, some families gathered sacks of piñon nuts that they traded to local ranchers or the trading post for store-bought commodities. Many men and older boys earned income by hiring out to ranchers as herders, cowboys, and fence builders. A most important development came in the late 1880s when Nels and Ida Field settled in the area. Trusted neighbors, the Fields were ranchers and owners of a small trading post, and in these capacities provided some seasonal employment for the men and a reliable outlet for Navajo rugs. Another source of income was Datil rancher Ray Morley. Beyond hiring the Navajos as sheepherders and fence builders, around 1920 he opened the Navajo Lodge on the Ocean-to-Ocean Highway (today's US Highway 60) and, in a scheme to attract tourists, invited several Navajos to set up camp within view of the lodge, where the Navajo women could be observed weaving rugs available for sale at Morley's establishment.[47]

The Alamo Navajos' twentieth-century struggle for survival took place against the backdrop of three important developments. In 1912, P. T. Lonergan, superintendent of the Southern Pueblo Agency in Albuquerque, discovered the "Lost Band of the Navajo." As Lonergan describes it,

> I was informed . . . that there was a band of Navajo Indians located near Puertocito, New Mexico, who were being imposed upon by their White neighbors; that their land were being taken from them; that they were forbidden to graze upon the public domain where they had the same right as their White neighbors, and that as a consequence their flocks were diminishing to such an extent that they were not capable of self-support. On April 20, 1912, I visited the vicinity where the Navajos are. . . . I found that the stories that had been told me concerning the injustice done these Indians were true.[48]

Shortly after his visit, Lonergan secured 160-acre allotments for each family, thereby establishing the band's legal claim to its land. In the coming years the Alamo band's relationship with the Office of Indian Affairs (later renamed the Bureau of Indian Affairs, or BIA) was uneven because it was bounced from one agency jurisdiction to another, finally ending up at the Eastern Navajo Agency in 1968. But government support made the difference. When the BIA got word in the winter of 1928 that the Alamo

Navajos were butchering their horses to stave off starvation, the agent sent emergency relief rations of flour, sugar, coffee, baking powder, beans, salt pork, and blankets—along with more horses![49]

A second development was the Alamo Navajos' success in holding onto their land base in the face of ranchers' efforts to remove them from the region. In a statement written years after the episode, Ida Field recalled that in the late 1890s José Chávez, a prominent sheep rancher, circulated a petition calling for the Alamos' removal. The Fields, who had developed warm relations with the Alamo Navajos, refused to sign. Alamo elder John Guerro recalled years later the Fields' opposition to the petition. "He said to leave the people alone and not to bother them. . . . During that time the ranchers really did hated the Navajos." Perhaps because of the Fields' opposition, but more likely because of Office of Indian Affairs opposition, the petition failed in its design.[50] In 1913, shortly after the Alamo Navajos received allotments, ranchers made another attempt to accomplish the band's removal, this time apparently with the support of US senator Albert B. Fall. Again, the effort failed.[51] But this second effort did have one result—a new name for a local geographical feature. According to one Alamo man's recollection, in the middle of the controversy several ranchers initiated a meeting with Alamo leaders, hoping to convince them to relocate. Surely the government (it was probably argued) would assist them in some sort of beneficial land exchange. Perhaps the Alamos would like to move up north with the Big Navajos? But it was soon evident that the assembled Indians were not budging. At the end of the confrontation, memory has it that one of the disgusted ranchers uttered, "Ah, shit." So the rocky peak was given a name by one of the Navajos—Ah Shit Mountain.[52]

A third development brought the Alamos into closer political alignment with the Big Navajos up north. In 1918, the Alamo band formally elected its first chairman, José María Apache. In the 1920s the band became a voting "chapter" of the Navajo Tribal Council, a status reaffirmed in 1938 during Commissioner of Indian Affairs John Collier's so-called Indian New Deal. In 1943, the Alamo Navajos adopted a formal chapter constitution.[53] Indeed, during the New Deal years, the band allowed itself a hopeful feeling about the future. In 1944, speaking at the new day school built by the Alamos under the auspices of the Civilian Conservation Corps (CCC), Olson Apachito recounted for visiting BIA officials the change in mood. "Up until 1939 we had face the hardest time we ever have to," Apachito related. "There was no job to earn money to take care our families. The summer season was dry. No crops of any kinds and nowhere to look for help to made that year. We all come to the end of the road, we thought." But now, under their new agent, Dr. Sophie Aberle (at the United Pueblo Agency), someone was listening. Perhaps now their checkerboard allotments could be "block together" and more land acquired for a growing population; perhaps now the BIA could help them with water and irrigation; perhaps now the new school and its "good teacher" would lead their children to a better future. One thing was for sure: "We don't want to stop."[54]

Calamity's Dream

By the late 1880s all roads in western Socorro County led to Magdalena. What had once been a raw-boned frontier settlement was now the regional shipping point for cattle, sheep, wool, and mineral ore. The sound of bawling cattle in the stockyard, the sight of evening campfires on the surrounding hills as sheepherders and cowboys awaited their turns to bring in their herds, the blast of the locomotive whistle, all bespoke Magdalena's bright future. After all, this was the West, where all things were possible. The almost daily arrival of homesteaders, the growing number of business establishments, the territory's transition to statehood in 1912—all these reaffirmed the enthusiasm of the town's boosters.[55]

The town's growth was reflected in the region's population figures. In 1900 Magdalena, with a population of 300, was the fourth-largest settlement in western Socorro County, surpassed by Kelly (616), Santa Rita (536), and Mangas (400). By 1910 Magdalena was the largest of the four at 1,226, followed by Kelly at 1,015. By 1920 Magdalena was still climbing at 1,960, whereas Kelly had slipped to 407.[56]

The 1920 US census figures reveal much about the demographic makeup of the town. First, approximately 60 percent of Magdalena's population was Hispanic, with Anglos constituting almost all of the balance. Second, the census information on the nativity of Magdalena's citizenry reflects a general New Mexico pattern. The census taker recorded that of the 1,156 Hispanics, all but 55 were native New Mexicans. On the contrary, although the overwhelming number of Anglos were born in the United States, only one-fourth had been born in New Mexico. By region, the southern plains, followed by the midwestern and southern regions, were the largest contributors to the Anglo population. Texas, the largest single-state contributor, accounted for slightly more than one-fourth of the Anglo population. Some 43 Anglos were born in Europe. Third, nearly half the residents (916) were below twenty years of age, with Hispanics accounting for roughly two-thirds of this number. Magdalena was mainly a town of families—and of special significance for this study—a town full of children.⁵⁷

Meanwhile, Magdalena's cash registers were singing the song of progress. In 1916 a young local poetess, perhaps a high schooler, calling herself Calamity, caught the boom spirit when she sent to the *Magdalena News* a ten-stanza prophetic vision of the town's future. "The Day When Dreams Come True" begins with:

> I had a dream the other night
>   When everything was still,
> I dreamed I took a pasear
>   To the top of Baldy-Hill

From Baldy, Calamity gazes down upon a Magdalena transformed from a bustling frontier town to a modern community. Electric lights twinkle up and down the main street, lighting up many of the older stores, now grown into major commercial enterprises. Cabarets and movie theaters now bask in the glow of city lights. Magdalena is a cow town no more. When the dreamer finally awakens she is so enthralled with her vision that she "promptly went to sleep again," hoping to "dream some more."

> But my vision had passed away,
>   But I'll make a bet with you—
> Fifty bones to a doughnut that
>   This dream will sure come true.⁵⁸

But it never did, really. Like so many frontier towns, bust followed boom. Between drought, overgrazing, market fluxes, played-out mines, and economic depression, Magdalena slipped into slow decline, gaining the reputation as a "has-been" cow town with a violent past.⁵⁹ But through it all, generations of children would go about the business of making sense of the world they were born into, a world where the crosscurrents of race, class, gender, and religion cut in ways both predictable and surprising, a world where the processes of negotiating identity, social space, and power relationships unfolded in an ever-changing social universe.

To this story we now turn.

PART ONE
CULTURES AND THEIR SCRIPTS

CHAPTER ONE

FAMILY AND RELIGION

Fred Billings's earliest memory is of a screaming, bucking wild colt. With his rancher father away on spring roundup, Fred's mother, Maureen, decided to pay a visit to their nearest neighbor, a homesteader family 15 miles away. Fred's mother saddled a horse, and with five-year-old Fred behind her and his younger sister in front, the trio set out, making their way up the dry riverbed of the Rio Salado. Shortly they were joined by Bob McCoy, the husband of the very family they were going to visit. McCoy was agitated. He announced that he had just seen about thirty wild horses head up a draw where they would be trapped in a complex of canyon walls and fences. McCoy was determined to rope one of the horses, and he excitedly hatched a plan. He directed Maureen to deposit the children on the riverbank, ride up the draw, and then run horses down to the riverbed, where McCoy would be waiting. With the horses partially winded and running in the sand, he would be able to rope a choice colt. So the two children watched the drama unfold. With his "loop built," McCoy sat a short distance away, hidden under the shadow of the riverbank. Suddenly Fred saw the horses hit the riverbed with his mother close behind. McCoy galloped into the frantic herd and roped a good-sized colt. The boy would never forget the sight of the colt fighting the rope. But mostly it was the sound, the violent squealing, that got to him. "Us kids thought that was pretty bad. That colt was squealing and bucking and we didn't like that." His sister was crying out, "Turn him loose. He needs to go to his mama." For the boy there were so many compelling images: the horse fighting the rope, his mother's equestrian skill, McCoy's skill at capturing a wild horse. In time, he would grow accustomed to the squealing. It came with the territory.[1]

When Candelaria García thinks about strong-willed Hispanic women, she thinks of her mother. The specific image that comes to mind is the day her mother beat her father and two uncles in a horse race between two ranches. Candelaria can still visualize her mother in her buttoned high-top riding shoes galloping down the road on her favorite horse, Diamonte.

Hooves pounding, dust flying, "I saw them coming. I could see mama WAY ahead of them, her *chongos* [braids] bouncing up and down, up and down. And we'd say 'Hurry up mama, hurry up!' and clap our hands." Reining in her horse at the gate, her mother laughingly taunted the men as they galloped in behind her. "*No es valido*," her father protested. "You started before we told you to go!" "No, I didn't," her mother answered. "*Derecho, derecho todo*." It was totally fair. In telling this story, Candelaria confesses that "every once and a while when I will get—I guess you could say depressed—I start to remembering back, and I always land on that story when mama beat the men horseback."[2]

The earliest memory of Benjamin Apache is of a cold morning in 1919 and his uncle leading him away from a hogan. Benjamin recalls wanting to look over his shoulder at the red glare that lit up the dawn sky, but his uncle kept urging him forward, all the time telling the boy not to turn his head. He could not be sure, but he thought it might have something to do with his mother:

> I never got to know my mother well. One thing that I have in the back of my mind ever since then was toward early in the morning some time, we were taken out of the hogan—my brothers and sisters—we were taken out a little ways and I kinda looked back and when I looked back there was a big fire back there. And I told my uncle, "What's that big fire?" "Well," he told me, "don't look back." And we just kept on.

Later, he would come to know the significance of his uncle's admonition. By Navajo tradition, when someone died, the corpse was ritualistically removed from a hole knocked out of the hogan's north side, the direction of evil, before being buried. The dwelling was then incinerated to protect the family from lingering ghosts or evil surrounding the dead. "That was my mother. So they were burning the hogan. I didn't know nothing about it. Later I found out what it was."[3]

The three stories above are stories about childhood in west-central New Mexico, a cultural borderland where one's ethnocultural ancestry shaped in fundamental ways the coming-of-age experience.

We begin at the beginning.

Getting Born

In September 1936 the Socorro Health Department announced that during the month of August thirteen infants had died, nine without any sort of medical care. If equivalent figures were projected over a year's time, the *Magdalena News* calculated, "a child born in Socorro County would have less than a 50 per cent chance of surviving to reach the age of one year." The paper went on to point out that the county had not only one of the highest rates of infant mortality in the state but also that it was nearly three and a half times the national average. Contributing factors included pervasive ignorance, poverty, indifference, and lack of proper sanitation. In what was probably a veiled criticism of Hispanic Catholics, the article also attributed the problem partly to the fact that "in a large proportion of our homes the number of children far exceeds the parents' ability to give them proper care."[4]

As a "frontier" region, west-central New Mexico lagged behind most other areas in the nation in making the transition from what one historian has called "social childbirth" to the more modern concept of "medically managed childbirth." Several factors explain the slow pace of the transition. First, although doctors were practicing in Magdalena as early as the 1890s, the unpredictability of childbirth combined with the remoteness of ranch life made the chances of procuring a doctor at a moment's notice a risky enterprise. Second, doctors' practice of charging rural families a dollar per mile introduced an economic dimension into the matter, especially for those living on the edge of poverty. Third, although theoretically there was a possibility of moving the pregnant mother into town to "lamb out," in practice this was a luxury limited either to wealthier ranchers or to those with kin in Magdalena. Finally, assisting in childbirth had long been the province of women. In the early twentieth century many women were still relying on midwives in their moment of need. For several reasons, Hispanic women were probably slower to abandon the practice: the age-old respect for *curanderas* as healers, traditional beliefs concerning female modesty, and fewer economic resources. In 1929, 29 percent of New Mexican children were delivered by midwives, another 14 percent "unattended," and the balance, 57 percent, were delivered by doctors. In western Socorro County the number of birthing mothers either unattended or assisted by a midwife was probably well over 50 percent.[5]

The birth of a child was a momentous occasion for any family. At the same time, during the birthing process, children in the family might either be kept in the dark as to what was transpiring or be given some role to play, depending on the circumstances. Anabel Howell recalls that when her mother gave birth in Datil in 1895 she and her sister were too young to be of much help. "My father put the two of us on a horse and took us down a short distance from the house and told us we were to count cows that came down the trail until he came for us." In time, he rode up and told the girls they had new twin sisters. Howell cannot remember who actually assisted her mother in the birth, but she does recall that "Grandma Patter" came from over the mountain to help care for the babies, one of which was scarcely three pounds. When it was time for Grandma Patter to leave, Anabel's father put the old woman on a saddled horse with Anabel behind her, the girl's responsibility being to bring the horse back. "He told me if I wasn't sure of being on the right trail to give 'Blue Dog' the reins and he would come home alright without my help, which was little comfort. I doubted I would ever see home again." But sure enough, Blue Dog got her home safely. As for the newborns, one would die within the year.[6]

At six years old, Margarita García had no idea that her mother was pregnant, or for that matter what pregnancy was. The birth of her brother was nothing less than traumatic. One day when the six-year-old came home from kindergarten for lunch, her mother, who appeared ill, firmly instructed her, "Go get Doña Luz." So the child ran to the woman's house and, out of breath, relayed the message, "*Doña Luz, Mamá te la necessita.*" The woman in the doorway knowingly responded, "*Bueno, vamos mijita.*" After she ran home, her mother immediately sent the child on another errand. Now Margarita must run to the school and fetch her older sister, Adelia. If she could not find Adelia, she should get her brother Benjamin to find Adelia. Running to school, the child was consumed with purpose but also panic. She had no idea where to find Adelia, or for that matter Benjamin; the small children never associated with the older children. Reaching the school, she went from classroom to classroom telling each teacher that her mother needed her sister and brother. Finally, she found Benjamin's classroom and hurriedly rushed up to him, announcing, "*Mamá te necessita que lleves a Adelia.*" Benjamin was aghast with embarrassment. "Ssssshhhh!" she remembers him saying. Leaving the classroom and uncertain what her brother would do, she waited outside the classroom, periodically peeking through the door. Finally, she saw the boy go up to the teacher, who gave him permission to leave. After Benjamin found the older sister, all three bolted for home.[7]

For Margarita the scene at home defied comprehension. Doña Luz was nowhere in sight. The girls rushed into the bedroom, where Adelia immediately came to the assistance of her mother. To Margarita it seemed a small doll was lying on some rags on the floor. Meanwhile, her mother was attempting to stand and had something like a cord tied to her big toe. "Get the scissors," her mother instructed Adelia. "And I thought: What does she want with a pair of scissors? And at that time she turned around and she told me to leave and close the door." While Adelia was cutting the umbilical cord and wrapping the afterbirth, Margarita went into the kitchen, where she announced to her brother: "*Una muñeca está en el suelo. Mamá se está sangrando.*" She had seen a doll on the floor, and their mother was bleeding. Apparently clueless himself as to what was transpiring, Benjamin simply informed his sister she did not know what she was talking about.

About this time, Doña Luz arrived, explaining that she had unsuccessfully gone in search of the children's maternal grandmother to assist her in care of their mother. At this point Adelia entered the kitchen, and as she handed a bundle of blood-soaked rags to the midwife, she announced, "We have a new baby!" Benjamin could only respond, "*Qué?* You're lying." It was in the midst of this confusion that another sister, Estella, arrived from school to hear the good news. After going to her mother's bed, she confirmed Adelia's announcement: "Yes we do, *un hombrecito.*"

For Estella, this *hombrecito* was one brother too many. "Let's throw him into the dump," she casually suggested. Horror stricken, Margarita went to her mother.

> So I opened the door and I went in the room and said, "Mamá? And she said, "Yeah, come on in." And I walked over there and I said, "The girls were saying that we had a little baby. May I see it?" And she said, "Yes, didn't you see it a while ago? I saw you creeping in here. And how many times have I told you, when the door is closed, you're not allowed to go in." . . . So she showed me the child. Oh, it was the cutest, little thing, and there were blankets and everything, not like what I'd seen on the floor. She said: "You want to hold it?" And I said "Yes." So I held it and I just loved it to death. . . . So I said, "Mamá, will you give me this child?" And she said, "Why?" And I said, "Cause Estella said she's gonna throw it to the dump!" So Mamá said, "No, you can't throw it to the dump because he belongs to us." And I said, "Well they are, they're gonna throw it to the dump because it's not a girl." And she says, "No, we're gonna keep it and we're gonna love it." And I said, "Okay, well, give it to me and I'll take care of it." And she said, "Okay, you promise that you'll take care of him forever."

And from that day forward Margarita took it upon herself to do everything possible for her little brother's welfare, including buying him his first pair of boots.

In the 1940s, Navajo children were still born in much the same manner as in the nineteenth century, which is to say that cultural prescriptions

FAMILY AND RELIGION : 25

governed many aspects of the event. There were, for example, the several taboos that an expectant mother should observe: she must never gaze at an eclipse of the sun or the moon; she must never look upon a dead coyote, bear, snake, or porcupine for fear the animal would take revenge on the baby; she must avoid certain religious ceremonies lest they make the baby ill; she must not eat piñon nuts because they would add unnecessary fat to the fetus and cause a difficult delivery; and for reasons that are unclear, she must avoid goat's milk. Near the time of delivery, cultural traditions continued to operate. Frequently ritual "sings" were conducted for women delivering their first child or for those who violated a taboo. At the time of delivery the birth mother kneeled over a sheepskin and took hold of a rope or sash hanging from one of the hogan's beams while a female relative pressed down on the abdomen. Another sat in front to receive the baby. In the more difficult cases, the mother might lie on her back while one of the other women molded the baby into position for delivery.[8]

After the birth, ritual and tradition continued to assert themselves. The newborn was sprinkled with corn pollen to ensure a long and healthy life. In some instances, the baby's head features were molded to enhance its attractiveness. After having its hair washed, the infant was bound and placed next to its mother, its head facing the East. Meanwhile, strict attention was paid to the afterbirth and the umbilical cord. In the instance of the former, it was carefully buried some distance from the hogan, out of reach of animals and witches. As for the cord, if the infant was a boy, it might be buried in the horse corral "so he will have many horses," and if a girl, in the sheep corral "to bring her many sheep." In the absence of a horse corral, male infants also had their umbilical cords buried in a sheep corral, a ubiquitous feature of Navajo camps.[9]

In a few days, when it was clear the child was healthy, it was placed in a 'awééts 'áál, or cradleboard, where it would spend several hours a day in the coming months. In addition to protecting the child from injury and providing womb-like security, when propped against the hogan wall or tree, the cradleboard enabled the infant to observe family activities. The cradleboard, moreover, enfolded the infant in a symbolic universe pregnant with meaning. The first cradleboard, according to Navajo mythology, was constructed for the Hero Twins, born to Changing Woman. Each part of the cradleboard represented some aspect of the natural world the Navajos inhabited, a world of earth, sunbeams, rainbows, and lightning. After being constructed, the cradleboard was sprinkled with corn pollen and prayed over. Any number of prayers might be used:

> I have made a baby board for you, my son (daughter)
> May you grow to a great old age.
> Of the sun's rays have I made the back
> Of black clouds have I made the blanket
> Of rainbow have I made the bow
> Of sunbeams have I made the side hoops
> Of lightning have I made the lacings
> Of sun dogs have I made the footboard.

As a final act, parents frequently fastened a small medicine bundle to the board to offer protection against harm.[10]

The cradleboard's protective qualities are revealed in one of the Alamos' most cherished stories. Sometime in the 1870s, when fear of the Apaches was still great, a party of Alamo Navajos was camped below a hill, where a sentinel was posted to look for possible enemies. When the lookout announced that a group of Apaches was heading in their direction, the Alamos, including at least one woman and an infant, quickly mounted their horses to avoid what might be a dangerous encounter. But in their hurried escape, the mother failed to properly secure the cradleboard to the horse, and the worst of all things happened: the cradleboard slipped from the horse and slid down an embankment. As one elder tells it:

> The Apache were comin' close. She was scared to get off to get the little baby and she thought the baby might be died when it hit the ground. So she didn't come back. But somehow they stopped at another place up there at a high place where they could watch. The Apache never follow them. So they spend the night there. In the morning the baby's mother was worrying about it. She didn't think about her baby being dead. She wanted to send somebody over there to check, to see if the baby still there. Well, they sent two boys to check on it. They went back and sure enough the baby was laying there in the arroyo and there was a great big cedar root. The cradle was turned over on top of the cedar root.

The two boys approached the face-down cradleboard, still expecting the worst. What they saw would provide many an Alamo storyteller a dramatic and satisfying outcome. "Finally, they turned the baby over. And the baby was smilin'. He been suckin' on the cedar root. You know that sap in the root? He liked that and just smiled. Not even a scratch on his face."[11]

In the end, this Navajo infant's ordeal was probably less traumatic than that of an Anglo infant forced to nurse from a goat. In 1919, when Susan

Lee and her husband Jesse were working on a large sheep ranch, Susan found herself cooking for twelve men, keeping house, all the while nursing her baby, Alice. Understandably, she was exhausted. Then one day someone happened to point out to her a goat nursing its kid. Susan recalls immediately thinking, "How much help it would be if the goat took over Alice and fed her."

> One day when the men were up at the commissary, I took Alice down to the pen where the goat was kept and put Alice down by her where she could see the goat's tit. Now Alice had never seen a goat before and was scared pink and started to cry, which scared the old goat and I couldn't get any cooperation. So I finally got irritated and threw the goat down on her back and grabbed Alice by the back of her neck and pushed her mouth down on the goat's tit and that really brought down the house. Alice went to screaming and pulling the goat's hair, which hurt and scared the goat so she started yelling.

When husband Jesse came to the rescue of both baby and goat, a frustrated Susan blurted out, "This stupid kid of yours hasn't sense enough to know a good thing when she sees it." Most infants and toddlers were blessed with a calmer setting.[12]

Almost immediately newborns began to take in the sights, smells, and sounds of their surroundings. Although some of these elements—the pungent smell of burning piñon logs, the sight of a blazing persimmon sunset, and the eerie sound of howling coyotes—were nearly universal, others were culturally specific. Mostly the Hispanic infants first smelled pots of simmering chili, caught sight of the sorrowful Holy Mother above the crib, and heard grandmothers reciting the rosary. Navajo infants propped up in their cradleboards saw their mothers weaving brightly colored blankets or glimpsed a grandfather offering a prayer to the rising sun. Anglo infants were most likely to hear the sound of bawling cattle or hear their mothers singing an old Texan country song. Into this mix of sensations and impressions came the languages, each conveying meaning and a way to make sense of an expanding world.

Ruffles and Rats

As we have already observed, in Magdalena there existed a general correlation between ethnicity and economic status, with Anglos largely occupying the upper echelons. Among Anglos, few could claim the status of the

Mactavishes and the Morleys. John S. Mactavish was born in Scotland in 1867, then sometime in his twenties migrated to the United States, ending up in the New Mexico Territory. After clerking for several years in Albuquerque, he returned to Scotland, where he wed Bessie Cameron. In 1897 the Mactavishes moved to Magdalena, where John assumed management of the Becker-Blackwell store, soon to emerge as the town's major mercantile establishment. In a few years he was the major partner in what came to be known as Becker-Mactavish. By 1910 he was president of the Magdalena Bank, an investor in several business enterprises, a trustee in the Presbyterian Church, a high-order Mason, and one of the chief boosters of the town's fledgling school system. Until the 1930s, when Becker-Mactavish went belly-up, Mactavish devoted most of his time running his store, which sold everything from cartridges to fashionable dresses. When ranchers came to town for six months' worth of groceries, Becker-Mactavish was always a destination. At shipping time many ranchers paid last year's account and started a new one. Mactavish was a willing creditor and a friendly conversationalist.[13]

As Magdalena's biggest promoter and a pillar of the community, Mactavish saw himself as the harbinger of progress, a civilizing force in a rough-hewn frontier town destined for great things. If the Mactavishes were not at the very apex of the Anglo social pyramid, there was not another family with a greater claim to it. A Mactavish childhood, moreover, was not like most. Mactavish possessed an extensive library, and his habit of reading late into the night spoke volumes about the value placed on education. Daughter Christina practiced piano several hours a day and was sent off to Los Angeles and Great Britain to polish her skills. Although grandson John attended the Magdalena schools for a time, he also was sent off to a Presbyterian boarding school in Santa Fe for part of his education. On the Lord's Day, growing up a Mactavish meant studying your Sunday school lesson and foregoing the pleasures of playing cards or dancing. It meant completing your homework in the winter and being home on summer nights by the time the street lights blinked out. The Mactavishes were "very, very class conscious," recalls grandson John. If a playmate's last name was not "high-powered" enough, the children were encouraged to look elsewhere for companionship. "We just had a whole different set of values." There were also strict prescriptions for public behavior. "We couldn't laugh real loud, you know. It was uncouth if you laughed real loud in public. So we couldn't laugh, we couldn't just let our hair down." At the same time, there was a natural curiosity about Magdalena's commoner elements. Periodically, the family would climb into the 1930 Studebaker and "sit in front of the old store and watch the people go in and out of the old Silver Bell bar and see who had a little too much to drink or who was dancing with whom. Sit in the car. We weren't out in the middle."[14]

What the Mactavishes were to Magdalena, the Morleys were to the Datil region. Ada Morley and her three children arrived in Datil in the winter of 1886. She had been widowed three years earlier when her husband, William Raymond Morley, a prominent railroad-building engineer and one-time manager of the famed Maxwell Land Grant, was accidentally killed in an "unloaded" rifle accident. In a disastrous second marriage, Ada deferred to her husband's advice to invest in a New Mexican cattle ranch in western Socorro County. Shortly after she and her children arrived in Datil, she soon found herself abandoned by her new husband and on her own. As Ada's daughter, Agnes Morley Cleaveland, later described the situation, "She who believed more than anything else in education and culture found herself marooned with three young children on a desert island of cultural barrenness, with no means of escape that would not sacrifice her entire investment." Ada Morley was entirely unsuited for the role of "cattle queen." A college graduate, she was convinced that women had an important role to play in solving society's ills. In the coming years she would spend countless hours writing letters from her Datil ranch on behalf of reform movements dear to her heart: woman's suffrage, temperance, and the prevention of cruelty to animals.[15]

In 1886 Ada Morley was primarily concerned with how to civilize her three children, Agnes, Ray, and Loraine (ages twelve, ten, and eight), in the wild-and-woolly West. Strong-willed, Ada proved up to the challenge. The crude log cabin was expanded to a ten-room house, a virtual mansion by frontier standards. After the house was completed, it was furnished with walnut and rosewood furniture, a Steinway piano, and boxes of sheet music. The library grew by the week. "Books came out to the ranch in wagon-load lots," recalls Agnes. When it came time for the children to be educated beyond the rudiments, they were sent off to either East or West Coast environs. The social distance between the Morley children and others in the area was never in question.[16]

Some Hispanics also grew up in privileged environments. Prominent among Magdalena's leading citizens was José Y. Aragón, whose extensive investments included a large sheep ranch and one of the town's major hotels. Aragón was also vice president of the First National Bank of Magdalena. Ruben Maiz, a physician; C. B. Sedillo and Maurice Miera, both lawyers;

and Adolfo Torres, storeowner and president of the Magdalena School Board, were also among Magdalena's Hispanic elite.[17] Nearly all Hispanic males in the upper echelons of Magdalena were members of La Alianza Hispano-Americana. Founded in 1894, La Alianza was a mutual-aid society and fraternal organization devoted to the threefold aims of assisting those in dire economic straits, promoting self-improvement through knowledge, and advancing individual and community morality. Until the early 1940s the society also embraced language maintenance, which it reinforced by publishing its magazine solely in Spanish. Local lodges (eventually numbering some 300 across the Southwest) also sponsored social gatherings, including dances. In 1918, for instance, the local Magdalena-Kelly Lodge built a two-story building for the Kelly community, a structure the *Magdalena News* described as being ideal for "public gatherings" and possessing "an excellent floor for dancing." Thus, although fewer Hispanic children enjoyed the same economic advantages as their Anglo counterparts, a good number benefited from community-enhancing and supportive efforts of prominent men.[18]

One Hispanic woman who grew up in a privileged environment was Esther Peralta. Esther was raised in Kelly by her grandparents, her grandfather's income coming from a profitable zinc mine and a general merchandise store. In the 1920s the Peraltas lived in one of Kelly's finest houses, and to the child it was an enchanted world. The parlor, reserved for weddings, funerals, and other special occasions, was furnished with velvet couches and drapes and an elegant carpet. Unlike most Hispanic families, the Peraltas had domestic help. Every evening in the thickly draped dining room the family dinner was set on a silk tablecloth under a cut-glass chandelier. Children were encouraged to join in dinner-table discussions on subjects as varied as the price of zinc, European politics, and the boxer Jack Dempsey. After dinner the family adjourned to the living room, where Esther's grandfather might read aloud from *Don Quixote*.[19]

Still, viewed through the lens of occupational status, it is clear that Magdalena was a community where ethnic differences generally intersected with economic status (see Table 1.1). The breakdown of occupational categories in the 1920 US census and 1930 US census reveals that whereas Anglos dominated the higher-income categories, Hispanics were overrepresented in the labor and service sectors. The fact that Anglos generally commanded higher incomes and had smaller families meant that more Hispanic than Anglo children grew up in struggling households. It was Hispanic children who generally made the rounds selling the excess egg

Table 1.1 Occupational Status in Magdalena, New Mexico, by Ethnicity, 1920, 1930

	1920 Anglo	1920 Hispanic	1920 Other	1930 Anglo	1930 Hispanic	1930 Other
MERCANTILE/FINANCIAL	26	6	5	20	6	4
PROFESSIONAL	11	2	–	7	1	–
CATTLE RANCHER	20	20	–	15	6	–
WHITE COLLAR/TECHNICAL (MINING)	16	–	–	2	–	–
SALES/CLERKS	49	26	–	44	23	–
CONSTRUCTION/TECHNICAL	33	7	–	8	4	–
CRAFT WORKERS	3	2	–	4	3	–
TEACHERS	13	4	–	12	4	–
MINERS	14	59	–	8	5	–
FREIGHTING/TRUCKING	13	18	–	9	14	–
HERDERS	8	37	–	15	145	–
PERSONAL SERVICE	14	32	–	9	65	–
LABORERS	48	153	–	34	29	–
MISCELLANEOUS	22	28	–	5	3	–

Source: US Census, New Mexico, 1920, 1930.

production of backyard hens and the family milk cow. It was mainly Hispanic mothers and their daughters who filled the demand for domestic labor. The full significance of these disparities will be revealed later in this study. For now this generalization will suffice: class, because it operated within as well as across ethnic boundaries, was both a significant and complicating factor in shaping Magdalena's social relations.[20]

If Hispanic children generally lived a leaner existence than Anglo children, the Anglo children of Pie Town, a community of mostly dry farmers out of Texas and Oklahoma, also knew the meaning of material struggle. Among the last wave of Pie Town settlers, Alma Giles and her husband homesteaded in the area in 1934. "It was the Depression days and life was really hard," she recalls. "When we arrived at Pie Town, we had two horses, two cows, two children, and two dollars, so two was our lucky number." The two children, ages eight and three, spent four years living in a "half dugout." Built approximately 5 feet below ground and 3 above, lined with logs, and then topped with a roof of dirt and straw, the dugout was often the homesteader's dwelling of choice until circumstances allowed otherwise. Dugout living involved waging a constant war against dirt. Most families strung a sheet of oilcloth under the roof-supporting beams to catch the sifting dirt. Because most families had to haul their drinking water, they used the laundry rinse water to sprinkle and pack down the floor. Store-bought cabinets, bedsteads, and dressers were something of a rarity.[21] When money was particularly scarce, deer and rabbit meat were crucial food sources. Often there was more than hunger to fend off. One Pie Town girl recalls, "Our house was not very well built—just had mud between the logs and as it dried and shrunk, the rats would come in. Daddy would sit up and wait for them to come out. They would get in the shadow of the water bucket, thinking they were hid, then he shot them with his .22." One Pie Town mother recalls that the family's mud-and-brush ceiling was so infested with rats, "It came to the point where we never sat down to dinner without the 22 rifle at the table." On one occasion, spying a huge rat, "I reached over carefully and slowly for the gun and shot the rat, which fell in the middle of the table ruining our dinner."[22] As meager as the material circumstances might be for Pie Town children, a certain measure of security flowed from the fact that they were being raised in a stable community where economic struggle was the norm.

Of the three groups, surely the Alamo Navajos suffered the most. Looking back, Gilbert Guerro wonders how he survived a childhood of herding sheep without shoes and a daily diet of just two tortillas. What saved him was one of the she-goats and a rusty can he used to collect her milk. Martíniano Apachito recalls that children sometimes died of starvation, and those that did not went around in ragged clothes washed only once every two or three months. Many children suffered from head lice. As Apachito expresses it, "People had a hard time to struggle against bugs which were commonly known among the Alamo people." About growing up, one Navajo woman recalls thinking to herself: "Are we going to live like this forever?" It was a question many children, Anglo and Hispanic as well, asked.[23]

Families

Because the family was the earliest and primary social unit shaping the children, in this institutional setting they first began to make sense of their physical and social surroundings. Here, children first came to perceive the nature and obligations of kinship. Here, they got their first taste of what it meant to grow up male and female. Here, they began to communicate in their parents' language. Here, they received an introduction to those essential values and beliefs that made them cultural beings.[24]

To grow up a "traditional" Navajo meant growing up in a matricentered society. By tradition, Navajos were both matrilineal and matrilocal. In the first instance, this meant that the child's lineage was mainly traced through the mother's line. In the latter it meant that upon marriage the husband moved into the bride's hogan, one of several dwellings in her family's "outfit." In Navajo society women owned property, including the hogan and their portion of acquired livestock. Although women's main realm of responsibility was domestic, including child raising, they also worked gardens and herded sheep. Moreover, it was usually maternal aunts and grandmothers who stepped in to raise a child whose parents were unable to do so. As one scholar observes, "Navajo women have a great deal of control over their lives. They do not need to wrest power from others who hold positions of authority or attempt to influence decisions that are not theirs to make." At the same time, fathers were usually viewed as "heads of the household" and had primary responsibilities in the realms of politics, hunting, religion, and acquiring livestock. In addition to bringing essential income into the household, they served as male role models and frequently formed strong emotional ties with their children. Still, even in this realm matrilineal connections were operative. Maternal uncles, for instance, had primary responsibility for administering serious discipline.[25]

Before the age of ten, Alamo Navajo children were learning the intricacies of kin relations and the appropriate behavior each connection required. There were relatives with whom one could be at ease; there were others with whom one must be more restrained. There were some to whom one had lifelong obligations; there were others—especially after puberty—to be avoided.[26] It was also about this time that the children were coming to understand that the boundaries of kinship went beyond the recognizable boundaries of their nuclear and extended families. That is to say, at some point the importance of clan membership came to be understood. By Navajo belief all children are "born into" their mothers' clans and "born for" their fathers' clans. Consistent with the principle of matrilineal descent, the child's link to the mother's clan was the primary one. Clan affiliation was all-important to traditional Navajos for the simple reason that all Navajos belonging to the same clan were considered relatives, however distant or fictive the actual connection might be. One implication of this connection was that Navajos were obligated to show special politeness and hospitality to fellow clan members. Another implication was that marrying a clan relative, especially on the mother's side, was strictly forbidden. Although more than fifty clans have been identified across Navajo country, a few clans are dominant in some communities, and such is the case at Alamo. In 1950 the primary clan affiliations were Apache, Salt, Two Come after the Water, Standing House, Dirty Water, and Big Bucket.[27]

Alamo Navajo children were also beginning to internalize the intricacies of the *Diné* (People's) language. Indeed, through language the child's understanding of the world took shape; experience took on meaning.[28] In the beginning it allowed children to name things, including their physical and geographical universe. In each name there was a story. For instance, elders said that on *Tsé dah azkání,* or Rock Mesa, a large lizard or snake made its nest. By some accounts, this reptile was so powerful it could suck birds out of the air. Obviously, it was a place to be avoided. Then there was the mesa children came to know as "A Blind Man Fell Off." In one version the name derived from the ill fate of a man neglectful of the time-honored rituals associated with acquiring ceremonial turtle shells.

> There was a certain medicine man long time ago. He used to take shells off turtles in such a way that he didn't endanger himself or the turtle. He did that to put into his medicine bundle. He did it not only for himself but for other medicine men. He was holy enough to know how to do this the right way. Before he took the shells of a live box turtle, he sang a song (prayer) for that purpose and put corn pollen and other kind of things for that. After he finished that part, he took these shells off, and let the turtle loose back into the water. As soon as it gets into the water, it regrows the shell back. This was a sign that he did it correctly and he did not harm anything. The man who became blind decided to try doing this. He was not a medicine man. He took off the shell without any prayer or singing. As soon as he took the shell off, the turtle went to the water and did not grow back the shell. Not too long after that, he became blind . . . and fell off the cliff.

Stories like the above were invaluable for transmitting Navajo values. In this instance, the message was broader than about how to treat turtles: it was also about the importance of doing things in the right manner, and perhaps as well, about the consequential significance of ritual violation.[29]

In the course of growing up Alamo Navajo, children internalized several core values: reciprocity, cooperation, generosity, politeness, the inviolability of the individual, and the importance of industriousness. Like most cultures, traditional Navajo culture contains within itself tensions and areas of conflict. For instance, the freedom accorded individual action—exhibited in the oft-heard phrase *t'aa bee boholníih,* or "it's up to him"—sometimes comes into conflict with the value of cooperativeness. Industriousness, when manifested in the accumulation of material goods in disregard of one's obligation to relatives, was sure to invite condemnation for being stingy. Learning to negotiate these tensions was part of growing up Alamo Navajo. As *Diné* poet Jim McGrath writes, "I am paradoxical as coyote."[30]

Children learned to be Alamo Navajo in multiple ways. In the day-to-day routine of hogan life and interaction with relatives, children acquired the nuances of language, the skills essential to the family's subsistence, and the knowledge of a wealth of taboos. Among the latter: playing with string in the summer would surely result in spider bites; killing grasshoppers would give you nosebleeds; going near livestock during a rainstorm increased your chances of being struck by lightning; girls should not cut their hair, or it would cut short their life. Storytelling was a second source of cultural knowledge. During winter nights elders told ancient stories about the *Diné* emergence, Changing Woman, and the adventures of the Hero Twins. Stories of the trickster Coyote were always a favorite among the children. "Grandma, tell us a story about Coyote, and the world," one Alamo man recalls calling out. Coyote stories, he remembers, were a source of both entertainment and instruction. "See Coyote always wrong. See, that what they teach them. They were lessons. So the child say, let's not be like Coyote." A third source of knowledge came from the rich tradition of ceremonies, ritual observances, songs, and prayers upon which the elders drew to protect family and livestock from harm. Whether it was observing grandfathers greet the dawn with prayers and corn pollen, learning a sweathouse protection song, or being taken to a medicine man for a cure for an ailment—perhaps brought on from the violation of some taboo—Alamo Navajo children learned that the world was filled with wonder but also danger.[31] Little by little, they were becoming *Diné*.

Extended family connections were also an important part of the Hispanic child's upbringing. Beyond the network of grandparents, uncles, and aunts, the age-old tradition of *compadrazgo,* or the godparent tradition, was of special significance. Ritualistically sealed at the time of the infant's baptism, the implications of this wider familial connection—which might be biological or fictive—were substantial. In an examination of the tradition during the Spanish and Mexican eras, Ramón A. Gutiérrez explains:

> The obligations of compadrazgo were initially primarily moral, but in time they also became material. Godparents were supposed to counsel and guide their godchildren, leading them to eternal salvation and God by ensuring that they complied with the laws of the church. . . .

But godparenthood could also entail material succor. If one's parents died, for example, it was the godparents' responsibility to care for the orphaned child. In times of economic distress or if there were a stark economic inequality between the godparents and their godchild, it was common for godparents to assist their coparents with resources, to guarantee loans, and to offer introductions, social connections, and even the marriage-validating gifts necessary for their godchild to marry well.[32]

In the family, then, children began their journey into life and identity. In the family children witnessed their mothers praying the rosary, learned the names of saints, acquired their first notions of right and wrong, and came to see their father as the main authority figure in their households. In the family, moreover, children first heard the melodic sounds of Spanish and the seemingly endless number of *dichos,* the value-laden proverbs with which elders regularly laced their everyday conversations.[33]

Although Hispanic families were in the main patriarchal, it would be wrong to overemphasize the point. The role and status of Hispanic women was in fact substantial and derived from several sources. First, women had primary responsibility for running the household and rearing the children. Indeed, a woman's social position in the community was in large part determined by the character and deportment of her children. Second, through various social activities carried on largely in the context of the family, friendships, and church association, women played a central role in building and sustaining what sociologists call "social capital," the connective relationships that over time create a sense of community. Mainly women looked out for other families' children, cooked foods for church gatherings, and shared information across kitchen tables on some development at the school. Finally, women played a vital role in what one historian calls the domain of "labor and production." In addition to cooking and cleaning, women tended gardens; milked cows; raised chickens; butchered livestock; plastered adobe; and took in sewing, laundry, and ironing. Moreover, when one considers the number of Hispanic men categorized by the census taker as either "laborers working out" or "herders," it becomes clear that for all practical purposes many women were the heads of the household for several months of the year.[34]

A large part of Hispanic women's social standing stemmed from their moral character. Partly a throwback to the Spanish colonial heritage, when public knowledge of an unmarried daughter's loss of virginity brought dishonor to the family, the ideal of moral and sexual purity held sway in

Hispanic households well into the twentieth century and still does in many families. "If a man got a girl into trouble," according to one woman, "they would say 'he spoiled her, ruined her.' . . . People just had an opinion that she was like a piece of goods that had been handled too much." When a rumor came back to parents that a daughter had been seen committing some small act of affection toward a boy, she was sure to be met with, *No tienes vergüenza!* To tell a daughter that she "had no shame" was to warn that her behavior was bringing shame down on the whole family. Parents who joked to one another, *Sujeten sus pollos que mi gallos andan libres* ("Control your chicks, for my roosters are free") knew perfectly well that raising daughters could be fraught with peril. Mainly it came down to the strict curtailment of pubescent daughters' exposure in the public sphere and the constant reminders that a single indiscretion might result in tragic consequences.[35] Indiscretions did, of course, occur. The ideal of female virginity was just that—an ideal, which some Hispanic females found difficult to live up to.

Mainly it was the classic case of the double standard. Still, Lorenzo Ortega insists that most men grew up holding women of high moral character in high regard. "We respect our women," Lorenzo insists. "We don't dominate our women—especially in the house." The distinction between the house and world outside was a crucial one. Lorenzo, who grew up working on ranches, recalls, "My uncle always used to tell me, look son, you're wild and you're learning to cuss. When you get to the barn, you unsaddle your horse, you put your saddle up, and the language stays THERE." However, Lorenzo remembers that shortly afterward he violated his uncle's admonition. One day when his mother questioned him about his disregard for his school studies, he unthinkingly responded with, "Well, that's alright, I want to be a piano player in a whorehouse." The remark, he explains, had a certain logic to it.

> All the old cowboys, that's all they used to talk about—piano player in a whorehouse. They always wanted to do that. . . . Hell, that was the job to have. I had to have it, because they said it was. Can you imagine being a piano player in a whorehouse? Sounds pretty good while you out there freezing your ass off, dirty, hungry. Hell, a piano player in a whorehouse, they even bring his food to him, his drinks, everything. The way they talked it was PARADISE.

Paradise or not, his mother was not impressed. "God-damn, did I get the hell beat of me."[36]

Generally speaking, discipline in Hispanic households was strict. Candelaria García remembers the time when her family was having dinner, and her father instructed her to refill the milk pitcher. Candelaria, who had been taught to see to the needs of the dinner table, saw no reason on this occasion to respond to her father's request because they now had a young girl working for them. So she replied, "Why can't Sinforosa get it?" It was a mistake. "I didn't say it twice. Daddy came at me, SLAP, like that on my behind. . . . Nobody said anything. But that was the lesson daddy gave me. I was naughty. I know I was. I shouldn't have rebuked my daddy that way. It wasn't my business." In addition to getting slapped, there were other considerations to keep in mind. Some children were given to understand that disobeying their parents could result in supernatural retribution—the child's hand shriveling up, or worse yet, "the ground would open up and swallow you."[37]

The strict discipline came from two motivations. One was purely practical. *Cria cuervos y te sacarán los ojos,* Magdalena parents reminded each other. ("Raise ravens, and they will scratch your eyes out.") But another motivation sprang from a deeply held sense of religious obligation. "What account will I give my Lord about my children, my family, when my dear Lord asks me to account?" one Hispanic woman remembers her mother saying. "What will I tell Him? Did I do right? Did I do wrong? God loaned me those children; I have to do to the best of my knowledge to raise them and protect them and give them a good raising. If I do wrong, God will say I gave those children to you to raise in My image."[38] It followed that conscientious parents strived to implant several key values. Central among these were showing respect to elders, honoring community mores, balancing the importance of hard work with recognition of the role of fate, and showing kindness to the less fortunate. Showing respect for elders was instituted at an early age. One woman recalls that she grew up prefacing all references to her older brothers and sisters by the formal words *hermano* or *hermana,* denoting their higher place in the family hierarchy.[39] Children were also expected to show the utmost deference to older relatives and visitors. The request for a glass of water, for example, elicited a prescribed ritualistic response of handing over the glass and then waiting patiently to see if the visitor wanted another.[40] In some households the child was expected to kneel down and cross his hands during the ritual.[41]

Given the importance placed on *respecto,* it is remarkable that five-year-old Candelaria escaped a whipping the day a tobacco-chewing family acquaintance, known for his crudity, came to pay a visit on a day her father was away and her mother had just finished scrubbing the floors.

Candelaria's father chewed tobacco, but when he did so he always brought in the *cubeta*, or pail, to set beside his chair. Later one of the children would dump it in the arroyo. On this particular day the visitor sat down, periodically spitting tobacco juice directly on the freshly washed floor. Observing the scene, Candelaria quickly rushed outside to fetch the pail. Placing it beside their guest, she pronounced, *Aquí está la cubeta por favor. Escupa en ella. No escupa hasta abajo en el suelo.* ("Here is the pail. Please spit in it. Do not spit on the floor.") At this juncture, Candelaria's mother might have censured her daughter but chose not to. The result was that their guest spat in the pail, not on the floor. Moreover, on subsequent visits he always remembered to ask Candelaria to bring him the *cubeta*.[42]

Hispanic families also emphasized conforming to community mores; personal desires must be weighed against the obligations to the larger secular and religious community. What one's neighbors thought of you counted for something. Thus, *Qué dirá el mundo?*, or "What will the world say?" was a constant refrain in many households.[43] It followed that children were pummeled with the importance of choosing their friends carefully. In this regard, parents possessed a rich treasury of *dichos* to draw upon:

> *El que entre los lobos anda, a aullar se enseña.*
> ("He who walks among the wolves learns to howl.")
> *Una mala res descompone un atajo.*
> ("One bad cow disturbs the whole herd.")
> *Juntate con un bueno te haras mejor que él; juntate con un malo te haras mas malo que él.*
> ("Going with good company, you will become better than him; going with bad company, you will become worse than him.")[44]

As the above suggests, *dichos* also expressed concerns over social status. One woman recalls learning to sew by hand from her grandmother. "She used to make us do tiny, tiny stitches, and if we got big stitches, SLAP! She'd slap our little hands and say, 'You're not sheepherders.'"[45]

Industriousness was another key value. It followed that its counterpart, laziness, was seen as a character defect and a guarantee of *pobreza,* or poverty. As we shall see in the next chapter, Hispanic children, like Anglo children, were expected to perform daily chores and sometimes hard labor on a routine basis. For now, it is sufficient to call attention to this value and note that it was frequently referenced in the *dichos* that laced family conversations. Children were reminded that a sleeping cat failed to catch the mouse, and that a timorous Apache would never acquire a herd of horses.

In this area too, one could learn from another's example. *Cuando mires a tu vecino lavar, por la tuya a remojar,* mothers could be heard saying on occasion. ("When you see your neighbor washing, begin to soak your own.") Whether it was in the daily chores or the value-laden utterances of well-worn proverbs, children could not help but get the point that hard work was an essential ingredient of success.[46]

At the same time, there was a measure of ambivalence with the idea that individuals were the *arquitectos* of their *destinos*. Too many parents had learned firsthand that concentrations of economic power and ethnic discrimination were all too often barriers to upward advancement. Moreover, in an age when the increased importance of education—namely, a high school diploma—was becoming ever more evident, many children strapped for money were forced to drop out of school. Then, too, a degree of cosmic fatalism—expressed in the oft-heard phrase *lo que Dios quiere* ("what God wills")—framed the outlook of some families.[47] Partly for these reasons, but partly too because of community and religious claims on one's personal wealth, most families stopped short of conveying to their children an economic outlook of unbridled individualism. Personal economic advancement had to be balanced with compassion for those less fortunate, a belief one study of a New Mexico village characterizes as *misericordia*.[48] Adelita Chávez recalls that when her family butchered a sheep or cow, "I was all around the neighborhood taking everybody plates." On one occasion she remembers her *madrino* tucking a chicken under her arm and delivering it to the priest. According to another woman, whenever her father butchered a large calf, before cooking it, he "would always cut a piece and divide it among the poor people of town. He always helped the poor people."[49]

Hispanic families, then, were part of a larger ethnosocial network. When the teachings of home converged with those of the community and church, as they often did, the world seemed somehow to cohere. Eduardo Jaramillo remembers,

> We were all in our Sunday best and we'd go to church. And then after church, about half a block from there . . . this lady had a boarding house, and we'd all go there after Mass, to eat there. I can picture it like it was yesterday, LONG tables. My mother would tell us where to sit. The people sitting across the table might have been the Bacas or the Chávezes. By the time we got there, maybe there was no place here or there, so someone would sit here, and someone over there. So there was the come-togetherness—this conversation.[50]

As the days, months, and years piled up, such moments built culture.

The makeup of Magdalena's Anglo families was unique in two respects. First, whereas Navajo and Hispanic families were by definition structurally extended, Anglo families largely migrated into the area as detached nuclear units. Certainly there were exceptions to this pattern, but in the main the generalization holds. Second, Anglos tended to have fewer children than Hispanics. (The data on the Alamo Navajos are unreliable on this score, but the overall population growth after 1920 suggests the same.) In 1920, for instance, the census figures show that in Magdalena the average number of children under eighteen in Hispanic families was 2.84, whereas for Anglos it was 2.28.[51] At first glance, this difference seems a modest one. But when considered alongside the fact that Anglos possessed significantly greater economic resources, the difference looms larger. In larger, poorer families, for instance, the likelihood of children dropping out of school to earn income was greater than in those families less strapped for cash (a subject to be addressed later).

As the myth of the frontier would have it, the West was essentially an Anglo male enterprise. First the trapper and the backwoodsman untethered by the constraints of civilized society entered the untamed wilderness. The story moves on to the Santa Fe bullwhackers, California Argonauts, Indian fighters, and finally, the horseback cowboy. The story gets a little more complicated when one considers Caleb Bingham's painting of the Boone family at Cumberland Gap, the diary entries of women on the Oregon and Santa Fe Trails, or the photographs of Kansas sod-house settlers—for these remind us that women played a central part in the settlement and building of the West.[52] If the myth of the West mainly revolves around men, the reason is simple enough. Stories about chasing wild horses and cattle stampedes are inherently more exciting to some audiences than those of raising children and baking bread. To be sure, migrant women's lives in the West were more constrained than that of men. The ideology of domesticity and conditions on the livestock frontier deemed it so. Many, moreover, regretted moving away from the kin and friends they left behind in more settled communities.[53]

We shall never know how many women settlers in west-central New Mexico found the country unbearable. For Mary Quinn Hobson, it was mainly a matter of her children's welfare. Mary and her two children arrived in Magdalena by train in 1886, after which they immediately pushed on into the high country to join her husband, who was working in a lumber mill camp. Although living conditions were primitive, the view from her cabin door at first made up for it—"the long vista of the green valley between the mountains, the exhilarating air and soft breeze, the fragrance of pine and juniper."

But the beauty soon began to wear thin. Shortly after their arrival, her little girl, Louisa, was attacked by monstrous ants, so vicious they left her covered with blood marks. "That must be the kind," her neighbor informed her, "that chewed old man Erie. He was chopping trees, one fell on him, and the ants chewed him head to foot." One night when logs were burning in the fireplace, she heard a bone-chilling scream just outside the window and saw a mountain lion looking in transfixed by the flames. In the daytime she feared the "great bald eagles that soared over our heads, flapping slowly and mysteriously, or sailing along looking down at our chickens and our children." Then, of course, there were the wolves, grizzlies, and rattlers. When Louisa wandered off into the freezing wilds one January morning, Mary was paralyzed with numbing fear. Kate, her faithful neighbor, sprang into action, alerting the lumber mill to initiate a search party. When Mary, standing in the cabin doorway, saw a lumberjack come off the mountain holding the safe child over his head, she thanked heaven and waved her shawl. Then "the mountains began to spin around me, and I went down, crumpled in a heap of unconsciousness."[54]

Beyond the dangers of nature, there were cultural and educational considerations. One day when Louisa gained permission to go out and play if she promised not to run off, she assured her mother she was a good girl by responding, "*Gracias, soy una buena muchacha.*" One night Mary found herself pleading with her husband to return to Missouri where her father, in a recent letter, offered to help the family make a "fresh start." "You see?" she began, "we simply must *not* stay here permanently and rear two children among Mexicans, Indians, and wild animals. Don't you want them in churches and schools? Don't you want them in an atmosphere of music and refinement?" After a long night of discussion, her husband, who had moved the family several times, conceded that it had been a "hard pull." New Mexico was soon to be just a memory.[55]

But it would be a mistake to judge women's experiences in the West as those of unrelenting loneliness, drudgery, and psychological deprivation. As more than one historian has reminded us, the West was a complicated place where new beginnings frequently redefined inherited conceptions of woman's domain.[56] It did so in several respects. First, some found spiritual sustenance in the dramatic beauty of the landscape and its wildlife. Second, others found a new sense of freedom and independence in the opportunity to break out of the constraints imposed on women by the ideology of domesticity. In this regard, one historian makes the important point that ranch women were not like farm women, a key factor being their access to horses. "Unlike other frontier women who were practically prisoners of their homes, cowgirls were mobile, and therefore not only could master ranch chores and be full partners to their husbands, but also could achieve a new identity."[57] Third, and this point cannot be emphasized enough, longings for the homes left behind were mostly the laments of the first generation of women settlers. Children saw the world completely differently; they knew the landscape as home. The first words out of young Agnes Morley's mouth when she scanned the horizon of their new ranch in Datil Canyon were "That's my mountain." Each of the three children laid claim to a portion of the landscape—a landscape to write stories upon.[58]

In the main, growing up Anglo meant subscribing to the values of rugged individualism, self-reliance, the Protestant work ethic, a deep belief in personal freedom and, all too often, a belief in group superiority.[59] For male children raised on ranches these values were on resplendent display in both their fathers and the cowboys they encountered. In that connection one can only wonder if young males managed to make the insightful distinction that historian Jacqueline M. Moore makes between "cattlemen" and "cowboys." By this account, cattlemen were owners and managers of ranches, built families, were more attuned to "success," and generally were more civic minded. Cowboys, on the other hand, were hirelings, led a more footloose existence, and generally held little interest in building community institutions—such as schools. Still, both had two things in common: a strong individualistic outlook and long experience working with livestock. Thus, ranch children probably tended to admire both their fathers and the cowhands they employed. Indeed, as Moore suggests, as the mythic image of the cowboy became increasingly more burnished in the public mind, cattlemen often forged an image of themselves that merged the cowboy and cattleman personas.[60]

The smoothness of a youngster's passage into a value system that emphasized self-reliance depended in part on the circumstances of the family into which he or she was born. Consider the story of Jack Foote. Foote spent his early years in West Texas. After his father died of gunshot wounds, it fell to his mother alone to raise Jack, his sister, and his brother. One day when he accidentally knocked his younger brother unconscious while roughhousing, his mother sent Jack out to the barn to get the buggy whip.

> I went out and got the buggy whip. And she sat on the bed and whipped me. And I wouldn't dot an i—I mean I didn't cry. I just stood there and gritted my damn teeth and she beat me. She hit me harder than what she intended to. And she cut the blood. So that night I went to bed and

I couldn't pull off my shirt. My mom came in to check us, you know, and wanted to know why I had on this shirt. And I said, well, it stuck, mother, to my back. It hurt her worse than it did me. Why didn't you cry? I said, well, I don't know, mother. So she took me in and bathed me and got that loose—that blood—and pulled my shirt off. Gave me another nightshirt. And so, I never got any more whippings from mother.[61]

After the death of his mother, the children were separated, with Jack, now twelve, going to his uncle and aunt's home. The uncle was all right, "but my aunt was a hellcat—nag, nag, nag, all the time. So I ran away two or three times, and they'd find out where the hell I went, and they'd beg me to come back. And I'd go back a while, then they'd start nagging again." One day, just after Jack had wrenched an ax handle from his aunt to avoid a clubbing, his uncle entered the house angry over the boy having left a quirt lying in the yard all day. Ordered to retrieve the quirt, Jack presented his uncle with it, whereupon his uncle used it as an instrument to whip him. At this point, Jack pulled a pocketknife, "fixin' to put him down about my size." This put an end to the beatings, but the boy had had enough. At the age of fourteen he ran away and never looked back. First, he joined a Wild West show. When the show went into winter quarters, he caught "a hand full of box cars" and landed in New Orleans, where he worked as a janitor in a casino. He spent that Christmas Eve working in a ship's hold loading and dumping barrels of oil sludge in the Mississippi. Soon he was working as a deckhand on a barge headed for St. Louis. But all this was preface to heading back to West Texas, where he would spend his young adult years working on ranches as a cowboy. Finally, one day he saddled his horse and lit out for Magdalena, where he heard they were looking for good cowboys.[62] By the time he rode across the state line, Jack Foote had learned a thing or two about self-reliance and survival, values he would pass on to another generation.

Children and the Supernatural

Religion serves a number of functions. By creating a mythic order out of seeming chaos, it gives meaning and coherence to human existence; it offers an explanation for and a shield against the terrors of life, including a child's death; and it offers the possibility of transcending the purely material in the pursuit of spiritual fulfillment. Beyond these commonalities, some religious traditions are unique for the role they play in reifying a culture's social institutions and ideological outlook, the emphasis they place on physical wellness or the promise of an afterlife, or the attention they give to articulating a code of moral conduct. In the cultural mix of New Mexico, where life could be both harsh and unforgiving—where drought, death, and social conflict stalked the land—the certitudes of religious belief and ritual often exerted an immense influence over the lives of adults and children alike.

When the mostly Protestant Anglos moved into the largely "Mexican," Catholic Magdalena, they brought with them not only their bibles and faith but also a deep sense of religious superiority. On a personal level, religion was a great source of comfort and joy and a natural component of children's upbringing. During the Hobson family's brief stay outside of the "rip-roaring cattle town" of Magdalena, one of the few consolations was that the family could attend the log cabin Methodist church regularly. "And an organ—we had an organ! Gol-lee! I was so glad when they asked me to play it!" The highlight, however, came during the Christmas program, when Mary Hobson saw her little Louisa lifted up onto the organ, where to the accompaniment of her mother, the child sang:

> Beautiful the little hands
> That fulfill the Lord's commands,
> Beautiful the little eyes,
> Kindled with light from the skies.[63]

Within the first two decades of the twentieth century, Presbyterians, Episcopalians, Methodists, and Baptists were all vying for Protestant souls, although for most, doctrinal differences were probably a matter of little consequence in the face of the larger number of Catholics.[64]

The spirit of Protestantism bore in on children's consciousness from several directions: church sermons, Sunday schools, camp meetings, and home instruction.[65] The grandson of John Mactavish, a staunch Presbyterian, recalls that his grandfather nightly gathered three generations of the family together in the "big house" for bible reading, prayers, and hymn singing. Norman Cleaveland, the grandson of Ada Morley, recalls that his grandmother was a constant source of religious instruction. He recalls one day leafing through an illustrated copy of Dante's *Inferno*. "I can remember thumbing through that and seeing what was in store for me if I didn't mind my manners." Another memory was lying on his back "watching these big clouds go by, sure that God was on one of them. . . . He was keeping an eye on me. I'd better watch out. He'd catch me on something." Thus even on remote ranches, where church attendance was rare, religion could still be a factor in children's upbringing. A son whose father was one of the region's largest ranchers recalls that his mother read to the children from the bible nearly every night. Indeed, the religious impulse was so strong that even though the family was Protestant, she periodically took the children for services at a Hispanic neighbor's ranch, where a small chapel existed. When his mother moved the children to town for schooling, church attendance became routine.[66]

On the scattered ranches of cow country, most religious devotion appears to have taken the form of bible reading and prayer recitation in lantern-lit rooms before children were tucked into bed. Occasionally, however, children's religious education benefited from itinerate cowboy preachers who rode horseback from ranch to ranch on behalf of the gospel. When a certain Reverend Moody visited the Field ranch, Bessie Field recalls he taught the children songs as he worked a small accordion and her mother played the harmonica. From his saddlebags he passed out cards with pictures of Mary, Jesus, and the disciples. Staying overnight at the ranch, Moody even found time to bless Bessie's calf. "We took that little calf down to the tank and asked Reverend Moody to baptize her like they baptized my mother in Missouri." The reverend obliged the request and gave the calf a name from the bible: Esther. Bessie observes, "Mama at that time was a Baptist and father was a Catholic. But my father never followed his religion at all. He didn't have any particular thing about religion. He was just a cowboy, and he worked hard with his cattle. He worked hard keeping his family with shoes and clothes."[67]

Many ranchers were lukewarm on religion. One old rancher recalls, "Most of the cowboys that I knew, they don't know anything about the Bible and churches."[68] But there were exceptions. Perhaps the most notable one was the Dub and Beulah Evans family. Baptists from West Texas, the Evanses played an active role in the organization of revival meetings, which by the 1920s were an annual event held on the outskirts of Magdalena. Both religious and social gatherings, camp meetings were opportunities for singing, praying, and seeing old friends. It was also an opportunity for cowboy preachers to conjure up sermons that made a direct connection between the bible and the cattlemen's more basic concerns. These kinds of connections are reflected in the writings of Joe Evans, a West Texas rancher-preacher who, as brother to Dub Evans, was a frequent visitor in New Mexico ranch circles. In "Abraham—God's Cowman Partner," Evans argued that a close reading of Genesis showed that next to humans, God's two most important creations were grass and cattle. According to Evans, in chapter 18 of Genesis, "when the Lord and two angels came to Abraham's cow camp," he instructed Sarah to fix dinner for their guests while he "ran unto the herd and fetched a tender calf, the best he had." Because the scriptures speak of all this being done with great "haste," Evans was convinced that Sarah served his guests nothing less than T-bone steaks. "They didn't have the time for a beef roast or bar-b-que." Moving to contemporary concerns, Evans pitched the Christian message at a level difficult to resist. In the "Cowman's Prayer" the booted supplicant prays,

> As you, O! Lord, my herd behold
> They represent a stack of gold.
> I think at least ten cents a pound
> Should be the price the whole year round.[69]

Most ranchers, however, remained cynical about God's role in the cattle business. Thus, one old rancher still recalls his father's bitterly sarcastic comment about a wealthy rancher known for his liberal contributions to the Methodist Church: "He got all the rain because the son-of-a-bitch built a church."[70]

The children of the Pie Town region were the most exposed to religious influences. In an area heavily settled by Texans, Baptists were the largest group, although Methodists and followers of the Church of Nazarene were well represented. Given the distance between homesteads and the primitive state of transportation, outlying families frequently gathered in schools or ranch houses regardless of their church affiliations, a pattern that gave rise to a general religious outlook that was (within Protestant boundaries) at once fundamentalist and ecumenical. Between hearing the Lord's word preached "right from the bible," praying, hymn singing, and "dinner on the ground," Sunday worship was frequently an all-day affair. Periodic revivals also ratcheted up religious enthusiasm.[71] Many Pie Town children, it appears, soaked up the spirit of plain-spoken, primitive Protestantism, sometimes beginning their spiritual journey by being baptized in a rancher's stock tank. One Pie Town settler will never forget her first church service, where she witnessed the scene of a four-year-old boy "puffing clouds of smoke from a huge pipe while the preacher brought the word of God to the small congregation of the Mountain peoples." Another Pie Town mother recalls how the family walked 3 miles to church until the birth of her son, whereupon they rode horseback. "I would put a pillow in front of me on the horse, then lay Douglas on the pillow. He grew up going to church horseback." It took: "He now preaches the good news about Jesus."[72]

But for at least one child, it was not a bible-thumping preacher that defined the essence of the spiritual realm but rather the land itself—the dramatic vistas, the scent of desert flowers, the blazing sunsets. "I guess I was kind of a strange child in a lot of ways," one old ranch woman recollects. Riding for miles on her favorite horse, she would drink in the landscape and consider the wonder of it all. "I had lots of thoughts I still have. But it seemed like there was something other than just everyday life to me. I mean I don't like to talk about it, but I don't believe too much in the bible per se, you know. I really don't, word for word. And I haven't since I was real small." Still, the young girl sensed a transcendent "presence" upon the land: "Yeah, I sensed something." What that something was, she could not be certain. Perhaps all life was part of a grand scheme. She even wondered about the possibility of reincarnation. "I used to wander way out away from the house, you know, and just wander. And I didn't want anybody around. I didn't think about it. I did. I loved it."[73]

For Hispanic children, nearly all raised Catholic, the religious experience was altogether different. Whereas frontier Protestantism was characterized by democratic localism, New Mexico Catholics were inheritors of a religious tradition centuries old in its hierarchical structure, doctrinal outlook, and ritual prescriptions.[74] Moreover, given the church's entanglement with all things familial and social, it is little wonder that on a day-to-day basis, Hispanic children were probably more shaped by their religion than most Anglos. In Magdalena the center of Catholic life was the Church of St. Mary Magdalene, which in the town's heyday had a full-time priest. As for churches in the outlying communities, the priest might appear once or twice a month. Occasionally, priests visited distant ranches with small chapels to baptize babies, hear confessions, conduct mass, perform marriages, and pray for those recently deceased.[75]

In learning to be Catholic, some children may have discerned that their mothers' attachment to the church was more pronounced than their fathers'.[76] Indeed, other than the local priest, it fell mainly to mothers and grandmothers to inculcate children with the precepts and worldview of the one true faith. "We prayed the rosary every night," one Kelly woman remembers. Another woman recalls how when her grandmother took her every morning to church, "she'd kneel down before she'd get inside—kneel all the way in that long black skirt. She'd go kneeling all the way to the altar." Also part of her memory is the sound of the priest coming from the rear of the church and her grandmother's admonition not to look back. But the temptation was simply too great. "I'd hear the Father come in—shoosh,

shoosh, with the long skirt—and I'd look. I always had to look back. And of course my grandmother pinched me."[77]

The most important event in the young Hispanic's religious development was First Communion. Preparing for the ritual event entailed committing to memory the central articles of the Catholic faith as embodied in the Baltimore Catechism and various prayers, including the "Lord's Prayer," the "Apostles' Creed," and the rosary ritual.[78] Instruction in these areas might come from the priest himself, but in most instances the training was entrusted to women who taught classes either at the church or in their homes. On ranches, the responsibility often fell entirely on the family, usually the mother. One woman recalls her mother painstakingly teaching her the catechism and prayers. Each day there was something new to commit to memory. "I would stand in the door, and Mama would catch me by surprise. '*Reza el Padre Nuestro.*' I had to repeat the whole thing, the whole 'Our Father.'" While making the beds, sweeping the floors, or washing the dishes, the girl rehearsed her responses to the queries the priest might put to her on the upcoming day. Who is God? Who made you? What purpose do you have in the world? For some, the scripted responses were no more than that; for others the words opened up a world of faith and obligation that would sustain them the rest of their lives.[79]

As the day of the ritual approached, children had different emotions. Lorenzo Ortega ran away rather than undergo the ritual. "I took off from the house. I didn't go. So you can imagine how upset my mother was. . . . I think I was nervous and I couldn't go THROUGH with it." Later, when he completed it at the age of twelve, there was the additional embarrassment of being the oldest in his class. Beyond the fear of forgetting the words to the "Apostles' Creed," some worried about how they would survive the priest's interrogation on essential points of church doctrine. Then there was the anxiety of making their first confession to the priest—an obligatory act carried out in conjunction with the ceremony. Usually on the evening before taking the "consecrated host," they made their first confession. For many it was a struggle to come up with a heartfelt example of sin. Small acts of disobedience, disrespect, or lying were the normal sins confessed by a seven- or eight-year-old. One year, the rumor spread through the ranks of the children that an inadequate confession would result in the priest shoving a hot, boiled egg in their mouths. One can barely imagine the extent of Carlotta Madril's fears, age five, when her mother forced her to undergo the experience. The priest, she remembers, had on a purple robe and a cap. "When I saw him—ugh!" When Carlotta burst into tears, the priest "took

Lucianita Pino (on the left) and friends on First Communion day, ca. 1940. (Courtesy of Magdalena Public Library.)

me on his lap. So my first confession was in the priest's lap." The good news was that the priest refrained from sticking an egg in her mouth. The bad news was that she had to return the next year. At five years old, the priest declared her too young to make her First Communion.[80]

But many children looked forward to this rite of passage with excitement. One man claims that making his First Communion was the happiest moment of his young life. "I was lookin' forward to it. I was very dedicated to religion." The care mothers took with their children's attire signaled the importance of the occasion. "I remember very distinctly," recalls another. "The style of pants, they just came below the knee with a buckle. Of course we wore the white shirt. The material . . . under the collar, kind of puffed out under your chin—just like a tie." He also remembers having a small, white handkerchief with his initials embroidered on the corner. Candelaria García recalls that her mother cut up her silk wedding dress, also using the veil, to fashion her daughter's dress for the special day. The only

FAMILY AND RELIGION : 51

store-bought items were the white stockings and the black shoes. "I was nervous at first that I might do something wrong," continues Candelaria, "but in another way I was happy because I was going to receive God for the first time in the form of bread—you know, in a consecrated host."[81]

In addition to their First Communion, other aspects of Catholicism also bore in on the children's consciousness. One of these was the attention paid to saints. As intermediaries between God and believers, saints had it in their power to protect, guide, or answer the prayers of devoted supplicants. For Hispanics, Mary, the Blessed Mother of Jesus, reigned supreme in this regard. Among the other saints most honored were San Antonio, San Lorenzo, and San Isidro.[82] The importance of saints was brought home to children in various ways. The daughter of a Kelly miner recalls that her father always carried a small statue of Santo Niño and a little box of dimes in his lunch-bucket. "At the end of the day, he'd open the bucket and say: 'Oh, look what the Santo Niño brought.'" But saints were capable of bestowing much larger gifts than small coins. One woman recalls:

> I still remember one time when I was very young and still living at the ranch. We had a bad drought at one time. We would get together and pray for rain as a family. The day before, my mother said, "Tomorrow after we get our things done here at home, we are going to go out and pray for rain." So we took a statue of our Blessed Mother and we walked praying the rosary out in the field. I still remember. This doesn't even sound true. It's so vivid in my mind. There were no clouds when we first started out. We walked quite a distance and we came back home. We hadn't been home but maybe ten minutes when it started to rain. To me that was sort of like a miracle that happened. It made my faith grow.

Along a similar vein, in Santa Rita every June 15 villagers made a procession and moved from garden to garden carrying a statue of San Isidro, praying for the crops to grow. Along the way they sang hymns such as "Corazón Santo" and "Ave María."[83]

To the extent there was religious skepticism, it nearly always resided with the men. Looking back, Alfredo Bustamante observes that his father's participation in church rituals was "because of habit, not because of conviction." Perhaps out of deference to the boy's mother, he "never said anything against the Church but he was so skeptical about all kinds of superstitions and beliefs that I think in his heart he was very skeptical about all kinds of teaching of the Catholic Church—but he never uttered it." Somehow his father's disposition rubbed off on his son. When the archbishop came from

Santa Fe to Quemado—an extraordinary event given the fact that a priest only made it to the village three times a year—ten-year-old Alfredo refused to join in the procession to kiss the archbishop's ring. "My dad took me by the hand and dragged me over there and oh golly I almost puked. But he made me do it you see. . . . He had to drag me over there kicking and screaming to kiss the bishop's ring." Years later, when the bishop returned, Alfredo joined the procession, but "when he put his hand up for me to kiss it, I flung it aside and went on." In time, he would regret the act. "You shouldn't insult anybody like that."[84]

Because of her grandfather, growing up Catholic for Esther Peralta was an intellectual as well as a religious experience. Whereas most children were taught to memorize prayers and the catechism, Esther's grandfather insisted that the children of the household reflect critically on church teachings. With respect to confession, for instance, he insisted the ritual was just that—a ritual.

> He would say, there's people that live without churches in places where there is no church. Do you think those people have to carry their sins until they find a priest? No, God is where you are and confession is yours. You don't have to worry if we didn't go to Magdalena this week and feel guilty. No, because God was here. The ritual is that we love community and we like to go. But religion didn't stop because we didn't go to church. He would say to us, take a moment and think. Forgiveness is for YOU to ask for. You didn't have to go and ask the priest to give you penance. You do it. YOU feel your penance. If you felt you were wrong, your penance will be YOURS—you with your conscience.

On one occasion, Esther came home after confession worried that she had forgotten to use the words, "Bless me father for I have sinned." Her grandfather's response put her at ease. "It doesn't MATTER. What did you go for? To ask God to forgive. . . . If you say it and feel it, already you know you did well."[85]

To be sure, children understood religion at different levels. Margarita García remembers how she witnessed God's power to exact retribution against the sinful, in this instance against none other than banker-businessman John Mactavish. In the midst of the Great Depression, when Mactavish announced that the bank was broke, many Hispanics, whose savings were wiped out, suspected the old man was holding money back. Only five or six years old, Margarita recalls the moment when Herman Contreras came to the house and urged her father to join him in confronting Mactavish with pistols, a proposal to which her mother took immediate exception. There was no need for violence, her mother insisted. "He [Mactavish] will have suffering. God will punish him. What he has taken from your kids' mouths, he will have to suffer with his hands." In the face of his wife's objections, Margarita's father decided against the plan. (Contreras later claimed he got his money by threatening Mactavish within an inch of his life.) But the girl could not forget her mother's prediction. Could it in fact be true that the banker would "suffer with his hands"? Over the course of time the girl would go down to Mactavish's store to buy candy, always looking at his hands "to see if God had really punished him. I would look and look, just to see him, just to see his hands." Then one day she noticed that his hands were "really getting crooked." Rushing home, she remembers announcing, "Mother, God DID punish him. Look at his hands. He can't pick up a dime." In the youngster's mind the connective association between the old man's knotted knuckles and divine justice was self-evident.[86]

Children's capacity to misread some aspect of church doctrine or practice is nowhere better illustrated than in Juan Jaramillo's recollection of how he overstepped his bounds when serving as an altar boy under Father Stoffel. The situation arose one morning when, just prior to mass, the priest was called away to take confession and administer last rites to a dying man. Before rushing from the church, Father Stoffel instructed Juan and the other altar boy, Willie, to make certain everything was in order for the service. But shortly afterward, an unexpected crisis arose. A woman coming into the church pointed out that there was no Holy Water in the *pila*. Worse yet, the boys discovered, there was no water blessed by the priest in the small barrel kept in reserve. At this point, Juan concluded there was only one thing to do: he must bless some water in the priest's absence. He had observed the ritual numerous times. So while Willie filled the barrel with tap water, Juan slipped into Father Stoffel's robe, acquired a pinch of salt, and then uttered the appropriate words. The blessing completed, the boys filled the *pila* and replaced the newly filled barrel in the proper location. Shortly after that, Father Stoffel returned and conducted the mass. It was a month or so later that Juan's ingenuity was revealed. Ironically, it was the same woman who entered the church complaining—this time to the Father—that there was no Holy Water. After the Holy Water was fetched, the now suspicious priest inquired of the boys why the previous supply had lasted two months. "And Willie had to open his mouth. He says Father, you remember when you went to confess [that man]. Well, there wasn't any, but Juan blessed some."

The good father was not pleased. Turning to Juan: "YOU! YOU blessed the water?" Juan, in turn, conjured up the best response he could think of: "I says, Father, when you weren't here and you says to help you when you're not here. Well we have to do it. Father, don't get mad. You're the first one kickin' about it. You already baptized five kids and the people have been using it every day. Nobody has kicked—only YOU. He says, GO! Ring the bell! Go! We was afraid. We didn't say anything." It was just as mass was beginning, when the good father made the mistake of glancing over at his two altar boys. "And I don't know how he looked at me, but he couldn't hold it. He started laughing. And he said, both of you, go to the sacristy. So we got out of there. And I says to Willie, boy, he's going to be mad when he gets out of there." As it turned out, Father Stoffel was no longer upset. On further reflection the priest admitted that Juan had a good point: "I'm the only one that's kicking about it."[87]

Some consideration must be given to the role of superstition in children's lives. Some might argue, of course, that all religion is, to a large extent, superstition. But our attention here is on those beliefs and practices that were for the most part aberrational or offshoots from the mainstream of religious belief. In the instance of Hispanics, it was the inheritance of centuries-old New Mexico folk beliefs. One of the region's oldest folk superstitions was that of La Llorona. As the story was told, La Llorona was an old woman mourning for her lost or dead children. While crying, the legend goes, she wandered the canyons and arroyos at night, the sounds of her eerie wailing carried on the winds circling around darkened adobe houses. Although few in the Magdalena area claim to have actually seen the apparition, some reported hearing her pitiful cries while lying in bed at night or walking home after dark. One woman says, "She was a woman with long hair. She'd come out of the arroyo every night and go around crying. I guess she was a soul in torment. Of course, if you were bad she'd get you. It was scary."[88] But the story of La Llorona seems not to have resonated in the Magdalena area the way it did elsewhere. As one woman explains, because of the town's late settlement, "everything was new and fresh." Thus, La Llorona appears to have functioned there more as a convenient device available to parents to enforce curfews than a deeply held folk belief.[89]

Similarly, western Socorro and Catron Counties were not centers for Hispanic belief in *brujas*—witches who used their powers for evil ends.[90] Still, children grew up hearing stories. There was the *bruja* who brought an old man a bowl of rice pudding that shortly turned into a mass of worms. There was also the story of the several men living south of Datil who, after identifying an old woman as a witch, proceeded to carry out a ritualistic removal of the supposed threat. They selected three men with the name of John who, after putting their clothes on backward, tied the accused up "and beat the hell out of her." Still another involved Magdalena's night watchman, who, while making his rounds, saw a chicken suddenly appear before him. Thinking it strange, he was just about to kill it with the butt of his rifle when the bird spoke to him: "Don't kill me. It's your *comadre*." Disregarding the appeal, he quickly killed the chicken. The next morning he learned that about the same time he had killed the chicken, a woman widely suspected of being a *bruja* dropped dead at the town dance.[91]

In contrast, the superstition of *mal ojo*, or the evil eye, had more local currency. *Mal ojo* involved the power of some persons (whether deliberately or not) to cast an evil spell on individuals. Children, especially babies, were prone to the evil eye, and victims of it became very sick and might even die. Thus, when a newborn was seriously ill, Hispanics of a superstitious bent immediately began considering who might have cast the spell. There were different ways of discerning this. One was to crack an egg and look in the yoke for an image of the guilty party's face. Others contended that the image would show through a whole egg placed under the bed of the sick child. Frequently, an individual who had looked too admiringly at the child, perhaps out of jealousy, was believed to be the source of the spell. When the spell-caster was identified (usually a woman), she was brought to the house to perform the prescribed ritual for erasing the curse: spitting on the child's forehead and making the sign of the cross.[92]

Sometimes even those who put little stock in superstition felt compelled to go along with such rituals in order to prevent bad feelings and allay suspicions. Candelaria García recalls the time when as a young girl she was asked to go the extra mile to satisfy a distraught family's suspicion that she was the source of their child's sickness. The day before, Candelaria had gone to their home and lavishly praised the baby's beauty. The next day, when the baby took sick, the mother appeared at the García's door suggesting that the girl had brought harm to the child.

> She wanted me to come over to their house to . . . make up for what I had done, what I had been accused of. And so my mother said that I should go, even though my mother was not at all superstitious and knew that I had nothing to do with the sickness of the child. And so I went over to the house, and then I made saliva on my finger and I made the sign of the cross on the child's forehead. And then they asked me to actually get into bed with the child and hold it. And they wrapped the child in two or

three blankets, and I laid down with it. I felt terrible about doing it, about being in bed for that reason. But my mother said that I should do it, so I did it. And after a while the child went to the bathroom in the blankets. And then it began to feel better and a brightness came into the baby's eyes again and they thought for that reason that I had removed the spell.

Thus, there were times superstitions had to be accommodated, as one woman explains, "to keep peace among friends."[93]

In the Navajo language there is no word for "religion." The reason for this is that for traditional Navajos all realms of the natural world and daily life are to some extent permeated with the supernatural. As noted earlier, the concept *hózhó,* or harmony, is central in the Navajo worldview. When both the supernatural and the human relationships are in harmonious balance, life is good. The sheep and horses reproduce, the corn grows tall, and family relations are peaceful. However, when disharmony prevails, when some violation of the supernatural order occurs, dangerous forces are unleashed, posing a grave risk to the individual's physical and psychological well-being. Thus, to maintain the proper order of things, individual Navajos rely upon a wealth of rituals, songs, and prayers handed down by the Holy People and enshrined in the mythological past of the *Diné*. In drawing upon these sources of supernatural knowledge, Navajos strive, as the prayer says, "to walk in beauty."[94]

On a pragmatic level, the overall emphasis of Navajo spirituality is on the avoidance of and curing of sickness. As traditional Navajos see it, at the root of nearly all ailments are supernatural causes. First, although contact with bears, coyotes, snakes, and deer is natural, under certain circumstances these and other animals can pose a serious threat to one's health. Dreaming of an animal, being attacked by it, and violating prescribed hunting rituals are especially dangerous. Second, all manner of taboos govern Navajo behavior, the breach of which can cause serious harm. As we have already seen, these shape pregnant mothers' behavior as well as young children's upbringing. In fact, a whole range of "thou shalt nots" shapes behavior throughout one's life, ranging from not telling Coyote stories in the summer to not "cussing the wind." Finally, Navajos have long believed that sickness can be brought on by witchery. Witches, as one scholar explains it, "murder their nearest and dearest friends and relatives, practice incest, handle corpses freely, robbing them of their burial jewels and using parts of their bodies for their incantations." Like their northern brethren, Alamo Navajos have traditionally taken great care to bury hair and nail clippings to deny witches items through which to work their malignant power.[95]

Traditional Navajos suffering from a physical or mental disorder seek a cure by having a "sing" or ceremony conducted for them. One of the unique aspects of Navajo spirituality is its ritual complexity. (By one account, the Navajos had at one point some thirty-five major ceremonies.) The treatment of the stricken individual's ailment normally begins with a "hand trembler's" diagnosis of the particular malady to be treated. Sometimes working themselves into a trancelike state, hand tremblers divine the origin or source of the problem and then recommend the appropriate ceremony to be "put on" the patient. Because sings normally last from one to four days and may call for chanting by memory thousands of lines from myths and prayers, as well as the knowledge of specialized rituals such as sand paintings, singers (more commonly known as medicine men) are seldom able to perform more than one or two kinds of the many ceremonies.[96]

This leads to an all-important point with respect to the Alamo Navajos. Because the Alamo Navajos were a small, isolated band, for all practical purposes cut off from the main branch of the *Diné*, and because Navajo spirituality, to function fully, requires the existence of numerous singers, each one a specialist, the Alamo Navajo band never had access to the full range of Navajo ceremonies. To be sure, the band had two or three practicing singers. Elders, moreover, offered corn pollen to the morning sun, sang sweat-lodge songs, and told stories of Changing Woman.[97] But taken together, the small number of ceremonies available to the community fell short of the full-blown system up north. One consequence of this was that the Alamo Navajo band was particularly vulnerable to Christian missionaries.

Still, in the early twentieth century many Alamo Navajo children grew up acquiring knowledge of and appreciation for the general Navajo outlook, observing and participating in ceremonies conducted not only by local singers but also by singers imported from other communities such as Ramah, Fort Wingate, and Cañoncito.[98] Older members of the Alamo band have distinct memories of several ceremonies being conducted in their community—Evil Way, Enemy Way, and *Kinaaldá*—although it appears others were occasionally performed as well.[99] One woman says that as a child, "I had a lot of singing done on me. I was told it was sacred and it was very meaningful and important to have these singings done for me." On one occasion, "The medicine man made sand paintings resembling the moon, saying they would heal me." Margaret Secatero recalls,

> I somehow got sick so they had a sing for me and I was told not to eat certain parts of sheep or goat's meat. And a little round shell with a hole

was tied to the string for my bun. So every morning my mother tied my bun, made sure I wear all the time. And later I forgot about it when we went herding sheep and I was playing around I lost it. My mother made me look for it. I look everywhere, started from the sheep corral to where we played but I couldn't find it. I was so scared and I was crying. So the next few days my grandmother and mother had the medicine man. And they had a sing over me. I remember staying up all night and the medicine man cook some kind of mix weed and small bits of different kinds of meat and I had to eat it. That was because I lost a little shell. And he told me to go ahead and eat all parts of sheep.[100]

The clearest memories are of *'Anaa'jís*, or Enemy Way, commonly associated with *Ndáá'*, popularly known as the "Squaw Dance" because of the dancing and social activities carried on simultaneously with the Enemy Way rituals. Enemy Way was performed over four days and nights to cure sickness induced by having contact with the dead or with an enemy. Returning warriors, or individuals exposed to ancient ruins (where ghost spirits are thought to linger), are the most likely ones to require the ceremony. One Alamo Navajo man recalls attending a ceremonial gathering in Ramah when the sickness hit him. Two days into the ceremony he was struck with terrible cramping in his legs. "So I went over to the main area where they were cooking and I told some of the people there something happened to my legs." Those who knew about the ceremony told him that this frequently happened to someone who had been in contact with Anasazi ruins. He explains, "Somehow I was in contact with them. Maybe I've been to the area where they used to live, or maybe I pick up some of their pottery, or maybe I just walked over something they used." In any event, it was decided he should join the balance of the ceremony as a patient. He did, and the pain left him.[101]

But sometimes the ceremonies failed. When the flu epidemic of 1918–1919 struck the Alamo Navajo population, all the curative rituals in the community's arsenal failed to make much difference. Those who lived through the period recall that people were dying everywhere.[102] Bessie Baca, an Anglo woman who later married a local Navajo, would never forget the night she attended a ceremony for a sick child, probably in the 1930s.

They built this new hogan where they brought that little sick boy. They laid him nude on the floor. And after a while I went to the grandparents of the little boy and asked them if I might hold the baby—pick it up off the ground. I didn't like to see it lying on the dirt. So I went in and picked him up. Oh, he was burning up with fever—my God, I hadn't any idea. It was terrible. He was so near death. So I asked for a bowl of cold water and I bathed his face. They all sat lookin'—watchin' me to see what I was doin'. I bathed his face. I could gather from the pulse that he was runnin' a temperature about 104. He was a little bitty kid; he was just learnin' to walk. He died in my arms. I closed his eyes. He didn't have nothin' on but the blanket around him. I had to break down and cry. I felt horrible that I couldn't have taken him to a hospital. If they would've consented I would have taken my car immediately and taken him myself to Dr. Peppers at the Indian school hospital—is what I would have done. But they wouldn't consent. The husband—they wouldn't consent at all.

Nels and Ida Field, Bessie's parents, provided the materials for the casket, and Bessie furnished the cloth to line it. At the burial service, scripture was read from the bible. "There wasn't anybody that went but the ones that buried him. Folks didn't go. I've often wondered because of my holding that boy they didn't go to the funeral. Do you suppose?"[103]

Besides having medicine men sing over them, Navajo youth also grew up hearing tales of witchery and the *yenaldlooshi*, commonly translated as skinwalkers or wolf men. As practitioners of witchcraft, skinwalkers are the antithesis of the healing medicine man or singer. In a culture where elaborate ceremonial activities are devoted to promoting order, harmony, and good health, skinwalkers symbolize the opposite—chaos and sickness. Dressed in coyote skins, skinwalkers are said to attack their victims in several ways: blowing corpse dust through hogan smoke holes, shooting small foreign objects into the body, using some representation of the person—hair clippings or a photograph—through which to channel their witchery. Because skinwalkers are most active in the night, most Navajos grow up having an exorbitant fear of the dark.[104]

Fear of skinwalkers was generally common among the Alamo Navajos. Among those stories the renowned anthropologist Clyde Kluckhohn collected for his *Navajo Witchcraft*, published in 1944, were two witchcraft stories from the Alamo Navajo region. One of Kluckhohn's informants claimed that a group of Navajos in the area once caught and burned a skinwalker on a pile of logs 8 feet high. On another occasion an Alamo Navajo man "shot a woman dressed like a wolf in the rump. The very next day a woman died there [Alamo]. And they say she had a gunshot wound in the rump." Perhaps the following story, still told on the reservation, is another version of the second story, or perhaps a combination of both.

See, these two hunters were hunting up there east of the reservation. They were separated from their camp. And these persons was walking. And as they was walking along there was a lot of trees, like these small cedar trees. And they had no idea that there was somebody behind it. Then all of the sudden they saw a lady, half-dressed from the waist down, nothing but animal on top, wolf or coyote from the waist up. The hair went straight down. A lot of jewels on herself, bracelets and rings. All of a sudden this lady started beggin' the hunters. Please don't tell anybody. Please don't kill me. This hunter was about to shoot that lady, and that lady start to beg him not to shoot. I don't know what happened. Maybe he heard some kind of stories about that—if he see one of those with a naked eye somewhere, all you do is just shoot it. Don't let it go. He know that story. So what he did was he shot that lady there. Killed that lady. And then what he did was built a big bonfire and threw that lady in and burned her up.[105]

Stories of witchery were passed on generation to generation, fueling children's fears well beyond the 1940s. "I was even afraid to step outside the hogan at night because I feared that there was something waiting for me," one man recalls. Another man grew up hearing from his parents that he should always treat others with politeness, partly as protection against witchcraft. "They used to say that you should not get mad at any person. Let them say what they have to say, but do not say anything to them. When you leave them they will do something which the witchcraft people do. They do this to get even with you."[106]

Growing up Navajo, Hispanic, or Anglo in west-central New Mexico in the early twentieth century was a culturally distinct experience. By any measure, being reared by Anglo, English-speaking, Protestant homesteaders was simply not the same as being raised by a Hispanic, Spanish-speaking, Catholic family living in Magdalena. However, as different as the cultural influences were on Hispanic and Anglo children, they paled in comparison with those shaping the Navajo children, where definitions of kinship, gender roles, and the supernatural were outside the Euro-Christian tradition. Still, to the extent that Anglo, Hispanic, and Navajo children internalized the values, knowledge, language, religious worldviews, and stories of their elders, they emerged as genuine cultural beings, possessing distinct ways of knowing and acting upon the world around them.

The above is not meant to argue that culture was destiny. First, as we have already observed, the disparities in families' economic resources and social class consciousness were important aspects of growing up Anglo and Hispanic, although in the latter case Catholic values probably ameliorated the differences somewhat. In the material realm, Alamo Navajo children, of course, suffered the most. Second, intragroup occupational differences and settlement patterns complicate a purely cultural interpretation. The Anglo children of Pie Town farmers and Magdalena cattle ranchers were not exactly cut from the same cultural cloth, just as the children of Hispanic sheepherders and miners were not. Finally, we should remember that culture is not race—a distinction some found difficult to make on the "racial frontier" of west-central New Mexico, where assumptions about race, race hierarchy, and culture were sometimes hopelessly intertwined. As we shall see in subsequent chapters, when these misunderstandings interacted with national agendas, institutional policies, and power relations, children's attempt to negotiate the ethnocultural landscape was a precarious undertaking.

But we get ahead of ourselves. Before bringing the three groups together, we shall mostly keep them apart as we explore other domains of their cultural experience.

CHAPTER TWO

WORK AND PLAY

"Put a kid on a horse" was a frequently heard refrain in frontier New Mexico. This explains why five-year-old Norman Cleaveland found himself one day in 1906 riding an old horse 3 miles to the Datil Post Office to fetch mail for his grandmother, Ada Morley. He had made the trip before, but this day turned out to be unusual. As Cleaveland later recalled, "I spotted a six-shooter, complete with holster and belt, lying alongside the road. I slid off old Block and pounced on my find—beside myself with excitement at the thought of having a six-shooter for my very own. To me that was the most desirable thing in the world." Knowing that his grandmother would confiscate the gun if she knew about it, when Norman returned to the ranch he rode in from behind the barn and stashed his miraculous prize in the hay. In the coming days he would slip away to the barn, retrieve the six-shooter, and play at fending off Apache raids and quick-draw gunslingers. The boy knew better than to pull the trigger; besides the report giving away his secret, he had seen the way pistols could kick when the cowboys fired them. So he reveled in his imaginary world of fighting off all manner of western varmints—that is until a sister and cousin caught him with the pistol and reported the news to Grandmother Morley, who promptly took away the weapon.

To lessen Norman's despondency over the loss of his Colt 45, Ada Morley announced that she would order him a Daisy Air Rifle from the Montgomery Ward Catalogue. Brightened by the news, he quickly agreed to the precondition that he would shoot only at targets such as tin cans and fence posts; living objects must never enter the rifle's sights. (Ada Morley was known widely for her opposition to animal cruelty.) After the rifle arrived, and Norman was instructed by one of the working cowboys on safety, he ventured off to shoot at a few fence posts. He was hardly out of sight, however, "when what should hop out onto the road and pause in front of me but a cottontail rabbit. Without hesitation I aimed and fired and was overwhelmed with excitement when I knocked off the major portion of the rabbit's tail." Momentarily forgetting his pledge, Norman bolted for the house to show everyone what a superb marksman he was. "My joy was short-lived. Granny descended on me in all her wrath." Once again, the boy lost his weapon. But all was not lost. After an appropriate period, Norman's uncle, Ray Morley, lifted the boy upon his saddle and rode a mile or so away from the ranch house. "Here he broke out a single shot 22 rifle. After further instructions, I went forth to ping at tin cans, bottles, and fence posts. Never did I shoot at any living thing."[1]

In several ways, Norman Cleaveland's story serves as a fitting introduction to the subject of work and play. First, it suggests just one of the ways children at a tender age were expected to be useful, productive persons in the frontier environment. "Put a kid on a horse" was but the opening refrain of a western outlook that viewed children's labor as essential to a family's economic status, even its very survival. Second, it illustrates how in the West the realms of work and play were often intertwined. It was no doubt exciting enough for the errand-running five-year-old to ride a horse 3 miles to the post office, and it became all the more so when he found the six-shooter, which then served as a prop for imaginary standoffs with pistol-packing varmints. Third, the boy's experience reminds us that in the West both work and play were often suffused with dangerous possibilities. Even if one removes the six-shooter from the story, there is still the fact that a five-year-old was being sent alone some distance on a horse, not always the most predictable of animals.

Although Norman's story is revealing, it is only suggestive. It tells us nothing, for instance, about the role class played in the realms of work and play. Growing up a Morley meant that Norman grew up in a social stratum where dropping out of school to support the family was unimaginable. Norman would grow up having his share of experiences with cows and horses, but they never framed the contours of his long-term work experience as a mining engineer. The story is also silent on how the domains of work and play often challenged prevailing ideas about gender. Third, how did children's experiences in these realms affect their emerging value orientations and overall social outlook? Norman Cleaveland tells us that the experience with the six-shooter taught him the importance of keeping one's word, in this instance, the promise not to kill any living being. But as we shall soon see, the very nature of his errand was part of a larger western outlook rooted in the frontier values of self-reliance and survival of the fittest. Finally, the story of the boy on a horse tells us little about the extent to which work and play were culturally specific.

Before we turn to these subjects, the sheer variety of children's play experiences must be emphasized. Running races, playing tag and hide and seek, and romping with pets were ubiquitous activities. In the 1920s Hispanic boys spent hours playing *tejas,* a game that entailed pitching steel washers into a pit several yards away, and *jalapia,* a game where blindfolded players matched skills tossing a pocketknife in an attempt to bury a matchstick planted in a mound of dirt. Raised on a ranch, Margarita García had glorious times playing barefoot in a nearby arroyo where thick-skinned wildflowers grew to a height of several feet, making them ideal hiding places. After a rainstorm the arroyo was thick with mud, perfect material for molding miniature adobe houses, cars, and trains. Rocks, bottles, and tin cans were also put to use, often as targets for homemade slingshots. For Hispanics and Anglos, searching for arrowheads in anthills and old ruins was a favorite pastime. (Navajos would have gone out of their way to avoid ancient sites owing to the possibility of ghosts.[2])

In Magdalena and Kelly, children had more resources to draw upon. One Hispanic man, whose father ran a general merchandise store, recalls that discarded packing crates made ideal chassis for constructing automobiles. When winter snowstorms blew in, children constructed sleds, sometimes aided by the local blacksmith, who cut strips of iron for runners. (In Kelly, Esther Peralta owned a pair of roller skates but had scant chance to use them because the mining town had neither paved roads nor sidewalks.) Adult-supervised recreation in Magdalena was mainly limited to a Boy Scout troop and church activities. Diego Montoya fondly remembers Father Stoffel taking the Boy Scouts camping. "At night we would cook and sleep out in the woods. At night we would all sit by the fire, look at the stars, and tie knots and tell stories." Hunting rabbits and digging up Indian pots and *metates* also made for great fun. At the end of the adventure, the priest "would take each one of us home to our parents and tell them how much fun we had, and that he really enjoyed being with us."[3]

Store-bought toys were a rarity in the early decades of the century and virtually nonexistent among the Navajos. Fortunate indeed was the child on Christmas morning who found a toy under the tree either purchased from Becker-Mactavish or ordered from the Montgomery Ward Catalogue. Recalling how "skinny" her father's wages were when he was managing a ranch for stock magnate Charles Ilfeld—her family lived in a two-room adobe grain storehouse—Bessie Field remembers how her father on Christmas Eve appeared with a small cedar tree that the children decorated with pictures from an old catalogue while her father cut a star from a tin can to hang from a beam over the tree. At night the children hung their stockings—"they had more holes than anything you ever saw"—which in the morning were filled with oranges and apples their mother had saved from Ilfield's last visit.

> Oh yes, and he brought out a stone jug of grape juice. I remember that because it played out awful fast. We children had never taken grape juice. That was our Christmas. There was no toys. And I remember my father was crying—he was very sensitive about his children—when he had to lie about Santa Claus getting lost. . . . I remember wakin' up and there was just a sprinkle of snow on the ground. Papa said he guessed Santa Claus couldn't travel down there because there wasn't any snow deep enough to run a sled on. So we let it go. Santa Claus didn't seem to stick with me very much.

On another Christmas their neighbors, Ray and Agnes Morley, brought over some store-bought toys for the girls. "There was little toy plates and little tin cups. I thought those was the most beautiful things in the world."[4]

For Anglo, Hispanic, and Navajo children alike, play was characterized by five general traits: its rootedness in the culture and economy, its connection to nature and dependence upon animals, its earthy pranksterism, its dangerous quality, and its connection to work.[5]

The cultural embeddedness of play is nowhere clearer than in the livestock economies. Anglo and Hispanic youth growing up on cattle ranches watched older men roping cows and breaking horses. Small wonder that they aspired to do the same. Lorenzo Ortega recalls, "My uncle was a hell of a bronc rider, a beautiful bronc rider." Thus, Lorenzo's childhood aim in life was "to ride the hell out of a bucking horse." Sometimes children went to extraordinary lengths to reenact imagined scenes from cowboy life. One woman recalls how several children got together and recreated an old-time cow camp, including building a fire and boiling some coffee. When one of the youngsters announced he had a box of .22 shells, "we decided it would be fun if we just threw all these bullets in that fire and hide like someone was shootin' at us." The subsequent sound of the bullets exploding as they ricocheted around the camp, they shortly concurred, was quite realistic.[6]

Because roping and branding were at the heart of the ranch economy, these activities also found their way into the play experience. When milk calves were not available for torture, a child sometimes volunteered or was selected to play the unenviable part of a "busted" cow. Not surprisingly the possibilities for things getting out of hand were immense, as they did on one occasion when a group of Hispanic and Navajo boys were playing on a ranch near Santa Rita. In this instance it was decided that one of the boys was a particularly "mean cow" that called for special treatment. After the "cow" was roped and wrestled to the ground, one of the imaginative youngsters decided that the cow's horns should be broken off to prevent it from goring the ranch hands. It was at this point that someone picked up a slap of wood and struck the "cow" alongside of the head. Not surprisingly, the game ended in a ferocious fight. Another instance of children playing at branding was when Fred Billings talked his six-year-old sister into being the calf. Mounted on an old pony named Star, "I roped her and jumped off and tied her down . . . real good and tight with a piggin' string. I had a branding iron and some sticks stacked up like a fire. So I was branding her and she was bawling like a calf. . . . The rope I had on her was also tied to the saddle horn." All was going well until the horse, nibbling on weeds, stepped across the rope, which pulled up between its legs, causing it to spook and take off at a full gallop for the ranch house—Fred's sister bouncing along behind. Running helplessly behind, Fred breathed a sigh of relief when he saw the girl's head clear a dangerous gatepost before the horse headed for the corral. Next, there was the dangerous prospect of the girl's head striking the corral gatepost. "I just knew she was going to get hurt bad on that post." But miraculously, "her little ole fat butt hit the post and she bounced around it and into the corral he went with her." At this point Fred's mother appeared on the scene and administered a severe whipping. "She liked to beat me to death with that rope. Dang, I never will forget that. I was so scared though, I didn't need a whipping. I was scared."[7]

In most instances the fantasy of the cowboy life manifested itself in less perilous ways. West of Magdalena, Bernadyne Powell and her friends spent summer days imagining they were driving cattle over a patch of land named the "Old Chisolm Trail," using some old cow horns to make up the trail herd. "We rode stick horses. Mine was an oak sucker rod and I could vault on it. I was the envy of the other cowhands." Vaulting aside, the children did their best to simulate an imaginary trail drive. "It was an awful drive! So we had to camp and we had a tin can to boil our coffee. Our coffee was buck brush leaves. It was awful, but remember we were tough." Burt Halsey was only six years old when he decided he would build his own herd of cows and some horses out of barrel stays, cottonwood logs, and miscellaneous sticks. "I got me quite a herd of horses and cows," he recalls. "Then I decided someone might swipe 'em so I branded them." That was his mistake. "The next mornin' I went out there and I didn't have nothin' left. They just burned up. Cottonwood, when you put a hot iron to it, it starts to smolder. It don't look like it's a burnin', but you can't hardly put it out. It took me awhile to get my herd built up." Next time Burt carved his brand with a knife.[8]

Navajo children also drew on cultural references for play. Sometimes this took the form of constructing miniature hogans for "playing house" and corrals for penning sheep. The wet clay along the banks of the Rio Salado was ideal for molding sheep, goats, and horses. Failing this, small white and black rocks were sometimes collected to represent the two colors of sheep. Imitating adult life sometimes extended to slaughtering animals. When playing in an arroyo, one man recalls how he and his friends would imagine the cedar bushes were sheep. In keeping with what they heard adults say when selecting a sheep for butchering, the children would call out in Navajo, "Get the fat one, get the fat one!" After the butchering, they would munch on the salty cedar bark. Tennie Guerro went a step farther. By the age of eight she had already attended a number of sings and so one day decided to play at being a medicine man. Knowing that ceremonies always entailed feeding those in attendance, she talked several friends into actually butchering one of her grandmother's lambs. The old woman was not impressed with her granddaughter's hospitality.[9]

A second attribute of play—particularly in the case of isolated homesteads—was its connection to natural surroundings.[10] Mountains, canyons, and creeks offered children an enormous playground for exploration and adventure. The children in a Hispanic family living outside Magdalena found the mountains in their "backyard" a consistent source of adventure, whether it was climbing them in the summer or sledding down them in the winter. In the summer, "we'd fill a can with prickly pears and go find an arroyo that had smooth sand and we'd rub the pears on the sand to get all those stickers off, and then . . . we'd eat them." Then there was the time that the two brothers spied an eagle's nest on the side of a deep arroyo. With one of the boys holding the other by the feet, they snatched one of the bird's eggs and scurried home to place it under a setting hen. To the delight of the boys—and to the horror of the chicken—it eventually hatched. Some of the sweetest memories of childhood for Kathryn McKee of Pie Town are of those long summer days spent wandering through fields of sunflowers and patches of Indian paintbrush. From the latter, "we

Mixing work and play, Fred Martin Jr. mounts a heifer during branding, 1937. (Courtesy of Fred Martin Jr.)

plucked the little blossoms and sucked the honey from them just as the little hummingbirds did."[11]

The main sources of play, however, were animals. Mainly for Navajo and Hispanic sheep-raising families, frolicking lambs were entertaining playmates. For aspiring cowboys and cowgirls, milk calves were ideal substitutes for imaginary rides on rough stock horses. "I broke all the milk pen calves to ride," recalls one rancher's son. "I started when I was about five years old. Ever new calf that got put into the pen, I'd make a saddle horse of him." Girls also delighted in the activity. "We rode burros, we rode calves, we rode steers, we rode anything we thought we could set on," recalls one woman.[12]

But horses were at the center of the play universe. For children growing up on ranches, horses were at once economic units, objects of beauty, and mythic symbols of power and freedom. Few children grew up in west-central New Mexico without being infected with the desire to ride a galloping, fleet-footed horse across the windswept plains and mesas of the region—and many did. Early on, therefore, children learned to pay a great deal of attention to horses, so much so that when a horseback stranger passed through the country, the memory of the horse remained much clearer than that of the rider. "Anytime they probably won't remember his name or where he was from, but they can tell ya what horse he was ridin'.

They'll say, remember that guy that come out that time? He was ridin' a real good bay horse. Or, they'll say, remember, he was on that ole sorry Appaloosa." Agnes Morley Cleaveland makes this same point: "Horses' personalities were even more vivid in our minds than the personalities of our human associates. The mounted stranger yielded first place in interest to the horse he bestrode. A year later we might have forgotten the color of the man's eyes, but never the set of the ears on his horse's head."[13]

Navajo youths spent innumerable hours chasing, breaking, and racing horses. With the echoes of sweathouse horse-riding songs in their heads, or perhaps even a song chanted by one of the mythological Hero Twins, they might have imagined they were astride a spirit horse carrying them across space unbounded by ranchers' fences.

> The turquoise horse prances with me.
> From where we start the turquoise horse is seen.
> The lightning flashes from the turquoise horse.
> The turquoise horse is terrifying.
> He stands on the upper circle of the rainbow.
> The sunbeam in his mouth for a bridle.
> He circles around all the people of the earth.[14]

But mostly they played at mastering the skills of horsemanship. One of the favorite sports was for several boys to take their mounts down to the Rio Salado, where they would look for a spot with "real fine silk mud." The game was to gallop into the mud and then "just put on the brakes and slide plumb across." With horseshoes, a horse might slide up to 50 or 60 feet. After a winter snow, the competition took place on fields of packed ice. Another favorite pastime was running down jackrabbits. One Alamo Navajo man recalls that some of his happiest moments as a child were spent with friends weaving ropes out of yucca plants for roping wild burros. One day, they would try their hand at roping wild horses on the San Augustine Plains.[15]

Although horses constituted the greatest source of play and entertainment, other animals played their part. Langford Johnston tells of the time in 1914 when he and several friends, including Carl Gatlin, were riding down a brushy canyon in the Datils when a bobcat jumped in front of them. Announcing that he was "going to catch that damn cat," Carl bolted up the trail with his rope in hand. It was a beautiful bit of roping; the rope sailed perfectly over the cat's head. But when the cat hit the end of the rope, it turned and sprang on the boy's hip, clawing and screaming, whereupon the horse "bogged his head and went for the sky." As Johnston relates it, "Carl was in a real tough spot, the cat snarling and spitting up his back, and the pony jumping high. But somehow Carl managed to slip the loop off the saddle horn before hitting the dirt, but he never saw the cat or his rope again." The whole fiasco, of course, prompted unbridled mirth among the horseback witnesses.[16]

Even bulls could be factored into play. Joe Evans, who was mostly raised in West Texas but also spent time in Dusty, New Mexico, recalls: "In my early boyhood days I spent a lot of time driving bulls together, to see them fight." He and his friends began by searching out a "bad fighting bull by his horns and size, and general makeup." After making their selection, they proceeded to engineer one matchup after another, the strongest bull being declared the "winner." Evans reflects, "I have spent many a day doing this and it was great entertainment to a bunch of boys who had no picture shows to go to."[17] It was also a lesson in natural selection.

A third characteristic of play was that so much of it was dangerous. This stemmed from two factors: the fact that children were often beyond the reach of adult supervision and that so much of it involved livestock. Bucking horses were, of course, the major threat to life and limb, and young cowboys delighted in nothing more than inciting a friend's horse to "bust in two." One of the favorite means of accomplishing this objective was to stick a branch under a horse's tail, a practice called "rim-firing."[18] But usually the thrills came from simply climbing aboard a bucking horse. "Oh, I've been throwed so high on a horse, I thought I never would see earth again—just throwed up there where the birds are," recalls Grace Higgins. "And then I'd land and all the breath would go out of me and I'd think, oh boy, I'm gonna die this time." Most memorable was her inability to ride Red Wing, a wild bronc her father bought from a cowboy in Magdalena. Grace thought the animal "was the most beautiful sorrel horse I ever saw, and I wanted him SO bad." After her father half-broke the horse, Grace was forbidden to ride him. "Why don't you make him gentle enough for me, Daddy?" she would ask, bowing to her father's pronouncement that Red Wing was too big—strictly a man's horse. So Grace bided her time, never giving up the hope she might sometime ride the beautiful sorrel. The opportunity presented itself one day when the adults were away, leaving Grace and some of her friends the run of the ranch. Grace commissioned a couple of conspirators to bring the horse over to the corral fence, from which she slid onto his back. "Oh, I just jumped off on him and I don't think I ever got a hold of him. I remember reaching for his neck. That's the last thing I remember." When she woke up, she was in the water trough, the gate open, Red Wing nowhere in sight, and all her fellow conspirators absent. Soaking wet, crying, and still dazed, she struggled to catch her breath and make sense of the situation. Later she discovered what had happened. Just as Red Wing was throwing her up "where the birds are," her friends spied a car coming over the hill, which they correctly surmised contained her parents. Knowing full well the ban on riding Red Wing, they opened the corral gate and skedaddled, abandoning Grace in the trough. Grace never fulfilled her dream of riding Red Wing.[19]

If riding horses could send children skyward, other dangerous sources of play threatened to pull them below ground. Children growing up in mining country found it almost impossible to abide by their parents' warnings to stay clear of abandoned mines. "We'd take a rope and we'd tie it to something and we'd go down in those old shafts. Daddy caught us one time, just comin' out of one, and we really got it," recalls one woman. Agnes Billings reports being three years old when her brothers dared her to sit atop an old well covered with rotten logs. She took the dare, whereupon she crashed through the logs, dropping into a dark chasm filled with freezing water. Luckily, the boys ran to the ranch house for their father (in bed with severe rheumatism), who, after directing a cowboy to fetch a horse and rope, dropped into the well. All Agnes can remember before she passed out is her father telling her to put her arms around his neck. Retrieved from the well, she contracted pneumonia and slipped into a weeklong coma.[20]

It was a sheep-dipping vat that nearly killed Bessie Field. Because the vat was nearly at ground level and had already been used for the season, on this particular day the dip's content was a murky mixture of standing water, chemicals, sheep manure, and a multitude of dead bugs and rodents—in short, polluted sludge. Still, Bessie and her playmates decided it would be great fun to fish out some of the dead rodents. But after Bessie climbed up on the ramp that led into the vat, her feet went out from under her, sending her head-over-heels into the vat. Recognizing the crisis, one of the children ran to the ranch house for help, while another did what he could to extricate Bessie from the filthy ooze. "Little Johnny Warren—God bless him—he grabbed my braids. I was strangling. He got me by the hair and pulled me. But he couldn't get me out, I was so soggy. Well, he was about to vomit, it was makin' him so sick, what he could smell." With Bessie's parents away, her older sister, Daisy, came to the rescue. After dragging Bessie from the vat, Daisy doused her with cold springwater from the horse trough, rushed her into the house, forced her to swallow a raw egg, and then stuck a finger down her throat to induce vomiting. "And I did vomit. Boy, I vomited up that ole stinkin' stuff." After vomiting until she was "pale as a ghost," she was taken to the bathtub, where she was scrubbed with lye soap. According to Bessie, "My hair and scalp was burning. My skin was burning all over. That dip was so strong." When her mother returned home to find entire patches of Bessie's scalp devoid of hair, a retelling of the day's events explained all.[21]

A fourth characteristic of play was the amount of energy expended on pranks, some of them Rabelaisian in their bawdiness and beyond the possibility of execution in urban, middle-class environments. There was the time Lorenzo Ortega and a friend were helping move cattle. "I was on drag; two of us kids were back. BORING, son-of-a-bitch, BORING. We had this ole lazy bull—Goddamned lazy son-of-a-bitch. We kept hittin' him with a rope. He'd lay down—didn't want to go. So we decided we'd try and rope his balls. You know, we'd take turns." Unable to get the loop between the bull's hindquarters but unwilling to give up on the project, one of the boys remembered his piggin' string, a short piece of rawhide all cowboys carried to tie down the feet of a flanked cow. "So I jerked my piggin' string off and I got off my horse and I got behind that old bull and made a little loop and Goddamn it did go between his legs and over his balls. I jerked it hard. And when I did, that son-of-a-bitch let out a beller and jerked that string out of my hands. And shit, every time he'd step on it, it would jerk his balls, and he would let out a beller. I mean every time he'd jump and step on it, those big ole balls would jingle down—BLAAH." In the end, the cowboys appreciated the stunt little more than the bull, whose painful bellowing "scattered the whole fuckin' herd. Oh, I got whipped that time. We scattered cows from one end of Catron County to the next."[22]

Only fifty years after the fact could Ray Bonner, the son of a Pie Town homesteader, confess to the stunt he and his brother pulled on a neighbor, a Mr. Howard, a recently arrived New Yorker whose pride and joy was a thoroughbred mare—something of a rarity in Pie Town country. When the Howards decided to take a summer trip, Mr. Howard asked the Bonner boys to look after his affairs. Under no circumstance, he emphasized, should his prize thoroughbred, coming into heat, be allowed to hook up with the shabbier ranch stock. Upon the Howards leaving, however, the Bonner boys immediately began to wonder if there was some way they could breed the mare with a neighbor's Shetland pony. It was a fascinating idea, and one, if successfully carried out, sure to guarantee a good deal of entertainment. Moreover, the coupling posed an intriguing engineering challenge, but, as it turned out, not beyond the ingenuity of the two boys. The strategy finally decided upon was to lead the Shetland on top of a dugout the Howards used to store fruit and vegetables. "We put the mare down at the end of the dugout and put the Shetland on top, because he can't reach it [the mare]." With the engineering problem solved, the enthusiastic Shetland rose to the occasion. Several months later, the boys' father made the observation to Howard that his mare appeared to be in foal. Howard declared it a flat impossibility. When the mare did indeed give birth to a runty, spotted colt, Howard was in shock. "Daddy told him it's that goddamned Shetland." Howard could only reply, "It can't be, it can't be. There's no way." While settlers in the region had a good laugh, the two boys kept mum. "We ain't tellin' Daddy what we done. Why would you jeopardize your LIFE? The man was MAD. . . . He was goin' to kill somebody. Goddamn, you might as well hand a man a rope to hang you." But Ray Bonner always suspected that his father knew full well the source of the mystery—"he had two sons that were damn rank."[23]

Even when boys were under adult supervision, things could get out of hand. Take for example the time that ranchers Guy and Birdie Spears took the Magdalena Boy Scouts on a trip to Carlsbad Caverns. As Lorenzo Ortega tells the story, sitting on the flatbed truck with their bedrolls, the boys got unmercifully bored as the truck bumped along at 40 miles per hour. To alleviate the boredom, they began to throw banana peels and apple cores at the passing cars. When this ammunition played out, they considered other possibilities. Meanwhile, the Spearses were oblivious to the antics being performed from the rear of the truck. But they soon appreciated the seriousness of the situation when they pulled up for a police roadblock. Guy Spears's first words were, "What the hell's the matter? Didn't my lights work? We're in compliance." "Yes, you are," the officer replied, before adding a bit of information that caught the Spearses by surprise, "but your boys are pissing on the cars." All Lorenzo remembers is Guy yelling out, "You little bastards," and Birdie trying to curb his language. "You don't talk that way to kids. They're kids, not bastards." Eventually though, the rancher took it all in stride. Recalls Lorenzo, "One thing about Guy, he wouldn't squeal on you. No matter how bad you got, Guy wouldn't squeal on you for shit."[24]

Finally, a good deal of the play emerged from work. Whether it was shooting rabbits, breaking horses, roping and branding calves, or responding to the call to "put a kid on a horse," children extracted much of their enjoyment from activities that in some small way contributed to the families' welfare. One woman recalls, "I had to rustle the milk cows and every other day, I had to ride 2 miles to the mailbox and get the mail—fun, fun!" Another woman recalls the fun children had in the cattle drives across the San Augustine Plains. The high point came when they met up with the sheep flocks coming in from the west. "We always look forward to that because they had these big pens over there where they put their burros . . . and they let us kids . . . buck 'em out at night. Didn't matter how tired we was; we always look forward to get to ride those bucking burros."[25] Herding sheep, Navajo children also sought out opportunities for mixing play with work. Playing with dolls and romping with lambs were common pastimes.[26] However, one woman recalls, "Sometimes my nephews and I would play without paying attention to the sheep [and] we would lose some. Towards evening, taking the sheep home we would start counting and if some were missing, my mom would get mad at us." Sent out to find the missing sheep, she, like all children in the region, was ever reminded that play must always give way to work.[27]

Work

Whether children grew up Navajo, Hispanic, or Anglo, it was work, not play, that shaped most of their daily existence. Because the labor of children was vital to the success of the family as an economic unit, both parents and children regarded it as the natural order of things. Although increasing numbers of children in turn-of-the-century, eastern, middle-class environments benefited from emerging theories that promoted childhood as a protected stage in human development, such notions had little purchase in the hardscrabble Rocky Mountain Southwest.[28]

Navajo children's introduction to the world of work is hardest to describe, owing to the fact that most were swept off to boarding schools at a very young age and therefore removed from traditional work patterns for a significant portion of their lives. Still, at an early age the Navajo work ethic asserted itself in various ways. Depending on their age, children performed simple chores, worked in gardens, picked piñon, chopped wood, hauled water, and most certainly herded sheep and goats. Because Navajos mostly lived in extended residential groups and placed a high value on cooperation, Alamo Navajo children learned early on to associate work with the greater good of the group.[29] The cooperative ideal was reinforced by the fact that young herders usually tended flocks composed of animals owned by various members of the outfit. When children were rewarded with a lamb or two of their own, their sense of personal responsibility took hold.

Alamo Navajo children enjoy garden harvest, ca. 1950. (Courtesy of José Guerro.)

By the early 1940s the Alamo Navajo population was nearing 300 with an annual per capita income of $60 or $297.85 for a family of five.[30] It followed that families were eager to find work off the reservation. Traditionally, Alamo Navajo men had long sought employment as sheepherders, cowboys, and fence builders, and these continued to be the main opportunities. Adolescent boys—especially school dropouts—joined their fathers and uncles in these endeavors. One man recalls being only twelve or thirteen when assisting his father in building fences for a "Mexican" in Puertecito at the wage of $20 a mile. Another tells of being only eleven when he rode his horse behind his father's wagon as the two set off for ranches to build fences. "I had four sisters and three brothers," he explains. "They was a lot younger, so you had to take care of them. So you had to go to work and get some money to buy whatever you need for the family."[31] A man born in 1904 recalls a different pathway into work:

> The way I was raised my mother was living with another man. My stepfather was treating me bad and almost killed me. So my mother told me to go to my grandmother. My mother said the man she was living with might kill me someday. So I went to live with my grandmother. As I was living with her I start thinking for myself. Then I knew I had a mind of my own. Then I went to work when I was still young. I used to take care

of the sheep as they had their young ones. I earned $5 a month for taking care of the sheep. That's how I worked. I was working for an Anglo in Datil. The Anglo's name was Ray Morley. Some Navajos used to weave saddle blankets for him. As I grew older I didn't live with my people. I stayed working for the Anglos. As I grew a little older, about fifteen years old, I came back to my people. Then I start learning more about my people and about Alamo. That's how I think about my young days, when I started working when I was young. I think about it all the time.[32]

In Magdalena and Kelly, Hispanic and Anglo boys found more opportunities for earning a few dollars. Storekeepers were in constant need of boys to run errands, make deliveries, and perform various odd jobs. One enterprising teenager put $3 down as credit for a new bicycle so he could get hired as a telegram delivery boy, earning 50 cents a day. "In the fall I'd deliver quite a few telegrams down to the stockyards to cattle buyers. I always thought that would be the greatest thing in the world to be a cattle buyer out at those stockyards." Years later he would achieve his dream. Another Magdalena youngster performed all manner of jobs. Rising at 5 o'clock in the morning, he washed dishes at one of the cafes before returning home to milk the cow and then set out for school. Following school, he would head for home, collect the milk, and make deliveries on the way to basketball practice. The most difficult job was as a janitor at one of the town's saloons, which entailed dumping and cleaning four brass spittoons. Given their vile contents, he remembers being barely able to keep his stomach together. "I'm telling you, they were BAD." Then one night the dreaded chore suddenly took on a new light. "I dumped one in the toilet and here was this dollar bill in it. So after that I got me a screen and I put it over the commode, so . . . it wasn't near as big a choke as when I first did it. I got several dollars out of that." In a couple of years the boy moved closer to the source of those spittoon dollars. "Gamblin' was open in Magdalena," he recalls. "I run a poker game down here at the Paris Tavern when I was fifteen years old."[33]

Because Hispanic families were generally poorer than their Anglo counterparts, their children generally entered the labor market at an earlier age. In Kelly this meant working in some aspect of the mining industry, where unskilled jobs ranged from handling mules to filling boxes with chunks of ore. In 1925, the New Mexico state legislature passed an anti-child-labor law forbidding employers from hiring children under sixteen for dangerous jobs, including mining, but various loopholes made the measure difficult to enforce. Precisely how many adolescents were pushed prematurely into

Lambing crew somewhere in western Socorro County. (Courtesy of US Forest Service, US Department of Agriculture, Albuquerque office, no. 39380A.)

the world of hard-rock mining is difficult to document, but in the early years of the twentieth century, it was not unusual.[34] A more common occupation for male youths was sheepherding. Sheep ranchers such as Solomon Luna and Frank Hubbell were always looking for *burreros,* or burro boys, to work alongside experienced herders. Boys no older than ten could earn $15 a month performing vital functions such as tending camp, caring for pack burros, watching for coyotes, and assisting the main herder in moving the flock. Although there was little future in sheepherding, one man recalls he had little choice in the matter. When his father died, the boy was only five years old, so by the age of twelve he was a *burrero.* More fortunate was José Ortega, who worked higher on the sheep-ranching hierarchy. Because his father owned 200 sheep and 30 head of cattle, by his early teens José was helping his father haul wool from the western country to Magdalena. By the time he was fifteen he was strong enough to drive two wagons pulled by six horses. In a few years he was earning the extraordinary salary of $55 a month punching cows for Ray Morley.[35]

 Outside of the Pie Town area, where children of dry farmers hauled water, worked the fields, and cared for chickens and livestock, mostly Anglo youth—but some Hispanics as well—came to know the world of work most intensely on cattle ranches. For some, their earliest memories are of seeing the world from the back of a horse. One recalls "ridin' behind my mother . . . to go out and gather cattle." Another recalls, "My dad would ride and prettin' near everywhere he'd go he'd take me with him," a tradition in cow country known as "sidin' his dad"—an image perfectly suited for the western poet:

> Now can't you remember when you was a lad
> And you started out ridin' along with your Dad.
> You first rode behind him. How awkward you felt
> When you grabbed at the saddle or hung to his belt.[36]

From their dads, ranch children mostly received their early education in the cattle business. Sidin' his dad, the youngster not only perfected his horse-handling skills but also learned how to match calves with their mothers, how to pull a cow out of a bog, and how to repair a break in a fence. It was also alongside his dad that the young cowboy began his schooling in the art of "reading" cattle. On one level, learning how to read cattle meant learning the language of brands. As Ramon Adams writes, "The reading of brands was an art. To the tenderfoot, brands were so many picture puzzles, and he was almost sure to misread them, and often dazed by their queer jumble of lines, letters, and curves." Because brands were the primary denotation of ownership, learning the myriad brands in the region (particularly before extensive fencing) was an essential part of the aspiring cattle rancher's education. Little by little, the cowhide script was decipherable. After they were conversant in brand language, ranch youngsters understood that an underscored letter M on its side was the "lazy M bar" and that a U atop the same letter, but inverted, might be known as a "whangdoodle."[37] The son of one rancher recalls, "I guess I learned about that [brands] before I knew anything; I knew that long before I started to school"—his introduction to literacy.[38]

But reading cattle was about more than brand recognition. On a more subtle level it involved knowing the particular marks, personalities, and habits of cows carrying the same brands, a vitally important skill required for gathering particular animals. One man recalls that at an early age he learned that "Ever' cow is just like a person, really. They have a different personality. They'll do different things." The young cowboy came to marvel at how his father knew hundreds of cattle by individual traits. One rancher recalls that at one point his father was raising 475 cattle, and "he knew every damn cow." Frequently, he would send his sons after a cow he had recently seen looking poorly, describing to the boys the animal's markings. "And we'd go and we'd ride and ride. We usually came back with the right cow. Once in a while we'd get the wrong one. And then we'd have to go back and get the right one. That was a learning process. But he'd tell you about her and he'd say, well, she's got a little spot on her head and she's got a lot of white on her neck or something. Said you can't miss her. You get over there."[39]

Early on, youngsters were also taught the trick of looking for "spotters," or cows that always grazed in a bunch. Melvin Akers recalls his father keeping an old red cow until "she was as old as the trees" simply because she was a good spotter. "When you're gatherin' and you don't gather her, you know you're out some cattle. And he was right. Ever' time you found her, she'd always have eight or ten head with her." But mostly it was knowing what to look for: the ability to scan the horizon and spot a cow amongst some distant scrub trees, to take notice of blue jays taking flight from a far-off piñon tree, or knowing a missing cow's favorite locale for "sneaking off."[40]

As the child matured, he aspired to mastering those higher-level skills displayed by his father or the hired cowboys. However many hours he had practiced roping fence posts or milk calves, it was usually years before he could rope calves from a horse, either "heeling" or "forefooting" them prior to branding. For the want-to-be cowboy, observing an experienced cowhand build a loop, twirl his rope, and sail it 20 feet over a calf's head was sheer poetry in motion. For now the youngster was expected to prove his worth in the branding pen as a "flanker," that is, display his ability at throwing the roped calf to the ground prior to it being stretched out, branded, and if a bull calf, castrated, or "cut." Actually, boys began flanking calves—or trying to—as young as seven or eight. One rancher claims he was only five when his uncle pointed out a calf and said he would make the boy a gift of it if he could wrestle it to the ground and tie it. "I guess it took an hour to do it, but I finally got it tied down." Learning to flank a calf was a public rite of passage of sorts, and the novice flanker knew he was providing onlookers entertainment. "They'd stand there and watch and laugh. The harder you got kicked, the more they'd laugh." Another recalls,

> I started when I was about twelve. The calf weighed more than I did—was stronger anyway. My uncle just delighted in that. . . . He'd get a live one and say, "Here's one about your size," and it would the biggest one. And then he'd stand back and the calf and I would have a free-for-all. And I'd finally get a hammerlock on him and throw him down. I finally learned how to do it more gracefully. But he'd say, "Here's one big for ya," and then he'd sit back and just roar with laughter while the calf and I would have it out.[41]

In time, the sights, smells, and rituals of the branding pen were second nature, bawling calves being thrown down in succession, the application of the scorching branding iron, the smell of burning hide, and the quick surgical removal of a bull calf's testicles.

Because the cattle economy depended on a large number of horses (during roundup season the cowboy might have several horses in his "mount" or "string"), skill at breaking horses was also highly valued. Here was another theater of activity where the realms of work, play, and masculine bravado were thoroughly fused. One rancher recalls he was fourteen when he regularly began breaking horses, and he still remembers the pride he felt when someone would turn a wild bronc over to him, saying, "Try and make a horse out of him." Paid $5 for every horse he broke, the boy discovered how he could combine breaking horses with school attendance. "I knew school was 5 to 6 miles from where we lived up to the schoolhouse. Well, that was just a pretty good ride for a horse that morning." Tying the horse to a tree, he would ride him home late in the afternoon, monitoring the horse's progress. Lorenzo Ortega recalls learning to break horses as a teenager when he worked for rancher Guy Spears. Spears would "snub" a wild pony up to his horse in the deep sand of the Rio Salado, and just before turning it loose with the boy aboard, he would say, "Are you ready, button?" Lorenzo would respond in turn, "Turn the son-of-a-bitch loose." So the contest commenced. "It would buck like hell on me," and every time "I started buckin' off, Guy would reach over and pull me over and say, 'ride that son-of-a-bitch, boy.' . . . I never hit the ground." In time, the young cowboy would take pride not only in his ability to stay aboard a bucking horse but also in his adherence to accepted cowboy protocol. Burt Halsey, for instance, recalls that when he first began breaking broncs, if he reached for the saddle horn, his father would "whip my hand with a quirt." As Halsey explains, "A cowboy didn't reach for the saddle horn. That saddle horn was to tie your rope to, not to hang on to. . . . It's just the principle of it."[42]

Some youths were also involved in running wild horses that, prior to the big "dry up" of the 1930s, populated the San Augustine Plains. Chasing wild horses was a dangerous enterprise, and ranchers engaged in it for a multitude of reasons: finding a good saddlehorse, selling off the good stock to willing buyers, and selling worthless stock to the "soap factory" in Gallup. In the early 1930s, Fred Billings was no more than ten years old when he joined his father, grandfather, and a cowboy named Shorty Claghorn in the operation. It began with driving a band of thirty or more horses off the ridges onto the plains, where, in relay fashion, the riders undertook to push the slowly weakening animals into a corral or horse trap. On one occasion this involved running the horses for more than 50 miles. As Fred relates the story, he fell in behind the horses late in the afternoon and was still pushing them hours later under a cold, moonlit sky. When the moon went down, he "pulled off to one side and built a little ole fire and went to sleep." At daybreak, the horses, being driven in a large circle, came into view again. His mount "could smell 'em. The winds was blowin' just right and he'd already smelled it. And he knew what he was doing." Falling in behind the flagging horses, he can still see a "wise old mare in the lead" and the stallion at the rear pestering and nipping the flanks of those falling behind. "Yeah, he'd keep 'em going," only taking the lead when they were "just about to get caught in a real tight place." After they were corralled, the horses were broken, sorted, and sold off. Sometimes, the boy helped run wild horses for six weeks at a stretch. "That was part of my schooling. Instead of getting to go to school, I had to go run wild horses."[43]

A part of growing up was making mistakes—sometimes big ones. Buddy Major was only eight years old and his sister two years older when they attempted to carry out one of the more noble dictums of cattle ranching: if you come across another rancher's cow and its unbranded calf, the neighborly thing to do was to throw the mother's brand on the calf.

> One time my folks were gone to town and they left us kids up here. There was a neighbor—ole man Bodenhamer—and we kids were ridin' over there about 3 or 4 miles on his land and we found thirty to forty head of cows and calves and the calves didn't have no brand on 'em. . . . We thought this would be a grownup deal and we'd go and brand these cattle for this guy. There wasn't nobody around to bother us so we were gonna do it ourselves. We were gonna do him a big favor. We chased 'em all over tryin' to get 'em together. We had cattle runnin' in every direction, up and down the canyons. We took 'em off his ranch and drove 'em all the way over to our ranch . . . and were gittin' ready to brand 'em. We were buildin' the fire and dad showed up, and boy, he jumped on us. "What in the world do you kids think you are doin'?"

The children explained they were just trying to do the neighborly thing, but Buddy's father was not overly impressed. As the children were made to understand, if Bodenhamer had seen his cattle being driven off his ranch, he would have naturally assumed cattle thievery to be the motivation. The children were directed to return the cows to their proper range.[44]

Buddy was about the same age when he and his two sisters discovered that being a good Samaritan could have even sadder consequences. The three were riding across Putney Mesa to gather the mail at the Fields' store (an activity they performed every two or three months) when they spotted a two-month-old orphan colt. The trio knew the land they were riding across belonged to a rancher recently killing wild horses because they competed with his cattle for the meager grass. The colt, they wagered, had somehow avoided the slaughter. At first they considered taking the colt on to the Fields' ranch but decided the animal was so emaciated it would never make it:

> He'd jist give out. We couldn't decide what to do. We wanted to put him out of his misery. So there was a big bluff about 200 yards from where we were at, so we decided we'd push him off that bluff. We all decided, all three of us was goin' to be responsible. There wasn't gonna be [just] one person pushin' him off. . . . So we pushed and we knew it was gonna kill him instantly. We couldn't git nerve to look down there, but we finally looked down and here the colt was kickin'. It didn't kill him.

What to do now? The broken colt lay kicking at the bottom of the bluff, and there was no way to descend it to "finish him off." So there seemed only one thing to do. Screwing up their courage a second time, "We got rocks and threw rocks down on that colt." Finally, the kicking and twitching stopped. For Buddy the day was turning out to be a sorry one all the way around. When they set off that morning, he was wearing his new Stetson hat, something he did on special occasions—like riding to the Fields' store. At some point up on the bluff the wind had come up and blown his hat off. "I never did git that hat. I guess the rats ate it or somethin'."[45]

For one Hispanic youngster a misstep resulted in outright humiliation. At the age of twelve, Lorenzo Ortega was working for his brother-in-law, whom he had observed numerous times performing the delicate procedure of cutting a cancerous eye out of a cow and then sewing it up tight. If the procedure was done correctly, the socket would be covered with solid skin, and the cow could be more easily sold. One day when a cow with a diseased eye was spotted, the twelve-year-old volunteered to perform the surgery himself. Yes, he assured his brother-in-law, he could perform the operation. So it was agreed: the boy should come back on his own and perform the procedure. It all seemed to go well. After getting the cow in the chute, he cut the eye out, stitched the lid shut with catgut, and turned the cow loose. A few days later, when the two went to check on the cow, Lorenzo recalls "she was lookin' good" except for the fact that the stitched eye was dripping pus and blood. Worried, his brother-in-law took the cow back to the corral, where he slit the cavity open and examined the wound. It was at this point Lorenzo received an unexpected assessment of his veterinarian abilities. "He said, you dumb little shit and he swatted me a good one. I told you never to cut the damn eyelid, top or bottom. You have to get fresh hide. The eyelid ain't never goin' to grow together. . . . You smart son-of-a-bitch, there'll always be a hole here." As his brother-in-law performed the surgery a second time, Lorenzo "felt terrible." The worst part of it was that word soon got around to other ranches what he had done. "Hey, button, do you want to come over here and work on some cancer eyes? We hear you're a good man." Or, "There's that dumb little shit over there." The old-timers, he recalls, "could really put the meat to you."[46]

Because fine horses were generally revered in the West, children were also rebuked for unnecessary rough treatment of the same. Lee Coker was only seven when he learned the lesson. One of the boy's morning chores was to wrangle the horses on a horse that was "high headed." The horse was simply too much for the boy to handle and was always running away with him. "I couldn't hold him. I couldn't. I was too little." But the boy did possess a pair of sharp-pointed spurs, so he began using them to punish the horse.

> So I come in one morning and my dad said, you been spurrin' that horse in the shoulder? And I said, yes sir. He said, the next time you spur that horse in the shoulder, I'm goin' to give ya a good lickin'. Well, it went on for about a month or two and I went out one morning . . . and this ole thing run away with me, just stuck his head and took off. I couldn't stop him. So I just really give him a good rakin' . . . and there was blood runnin' out of his shoulders. And I thought, oh damn. So I got down off of him and throw'd dirt up on his shoulders. And damned, when I got into the corral with these horses, he [Dad] was standin' at the gate. I was hopin' he wouldn't see it, but he saw it. And he said, well, I see you've been spurrin' that horse in the shoulder again. Yes sir. You remember what I promised you, don't you? Yes sir. Well go ahead . . . to the house and git your breakfast. So anyway, I eat a little cold gravy and biscuit, and took off. And I worried about that all day. He let me worry about it all day—that whippin'. So long about 4 o'clock, when we come in, I thought maybe he'd forgot it. He hadn't mentioned it. AND I SURE HADN'T. I unsaddled and turned the ole horse loose, and started for the house right quick. He said, HUP, HUP, come back here. I think I promised you

somethin' this mornin'. And he took my bridle reins and he whupped me where I couldn't sit down for three days. But I didn't spur a horse in the shoulder anymore."[47]

Not only the distinctive nature of ranch work but also the extreme conditions under which children labored placed it outside the bounds of emerging national sensibilities. One rancher recalls, "I remember . . . my dad always waited 'til Christmas—when I was on vacation from school—to help the cowboys get the bulls in. It was ALWAYS cold. Every time I got off a horse—you could hardly get off, your feet would be so numb—I could hardly pull the reins out from my hands they was so froze." By the age of thirteen, Pete Evans spent several weeks at a time with three other teenagers at a cow camp, from which they ventured forth to dig postholes and string wire. At the age of eight, Cecil Taggert drove a team of horses and wagon 20 miles to Socorro for a load of hay. At the age of fourteen, he stayed in a cow camp by himself for six months branding mavericks, riding fence, and breaking ice on waterholes, coming home only for Christmas.[48]

After children were socialized into believing that such work responsibilities were the natural order of things, they became matter-of-fact. Again, Cecil Taggert recalls that he and his brother were scarcely more than ten when they were expected to brand maverick cattle they might come upon. On one occasion, it was near the end of the day when the boys came across a year-old maverick. Even though it was getting dark and the two were exhausted, it was a "necessity" that they brand the unmarked cow; they might not see it again for months before another cowboy threw someone else's brand on it. So the boys did what was expected of them: roped the cow, jerked it down, tied it, built a branding fire, and slapped their father's brand on. "You did what you had to do. And that's one of the things that was expected of you. We didn't think there was a big deal about it. We'd come in and tell our dad we branded a yearling over there."[49]

Children sometimes hired out. During World War I, when there was a shortage of cowboys, Ray Morley was forced to rely almost completely on teenaged hired hands—a group dubbed the "kindergarten outfit." One man claims he was only six years old when he decided to earn the necessary $19 to buy a saddle. "I'd go chop wood for anybody I could. I'd walk as much as 5 miles to chop wood all day, and then walk home." Earning 50 cents a day, he had the saddle within the year. ("You couldn't depend on your parents to get it, because they didn't have nothin'.") The best prospect for employment was to hire out as a horse wrangler. Melvin Akers was twelve years old when he convinced Cole Railston, manager of the V+T ranch, to hire him.

He was a friend of my daddy's. I guess that's the only reason he gave me the job, because I wasn't hardly big enough to do anything. . . . I went out there and went to work wrangling horses, which wasn't hard to do cause I could ride good. They was gettin' ready to bring a bunch of cattle to Magdalena to ship. It was in the spring of the year. The cattle was real poor. I guess they'd had a hard winter. What I did was bring in the remuda, the horse herd. I'd follow the chuck wagon, drive these horses, take 'em in front of the cattle and give 'em water wherever we stopped, and then take 'em out a ways and graze 'em 'til it come time to change horses or bring 'em in. That was my job, takin' care of the horse herd.

Melvin also helped the cook by chopping wood, loading the cowboys' bedrolls, and hauling water. Although horse wrangling was often the young hired hand's first foray into the cowboy labor market, fence building, breaking horses, and assisting at branding time were other ways in which youths proved their worth to cattle ranchers.[50]

To contemporary eyes the most jarring aspect of children's work experience was the danger involved. So much could go wrong, and more often than not, it involved horses. One Hispanic woman recalls the time she was pulling garden weeds with her mother and sister while her father and twelve-year-old brother were breaking a colt in the corral. She remembers how they were stricken with fear as they saw the father walking toward them carrying the boy in his arms. "*Aquí está tu hijo. Pienso que lo mate*," the father announced to his wife. "Here's your son. I think I killed him." Miraculously, her mother revived the boy's breathing. Later her parents argued over the fate of the horse, her father wanting to kill the animal, her mother placing the blame elsewhere. "No, it's not the horse's fault, it's yours. The boy is too young and too light."[51]

Getting knocked unconscious was not exactly a rarity. Melvin Akers was just fourteen and horseback when he made the mistake of roping another horse running by him. "It was a dumb thing that I had done, because I knew better. I just sat there. And when he hit the end of that rope, he just jerked my horse down on top of me." It would be three days before Melvin could walk. Similarly, a Datil rancher recalls the time his younger brother was breaking his first colt. When the horse ran away with him and headed for the fence, a hired hand quickly used his own horse to divert the colt away from the fence. The result was a "big ole wreck." The runaway horse crashed to the ground with a broken leg, and the boy was thrown sideways and lay unconscious. Two distinct memories remain forever in the older brother's recollection of what happened next. One was of someone shouting, "Come on, git the gun. We gotta shoot the horse." The other was of his mother rushing to the scene. "It was pourin' down rain, and her hat was all [hanging down] because of the rain. And she was carrying Mike in her arms in the rain, and he had blood all over his face, and mom was crying." The boy was taken to the hospital, where he was diagnosed as having a concussion. "What was weird was that a piece of his tooth was knocked clear up into his nose. But he was okay." The horse was not.[52]

According to Agnes Morley Cleaveland, "The disaster we most feared was a horse falling and disabling us." Two major causes for concern were a horse stepping in a prairie dog hole and a horseman getting "hung up" in the stirrup. Frequently sent out alone on some errand, children were always at risk in these regards. Tom Locke was just thirteen when a ranch foreman told him to ride over the mountains some 20 miles and spend a couple of days checking on some horses. Years later, he cannot believe so little thought was given to his safety. If the horse had fallen and broken his leg, the boy probably would have been finished. "Any little thing would be fatal."[53]

Nothing sparked alarm more than the sight of a riderless horse limping back to the ranch house. Pete Evans remembers as if it were yesterday the tragedy that occurred the time neighboring ranchers sent their son, Deming Inman, over as a "stray man" to help the Evanses brand cattle. While helping out with the branding, Deming was to keep an eye out for any strays from the Inman herd that had gotten mixed in with the Evanses' cattle. On this particular day, just before the branding commenced, Deming was sent some distance to a spring to bring back a bucket of water. When the horse came back riderless and soaking wet, the branding crew immediately was worried. Tracking the horse back to a dirt tank, they found no sign of the boy. By reading the signs in the trail, the cowboys constructed a theory as to what had happened: Deming's horse had started bucking, the rider was thrown with his foot hung up in the stirrup, the frightened horse ran into the dirt tank and drowned the boy (or alternatively, he was dead before being dragged into the tank), the foot came loose, and the horse came home. For nearly two hours those who could swim dove into the muddy water looking for the body. When they finally pulled him out, he had a large gash on his head. At fourteen, Pete Evans was seeing death for the first time and under ghastly circumstances. Pete's mother recalls that the cowboys brought Deming's body back to the ranch, where someone "set up with him all night." The next day his body was taken into Magdalena for burial, after which the boy's parents came back to the Evans ranch to spend the night. "The next morning I can still hear Mr. Inman, the father of the child. He hollered out at my husband, 'Dub, kill ole Paint.' That was the horse that drowned the boy."[54]

A good number of accidents occurred while children were chasing wild cattle. Particularly dangerous was rounding up the wild mavericks that inhabited the piñon-and-cedar-studded mountain terrain so common to the region. Burt Halsey was only twelve when he "jumped a bunch of wild cows." In this instance, his horse bolted "between a couple of trees and there wasn't enough room for me to go through with him. Caught both knees on the trees." Burt was left sitting on the ground with two broken kneecaps. Tom Locke was working on the Morley ranch when one day he was riding up a narrow crevice of a steep mountain in pursuit of a wild cow. At the time Locke thought his horse could make the grade, but as the horse suddenly made an attempt to turn around, Tom realized too late that he had overestimated the horse's ability. In the process of turning around, the horse fell over backward and toppled down the mountainside. "Down the mountain we went. There was a rock about 5 feet high, and about 4 feet from the rock was a little ole cedar bush. His back went right down between the rock and this cedar bush—layin' on his back . . . and I was settin' up on his belly amongst them feet." Fortunately the horse "settled," and a nearby cowboy came to the boy's rescue.[55]

Ray Bonner was just ten when his parents left him in charge of the homestead for several days. The boy was to be five days by himself, the parents explained, and then his uncle would come and stay with him. It all went smoothly until the fourth day, when the family cow came into heat and "went to bullin'." Saddling his horse, the ten-year-old set out to find her. Just before sundown he spotted her in the mountains with a bunch of wild cattle. He proceeded to cut her out and was making progress pushing her out of the mountains when the cow saw another bunch of cattle and took off again. Ray spurred his horse and then saw too late the badger holes up ahead. The next thing he knew the horse was tumbling forward.

> When I come to, there the horse was standin' there. So I grabbed them reins. I can't get up. My leg is paralyzed. So we're about 4 miles from home and about 12 miles from the neighbors. I'm tryin' to coax the horse to stand still, but when I talk to him, he backs up. Well, I figure I'm in trouble. So I take those reins and tie 'em to my arm. Because I think my leg is broken. I just think to myself, well, in two or three days this horse will get thirsty enough, he'll drag me to water. I can't walk. I can't move. So I kept talkin' at the horse, and hangin' onto these reins.

Finally, I got up on my feet. He let me pull myself up on my feet—this is after dark—and I kept pettin' him and pettin' him, and talkin' to him, and pulled myself up and layed on that horse on the pommel. But my leg was in such shape I couldn't pull it over. So I turned him loose and he takes me home. When he got home, my uncle took me down.

As it turned out, the leg was not broken, just temporarily paralyzed. The next day in bed he was able to move his toes. Soon, he was horseback again.[56]

In addition to bucking horses, badger holes, and wild cows, there was also the possibility of getting bogged down in quicksand. "My dad had always told us kids," Lee Coker explains, "if the horse gets in the quicksand, don't try and get off him. Stay on him 'til he goes out of sight." Fortunately, the boy tucked away his father's advice. Shortly thereafter, when Lee and his older brother were returning from rounding up a couple of cows, Lee's horse got trapped in quicksand. As his brother rode the 2 miles to the ranch for help, Lee kept calm, sitting on the horse as it struggled and slipped ever deeper into the mire. It was nearly dark when his father showed up. By now the horse's head was underwater, its body had all but vanished, and the stirrup leathers were splayed out over the murky water. But sitting on top of the saddle was the six-year-old boy. He had not panicked.[57]

Dangers aside, growing up in ranch country had its share of rewards, both psychological and material. Compliments from a parent or cowboy instilled in children a growing sense of self-worth. When the child's accomplishment resulted in some material reward, so much the better. Jack Russell was only six when his father sent him out to look for an old bay mare and her colt, both of which the father surmised were dead because his own efforts had failed to turn them up. When the boy succeeded in finding them, the father was more than a little impressed. "You didn't give up, did you? You just stayed with it. You finally found her." For the boy, hearing these words "was the greatest thing that there ever was." To top it off, his dad gave him the colt.[58] Indeed, few things engendered responsibility more than giving a child a calf or horse. Even more satisfying for children—girls and boys alike—was to be rewarded with their registered brand. One youngster's aunt officially got him started in the cattle business when she gave him her brand and eight cows. Another recalls that at the end of shipping season his father usually gave each of the children a heifer in payment for their labor. With the aid of a bull, "pretty soon you got a cow and a calf. Pretty soon you got two cows with calves." By the time he and his sister were in their mid-teens, they were partners with twenty-five cattle "under the same brand."[59]

Short of being given a cow, the supreme compliment was hearing a rancher or foreman say you were "good enough to take along." Jack Russell was thirteen when he met this standard. He and his father happened to be in Magdalena when Ray Morley was hiring cowboys to gather upward of 1,500 steers. The wages were good, so Jack's father signed on and offered that his son would also "make a hand." Morley agreed to take the boy on. The first few days were boring, young Jack being assigned to "day herd," which entailed no more than grazing those cattle already gathered. Then one day Morley asked, "How'd you like to go on a drive today?" The boy jumped at the opportunity. Morley then announced that he wanted Jack to ride a little roan horse that liked to buck. "Well, that's what I wanted. And I says, well, I can try. So we saddled up and I got on my little ole horse and turned him around and rode off and he never humped up." For two weeks, Jack proved he could do a man's work, pulling down $2 a day, "big wages." Meanwhile, Morley took notice of the boy's attire, his worn-out boots, old slouch hat, and raggedy clothes. When they reached Magdalena, Morley outfitted him in boots, socks, pants, shirts, jacket, and a new hat. Jack recalls plainly Morley informing the salesman, "I'm abuyin' this for the kid. That kid made a hand and I'm abuyin'."[60]

The cattle drive—one of the truly mythic moments in the storied cowboy West—brought its own satisfactions, although sometimes actually experiencing the event was devoid of romance. Ralph Hickle was just starting to grow whiskers when, during a fall drive across the San Augustine Plains, the weather turned brutally stormy and cold. With the snow blowing in blustery sheets, "ever' so often, I'd have to reach up and break the ice off my whiskers." At night, when it fell to Ralph to stand night guard over the herd from 10 o'clock until midnight, the sky was so black that the only light was a small campfire. "One old cedar bush about 4 feet high was just at the edge of the firelight. It looked just like a cow movin' out and headin' out toward Dusty. I turned that bush back four times in those two hours."[61]

Although a cattle drive entailed monotonous hours in the saddle, suffocating trail dust, and temperature extremes, it also served up adventures and scenes worthy of the myth. Jack Russell, who counts making eight drives from Dusty to Magdalena in just one summer, will never forget one moment when he paused at the top of the divide west of Magdalena. Looking back across the expanse of the San Augustine Plains, he counted some seventeen herds being driven to Magdalena. The next night, when the herds covered the hills surrounding the stockyards, the glimmer of campfires could be seen all around as each outfit awaited its time for loading. And just imagine the rush of excitement thirteen-year-old Burt Halsey experienced during a cattle drive when a lightning storm triggered a stampede in the dead of night. Galloping at full speed in pursuit of wild-eyed steers in the thundering blackness—broken only by the periodic bolts of lightning—was memorable enough. But then add to this another element in the experience—a scene few cowboys witnessed in their entire lives: the tips of the stampeding cattle's horns ablaze with balls of fire, the spectacle induced by the electricity in the storm. Here was a moment to tell one's grandchildren about, an entire herd of crazed, electrified cattle lighting up the blackness. Making it more surreal was the smell of something like burning sulfur. Truly, "it was another world."[62]

Depression

In the end, the cattle economy depended on grass and water. When the natural aridity of the region asserted itself, as it did in the 1930s with a vengeance, livestock suffered and began dying. At one point, ranchers were so desperate that a local preacher convinced them to remove their hats and bow down in the middle of the street and pray to the Lord Almighty for rain. Meanwhile, western New Mexico benefited immensely from the New Deal's alphabet agencies, which pumped money and relief programs into the region. While the Works Progress Administration (WPA) built schools, the Civilian Conservation Corps (CCC) set up camps for men aged eighteen years and older to carry out various projects including erosion prevention, fence building, forest fire suppression, road building, and rodent control. Stockmen especially benefited from the CCC's work in constructing the so-called Magdalena Stock Driveway, a 100-mile stretch of fenced trail (including corrals and wells) to facilitate the movement of livestock to Magdalena. When signing up for the CCC, enrollees agreed to send $25 a month home to their families and to abide by the regulations and discipline of camp life. In addition to instituting much-needed public works projects and infusing income into cash-strapped families, the CCC boosted enrollees' educational skills by offering courses in both basic and vocational education. Because many of those who signed on were high school dropouts, the camp classes offered them a second chance to advance their marketable skills.[63]

As the drought deepened, many ranch youths must have wondered if there was a future in the cattle business. By 1934, talk around the kitchen table was about a New Deal initiative, the Federal Surplus Relief Corporation, that in conjunction with the New Mexico Relief Administration was purchasing drought-stricken cattle. The program only paid a few dollars for each animal, but it was something. It was understood that those animals too emaciated to be preserved or used for food would simply be destroyed. Hard pressed, many ranchers signed up for the program.[64] For both adults and children who witnessed the slaughter, it was a heartbreaking event. "I can just see those guys standin' on the banks of this arroyo and shootin' down there and killin' those cattle," one youngster of the era recalls. "I guess the point of shootin' 'em in the arroyo is . . . they'd lay and rot. I don't ever remember 'em coverin' 'em up. They may have had a tractor there and covered 'em up. I don't remember." Pete Evans was just a boy when he helped drive some cows into Magdalena for the shooting. After the slaughter began, he was "scared to death." His responsibility was to "hold the cattle," that is, keep them from stampeding in the midst of the mayhem. When it was all over, "there was dead cows all over that hillside." Burt Halsey was scarcely more than a toddler when they shot cattle in a remote canyon in the Dusty country. He can still recall the stench of the killing field weeks thereafter—especially when the wind kicked up.[65]

But occasionally grit and ingenuity outwitted the forces that drought and depression set in motion. When the bank foreclosed on the Red Lake Ranch, a mother and son on a neighboring ranch turned the development to their advantage. Fred Billings, who was only ten at the time, says his mother knew from experience that in the process of driving 4,000 cattle over the space of several days into Magdalena, a number of starving calves would never survive the drive and would simply be abandoned along the trail. With his father away on business, his mother hitched a team of horses to a wagon, and the two fell in behind the repossessed herd, the cattle doing so poorly that the cowboys could only push them 6 or 7 miles a day. As the boy remembers it, "We just went down there and come along behind them . . . and picked up all those calves. We had a high sideboard on that wagon. We put those little give-out dogie calves in that wagon and took 'em home." Mother and son managed to rescue eighteen calves in all. They spent the summer bottle feeding "the little boogers" before breaking them to feed. Because of the boy's part in the operation, "Nine of them was mine, and nine of them was hers."[66]

Of the three groups, the Alamo Navajos had the fewest resources to fall back upon. For starters, the *Diné* sheep flocks—the central measure of individual and family wealth and sustenance—were greatly diminished as the drought settled in. In July 1936 Nels Field reported in the *Magdalena News* that some Navajos were "going to town with some sheep to try and sell, as there is no feed on their places for them." Moreover, with the surrounding livestock economy in peril, fewer and fewer Indians found employment as fence builders, cowboys, and sheepherders. This, combined with the fact that the drought degraded even further the traditional sources of nourishment garnered from hunting and gathering, translated into thinner wages and depleted larders. Presumably, some parents found solace in knowing that their children away at boarding school were better clothed and fed than those at home. By the late 1930s, however, two developments did marginally improve conditions: the jurisdictional transfer of the band from the Eastern Navajo Agency to the United Pueblo Agency and John Collier's Indian New Deal, which resulted in the establishment of a day school, an expansion of the Alamo land base, and a livestock improvement program.[67]

Hispanics fared somewhat better. Many families had a cow or two and a household garden. Those higher on the income scale helped those less fortunate. According to Esther Peralta, after the mines closed in Kelly, "my grandfather kept the store open. And I heard my grandmother say to him: 'you can't go on clothing the whole town. You have your children. Look at your children.' . . . And he'd say: 'These people came to work here. I have to clothe them, feed them, and help them get back to where their families are.'" After the banks collapsed, the conversation continued in the same vein but with a new urgency on the grandmother's part. "You can't go on feeding the whole world. You can't do it." Her grandfather continued to insist, "There will always be enough. I've got to take care of these people." For the longest time life seemed normal to the granddaughter. Every night the family ate dinner under the chandelier. Finally, when the miners were all but gone from the town, the store closed.[68]

Even Anglos such as the Mactavishes were hit hard. By 1934, John Blackburn, the grandson of John Mactavish, was wearing hand-me-downs. The old man, who had been to Scotland twelve times, could be heard muttering, "Oh, how the mighty have fallen." Still, Mactavish continued to give credit to those who had little chance of settling their accounts. Grandson Blackburn remembers that his grandfather "was not about to let them go hungry." Further west, out Pie Town way, the drought played havoc with the dreams of struggling homesteaders. Ray Bonner spent the twelfth summer of his life working for a neighboring rancher who paid him $15 a month in addition to room and board. "My mother and dad never bought me a shirt, a pair of socks, or a handkerchief until I was fourteen." Dropping out of school after eighth grade, he saw no alternative other than striking out on his own. "I rode freight trains. I heard about a job in Las Cruces. I hitched a freight tryin' to see about that job on a ranch." When that did not pan out, he hitched one headed north:

> And they switched us off here at Socorro. I was sittin' out here under a bridge. Goddamned, I could draw you a picture where it was. I was about sixteen or seventeen. It started thunderin' and lightnin'. I didn't have no money. I didn't have nothin' to eat. And that's the only time I ever called to cry. But I was under that viaduct about 4 o'clock in the morning. I didn't know where to turn. After it got daylight, the sun come out and it cleared off. Two or three hobos up town bought some grub and fixed some breakfast, and hollered to me to come down and eat with them—I didn't have a penny. The sun come up. Hell, I was alright. I made it![69]

He did, and he would.

Gender

Just as work constituted an important element in the life of boys, so it did for girls as well. To be sure, much of the time growing up female and Navajo was spent on domestic chores of hogan life: cleaning, cooking, and assisting to rear younger siblings. Although the division of labor in Navajo society was fairly flexible, with both males and females performing such chores as planting, weeding, and harvesting gardens, the hogan was strictly the women's domain. By the time daughters achieved puberty they were accomplished at grinding corn, preparing mutton stews, turning out tasty fry bread, and cooking all manner of corn dishes, including blue corn tamales. The hogan, daughters were taught, was the women's dominion, a symbolic expression of women's central role in bestowing sustenance and fostering harmonious relations.[70] In this connection, Alamo Navajo daughters on the verge of marriage most likely took to heart the sentiments of various hogan songs their cultural cousins sang up north, one of which proclaimed:

> Beauty extends from the rear corner of my hogan,
> it extends from the woman,
> Beauty extends from the center of my room,
> it extends from the woman,
> Beauty extends from the fireside of my hogan,
> it extends from the woman,
> Beauty extends from the side corners of my hogan,
> it extends from the woman,
> Beauty extends from the doorway of my hogan,

it extends from the woman,
Beauty extends from the surroundings of my hogan,
it extends from the woman,
Beauty radiates from it in every direction, so it does.[71]

Young girls also spent considerable time herding. Tennie Guerro remembers all too well the price of losing track of a sheep or two when her grandmother sent her and another child to herd some 500 sheep and goats (an exceptionally large flock by Alamo Navajo standards). At the end of the day, when the girls brought in the flock, her grandmother stood waiting to check for missing animals. With two pockets, one filled with white pebbles and the other with black ones, she rapidly counted the returning sheep, dropping the black and white pebbles into two coffee cans. "If we'd lose one sheep or goat, she'd say, go look for it. So we don't never answer back or say no. We do it. Just go straight over there and look for it."[72]

By the age of ten, some Alamo Navajo girls were also learning to weave saddle blankets and rugs.[73] In the early twentieth century a nearly ubiquitous scene in Alamo Navajo family units was that of a baby propped up in a cradleboard observing his or her mother seated before her loom giving birth to brightly colored rug patterns spun of traditional designs and the weaver's imagination. Young girls showing interest and promise as weavers were generally encouraged to develop their skills, for a handsomely woven rug could be bartered for bags of flour, coffee, and canned goods at the Fields' trading post or sold to Ray Morley's tourism establishment. The young weaver was painstakingly taught all the steps in the production process: shearing the sheep, carding and spinning the wool, making dyes, and finally, the precise art of weaving itself. One of the reservation's premier weavers recalls that she was fourteen when she completed her first rug, a diamond design 18 inches by 2 feet in size, an accomplishment of which she was immensely proud. Both her mother and uncle urged the girl to "stick with that weaving," advice that in time enabled her to produce stunning works of art while helping to feed the family.[74] In Alamo Navajo country the connection between women's labor at the loom and the family's material welfare was a long-established fact of life. In 1902, rancher-trader Nels Field reported to the *Socorro Chieftain*, "The Indians [who] lost their crop by the drouth manage to make blankets enough to live by." Nearly thirty years later Field informed readers in Magdalena, "Indians have come every day from Alamo to buy supplies at the Fields' store. We have quite a collection of Navajo blankets."[75] Weaving would remain an important source of income for years to come.[76]

Rita Mexicano at loom, Datil, New Mexico, ca. 1930. (Courtesy of the Wheelwright Museum of the American Indian, no. WW2-4.)

Hispanic and Anglo females also performed a number of domestic chores: cooking, washing dishes, cleaning, caring for younger siblings, filling kerosene lamps, straining milk through a cloth, making butter and cheese, emptying chamber pots, and canning. One Hispanic woman recalls that her mother organized the work week into a strict routine: Monday was wash day; Tuesday was ironing; Wednesday was sewing and mending; Thursday was house cleaning; Friday was catching up on unaccomplished projects; and Saturday was devoted to baking, which in this instance was done in outdoor ovens. Whatever the pattern of the work week, young girls spent hours washing clothes over tubs of boiling water, scrub boards, rinse water, and primitive ringers. Ironing was a major operation. All clothes were soaked in a pot of starch. Heavy irons were heated on the stove; as one cooled with the pressing and crease making, another was reached for. "My mother really took pride in her laundry," Lucianita (Lucy) Pino remembers. Even for the Levis, "the crease had to be absolutely perfect."[77] Older daughters, after they learned to sew, made clothes for the younger children, frequently from discarded flour sacks. One woman recalls the special day her father brought home store-bought cloth for the children. "My dad told my mother, 'Now you let them make a dress. If they ruin that material, that's fine. Just let them. I know how you are; you want them to be perfect the first time. Let them do it.' Boy! That really made us feel good. So the dresses fit okay. We made our own patterns. I used that dress for the fiestas that year. I don't know how well it was made but I was very proud and I wore it."[78]

Work responsibilities frequently extended to the outdoors. Throughout New Mexico women regularly tended and harvested gardens, fed chickens, milked cows, chopped wood, and hauled water.[79] Bernadyne Powell Brown says, "Milking time was always after night—I can't remember why, unless the cows had not come in, but I remember I went after the cows at night. . . . We always milked eight or ten cows." Often outdoor work was a family affair. When Lucy Pino's mother decided to enlarge their adobe house, Lucy was enlisted to mix and mold adobe bricks. The entire family went into the mountains to gather wood and pick piñon. For Lucy, the latter excursions were especially memorable. "I loved that because my folks would build a little fire for me . . . so I would stay warm, and we slept outdoors, and my mother used to cook beans in a big Dutch oven, and biscuits on top." On one occasion, Lucy filled a 100-pound bag, enough for her mother to buy her some fashionable white boots and some sewing material for a blouse and pants.[80]

On ranches, however, the gender boundaries came closest to collapsing—especially when sons were in short supply. In addition to wrangling horses, girls, like boys, helped with roundups and branding, jerked cows out of bogs, and rode the fence line.[81] Josefia Leyba, born into a family of mostly girls, was only ten in 1933 when she helped her father and sisters drive sheep and cattle across the San Augustine Plains to the shipping pens in Magdalena.[82] The challenge facing eight-year-old Grace Higgins was that of "getting up the horses" each morning. The problem was that her horse, Midget, a part-Shetland horse her father had purchased for her, balked at performing the predawn chore. Grace could saddle and bridle the horse, but the minute she rode the horse over the ridge out of her father's sight, it routinely bucked her off, forcing her to wrangle the horses on foot. Meanwhile, the savvy Midget waited by a distant water tank until the horses were headed for the corral, whereupon he compliantly joined them. After several days of seeing his daughter walk back to the corral covered in scratches, Grace's father decided to put an end to it. One morning, as the girl was saddling her horse, her father laid a freshly braided quirt over the saddle and asked: "Do you know what that's for?" Then he proceeded to explain.

> You take that horse and you go get them horses. And if that horse throws you off and comes home without you, when you get home we're going to

use that quirt on you. This is the time and you learn who's boss. Don't let her get away from you. You have been taught enough; you have watched all your life; you've seen me break horses. You've been in the corrals with the cowboys all your life. And this little bitty horse—you make up your mind—is she goin' to boss you or what? But if she comes home without you, I'm going to use that quirt on you.

The moment of truth had come: it was either stay on the horse or be whipped. Fearing the consequences of being thrown, Grace rode Midget over the ridge that morning with renewed determination. She also remembered her Dad's last words: when the horse began bucking, get hold of the bit and hold on; grabbing hold of the reins would only burn her hands. "So I did. I jerked her head around and got hold of that bit and off I went. But I never did turn loose. And I got the quirt and I whipped her. And I whipped her until she cried." After handing out the punishment, the eight-year-old climbed aboard again. "I rode all day and didn't have no trouble. And she never did pitch no more."[83]

Candelaria and Margarita García had a strong role model in their mother, who often assisted in the roping and branding of calves. With singular clarity, Margarita recalls her first experience with branding. With her father away, her mother, armed with a .38-caliber revolver in one chap pocket (for emergencies) and a knife in the other, directed the operation. Margarita's assignment was to build the branding fire and pass the hot irons to her mother as called for. At eight years old she had never before seen the operation close up, let alone played such an important role. "*El hierro derecho*" ("iron on the right"), she remembers her mother calling out, and then, "*Dame la eso*" ("the other one"). But for the eight-year-old the smell of the burning hide was too much to bear, and she started to vomit, at which point her mother "turned around and looked at me, continued to finish her job, then backslapped me so hard that I nearly fell over. She never said a word, but from that day on I never lost my nerve in front of her." For the girl the message was crystal clear: she must never cringe before a whole way of life. The only thing her mother protected her daughters from was the castrating. When it was time to castrate a colt, the girls were not allowed to watch. "She always said it was too much to witness."[84]

Most families appear to have shielded their young daughters from participating in branding and especially castrating. Indeed, Agnes Morley Cleaveland wrote, "The one phase of life, however, which I refused to face directly was the branding itself. However much of an accessory to the crime

I may have been in the matter of rounding up or even roping the calf, when it came to the actual applying of a hot iron to sentient flesh, I couldn't do it." Families adopted different postures on the degree of female involvement. Some sought to keep their daughters from witnessing the operation altogether. "Whenever they went to castrate the cows and the horses," recalls one woman, "us girls just didn't go near it—just my dad and the boys. We didn't even know about it." However, some ranchers adopted a middle position, expecting their daughters to help in the branding short of actually applying the hot irons or wielding a castration knife. "I used to get stuck tallying," remembers one Datil woman. "I'd sit upon the fence and tally the branding 'cause I couldn't physically get down there and wrestle animals. I didn't have the size." Girls also helped out in other ways: building branding fires, handing men the hot irons, dehorning, and vaccinating.[85]

Gender work roles were all but obliterated on those ranches where a shortage of sons forced daughters to be full-fledged "cowboys." Nowhere was this more evident than on the Fields' ranch, where Nels and Ida Field's offspring consisted of nine girls and no sons. Bessie Field recalls her father's frustration. "He always hoped that the next baby would be a boy. He used to say, 'Mother, I just have to have a boy in this family to run things.'" But it was not to be, with the consequence that several of his daughters grew up as genuine cowgirls, none more so than Bessie, whom Nels affectionately called his "foreman." Born in 1902, Bessie grew up hearing her father's stories of how as a youngster he had driven cattle up the Chisholm Trail. Bessie wanted the same life, a life of cattle and horses. Indeed her association with horses began at birth. Because her mother had pneumonia and the family was without a milk cow, Bessie was fed bottled mare's milk. Some of her earliest memories are of livestock. "It was just an everyday thing. I was just toddlin' around and I could hear cattle bawlin'." She commenced riding horses as soon as "I could sit up on a horse with my father," and she was soon begging him to take her with him as he rode out to check on stock. Bessie did her share of housework, but her passion was the outdoors. "I'll tell you what I used to do. I'd get up when mama got up to start breakfast and I'd go in there and I would tell her—now this wasn't lyin'—I told her I was going up there to feed my horse. . . . Well, I'd go out to the barn, and the next thing she knew I was gone."[86]

It was only a matter of time before Bessie proved herself the son Nels never had, whether it was riding 15 or 20 miles in search of a stray or helping her father build "miles and miles of fence." One year, Nels put Bessie and a sister in charge of a remuda of about seventy horses when several ranchers threw in together to make a "big loop" looking for stray stock. For fourteen days the girls herded the horses as the men periodically came in for fresh mounts. After two weeks in the saddle eating trail dust, "we were hard lookin' characters." By the age of fifteen, Bessie was helping her dad drive cattle to Magdalena. "I seen many a carload of cattle goin' out of Magdalena—hundreds of carloads of cattle. . . . I would just stand there and cry, tears running down my face. Us girls just cryin' cuz we just hated to part with those cattle. I guess we knew every cow papa had." But such scenes never dampened her enthusiasm for being a part of the drive. "I worked with herds right out there with the men, cuttin' cattle out, separatin' the brands." Whereas Agnes Morley Cleaveland could never bring herself to apply a red-hot iron to the side of a cow, Bessie felt no such inhibition:

> I could put a brand on as good as my Dad. I could tie a calf as good as any cowboy with a piggin' string. . . . I learned to castrate my first bull calf. And it wasn't any problem. It was something that had to be done. And I'd come home so dirty and bloody you couldn't tell me from a fresh butchered animal. But to me it was the happiest days of my life.

Bessie remembers the first time she slaughtered a cow. With her father away in Santa Fe fulfilling his obligations as state land commissioner, Bessie spent the winter living at the ranch with her mother and younger sister, Katherine, who was disabled by polio at the age of four. Bessie thinks it was about Thanksgiving when her mother said, "We've got to have meat of some kind or another. We can't live on bacon. I'm so sick of bacon." There had been a few chickens, but "by the time the skunks, bobcats, and the coyotes got through with 'em," there was little sustenance to be had in that direction. Something had to be done.

> So mama gave me papa's rifle and told me to go lookin' for a beef. So I took the rifle with me and the scabbard . . . and found a cow and a calf that I could drive home. The calf was about, well, he was still nursing his mother—about eleven months old. I had a little struggle there tryin' to get him to the house in the corral. Then I had to get ready to do my slaughtering. So my mother got the dishpan and the butcher knives and the big knife that papa always used to cut its throat. Well, I went up there—mama was there, right there aside me—and I walked in the corral. It took a lot of nerve; I shot that calf right square, one shot, and dropped it. So I went to work askinnin' that beef. I quartered it up, hung up the hide over the fence, and I carried the meat down in the

Bessie and Katherine Field display their success at trapping coyotes, ca. 1915. (Courtesy of John Guerro.)

wheelbarrow down to the house. Papa had meat hooks on the north side of the bunkhouse, and I hung the meat up and let it cool off that night.

When Bessie wasn't digging postholes or hunting up strays, she was earning a little money trapping coyotes for their hides, which, depending on the market, brought in a little money. Occasionally she caught a timber wolf that "was no problem to sell." Bobcat fur also was worth something. Trapping coyotes entailed baiting the iron trap, periodically checking it, shooting the captured animal between the ears with a .22 rifle, skinning the hide, and then drying it on a cedar stretcher. Nels packed the skins and sent them off to Denver, which paid top dollar. When the price of coyote skins dropped out of sight, Bessie settled for a lesser amount paid out by the state for the pest's ears. In the end, all these activities earned Bessie enough money to buy a horse, saddle, boots, spurs, and some lariats.

Bessie's helper in these operations was none other than her younger, polio-stricken sister, Katherine. With Katie only able to walk with crutches, Bessie devised special stirrups for Katie's "crippled legs" and tied her to a specially designed saddle, thus enabling her to join her older sister on the "coyote trail." Katie's share of the profits apparently went to support what was emerging as her special talents as a sketch artist, especially her ability to depict scenes from ranch life. Years later her sketches would appear in livestock publications and on western calendars. In many of these efforts she teamed up with western poet Bruce Kiskaddon. In one such collaboration she rendered a sketch to accompany a poem, "Daddy's Boots," which began:

> This baby is wearin' her daddy's big boots
> She is makin' believe they are hers.
> She is ridin' a stick that's a terrible brute.
> She stomps and she rattles her spurs.[87]

Daddy's Boots, *sketch by Katherine Field, 1939. (Courtesy of Laurie Taylor Gregg.)*

Katherine Field standing with horse, ca. 1925. (Courtesy of Tom Barrington.)

For the daughters of Nels and Ida Field, filling their "daddy's boots" clearly held more allure than the drudgery of ranch house chores. Indeed, Katherine Field, the girl who despite her disabilities rode the "coyote trail," sought to convey in poetry the romance of coming of age in a land where gender boundaries might be suspended—temporarily at least—even for a girl on crutches. Writing for the local newspaper in 1929, Katherine, now an adult, reminisced:

> Sometimes I see a windin' trail,
> Leadin' across th' ol' home range,
> An' once more I'm on my blue-roan horse,
> The blood leapin' in my veins.[88]

Work and Play

In western historian Elliot West's account of childhood on the Anglo frontier, he takes note of "one of the most delicious ironies of the children's story," namely, that as pioneering families "moved forward in space," they actually were "traveling backward in time," where earlier patterns of living held sway. About the same group, another historian writes, "For many children the western adventure was a nightmare from which they longed to awaken."[89] True enough, when children's lives—Anglo, Navajo, and Hispanic alike—were dictated by endless toil and crippling poverty, the hardscrabble West stood in stark contrast to "modern" ideas of childhood emergent in an urban, middle-class culture where the virtues of play were extolled and child labor deplored. The contrast was nowhere greater than in west-central New Mexico, where children, depending on their ethnocultural status, spent hours "busting calves" or setting out in the early dawn to herd sheep.

But the larger picture tells us that children's lives were more than this. For one thing, children often found meaning in their workaday lives. Whether performing household chores, helping in the gardens, or herding sheep, they took solace in the fact that they were contributing to the family's welfare. When a young Navajo girl began learning to weave a fine rug, she knew the skill potentially offered a source of income for her family. Looking after her grandmother's sheep, moreover, would one day result in her having her own animals. Without doubt, coming of age in the cattle economy had its special rewards. The fact that the work was horseback and enshrined in the cowboy myth brought its own unique satisfactions. For some, the pronouncement that young Billy or Jimmy would "make a hand" or was "good enough to take along" made the miles of trail dust and early morning horse wrangling as satisfying as $1-a-day wages. Finally, endless hours of working with livestock helped these youths sort out their futures. If some might look for ways to escape it, others took to it. Melvin Akers, for instance, recalls, "When I was big enough to walk up and put my hand on a horse I knew what I wanted to do from there on. I never had no problem with wonderin' if this was what I wanted to do. I knew it. I wanted to be a rancher. I wanted to be a cowman, or cowpuncher."[90]

Three other observations flow from these stories of work and play. The first is the extent to which the two were often intertwined. Certainly there were times when children experienced the joy of play unburdened by the responsibility of work. Most children found time to engage in adventurous exploration, playing with homemade toys, sledding down snow-covered mountains, running races, and romping with livestock. Navajo children molded clay hogans and sheep corrals in the Rio Salado river bottom, and like ranch children in the region, raced and galloped spirited horses across the land. In a time and region where children's labor was deemed both necessary and ordinary, they could be endlessly inventive in extracting play out of work. So often, it began and ended with animals. When a child was horseback, the worlds of work and play melded. Looking for a lost cow was work of sorts, but it also opened up the gates of adventure, a chance to drink in the landscape and imagine stories about your life.

Second, mainly Anglo ranch children internalized a social outlook informed by exaggerated conceptions of rugged individualism and personal freedom. As noted earlier, self-reliance was an important value in both Navajo and Hispanic cultures as well, but in both instances kinship and religious traditions worked to temper the more severe strains of individualist thinking. Unfettered by these constraints, Anglo youths' work experience—the long periods alone horseback, the assumption of adult work roles at an astonishingly young age, and the death-defying brushes with danger—contributed over time to a leaner, more survivalist frame of mind. More than either Navajos or Hispanics, Anglo ranch children were natural social Darwinists (in spite of the federal New Deal policies in which cattle ranchers readily participated). Reflecting back on his youth, one rancher remembers all the times "you're kinda out on your own. You go off on a horse. You gotta figure out how to survive by yourself or you don't get back. Things happen. Your horse falls with you or gits away from you." A woman rancher offers, "Just the strongest ones were the ones that lived. That's all there was to it." Another rancher opines, "I'm still believe in the survival of the fittest."[91] Children saw this easily enough and frequently grew up disdainful of government programs—especially federal—that impinged on their freedom of operation or those deemed "handouts" to those undeserving of government largess.

Finally, one is struck by the flexibility of gender roles. If in Navajo society the domestic worlds of the hogan and rug weaving were women's realm, herding sheep fell to both genders as did the maintenance of gardens and butchering. In ranch country, "Put a kid on a horse" was hardly gender specific. Think of the Field sisters' eagerness to fill "Daddy's boots," and in particular, Bessie Field's desire to be "good enough to take along." As one historian observes, there is a "sad paradox" in growing up in the frontier West—namely, that "pioneer childhood offered the most liberating possibilities for young girls, only to snatch them back as they reached their adult years."[92] In the main this was true. But in the meantime, young females such as Bessie were claiming a piece of the frontier myth, and for Bessie it continued after marriage. In August 1929, Nels Field sent this news item to the *Magdalena News*: "Bessie Field Scott is our official bronco rider.... Bessie purchased a black colt Monday and has been busy breaking him. During the branding work a few weeks ago she rode one that made her dizzy."[93] For Bessie the smell of saddle leather beat altogether the scent of perfume.

CHAPTER THREE

PLEASURES AND TRANSITIONS

Growing up in west-central New Mexico necessarily involved two kinds of transitions. The first involved space. The most dramatic in this regard was the geographical displacement forced on Alamo Navajo children occasioned by their removal to distant schools (a subject to be examined later). A much more pleasing journey was that made by Anglo and Hispanic children living on isolated ranches and homesteads to the bustling town of Magdalena, a town that by 1920 laid claim to a population of nearly 2,000. Where else could one see automobiles chugging alongside horseback cowboys and freight wagons, watch herds of bawling cattle being loaded into boxcars pulled by a puffing locomotive, witness the wonders of electricity, attend a moving picture show, gaze upon the riches for sale at Mactavish's store, and take in a first-class rodeo with bucking horses of regional fame? For freshly paid cowboys and sheepherders there were the sensual pleasures to be had at one of the town's several brothels.

There were also the transitions wrought by time. In this instance time was not historical nor strictly chronological, but rather biological—namely, the changes that came with the onset of puberty. The fact that postpubescent youths might engage in all manner of intimate relationships made this one of the most consequential and perilous periods of their lives. It followed that each ethnocultural group had its own rituals and normative prescriptions for guiding tempestuous youths through this dangerous phase of their lives, which, if successfully negotiated, might well culminate in a successful lifelong union. Because the stakes were especially high for females, their behavior received a disproportionate amount of attention. In the end, instruction in the rituals and mechanics of female-male social interaction came from many directions and played out in a multitude of settings. Along the way, Navajo chantway singers, black-shawled Hispanic grandmothers, and square-dance callers played their part.

Magdalena Town

On average, ranchers and homesteaders living in the far country made the trip to Magdalena twice a year, either to ship livestock or buy supplies. Sometimes entire families made the journey, the town offering a welcome relief from the isolation and exhausting work of frontier living. For men there were the multiple satisfactions of selling and shipping livestock, settling up accounts, and the chance to do a little drinking and gambling. For women the satisfactions were those of eating in one of the hotel restaurants, socializing with other women, and perusing the merchandise stores, the latter activity eminently more rewarding than gazing at the pages of a Sears and Roebuck or Montgomery Ward Catalogue. Selecting which 50-pound bag of flour to purchase had its own pleasures—the cloth bags, coming in a variety of colors and patterns, perfect for dressmaking. (When women remained at the ranch, it fell to their husbands to make the choices. "I can remember daddy standin' there lookin', and goin' through big stacks of flour to pick out the ones that would make the prettiest dresses.") For children, especially, visiting Magdalena was an introduction to a wonderland of discoveries. One homesteader's son recalls, "Treat? Goddamned, it was unbelievable—a town with electric lights, running water, bathrooms. Hell, I didn't know what it was." However much the children of the far country might love the limitless vistas of sky and mesa, all anticipated the sights and experiences awaiting them at the trail's end.[1]

One of the first things that caught young Bernadyne Powell's attention when walking down Magdalena's main street was the red-and-white-striped pole in front of the barbershop. Never having seen such an apparition before, and entirely ignorant of the business within, Bernadyne's childhood imagination told her the pole could be only one thing: a giant stick of peppermint candy. There was only one thing to do. To the "horror and embarrassment" of her mother, the girl attacked the pole and began vigorously licking it. Candy, it turns out, was one of the chief attractions of the town for children. Every time Cecil Taggert's folks came to town to buy supplies, one of the store clerks could be counted upon to present the children a small bag of candy. "Oh man, that was the GREATEST thing in the world. This candy wasn't worth maybe a penny in them days, but for us that was a GREAT EVENT."[2]

When parents gave children a coin or two the horizons of pleasure expanded. The first item on one Dusty youngster's list was a Coca-Cola. The rest of the money he spent on a cap pistol and ammunition, whereupon he proceeded to shoot up the town. Strapped for cash, children might try their hand at acquiring goods in the manner of their parents, that is, merely instructing the store clerk to add the purchase to the family account. When the daughter of a prominent rancher spotted some lace and velvet perfect for making doll clothes, instructing the clerk to charge it to her daddy's account, the clerk happily obliged. But this practice only occurred once. The next time her father was in town he informed the store "not to give me as much as a spool of thread without a written order." The restriction held until marriage.[3]

Six-year-old José Ortega made two wondrous discoveries the first time he visited Magdalena. The first was when his father took him to a drugstore with a soda fountain. The boy was mesmerized by the bursts of the soda dispenser and was then confounded by the soda jerk's question: What flavor did he want? Stupefied, José responded that he wanted a soda. When he finally understood that he must choose a flavor, he decided on vanilla. "It taste pretty good." But even more exciting was seeing his first moving picture show. By 1920, Magdalena had one, possibly two, movie theaters. Although the films themselves were silent, the theaters were anything but quiet—for the simple reason that many of the Hispanics in the audience, still struggling with English, read the subtitles aloud. But subtitles were the last thing on little José's mind when he stepped into the darkened theater and saw the dramatic action flashing across the screen. "The first thing I saw this guy on a pinto horse with a six-shooter. I got SCARED. I thought he was comin' for me. I tried to get up the stairs." Interrupted midway in his escape, he received an explanation that the cowboy on the screen could not shoot him. After receiving this good news, José sat down again and began to enjoy the story. "I remember a rattlesnake bit a guy and another cowpuncher took a knife, cut it, sucked the bite and spit the poison out. But the first time I saw that guy comin' on that pinto horse, by God, I thought he was goin' to shoot me."[4]

If José had been a few years older, and it had been a few years earlier, he might have witnessed an even more amazing sight—the beer-drinking bear! According to rancher Tom Kelly, around 1910 his dad captured a couple of bear cubs and months later sold one to a local saloon keeper. "The owner kept the bear chained to the rail at the bar. The bear sat on a stool and drank beer like a man. He'd drink until he passed out. That saloon made a lot of money out of that bear. He was a big drawing card."[5] Surely he was. How long the stunt—or for that matter the bear—lasted is not known. Nor is it known what happened to the other captured cub. Nor is it known how many teens slipped through the saloon doors to see the spectacle. Meanwhile, the story only served to burnish the image of Magdalena as a place of marvelous discoveries, however questionable the moral quality of the experience.

No attraction matched that of the annual rodeo. This history of rodeo is a disputed subject. What is not disputed is that the core events of rodeo—roping and equestrian contests—grew out of the cattle economies of the West. Before the arrival of Anglo Americans, Mexican *vaqueros* periodically participated in *charreadas,* often held in conjunction with fiestas, where they competed in events that tested their skills in horsemanship, tossing lassos, wrestling steers, and riding bulls. After the arrival of Anglo Americans, the rise of the cattle industry, the popularity of "wild West" shows, and finally, the emergence of the cowboy myth, rodeos became the West's most distinctive and popular sport, in which cowboys displayed the skill and quiet courage thought synonymous with the "winning of the West."[6]

The high point in Magdalena's rodeo history was in 1918, when Tex Austin brought one of the country's biggest professional rodeo shows to town. On the eve of the event, the *Magdalena News* announced, "Every train for the past ten days has been overloaded with parties coming to the 'Big Doins,' while hundreds of people have been coming overland." Everything was set for the big show. "The buckingest broncs and the wildest steers are here ready for the fray. And hundreds of cowboys and cowgirls, steer riders, and riders of all kinds are here ready to do their part in entertaining the thousands of visitors." Unwilling to concede first place to Santa Fe or Albuquerque, the reporter went on to claim, "It will be the biggest entertainment of this kind ever staged in the state, and the crowds attending will be the largest ever attending an affair of this kind in the West." How many of those in the crowds were children is impossible to know, but those who attended could not fail to be thrilled by seeing famous rodeo stars such as Leonard Stroud, Shorty Kelso, and Hugh Strickland compete for honors and purses. Mabel Strickland, champion trick rider and steer roper, and Mildred Douglas, bronc and steer rider, were also part of the Austin program and served as flesh and blood role models for young cowgirls in the audience.[7]

The Austin show was a onetime event, but Magdalena's rodeo tradition gained new life in 1924 with the "Annual Round-up."[8] Now the contestants were largely range cowboys, a few of whom went on to national fame. But whether it was Austin's extravaganza or Magdalena's regional contest, the sight of cowboys riding bucking broncs and wrestling steers fired the imagination of youth. Legendary "outlaw" horses were also objects of fascination. At the Austin rodeo the focus of attention was on Done Gone, a local horse billed as the "world's worst pitching horse." When bronc rider Ed Wright put the horse "through his poses," the reporter wrote, he "put up a pretty exhibition of fancy riding" before the powerful dun sent him flying. Such sights left indelible impressions on young cowboys, as evidenced by Langford Johnston's recollection of Angelo Hughes's near-fatal effort to stay aboard Done Gone. Johnston recalls that the outlaw horse "came out jumping high. After two jumps he reared high in the air, almost straight up on his hind legs, and swapped ends. It seemed to me that Hughes's feet went 20 feet high" before he hit the ground and lay motionless. The rider was carried off on a stretcher but survived to ride another day. Between events Johnston was astonished to see a small girl riding the famed bronc down the street as tame as could be.[9]

Young or old, those who attended rodeos did not leave disappointed. Imagine the thoughts of the crowd in 1918 when Austin unveiled a new event that weirdly meshed steer wrestling with the automobile—auto bulldogging. As the reporter described the action, the stunt involved daredevil cowboy Tex Parker standing on the running board of a Paige racing car, chasing a panicky steer. The first go-around did not go that well. "In the first attempt the steer was killed by the car running over the animal." In the second attempt, however, Parker successfully leapt from the car, grabbed hold of the steer's horns, and then went head-over-heels turning a double somersault with the animal in tow. Onlookers had little reason to doubt the newspaper's assessment that it was the "most reckless exhibition ever pulled off at an affair of this kind."[10]

Children looked upon Magdalena as a mecca of peppermint pleasures and eye-popping adventures. Bernadyne Powell recalls that when her family members made the trip to Magdalena in the 1920s for the annual rodeo, they stayed in the Bartlett Hotel. This and taking in the sights were special treats. But mostly, "I loved the rodeo, the pitching horses and bucking bulls, even though it scared me to watch." When her father made the occasional trip to town by himself to buy the year's supply of staples, the railhead town still served as a symbol of civilization and anticipated delights. The returning wagon almost always contained clothes (purchased ahead by catalogue), powdered and brown sugars, a bit of chocolate, and quantities of dried peaches, apples, raisins, prunes, and apricots. "We always were waiting for my dad's return and as soon as we would see him coming, mama would get the skillet out to fry the baloney [sic] my dad would always bring. What a celebration we would have."[11]

Seedier Pleasures

In 1906, five-year-old Norman Cleaveland made his first memorable trip to Magdalena with his grandmother, Ada Morley. In the midst of his grandmother's social calls, the two somehow became separated, whereupon little Norman "set off to see the sights." Shortly, Johnny Higgins, a local cowboy and friend of the family, spotted the boy and invited him to join him in Jerry Wheeler's saloon. When they entered the establishment, several cowboys turned to say hello, addressing him by name:

> I tagged along as Johnny Higgins threaded his way through the tables to where a crowd was gathered around a roulette wheel. They opened up and made room for us. I kept peeking up over the table trying to see everything going on as the wheel spun and the little white ball spurted and jumped around until it finally landed in a slot amidst shouts and groans of the players. I was trying so hard to see everything that somebody finally perched me up high on a stool. When all the bets were down, I was invited to spin the wheel. Then the croupier flipped the little white ball into the spinning wheel and it began its jumping and skipping from one slot to another as the wheel went round and round. Every eye watched the wheel, and the room was suddenly silent. Then the wheel slowed and stopped and the little white ball fell into its final slot—and a yell went up from the winners.[12]

Understandably, the five-year-old was swept up in the moment. "I never before experienced such excitement. It was the high point of my life, and I was the center of attraction as I was acclaimed by the winners and frowned on by the losers. Then, all of a sudden, the shouts and laughter ceased, and men nodded their heads or signaled with their eyes toward the front door of the saloon." Following the cowboys' collective gaze, Norman spied the source of the sudden hush—Grandmother Morley, "standing there hands on hips and her eyes full of fire, just ready to explode." As president of the New Mexico chapter of the Woman's Temperance Union, Ada Morley saw saloons and gambling as responsible for much of society's moral and social wreckage. The sight of her grandson—still in the innocence of his childhood but spinning the roulette wheel in the midst of whisky-drinking cowboys—was the worst of all imaginable visions. Little wonder that she exploded, delivering a "blistering denunciation" of all those contributing to the boy's fall from grace. Meanwhile, young Norman was given over to humiliation and "wails of anguish" as he witnessed the tongue-lashing being unleashed on his newfound gambling companions.[13]

For those parents kept awake at night worrying about their children's moral development, there was much to fret about. Saloons and gambling houses were a ubiquitous feature of frontier communities, and Magdalena did not disappoint in this regard.[14] Particularly during shipping or rodeo season, thirsty ranchers, cowboys, and sheepherders flooded the drinking establishments to celebrate, let off steam, gamble, "spin windies," and generally raise a little hell. Well into the twentieth century, scenes of a "well-oiled" cowboy riding his horse into a saloon or a slugfest between drunken ranch hands were not that unusual. When things got out of hand, the town marshal, who one cowboy remembers having a stutter, would enter the establishment with his two-barreled "talking machine" and announce, "You boys b-b-b-better git a little bit quieter." Normally, that was enough.[15]

Youngsters in their teens were frequently witness to such scenes. As one local recalls, "If they were big enough to walk up to the bar, they were big enough to drink." Langford Johnston was only fifteen when an old cowboy "bought me a shot." Because the boy was already a working cowboy, neither the old-timer nor the bartender thought twice about the propriety of it. In one of the town's watering holes, Bud Medley was seventeen when an elder cowboy made a crude remark about his sister. Defending his sister's honor, young Medley hit the cowboy so hard he sailed through the establishment's front window. The brawl continued in the street, where the seventeen-year-old proved strong enough to carry the day. Although alcohol had much more appeal to youngsters than gambling, this too was not a foreign country.[16]

When young cowboys neared the end of a trail drive, the town's moral elite liked to imagine that the dusty herders' thoughts were of innocent pleasures—on the order of ice cream. Sometimes they were. After Cecil Taggert and two other young cowboys (all in their teens) delivered a herd to the stockyards, each of the pleasure-hungry trio bought a quart of ice cream to take back to the camp outside of town. "We'd come back and sit out there by the campfire and eat it, ate that whole damn quart of ice cream, shiverin', shiverin', and shiverin', in November. . . . That was a BIG TREAT. That was a BIG DEAL."[17] What worried those who feared for youths' moral character was that over time the desire for ice cream might give way to pleasure-seeking in less reputable quarters, like one of the town's saloons, or worse yet, an establishment devoted to slaking thirsts of a more carnal nature.

Like saloons, houses of prostitution were commonplace in the West. In its heyday, Magdalena had four such establishments. Known by sobriquets such as "soiled doves," "fallen angels," "daughters of joy," or simply harlots, prostitutes catered to mostly unmarried cowboys, sheepherders, miners, and visitors passing through town.[18] For the town's moral guardians the presence of "cat houses" constituted a pernicious threat to both the town's image and youths' moral development. With these two concerns in mind, city officials announced in May 1918 that the "houses of ill fame" must close down. A month later, the village ordinance laid out the particulars. Henceforth, it was unlawful for prostitutes and "suspicious females" to congregate either in public places or the streets and alleys of the town between midnight and 6 o'clock in the morning. Second, any female's presence in a house of prostitution would be deemed "prima facie evidence of her character as a lewd woman or common prostitute." Third, such females were forbidden to ply their trade in any public place, a prohibition that included making lewd and boisterous comments on the street or calling out from windows and doorways. The penalty for such crimes ranged from $5 to $50, and for those unable to pay, a combination of thirty days in jail and public works.[19]

But the ordinance was rarely enforced. The demand for the sexual services was simply too great, especially at shipping time, when freshly paid sheepherders and cowboys hit the town. Locals can still point out the locations of the houses: Casa Grande, the Green House, and the West Hotel. At the trail's end, according to one account, cowboys "would take a bath, buy a new pair of Levis, a quart of whisky and away they'd go." The town's daughters of joy also proved endlessly creative in their outreach activities. In an attempt to get a jump on the competition, some set out to meet herders the minute they delivered their livestock for shipping. "I remember the whores even when I was little," remarks one Hispanic man. "They used to leave Magdalena to come out to meet the herds—to get the money right away before they spent it in the bars."[20]

Both Hispanic and Anglo girls worked as prostitutes. However, one rancher who frequented brothels as a young man relates, "The cheap ones were Mexican. There was two or three houses there that had white girls in it. The goin' price was two bucks. But most kids didn't have that much money. So if they was inclined that way, they had to go to a cheaper place." Fifty cents, he recalls, would "git the job done." Two of the establishments were managed by madams, and in at least one of the houses the girls were periodically rotated and examined by a doctor for disease. In "Mother Watson's" establishment, when a cowboy became too unruly, Watson had him thrown out. But according to Melvin Akers, most cowboys "had great respect for prostitutes . . . ; it was just second nature to be respectful to 'em. I don't say they all was, but the great majority was." Perhaps so, but for those high-minded citizens devoted to improving the town's moral climate, the brothel element was an embarrassing stain on the community's image.[21]

Youths had varying degrees of familiarity with the town's sex traffic. Candelaria García recalls asking her mother about a restaurant-fronted brothel from which there seemed to be an unusual number of pretty women coming and going. Her mother's response: "*Este es el restarante de las mujeras bonitas,*" or, "It's the restaurant of the pretty ladies." One day, while she was kicking a rock down the street, Candelaria observed yet another house inhabited by "pretty ladies." What confused the child was that the pretty ladies were being visited by an unusual number of men, some of whom she recognized. "That's what I couldn't figure out. See, I couldn't put the two together: why the pretty ladies, and why the men I knew were going in there, because they were family men, and I knew them." When she grew to be fourteen or fifteen, her mother explained the true nature of the pretty ladies' business.[22]

For those young Hispanic females entering the workplace as waitresses, dishwashers, and chambermaids, they were no longer under the protection of the family. When one young woman took a job in one of the town's hotels, her mother, without explanation, gave her strict instructions: she should only work in the dining room and the kitchen; under no circumstances should she ever go upstairs or leave the building. After she was on the job, the daughter did observe some strange goings-on. For inexplicable reasons some of the female help were going upstairs, and then there was the mystery of why the doctor made regular visits to the rooms. Naïve as to what all this meant, she finally got "nerve enough" to ask her mother what was going on. Her mother's answer revealed a side of Magdalena's social life far seedier than her sheltered daughter had ever suspected. For another young waitress working at the same hotel, the revelation was even more startling. It came when one of the hotel guests asked her to bring a pitcher of ice water up to his room. "So I got the ice water and ran up to the room and knocked on the door. He says, are you the girl who is bringing my ice water? Yes sir. Come on in, honey. I'll never forget he had the window shades drawn by moving from the breeze. So he's lyin' there without a thing on. I don't know what happened to the water. Shoo!—and I flew down the stairs."[23]

Certainly adolescent boys with a strict religious upbringing, Protestant or Catholic, avoided these scenarios. One Hispanic man confesses that it

PLEASURES AND TRANSITIONS : 115

was the moral influence of his mother that kept him away from such pastimes. "I didn't go there at all. And you know why I didn't? My mother. It goes back to her."[24] But apparently many pubescent males had no such compunction. Indeed, for some adolescent males, visiting a brothel served as a sort of rite of passage into manhood.

> No problem. If you had the two dollars, you was in business. Ole Mother Watson, she was a big ole fat gal. We always called her Mother Watson because she was the matron. I took my youngest brother up there when he was gittin' up there in years. I thought he had to learn sometime. I'd been in there several times before. He was shy and bashful, probably about fifteen. He was just standin' there. We had to pretty much pick him up and drag him in there. All the rest of us was lookin', gigglin', pushin', and everything else. I don't know why he didn't kill us. Embarrassed him so bad. Finally, she drug him off in there in the room.[25]

How many youngsters underwent this initiation into adulthood is hard to tell. For those who did, the price could be high. Indeed, the above informant claims that one of Mother Watson's girls—"she was a good-lookin' ole gal"—sterilized four young men. He remembers like it was yesterday accompanying one of his teenage friends as he confessed an embarrassing problem to his father. "Papa," the boy blurted out, "I've got the gonorrhea." This met with the response, "You've got the WHAT?" When the boy made his situation clear, the father's only response: "Gee whiz, you'd better go see a doctor." When the local doctor could not cure him, he went to Silver City for treatment.[26]

Puberty, Forbidden Knowledge, and a Rite of Passage

The onset of puberty marked a definite alteration in youths' evolving physical and psychological being. Usually these changes were accompanied by a growing cognizance of the mechanics of copulation and procreation, but also the implications of this knowledge for one's behavior toward the object of one's desire. Generally, knowledge of the former came more easily to boys than girls. In this connection, breeding livestock, bawdy cowboy talk, and the schoolyard braggadocios accomplished this education. But for both Anglo and Hispanic girls this knowledge appears to have been dribbled out more sparingly, and however dispensed, it was almost always laden with stern admonitions on sexual conduct. Only in the instance of Navajo girls was the onset of puberty acknowledged publicly in a formal rite of passage, an elaborate ceremony signifying her changed status and responsibilities as a *Diné* woman.

For many girls, acquiring knowledge about the "facts of life" meant entering forbidden territory. Even for those raised around livestock, the subject of "where babies come from" was often not a fit subject for discussion. Betsy Crawford learned this the hard way on a cold and rainy spring night when she assisted her father in helping her pet goat give birth to two kids. When Betsy returned to the house and washed up, her older sister (who wanted no part of the operation), asked, "You saw it?" Betsy replied that she had indeed seen everything, and then made the mistake of adding, "And I'll bet you that's the way babies come." The words scarcely slipped out before "I got lifted with a good one, right on the backside, and my mother just gave me a good whipping. Oh, she slapped my butt. She beat me." Her father, she remembers, disapproved of the whipping, but the lesson was learned: even though she was expected to work in "nature," she was "not allowed to talk about it." Later, the lesson was reinforced. After some "fancy-lookin'" visitors left the ranch, Betsy offered the observation that the couple most likely "wouldn't know a bull from a cow." Her mother was once again horrified that her daughter would actually utter the word "bull." Betsy's explanation for her mother's objection was that she was "hard-shelled with religion."[27]

Betsy's experience might not have been that much out of the ordinary. One ranch woman who saw her share of livestock breeding and calves being born observes, "I've seen those things ever since I can remember.... But I never talked about it." Another woman concurs, "No, no, no.... We just knew better than to talk about it in the first place." Still another claims, "If I'd have walked in the house and said the word sex, my dad would probably blow the roof off." Although as a child she had raised lambs on a bottle and cared for dogie calves, her father had never permitted her to see the animals born. In fact it was not until she was in her fifties, when a rancher asked her to help him "pull calves," that she witnessed the birth of a calf.[28]

Hispanic females were also protected as long as possible from sexual knowledge. Candelaria García, for instance, never thought to resolve the contradictory explanations as to the source of newborn lambs and calves. On the one hand, her mother said that "God sent the animals"; on the other hand, she remembers hearing, "If we don't have a bull for that mother cow, we cannot have baby calves." For several years, the contradiction was never resolved. Children had too much respect for their parents to press the subject. The veil of secrecy was even stronger as to where human babies came from. "Of course in those years, we all shared the same bedroom, but . . . we never saw anything going wrong with my mother and daddy." Moreover, when her mother was pregnant, "we never questioned why our mother was getting big." The loose clothing also served to hide her swelling abdomen. When the baby came, it was somehow God's doing. In later years, her mother "finally broke down and gave us more details."[29]

On the precipice of womanhood, many Anglo and Hispanic girls watched the changes in their bodies with a mixture of ignorance and foreboding. One anthropological study of a village in northern New Mexico probably captures the state of a Hispanic girl's understanding of her changing physiology: "She is not given instruction by anyone, unless an older sister takes pity on her ignorance. So menstruation comes [as] a surprise, often a shock to her." At the same time, daughters were constantly subjected to strict admonitions on how to conduct themselves in the presence of the opposite sex.[30] Given the rich fund of *dichos*, mothers possessed a seemingly endless supply of instructive homilies designed to protect their daughters' honor—that is to say, their virginity—before matrimony. In this sense, mothers took seriously another mother's joking remark, "*Sujeten sus pollas que gallos andan libres*," or "Control your chicks, for my roosters are free." Later in her daughters' development, a protective mother might slip into her conversation valuable information like: "*Los hombres son como la vibora. Pican!*" ("Men are like rattlesnakes. They bite!") Upon hearing this warning from her mother, one Hispanic woman recalls taking it to heart even though she never was given to understand how men actually bit. But the message was clear enough. The double standard to which females were held was emphasized time and again. Following a sexual encounter, it was understood, "*El hombre siempre queda bien y secuda su leva*," or, "The man always walks away and brushes off his jacket." Not so for the woman. "*La mujer siempre está con su pecado que hizo*," or, "The woman always lives with the sin she has committed."[31]

In one instance, a young Hispanic female's source of sexual knowledge was the town priest. As in many households, Tomasita Gallegos grew up holding members of the Catholic clergy in awe. "When you saw a priest, you'd get all embarrassed. . . . You couldn't talk to them or look them in the eye." In this instance, the child's relationship with the priest was especially intense. When Tomasita went to confession, "I always confessed the same thing—things I didn't do sometimes, just to have things to say." One time when Tomasita was exiting the church alone, she imagined the priest had locked the doors on her. "I tried to push it open. I got scared. I thought he was going to grab me. I don't know why I thought that." Approaching the panic-stricken girl, the priest asked what the problem was, and then proceeded to show her that it was just her imagination: the door was not locked. Then he said, "Let me look at your eyes." At this point Tomasita was "shaking all over," and she "tore out of the church."[32] When she was fifteen:

> There was this guy, we were friends. And he said, have you ever been kissed? And I said no. They were very strict at home. He said, you want me to teach you how? I said, I don't think so. And he said, if you pay me 25 cents I'll show you. I said, let me see if I have 25 cents. So I did. I gave him a quarter, and he kissed me. I felt guilty about it, too. My mother kept saying girls shouldn't do this; it's a sin to kiss and all that. I couldn't STAND it. So I went to confession. The Father heard me crying and asked me why. Because I have sinned I told him. I had 25 cents—I told him the whole story. I told him I sinned. . . . I said, I don't know whether I'm gonna have a baby or not. But anyway I SINNED.

By this point the priest was out of the confessional and laughing. Merely kissing a boy, he explained, was not a sin; furthermore, babies were not made in that fashion. When Tomasita went home, she told her mother what she had learned, and *where* she had learned it. Her mother "didn't go to church for about a month. She was embarrassed mostly because she hadn't explained to me the facts of life and because the priest knew who I was and who she was." Shortly thereafter, the priest pulled Tomasita aside and presented her a pair of earrings and some lipstick. "No, I said. I can't take these. Because of my mother. If you talk to my mother, it's fine." He did, and it was.[33]

From all appearances the Navajo girls' transition to womanhood was less torturous, in large part because the moment was publicly marked by ceremony and rejoicing. As one scholar observes, "One cannot overestimate the importance of this rite in creating a positive self-image in a young girl."[34] By Navajo tradition, Changing Woman was the first to undergo the puberty rite of *Kinaaldá,* an elaborate ceremony lasting four days and nights and conducted as closely as possible after the appearance of menstrual blood. Navajos give several reasons for the rite in addition to its sacred origins: its public announcement of a young woman's eligibility for marriage and capacity for childbearing, its educational function in reinforcing the cultural ideals and norms governing Navajo womanhood, and finally its mythic role in guaranteeing a young woman's long-term health and prosperity.[35] Because there is no single version of *Kinaaldá,* the task of describing the

Alamo Navajo Kinaaldá *ceremony in process, ca 1920. (Courtesy of Rudy Latasa.)*

Alamo Navajo girls' precise experience is nigh impossible. Still, with the aid of Alamo Navajo recollections and the secondary literature, it is possible to identity several ritualistic moments in the four-day ceremony.

Let us imagine a fourteen-year-old named Agnes. The first day Agnes is dressed by an older, respected woman and has her hair fixed in a fashion reminiscent of Changing Woman's. As one song records:

> Before her, it is blessed,
> Behind her, it is blessed,
> Now with long life and everlasting beauty,
> Now she is dressing her up.

Also, on the first day, Agnes lies on a blanket, where an "ideal" woman proceeds to "mold" her into the shape of Changing Woman, thereby enhancing her strength, character, and beauty. During the first two days, Agnes spends much of her time grinding corn, symbolic of her preparation for marriage and motherhood, when the responsibilities of caring for and feeding her family will constitute a major portion of her day.[36]

A central element in the *Kinaaldá* is the morning race. This daily activity is to test Agnes's capacity for strength, health, and energy—all necessary ingredients of a productive and long life. Because the ceremony is a social event, any number of guests might join her in the race. As one Alamo

Navajo woman explains: "If the people wants to run with you, they run with you, but you never pass her—behind her all the time. I don't know what they do to you if you pass her. They never tell us that story." Agnes begins her race in the direction of the rising sun and charts her course to circle around a "young tree" that, like a girl entering the domain of full womanhood, is still growing. While running, Agnes and other runners send up shouts to the Holy People, signaling them that they are carrying out the sacred rite. As one of the ceremonial racing songs proclaims,

> Before her, it is blessed,
>   she starts off shouting,
> Behind her, it is blessed,
>   she starts off shouting
> Now the girl can endure much without tiring,
>   she starts off shouting.[37]

The culmination of *Kinaaldá* comes on the fourth night and following morning. Over this span of time Agnes hears many sacred songs, is lectured on her responsibilities as a woman (including the importance of not showing anger or spreading gossip), is blessed with corn pollen, runs her last race, distributes a special cake made from cornmeal ground by herself, and has her face painted in such a manner as to ensure she grows into a healthy woman. During the last hours of the rite, she reflects upon whether she has conducted herself properly over the four days. Has she been respectful to her parents, relatives, and elders? Has she demonstrated strength and endurance? Has she avoided the taboos? In the last regard, Agnes might have been instructed in any of the following: if she scratched her head, her skin would be scarred; if she laughed, she would get wrinkles; eating canned fruit would make her too weak to cook and weave; grouchiness would result in an ugly personality. But if all has gone well with *Kinaaldá,* there is much reason for gratitude. As the major chronicler of the ceremony writes, "It is almost as if the girl, in becoming a woman, has been physically and mentally reborn and is passing through several days in which both her body and her personality can be reshaped by the people around her, so as to correspond more closely with the cultural ideal."

> With beauty before me, I am traveling,
>   With my sacred power, I am traveling,
> With beauty behind me, I am traveling,
>   With my sacred power, I am traveling,

With beauty below me, I am traveling,
   With my sacred power, I am traveling,
With beauty above me, I am traveling,
   With my sacred power, I am traveling,
Now with long life, now with everlasting beauty, I live.
   I am traveling,
   With my sacred power, I am traveling.[38]

Fairs and Dances

In the course of making the transition to adulthood, youths were taking note of the opposite sex in a variety of social gatherings: Navajo fairs, Hispanic fiestas, and ranch house and town dances. Although the primary function of these events might not have been to spark amorous unions, they still provided youths ample opportunities for doing just that. Whatever their potential in this regard, community gatherings were vitally important as theaters for learning the culturally prescribed rituals and behaviors for engaging the opposite sex.

For Alamo Navajos, one of the primary opportunities for this came in the form of the "Girl's Dance," usually held in conjunction with the considerably more solemn Enemy Way ceremony. One elderly woman recalls sneaking out to observe such a dance in defiance of her parents' forbiddance. Stealing out at night, she and her sister watched the dancing from a distance for several hours before slipping home in the early morning, where they acted like "we didn't go anywhere that night."[39] Writing in the 1940s, anthropologists Clyde Kluckhohn and Dorothea Leighton observed that the chief function of the Girl's Dance was to provide an opportunity for marriageable young men and women to "look over" one another. "Most of the girls who dance are brought there to announce the fact that they have recently become, or still are, of the right age to marry." In that regard,

> The parallel to the debutante ball in white society is inescapable. Everyone—particularly members of families who are considering a marriage alliance—dresses as well as possible and appears with his best horse, wagon, or automobile. Putting up a front through borrowed jewelry and other finery is not unknown. Navaho mothers, a trifle franker than is usual among whites, literally push their daughters after a "catch," saying: "Go ask that boy. His mother has 2,000 sheep." At last even the shyest girl is induced to choose a man, and the dance goes on until morning.[40]

The other occasion for pubescent males and females to "look over" one another was at the annual August fiesta. The two-day event was something on the order of a fair. Although it was hosted and mainly attended by the Indians, a few Hispanics and Anglo ranchers also joined in the festivities. During the day, men and women competed in all manner of events. One of the most popular was the chicken pull, where horseback males ran at full gallop at chickens buried up to their necks in the sand, the aim being to extricate the bird with one sweeping arm motion. Men and women generally competed separately in horse racing, bronc riding, sheep roping, and other events. Older girls and women also engaged in contests of sheep- and goat-tying and tug-of-wars. At night, against the background of drums and singing, the dances began.[41] The most popular of these was a version of the Round Dance, which was women's choice. Here was a perfect opportunity for a young woman to show her interest in a young man. If not overly shy, she approached the man in the crowd and asked him to dance with her in the circle. Accepting or not, he was obliged to pay her a coin or two. For many years the Alamo Navajo fiesta was the largest community gathering on the reservation. Until it was abandoned sometime in the 1950s because of excessive drinking and fighting, it served as an ideal setting for young women and men to show off their athletic prowess, display their finest clothing and jewelry, dance, flirt, and eye one another as potential mates. (But as we shall see shortly, the last consideration was not entirely in their control.)

The express purpose of the Hispanic fiesta was ostensibly to honor the patron saint of the village and church. This much-anticipated event spanned two or three days and combined religious observances with feasting, socializing, and recreational activities such as foot and horse races, baseball games, cockfights, and a performance by the Kelly Miners' Band. For many, the highlight of the fiesta was the *baile,* or dance. According to the *Magdalena News,* "All afternoon and until midnight the Barrowdale Hall was a jam with dancers," the couples stepping out on the floor to perform a *chote, polca, varsoviana, walse,* or *cuadrilla.*[42] In addition to special occasions such as feast days and weddings, community dances were periodically held in the larger towns of Magdalena and Kelly. In more remote areas society-starved families periodically piled into wagons, buggies, and autos and headed to all-night gatherings at a *rancho,* where, after the socializing and eating, the furniture was moved back to make space for the dancing. Depending on the setting, the music differed widely in nature and quality. Often a guitar, violin, and perhaps an accordion were the instruments. One man recalls that in Kelly the postmaster's phonograph sometimes served

Mangas Fiesta, 1904. (Courtesy of Eliseo Baca.)

the purpose for weekly Saturday night dances. On special occasions a dance band was coaxed up to the mining community.[43]

Because families often traveled considerable distances to dances, children were often in attendance, although their freedom of participation differed greatly, with gender and age being the primary determinants. At the bigger dances, older children looked after the babies while the younger ones sat on the benches watching their parents display their dexterity on the dance floor. Some of the dances were indeed entertaining, such as the *Baile de la Silla,* or "Dance of the Saddle," which called for dancers to interrupt the dancing at designated moments to tell a joke. As the night wore on, the youngest children searched for a spot under the benches to sleep, the high-stepping, swirling dancers carefully avoiding the growing collection of slumbering children strewn along the floor's perimeter. At ranch houses, where the dancing carried on until dawn, children fell asleep in a bedroom or retired to bedrolls spread out under a star-studded sky, drifting off to sleep to sounds of singing guitars, thumping boot heels, and the occasional burst of laughter.[44]

During the early hours children joined in the dancing. Mostly these were happy moments but not always. One man who grew up in Kelly painfully remembers, "The first memory I have is that I liked to dance. I was always looking forward to that Saturday night dance. And then there was a man there by the name of Julian Cordova and he used to make fun of me. He said I was out there like I was nursing the ladies. I was about eight years old [and only came breast-high to the woman]. And that gave me an inferiority complex to where I didn't dance anymore. And I think I would have become a good dancer. It affected me to where I couldn't dance. It hurt my mother too."

Esther Peralta's memories are much fonder. When she was just five or six, her grandfather took her to the Kelly dances, where she danced on his shoes. After a while, she and the other children were escorted home, where "all of us would sit out on the porch and listen to the music. . . . But we knew we would go someday." As it turned out, "someday" never came. When the Depression came, the mines closed. "There was no dance by the time I grew old enough. Kelly wasn't there."[45]

As noted earlier, after Hispanic females were in their teens, most families closely monitored their daughters' relations with the opposite sex. One man recalls that his sisters were not allowed to date before an actual marriage proposal. In another family, the daughters were not allowed to date until they turned eighteen. When teenage girls were allowed to attend one of the town dances, it was usually under the chaperonage of their parents or a close relative. One woman recalls that it was a settled matter that their brothers were their dance partners for the first and last dance of the evening. "In those days [1940s] a girl who rode in a car was bad. You wouldn't even talk or wave to a boy in public," remembers one woman. Indeed, her parents were so strict they "wouldn't let me go to any dances or movies. I wasn't allowed to go to dances unless I worked all day, and my aunt used to take me. I didn't know what a movie house was until I was of age to get married—eighteen. Even then they went with me and my boyfriend to the movies. I was not let to go anywhere alone until I got married."[46]

Why such restrictions? Clearly the main explanation is cultural and historical, a throwback to old Hispanic-Catholic tradition that associated family honor with a daughter's virginity at the juncture of marriage. There was also the practical reason that fights sometimes erupted at the town dances, mostly on those occasions when unwelcome Anglo cowboys attempted to cross the ethnic divide but also when Hispanic males did the same. Of course the old *dichos* carried traditional warnings: the woman was of the house, the man of the street; watch your chicks for my roosters are on the loose. So they were. One Hispanic rancher says he came to learn early on how to distinguish between those to whom he tipped his hat and those he took to bed—a talent he describes as knowing how to "split the herd."[47]

But the times were changing. As modern attitudes infiltrated households, it was ever more difficult for families to regulate their daughters' behavior. One of the major reasons for this was the growing influence of the institution of the school relative to that of the family and the church. One can see this in the following account of how Victoria Martínez cleverly outwitted her mother's attempt to control who her daughter should date for the eighth-grade prom. Her mother knew that a very fine boy had asked her daughter to the dance. "My mother said he's a nice guy. You can go with him. He'll pick you up and bring you back at a certain time. You are to go with him, that's that!" This, Victoria explains, was a most unsatisfactory prospect. "I wanted to go to the prom, but I sure didn't want to go with him because I didn't like him." When the boy pressed his case, emphasizing that he had her mother's approval, "I said, I know, but you know something? I'll go with you but you leave me there and you WAIT for me. Well, do you [still] want me to go with you?" Remarkably, the boy accepted the terms. He picked her up, dropped her off at the prom, where a date of her own choosing met her at the door, and then "stayed waiting for me 'til it was time to go home," her mother none the wiser.[48]

When Anglo children grew up in isolated homesteads, they too experienced opportunities for socializing with the opposite sex. In a region where many families might go months on end without seeing their neighbors, the desire for community was immense. In the close-knit community of Pie Town, where homesteads tended to be smaller and the opportunities for social gatherings greater, families, in addition to Sunday worship, periodically came together for box suppers, group singing, and meetings of the Literary Society, which entertained old and young alike with plays, recitations, and an occasional debate on some stirring topic—such as the relative importance of the dishrag and the broom to civilization. Viewing an occasional movie at the Pie Town Farm Bureau building was also a high point in a region where motion pictures were a rarity.[49] But the most joyful and exuberant expression of social life in Pie Town—and the more sparsely settled ranch country as well—was the local ranch house or schoolhouse dance. Anabel Howell, a schoolteacher at Dusty in the late 1920s, recollects, "The entire population found their greatest pleasure and relaxation in attending dances. People came from a radius of 200 miles, by automobile, truck, horseback, wagon, and even by foot. The entire family from tiny babies to grandparents attended."[50]

There were the predictable holiday dances such as on Fourth of July and Valentine's Day, and there were the invented occasions such as Ray Morley's "Cow Thieves' Ball," when the price of admission was offering proof of cow stealing. But mostly no reason was needed, simply a yearning to reach across the expanse of miles to enjoy one another's company, for men to talk about cattle prices and the weather, women to trade stories and share recipes, and children to play games and race horses. "For any excuse we could think of we'd have a dance." After a dance was planned, word traveled quickly. "We'd just all get together and go around on horseback and tell them there's goin' to be a dance at the schoolhouse and bring anything you want," one homesteader's daughter remembers. One elderly rancher recalls, "I've rode 25 miles to a dance horseback. It killed half a day if you rode a good horse." His wife, recalling her youth, remembers riding 14 miles to a dance, where she danced "all night long until sunup." As Agnes Morley Cleaveland remembers these affairs:

> High-heeled boots pounded out the rhythms on rough floors; the lighter tap of feminine feet played treble accompaniment. . . . Toward morning the sufferings of my sex would become acute. Dazed with fatigue, I have dragged myself through the last hour of many a dance, praying for the sun to rise and put an end to my misery. A cowpuncher who would have gone to fantastic lengths to save a lady from discomfort in any other circumstances would be inhuman in his insistence upon "just one dance more."

But that was the point: to make the most of it—to dance schottisches, varsouviannas, polkas, waltzes, and square dances throughout the night to the music of a fiddle, a guitar, and perhaps an accordion, only taking breaks to feast on platters of beef, beans, pies, and cakes—and to gulp down coffee. "We had a grand time," one woman recalls. At the crack of dawn the footsore celebrants mounted their horses, cranked truck engines, and climbed into wagons filled with children asleep in their bedrolls, heading for home. That is assuming they did not injure themselves. In 1934 the *Magdalena News* reported, "Miss Joy Smith, of Beaverhead, was brought to Magdalena early Sunday morning and it was found the wrist of her left hand was broken, the result of a fall on a dance floor at a dance held in the Beaverhead district Saturday night."[51]

Children no less than parents enjoyed these occasions. In the early hours there was ample time for playing games, and when the dancing began they participated as much as their age and desire allowed. Fathers danced with their daughters, mothers with sons, and occasionally a sister coaxed her brother out onto the floor. By one account, "We danced everything that the grown people did. We learned and danced with the big people. They taught us." When the children were overtaken by sleep, they passed out in any available bed, or failing this, climbed into bedrolls in the family wagon, falling asleep under the stars, the night air filled with sounds of fiddle, guitar, and shuffling boots as a caller put their parents through the paces of a favorite square dance.

> Caller let no echo slumber
> Fiddler sweatin' like a steer;
> Hoof a poundin' at the lumber
> Makin' noise the stars could hear.[52]

One can only wonder what the coyotes thought of it all.

For those able to stay awake, there were dramas galore. Some adults took great pride in demonstrating their dancing prowess, as evidenced by Anabel Howell's description of an old ranch couple she identifies as the Moores. "Theirs was a very fast, intricate step on the order of a polka or a 'stomp,' and it was obvious they enjoyed showing off their skill." The performance was made all the more memorable by the fact that Mrs. Moore "danced with a gaping smile, showing her three remaining teeth." More to the liking of young ranch boys was the occasional fistfight. At one dance those in attendance witnessed a falling out between the fiddler and guitar player, both tipsy from imbibing moonshine. After trading insults for several minutes about each other's musical abilities—"If you could play, by God, it would be easier to keep time"—the two men laid down their instruments and took their argument outdoors. After exchanging several blows, they fell down and rolled over a half-dug well covered with planks, which immediately gave way under their combined weight. Pulled from the well, the two washed off in the horse trough, and after some persuading, agreed to take up their instruments for the sake of the dance. Somewhat sobered now, each was much more impressed with the other's musical ability. For one youngster, "That dance really stood out."[53]

Children asleep while their parents square dance, Pie Town, New Mexico, ca. 1944. Photo by Russell Lee. (Courtesy of Library of Congress, no. LC-USF34-036884.)

Square dances both reflected and reinforced the social norms and economic values of cow country. Performed by four couples who followed the directives of a "caller," square dances carried titles such as "Adam and Eve," "Ocean Wave," "Cheat and Swing," "Bow and Kneel to That Lady," "Don't Touch Her," "Bird in the Cage," and "Take a Little Peek." Moving through scripted steps, couples split apart, dancers left their partners to "visit" the opposite sex—"swing that gal"—but invariably were instructed to circle "home," prompting one scholar to observe that square dances were mostly scripted "depictions of controlled visits, stable homes, and monogamous male and female relationships."[54]

> Now swing you opposite across the hall,
> You haven't swung her since last fall.
> Now trot home and swing your own,
> And thank your stars the bird ain't flown.
> Now promenade.[55]

The culture connection is clearly evident in the so-called patter of square dances, the rhymed lines with which local callers introduced, ended, and laced their calls. Locally invented patter was laden with references to the material and cultural life of the region, and might even make light of forbidden behavior:

> First lady to the right;
> Swing that man that stole that sheep,
> Now the one that hauled it home,
> Now the one that ate the meat,
> Now the one that gnawed the bones.

Livestock theft was, of course, a touchy subject. Dancers were more likely to hear something on the order of:

> Rope that calf,
> Jerk the slack,
> Meet your lady
> And turn right back

Or:

> Rope your cow and brand your calf,
> Swing your honey an hour and a half!
> Here I come with the old mess wagon,
> Hind wheel broken and the axle draggin'.
> Meet your honey and pat 'er on the head,
> If she don't like biscuit give her cornbread!
> Promenade, boys, promenade![56]

In addition to alleviating loneliness, providing recreation, and forging community bonds, dances were important venues for postpubescent teens to explore the world of romance. Agnes Billings looks back on her fourteenth birthday—an occasion celebrated with a ranch house dance—as a "turning point in my life." The symbol of this transition was a black dress her mother allowed her to wear. "To me the only thing that was important to me that night was this long black dress. It wasn't the fact that I was fourteen, or goin' to be grown up. All I thought of was that mother finally consented to me wearing it—a long black dress." From now on, the ranch teen would regard herself differently, as would the young cowhands of the territory who took new notice of her.[57]

Just as entire families traveled long distances to dance, so young cowboys got "slickered up" and rode their ponies for miles to meet and dance with eligible females. Early in the evening a certain shyness might prevail, but as Ramon Adams notes, the spirit of the dance eventually worked its magic:

"The whining of the fiddle, the shouts of the caller, the stomping of high-heeled boots got into the blood and dispelled all traces of self-consciousness. Soon everything was a continuous noise and action that seemed to cast a spell over all." Out in Datil country, the caller urged cowboys to:

> Chase that rabbit.
> Chase that squirrel.
> Chase that pretty girl
> Around the world.[58]

The draw of the dances for teens is clearly apparent in Agnes Billings's story of the time when she (at sixteen), a wannabe boyfriend, and her older brother set out in a Model A for a dance at a newly built school somewhere out on the San Augustine Plains. But exactly where? That became the crucial question as they drove the multiple crisscrossing rutted roads, none of which led them to their destination. Making the situation worse was the fact that a heavy rain had turned the roads to mud, requiring the trio to periodically extricate the stuck car from the muck. But the bigger challenge was locating the dance. Finally, they came upon a strategy. Every now and then they turned off the engine and listened for the faint sound of the fiddle wafting across the plains, allowing them to reset their course by the music. "But when we'd get back in we couldn't find it, and we'd drive around and around." Finally, mud-covered, they struck the dance. They might have enjoyed themselves, too, if Agnes's date had not derisively announced in earshot of the dancers, "Looks like a nester's [homesteading farmer] reunion to me."[59]

But most young cowboys could not afford to be so dismissive of small homesteaders—especially their daughters. In the early years, the sex ratio significantly favored females. "Hell, there wasn't any women in that country," one old rancher recalls. When a rancher had an eligible daughter, "she didn't last long." Then too, hired cowboys earning $30 a month had little reason to look askance at courting a Pie Town farmer's daughter. Thus, one local remembers one dance where several males "just gettin' about growed" took turns wearing one pair of "Sunday boots" so as not to embarrass themselves in front of the girls. "One of these boys would go in there and dance a while, then he'd come back out and trade boots with this other boy, and then he'd go in and dance awhile."[60]

> Now step right back and watch her smile,
> Step right up and swing her awhile.
> Step right back and watch her grin,
> Step right up and swing her again.

Lest all the responsibility for initiating a romantic interest fall solely on a bashful male, dances provided other ways for fostering couplings. One of these was the ubiquitous "box" or "pie supper," at which cowboys bid on unidentified boxes prepared by young women in the area. The highest bidder not only got the box but had the opportunity to share it with the girl whose name was revealed within. Box suppers served several purposes. When the dance was held at a schoolhouse, the proceeds from the bidding went to improving the school. The auction itself was frequently a great source of entertainment. One of the favorite pranks was for a group of cowboys to drive up the price of a box by bidding against a friend determined to buy the box rumored to have been prepared by a budding sweetheart, or on a crueler note, to spread a false rumor as to the given box's preparer, almost always someone deemed less than desirable company.[61] But box suppers were more than fund-raising and comedy—they were also a safe setting where young men and women could get to know one another. The results were various. Eunice Stokes still remembers how she felt when her mother instructed her to ask a Jack Blanton, who had purchased the girl's pie, if he would like to share it with her. The problem was that Jack, in an apparent effort to hedge his bets, had actually bought two pies, and replied that he would be eating his pie with another girl. "I was a shy girl back then, and I sure hated to go ask if he wanted to share my pie, and was I glad when he refused!"[62]

Naturally some girls commanded more attention than others. Sixty-five years after the fact, Langford Johnston still recalled a strikingly beautiful girl in Datil country who was an especially graceful dancer. "The cowboys would run over each other to get a dance with Mary." Maybe so, but there were also ways to foster a more democratic allotment of romantic-minded cowboys. In some instances the dance itself worked at the distribution. In the "broom dance," a lone dancer danced with a broom around couples before stepping on the straw end with his foot and snapping the handle on the floor, a signal for everyone to trade partners. Sometimes a "ladies' choice" did the trick. In 1936 some teens took the initiative to organize a "Leap Year's dance," where boys brought the cakes and had to abide by the rule of "ladies' choice" until midnight, after which it was "gents' choice."[63]

Generally speaking, it appears Anglo teenage girls operated in a less restrictive environment than their Hispanic counterparts, where the chaperone tradition was still fairly strong. At the same time, ranchers and homesteaders mainly held to a common set of sexual mores designed to protect their daughters from lusty cowpokes. This, together with the fact that ranch and schoolhouse dances were essentially family affairs, meant that pubescent daughters' activities on or off the dance floor could be carefully monitored. What one historian says of the cultural pressures operating on the young single women of Sweetwater County, Wyoming, during the early decades of the twentieth century might be said of their sisters in west-central New Mexico: "The stable and homogeneous community that made chaperones unnecessary also held the threat of public shame and social isolation for those who veered from its rules. In rural areas where everyone knew and judged each other by a double moral standard, single women's reputations hung in the balance."[64]

Occasionally, however, a rancher's daughter could show an amazing degree of independence in the pursuit of a dance date. When Betsy Crawford and a friend learned that their dates were locked up in the Magdalena jail for drunkenness, she passed word to the prisoners through the barred windows that the two girls would concoct a jailbreak. This they proceeded to do. Noticing the "Hughes boys" were in town delivering lumber, they persuaded them to back their truck up to the jail window, whereupon logging chains were attached to the bars. The plan worked beautifully. A little pressure on the gas pedal, and the windows ripped free. The two prisoners "just walked out." Remarkably the town marshal was never able to solve the crime, or chose not to. Whether the ex-cons ever made it to the dance is not clear.[65]

Although the two girls' engineering of the jailbreak is clearly the exception, it is also clear that more modern conceptions of female freedom were also creeping into the region. Consider the dynamic of the biannual dances hosted by a local Civilian Conservation Corps (CCC) camp in 1937. Lest the camp enrollees be without dance partners, the camp inspector reported, "one army truck is utilized to transport feminine guests who cannot be conveyed in private vehicles."[66]

Marriage

Velma, an Alamo Navajo woman, says that her mother died when Velma was just five years old. Her memories of her mother are therefore hazy. There was the time, after the child's pleading and crying, that she allowed Velma to herd sheep with an older sister. There was the time she helped Velma build a miniature hogan in the arroyo. She can also recall certain things her mother said to her. The trouble is she cannot attach those memories to an actual image of her mother's face. "Every time I think about it, it always comes out blank." Following her mother's death, Velma and two younger brothers were shuttled between the households of two married sisters and a grandmother. But none of these arrangements was satisfactory. When she was seven, Velma and her brothers were shipped off to the Albuquerque Indian School because there was not "anybody to take care of us." Meanwhile, her father remarried. Home from school for the summer, the children looked forward to living with their father and new mother. But their expectations were soon shattered when they discovered that their new mother resented their presence. The memories still sting. There was the time her father brought Velma a piece of velvet cloth for making a blouse and skirt. But her father's gesture provoked a crisis when the woman "got mad at my Dad for buying me that material. She wanted the material for herself. So they got into a fight." Somehow the argument resulted in her brother receiving a whipping. Another painful memory comes from the time when the children were told "we weren't going to eat with them." After two weeks of segregation, they took off again for their grandmother's. Then it was off to school again. Boarding school brought its own pain and trauma, but at least it provided the serenity of routine and three meals a day. At the same time, it never could satisfy Velma's craving to be back at Alamo. So when she returned from school one summer, she decided to stay. "That's when I got married to my stepmother's brother. I guess he felt sorry for me. I got married when I was twelve years old. My husband taught me how to cook and sew. I guess you would say he raised me."[67]

As Velma's story illustrates, coming of age cannot be rigidly defined by chronological age. Velma was scarcely more than a child when she entered into marriage. In fact, one might argue that she came of age *after* her marriage. In any event, her story suggests that the connection between young females' age attainment and the circumstances that pushed them into marriage were marked by complexity. It also raises several questions with respect to all three groups. How did the marriage age of females (and males) change over time? What factors accounted for these changes? Finally, what role did culture play?

For the first half of the twentieth century, information on the age of Alamo Navajo couples getting married is extremely sketchy. For most of this period, traditional marriages were the rule, leaving no legal documents for the benefit of historians. However, a 1930 US census recorded that out of the twenty-eight known marriages in the community, eleven, or 39 percent, of the women had married by the age of sixteen. Interestingly, nine of those eleven marriages had taken place before 1920. In a study of Alamo Navajo kinship conducted in 1949, the author concluded that the community viewed the marriageable age for girls to be between fifteen and seventeen, and for boys between nineteen and twenty-one. Several factors contributed to the gradual increase in marriage age: the impact of missionaries, greater contact with the outside world, state age requirements for legal marriage, and the role of boarding schools. The role of the latter is reflected in Fred Apache's efforts to acquire a wife. When his desired girl's parents were approached over the summer with a marriage proposal, they responded that their daughter was only twelve and would be returning to boarding school. Fred was "worried and upset" but decided to wait for the girl's return, at which time the girl's family was approached a second time—this time with success.[68]

Navajo culture shaped every aspect of this all-important rite of passage. For one thing eligible marriage partners were restricted by clan affiliations; a child was not permitted to marry a member of either the mother's or father's clan. Given the small number of clans at Alamo, this incest taboo ruled out any number of possible couplings.[69] A second feature of early Navajo marriages during this period was the extent to which they were arranged. Usually, but not always, after consulting a daughter or son about a prospective marriage partner, the boy's father or girl's mother approached another family about a proposed match. The consequence of this system was that partners sometimes hardly knew one another before marriage. One woman married at the age of fourteen in 1919 and recalls that she had "hardly seen" her husband when her mother arranged the marriage. Similarly, for one World War II veteran, "My relatives say that I was old. I was about thirty-four. And then my nephew's wife told me she knew a girl out here, so they went over there and asked her. . . . She'd seen me a couple of times, so she knew me. So they asked this girl if I could marry her and the girl said yes." Probably the marriage contract was sealed with a "bride price" or gifts to the girl's family in the form of sheep, jewelry, or horses.[70]

Couples were married in one of two ways. In a few instances the young man and woman simply began living together. Most, however, were married in a traditional ceremony. This description of an Alamo Navajo wedding sometime in the 1940s outlines its essential features.

> When it was dark in the evening, about twenty persons came to the hogan where his [the groom's] wife-to-be was staying. All came inside the hogan. Then some mutton and bread, which had been brought by the woman's relatives, was brought out for the guests to eat. The groom sat on the north side, and the woman on the south side. A basket filled with

Alta Secatero on her wedding day, ca. late 1930s. (Courtesy of Clara Winston.)

corn mush was placed between them. Then a line of corn-pollen was drawn from East to West, and another line drawn from West to East on the mush. Then a corn-pollen line was made from South to North, and back from North to South. Then starting at the East a circle around the edge of the basket was made. Some water was put into a gourd cup and poured on the man's hands and the man washed his hands; the same was then done for the girl. After this the man started to eat the mush, scooping it out with four fingers, first from the East, then from the West, North, [South], and middle. Next the girl did the same thing. The remaining mush was eaten by the man's relatives.

At the conclusion of this ritual, the two were lectured by an elder on their respective responsibilities as husband and wife. The man should plant a garden, look after the livestock, and generally work to support his family; the woman should care for the hogan, be a kind mother, and help support the family through weaving, sheepherding, and helping to tend the garden. Both husband and wife were urged to respect one another and "make a good life."[71]

But as already noted, outside forces were gradually altering tradition. Thus, one woman recalls that Baptist missionaries "help us get our marriage license, which I still have. They also help other people get their license too." In this instance the couple waived a traditional ceremony but still received a marriage lecture from the chapter officer. Other couples no doubt combined getting a license with a formal traditional ceremony. Meanwhile, the age of girls entering marriage was creeping up. Increasingly it was becoming rarer to hear comments like this woman's recollection of another woman's fate early in the century: "When she was a young girl, she was given to him."[72]

Tracking the marriage age of Anglos and Hispanics is much easier. Table 3.1 reveals two discernible patterns. The first is the persistent disparity between the female marriage age. As shown, for the years 1905–1914, 35 out of 146, or 24 percent, of Hispanic females were married by the age of sixteen, compared with 5 out of 61, or 8.2 percent, for Anglos. The disparity closes somewhat for the years 1945–1954, when the disparity drops to 15.5 percent to 9 percent. A second pattern is less surprising: on average, both Hispanic and Anglo males married later than their female counterparts.

But our focus here is on the marriage age of young females who, although grown up physically, had scarcely left the world of childhood in less tangible ways. What, then, are the reasons for Hispanic females marrying at a younger age? Three explanations seem plausible. First, if arranged marriage was no longer the norm in the early-twentieth-century Hispanic communities, it was still operative in some families. Second, the school dropout rate was higher for Hispanic females (for reasons addressed in a later chapter), thereby making them available as marriage partners at an earlier age. Third, class certainly played into the equation; it was easier for Anglo females to postpone mate selection until both economic and romantic stars were aligned.[73] Any one or some combination of these factors might have been operative in individual situations.

The changing patterns of marriage in Hispanic society can be seen in the following three stories. Esther Peralta's grandmother was only fourteen

Table 3.1 Marriage Age of Magdalena and Kelly Hispanics and Anglos by Sex and Surname, 1905–1914, 1945–1954

	1905–1914				1945–1954			
	Hispanics		Anglos		Hispanics		Anglos	
Age	F	M	F	M	F	M	F	M
12–14	0	0	0	0	0	0	1	0
15–16	35	0	5	0	17	1	6	0
17–18	47	6	13	0	23	11	28	2
19–20	22	13	7	0	22	19	12	10
21–22	8	40	7	4	20	28	7	4
23–24	9	29	8	15	10	17	7	17
25–26	3	14	4	12	8	7	5	6
27–28	2	12	1	3	3	7	2	7
29–30	1	4	4	5	2	6	0	2
31–32	2	5	4	1	3	2	0	7
33–34	1	3	0	7	0	1	1	3
35–36	4	2	4	2	0	1	1	1
37–38	1	1	4	1	0	2	3	2
39 +	11	17	3	13	2	5	5	8
Total	146	146	61	63	110	107	78	79

Note: The table does not include those persons for whom ethnic status could not be determined.
Source: Socorro County marriage records, Socorro, New Mexico.

when she married a much older Kelly man she hardly knew. Esther remembers asking her grandmother, "Couldn't you have said no?" But as her grandmother explained, such a thing was absolutely out of the question. It never entered her mind to object to her parent's judgment.[74]

A less extreme example of the role of parents in fashioning marriages is Candelaria García's account of how her parents—let us call them Alberto and Josefita—came to be married. As the story is told, when Alberto came to ask for Josefita's hand, her father asked his daughter, who was in another room, if she wanted to marry this man. Josefita replied she had not the slightest interest in the proposal, stating, "I don't even know the gentleman." So Alberto was sent on his way. The following year, however, the persistent Alberto wrote the girl's father that he was coming to the ranch to ask a second time for Josefita's hand, and her father replied that he was welcome. In anticipation of the visit, Josefita repeated her lack of interest in the man—"I don't even know him." Her father's response: "Well, I'm not telling you to marry him, but I'm telling you he comes from a good family, and evidently he has seen you somewhere. He knows of you, and he thinks you would make him a good wife." Her father added that he liked the man and respected him for coming by himself. "He doesn't bring somebody else to do the talking for him." In any event, his daughter should give the man her final answer on a certain day when he was returning for a third time. On the appointed day, Alberto once more spoke to Josefita's father and declared his desire to marry his daughter. After the two spoke for a while, Josefita was called into the room, at which time Alberto said, "I guess you already know why I'm here. I would like you to be my wife, my bride," to which she replied, "I'm going to say yes because my father and mother approve of you. I'll be your wife. I'll be your bride. But they are the ones that know you. I don't know you." Years later, Candelaria recalls how her parents would tease each other about how they came to be married. "I got married because my father and mother liked you and approved of you, not because I knew you," she would say. Then her father would laugh and ask with a knowing grin, "Haven't you lived happy and good?" Smiling, her mother confessed, "Yes, I'd made a good choice." Over the years it was a playful ritual of sorts, one the children never grew tired of hearing.[75]

But tradition was rapidly giving way under the pressure of modernity. One can see the forces of change in operation in Juan Jaramillo's account of José Aragón's inability to arrange a marriage between his granddaughter, Carla (pseudonym), and Juan. From a purely economic perspective one might think that Juan, a carpenter, would have jumped at the prospect of marrying into one of Magdalena's most prominent Hispanic families. From José Aragón's perspective the young man's economic credentials seem not to have mattered so much. Juan was a hard worker, of strong character, and possessed a winning personality. Juan's father also favored the union. The next development was when Aragón invited him over to his house to make his case for the marriage. He began by reminding Juan of the economic status of the family he would be marrying into. Had the young man noticed that Carla wore expensive rings and drove a nice car? Then he pointed to his own ring, one with eleven diamonds and a ruby. Should the marriage take place, the old man promised to give the couple a ranch and put money in the bank for them. Through it all Juan was noncommittal. Finally, Aragón instructed Juan to fetch the bottle of whisky and two glasses on a nearby cabinet. After the pouring, Aragón raised his glass saying, "Hit the clinches!" Upon departing, Juan promised he would think the matter over.[76]

In a few days, Aragón invited Juan over for another glass of whisky, and after "hitting the clinches" two or three times, again broached the subject of the marriage. Juan, who had been sipping just a single glass all the while, began by saying that he knew Carla to be a "good girl." He knew her from school. But no, he had decided against the marriage. Addressing him as Don José out of respect for the man's age and position, he explained the reasons for his decision. "The first thing, Carla don't even know how to cook an egg. She don't know how to mend or put a button on anything. I don't know if she can take a bath by herself. I know how to mend. I know how to cook. I know how to work on anything." Furthermore,

> She is going to be the one that's got the money because it's coming from your side. And any day, if she likes somebody else, she's got the key and she'd tell me, "You sleep in that shack over there because I'm going to sleep with HIM." If she knew what WORK is, it would be a different deal. I don't have anything against Carla, but only that she wouldn't be a WIFE. She'll be ridin' in that car like she does every day. . . . I got to marry somebody that is [working] right WITH me.

At this point, Juan remembers the old man having tears in his eyes, prompting the young man to plead, "I don't want you to be mad at me." Don José replied he would never hold it against him.[77]

Shortly thereafter, Juan met Maria, age sixteen. Juan remembers the moment. He was driving to his Datil homestead and saw her and a brother plowing a field, each driving a separate team of horses. He knew her slightly, so he pulled his car over, and the two talked over a fence post, the brother still continuing to plow. Juan was falling in love. Soon Maria and her brothers were helping him plaster the new house he was building. It was not long before he proposed to her, and the two were married. Not long after, the couple paid a visit to José Aragón. Don José was effusive in his congratulations. "I'm really proud of you," he told Juan, then hugged the two of them. To show there were no hard feelings, he went to his desk and wrote Maria a check for $500 and Juan a check for a $1,000 and then gave the couple a table and chairs. So it all ended well. Juan not only had a wife he loved but one who could cook, plaster a house, plow a field, ride horseback, and even bulldog a calf. "So we started very, very nice." Now an old man and widower, Juan reflects, "If you haven't got love, what's the use?"[78]

A Special Wedding

Most likely Juan and Maria's wedding was a modest affair, befitting a carpenter-homesteader and rural farm girl. For the young bride, all of sixteen, this rite of passage marked a turning point in her life, a day marked by solemn ceremony and joyful celebration. Just imagine, her husband had turned down land and riches from one of the wealthiest men in Magdalena to marry her. Meanwhile, Juan acquired a wife he loved, whom he could count on to work beside him in the struggles ahead. Marrying for love was not new for Hispanics, but neither were unions that, by design or happenstance, reinforced elite economic status.

One only has to turn the clock back to 1900 to see the process at work. We can never know whether the marriage between Encarnación Abeyta, age sixteen, and Lorenzo García, age twenty, was arranged or not. What is clear is that Encarnación's rite of passage into matrimony was not of a sort most Hispanic females could fathom. As described by the *Socorro Chieftain*, the groom was the son of Juan García, one of Magdalena's richest sheep ranchers. The bride was the daughter of Abran Abeyta, one of Socorro's most prominent businessmen and Republican officeholders.[79] The grand event began with a wedding procession moving from the "handsome" Abeyta residence to the town's old church, accompanied by the strains of the San Miguel Band. The groom wore the "conventional black fall dress suit," and the bride, appearing "more beautiful than ever, was arrayed in a rich white corded silk trimmed with satin and Spanish lace, was made with full train, and had on the regulation bridal veil and orange blossoms." The guest list numbered more than 1,500, including the "who's who" of the region, and following the ceremony "ate and supped at the banquet tables."

> The following orders for the banquet will give some idea of its magnitude: 50 gallons each of Roman punch, claret punch, lemonade, ice cream, and claret wine; also 500 bottles of beer, 500 bottles of wine; 500 pounds of fine nut cake, 500 doz. assorted cakes, besides the fowls, meats, vegetables, candies, fruits, and nuts. . . . No expense was spared to make it what it was, the greatest wedding that ever took place in the territory.

Meanwhile, the wedding gifts were "numerous, costly, and handsome," the tables groaning under the weight of silver sets, china dishes, decorative vases, lamps, crystal, a Persian rug, and scores of other items.

On the surface, the García-Abeyta wedding speaks to the historic place of marriage in perpetuating the Hispanic social hierarchy. But a closer look reveals something else—namely, the extent to which it crossed ethnic boundaries. Consider the guest list, which along with names such as Baca, Abeyta, Sais, and Sanchez, also included names such as Duncan, Leland, Eaton, and Stapleton. Consider, too, that Lorenzo García's groomsman, Frank Hubbell, was one of the most prominent Anglo sheep ranchers and politicians in the territory. (The reporter for the *Chieftain* could not resist noting, "We predict if he makes the friends of the national Republican convention at Philadelphia that he made at the grand wedding he can name the man who will receive the nomination.") The bridesmaid, Ann Thomas, was also an Anglo, at least on her father's side. Finally, the bride herself, it turns out, was the product of a cross-cultural marriage, her mother being Amelia Stapleton before her marriage to Abeyta.

The García-Abeyta wedding is revealing in a couple of ways. First, the resplendent nature of the event is a window on how social class factored into shaping social relations, including that of marriage. Second, it suggests just how complicated the social landscape in the region really was—that however much the coming-of-age experience involved taking on distinctive ethnic and cultural identities, so too it involved periodic encounters with the "other." At such moments Navajos, Hispanics, and Anglos realized that their lives, like it or not, were hopelessly intertwined.

PART TWO
BOUNDARIES AND BORDER CROSSINGS

CHAPTER FOUR

POINTS OF CONTACT

In 1886 Agnes Morley Cleaveland was twelve years old when she first encountered the Alamo Navajos. Exploring the country north of Alamocita Creek on a buckskin pony, she emerged from a thicket of junipers on an open plain and quickly noticed a group of mounted Indians emerging from the opposite timber. The Indians were headed directly for her. "Arriving at the spot where I waited—for I had stopped when the first Indian appeared—the leader of the band looked at me with an air of puzzlement and then circled his horse slowly around me. Each Indian that followed did the same: in a moment I was the center of a ring of horsemen who rode slowly around and around. Even though I had heard of this encircling maneuver as something Indians did before they attacked, it still did not occur to me to be frightened. I was as interested in the Indians as they were in me." The object of the Indians' curiosity was soon apparent: the cascading waves of wind-loosened blond hair flowing down her back. "After some moments of this silent riding in a circle, during which no word had been spoken on either side, the leader broke the ring and resumed the straight direction in which the group had originally been traveling, followed each in his place by the whole forty of them. I had even taken time to count them."[1]

Compare the above scene with Gilbert Guerro's memories of the first time he encountered whites. In 1918, Gilbert was five years old when rancher Nels Field drove a wagon up to the hogan to recruit his father for work:

> One day he came there with the wagon and beautiful horses, and he brought three girls. And by golly, I thought, the first time I saw white girls. . . . And then they tried to talk to me, and I don't understand. . . . And then I began to wonder. Where in the world? There must be another kind of people. Must be. That's what I was thinking. Couldn't realize where in the world these three girls coming from! And they cannot

speak Navajo. They can't talk my language; I can't talk their language. I was really completely confused because they different kind of people. They white; I'm brown. And they have different language. And then beginning to realize. And how come my father and mother didn't tell me? And then one day my father come back in from work. First thing I thought I wanted to ask him question. Well dad, I said, I ask him how I would like to learn how to speak the language those girls talked to me because it sounds so good, so nice, so sweet, so beautiful. How can I learn that language?[2]

Both Agnes's and Gilbert's stories are about the discovery of the "other." There are differences, to be sure. Gilbert was much younger than Agnes at the moment of the encounter. Whereas Agnes had heard about Indians before actually meeting them, there is no evidence that Gilbert knew about the existence of Anglos. Although Agnes expresses interest in the Indians, Gilbert, conscious for the first time of his brown skin, expresses the desire to actually reach across the ethnocultural divide to the point of learning the language spoken by the light-skinned Field girls. One day, this penchant for border crossing would culminate in his marriage to an Anglo woman.

Until now this study of coming of age has emphasized the cultural distinctiveness of children's upbringing. But as the stories of Agnes and Gilbert suggest, children in the region did not grow up entirely encapsulated in a closed universe. Like all regions characterized by ethnocultural diversity, west-central New Mexico was a land where, to use one historian's terminology, "points of contact" were sometimes commonplace. Children, moreover, were frequently involved in these encounters and played their part both in reinforcing long-standing boundaries and forging intergroup connections of the deepest kind.[3]

Hispanic-Navajo

In the early twentieth century Alamo Navajo children generally avoided contact with Hispanics in the area. With the coming of the Anglos, the inherent Navajo suspicion of outsiders became more generalized. "When we were kids," one old man recalls, if "an Anglo or Spanish person comes by our hogan, we'd all hide behind our mother's skirt or over the hills." Another adds, "The feeling the Navajo people first got seeing a Spanish or Anglo was fear." Thus, when children herding sheep saw a rider on the horizon, they were taught to head in the opposite direction. "If we talk to a person that's not Navajo, we had to talk to the medicine man about it."[4]

In time, the Alamo Navajos came to regard both Hispanics and Anglos with equal suspicion, but in the late nineteenth century the antipathy toward Hispanics appears to have run deeper, owing to the fact that it was of a more ancient order. Although Anglo ranchers lost no opportunity to acquire rangeland at the Navajos' expense, Hispanic sheep ranchers were the first to move into the country west of the Rio Grande. As a young boy, one man recalls, "I would herd sheep and the sheep would go off too far and the next thing I notice is a Spanish man would be herding, chasing our sheep . . . back over to where I was. I didn't know I was trespassing on their land. We were here first. I was always afraid of this Spanish man so I would hide from him."[5]

Stories of murders and poisonings exacerbated children's fears. In the former instance, one story in particular held children's attention. Near the end of the nineteenth century an Alamo Navajo man and his dog, while walking to Magdalena, came across a Mexican sheep camp. One account claims the Indian had recently discovered some old Spanish gold and had several coins on him when he encountered the sheepherders. In any event, he stayed on at the sheep camp and was soon gambling and drinking with his Mexican hosts. At some point, the joviality turned sour, and sheepherders turned on the Indian, beating him to death with a shovel. After burying the body in the sheep corral (a well-known method employed to disguise a grave by the constant tamping of the sheep), the sheepherders moved on toward Magdalena. When the dog returned to Alamo alone, concern led to a search party. The searchers headed in the direction of Magdalena and on their way encountered the sheepherders, who claimed they had never seen such a person. Queries in Magdalena produced the same response. Baffled, the Indians returned home. At this point the missing man's family engaged a hand trembler to solve the mystery. Working with a piece of the man's clothing, the woman worked herself into a trance. All she was able to make out, she said, was an image of branches twisted and entwined with one another. To the search party it sounded like the sheep corral they had passed on their initial foray. Returning to the corral, they spotted long strands of hair, perhaps signs of a struggle. Also, in spite of the murderers' attempt to hide the grave, a more careful inspection now revealed a slight mound in the ground; the grave was too shallow, and the heat was causing the body to swell. Discovering the truth of the matter, the searchers pushed on to Magdalena and overtook the Mexican herders. Two of them were immediately shot. The third, a young boy, managed to escape on a horse but was shortly thereafter captured. After he confessed the true fate of the murdered Indian, he too was shot. Returning home, the search party surely underwent ceremonial protection from contact with enemies, blood, and the missing man's corpse. Fearing retribution, many families moved into hiding for a period.[6]

There were also stories about attempted poisonings. "The Spanish people," one man asserts, "they kill a lot of our Navajo people. They poison by putting something in the food they sold to our people. A lot of our people died because of that." One such story involves Juan Guerro (for many years the community's headman) and another Navajo, each given a cookie by a Hispanic rancher in the Puertecito area. As one man tells the story, Juan was "a smart man," and because he was apparently suspicious of foul play, rather than eating the cookie, he slipped it into a pocket. "But the other guy ate it and he got sick right then. About three days after that he died." Another story tells of a Hispanic store owner who sold an Alamo Navajo man poisoned cheese, which he took back to his family. A day or so later, some Navajos spotted a boy in the family running around some distance from the family's hogan. Upon investigation they found everyone in the family was afflicted with high temperatures and dying. Only the boy who had never eaten the cheese survived. Interestingly, in both stories the poisonings were immediately ascribed to Hispanic malevolence rather than simple food poisoning. Misdiagnoses or not, many children grew up believing "the Spanish people around here almost kill off our people."[7]

But fear and suspicion cut both ways. The legend of how Magdalena got its name, it will be remembered, told how Spanish soldiers and a priest, fleeing attacking Indians, found protection beneath the mountain image of Saint Mary Magdalene. In the early twentieth century, Hispanic grandparents still told their grandchildren stories of "savage" Indians taking children captive. Some children may have heard the old ballad of *Marcelina*:

Marcelina, the captive,
She is leaving, they are taking her
She is leaving, they are taking her
She is leaving, they are taking her
To eat horse meat.

As they passed by Puertecito
She looked back, sighed, and said

She looked back, sighed, and said
She looked back, sighed, and said
Oh, little brother of my heart![8]

Most of the stories were about Apaches, but it is difficult to imagine that young listeners, or for that matter, the storytellers, made fine distinctions between Indian groups. One woman remembers hearing how her great-grandmother at the age of seven was kidnapped by Indians north of Socorro. Fortunately, by paying a ransom of beans, corn, and "whatever they had," her family members were able to retrieve her. Another woman recalls how her grandmother, also from the same area, "used to tell us how they were always in fear of the Indians." The fact that the woman's own uncle was once taken captive only deepened her anxiety. "The Indians held my uncle for a long time and they got to where they trusted him more and more." In time, he was able to escape and returned to the village, whereupon a mass of Thanksgiving and celebration was held. Still another woman grew up hearing about her grandfather's brother being taken captive by the Apaches. "Efforts were made to bring him back, but once he grew accustomed to their way of life, he no longer wanted to return home." The same woman claims one of her father's uncles, as a child, was killed by Indians outside of Magdalena for a red belt the boy was wearing.[9]

Hearing stories of Indian treachery, it is little wonder that parents sometimes employed the threat of an Indian attack as a way of governing children. Just before sundown, one man remembers, "My mom would go out and say, 'Hey, you boys come in here. There's some Indians out there in the woods. I can hear them singing.' My brother and I would run into the house and we'd be real quiet." Little wonder, too, that scalping "savages" sometimes stalked children's nightmares. According to one woman, "I dreamed that the Indians had taken me away from home and cut me up into tiny pieces. I could see the cutting board and knife in my dreams."[10]

But relations between the two groups were not always contentious. Cultural borderlands are complicated spaces where, depending on the circumstances, groups often develop cooperative relations. The fact is that Hispanics and Navajos in the region had strong economic motivations to reach some sort of accommodation. Exchanging agricultural products and other goods was one such pattern. Moreover, depleted food stores and empty cooking pots were a strong motive for Navajo men and boys to hire themselves out as herders and wool shearers. Ranchers were happy to have their work.[11] This relationship, in turn, resulted in Navajo workers acquiring a working knowledge of Spanish. One Alamo Navajo man says that as a small boy, "I used to go with my dad herding sheep for a Mexican. I learned Mexican pretty good to get along, to work for somebody."[12]

Those Alamo Navajos living in close proximity to Hispanics also found that their neighbors were capable of small acts of charity. One Hispanic rancher recalls,

> There was this old [Navajo] lady. I remember she had grey hair, and she come on a donkey. One time she came in October because my father always had a little garden. They had picked all the chili and watermelons. There wasn't too much [left]. My mother asked the old lady if she wanted to pick some of the chili that was not too good. The old lady, she didn't have a sack; she had a shawl. She put it on the ground and she made a pretty nice pile. She made knots and then she hang it on her neck. Oh, she was so glad. She said "Gracias, gracias. God will pay you." She was very glad because they were very poor people.[13]

As the Navajo woman's response reveals, she knew something about the language and religion of her Hispanic neighbors. Did they in turn know something of Navajo ways? Acculturation can be a two-way process, but in circumstances where power relations tip dramatically in one group's favor, the weaker or dominated group frequently adopts a strategy of adaptive acculturation. Thus, on the Hispanic-Navajo frontier (and as we shall see even more dramatically in the instance of Anglo-Navajo relations), the colonized group was doing most of the adapting.

But not entirely. Because children are generally flexible and willing learners, Hispanic youths picked up bits and pieces of Navajo culture, including language. The son of a sheep rancher recalls how his father would send him out for months on end as a camp cook with an Alamo Navajo herder, Casamira Apachito. The herder spoke Spanish, but the long nights around the campfire gave the boy ample time to learn something about the cultural ways of the herder. So it was that the boy "learned how to talk Indian pretty good." The son of another rancher, Juan Jaramillo, even asserts, "I used to speak their language just the same as them—all of it." The cross-cultural learning took place in more settings than ranches and sheep camps. Because Hispanic ranchers in the area were welcome participants in the annual Alamo Navajo fair, their children enthusiastically entered into the rodeo contests and joined in the night dances. By the time he was fifteen, Jaramillo claims, "I could sing with them too." When the drumming and dancing started, Jaramillo recalls, Alamo Navajo girls regularly pulled visiting adolescents onto the fire-lit dance ground, where the couple danced in back-and-forth fashion until the boy paid up with a nickel or piece of gum. "Then she'd turn you loose. But if you didn't pay, you could dance all night."[14]

Hispanic-Anglo

Nowhere was the social landscape more complicated than in the instance of Hispanic-Anglo relations. Several factors shaped the dynamic. First, there was the long-standing attitude of many Anglos that "Mexicans" were a "mongrel race" and therefore unfit candidates for full incorporation into the national polity. It followed that during the last phases of the push for statehood, both Anglo and Hispanic boosters undertook a concerted campaign to reconstruct the Hispanic image in the national mind. *Nuevomexicanos* were not from a "mongrel" race, it was argued, but pure-blooded Spanish. As descendants of European colonizers—that is to say of Spanish *conquistadors*—they were in fact *white*. (During this period Hispanic self-referents such as *mexicanos* and *nuevomexicanos* increasingly gave way to terms such as Hispano-Americans and Spanish Americans.) As historian Charles Montgomery has observed, both *ricos* and poorer Hispanics stood to benefit from the campaign. For *ricos*, the reformulation would solidify their racial status; for *paisanos* it offered a pathway out of socioeconomic marginalization. Both Anglo and Hispanic boosters viewed the movement as a crucial step in furthering the state's economic growth. No one supported the rebranding more than the nascent tourist industry, of which the Santa Fe Railroad was a major sponsor and beneficiary. For these reasons, New Mexico Hispanics' public identity—an identity rooted in both history and myth—was deployed along more politically and economically promising lines.[15]

But this effort never fully succeeded in Magdalena. For one thing, west-central New Mexico was far removed from the political and cultural councils of Santa Fe. For another, the Hispanic elites who had historically laid claim to *limpieza de sangre* (purity of blood) were largely in the northern regions of the state. Such claims in the southern part of New Mexico were met with more skepticism. Then, too, Magdalena was devoid of Santa Fe's architectural forms and public ritual dramas suggesting it had once been a thriving center of Spanish colonial settlement. Finally, a disproportionate number of the Anglos moving into the Magdalena region were from Texas, a state where the referent "Mexican" had historically triggered notions of Anglo superiority and hierarchy. For Anglos, then, the politics of Hispanic identity were not a settled affair.[16]

A second factor shaping relations was the demographic makeup of the state generally and the region specifically. In 1940, Hispanics were still 70–80 percent of Socorro County's population. This disparity, along with long-standing economic alliances between Hispanic *ricos* and Anglo business interests, forced Anglos into a strategic political accommodation with Hispanic leaders on the state, county, and local levels. This usually took the form of a "gentlemen's agreement" that, as historian Juan Gómez-Quiñones observes, consisted of two parts: apportioning a certain number of state offices to Hispanics and minimizing contests that pitted the two ethnic groups against each other. Thus, although Hispanics were still underrepresented in elected offices across the state, their influence was still substantial.[17] The pattern can be seen in 1918, the year Magdalena elected its first municipal officers: of the six offices on the ballot, Hispanics captured four, including those of mayor, two trusteeships, and city clerk.[18]

A third factor was the growing sense among *nativos* that New Mexico was a "lost land." The most obvious manifestation of this was the new political and legal order undermining traditional patterns of land use and ownership. Just as disheartening was the invaders' cultural assault on Hispanic beliefs, norms, and folkways—a threat that found its expression in such varied forms as market capitalism, mass consumer culture, "modern attitudes," and perhaps most especially, the public schools. Thus, however skillful Hispanic leaders were in commanding a certain level of political influence, the cultural demarcations of what constituted Hispanic identity would have to be continuously defended. As Marc Simmons wrote, Hispanics "managed with some success to cling to the core of their culture and language during the early decades of the twentieth century.... But after 1940, the modern world—swiftly, inexorably—began closing in, with its powerful pressures for assimilation into the dominant stream of national life."[19]

Finally, there was the ongoing conflict between cattle and sheep stock growers, which, more often than not, intersected with ethnic status. The numbers in Socorro County tell the story. In 1914, aside from the large stock companies, the total number of Hispanics listed as sheep growers compared with Anglos was 88 to 13; the disparity between Hispanics and Anglos owning cattle was 194 to 340.[20] These numbers translated into an ongoing conflict between mostly Hispanic sheep growers and mostly Anglo cattle growers over grazing lands—a conflict that in frontier Socorro County could easily turn violent. In an anonymous letter to the *Socorro Chieftain* in 1900, under the title "The Cowman's Grievance," one rancher claimed that unless cowmen were protected "from being run over by large herds of sheep, there will be bloodshed." Furthermore,

> I find that these cow men only want from 4 to 8 miles around their homestead and they are going to have it or have serious trouble with the sheep men. The sheep man nowadays only respect[s] a man's patented land. He will move his herds in on the cowman's range and eat off the grass and tramp it into dust; then it seems he will hunt some other poor devil who has a few cows and serve him likewise. If you go to a sheep herder and ask him to kindly move off of your range he will say, "I am on government land, and you go to h___."[21]

In the above letter there is no mention of the ethnicity of the disputants. But readers could read between the lines, or at least thought they could. In the following news story there was no doubt as to the ethnic makeup of those involved. "Quite a skirmish ensued near Magdalena," the *Socorro Chieftain* reported in early 1900, "between the herders of Juan García's flocks and a man by the name of Downing." The confrontation apparently began when Downing ordered the sheepherders to move off the rancher's range. The order of events is not all that clear, but things quickly got out of hand when Downing or one of his cowboys shot two sheep. At some point in the fray the sheepherders captured Downing's horse, after which "all parties came to Magdalena for reinforcements and the battle was renewed with energy, and although thirty or forty shots were fired no injuries were sustained by either side."[22]

Interethnic violence was hardly new to the region. Just twenty years earlier, tensions in Socorro took a violent turn when the Anglo editor of the *Socorro Sun* was murdered, and an all-Anglo vigilante committee, convinced that the Hispanic guilty parties would never receive "justice" from a "Mexican" jury, took matters into its own hands and lynched the chief perpetrator of the crime on a corral gate.[23] Perhaps because the episode provoked fears of a general "race war," cowmen thought twice about being overly aggressive in settling range disputes. Demographics argued against it. Thus, in early 1901, when cattleman L. V. Medley wrote to the *Socorro Chieftain* protesting the invasion of Hispanic sheepherders, he also acknowledged that an overly aggressive response by the cowman would most likely result in his being "tried by a Mexican jury and sent to the penitentiary for a term of from five to fifteen years." Partly for this reason, Medley reasoned, "let us make violence our last resort."[24]

Such was the mix of contextual factors that shaped Hispanic-Anglo relations in turn-of-the-century west-central New Mexico. When one adds the element of religion to the mix, one can see that the region was beset with potential conflicts. It began with terminology—that is, the terms the two groups used to describe one another. Early in the twentieth century, Magdalena's Anglo political and business leaders were careful to use the term "Spanish American" when referring to prominent members of the Hispanic community. The 1915 "booster" edition of the *Magdalena News*, which devoted several articles to business leaders, describes José Y. Aragón as "one of our oldest and most prominent Spanish-American citizens." In deference to Hispanic sensitivity, the term also surely found its way into various social situations where polite discourse was the order of the day.[25] As Montague Stevens, an early stockman in the Datil region, observed years later: "The old Spanish people here were very particular about saying they were Spanish, not Mexican. In fact, you hurt their feelings if you called them Mexicans." A Hispanic woman raised in Magdalena concurs: "People here in town do not like to be called Mexican. Mexican to them was a bad word." It followed that Hispanic parents did their best to imprint their children with their Spanish ancestry. Around 1920, one woman recalls, "When I went to school for the first time, they would call us Spanish people Mexicans. And Mama told us never to admit you're a Mexican because you're not. You were born under the American flag and you're a Spanish American. And you're not a Mexican; you didn't come from Mexico in the first place, and you don't have Mexican blood. So that's the distinction."[26]

The problem was that not all Anglos were willing to grant the distinction. Indeed, the manner in which Anglos and Hispanics chose to name each other served to either ameliorate or reinforce existing or latent antagonisms. For decades, Hispanics were recipients of the epithet "greasy *mexicano*," a reference to their supposed filth and laziness. Hispanics, in turn, responded with the appellation that Anglos were "gringo *salados*." (Any one of several connotations for attributing saltiness to Anglos was implied: their chalky whiteness, their propensity to perspire, or the allegation that dirt-poor homesteaders were always borrowing salt from their Hispanic neighbors.)[27]

The two groups, moreover, largely moved in distinctly different social worlds. "There was a strong division among sections of the town," one Anglo who grew up in the 1920s remembers. "You had the Spanish sections, we had the Anglo sections."[28] Although census figures reveal a more complicated picture, the generalization holds true in the main. In fact, the separation extended beyond residential patterns. Hispanics almost exclusively attended the Catholic church, whereas Anglos attended one of the Protestant ones. Membership in Magdalena's several social clubs and fraternal orders was also along ethnic lines. Likewise, guest lists for weddings—and especially significant for this study, children's birthday parties—reflect ethnic social boundaries (although it should be noted that newspapers paid much less attention to Hispanic rites of passage).[29] Similarly, Hispanics would have been the exclusive attendees at a 1915 lecture sponsored by the local Alianza Hispano-Americano, and the same year, a dance sponsored by the same organization. The Kelly Miners' Band, it appears, was composed entirely of Hispanics, as was Magdalena's "Spanish American" baseball team—the Aragóns.[30]

As noted earlier, in the early decades of the twentieth century, Hispanics and Anglos also generally patronized their own dances and drinking establishments. "They had Mexican dances and they had gringo dances," recalls one Anglo man. If Hispanics joined Anglo cowboys in the bar, "they didn't go back and dance.... They went to their own dances." By another account,

> It was a clannish thing in them days.... If a whole bunch of cowboys went to town and there was a big dance goin' on, why we'd dance and everything, and if the Mexicans showed up and after a while if they danced with our girls a little too much, we'd tell 'em to beat it. And of course most of 'em didn't and we'd have a big fight and run 'em off. The same thing would happen if we went to Kelly. We'd go to Kelly to a big dance. Everything was fine as long as we danced with our own girls, but if we went to dancin' with the Mexican girls they'd balk. I remember many times—we had an old Model T touring car—rocks would be bouncin' off the top of that thing when they ran us out of Kelly. That was a fact of life. But the next day, the Mexicans and us, we were friends. It was just a social thing. You jist didn't mess with the Mexican girls.

Another cowboy who came into the region in the late 1920s concurs: "The Spanish could be a little bit salty when it came to mixin'.... It could cause fights lots of times. If you'd go off to a Mexican dance, you might come back with a black eye ... if you came back at all."[31]

Curiously, interethnic social gatherings, including dances, were more likely in rural areas. According to Cecil Taggert, "If we had dances at our house they'd come over there and dance up a storm and there was no friction. No way in the world." Even if a "grizzly old Mexican man were to ask you [a girl] to dance you didn't refuse him because that was an insult."

Several explanations account for the difference. According to Taggert, much of it had to do with "old world courtesy," recognition of traditional ideas of honor and respect. Taggert's sister attributes the difference to ranch families' isolation, thus the deep longing for connection. "I think there was a need . . . to be close to somebody, because we were so far apart—like maybe 10 or 12 miles to your nearest neighbor. You want that feeling of closeness with somebody else." A third reason was that ranch house gatherings, unlike town dances, were less likely to attract potentially aggressive males (cowboys being a prime example), individuals with less stake in respecting established norms of behavior. Whatever the reason, some children on ranches participated in the mixed social gatherings. Fred Billings, who as an adolescent rode more than 20 miles with his father to the fiestas held in the small rural community of Santa Rita, recalls, "We'd stay with those people. Oh, they treated us good. They sure can—they know how to celebrate."[32]

If females were the focus of conflict at town dance halls, long-eared burros were enough to spark violence in dustier realms. Although the "Magdalena Burro Wars" hardly capture the full range of interethnic relations, they illustrate the extent to which age-old antagonisms might find expression in a younger generation. The burro wars were actually a series of skirmishes between the children of Kelly miners (mostly Hispanics) and Magdalena youths (mostly Anglo) over the capture of burros that on weekends wandered loose in the foothills separating the two towns. Although some of the animals were owned and simply unpenned, many were abandoned by western sheep ranchers, who, after driving their sheep from as far away as Arizona to the railhead at Magdalena, chose to simply turn the animals loose rather than drive them back west. Pack burros were cheap and easy to break.

The burro wars, which took place in the early 1930s, erupted every Friday after school when both gangs spread out to capture the animals. One veteran of the wars observes, "During the week the Spanish and the Anglos went to school fine. Weekends, that was fightin' time." The burros were prized for two reasons: they could be used as pack animals for weekend camping trips or simply be ridden around town, partly no doubt as a taunt to those who had lost out in the scramble for the animals. Around town, "there'd be five or six of us riding burros. And then these other kids would catch us, and by God, they'd take them away from us. . . . And whoever was the toughest got to keep the burros. And boy, we had some big wars over that." At times, it appears, gang membership was not strictly along ethnic lines but between the children of ranchers and miners, Kelly and

Magdalena, or neighborhood and neighborhood. An indication of how other loyalties could come into play is Fred Billings's explanation of how one Hispanic boy came to align himself with mainly the Anglo side. According to Billings, "This Ed Gomez kid, he was a sheepherder's son, so I had known his dad. . . . I'd met him out at the sheep camp." Similarly, a member of the Hispanic gang was an Anglo who lived in "Mexican town" and spoke Spanish. "He was just like one of them—couldn't tell him apart." But Billings is quick to assert that membership in the two battle groups was mostly along ethnic lines. Those on the other side were largely the children of "low-class" sheepherders and miners—"We called them Mexicans."[33]

The main objective of the wars was to round up the burros and prevent their recapture by the other side. When possible, an abandoned shack or barn was the preferred penning area, for it provided ample protection against the onslaught sure to come. While the burros munched on hay provided by the boys, an arsenal was readied. If the Anglos had the burros, the assault came from the "Mexican side"—distinguishable by the red bandannas tied around their heads. Also in full view were sticks, clubs, and slingshots. Meanwhile, those inside were well armed with piles of rocks and their "nigger shooters" (a popular Texas term for slingshots).

> Hell, I could shoot one of those things better than I can a rifle. Damn right. We used to go down and buy for a nickel . . . a sack of those tarpaper nails. They're about . . . three quarters of an inch long, and they got a big head on them. Well, we'd take every one and get them on an anvil with a hammer [and] pinch that head together just a little bit. And you pull that back with that nigger shooter, you can nail his britches on, stick him about three quarters of an inch deep.

On one occasion, two of the boys built a catapult using an old windmill spring. It took three boys to pull the arm back, after which they set the trigger and loaded the cup with a mountain of iron nuts. The shower of nuts kept the attackers at bay.[34]

Both sides had their victories. On one occasion the Anglo gang was inside its fortress and still planning the defense when "the next thing we knew they were there and they beat the hell out of us." On another occasion the "Mexicans" exacted a different sort of pain. As one of the Anglo combatants remembers it, he had developed considerable skill at slinging fist-sized rocks from netted ropes. "Boy they would sail." The problem was that he never had much directional control over the hurling rocks. One day in the heat of battle, "I was rockin' away and I throw'ed one through the

Catholic church window. I can tell you, that was taboo. The Spanish kids turned me in right away—that I broke the window out of the church. I had to pay for that."[35]

But the story of Hispanic-Anglo relations is about more than conflict. It is also a narrative about accommodation, adaption, and border crossings. However much Hispanics might have resented the Anglo invasion, in the end the two groups had to learn to live with one another. "Don't ever judge a man by where his ancestors came from," Alfredo Bustamante grew up hearing his father say, followed by, "Judge him by what he IS." A more pointed acceptance of the ethnic mix of Magdalena was displayed by the town's Anglo marshal's response to a visiting Texan, who, after looking up and down the street, queried, "Don't any white people live here?" The marshal, who was married to a Hispanic woman, replied; "No, only Mexicans and Texicans."[36]

The fact is, although Anglos and Hispanics moved largely in separate social spheres, there were also occasions when they interacted in the spirit of polite acceptance and even genuine friendship. In the process of forging interethnic political alliances, conducting business, drawing wages, applauding local bronc riders, attending ethnically mixed school performances, or encountering each other casually on the street, the two groups were gradually learning more about each other. On a ranch, Cecil Taggert recalls, "If you needed help, they'd come, and if we needed help, they'd help us. Like when we had a roundup or something, they'd come help us round up our cattle and brand calves." Candelaria García remembers how an old Anglo woman who had chickens would bring eggs to her house to exchange for milk and cheese obtained from the family milk cow. Her mother would always insist that the woman not bring the eggs; the García cow gave more milk than the family required. But the old woman insisted on making the exchange. "Mama didn't know English, and she [the old woman] didn't know Spanish, but they communicated." West of Datil, when word got out that a homesteader's daughter needed fresh eggs, it was a Hispanic family who responded. "The Chávez family had heard my sister needed eggs," Bernadyne Powell remembers, "so one day four or five of these young people came down the hill behind the house on horses. Around the horses' necks hung what would appear to be a beaded necklace. I couldn't believe my eyes! The necklaces were stockings filled with eggs! There was a string tied between each egg preventing them from breaking."[37] In the face of considerable evidence to the contrary, one old Hispanic even asserts there was "no prejudice between the Anglos and Spanish people. We got along together."[38]

Children were instrumental in breaking through boundaries. As one Hispanic man whose family had a ranch near Datil explains, when Anglo homesteaders began moving into the area, "we needed to communicate with them. One of my playmates then couldn't speak Spanish and I spoke very little English." Within a week the two had learned enough of each other's language to become fast friends. Another fondly remembers all the times children of the two groups in Magdalena played in the snow and skated together around the Magdalena Hotel. "We got along nice." Thus, for all the interethnic tensions and antagonisms, childhood associations held out the possibility that relations between the two groups might one day improve.[39] Meanwhile, the social distance between the groups was gradually shrinking, although as the following story illustrates, class as well as ethnicity might have played a part.

While growing up, the García sisters loved to dance. Although their mother never allowed them to have boyfriends, she saw nothing wrong with the girls enjoying themselves on the dance floor. The problem was that by the 1940s, the only steady opportunities to dance were at either the Silver Bell, patronized by Anglos, or the dance hall adjacent to the West Bar, almost exclusively Hispanic. Given the fact that the West Bar was owned by a close relative, one might think that the girls' mothers would have taken them to this establishment. But Mrs. García wanted her girls to stay clear of the place. "You'll never go there. I'll never take you there!" the girls remember their mother exclaiming. In such moments their mother drew upon her boundless cache of *dichos,* letting loose with something like: "*Dime con quien andas y yo te diré quien eres*" ("Tell me with whom you associate, and I'll tell you who you are"). Recollecting her mother's attitude, one of the daughters thinks, "She didn't want us to associate with those Spanish people, or maybe they were just not up to her level." In any event, there was only one alternative. One night the girls' mother, with her daughters on arm, walked into the Silver Bell and announced to the proprietor, whom she knew slightly, "My girls are going to dance," and then proceeded to escort them through the bar to the dance floor in the rear. "I guess we were the first Spanish to ever go to those dances. Mother just walked right in and she took us to the dance. We danced, we danced, and we danced." Hours later, "she came and got us and out we went, right through the bar." A few weeks later, two young Hispanic females from another family appeared at the Silver Bell and attempted to duplicate the García sisters' experience. When the same proprietor refused them entry, they were heard to remark, "How come the García girls are in there?" The response: "That's my business, not yours."[40]

The story raises two questions. The first and obvious one is why the García sisters were admitted to the dance and the other two girls denied. One possibility is that the proprietor knew Mrs. García. But as the story is told, this appears not to be the major reason. Issues of class and perhaps degrees of "whiteness" also appear to have been involved. Given the construction of race in New Mexico, a geographical and historical space where the borders between "Spanish" and "Mexican" counted for something, the García sisters, but not the other pair, were clearly accorded higher status, at least by the proprietor, who in both instances was called upon to make a snap judgment. The second question is suggested by the dance itself. As we have already seen, because music and dancing are natural pathways to desire and intimacy, both Hispanic and Anglo males sometimes went to considerable lengths to exclude each other from their dances. The García sisters, then, were engaged in another sort of border crossing, one pregnant with possibilities. Although there is no reason to believe that their bouts of dancing—well monitored by their mother—led to romance, it does raise the question of how many Hispanics and Anglos traversed the social distance from "otherness" to the marriage bed.

Anglo-Hispanic marriages were hardly a rarity in New Mexico. In the nineteenth century the sex ratio imbalance among Anglos prompted many men to take Hispanic women as brides. The possible motives were romance, sexual desire, the need for a helpmate, and a strategy for gaining acceptance in a largely Hispanic community—partly for business reasons. (During the Mexican period, there were also certain legal advantages to such unions.) For Hispanic females, especially those of poor or modest circumstances, improvement in social status was likely an important reason for entering into a cross-cultural marriage. One historian estimates that between 1820 and 1858 as many as 50 percent of Anglo males entered into marriage or common-law unions with Hispanic women. Another points out that of the twenty-six Anglo men living in Socorro in 1880, sixteen were married to Hispanic women. But times were changing. By the turn of the century, when the Anglo gender ratio was coming into closer balance, would-be suitors were less inclined to challenge the growing social pressure against mixed couplings.[41] One study estimates that the number of mixed marriages in Albuquerque between 1890 and 1920 hovered between 6 and 11 percent of all marriages. Another puts the number in Bernalillo County between 1924 and 1940 at around 15 percent.[42]

What then, was the level of cross-cultural marriages in Magdalena? Examination of marriage records of Magdalena and Kelly by surname for two decades (1905–1914, 1945–1954) is revealing. Between 1905 and 1914, a period in which 214 marriage licenses were issued for couples in Magdalena and Kelly, some 18, or 8.4 percent, were of a mixed nature. Jumping to the years 1945–1954, 15 out of 185 marriage licenses issued, or 8.3 percent, were of Hispanic-Anglo mix. By these measures, the intermarriage rate remained essentially the same, below 10 percent over a fifty-year period.[43] These figures essentially conform with the memories of those who grew up during these periods. One Anglo recalls how "in those days there was very little intermarriage." It was all about "blood," which he adds, "meant something—or we thought it did." Another older Anglo recalls, "No Anglo girl would marry a Mexican guy." Even years later, when just such a marriage was announced, the woman remembers that her family "just liked to croak." Although it was more common for Hispanic women to marry Anglo men, these unions too could provoke consternation on either side of the ethnic aisle. When one woman announced to her parents whom she planned to marry, "Dad cracked because he [the groom] was an Anglo."[44]

As we shall see later, objections to mixed unions would eventually be less severe. But our concern here is assessing the social and cultural implications of such unions for children. On the one hand, it seems safe to say that in those marriages between Hispanic women and Anglo men—a slight majority—the Anglo influence was probably dominant. Certainly children raised in interethnic familial settings had an advantage in adjusting to mainstream Anglo culture—namely, school. Unfortunately we can never know how many families underwent the experience that occurred when this woman married an Anglo: "My husband told me that we had to speak English when we got married because he wanted the kids to learn English first and then Spanish." This arrangement turned out to be more than a little difficult when she and the children were in mixed-family gatherings. For her grandmother, who spoke no English, "it was like a mortal sin for us to speak English in front of her."[45]

But interethnic unions rarely acculturated children in just one direction. Family and cultural politics are inherently complicated affairs, as the foregoing example suggests. The husband in this case was not absolutely opposed to the children learning Spanish; he wanted only that they learn English first. Moreover, the wife's grandmother, and presumably others in the family as well, had something to say in the matter. Furthermore, it is important to remember that ethnic identity is not entirely freely chosen but is also shaped by how others see us. One sees the latter side of the equation in the 1915 marriage between Elena Drinkhouse and her groom,

Dolores Montoya. As Elena's surname indicates, her ethnic heritage was at least partially Anglo, yet the *Magdalena News* notes that the bride "is well known here in Spanish-American circles" and later that the couple consists of "two of our well-known and popular young Spanish-Americans, having spent the better part of their lives in Magdalena." Readers also learned that following the ceremony "a *baile* was given at the Barrowdale Opera House . . . which was largely attended and the light fantastic was the order of the evening."[46] Presumably, the guests drew from both the Hispanic and Anglo communities. We can never know what cultural struggles and compromises took place in the Montoya-Drinkhouse household or the way they shaped the ethnocultural identities of any children they might have had. Perhaps there was no struggle at all.[47]

Anglo-Navajo

If the ethnocultural divide separating Anglos and Hispanics was gully sized, the distance between Anglos and Navajos was a gaping canyon. Viewed through Navajo eyes, Anglos were essentially a second wave of invaders, Spanish conquistadors and Mexicans being the first. Whereas before mid-century the threat to the Alamo Navajo band had come principally from Hispanics in search of slaves and livestock, by the latter part of the century, ranchers of both groups were squeezing the band into an ever smaller geographical space. Although land allotment in 1912 and the increasing attention of the Bureau of Indian Affairs (BIA) guaranteed the Alamo Navajos a modicum of protection, ultimately the group's future depended on its members' capacity to adapt to the changing economic and political realities bearing down upon them. Chief among these was the growing power and influence of Anglos in the region. Over the years, the Alamo Navajos would come to know them in a variety of contexts as neighbors, employers, missionaries, and schoolteachers.

On the Anglo side of the chasm, the dominant image of the Alamo Navajos was that of a renegade band of pagan Indians culturally stuck on the lowest rung of civilization. However valuable Navajos might be as sheepherders and fence builders, however much neighboring ranchers might come to know and respect individual Indians, the general image of the Alamo Navajos was that the group was essentially mired in savagism, perhaps capable of being civilized over time by missionaries and schoolteachers, perhaps not. Time would tell. Because in the early decades the Indians rarely made an appearance in Magdalena, most points of contact took place on ranches near the Alamo Navajo community. Meanwhile, those in town were mostly fed derogatory stereotypes that solidified age-old conceptions of the Indian "other." Two examples make the point.

The first comes from a 1907 article under the headline "Navajo Did Not Sabe [Know]" in the *Socorro Chieftain*. The article relates the story of how on a Sunday morning the leader of a group of Navajos invited to perform at the Socorro County Fair knocked on the door of the ranch house outside which the Indians were camped. When W. E. Martin opened the door, the Indian "began gesticulating and in very broken English" communicated that he must see José Montoya, the individual responsible for bringing the Navajos to the fair. When Martin explained that Montoya was at his own ranch several miles to the north and would not return to Socorro for several hours, the Indian became very agitated and insisted he must speak to Montoya immediately. At this point Martin thought of the phone, so he coaxed the Indian into the house, whereupon he had the local operator ring up the Montoya ranch. When Montoya answered,

> It was with great difficulty that Mr. Martin got the receiver to the red man's ear and it was a still more tedious job to get him to talk into the little box. The Indian would drop the receiver and step back, surveying the wall and even looking into the dark corners of the room, for the owner of the mysterious voice. He listened in blank amazement. He called the other Indians in and each one took a turn at the receiver, and all were mystified and none of them satisfied that Montoya was really at his home 3 miles away but thought that he was in the wall or on the outside. They went out to see and some stood watch on the outside while others listened to the voice in the telephone.

In the end, the "Navajos left more puzzled than when they came," so Martin arranged for the Indians to visit the telephone company for a further demonstration and explanation of the "black box." After talking to a man the Indians knew to be 28 miles away in Magdalena, they were still mystified and "left the office still very uncertain as to what kind of a game the paleface was trying to play on them."[48]

If the above news story reinforced the notion that the Alamo Navajos were premodern primitives, a second story played to the image of the Indian as a drunken sot. As we will see later, the Alamo Navajo community was indeed to be plagued by the problem of alcoholism, but early accounts of the subject did little to raise the status of the group in Anglo eyes. In 1907, Nels Field, who periodically sent news items to the *Socorro Chieftain* under the name "Navajo," reported: "We are getting quite civilized; haven't seen or heard of a drunk Indian for more than a week." But two years later, under the title "One More Good Indian," Field reported:

> One of [Ray] Morley's sheepherders, a Navajo by the name of Capitan, got a little too much booze on the night of the second and on returning to his camp lay down by the fire. In some way his clothes caught in the blaze. All the lower part of his body and his feet and legs were so badly burned that in spite of all the efforts of Dr. Parvis and another he died within two hours. Mr. Morley had the body put into a coffin and sent to Capitan's former home near Alamo. About six years ago the Indian's old father also fell into the fire while drunk and was badly burned.[49]

Stories like the above reaffirmed the view that the Alamo Navajos were a miserable and degraded people. As one old Magdalena resident opined in the 1980s, the group was a "low class of Indians." Another offers, "I heard they're a lazy breed." On the other side of the ledger, the Alamo Navajo people had good reason to distrust Anglos, much of it having to do with land loss. Navajo children growing up in the early years of the century heard stories from elders on how the land had been free of fences before "settlers started comin' in grabbin' the land." One old man offers, "We been holdin' that land—big ones—but they take it anyway. So they put us in a bad place." The loss of land not only threatened traditional subsistence patterns but also meant the loss of freedom to move across it. One man never forgot his father's bitterness: "My father never got over it. He was hurtin' inside, because he cannot go wherever he wants to go. . . . 160 acres, that's all. No place to go."[50]

Because the Alamo Navajos seldom ventured into Magdalena until the 1940s, most of the intergroup contact was in the checkerboard area where Anglo and Hispanic ranches butted up against the Alamo Navajo population, which provided ranchers a reliable source of sheepherders and cowboys. As noted earlier, the Fields' store and Morley's Navajo Lodge were also points of contact, the former serving as a place for purchasing or trading for supplies, the latter a location where the "Indian camp" attracted tourist dollars. But some Anglo children gained their first impressions of the Alamo Navajos in tension-filled encounters. The son of one Datil rancher can still recall the time when a party of agitated Navajos woke the family in the middle of the night to inform his father that the tracks of a bunch of stolen horses led directly to their ranch. The boy remembers his father patiently explaining that he knew nothing about the horses but that the Indians were welcome to look for them. (As it turned out, they retrieved the horses from some rustlers who had passed through the area.) Also a woman from the Datil region still recalls her fear when riding up to the ranch house with her brother and finding it surrounded by Indians. Spotting the children, the Indians rode out to meet them. "And they circled us and had us scared to death." Looking back on the episode, she realizes she was really in no danger. Again, the purpose of the visit was lost horses. She muses, "The Indians were always a great hand at looking out for their horses."[51]

One of the first impressions Fred Billings had of the Alamo Navajos came from the periodic ranch house visits of an old man:

> He was a little old Indian—real old. And he was always trotting. Every place he was going, he was trotting—kind of trotted everywhere. Half Apache. And he'd been just a kid when Victorio was doing all his depredation. He'd been along. He'd seen a hell of a lot. He talked real good Spanish. He'd always come to the house and mother would always invite him to eat. But she'd have to watch him real closely because he'd steal silverware. They called him Cuchara; it means teaspoon. He made rings out of them. And he'd sit there and eat, and she'd talk to him in Spanish. And if he wanted to, he'd answer. If he didn't he wouldn't. And when he'd get through, he'd always . . . sing a little song in Navajo. Then when he'd get through, he'd lay down on the floor and take a nap. Just right by the chair he'd fall down on the floor and go to sleep for a little while. And pretty soon, just take off. And never knocked. He never did knock. None of them ever knocked. You'd look around and they were there. That just was the custom; they just didn't knock.[52]

Sometimes firsthand contact did more to encourage distrust and reinforce old prejudices than reduce them. Buddy Major was just seven years old when he thought he had made a pretty good bargain for a horse with a local Navajo man. The boy encountered the Indian and the horse in the corral near the small store his father operated for local ranchers and Indians. When the curious child wandered down to the corral, the Indian asked the boy if he might want to trade for the horse. Buddy, who had seen his father haggle over horses numerous times, had just gotten a new pair of gloves for Christmas, and he offered the Indian the prize gloves. The bargain was finally struck when the boy was also coaxed out of a pair of spurs and a rope. Proud of his purchase and excited, Buddy ran to the house and begged his mother to see his acquisition. Walking to the corral, his mother could not help but notice that the Indian was gone. Then the two turned to survey the horse. "I tried to give him a little bit of hay and he'd just walk over the hay. He wouldn't drink. He was just loco." When they turned the horse out to graze, he still would not eat. "About four or five days later we found him dead out there." As for the seller, "that Indian wouldn't come to that store for two months."[53]

Lee Coker's childhood contact with some Alamo Navajo children also did little to foster positive attitudes. Growing up near Morley's Navajo Lodge, Lee sometimes ventured over to the Indian camp to play with the children. "Damned if I didn't get head lice." Soon he carried it to the children at the local schoolhouse. At first his parents "wondered what the hell was wrong. They had to shave my head. They used lard and sulfur to git rid of it. The only cure they had for it was to shave your head. . . . I had this wavy hair and it about killed me when they shaved my head. I thought I was ruined for life."[54]

But bad experiences cut both ways. Even when Anglos joined the Alamo Navajos for their annual fiesta, some of the Indians learned to be wary of them. "We'd rodeo all day and dance all night," recalls one man who grew up near the Alamo Navajos. Amidst the sounds of drums and singing:

> The Indian squaws would go around and get the menfolk and dance with 'em. You'd dance around the fire, us kids, us young boys, we thought that was a big deal. The squaws would come and git us, and whenever they stopped their drum music and their singin', well you had to pay the squaw to git away from her. If you didn't pay her, you had to dance with her the next dance. Course us boys were broke . . . , so what we would do, we'd just stay dancin' as long as we could—until some of the Indian bucks told us, "Alright you boys, you dance with that squaw all night and you have to marry her in the morning." So that put a stop to that!
>
> But the boys struck upon an ingenious solution to their dilemma. One of the items sold at the Fields' store was Crackerjacks, each box containing a toy or counterfeit coin. "So we got over there to the dance and we got to givin' these coins to the squaws because they [the coins] weren't worth anything. So anyway, the squaws finally caught on. So before they let us go they'd check the coin to make sure it was real. But we pawned off a lot of those false coins."[55]

The Alamo Navajo fiestas were generally good-natured affairs where the Indians and their neighbors competed in all manner of contests in the day and then danced at night. If a couple of ranch boys passed off Crackerjacks coins for real ones, the Navajos also indulged in trickery. Because this story comes from the same dancer passing out counterfeit coins who related the story above, one wonders if there was a little playful retribution going on. In any event, on this occasion the boy's father and mother entered a sheep-roping contest. The idea was for his mother to rope a ewe and then for his father to rush to the animal and fill a bottle with the ewe's milk. But on this occasion, "the Indians wanted to play a trick on my dad, so they put a dry sheep out there and he roped this dumb sheep and tried to git milk—but no milk.... My dad worked and worked and worked tryin' to git that dry sheep to give milk. Course the Indians were sittin' around on the fence just breakin' up laughin'."[56]

Thus, much of the contact between the two groups was marked by genuine friendliness. In the early years the Indians had no greater friend than the Morleys. Ada Morley, her grandson observes, "was a great admirer of the Navajos," an attitude derived from her advocacy of women's rights. "She judged them—or anybody else—on how they treated the women.... The Navajos were a matriarchal society, which my grandmother thought was a great idea. They had something going, see. The Navajos were unique. And she figured by that standard they were better than the white man. They were human beings entitled to respect." Over the years, Ada's children—Ray, Agnes, and especially Loraine—would continue advocating for the Alamo Navajos and in small ways reach out to them with acts of benevolence. Preparing for a community Christmas celebration in 1928, the occasional columnist from Datil (no doubt one of the Morley children) reported that part of the money raised by a recent box supper and dance was being spent on Christmas presents for the Navajos. "We owe it to our less fortunate brothers to express kindness at Christmas. We have with us fifteen Indian children under the age of twelve, and we will ... have some simple toy for them all."[57]

It is not altogether clear, however, whether one ranch couple's adoption of a Navajo child was an act of benevolence or a bad joke gone wrong. As the story is told by the son of an Anglo rancher, his father, leading a horse he had just acquired in trade, stopped to say hello to "Old Pedro," an elderly Navajo that lived nearby. As he was talking to the Indian, a small child wearing a dress ran out of the hogan. Thinking the child a girl, he was surprised when the child jerked up its dress and revealed that he was actually a boy. At this point the rancher offered, "That's a good-looking boy. I'll trade for him"—to which Old Pedro responded, "What'll you trade me?" Continuing the good-hearted banter, this question met with the response, "I'll trade you this pony for him." At this point Old Pedro reached for the rope and started to lead the horse off, which immediately prompted the rancher to say, "Oh hell, I was just talkin.'" Old Pedro, however, said the bargain was completed. "Naw, you traded. Anyway, that one, he got no mama, no daddy, no nothin'. You take him." So the rancher set out for home with the child sitting behind him "like a little hoot owl." At this point in their marriage the couple was childless, the reason the rancher might have been thinking his wife might welcome this new addition to the family, this boy they would call Anthony.

> So he took him home to mama. She deloused that little sucker and put him in that bathtub and cleaned him up, gave him some clothes. And then when she got a chance, she bought him some clothes. And they kept him until he was about fourteen when the government come got him and took him to the Indian school. As soon as he got out of school, why I guess he was about sixteen when he come home, come back to us. So he just grew up there at the ranch with us.

In the coming years, Anthony returned to the Alamo Navajo community, served in the US Army during World War II, and upon his return, fell in love with a young Alamo Navajo woman, whereupon he presented the bride-to-be's parents with four horses, more than fifty cattle, and the promise of a year's labor. Meanwhile, the years in the Anglo rancher's home, coupled with his years at school and in the military, ideally prepared him for the role of cultural broker, a valued resource for a people increasingly encroached upon by the outside world.[58]

If an Anglo couple adopting an Alamo Navajo urchin was a border crossing of sorts, a more dramatic one—albeit a rare one—was intermarriage between the two groups. The Anglo pioneer in this regard was none other than the indomitable Bessie Field, one of Nels and Ida Field's several daughters. Growing up on the edge of the Alamo Navajo community, Bessie spent endless hours with the family's Navajo neighbors. At the trading post, "I was always playin' with the little children. I'd pick up those little kids in their cradleboards, sit and play with them and hold 'em. When one would cry, I'd cry too. They called me the word for grandmother—*hamá sání*. When a baby cried, they'd call for me to go attend the baby. I was supposed to be the grandmother."[59] When Bessie's mother was away one summer with Katie, who was being treated for polio at a sanatorium in St. Louis, and her father, who, as state land commissioner, was away performing his duties in Santa Fe, Bessie and another sister were left under the care of an old Navajo named José. "And we stayed out at the ranch with that old Indian alone. And he combed our hair, braided our hair, washed our hair. He'd bring in water and heat it on the cookstove, poor it in an old washtub, and then tell us to go in there and bathe. We had to wash and dry ourselves. And he'd inspect us to see if we were clean, because he himself was very clean. And he cooked our meals and he fed us good. We all got pot-bellied."[60]

As noted earlier, Nels Field regularly hired Navajos as cowboys. In fact he favored them for several reasons: they were superior workers, it made for good relations with the Navajos, and they commanded a "skinnier" wage. But there was another reason as well—namely, he could trust them around his several daughters. Bessie explains, "He wouldn't hire any white person because of the girls. His belief was that Indians wouldn't bother girls. He didn't know me though—heh, heh. Trouble was, he was watching his older girls and wasn't payin' attention to the younger ones." During a big roundup, when several ranchers in the area threw in together to collect and sort stray cattle,

> Many times we girls went along, cuz papa wasn't afraid of the Navajos doing anything to the girls, cuz they had respect for the girls, and he didn't mind them mingling. But he was a little leery of the other ranchers who joined the chuck wagon and their crew—a bunch of white guys and mixed people that they brought in as cowboys. My father always put his bed between the other men's outfit and his six-shooter right about under his pillow with his hand on it so if anybody come toward the girls. He was very protective. And the Indians were just as watchful. I can remember old Sacarino movin' his bed right in front of our door, and I can tell you, nobody was gonna come around our camp.[61]

It never crossed Nels Field's mind that his daughter might find Navajo boys to her liking. Even when the Fields moved to Santa Fe during his tenure as land commissioner, Bessie frequently saw some of the Alamo Navajo students attending the Santa Fe Indian School. In Santa Fe she took notice of a boy named Ayshia. "He was younger than me but I thought he was a pretty swell, good-lookin' guy. But he was very shy." As circumstances would have it, Bessie married a Cherokee Indian briefly before eventually marrying Ayshia. How did Nels feel about her marrying an Indian? Bessie laughs, "Heh, I wouldn't say they were exactly charmed. . . . Course I was old enough to do what I wanted to do anyhow. I had some in-laws that thought I had ate poison and become contaminated, I guess. But I didn't pay no attention to that. It wasn't their life. It was mine." Nels Field got a double jolt when his artist daughter, Katie, also married one of the local Navajos.⁶² Confirmation that the Field family was not "exactly charmed" with this second marriage is borne out by a comment several years later in a letter written by one of the Morley daughters to an acquaintance regarding Katie's marriage: "You have no idea of the ill will toward Katie for having married 'an Indian'—her own people didn't speak to her for years, some of them. You can't imagine how these Texans feel."⁶³

Although the marriages of the Field girls to Indians are stunning examples of how boundaries could melt into border crossings, they were also glaring exceptions. Much more significant was the arrival of the missionaries.⁶⁴ The Alamo Navajos' first contact with Christianity appears to have come early in the century in the form of Catholic priests who periodically made their way up the Rio Salado from Socorro to conduct mass for Hispanic ranchers, but they also took the opportunity to baptize any Navajos curious about the religion of the *'éé neishoodii be'éé' danineezígíí* (literally, "those who drag their garments about"). Juan Jaramillo recalls that his grandfather's ranch (located near the present-day Alamo Navajo chapter house) had a large room with an alter in it where nearby ranchers and Navajos periodically gathered, called to mass by the ringing of a large bell mounted on posts in front of the house. "There was a lot of people baptized then," observes one old Alamo Navajo man, "but they didn't know what Christian is. They just been baptized, that's all."⁶⁵ In 1932 the Southern Baptists entered the field, and this Protestant denomination would have the greatest impact on the Alamo Navajo community's religious outlook. Two young Navajos helped build the church, and it soon had forty-one charter members. The founder of the mission was a "Brother Burnett," but locals have more vivid memories of George Wilson (an Oklahoma Indian) and his wife, and especially C. W. Stumph, whom the Indians called *Bits'iiní*, or "Skinny." But the resources to support the church were themselves "skinny," so for most of the coming years the missionaries, who lived in Albuquerque, made only periodic visits to Alamo in their Model T, as road conditions allowed.⁶⁶

But Catholics were not prepared to abandon the field so easily. In an unpublished essay, Agnes Morley Cleaveland describes a fascinating moment in the late 1930s when Magdalena's local priest, Father Stoffel, drove a pickup out to the annual Alamo Navajo fiesta to win converts. As darkness descended, after a day of horse races, goat tyings, and other sundry competitions, the priest hoisted a wagon sheet, unveiled a battery projector, and proceeded to show slides of "the great masterpieces of historical religious art." Cleaveland correctly surmised that the priest's heavy Belgian accent only added to the confused reception of his message.

> In any event, he was unmistakably a stranger in a strange land, speaking a strange tongue—hopeful that the spirit itself would suffice. A Navajo interpreter and no mean orator, he stood at the young priest's side and turned the halting English into Navajo—with unction and with—I gravely question the accuracy—oratory. From the Annunciation to the Resurrection, the physical record of the Christian faith unfolded as the great masters, from the forerunner Giotto to Michelangelo, Ribera to Rembrandt, had conceived and immortalized it with paint on canvas. The Indian audience sat stolidly silent. Whatever emotions stirred them showed not at all in their faces.

The Alamo Navajo interpreter (no doubt a returned boarding school student) helped, but "it was a long session," she continues. "I hadn't realized how many old masters there were who painted biblical scenes. Before the last one was through on the screen, the younger Indian males had, one by one, drifted out, and the flicker of the great bonfire they had lighted brought into sharp focus the fact that Christianity had not yet wholly triumphed in its contest with paganism."[67]

The Southern Baptists had more success. On Reverend Stumph's visits, he preached the word of God, told the assembled how Jesus Christ had died on the cross to save their souls, and led the congregation in hymns such as "Holy, Holy, Holy" and "What a Friend We Have in Jesus." Baptism, at least from the missionaries' perspective, marked a signal moment in crossing the threshold from paganism to Christianity, and because it involved thrusting the individual completely under the water, no doubt left a powerful impression on the baptized. In 1936 Nels Field informed readers of the *Magdalena News* that Reverend Stumph "was over to our little church yesterday, but could not find water enough to baptize anyone, so will make another call soon." Actually, the baptisms took place in the artesian well at the Fields' ranch. One man recalls he was about fifteen when he took the step. "I remember the day. It's good, it's good. They put your head under the water."[68]

The missionary visits combined religious instruction with holiday celebrations and social activities, and these activities most appealed to children. "Every Christmas they used to come over there and bring some little things to pass out to the people," one old man recalls. "The first time I . . . go to church I don't even think I goin' to church. I go but I don't even think what I was doin'. . . . I just want to go over there and pick up some candy." During the summer the church was a regular site for social activities. With the aid of sewing machines, women made clothes for their families and cut and stitched quilts, and small girls made potholders and pillowcases. Because religious instruction for the children was accompanied by drawing, cutting and pasting pictures, singing songs, and playing games, many regarded it as a welcome alternative to herding sheep. A pot of boiling pinto beans and stacks of fry bread were also enticements.[69]

During the first years, the Alamo Navajos' understanding of Christianity was marked by confusion. One man recalls, "We would ride our horses over there and listen for a little while, but we didn't know what he was talking about. They would just preach to us, but we didn't know what he was talking about. We would just go for a little while and listen." To facilitate understanding, Reverend Stumph, like Father Stoffel, used translators, but as Cleaveland suggests, even when translators were able to rework Stumph's words into a rough approximation in Navajo, listeners had a difficult time comprehending a religious worldview so foreign to the Navajo outlook.[70] Bessie Field, ever concerned about the Indians' welfare, remembers being alarmed about how Stumph and others "were baptizing these people and they didn't know what they were getting into." On one occasion she even confronted the missionary: "Lookie, don't be comin' to these people for donations to the church until they know what it's about." Looking back on these years, Bessie observes,

> You've got to know what's in the Bible, what the teaching is, and what it's all about, and absolutely know what it is before you become a Christian. . . . Reverend Stumph tried awful well. He tried. But they didn't know how to interpret the Bible even though they got an interpreter. . . . They tried to get really educated interpreters. But it [the translation] didn't fit the Bible. The words in the Bible are different from what words you hear when you talk [Navajo].[71]

By one Alamo Navajo man's account, the early missionaries shrewdly avoided a head-on assault on traditional beliefs:

> I used to attend their services with a man by the name of Julio. The reason why we attending these church services was because these people never said anything against our Navajo ways, our beliefs. Even if they pray for you or baptize you, they didn't tell you we had to give up our Navajo ways, or had to keep going to church in order to be saved or know God. Nowadays when you go into church that's all you hear . . . people

talking against our beliefs. So I didn't go to church anymore but still believe in our ways.[72]

Students of Navajo culture have long observed that one of the distinguishing features of the *Diné* has been their adaptive capacity to incorporate new beliefs and practices while remaining essentially Navajo. Certainly the early Alamo Navajos' response lends credence to anthropologists' insight that acculturation can be additive as well as substitutive in nature.[73] Although the missionaries were clearly making inroads in the 1930s, a good many of the baptized were not ready to abandon traditional ways. One man, after recalling this period, says, "I was just in the middle. I don't even think about it. . . . I just go over there [to church]. I was not even a Christian. Just like I say, Navajo way, the white way—I just stand in the middle." An old woman concurs, "If we were baptized we were still running to our medicine men, so you can see I was just in between. And I didn't really favor one or the other."[74]

As the following story indicates, although many were "trying on" the new religion, others were adamantly holding on to the old faith.

Some people got after me for not going to church. I told them going to church was pretty hard because you have to keep your soul clean. It's a lot harder than going to school to learn how to read and write. They argued with me saying God, God, all the time. I told them when you say God, where does the word God originate? It is not in the Navajo vocabulary. It came with the first white people that came to this land. We didn't say God then. We have our own saints. God is a foreign language. We call it the Holy People, Diyin Din'é. We say "the Blessingway will come around."[75]

But the fact is, many in the community were entering new spiritual terrain, engaging in a sort of cultural border crossing that, next to white education, would have the single greatest influence on their response to the outside world now closing in upon them with inexorable force.

But the question remains: What was the attraction of Christianity to begin with? There are several plausible explanations. First, the Alamo Navajo ceremonial system was never a fully developed one. As noted earlier, Navajo religion is connected to the performance of a broad range of chantways and ceremonies directed by "singers," each possessing specialty knowledge for one or two ceremonies. Because the Alamo Navajo community was small, never claiming more than two or three medicine men, individuals stricken by some physical or psychological malady frequently required a ceremony not available in the local community. Thus, for many years locals were forced to import medicine men from Ramah, Cañoncito, and even further north to restore the ailing patient to health and *hózhó*. In short, however much the Alamo were Navajo in their spiritual outlook, the lack of available ceremonial specialists made them particularly vulnerable to the teachings of missionaries, which for all their strangeness, offered believers a full-blown religious system. A second reason has already been noted: the oft-cited *Diné* capacity—in the service of adaptive or pragmatic ends—to embrace two seemingly dichotomous belief systems. A third reason involved the implicit attraction of the Christian message. Navajo religion, for all its complexity and richness, never offered believers the promise of an afterlife in a mystical kingdom called heaven. The missionaries' promise of the celestial rewards awaiting the "saved" under Christianity must have been terribly inviting. Finally, some converts must have been drawn to a religion in which the believer's deep personal relationship with the deity was at the very center of the faith.

Whatever the reason, Alamo Navajo adults were taking tentative steps in the direction of Christianity, steps that in time would not only dramatically recast their own lives but their children's as well. But for now, it appears that most in the community were living in a state of "in between," one day attending a Baptist meeting and the next "running to our medicine men." More than Bessie Field's marriage to an Indian, more than young cowboys dancing with Navajo girls at a fiesta, and more than a local rancher adopting a Navajo toddler, the specter of Reverend Stumph's Model T—stuffed with hymnals, sewing machines, pinto beans, and bags of candy—kicking up dust as it made its way down to Alamo, was a much more consequential agent of cultural change. For however careful the missionary—more clever than the trickster Coyote himself—might be in not attacking the Navajo religion directly, the good reverend's intent was never in doubt—to send the Holy People packing and make way for Jesus Christ, who had died on the cross for the Navajos' sins.

Contact and Separateness

In the early decades of the twentieth century, outside of school, which would emerge as the chief point of intercultural contact for children in all three groups, Anglos, Hispanics, and Navajos largely moved in separate ethnocultural worlds. The Alamo Navajos, although just 30 miles from Magdalena and introduced to Christianity, continued to live their lives essentially as they always had. In Magdalena, where Anglos and Hispanics had much more contact, in the important domains of family, church, and ethnic social gatherings, they too principally moved in bounded cultural settings.

One only had to hear the ringing of the Catholic and Presbyterian church bells on Sunday mornings to be reminded of the Hispanic-Anglo divide. Everyone knew the story. Early in the century John Mactavish and José Aragón, two of the town's leading citizens, had boarded a train to St. Louis to purchase the bells. Apparently by prior agreement, the bell purchased for the Catholic church was to strike the note of G, and the Presbyterian bell the note of G sharp. "If you ring them at the same time," Mactavish's grandson explains, "you get a sort of discord because there's only a half-step between the two."[76] Perhaps Mactavish had made the concession—that the Presbyterian bell would sound the disharmony. After all, the Anglos were the latecomers to the country and a distinct minority in the town. In any event, for many years to come, when the mostly Anglo-Protestant and mostly Catholic-Hispanic children went off to church in their separate directions, the air resounded with the ringing sounds of dissonance, a musical reminder of the larger social distance in Magdalena.

CHAPTER FIVE

ANGLOS AND HISPANICS AT SCHOOL

In the fall of 1917 Juan Jaramillo and his younger sister Victoria set out for their first day of school. Like many ranchers, their parents had built a second house in Magdalena so the children could acquire a proper education. For the two children the first day would be full of surprises. The first came the moment they entered the classroom. Their teacher was none other than Rosa Barreras, who had grown up on a neighboring ranch. "*Mira quien está aquí. Rosa está de veras la maestra*" ("Look who is here. Rosa is actually the teacher"), Juan recalls his sister saying. Rosa, meanwhile, seemed not to recognize the two children. Then what might have been a pleasurable day quickly turned sour. For some incomprehensible reason Rosa walked down the row of seats (empty dynamite boxes served as chairs) and began pointing in Victoria's face and speaking loudly in English, a language neither she nor Juan understood. Surely, Juan thought, this Rosa Barreras meant to do harm to his sister. As her older brother, he must protect her. So Juan leapt onto Rosa's back, knocked her to the floor, and began shaking her by the neck. ("She was just a little bitty thing.") Victoria also got in a few licks before the two bolted for home. Their mother was doing the washing when the children returned, and Juan explained why they had come home so soon. "You know who is the teacher over there? Rosa Barreras. But she don't talk like we do any more. We don't know what she WANTS." Then Juan proceeded to explain how the two had "whipped her." Juan's mother, who had never been to school, agreed that the children should stay home until she talked to their father that evening. Upon hearing from his wife what had transpired, the children's father said nothing, but after dinner the children observed that he left the house and headed for town.[1]

Later in the evening his father called the children in from outdoors. "Pucha! When we walked in and saw the whole crew [board of education] there and Rosa, we didn't know what was going to happen." José Aragón, one of the board members, immediately took charge.

> So when we walked in and old man Aragón said, "Vengan por acá, hijitas." Come over here. So he got me on one side, Victoria on the other. He says, you came to school today—he said it in Spanish—to learn how to read and write and learn ENGLISH. I don't know nothing. And Ben Beagle [here], he is a gringo, but he knows both Spanish and English. And that's why you have to learn. I didn't have school in my days, but that's why they brought you over here. And you don't have to fight again. Rosa will know better now. Rosa, you come over here. So Rosa came over. He said Rosa, when you say something in English, start telling them in Spanish so they'll know what you mean. While they have known you all their lives, they don't know that there is such a language [as English]. It's hard for me, an old man, already. Well, it's rougher for them. So that's what you do . . . and I think that they'll do good. She said, sure. So she hugged both of us. She says, I want you in school tomorrow and we're not going to fight anymore. We says, fine. Mr. Aragón says, well now you can go play. So he turned us loose and we got out.

One of the most consequential influences on children's lives was school. In addition to expanding their cognitive worlds and perhaps their economic futures, schools also had the capacity to shape their beliefs, values, and very identities. Just as political and educational authorities had historically turned to the public school as the most promising instrument for incorporating ethnocultural minorities into the national polity, so they did in New Mexico, where the majority Hispanic population still existed largely outside the national cultural fold. It followed that Magdalena's classrooms were contested spaces where cultures collided, where group boundaries were fortified and challenged, and finally, where the promises of education were both realized and unfulfilled.

The Politics of Culture

As noted earlier, one of the reasons for New Mexico's prolonged territorial status was the feeling among some Anglos that the territory's mostly "Mexican" or "mongrel" inhabitants were unfit for enlightened self-governance—a judgment buttressed by reports of the population's general illiteracy. Whatever the racial status of Hispanics, the education question had to be addressed. The early years brought little "progress," in the eyes of Anglos. Following the defeat of an 1856 referendum on an education tax bill in which four largely Hispanic counties (Taos, Rio Arriba, Santa Ana, and Socorro) voted the measure down by 5,016 to 37, W. W. H. Davis, territorial governor, pronounced "that the people are so far sunk in ignorance that they are not really capable of judging of the advantages of education" and loved "darkness better than light."[2] In 1870, an almost 80 percent illiteracy rate in either Spanish or English among adults did little to inspire optimism on the matter. Historians have cited several factors for the slow growth of public schools: the weak public educational legacy of the Spanish and Mexican eras, congressional neglect of the territory, local opposition to school taxes, Catholic opposition to nonsectarian education, the legacy of peonage, and finally Hispanic opposition to the culturally hegemonic aims of public school supporters. But gradually inroads were being made. By 1910 adult illiteracy had dropped to 24 percent, and the school-age population attending school was up to 60 percent. The foundation of a modern school system was in place.[3]

Not surprisingly, in a region where Hispanics possessed considerable political power, the issue of culture, specifically language, was a major area of contention. The landmark 1891 school code stated that schoolbooks could be "in both English and Spanish," and in those districts where only Spanish was spoken, "the teacher shall have a knowledge of Spanish and English." (The same year Socorro County adopted several Spanish- as well as English-language texts.) But some Hispanic educators were conflicted on the question. In 1891, the territory's first superintendent of schools, Amado Cháves, declared that English should be the sole language of instruction. Five years later he was singing a different tune. "English and Spanish should walk hand in hand in the schools. . . . There is not a child in all this Territory that does not understand English more or less, but at the same time this child uses and listens reverently to the sweet sounds of the mellifluous language in which his adored mother taught him his first prayer. Is this a crime?" For much of this period, then, local communities had considerable flexibility in determining the language of instruction, although the long-term intent of most educators was to increasingly move Spanish speakers to English. In 1890, James P. Chase, Socorro County school superintendent, reported that of the forty-seven schools in the county, fifteen were taught in English, seven in both English and Spanish, and twenty-five in Spanish. Meanwhile, Chase asserted that the "growing desire is plainly manifest in a majority of the Mexican districts to have the children instructed in the English language. It would be well to encourage this desire, and when practical every encouragement and possible aid will be extended to that end."[4]

In the coming years, both state and local language policy, though marked by inconsistencies and ambiguities, increasingly shifted toward English-only instruction. The 1910 state constitution, for example, stated that schools "should always be conducted in English" but also held that teachers in rural areas should be trained to become "proficient in both the English and Spanish languages, to qualify them to teach Spanish-speaking pupils in public schools." In 1919 the state legislature again stipulated bilingual instruction as established policy, but the same year, the state board of education passed a resolution emphasizing its opposition "to the establishment and maintenance of primary schools where all branches of study are taught in a foreign language, and where the language of our country, which is the English language, is only incidentally taught." Clearly the shift was on. By 1923, provisions calling for bilingual instruction were absent from the school code, and by 1930 the state course of study called for the direct language method, that is to say, immersion.[5] When Adolfo Chávez, a member of the Socorro Board of Education, spoke to a county teacher's institute in 1924, his remarks were in keeping with this new direction in policy: "The teacher should not permit his pupils during the school day period either in the school or on the school grounds to converse with each other in the Spanish language but should at all times insist that the only language permissible at such places is the English language. Teach them to forget the Spanish language while in the school and to learn to think in English only."[6] Magdalena educators took the message to heart.

Attitudes toward Education

Anglo Tom Locke reckons he was fourteen the first time he saw Magdalena. The year was 1926. The family's long journey began in Texas two years earlier, after his father went broke dry farming cotton. "The weather and the market was against him," Tom recalls. So with $20 to their name and a string of horses, the Lockes loaded their nine children and belongings into a 16-by-6-foot covered wagon and set out to file on a homestead further west. They were only a quarter mile from home when the overloaded wagon sank in a bed of sand, requiring a neighbor's team of horses to pull them out. For the next 200 miles it went well, the Lockes making about 30 miles a day. Then around Roswell, the horses took sick from drinking alkaline water, so the Lockes decided to camp for two weeks and hire themselves out picking cotton. This allowed them to spend the winter in a two-room house. The house was without plumbing, a quarter of a mile from water, and without heat, but it surpassed spending the winter living out of a wagon.[7]

In the spring the Lockes headed for the Hondo Valley, with Tom's main job being to drive the ten horses, including three new ones acquired over the winter. They were making about 25 miles a day until the "hard pull" up to the valley caused one of the four horses pulling the wagon to drop dead. After three days' rest, with three horses "in a breast," the Lockes limped into the Hondo Valley. Short of cash, they stayed a month earning $5 a day putting their horses to work plowing. Then it was off to the Rio Grande and western New Mexico. When they passed through Magdalena, his mother traded some prize chickens tied on the wagon for a sack of grits. "It wasn't exactly horse food. It wasn't exactly human food. You could boil it and make a type of cereal out of it. And that's about all the grocery we had to eat for the next few days. And the horses were underfed and getting weaker."

Somewhere along the way, Tom's dad decided that Arizona, not New Mexico, should be the family's destination. Crossing the border into Arizona sometime in May, they settled on a piece of land and "put in a patch of beans." Meanwhile, Tom found work. "I got a job workin' for a guy puttin' in an irrigation system, hookin' up four mules to a fresno. I was fourteen years old and I'd hook up them four mules to the fresno and run it all day. Done that all summer, but Arizona laws caught up with us and said I had to go to school." Because the family was barely surviving with Tom's wages, their loss prompted the decision to turn back toward New Mexico. "My job on this wagon trip—we had a saddle bronc—was to ride that pony along the wagon. So I rode all the way, ridin' along slow. I seen the country, I guess as good as anybody did see it." Passing through Datil, the Lockes ran into some settlers on the San Augustine Plains.

> Got over there to Augustine, these people got to talkin' to him [Tom's father]. These people in them days wanted to send their children to school. They would work hard to build a schoolhouse. They had to have ten kids because they had to have an average attendance of eight, then the county would furnish a teacher. So my dad come through with that wagonload of kids and these guys got to talkin' to him about showin' him a good section of land over there he could file on. So we went over there and filed on that.

The Locke's homesteading story is interesting on several accounts, not the least of which is the reason for their final landing spot—surrounding families' desire to establish a school. By the time Anglos began settling west-central New Mexico, the one-room schoolhouse was an iconic feature in frontier communities, an architectural reflection of the near-national consensus that all children should receive a modicum of schooling. For those lacking such belief, ever more stringent school attendance laws helped provide the motivation. So it was that homesteaders streaming into western New Mexico began building schoolhouses with names such as Divide, Greens Gap, Mountain View, and Sally's Pine. When the Lockes entered the San Augustine Plains with a "wagonload of kids," the families in the area were only too happy to see them.[8]

Most Hispanics' initial attitude toward formal schooling is harder to gauge. Among *los pobres* the short-term economic value of their children's labor all too often outweighed the risky long-term advantages of schooling. *Rico* sheep ranchers, moreover, had little to gain in raising the educational aspirations of a labor pool seemingly content in their condition. One woman recalls the town priest remarking to her father: "Mr. García, you won't be able to get a sheepherder when these people get educated."[9] More than counterbalancing these attitudes was the growing belief among Hispanics that schooling was central to their children's future opportunities.

In some families this belief was rooted in a preexisting deep appreciation for education. Esther Peralta, who grew up listening to her grandfather read from *Don Quixote,* remembers how the importance of learning was constantly drilled into the children. "The most important thing is that God gave you a brain. Everything is learning," he admonished. The extent to which he took this principle is revealed in this astonishing story:

> We had a cow that was going to have a calf. We knew that. . . . So he woke us all up. And we went in our nightgowns. It was spring. It was early. The sun was just coming up. And he had the cow on a slab on the ground. The cow died and my grandfather cut her open. He wanted us to see. And he took the calf out. And grandmother had a blanket. And grandpa wanted us to see where the baby, where the calf was. He had to cut her to remove [the calf]. And we were crying for the cow. But he showed how the magic of where the calf was. And he took it out and handed it to grandma and . . . she cleaned the little calf and she fed it. See what kind of person he was. He wanted the children [to know] the magic. He gave us so much magic. So we had no doubt about how big

the little calf was. The cow died. Death, love, care—[that's] the way it was taught to us. The way it was taught to us was just the way we lived. It wasn't a lesson; it was living. We were crying because the cow died, but grandpa told us: death was living. The cow gave us milk. We brought her in; we loved her. She's gone, but look what's here—the calf. This is how we learned. And that's what he meant—think, think, think. That's how we learned.[10]

Other locals also tell of the older generation's support for education. One man whose grandfather settled in western Socorro County in 1893, when schools were still nonexistent, says the old man sent his children to board with families elsewhere so they could attain some schooling. His grandfather's reverence for learning was apparent by his habit of reading throughout the night. "It wasn't at all unusual for everybody to go to bed at night and he'd be reading, and when breakfast was ready, they'd call him from where they left him the night before—reading." The son of a Magdalena merchant says, "My dad was always stressing the advantages or importance of education" and constantly regaled his son with the story about how, as a small boy, he had daily carried an armload of firewood to the Catholic school in Socorro in lieu of paying tuition. At a tender age, his father explained, he had already discerned that "the one with the education didn't have to work so hard." When verbal persuasion failed, parents might resort to stronger motivational measures. After one mother was informed that her son had twice played hooky, "she came home and gave me a good whipping, make me clear the yard, and chop a half wagon of wood without stopping, and she didn't feed me the next day."[11]

At the same time, the older generation was conflicted on the question of how much schooling girls needed. As one woman explains, her parents believed it "was not very useful for a girl to know much. . . . They thought the boy should go to school. They had the idea that men had to get out and work to support the family. A lady could get by just knowing how to speak English."[12] But such attitudes were slowly giving way to a broader view. Candelaria García recalls how sometime in the 1930s, shortly after she graduated from eighth grade, her uncle was mystified over the fact that his brother intended to send Candelaria on to high school. Why was a high school education necessary for a life of washing diapers and doing housework? Her father's response: "Eduardo, you have more education than I do because my mother and daddy gave you a little more. You can read and write English. I can't. I just know Spanish." Thus, he had come to appreciate the importance of education. Why must his daughter's horizons be limited to housecleaning and the scrub board? Times were changing, and for "a good job, they have to have an education."[13]

By the early decades of the twentieth century, then, many parents clearly began to look upon schools as essential to their children's future status. One woman born on a remote sheep ranch recalls how her mother constantly urged her husband to sell the stock and move the family to Magdalena, where the children could get a real education. As things stood, "Your children are going to be sheep, sheep, sheep! They're not going to even go to school—nothing. And I want my children and your children to go to school and learn something and don't be like you and I that do not know anything." Finally convinced, the husband sold his sheep and moved the family to Magdalena, where once the children were in school, the mother forever pestered them with *"No quiero que sean borrequeros"* ("I don't want you to be sheepherders"). The connection between schooling and economic status was even more dramatically made by another father whose sixteen-year-old son, after being delivered to a school in Albuquerque, immediately caught a ride back to Magdalena. The first word out of his father's mouth was a stern command to hitch up the family workhorse to the plow. Because the family had two plows—a walking plow and one on wheels that was easier to maneuver—the boy naturally chose the latter. Seeing this, the father ordered, "No boy. Hook the horse onto the walking plow. If you want to be a burro all your life, you pull the walking plow." After this was settled, the father sent his son out to plow 100 acres—like a burro.[14]

Hispanic support for education also derived from the belief that New Mexico was a "lost land" partly as a consequence of Anglos' educational advantage. "The old people always claimed what beat our people was the education," one man reflects. "Education beat them. They brought their language with them. The contracts were written in English. . . . What beat my people was the paper." Old Manuel Armijo, the son of a sheep rancher, recalls decades later his father's anxiety when picking up the mail. "Sometimes my father get a letter in English. . . . Nobody here knew how to read English. . . . So sometimes he say, 'I don't know what it says here.' I could tell how lonesome he look." Invariably, when receiving such a letter, his father saddled a horse and rode the 20 miles to Magdalena for a translation. Upon his return, when someone asked about the contents of the letter, the response was usually, "Oh, nothing important." Occasionally, the boy would hear his father lament, "My father, why didn't he send me to school? I wouldn't have gone this far for nothing." Manuel's father, who witnessed the invasion of Anglo cattlemen, knew all too well the importance of language and education in the new order of things. Eventually, he moved his wife and children to Magdalena for schooling, impressing upon young Manuel, "Learn all you can. Study hard. Otherwise, you can be a burro like me."[15]

Old-timers knew very well the old adage, *"In la tierra a que fuiste, haz lo que vista,"* which Anglos knew as "When in Rome, do as the Romans do."[16] Nuevomexicanos, of course, knew the difference. They had not ventured to Rome. Rome had come to them.

Ranch House Schooling

For some children living in the hinterlands of ranch country, early education took the form of home schooling, sometimes provided by a hired teacher or governess. For Hispanic ranchers, generally less wealthy than their Anglo counterparts, this solution appears to have been less of an option. But Candelaria García recalls that her first two years of schooling were in a one-room adobe structure at an uncle's ranch, where Maestro Lucero, who knew both Spanish and English, instructed a few children in the basics. Here she learned the *alfabeto*, learned to count, and began to put letters and words together—such as *El burro tiene sed* ("The donkey is thirsty"). Here she learned proper pronunciation and how to trill or roll the double "r" in words like *ferrocarril* (railroad). This, combined with her mother teaching her the catechism, constituted her early education. Similarly, Herman Trujillo recalls that his first years of schooling on his father's sheep ranch were from a woman who could "speak a little bit of English." In this instance, the schoolroom consisted of a dirt floor and canvas ceiling, the class just composed of him and three younger siblings.[17]

Anglo ranchers largely relied on two methods of educating their children. Some subscribed to the Calvert Course out of Baltimore, Maryland, which one man remembers contained the "whole shootin' match" needed for home instruction: lesson plans, books, pencils, notepads, and rulers.[18] Other ranchers hired teachers until all the family's children were of sufficient age to justify moving the whole family into town. This decision was prompted in part by the nagging problem of hiring and retaining good teachers. Most were young and single, and after a few months on a remote ranch, eager for greener horizons. "They could never last a year. They'd come in the fall and then it snowed in the wintertime. And when the train would come through, they'd leave and they'd never come back. They thought that [this] was the most isolated place they'd ever saw—which it was." Some female teachers also succumbed to romance and marriage, a young single woman being an attractive addition to ranch country. Ranch house dances and pie suppers helped the process along.[19]

Then, too, some teachers found that the ranch environment itself undermined their best intentions. Fred Billings still bristles when recollecting a certain Mrs. Fitz—"an old maid from Indiana"—who stuck it out three years. According to Fred, Mrs. Fitz fit all three of his mother's qualifications for a teacher: she was of good character, she was clean, and she was talented in music. It was the last department, namely Fitz's determination to teach Fred how to play the piano, that sparked Fred's resentment. "I thought nobody but a damned sissy played the piano. I was a cowboy; I didn't want to play the piano. I used to kick that piano every time I walked by. . . . I hated that thing." The everyday incidental noises of ranch life—the squeal of a bucking horse or the laughing of cowboys—were also disruptive. Looking back on her ranch house school days, Bessie Field says, "We weren't very good students. Just as a little excitement was occurring somewhere with the cattle or the horses, we broke the school up. We forgot the teacher. As much as she [the teacher] could yell and holler, we couldn't hear."[20]

Surely, the most interesting itinerant teacher was a man locals knew as "Walkin' Smith." Smith appears to have come into the region around 1915 and taught at several ranches for a decade or so, acquiring his name from his sole manner of transportation—walking—and for his habit of taking solitary strolls in the mountains and across mesas. By all accounts Smith, who is remembered for having a very "educated accent," was something of a mystery. "We didn't know anything about him," Cecil Taggert, one of his former pupils, observes. "Different people thought that they knew him. But they didn't know him. Nobody knew him. They didn't know where he came from or where he went." During the summer, Smith just walked off. "We didn't know where he was. Then come school time, here he'd be. He'd show up." According to Taggert, the manner of Smith's quitting was fully in keeping with his strangeness. "One night he jist walked away and we never seen him again. He just took his suitcase and his violin and jist walked off."[21]

Smith had a passion for music. Taggert recalls waking up in the middle of the night and hearing Smith playing his violin, the strains of the melody wafting up from the bunkhouse some 400 yards away. The trouble was that Smith was intent on teaching the violin to Cecil and his brother. "Just with a PASSION he tried to teach us violin. But of course he wasn't teachin' us

Walkin' Smith with a local ranch dog named Nigger, ca. 1918. (Courtesy of Vera Owsley.)

western music like we heard; he was goin' to teach us classical violin playin,'" which to the boys was "old scratchy stuff." Perhaps it was the boys' resistance that caused Smith to pack up and leave. But several years later, Smith turned up again. When Cecil's younger sister Alvira was living in Socorro with her grandmother, Smith appeared at the door, and in the course of visiting, asked the girl if she could play the piano. The eleven-year-old responded by playing "some little western song." Smith complimented her and then sat down and proceeded to play a classical piece. "My God . . . oh it was out of this world. I felt so humiliated. . . . I felt like a worm. And that was the last time I saw him." Smith just walked away.

Even before Smith had left Magdalena country, the rumor began to take hold that Smith was not really Smith at all—that in reality he was none other than Billy the Kid! Fanciful stories that the "Kid" had not really been killed in Fort Sumner and was hiding out somewhere in the territory were rife at this time. On the surface, at least, Walkin' Smith's mysterious ways and background made him an ideal figure for romantic speculation. The fact that Smith spoke with an "educated accent," knew classical music, and avoided horses (something the Kid had a passion for) seemed to matter little. However fanciful, the story circulated for many years that the territory's most notorious outlaw was tutoring ranch children in west-central New Mexico. After all, this was the West.[22]

The One-Room School Experience

Most ranch children got their first taste of schooling in one of the many one-room schoolhouses scattered across western Socorro and Catron Counties. In the early decades of the century, teacher salaries and in some instances textbooks were provided by the county, whereas the school building itself was often constructed by the community. During the 1930s, the Works Progress Administration (WPA), in conjunction with the Federal Emergency Relief Administration (FERA), also helped build schools and pay teacher salaries. Rural schoolhouses were primitive affairs, constructed of logs, lumber, or occasionally adobe. It followed that teachers and students sometimes found themselves in a setting that was a throwback to an earlier century. "When I first saw the school, the sunflowers were 4 to 6 feet high growing on top of the roof," one teacher in the region remembers. "For the roof they hewed the logs to flatten them for the ceiling and put several feet of soil on top of the logs." All through the day, "dirt would filter down our necks or in over our heads. No one seemed to mind."[23]

Just getting to and from school was sometimes an adventure. At age six, Jack Russell rode a burro 5 miles to school. Fred Billings mostly remembers the 6-mile ride he and his sister made in the winter. "You know it's dark at five in the wintertime. Boy some of those blizzards were cold. Worst part was you had three gates to open. And damn, those old hard-to-open gates, you couldn't hardly get them open." One teacher remembers how "one little girl rode a horse 7 miles to school every day. She was a timid little person, and I really admired her courage and determination. The older boys, seventh and eighth graders, helped her unsaddle and saddle the horse each day, and helped carry water for her to drink. If it started to snow early in the day, I would give the little girl . . . the assignment for a few days; we would load her and her books on her horse and start her home. Usually her father came to meet her on the trail. She never got lost."[24]

Because teachers taught all eight grades, the age of students in the room ranged from six to sixteen, one or two students in each grade. Over the course of eight years, if students were reasonably diligent, they learned the fundamentals of "reading, 'riting, and 'rithmetic" and acquired an elementary understanding of the cultural, historical, and moral foundations of the nation. In the early decades, McGuffy Readers and standard subject texts served these purposes well.[25] Pedagogy varied, but most teachers relied heavily on older students assisting younger ones, individual and group recitation—"We all had to say a poem or tell a story or do something"—and spelling bees. Because singing was an activity in which the entire class could participate, music also figured into the school day. By the 1930s, "meets," or interschool debates, were sometimes arranged at which students tested their wits on some selected topic. At one such contest the topic was the comparative value of the horse and the cow. After the defender of the cow listed its many useful properties, including it being the source of ice cream, a somewhat "tongue-tied" supporter of the horse lost the debate when he blurted out, "Who likes ice cream nohow?" End of the year and holiday programs were highlights, offering parents another opportunity both for socializing and for observing their children's progress.[26]

Teachers faced monumental challenges. In 1890, Agnes Morley Cleaveland was just sixteen and home from school in the East when some parents in the Datil community asked her to "learn" their children how to read, write, and "figger." Her account of the experience offers a colorful window on the educational disparity separating her elite education from that of her pupils. When little Elva, unable to give a definition of "island," was coached by Cleaveland as to whether she had ever seen a bit of land in the middle of a lake or river, the girl replied: "How could I . . . when I ain't never seen no lake or river?" Another student challenged the physiology book's assertion that a single drop of nicotine was injurious to a cat's health. "Tain't so," he protested. "When my Aunt Minnie chaws tobaccer, she swallers it. If it killed cats it'd kill Aunt Minnie." Things, however, began to look up when nearly all students seemed to know that George Washington was the "Father of our country," although one youngster confessed his doubts. "He must have left this here country before us'ns all come. Where'd he come from—Texas?" Cleaveland's mission to broaden her pupils' intellectual horizons was made all the more difficult by the occasional interruptions sparked by events outside the classroom. On the first day of school, the class bolted for a nearby sheep pen when a young boy announced that a ewe had just given birth to a six-legged lamb. The last day of the term ended with "tragic suddenness" when her pony "was pawed to death before our horrified eyes by a vicious stallion." Meanwhile, Cleaveland received twenty-three dozen eggs in payment for her services.[27]

From the Greens Gap School, south of Datil, settled mostly by homesteaders, one gets the clearest picture of the one-room school experience. Erected around 1917 and serving the community until 1940, the schoolhouse was a simple log structure and unlike most school buildings, had a small, attached "teacherage"—an enticement for prospective teachers who could be spared the trouble of "boarding around." The teacherage at Greens Gap contained a wood stove, bed with mattress, and a cupboard.

Bobbie Mathers and her class at Greens Gap School, ca. 1927. (Courtesy of Maud Rudder.)

One woman who as a child boarded with the teacher recalls that the living quarters were abominable. On cold winter nights the two stuffed newspapers between the quilts, the roof being so poor that "you could see the snow drift in on the bed." Helen Tipton, who taught at Greens Gap in the 1930s, found the home environments of her children nearly as primitive as the teacherage. "Never had I seen cats, dogs, hogs, and chickens going through rooms in a home." The first day at school, Tipton writes that the topic of discussion among the children was "who is going to get the itch first this year?" At year's end, she felt a special sense of accomplishment when one of her youngest students "lugged a heavy Montgomery Ward Catalogue to me to help him figure how much fencing he should order to keep the animals out of their home and the cats out of the cream on their milk pans in the kitchen."[28]

Among the greatest challenges facing Tipton was that she was preceded by the much-adored Bobbie Mathers. Before coming to Greens Gap, "Miss Bob" taught briefly in Reserve, New Mexico, where she was grievously missed. Shortly after she assumed her new position, one of her former pupils wrote her, "I don't have the blues only when I think of you. . . . This world is just coming to an end if you don't come and live here. I'm coming to get you one of these days on our old big horse." "Miss Bob" also quickly endeared herself to the fifteen to twenty students at Greens Gap, where she made every effort to adjust instruction to the background and interests of the children. The latter is illustrated in her efforts to find regional ballads for group singing—songs such as "Little Joe the Wrangler," "Billy the Kid," and "The Last Longhorn."[29]

Discipline problems were relatively rare, in part because Miss Bob set aside plenty of time for children to let off steam during recess and lunch hour. Indeed, when one parent expressed concern that students were allowed to bring tops and "nigger shooters" (slingshots) to school, and suggested that the children were being allowed too much play time, Miss Bob wrote the disgruntled parent, "There has been less trouble with tops and nigger shooters" than with other activities. Moreover, "the greater interest I can arouse in the children for play at recess and noontime the better I am pleased, for then they work much harder on their lessons."[30] Although it is not clear how many students completed all eight grades at Greens Gap, one surmises that the percentage was high. According to one former pupil, Miss Bob's influence lingered on for years thereafter. "Even after they got grown, the boys wouldn't let Miss Bob see them smoke, even if they was to go to a dance or a rodeo. We respected her and loved her that much."[31]

Other teachers in the region had a more difficult time. Rebellious pupils found countless ways to torture teachers and disrupt classroom routine. A teacher in the ranch community of Dusty, whom the students nicknamed "High Pockets," lasted only two months. "The kids just got so rank that he couldn't handle them. . . . We'd meet at the schoolhouse and we'd pull out." Other teachers followed, but like "High Pockets" suffered from all manner of abuse. Stunts such as smuggling a cat into the class and snapping a mousetrap on its tail, or sneaking a roadrunner into the teacher's desk, were guaranteed to create excitement. The teacher's reaction to the latter incident? "She just squealed and just hollered and fell over—turned her desk over."[32] But these were the tamer pranks. Consider the time the boys assigned the chore of filling the wood stove threw in a few .22 shells to make things interesting. "We had a lot of fun out of that," seeing the teacher jump every time a shell went off. Clearly a new policy was called for. Henceforth, the teacher announced, the boys would haul firewood up to the school, but the girls would be the ones to actually fill the stove. But as it turned out, the new arrangement only succeeded in stimulating the devilish imagination of one of the original offenders, to wit that he brought a bit and brace to the woodpile and proceeded to bore holes in the smaller logs, into which he inserted several .22 shells. To make things even more interesting, he then inserted a .20-gauge shotgun shell into one of the larger logs—all this apparently without the girls' knowledge. It was about noon when the explosion occurred. The children were outside having their lunch, and the "ole lady" was carrying out her daily routine, warming a bowl of chili on the stovetop. While she was in the midst of stirring the chili, the blast was of such force it "blowed" several caps off the roof of the stove; but miraculously the teacher suffered no serious injuries when she was knocked to the floor. When punishing the entire class failed to produce the name of the culprit, the teacher recruited an old cowboy to restore order in the school. With a holstered pistol strapped to his belt, he was an impressive sight. "We was real good kids that day." But by that time the year was nearly lost. Jack Russell recalls that his father decided his son had had enough schooling. The boy's time would be better spent helping on the ranch.[33]

A generation later, students at Dusty were still giving their teachers fits. On one Halloween, some boys disassembled the teacher's wagon and rebuilt it on the schoolhouse roof. Another time they shot arrows into the schoolhouse door with an attached note suggesting that the teacher should "leave the country" (which he did). On still another occasion, a boy brought his mother's six-shooter to school, which several youngsters employed for target practice. Little wonder that the teachers at Dusty reportedly "didn't make nobody study"—with one exception: Miss Anabell Howell. "That lady must have really known how to start kids to learnin'."[34]

Two conclusions on the Anglo rural school experience seem particularly apt. First, although it is clear that a number of children enjoyed school, especially when fortunate enough to have a Miss Bob as their teacher, it is also clear that many devoted a good portion of their energy devising ways to resist it. Sitting in the classroom within earshot of horses neighing, many students were more than a little anxious for the day to end so they could strike out for home. Second, schools such as Greens Gap, Plains, and Pie Town functioned as centers of community and belonging, social spaces where children and their parents came together for school programs, dances, pie suppers, 4-H meetings, and sometimes community worship. The school-community connection in such locations stemmed in large part, then, from the essential homogeneity of the population.

Compare this with the so-called Sánchez school. Located on the José Maria Sánchez ranch, the school drew its enrollment largely from surrounding Hispanic ranching families but also pulled in a few Anglos. Although fistfights were hardly uncommon in rural schools, at the Sánchez school they took on an ethnic dimension. Every day after school, Lee Coker recalls, "we'd either have to fight or pick up our lunch bucket and run like hell. The Spanish and the white didn't get along." Thus, the school never attained the cohesiveness of a Greens Gap or a Pie Town. In addition to the mixed ethnic composition, there was also the issue of cultural hierarchy. As rustic as Anglo students' lives were, they still attended a school that privileged their language and culture and therefore was more conducive to their academic success. One Hispanic who attended Sánchez for five years recalls the frustration he experienced learning English, and then later transferring to Magdalena, where he discovered he was "far behind" other students.[35]

Magdalena

In the early decades of the twentieth century, Magdalena's city boosters had every reason to be optimistic. The arrival of the railroad, the achievement of statehood, the thriving mining and livestock economies, the influx of land-hungry homesteaders, and finally, the growing number of businesses all spelled growth and prosperity. Nowhere could the town's progress be seen more clearly than in the evolution of its school system. The crowning development in this regard was the opening of Magdalena High School in 1917, a modern structure boasting classrooms, laboratories, a domestic science room, a manual training workshop, an assembly hall, and an auditorium. The town had come a long way since 1883, the year that Miss M. Bradford and Miss Jeanie Hawley launched the first two schools, one in the Methodist parsonage and the other in the Presbyterian church.[36]

This growth was reflected in enrollment figures. Between 1906 and 1924, school attendance jumped from 158 to 276 and continued climbing to a high point of 613 in the early 1930s before sliding downward to 449 in 1946 and 352 in 1952. Particularly noteworthy are the Hispanic-Anglo enrollment ratios. A rare snapshot of the disparity is a 1924 document listing all students enrolled in the Magdalena schools. Using surnames as a basis for calculation, it appears that 190 out of 276 students, or more than two-thirds, were Hispanic. (The 1931 county school census identifies 79 percent of Socorro County students as Spanish.) Interviews with older residents of Magdalena suggest that the county figures come much closer to capturing the ethnic disparity.[37]

Because Hispanics constituted the vast majority of school enrollment, it is not surprising that they were represented on both the school board and the faculty. Consistent with New Mexico's "gentlemen's agreement" in politics, competing slates of candidates for the school board were never constructed along purely ethnic lines. Typical is the school board election in 1919 when the "Parent-Teacher Ticket" (P. H. Argall, Jennie Knoblock, Jerry Gonzales, Caroline Mayes, and Juan A. García Jr.) defeated the "Citizens Ticket" (E. A. Mayo, Paul B. Moore, George Goze, J. Frank Romero, and Jesus Landavaso). The deciding factor may have been that the former, "progressive" slate included two women for five of the slots, its advocates recognizing "the God given right of womanhood to participate in all educational matters and so recognizing, gives the noble womanhood of this town representation on the ticket."[38] At the same time, although teachers before World War II could be either Anglo or Hispanic, the available evidence suggests that the great majority was Anglo. "Let me put it this way," one older man recalls. "From grade one through the eighth grade I did not have a Spanish teacher." In the list of teachers for the fall of 1921, for instance, only one Hispanic name appears, Rosa Barreras. By the 1930s more Hispanic teachers were in evidence, although still in the minority. It was an altogether different picture, however, in the rural schools serving Hispanic children. For the 1935–1936 school year, for instance, the Socorro County Board of Education's list of teachers in rural schools shows that forty-three of the sixty-four appointments were Hispanic.[39]

The curriculum of the Magdalena schools was typical of mainstream US communities. In the elementary grades, children were taught the essential skills of reading, writing, and arithmetic and were introduced to literature and history. The school's special obligation, in the eyes of most educators in the state, was to transform Hispanic children into English-speaking, patriotic Americans.[40] Four years after statehood, and on the eve of US entry into World War I, the *Magdalena News* opined that "there can be no greater menace to the safety of this republic than that of ignorance. It is the father of crime and the mother of treason." Although this pronouncement made no direct reference to Hispanics, it must be read in light of widespread suspicions that many *nuevomexicanos* had never fully abandoned their Mexican national identities.[41]

Magdalena High School required a set number of credits for graduation, with emphasis in the areas of English, history and civics, mathematics, general science, and Spanish. Consistent with the growing national movement to make high school more attractive to the less academically minded, courses in industrial training, domestic science, and commercial science were also offered.[42] Magdalena also offered a rich complement of extracurricular activities. At various times between 1920 and 1940, grade schoolers had opportunities to be class officers, work on the newspaper—the *Grade School Echo*—play on basketball and baseball teams, and join clubs in such areas as reading, weaving, home economics, music, and dramatics. At the high school level, additional clubs existed in the areas of debate, 4-H, pep, photography, Spanish, glee, and science. The first yearbook appeared in 1939, and by 1943 a school newspaper went to print under the title of the *Magdalena Steer.*[43]

The question naturally arises: Given the level of Anglo prejudice toward "Mexicans," to what extent did Anglo teachers believe that Hispanics' intellectual potential was equivalent to that of Anglos? Lack of evidence makes it impossible to answer this all-important question with any degree of certitude. Still, Anglo teachers probably entered their classrooms with one of the following outlooks on their Hispanic children's potential. Some no doubt held to the position advanced in the emergent "scientific" intelligence studies that pronounced some ethnoracial groups mentally inferior. In his 1916 book *The Measurement of Intelligence,* for example, Lewis Terman concluded that those of "negro," Spanish, and Mexican heritage fell into this category. "Their dullness seems to be racial, or at least inherent in the family stocks from which they come." This, of course, would have only reinforced the lingering view among some Anglos that "Mexicans" were indeed of inferior racial stock.

By the 1930s, however, a second explanation was gaining ground. It was not innate intellectual inferiority that explained Hispanic children's difficulties in school, the argument went, but the culturally deficient homes from which so many emerged—families ill equipped to support children's success at school, or worse, little desire to do so. But a third explanation was also emerging, culminating in the writing of New Mexico educator George I. Sánchez. According to Sánchez, the notion of innate Hispanic mental inferiority was sheer rubbish, a tragic conclusion drawn from the unwise use of intelligence tests. Although the socioeconomic status of poorer families and language were certainly relevant factors, Sánchez argued, the child's background should not be blamed for existing achievement disparities. The responsibility, rather, lay with the school.[44] Again, to what extent any of these explanations influenced teachers' expectations regarding Hispanic students' academic potential is not discernible. But surely their preconceptions counted for something.

Culture and Context

When they headed off to school for the first time, it is doubtful that children with names such as Ortega or Montoya could have anticipated the extent to which the classroom would emerge as a contested cultural space where success and opportunity presupposed accommodation to privileged ways of knowing and being. Terms such as forced acculturation and internal colonialism—terms social scientists would one day employ to describe the process by which dominant cultures subordinate or incorporate minority populations—were understandably foreign to them. Nor could they have heard the terminology employed to describe the psychological responses and social consequences flowing from such policies—constructs such as acculturation stress, cognitive dissonance, identity construction, boundary maintenance, cultural adaptation, agency, and marginalization. But they would come to know these processes and responses firsthand. The stories begin with language.

Like most Hispanic children, Victoria Martínez spent the first five years of her life enveloped in a world of Spanish. At home grandparents and parents spoke to her only in Spanish. At church, although the priest sometimes spoke in Latin, the hymns were sung in Spanish, reaffirming that this place of worship named after St. Mary Magdalene was essentially a spiritual home for Spanish speakers. At the age of six, when Victoria was running errands for her mother, these excursions were confined to Spanish-speaking neighbors or business establishments. Thus her first day of school was something of a shock. She had no idea what the teacher was saying. The sense of dislocation was so immense that when it came time for recess she bolted for home. Only after her mother began accompanying her to school, for several days sitting at the back of the class, did she begin to like school.[45]

The first challenge children such as Victoria faced was figuring out how to ask the teacher's permission to go to the bathroom.[46] One woman remembers, "So many times when I wanted to go to the bathroom, I didn't know how to ask. So I would cross my legs. . . . It was very hard." After conquering this basic physical concern, children could begin to concentrate on learning new words and stringing them together in sentences. The Magdalena schools were uncompromising in their efforts to convert Spanish speakers into English-speaking ones; speaking Spanish was forbidden not only in the classroom but on the playground as well. Whatever agreement was worked out that evening in Juan Jaramillo's living room about teachers first speaking to their new mono-Spanish-speaking students in their native language before giving an English translation appears to have been either forgotten or reversed (perhaps because most Anglo teachers could not speak Spanish). So although many are able to recall teachers who were sympathetic and caring in helping them make the transition to English, there are also painful memories.

> I'm just a baby in the first grade. My mother doesn't speak English, my father doesn't speak English. So I take the books home and I was DESPERATE. At school it only meant one thing: She [the teacher] would stop pulling my hair. They would pull my hair and slap me. It almost didn't have anything to do with learning. It had to do with if I learned they would stop pulling my hair. . . . By the time I went to second grade I wouldn't speak Spanish, even at home when I was talking to my father or mother.[47]

The price paid for speaking Spanish depended on the teacher or administrator noticing the infraction. "They would make us write down 'I will not speak Spanish,' like a hundred times. Yes, I had to do that many times. They would catch us on the school grounds. We could not speak Spanish at all—zero." By another account, "All the way up 'til about the fourth grade they were still paddling us." Meanwhile, Margarita García struggled with making two transitions at once, making the switch from writing with her left hand to her right and making the language switch. Violating the first meant getting her hands slapped, the second standing in the corner. Another woman, however, remembers the punishment for violating the English-only rule being less severe. "They sent you to the office and they would talk to you and that was it. You learned. You were careful next time."[48]

Herman Toledo, who entered school in about 1920, describes the cognitive processes involved. Learning English, he explains, was like having "two hotel rooms" in your brain—one for Spanish, the other for English. The challenge was training yourself to "travel" between the two rooms searching for equivalent words and meanings, and then formulating a coherent response. In Herman's case, the process was made easier by having daily contact with an Anglo neighbor.

> We learned to say table, and we knew that table in Spanish was una mesa. So that mesa was the one we had in that little room there to use whenever we needed it. But later on, talking to my neighbor, to my friend there at home, he'd say why don't you go over there and bring that box that's on top of the table? You see? . . . I would have to get that mesa to table, or table to mesa, to understand that he said table. I knew that [table] was a mesa but I did not know it was a table until I learned another word. So when you're speaking in English or Spanish you have a problem of two words meaning the same thing, while when you only speak English you only have one word. So your thought, your line of thinking, everything is quicker. Because many times I'd catch myself

saying: I know in Spanish it's a mesa, but what is it in English? And I have to start thinking, thinking, to get it out of this little room here, . . . to tell you it's a table, it's a mesa.

Whereas Toledo's acquisition of English was aided by living next door to an Anglo boy, he explained that most Hispanic children had no such advantage. When they left school "that was the end of thinking in English until . . . the next day."[49]

Compare Herman's experience with that of José Ortega. In 1915 José's father sold his sheep ranch and moved the family to Magdalena so his children could attend school. But the boy got off to a disastrous start when he smuggled a scorpion into the classroom, and another child shouted out: "Teacher, teacher, José has a scorpion." Whether it was the scorpion or a collection of other pranks, José was expelled from the first grade.

> So the next year she [his mother] brought me again. I stayed two or three months in the first grade. I never learned nothin'. So the third year they put me in the second grade—because I was bigger. But I don't know a damn thing—numbers and figures. Very hard time. It was difficult. I understood a few words, but most of the time I don't. The teacher get mad all the time. In that days you're suppose to read your lesson. They give them about an hour time and then they say read your lesson, and then you have to read it. And I couldn't read it because I only know a few words. She couldn't help me because she couldn't speak Spanish. And she wanted me to learn English. So in other words, I've never been in school.[50]

Herman Martínez, who started school in Kelly, never made the transition.[51] The possibility that the boy's struggle with English might have been connected to a learning disability, and that his father placed a high value on education, makes Herman's story all the more tragic. From the very beginning Herman's father was frustrated with his son's lack of interest in school. To emphasize the importance of education, his father, Herman remembers, "used to miss work and take me by the hand to school and [he] sat down with me there in the same chair. He put me next to the wall and he was on the other side." But the tension and confusion surrounding learning English only worsened. Recalling these moments of frustration, Herman says:

> I don't know what happened. I could get a book of ABCs. I could read them in Spanish and English, but I cannot pronounce the WORDS.

That's too hard for me. I know all the letters in Spanish and English—the ABCs. And my dad say, what's the matter, son? What's the matter with your brain? My dad, he got a Spanish book to read. He give me the lesson in the book. And I read it. And then my daddy close the book. He got one book and I got the other one. Let's see if you can do it. I opened the book. After a while he said what's the matter? I said, I don't know. That was the trouble. I can't pronounce the words. Can't connect everything. And then I close the book and told him I don't need the book. . . . I understood the words but I couldn't read [pronounce] them. I don't know what was the matter. I don't know what happened.

Herman made it through several grades before the crisis came. One day his teacher, as punishment for his not completing his work, kept him after school and instructed him to copy his lesson ten times. After producing three copies, Herman announced that he was going home. At this point the teacher announced that he was going to lock Herman in school until all ten copies were produced, adding, "I'm going to my house and I'm going to come back in thirty minutes. I don't give a damn if I have to hold you all night." This was when Herman struck the teacher with a chair and ran home. That night, the teacher and three school board members appeared at the house. Herman still remembers his father's plea. "He don't want the school. What am I going to do? I could put him in the mines." After some discussion, the teacher proposed a compromise: the boy could "tend to his lessons" at home for two weeks and then return to school. But it never worked out. At age sixteen Herman decided he had had enough and refused to go back. He recalls his father's reaction: "Ooh God, he took me out to the mines with a scrap of wood and he whipped me out there." Perhaps his father still clung to the hope that his son, confronted with the alternative facing him in the mines, might reconsider his decision. "My Dad say, you don't want the school, so work at the mine. And then he worked me like a goddamned donkey—like a burro. . . . My mom told him, you're working him too hard. My dad say, he didn't want any school. He has to work." After two weeks of hard labor, Herman recalls, his father repeated the choice—school or the mines. But the sixteen-year-old had made his decision. "I don't want any school."

But others found making the transition to English easier. Indeed, one is struck by the singularity of experience. Recall how Juan Jaramillo on the first day of school knocked his teacher to the floor when she began shouting in English at his sister and how the school board instructed the teacher, Rosa Barreras, to translate her English into Spanish? Following the new policy, Juan explained, everything changed. "We knew that if we go and ask the teacher, we could ask her in Spanish anything and then she'll repeat it in English. So we pick [English] up very EASY.... Boy, I used to like school. And my sister is the same way." The Jaramillo children, of course, had the benefit of the Magdalena Board of Education's directive that the teacher should make some accommodation for their total unfamiliarity with English. But even in those instances where no or little accommodation was made—the case in later years—some children experienced little difficulty. Esther Peralta, for instance, says, "We had no problem. It was so easy and so wonderful." Then there is Lucy Pino, who says she took special delight in school. "I hardly knew any English at all when I went to school, but I was very fortunate, I had some very caring teachers. I felt their love." Where some children would have been humiliated by the experience of the principal singling them out publicly for mispronouncing a particular word, Lucy took it in stride. "All of a sudden, he had me stand up and say it two or three times, and then he would correct me, and I would say it over again, and that stayed in my mind. It worked."[52]

Meanwhile parents employed various strategies for helping their children learn English. One approach, which relatively few parents had either the linguistic ability or willingness to employ, was to encourage speaking English at home. One woman recalls that her mother attempted to speak only English in front of her small children until others in the community "teased them for trying to be higher so they just spoke to us in Spanish after that." But some families stuck with it. Vicente Tafoya recalls that although his father knew little English, his mother regularly read the newspaper in English to her children and was constantly urging them to "read, read, read," with the result that when he entered school the language barrier was virtually nonexistent. Similarly, when Esther Peralta read in Spanish to her bilingual grandfather, he periodically asked her to stop and translate the main ideas into English.[53]

A second strategy was to encourage contact with Anglos. "My mother," one woman claims, "hired herself out to only English-speaking people as a housekeeper so she could learn it, so she could speak to us.... She used to take my little sister with her whenever she cleaned house or babysat so she could learn it." One man attributes his early success in school to the fact that his mother was always encouraging him to play with an Anglo neighbor his age. Merely by jumping the fence he found himself developing a greater facility with the language spoken at school. As the following story suggests, Hispanic parents in a changing New Mexico (in this instance

1915) could go to great lengths to improve their children's facility with English, and in the process, improve their ethnoracial status as well:

> My mother was very interested in me to learn, and my sister. She always told me, "Why you playing with those Mexican boys?" I don't know why. I guess because I didn't talk English. "You should play with"—she didn't say gringitos like a lot of people say—she say "Americanitos," little American boys. . . . She used to say, "You're not going to learn. You're just going to be a Mexican all your life." But I didn't care for what my mother say. Now I do care. She wanted me to learn English real good. I know if I'd obey her and play with those boys . . . I could have learned to talk just like them.[54]

A third strategy was to devise supplemental instruction techniques, no easy accomplishment in households where Spanish was the exclusive mode of discourse. A well-meaning but particularly unhelpful practice of one mother was to help her daughter's pronunciation of English vocabulary words by associating them with like-sounding words in Spanish—words with no corresponding meaning in English. "I remember the teacher used to tell us we would have to learn words by Monday, and my mother would try to give me some words in Spanish that would sound like the words in English." One word she still remembers is the one her mother suggested for the word "hat"—*ojete*. Not only did the Spanish word not match "hat" in sound, the Spanish word referred to a body orifice and was "not that beautiful." In any event, her mother's effort was of no use whatsoever in helping the child master the vocabulary list. Come Monday, the girl would endure the usual: "The teacher would hit me for not learning the words."[55]

More effective was to make use of an available source in the house containing pictures of objects that might serve as the basis for bilingual instruction. When Candelaria García went off to school she already knew how to read and write a little in Spanish, but having spent her early years on an isolated sheep ranch, her exposure to English was minimal.

> I didn't know a word of English when I started school. I would come home and tell Mama what the teacher would say. And Mama, in her broken English and with her Spanish accent, would try and tell me what the English words meant. When she didn't know, she would go to what she called the "Monto-go-mary" book. She couldn't pronounce Montgomery Ward so she said "Monto-go-mary." So the Montgomery Ward Catalogue was my dictionary. I would bring home a new word from school like "flowers." I knew the word but I didn't know what it meant. So I would

point to the picture in the catalogue and mother would say what it meant in Spanish—"flores." And then I would go to school the next day and compare what the teacher said with what mother said. That's the way I learned my English.[56]

The varied experiences of learning English suggest several observations. First, in spite of the school board's directive to Rosa Barreras in 1917 to translate English into Spanish for strictly Spanish speakers, the overall instructional approach appears to have been one of English immersion. Second, during the early decades of the century, it is evident that many Hispanic children experienced school as a site of social and academic marginalization, a place where a diminishing sense of self gave rise to a desire to escape to the worlds of family, church, and work. At the same time, for those blessed with some mixture of innate intelligence, psychological resilience, attentive parents, and caring teachers, schooling set them on the path to short-term academic success, and for some, long-term economic opportunity and even bicultural identities.

Enclaves of Preservation

In the early decades of the twentieth century, New Mexico educational authorities faced an ongoing and politically delicate question: In the face of the school's obligation to integrate Hispanic children into mainstream US society, how much attention should be assigned to recognizing and honoring children's ancestral culture?[57] As noted earlier, until the mid-1920s, state educational codes permitted the use of bilingual instruction. During this period, there were periodic public school programs in both Magdalena and nearby Kelly in which students were permitted, even encouraged, both to display their facility with Spanish and to honor their cultural heritage.[58] By the 1920s, the main forums for such expressions in Magdalena were the Spanish-language classes and clubs, the latter existing at both the elementary and secondary levels. (When Magdalena High School opened in 1917, the language offerings were German, Latin, and Spanish, but within two years German was dropped and Latin was offered only on an "if demanded" basis, thereby making Spanish the "foreign" language of choice.)[59] The most pronounced efforts on behalf of cultural preservation came in the form of school assemblies and community performances. In the spring of 1922, for instance, the *Magdalena News* reported that an entire high school assembly was devoted to singing Spanish songs, reciting Spanish poems, rendering Iberian legends, and performing a love scene from a noted Spanish drama.

Those in attendance "loudly applauded" the program. Similarly, in 1932 thirty-four students took part in a Saturday evening performance of three short plays: *La Plancha de la Marquesa*, *Mi Novio Español*, and *El Pupito del Diablo*. Interestingly, the proceeds went "for the benefit of the Catholic church of Magdalena."[60]

The ultimate opportunity for honoring Hispanic students' cultural heritage came in 1940 when the Magdalena schools, in conjunction with a statewide initiative, celebrated the Coronado Cuarto Centennial. Although the state commission charged with promoting the yearlong commemoration ostensibly called for recognizing New Mexico's tricultural roots, as the name reveals, the real purpose was to pay festive and symbolic tribute to the Spanish colonial heritage.[61] In Magdalena most of the responsibility for the celebration fell on Trinidad García, who over the years taught Spanish and US history and served as sponsor of the Spanish Club. Stanford educated, García at one point served as a research assistant to the noted scholar Aurelio Macedonio Espinosa (an ardent promoter of the state's Spanish colonial legacy), for whom she collected old-world Spanish *corridos, versos*, and *cuentos* from those living in the area. In short, García was eminently qualified to spearhead the school's efforts.[62]

Under Garcia's direction, Magdalena celebrated the Coronado Cuarto Centennial in various venues. The 1940 high school yearbook's opening page began with, "In 1540 Coronado, on the march in his search for gold and fame, kept a journal in which he recorded important events." Four hundred years later, the yearbook announced, "this document has become a key which unlocks the door to the ancient civilization of our state." The yearbook's section on the Spanish Club proclaimed that members looked to Coronado and his men "as their guiding spirit" and in this connection spent the year exploring "the field of Spanish life and customs." The Coronado theme played out in other activities as well: the junior-senior banquet, the crowning of the queen at the Coronado Cuarto Centennial dance, and a Saturday evening performance of Spanish folk dances.[63]

None of these celebratory markers was in the least bit controversial. But the Dramatic Club's May performance of the three-act play *Kearney Takes Las Vegas* was of a different character. Written by Aurora Lucero-White, one of New Mexico's leading educators and folklorists, the play was based on General Stephen W. Kearney's invasion of New Mexico in 1846. The script revolves around the planned *prendorio* (engagement) of Dolores, the daughter of Juan de Dio Maes, the *alcalde* (mayor) of Las Vegas, to Lorenzo, the son of a wealthy landowner, Don Feliciano Armijo. Following the

Mary Armijo, queen of the Coronado Cuarto Centennial Dance, 1940. Magdalena Yearbook, 1940. (Courtesy of John Blackburn.)

engagement, Dolores expects to return to a convent in St. Louis where she has been attending school.[64]

Scene 1 opens on the evening before the festive day, which will include a ritualistic exchange of gifts, a solo dance performance by Dolores, and a grand *baile*. In the opening scene, however, we find Dolores weeping in bed. We learn the reason for her despair in an exchange between Dolores and Juana, her *duena*: the marriage has been arranged, and she feels no love for her intended husband. Juana proceeds to defend the custom of arranged marriages, and in an aside to the audience, makes known her own explanation for the girl's resistance—namely, that Dolores (unknown to herself) has "foreign blood" running through her veins. "That comes of these mixed marriages. They never turn out right." A few lines later, Juana sighs (again, outside of Dolores's hearing): "The blood, the blood—what can you expect?" The next morning, the day of the engagement, Don Juan de Dios assures his daughter that he has made the right decision and then reveals the meaning behind Juana's unexplained comments to the audience on "blood." For the first time Dolores learns that her mother, whom she never knew, was an Anglo American. It was truly a love match, he explains, but his young wife found life on a New Mexico *rancho* unbearable so she returned to her home, whereupon shortly she died. "So, my child, you see I have a reason for having an aversion towards love. I prefer to see you married to one who esteems you." Dolores now understands why her *duena* has been virtually a mother to her, but more importantly, her father's admission convinces her that she must accept her fate—to marry a man she does not love. But it also prompts a question: Does her father hate Americans? To this query her father replies, "On the contrary. I respect them very much. Otherwise I would never have sent you to the convent in St. Louis."

Scene 2 opens with the *prendorio*. Following the formal exchange of gifts, the guests join in a promenade and a joyful *cuadrilla*. Then, in the midst of the moment all have anticipated—the solo dance by Dolores—there is a loud knock at the door. It is none other than General Kearney, accompanied by his nephew, Robert Kearney. The general announces that on the following morning his troops will march into Las Vegas, and he has come to attain the peaceful cooperation of Don Juan de Dios, the village *alcalde*. Kearney's announcement meets with the response, "I am at your service." Kearney then explains that he must return to his troops but requests that his nephew be permitted to stay the evening to prepare for the army's entrance the following day, a request that is quickly granted. Upon the general's departure, Don Feliciano enters the scene. Horrified that Don Juan is submitting to the US takeover, he announces that he and Lorenzo will leave for Mexico "this very night." As for the marriage, he suggests that the *padre* be immediately summoned and the marriage ceremony performed, then adds that as Lorenzo's wife, Dolores will be "subject to her husband's orders." Naturally, she must follow the Armijos to Mexico.

Lorenzo quickly concurs. He and Dolores should marry immediately. But Dolores strenuously objects, declaring, "I'll never marry a coward," asserting that Lorenzo is, in fact, "running away." Lorenzo's father protests this cruel judgment by stating, "We do not wish to be American citizens," to which Dolores responds, "And I do not wish to be a Mexican citizen." On that note the Armijos depart. The *prendorio* is over, the tables are cleaned, and the stage lights dimmed. At this point, the young and handsome Robert Kearney enters the stage and engages Dolores in conversation. She explains that Lorenzo is forever gone from her life because "I prefer to be an American," to which Robert responds, "Good, another American!"

DOLORES: What difference does one American more or less make?
ROBERT: But if that American is the most beautiful one on earth?
DOLORES: Well, that's different.
ROBERT: And if one has always dreamed about her?
DOLORES: Oh!
ROBERT: And if one has sworn not to live without her?
DOLORES: Why, Lieutenant!
ROBERT: Dolores! (Embraces her and kisses her passionately.)

Scene 3 opens with Don Juan and General Kearney standing on the *azotea,* or roof, of a home on the plaza, where a large crowd has gathered. Dolores climbs a ladder, from which she watches her father urge the villagers "to swear allegiance to this new government, which offers us protection in the free enjoyment of our rights to person, property, and religion." The scene is then given over to Kearney's actual remarks—a history lesson for the audience—in which he proclaims the Americans' goodwill, including the statement: "We come amongst you as friends, not as enemies; as protectors, not as conquerors. We come among you for your benefit, not for your injury." At the conclusion of his remarks the crowd shouts: *"Viva Don Juan de Dios! Viva el General Kearney! Vivan los Estados Unidos!"* Several Mexicans climb the roof to shake hands with the general and their *alcalde.* The commotion and crowding, however, cause Dolores to fall from her perch on the uppermost rung of the ladder. Anticipating this development, Robert dashes over, catches her in midair, kisses her, and in the spirit of the moment, declares that "the conquest is complete." When the general and Don Juan rush to the scene, Robert declares, "You see, the United States has taken New Mexico." But as Dolores jumps from his arms, she utters the last line of the play—and a surprising one at that—"No, New Mexico has taken the United States."

Kearney Takes Las Vegas is a complicated text, embodying themes of conquest, accommodation, resistance, gender status, and miscegenation. With a large portion of scene 3 given over to Kearney's rooftop address, the audience is reminded of the reasons New Mexicans offered so little resistance to the invasion: the invader's promise to respect their religion, his guarantees to protect their property and to provide security against marauding Indians, and finally his reference to the sheer futility of resistance. ("There goes my army.") Although the script, by contrasting the responses of Don Juan and Don Feliciano, acknowledges the divisions among *nuevomexicanos* on how to respond to the US takeover, the emotional weight of the play favors Don Juan, who the audience learns has always possessed a genuine affection for Americans, to the point of marrying an American and sending his daughter to school in St. Louis. Moreover, Dolores, faced with the prospect of an immediate marriage—an arranged one at that—to a man she does not love—and then submission to his willful intent to carry her off to Mexico, announces that she prefers American to Mexican citizenship. Hispanics, the scene seems to suggest, need not choose between surrender and defiance, patriotism and ethnic loyalty. Indeed, why not just marry the invader? In the end, Lucero-White's script is about ethnic border crossings of the most sensitive sort—blood mixing—still a touchy subject to many in Magdalena in 1940. It is reasonable to assume that some, mainly Anglos, were more than a little bothered by the last line of the play and its implications. Did it seem to imply that Anglo colonizers were becoming the colonized, that the Anglo conquest of New Mexico was more imagined than real? Fortunately, some must have felt, the school's celebration of the Coronado Cuarto Centennial was nearly over.

Hierarchy

That schools frequently reflect or reinforce socioeconomic and cultural hierarchies in the larger society is a well-established fact. Given the paucity of hard evidence, measuring the nature and extent of social and academic hierarchies in the schools of Magdalena is fraught with difficulties. Still, through analyses of graduation rates, the ethnicity of class and club officers, and finally, the memories of former students, it is possible to discern what it meant to be a student in an educational setting where history and power relations conspired to favor some students over others. A befitting beginning for this analysis is the explosive school crisis of 1904.

The crisis began when county school superintendent A. C. Torres decided to lecture Magdalena's Hispanic students on their poor educational performance. Unfortunately, there is no record of Torres's exact words, but they ignited a blistering protest in the form of a letter published in the *Socorro Chieftain*. Signed by seven parents and written in Spanish, the letter recounted how the superintendent had recently "insulted and provoked in an indirect manner all of the Mexican race in general . . . as he said with all his power that the parents of Mexican families have no other purpose than loading donkeys." By contrast, the "race of the foreigners was wise, great, and capable." Continuing with his insults, the superintendent then asked the question: "Do you want to be superintendent of schools, or a cashier, or a schoolteacher?"—a query he proceeded to answer with a resounding "No." Repeatedly, the letter charged, the superintendent stated that Mexicans were apparently only good for loading donkeys.

> Now we, the heads of Mexican families, take pride in being Mexican, we are not ashamed of it, and we are Mexicans of complete and sustaining faculty; we maintain that the aforementioned superintendent was completely mistaken and didn't speak the truth. Take a look at all the different counties in New Mexico territory—there are Mexican men and boys, natives of our country, the best of which wind up becoming cashiers. They are secretaries in offices from the lower courts to the Supreme Court, they are delegates to the Congress of America, and they handle any office in the New Mexico territory, except in the office of the superintendent—apparently there [are] no Mexicans for that work.

The signatories wondered if they had placed too much faith in their superintendent. "Now New Mexico friends, think hard on the benefit we get from taking care of a viper only to have it turn around and bite us." Then in a sentence that might be read either as a veiled threat or note of forgiveness, they promised to honor the superintendent with a *velorio* (wake) "when your time comes."[65]

What happened next is not entirely clear, but subsequent letters in the *Chieftain*—all signed by Hispanics—reveal that the superintendent also had his staunch defenders. Clearly, they argued, the intention of his remarks had been misunderstood. Throughout his career the superintendent had demonstrated his commitment to the "intellectual development of all youths in general." Furthermore, "how can it occur in the mind of any gentleman who has average intelligence that Mr. Torres has now forgotten that through his veins runs pure Mexican blood, and what would make us believe that he used offensive language against the Mexican children of Magdalena?" Meanwhile, it appears Torres also made overtures to his critics, either apologizing or asserting that his remarks had been terribly misconstrued by the offended students. In any event, the seven signatories to the original letter withdrew their complaint. "We remain satisfied with the apology that Mr. Torres gave, and at the same time we believe that it is a misunderstanding of the children, and presently we don't have charges against Mr. Torres."[66]

The superintendent's remarks to Magdalena's "Mexican" students reveal the ways class and race were intertwined in discussions of Hispanic educational achievement. Given the history of class stratification in New Mexico, his comments were more than likely a well-meant, if crude, attempt to goad students into recognizing the importance of education to improving their socioeconomic status. At the same time, the reference to uneducated sheepherders and burro tenders occupying the lowest echelons of society was clearly inflammatory given the number of children's parents employed in those same occupations. But the superintendent's remarks also struck the raw nerve of race. In the minds of protesters, the uncomplimentary comparison made between native "Mexicans" and Anglo "foreigners" only served to reinforce the all-too-common attitude of Anglos that New Mexicans were living in a cultural backwater until the US invasion. Indeed, the terms "Mexican" and "foreigner" in 1904—eight years before statehood and early in the campaign to equate *nuevomexicanos* with a romanticized Spanish past—suggest that some sectors of the population were hesitant to surrender their old identities. Surely, many parents must have thought, there must be a better way to inspire love of education.

For many years to come, the correspondence between ethnicity, on the one hand, and academic progress (as measured by years in school) on the other, was starkly evident. Although the Hispanic-Anglo enrollment ratio shifted over time, generally speaking, Hispanics constituted between two-thirds to three-quarters of the enrollment.[67] But as Table 5.1 reveals, 1920 and 1930 US census rolls indicate that the percentage of Hispanics leaving school between the ages of fourteen and eighteen was twice that of Anglos. Although Magdalena school records during this era are nonexistent, newspaper reports of nine graduating classes between 1928 and 1940 suggest

Table 5.1 Anglo and Hispanic School Attendance by Gender, Ages 14–18, 1920, 1930

	No. attending M	No. attending F	No. not attending M	No. not attending F	Total percentage not attending
1920					
Anglo	24	29	7	7	20.9
Hispanic	32	47	28	31	42.8
1930					
Anglo	15	24	5	6	22.0
Hispanic	33	28	29	29	48.7

Note: Not included is a select number of children either unidentifiable by ethnic surname or classified as "other."

Source: Fourteenth Census of the United States, 1920; Fifteenth Census of the United States, 1930.

the same pattern: fifty-one Hispanics to seventy-eight Anglos. The fact that these disparities mirrored, or were in some instances less stark than, statewide patterns, was presumably of little consolation to Hispanic school boosters.[68]

The reasons for this disparity were several, but four in particular merit comment. First, economic status disproportionately affected Hispanic families' ability to keep their children in school. For instance, one man tells how his father died when he was only six, compelling him to drop out of school at the age of twelve to herd sheep. Similarly, a woman, also fatherless, recalls how she was forced to quit school after the fourth grade to work as a domestic. ("I had difficulty finding work because they didn't want to hire me because I was so young.") Manuel Armijo made it to the tenth grade before dropping out. "I had to work. We needed some money to pay for the ranch."[69] Second, gender status also conspired against staying in school. One woman says she was forced to drop out of school after third grade to help her mother with housekeeping and to care for younger siblings. Another recalls that when the teacher offered to move her from kindergarten to first grade if her father would buy the next level of textbook, she knew making the request was futile, so she stayed with the younger children longer than necessary. In fifth grade, when she announced to the family that she might like to be a nun, her father pulled her out of school. Then there was the view in some households that girls, given their domestic destinies, needed less education than boys.[70] Third, there is reason to believe that some students were simply discouraged from continuing with school because of being forced to repeat grades. What Hispanic scholar George I. Sánchez said of this statewide pattern in 1940 undoubtedly applied to Magdalena. "In every grade beyond the first, more than 55 per cent of the [Spanish-speaking] children are more than two years over-age for their grade."[71] Finally, the assimilationist orientation of the school curriculum set some students up for failure. Language, as we have seen, played a special role in this regard. All too often, the difficulties learning English in the early grades translated into academic frustration and growing insecurity, sometimes contributing to a diminished sense of self. For these youngsters, the worlds of work, family, and church must have been especially appealing—worlds that reaffirmed rather than challenged existing identities.

Negotiating Difference

Schools are social as well as academic settings. More than arenas for acquiring knowledge and competing for grades, they are settings where children establish friendships, try on new identities, and sort themselves out in an oft-times bruising hierarchy. These aspects of education occur not only in the classroom but also in such forums as the hallway, the playground, school clubs, elections of class officers, and even the charged atmosphere of the dance floor. Because school was the main social setting where Hispanic and Anglo youngsters encountered one another on a daily basis, it was here that the ethnocultural identities inscribed in the larger social landscape were challenged, reconstructed, and reaffirmed.

But demarcations were not solely along ethnic lines. The old conflict between the sheep and cattle economies was enough to set students against one another. For Jane Stoddard the memories are vivid. "Fights and more fights. If somebody is a little different than they are, and if you have sheep and some of the others have cattle, the sheep and the cattle kids didn't get along for some reason. We didn't know the difference, but when we got to Magdalena, we learn't the difference. . . . You'd ride the bus, you'd be in fights all the time." On one occasion, after Jane's brother and sister exited the bus, two boys held her down while "Dave Martin knocked the soup out of me." When the bus driver attempted to break up the fray, the bully's sister began pummeling him with her lunchbox. On another occasion, when the bus driver drove up to the Stoddard ranch to pick up the children, the very sight of sheep was sufficient to spark the ire of the same Martin children. Before the bus had even struck the highway, the customary epithets "sheep bitch" and "dirty sheepherder" were hurled about. Soon "the hair was aflyin'."[72]

Intraethnic fissures also were the basis for conflict. José Ortega landed in school in 1922 when his father moved his mother and the children to town so the children could attend school. As we have already seen, José had great difficulty making the adjustment from a rural ranch setting to the strictures of school. As he remembers it, most of his problems with other students involved Hispanics.

> The Spanish children used to call me Wild Man . . . because I had come from the mountains. And [they said] that I wasn't born of a woman but from a mule, because my daddy had lots of mules. This made me mad, so we would fight until they didn't want to fight anymore—unless they could corral me with several of them. I was a good rock thrower so I could rock them down if I could, because I didn't care who they were or how big they were. . . . I never had any trouble with the Anglo children. The trouble was with the Spanish children, and I never have been able to figure out why.[73]

Two Hispanic women from the same region also recall the difficulties adjusting to "urban" Magdalena. Coming off a ranch, the García sisters discovered that they dressed differently, were allowed less freedom than other girls, and spoke a more classical Spanish. (They still recall the embarrassment produced the time one of them uttered the comment, "*Estoy enferma—enfermo,*" meaning to be ill or sick, but used by locals to mean pregnant!) Their acceptance was also aggravated by the fact that they were high achievers. The bigger Hispanics "would give me a whipping every day because I knew a little more than they did and they were in school here longer than I was." A younger brother confirms, "We didn't fit in. . . . It was kind of tough, always getting the shit beat out of you."[74]

But it was the Anglo-Hispanic division that loomed most large. One man who attended school in the 1930s recalls, "They [Anglos] didn't like to play with us. I don't know whether it was the kids themselves or the parents didn't want them to do it." Another says, "Magdalena was BAD then. Boy, I'm telling you, you were a Mexican and that's all there was to it." The usual epithets—"dirty Mexican" and "Mexican greaser" on one side, or "gringo *salado*" on the other—were enough to trigger vicious brawls. "All Anglos are Texans," one Hispanic grew up hearing. One day when the boy came home from school and reported he had been in a fight, his father, looking concerned, inquired about his opponent's name. When the answer revealed that the other boy was Anglo, the father's response was simply, "Ah, that's alright."[75] Similarly, when Candelaria García went home complaining about a boy who regularly called her and her younger brother "Mexican greasers" and took delight in threatening to "whip all them Mexicans," her mother rescinded her "no-fighting" rule and even instructed her daughter to embellish the old insult gringo *salado*. The next time the boy called her names, she should respond by calling him gringo *saladas nalgas peladas* (a salty, bare-butted gringo), in apparent reference to the belief that Anglo homesteaders were so poor they could not afford underclothes. (In this household the "salty" charge referred to the Anglos always wanting to borrow salt.) So when the next provocation occurred, Candelaria was prepared for it and succeeded in bloodying the bully's nose. In time, they would become the best of friends.[76]

According to Melvin Akers, Anglo disdain for "Mexicans" permeated the entire school environment. Relations between the two groups were simply "terrible." From his side of the ethnic divide, "Us gringos, we didn't have nothin' but contempt for Mexicans." In his early years, Melvin claims he had "Mexican schoolteachers who couldn't hardly talk English. They'd talk so broken that you'd have to be around them a while before you could understand 'em. And THEY was tryin' to teach US kids somethin'." Later, when a Magdalena principal married a local Hispanic woman, Akers claims the school official "lost the respect of some of the white kids—just because he married this Mexican. And she was a beautiful woman. Today, I'd say marry her. She was intelligent. There wasn't anything wrong with her at all—outside of blood." Even so, Melvin had a couple of Hispanic friends—those "that didn't like Mexicans. That was the only reason I liked them, because they cussed the Mexicans just as I did. They hated being Mexican." As for fighting, "Before school, after school, and at recess, I guess that's where I learned how to fight. It was a case of survival of the fittest. You had to either fight or run, and if you'd run, they'd catch you. But I always kind of liked to fight when I was goin' to school."[77]

Tensions carried over into the classroom. In the mid-1920s, Vicente Tafoya entered school already speaking English and quickly established himself as a stellar student. By the time he reached high school he had a keen sense of ethnic pride and personal achievement. Whereas he had once felt a degree of "inferiority" in the presence of Anglos, his performance in the classroom and on the basketball court liberated him from his earlier insecurities. But he still recalls the ethnic separation at the school and how strangely it functioned. On the basketball court he and an Anglo boy "were real good friends" but off court "forget it." Thus, one day in a class where he was the sole Hispanic, his temper flared as one Anglo after another taunted him with ethnic slurs. Finally, he exploded. "Right behind me there was a guy by the name of Joe Medley. WHAM! I socked him." As the teacher looked on in frozen puzzlement, Vicente turned to the others and offered to fight all of them, one at a time. But there were no offers. (Sixty years later, "we're good friends now.")[78]

Even more dramatic, Vicente recalls, was the time that word spread through the high school that the superintendent had derogatorily called a student a "Mexican." The particulars are vague, but the response it ignited among Hispanics is clearer. Moving from classroom to classroom, Vicente began mobilizing a protest march, and in a matter of minutes thirty or more students were in the hall and headed for the main door. When the superintendent tried to block their passage, "we told him to get the hell out of the way." Outside the building, Vicente led the protesters toward the law office of a young lawyer and family friend—Mauricio Miera. Miera, who would eventually become a leading political figure in the state, listened to the students' frustration. Sympathetic to their pleas, he took action. "You know what he did? . . . He went to school with us and he told that guy, you pack up your belongings and get out of here. You're fired as of right now." How the lawyer managed this feat in a flash is not clear, but the superintendent was soon seen heading for the train station, somewhat wiser as to power relations in the largely Hispanic town. With a new superintendent, "everything quieted down."[79]

School dances presented school officials a special problem. On the one hand, there was the political reality that some parents objected to interethnic intimacy of any sort; on the other, there was the progressive legacy that schools ought to serve as instruments for social advancement, including breaking down historic prejudices. In the early decades of the twentieth century, both Anglos and Hispanics seemed mostly satisfied with the status quo. "We danced with our own and they with their own," recalls one. But at some point an incident was bound to disrupt things. Grace Higgins's account of her own experience offers insight as to the difficulties progressive-minded educators faced when they chose to insert themselves into the existing ethnic divide.[80]

Grace's father had strong views about race mixing. As owner of one of the town's drinking establishments, he hung a sign over the bar: "No Mexicans, No Indians, No Pets." The irony of this was that Grace knew her father had a lot of "Indian blood" in him. Her "father was a fourth and

... mother was a half-blood"—mostly Cherokee, she thinks. Meanwhile in high school Grace was becoming friends with a "very good-looking boy" by the name of Ernest Sánchez. "There wasn't any of us girls that didn't want to go with him, [but] if I'd been caught with him, my dad would have killed me." Apparently the feeling between Grace and Ernest was mutual, and the two commiserated over the impossibility of acting on their feelings. Ernest's father also felt strongly over breaching ethnic boundaries. But unexpectedly something wonderful happened. The school was having a dance, and the superintendent, O. E. Ludlow, decided that the boys needed to learn to dance, and that the girls should teach them. "We thought, oh boy, we had it made, because I could dance with him and I could tell them I was teaching him to dance." So under the protective cover of the superintendent the two quickly paired off. After the first lesson, Grace was so confident she "went blistering home" to tell her family about the dance class, including her partner.

It was a romance-ending mistake. Her father's words are etched in her memory. "Absolutely not. You don't dance with him in public, and you don't go with him, and you're not teaching him in school how to dance for that superintendent or any other one." So the next day Grace reported to the superintendent that she could no longer participate in the dance lessons, explaining her father's strong views on the subject. Ludlow's response was simple and direct. "If your daddy is that narrow-minded, I'll just expel you." When Grace walked down to the bar and informed her father of her new status, he immediately set out for Ludlow's office and announced that Grace was coming back to school, and lest there be any misunderstanding about the matter, she would not be dancing with any Mexicans! After being confronted, the well-intentioned superintendent backed down and agreed to Grace's reinstatement on her father's terms. So the would-be couple only had the one dance. "Oh I guess if I had married a Spanish boy, he would have killed me. That would have been the end of my career."[81]

On the Brighter Side

But it would be wrong to characterize interethnic school relations in a purely negative light. In fact, one of the more intriguing aspects of older residents' recollections is the differing light in which they characterize social relations between the two groups. One Anglo rancher's son who attended school in Magdalena early in the century observes, "I don't remember that any of the kids had any particular grievances against the Mexicans." To be

May Day celebration at Roosevelt Elementary School, Magdalena, New Mexico, early 1940s. (Courtesy of Magdalena Public Library.)

sure there was some fighting—something he attributes to ignorance on both sides of the ethnic divide—"but ordinarily they got along good." Esther Peralta, who attended Magdalena High School in the 1930s, claims she experienced no discrimination whatsoever. Peralta admits that some of the poorer Hispanics may have suffered from prejudice, but for the most part she has little patience for their complaints. "I don't care what anybody tells you. THEY felt it, THEY had a problem." As for herself, she found high school a glorious experience. "The whole town came to plays—stage plays. I know because I had main parts."[82]

By the 1940s the social boundaries were gradually breaking down, in part, it appears, because of the extraordinary degree of intergroup mixing in school clubs and activities. The school yearbooks between 1939 and 1941 offer a revealing snapshot in this regard (see Table 5.2). Unlike in the earlier years when smaller Hispanic high school enrollments translated into less schoolwide recognition, clearly things were changing.[83] Hispanics were now major players in the world of extracurricular activities. In 1940, for instance, all three officers of the senior, junior, and sophomore classes were Hispanic. Also noteworthy in this regard (but not reflected in the table) is the wide participation of both groups in school athletics.

Thus, although Hispanics were still more likely to drop out of school, for those who made the full journey, Magdalena High School was becoming

Table 5.2 Club and Class Officers by Surname, 1939–1941

	Anglo	Hispanic
Yearbook staff	14	22
Class officers	13	24
Student council officers	4	6
Dramatics Club	10	–
Science Club	5	6
Spanish Club	–	12
Home Economics Club	7	8
Pep Club	4	7
"M" Spirit Club	2	6
Total	59	91

Source: Magdalena yearbooks, 1939–1941.

a more positive experience. The combination of small graduating classes, integrated classrooms, and the mixed association in school activities all played their part. Indeed, if we are to believe the 1939 yearbook, which catalogued in rhyme the individual talents of each graduating senior, Hispanics and Anglos had come to appreciate each other as individuals. For instance,

> Miguel [Chávez] ranks high among the students;
> He's another star among the Steers.
> No doubt you've seen his first-rate acting;
> He's an all-around Senior it appears.[84]

If Hispanics were having an easier time of it than in the past, Lucy Pino's experience suggests that family support was a significant factor in their success. From the day in 1939 when Lucy first entered school, she found she loved it. She adored her teachers, and she sensed the feeling was mutual. She had barely started school when she was picked to play the part of a small child in a school play. Because of her quick intelligence, her father easily convinced the principal that Lucy should be jumped in midyear to the first grade. She developed a passion for books and was soon spending an inordinate amount of time in the bathroom, because it afforded the one place where she could read undisturbed by requests to perform various household tasks. When she grew tall enough to reach the stove, she found the perfect chore—making tortillas. "I could make tortillas and read." The times spent devouring books and flipping tortillas were treasured moments.

So she continued to thrive at school—"I loved the spelling bees"—distinguished herself academically, and eventually moved on to college.

Lucy attributes much of her academic success to her parents. Her mother, she says, was a feminist before her time, and both parents valued education. Her father, who at various times worked in the Kelly mines, owned a grocery store, and once ran for mayor, periodically walked unannounced into the school to "check up" on his daughter's progress and talk with her teachers. At the dinner table, moreover, politics and other subjects were discussed, and "we all jumped into the discussion. . . . We discussed ideas." Her parents "praised us when we had an opinion. . . . That was their biggest wish, that we would be independent thinkers." On several occasions her father invited doctors, teachers, or mining engineers to dinner so the children were exposed to the tangible benefits of education. Meanwhile, religion played a secondary role in the family, constituting more of a social ritual than a defining worldview. "It was another costume for me," she observes. At the same time, her father "was a defender of Hispanic culture and definitely wanted all of us to continue our culture and respect it." The family spoke Spanish at home, and "he had me learning to read and write in Spanish all the time I was growing up." He was always "worried that we would lose our culture."[85]

Disobedience and Longings

If Lucy Pino relished school, it is also clear that many did not. Although Hispanics had special reasons for disliking school, many Hispanics and Anglos alike, especially in the early decades, were more than willing to forsake the dull routines of school life for the imaginary adventures awaiting them in a bustling frontier community. The stockyard pens bulging with bleating sheep and bawling cattle, the screech of the locomotive pulling into the Magdalena station, the saloons, the brothels, the dance halls, and the fiestas all made school—especially high school—somehow seem irrelevant. It is hardly surprising that the disaffected found ingenious ways of displaying their dissatisfaction and that school officials resorted to harsh disciplinary measures. Indeed, a school principal's ability to retain his position was in large part dependent on his ability to maintain discipline. In February 1919, for instance, the *Magdalena News* reported that A. T. Smith was forced to resign his post after a very "heated" meeting with the school board and the faculty. "It seems very evident that the Magdalena High

School has a few pupils that cannot be controlled by kindness and have forced the school board to engage a principal who will not 'Spare the rod and spoil the child.'"[86]

There were the usual acts of disobedience: playing hooky, firing spitballs, smoking on school grounds, and the occasional verbal missile directed at a teacher. Betsy Crawford recalls the time when the Latin teacher—"she was a war hog"—lost her temper and marched off to the superintendent's office but made the fatal mistake of leaving her hat on the desk. The next day she discovered it atop the school flagpole. Another remembers how a friend who was given to epileptic fits periodically faked one, which always brought the response from the teacher, "Get him out of here." The two conspirators would then retire to a hidden location to smoke.[87]

Fred Billings probably set the standard for incorrigibility. On one occasion he hooked one end of a large logging chain to the superintendent's Model A and the other end to a fence post. The wind was blowing so hard, the "crazy ole bastard" never saw the chain. When he started the engine, raced the motor, slammed the gearshift in reverse, and released the clutch, the car shot backward, leaving the axle on the ground. Another time Fred turned his destructive talents to a more challenging project. One night he led a group of students in a plot to disassemble a large ore wagon and then rebuild it in the study hall on the second floor of the high school. After reassembling the wagon, they "pounded the hell" out of the bolts and nuts, making it all the more difficult to disassemble. The result was "we went to school there for about a month with the darn wagon in the study hall. Goddamn, they tried every way in the world to find out who did that." Fred almost made it through high school. But just a few weeks before graduation,

> The damn principal caught me messing around with a schoolteacher is what happened. I was sixteen. Yeah, she was twenty-seven, twenty-eight, somewhere around like that. And he was kind of sweet on her. She was an English teacher, and we were havin' a play. She was the dramatics teacher too. So I'd go to her house at night to study. So she thought I was great. She wanted to give me extra training in this dramatics and all this bullshit. Anyway, that had been goin' on all winter. And I think my mom kind of had somethin' figured out—wasn't quite right. Good-looking new teacher, and everyone was wantin' to go with her, and she wasn't interested. So anyway, the Goddamned principal come over there. We was about half drunk. [We] didn't have any clothes on, and the

son-of-a-bitch hadn't locked the door. I thought she had, but she hadn't. So it was a lot easier to expel me than it was to fire her and get a new teacher.[88]

Fred Billings's school days were over.

Little wonder that school discipline was sometimes severe. One man who attended school in the 1920s recalls how the principal severely whipped him and a friend when they got caught planning an escape from school. His friend, who got the worst of it, "ran out of the school, ran to his house, got up in the attic. They couldn't get him down from there. He sure got a beatin'." Twenty years later, whipping was still school policy. One rancher recalls how when he was in the seventh grade, a female teacher regularly yanked off an available student's belt to deliver punishment to some particularly obstreperous boys. "We had about four big bullies in the class, and I think she must have whipped them three times a day on the average. She'd come back there and take my belt off and run them back there in the closet and beat the holy tar out of them. And it never did do any good. They were sixteen, eighteen years old—in the seventh grade." There were other standard punishments as well: standing in the corner, missing recess, school detentions, and of course suspensions and expulsions. One student from the period remembers, "If we were real naughty they would pull our pant legs up and make us kneel on small pebbles that were put down on the floor."[89]

In the history of education there have always been children who wanted nothing more than to be somewhere else. Children who grew up on ranches seem to have been especially miserable. The daily grind of spelling bees and grammar exercises simply could not compete with riding a half-broke horse or the easy freedom of searching for a missing steer. Periodically ranch children gained relief by virtue of the school's policy to release them during fall and spring roundup.[90] But for would-be cowboys such as Melvin Akers this was little consolation. "I had a problem at school all the time that I went. . . . I never did like it. I never liked to be inside a house. When the damn bell would ring it would prettin' near give me a heart attack to have to go in and set all day." A generation later, a Hispanic rancher recollects, "My grades would go to hell, especially in the spring of the year. Because I knew what they were doing out here [at the ranch]. You know, they were workin'. They were ridin' buckin' horses. They just brought 'em in, and all the horses were buckin'. Everybody havin' fun, gettin' skinned up and bloody. And there I am—stuck with a book."[91]

No one missed this life more than Bessie Field. While attending school in Socorro, "I kept awantin' to come home. I listened for some word that somebody was goin' to the ranch." Every time her father appeared, she pleaded, "Can I go home with you, Papa?" When Nels Field was state land commissioner and Bessie was attending Loretto Academy in Santa Fe, the prospect of escaping to the ranch was even more remote:

> It was awfully hard for me. The last days of school I don't think I learned a thing. I don't think I paid attention. I couldn't see my books. I was lookin' out the window. The sisters talked to me and tried to get my mind off of home. I remember Sister Lois told me one day, and so did Sister Mary, "You cry all the time for something." And I said, "I want my freedom. I want to go home. I want to be free. I don't want to be in the house. I don't want to be shut up. I don't want to hear things that are goin' on in town. I don't want to hear what's goin' on in the world. I just want to go home." It was a continuous thing.

Summer brought relief: "We immediately changed our clothes, and within a few hours we were out to round up cattle, brand calves, move other cattle, and gather all the horses that were scattered from here to yonder."[92]

Moving On

In early May 1937 the junior class organized a banquet for graduating seniors, a class composed of eleven Hispanics and ten Anglos. The decor for the affair, held in the school gym, was strictly in the cowboy, western mode. Saddles, chaps, cattle skulls, saddle blankets, and juniper and cedar boughs hung on the gym walls. The tables were arranged in the shape of horseshoes and decorated with images of cowboys and bucking broncos. On each table a booklet—designed in the shape of a ten-gallon hat—listed the menu items, senior and junior class officers, and local sponsors of the event. The evening's program, moreover, held to the cowboy theme. After a retrospective by senior Edith Schmidt titled "First Brandings," Dome Armijo, senior class president, followed up with remarks titled "Headin' for the Last Roundup." The songs "Ole Faithful" and "Home on the Range" were then sung, capped by a reading of the "Cowboy Ode." Superintendent Stinnett, as "range boss," closed the banquet with remarks under the title "Get Along Little Dogies." The evening concluded with a dance, the first band selections adhering to the western theme.[93]

That "Headin' for the Last Roundup" should serve as the evening's theme is hardly surprising. By 1937 the Kelly mines were closing down. Although the drought was a severe setback for cattlemen, stock raising was clearly the dominant sector of the economy. The myth of the West swept all before it. Metaphorically, the banquet images also spoke to the power relationships in a region where cowboys and ranching were becoming increasingly associated with Anglos, regardless of Hispanics' *rancho* and *vaquero* heritage. If many Anglo ranch children might prefer the fit of a good saddle to a school desk, the fact remains that the school curriculum was pretty much an Anglo affair, an exercise in ethnic and cultural hegemony to which Hispanics must accommodate themselves. At the same time, power relations were not entirely one sided. Just three years after "Headin' for the Last Roundup," Trinidad García was making plans for the Coronado Cuarto Centennial.

Raised mostly by her grandparents, Esther Peralta loved school, and it was always understood that after graduating from high school, she would move to Albuquerque or Santa Fe for further education. But when her beloved grandfather died (the day of her graduation no less) her aspirations seemed selfish. In good conscience, she thought, how could she leave her suffering grandmother? But one day later in the summer, the old woman pulled Esther to the window and directed her to look at the two young women sitting on the porch across the street. "See those two girls sitting over there?" she remembers her grandmother asking. "They dropped out of school. And do you know what their whole life is going to be—and is? Do you know? It's there. No member of our family is ever going to do that—sitting on the porch.... You have to go."[94]

And she did.

CHAPTER SIX

THE ALAMO NAVAJOS AT SCHOOL

Gilbert Guerro never forgot that day in 1918 when he first laid eyes on Anglo rancher-trader Nels Field and two of his light-skinned daughters. That was the day the five-year-old first realized there must be a "different kind of people." The boy was terribly frustrated by the fact that he could not communicate with the girls in their own language. So almost immediately after, he began pestering his father that he wanted to learn this other language. He wanted to go to school. To these pleadings, he remembers his father answering, "Well, son, you're going to go to school very soon." As soon as Gilbert was old enough to take care of himself—when he could tie his shoes, put on his pants, wash his face—he could go to school. So the boy waited.[1]

Then "the worst thing happened." His father and mother suddenly died, victims of the influenza scourge. "Now I was completely lost." Handed off to relatives, he spent the next seven years herding sheep—"day after day, year after year." Shoeless, half-starved, and poorly clad, he followed the flock and came to know, he claims, every rock, tree, arroyo, and spring on the reservation. Still, he nursed the dream. "I didn't give up on the idea what my father promised me." The problem was he did not know how to make it happen—"I don't know where to go." Finally, at about thirteen, he heard that a truck was coming to the Fields' trading post to take children to a faraway school. This was his chance. So on the appointed day, Gilbert showed up, climbed aboard, and waited for the truck's big engine to turn over. Suddenly the engine roared, and they were heading north. At this point, the older boy surely took notice of the younger children sobbing, anxious about leaving their families for the first time. As for Gilbert, he was happy to be going to a place where he could learn to speak the language of the trader's daughters. As the truck rolled on, the dust kicked up by the thick tires produced a haze, blurring the children's last views of the receding hogans scattered across the landscape. As for Gilbert, he was not looking back. As the truck bounced along, he settled in for the ride, satisfied that what his father had once promised him was about to become a reality.

Beginnings

Late-nineteenth-century federal Indian policy was based on a series of interlocking propositions deeply embedded in the nation's conquest and colonization of Native Americans. The first was fundamental to all that followed—namely, that Indian societies were essentially "savage" in their cultural makeup, standing in dichotomous opposition to Euro American, white "civilization." The gap between civilization and savagism, it was held, was revealed in a series of binary distinctions: individualism versus tribalism, private property versus communalism, agriculture versus hunting and gathering, patri- and nuclear-centered versus extended and matricentered families, and Christianity versus paganism. It made little difference whether these dichotomous attributes applied in all cases; the list of deficiencies was sufficiently long to fit the overall narrative.[2] This indictment led to the second proposition: unless Indians were lifted out of their barbaric condition, they were fated to perish from the continent. By the "law" of historical progress, civilization and savagism were irreconcilable states of existence; the latter must inevitably give way to the former. Once more, time was running out on American Indians. The whistle of the locomotive, the hum of telegraph wires, and the clink of survey chains all signaled the rapidly approaching disaster on the horizon. Plummeting census figures told the story. Unless something was done, and done soon, the race would be swept from the continent.[3] The final proposition: only a full-press assault on Indian institutions, accompanied by an aggressive policy of cultural uplift and incorporation, would save the race from extinction. Schools were an essential ingredient in this national project.[4]

The Alamo Navajos got their first taste of schooling early in the twentieth century, well after the federal system of Indian education was solidly in place. By the early 1880s, the Bureau of Indian Affairs (BIA) looked to three models of schooling to accomplish its educational mission: reservation day schools, reservation boarding schools, and off-reservation boarding schools. The first two levels of the system were in place by the 1870s. The first off-reservation school opened in Carlisle, Pennsylvania, in 1879, the brainchild of Richard Henry Pratt, who coined the phrase, "Kill the Indian and save the man." Carlisle removed Indian children from their reservation homes for up to five years, soon regarded as the surest approach for incorporating Indians into the national mainstream. By 1902, the BIA had established some twenty-five schools on the Carlisle model, including those in Albuquerque (1884) and Santa Fe (1890)—two schools the Alamo Navajos would come to know intimately. Alamo Navajo children also attended a boarding school at Crownpoint, New Mexico, located on the southeast corner of the "Big Navajo" reservation.[5] Although technically a reservation boarding school, for all practical purposes it was an off-reservation school for the Alamo Navajos.

The first evidence of the Alamo Navajos' contact with boarding schools is a 1912 letter from the Indian agent in Albuquerque to the commissioner of Indian Affairs in Washington, DC, requesting funds for the transfer of a blind boy named Luz from the Albuquerque boarding school to the New Mexico Institute for the Blind. The year before, the agent related, he had received word that a "band of Navajos of which Luz is a member was about to kill him because he was a burden to them and unable to earn a livelihood." Justly alarmed, the agent sent Rueben Perry, superintendent of the Albuquerque Indian School, to the remote community to investigate the matter. When Perry "found conditions as reported," he immediately enrolled the boy in school, where he was learning the trade of broom making. But the Institute for the Blind would be much more suited to his condition, it was reasoned, so he was requesting the boy's transfer to the more appropriate facility. Presumably the transfer was made.[6]

In addition to rescuing the blind boy from being killed (or so Perry thought), his visit to Alamo alerted the BIA that the children in this small band of Navajos were in need of schooling. In the following years, there were annual roundups of Alamo Navajo children to attend the boarding schools at Santa Fe or Albuquerque. Still, in 1926, BIA authorities were complaining that many children at Alamo were not in school. There were several reasons such was the case. One was the BIA definition of "school-age" children—five to eighteen. Some parents were understandably hesitant to surrender five- or six-year-olds to school officials. Avoiding school was also made easier by the sheer remoteness of the area and the manner in which children were collected. Some years, parents were simply advised to bring children on a certain day to a designated location, such as the Fields' trading post; in other years, a BIA official, assisted by the band's headman, drove a wagon from outfit to outfit collecting children. Neither system was foolproof. Then, too, many older children found long-term school attendance an excessive burden, especially if there was the prospect of earning dollars in the local economy. In the fall of 1928, Nels Field notified the *Magdalena News*: "The Indian bus was down from Crownpoint for the Navajo schoolchildren, but only got fourteen, as the old folks kept them to gather piñons. They believe in eating before school."[7]

Many Alamo Navajo parents and elders, however, supported the idea that youths should learn something about the larger world. Benjamin Apache vividly remembers the morning he first heard about going off to school. He and his six-year-old cousin were chasing birds from a cornfield when his uncle asked the boys if they would like to go to school. "He talked to us about it. He said, 'You could learn the English language. Me, I don't understand it. I can't speak it. Maybe you can—and deal with the white people more. And in that way you can bring their ways back to the reservation.' That's how he explain it to us, so we just said yes. He said, there will be a truck in a week because a whole bunch of us were goin'." Another man recalls a speech given by a medicine man to children on the day of departure.

> When you start you don't know nothin'. And then next year you go, and then you go the eighth grade, and then graduate. You keep goin', goin', goin'—until you go way up. And then you got a good education. And we old peoples, we don't know nothin'. We don't know what school means. . . . We old people go someplace over there and look for job. You know how to talk English? No. You know how to write? No. We don't get jobs. You, new generation. You got a lot of things to give, a lot of things to learn. And when you learn in school, you're gonna go out someplace and get a good job.[8]

In addition to the long-term economic benefit, some parents viewed boarding schools as an immediate, if temporary, escape for their children from crushing poverty. Although the idea of "orphans" ran counter to Navajo kinship tradition, the fact is that the influenza epidemic of 1918–1919 put a severe strain on extended families' abilities to provide for parentless children. By the 1920s many families were facing starvation, resorting to eating prairie dogs and horsemeat for survival. One man recalls, "My dad don't have much—very poor. . . . I was afraid all the time, because they told me I was goin' to school. They showed us pictures of fruit, that we were goin' to have lots of fruit to eat." Another remembers, "I was told I should go to school because there at school they have good shoes, good pants, good shirts. They told [us] at this school they furnished all these things, and that they will take real good care of you. I was told all these things that convince me to go to school."[9] In at least one instance, Alamo Navajo leaders turned to the BIA as a solution to the growing problem of juvenile delinquency. In

August 1944, three leaders from the Alamo Navajo community, including tribal chairman Larry Monte, walked into the United Pueblo Agency in Albuquerque with a request. "They were very much concerned," the administrator reported, "about four boys who gang together and destroy property. Neither the officers nor the boys' parents are able to control them. They are thirteen and fourteen years old and as yet have not attended school. They asked if it would be possible to send these boys to school in Crownpoint."[10] Whether the request was acted upon is not clear.

Thus, for a multitude of reasons—including the fact that the community would surely pay a price for resistance—Alamo Navajo parents were turning over a good portion of their children to the BIA. On August 31, 1920, Reuben Perry, superintendent of the Albuquerque Indian School, wrote the superintendent at Santa Fe that after the summer break, "the Alamo Apaches [note the mistake] have brought the rest of their children back and also two other very nice girls who have never been in school but who are very deserving." Requesting authorization to send the two additional girls on to Santa Fe, Perry added, "the Alamo people are good people, hardworking, and are sure the girls will get along alright."[11]

The Boarding School Experience

The journey to boarding school followed one of two paths. Most children were taken north by wagon or truck to Laguna Pueblo, then east to Albuquerque, and for some, north again to Santa Fe. But others were taken by wagon to Magdalena, where they boarded trains for the journey north.[12] Either way, the time of leaving was emotionally fraught. Although parents mostly offered encouragement, they also dreaded saying good-bye to six- or seven-year-olds. Children, on the other hand, faced the future with a mixture of fear, bewilderment, and excitement. "We sure pretty scared," one man recalls, "because we don't want to go. We don't know what school means in them days. A lot of these kids start cryin', cryin'. We all cried." But one man says that the fear and sadness were counterbalanced by anticipation of the adventure ahead, including learning about the ways of Anglos. "I was not the only one who felt that way. There was a lot of us." Bumping along in the back of a truck headed for Santa Fe, nine-year-old Bernice Apache was not sure what she felt. With her mother dead, she had already shed her share of tears. So while the children around her sobbed, she steeled herself for what lay ahead. "I didn't feel good and I didn't feel bad. . . . I just hoped everything would turn out okay."[13]

Children sent off to boarding school entered an institution possessing many of the characteristics of a "total institution"—a regimented environment designed to control every aspect of their being. As noted earlier, the original mission of the boarding schools was twofold: first, to strip away all visible and psychological identification with past cultural ways; and second, accomplish wholesale acculturation to the ways and outlook of mainstream white society.[14] The process began immediately with the cutting of the hair. Boys' heads were shaved and then splashed with kerosene to kill any lice. During these early years the barber left a knot of hair on the top of the head, known as the "BIA handle," that offered school staff a handy way to yank wayward children into line. One man remembers that he "sure was scared" as the barbers performed their tasks. Girls too suffered from the ordeal, even though the shearing was more modest. Although the assault on their hair (in the case of boys) was partly motivated by the long-standing association of Indians' long hair with savagism, another reason was the challenge of keeping several hundred children healthy in an institutional environment prone to contagion. It follows that after the shearing, the new arrivals were introduced to the "gospel of soap."[15] After they were bathed, they were issued new clothing. In the early decades boys received a military style uniform, one pair of knee-length corduroy pants with long stockings, one pair of overalls, one pair of Sunday dress pants, three shirts, and two pairs of shoes. Girls apparently received the equivalent in dresses—for class, for work, and for church—all serving as a portent of things to come.[16] How students felt about their new clothing is not clear, but they most probably found this aspect of their new existence a welcome change from their makeshift and poor clothing at home.

More mixed were the impressions of the food served up in the dining room. For those who had suffered from the thin offerings at home, boarding school was a blessing.[17] But not for all. Some found the food "strange" and hungered for mutton and fry bread. In addition to the difference in diet, there were the meager portions. "The food was awful. We git one potato with gravy and a piece of meat. No dessert. Nothin'. That's all we git. Two slices of bread." One woman recalls, "We hardly ever get enough to eat. Sometimes the older boys would just come up to us and take our bread, but what could we do?"[18] Younger boys also suffered this injustice.

> We would go to the dining room. We sat at the table. We were in the middle. In those days we say grace before we sit down to eat. Sometimes they used to tell us close your eyes, so we close our eyes. But then, when you open your eyes, the food is all distributed among maybe two or three

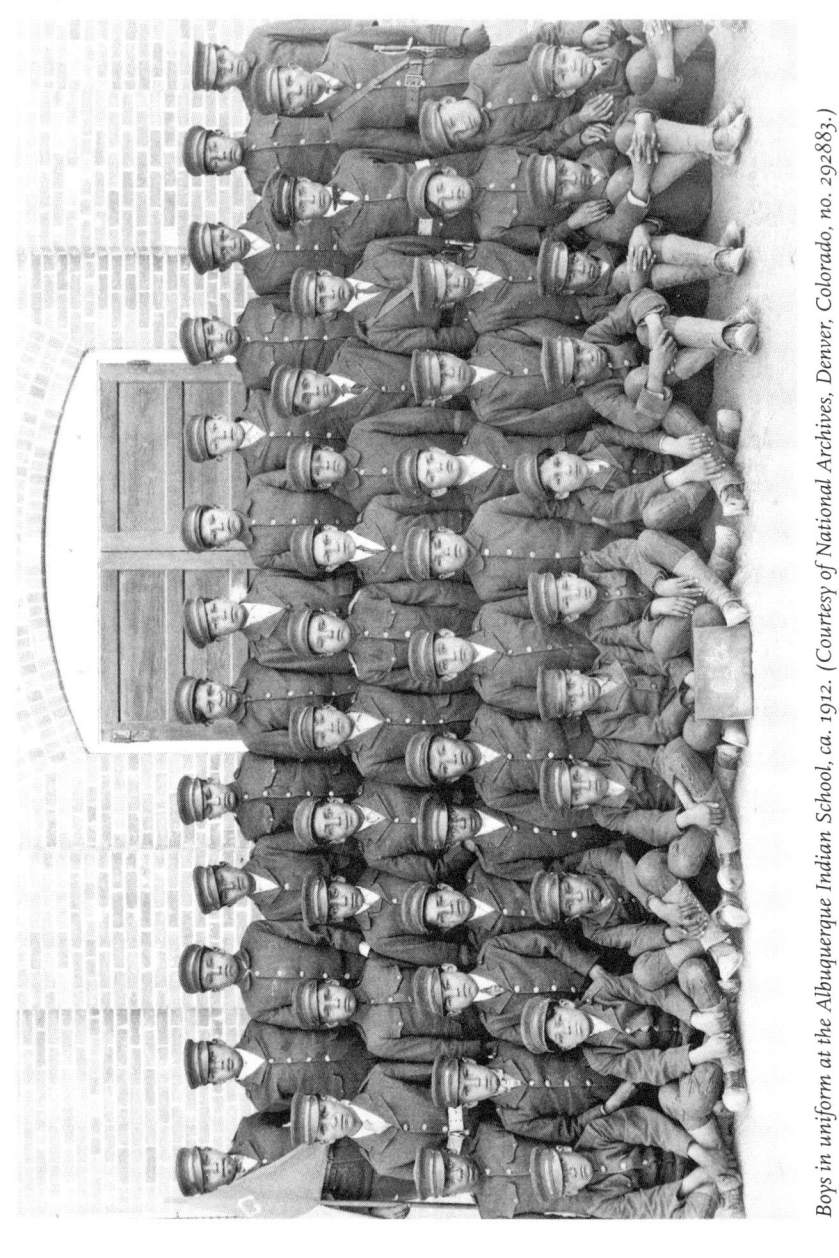

Boys in uniform at the Albuquerque Indian School, ca. 1912. (Courtesy of National Archives, Denver, Colorado, no. 292883.)

students and you're left without it. So then we try to go back up there to the kitchen to try and get some more. They say, what happened? Well, I can't explain it to them. That was hard.[19]

The last part of the induction process was settling on a new name. Renaming Indians was mainly driven by the fact that surnames, a vital component in tracking land inheritance, were absent in native society. Although much of the renaming was conducted at Indian agencies, a good deal of it also went on in schools, where an added motivation came into play—namely, the inability of teachers to pronounce names correctly. In choosing surnames, if the tongue moved easily over the native name, school officials sometimes retained the original or a shorthand version of the same. Hence, the frequency of surnames such as Begay or Yazzi among the northern *Diné* today. Sometimes the original was rendered into English, polished off with the addition of a new first name—the final product being something like Gilbert Running Horse. When such translations were impossible or impractical—one Alamo Navajo man's name translated as Hogan—the child was assigned an altogether new name.[20]

Renaming of the Alamo Navajos was relatively easy because most family heads had already taken on Spanish surname identities. Thus, upon arriving at school, children with names such as Apache, Secatero, and Guerro readily found a place on the roster. But not always. The 1915 Albuquerque Indian School roster is a snapshot of the renaming process in transition. Whereas several boys were enrolled with surnames such as those above, several girls were entered with names such as Ah Has Bah and Baggespah, that is to say, their original Navajo names (or an approximation thereof). On the same roster, however, another girl appears as Alta Has Bah Secatero, managing to retain her given Navajo name alongside her surname.[21] Children's assigned names also depended upon the efficiency of the school bureaucracy. Sometimes things worked out reasonably well. One Santa Fe memorandum sent to school staff in March 1924 reads, "It is hereby directed that the two girls heretofore on our records as 'Marie Alamo' and 'Dora Alamo' shall from this time forward be known and carried on our records as 'Marie Apache' and 'Dora Guerrero,' it having been ascertained that those are the real names of these two girls." But there were also mistakes. One man recalls how he should have gone into the roster with the surname Secatero, but "they had me mixed up" with another boy whose last name should have been Vicente. The two ended up spending the rest of their lives with each other's names.[22]

Occasionally children and parents successfully exercised a degree of agency in the naming process. A particularly poignant moment occurred when a group of children was taken by wagon to Magdalena before boarding the train for Santa Fe. Camping on the outskirts of Magdalena on the night previous to departure, the children sat around a campfire with one of the older girls, Dora Guerrero, who had already been to school. The children were all ears as Dora began telling them what to expect, including the fact that they would be receiving new names such as John, Benjamin, or Sally. Apparently in the midst of the telling Dora decided to assign them new names herself—which she proceeded to do. "That's how I got my name," one man recalls, "goin' to the train." But even arriving with a given name was not foolproof. When one seven-year-old girl arrived in Albuquerque and informed the registrar that her first name was "Angel," she was promptly told, "Navajos don't have that kind of name," whereupon a more plausible name was entered in the books, with which she went through life. One of the most successful efforts at name preservation occurred in 1929 when Olson Apachito surrendered his eleven-year-old daughter to the Santa Fe Indian School, apparently with explicit instructions on how she should be known. For whatever reason—because Olson was a veteran of the school, because he was a community leader, or because the BIA was getting increased criticism for its harsh assimilation policies—the superintendent abided by his wishes. His daughter officially entered the school as Bish-Ha-Dispah Apachito. A memorandum followed stating that teachers and staff should call her by her Navajo name.[23]

Meanwhile, new arrivals were in the throes of disorientation. "We don't feel too good," one man remembers. "We always lonesome. Don't know nobody there. A lot of different kind of Indians, but we don't know them. Lonesome all the time. You're always thinking about your family back home." It was one thing to maintain a pose of stoic bravery in the light of day; it was quite another when the lights went out. "We used to cry in bed at night. During the daytime, we'd think that we're tough. . . . But at night when we hide in bed, that's when our tears come out. The next day we don't tell anybody." The girl stripped of her name, Angel, remembers, "I cried almost every night for one month." Occasionally, children found relief in the company of a student relative. "Sometime at night I don't went to sleep alone. I go to my aunt bed and sleep with her. Around about 5:00 o'clock, she tell me to go back to my bed and sleep there." But this was a luxury because children were separated by age, and of course, by gender.

One woman arrived at school expecting to see two of her aunts at school, only to learn that the two girls were recent runaways.

> I was so lonesome I refuse to do anything because they separate us. I cried I don't know how many days. Also at the dorm at night I cried to sleep. I had a hard time sleeping the first few weeks because at night I could hear cars, trucks, trains passing by and also the crickets use to scare me. Once in while I would hear a dog barking that reminded me of home. I just cried to sleep.

Then there was the problem of bed wetting. In at least one of the boys' dormitories there was no bathroom, which meant that on cold winter nights some of the children, not wanting to make the trek to the facilities, tried to "hold it." The next morning, students only needed to glance at the number of urine-soaked mattresses hanging out the dormitory windows to see how many were unsuccessful. "I see lots of mattresses sticking out there for drying."[24]

For some, the adjustment was easier. One man recalls, "I don't ever mind it. I don't even think about home. . . . They feed us real good. They take care of us real good." The adventure of discovering a new world—flushing toilets, electric lights, moving pictures, organized sports—held its own pleasures. "At first I used to think about my family at home," one woman reflects, "then gradually I kind of forgot. There were girls that liked taking care of us small girls. So being under their care and my enjoyment of learning to read and write, I didn't mind being at school."[25]

One of the greatest adjustments was adapting to the strict military-like regimen. This aspect of institutional life stemmed from two factors. First, policy makers believed one of the cardinal deficiencies in Indian life was its chaotic nature. To be truly civilized, children must be taught to regulate their existence in smaller, more precise units of time—that is to say, "clock time"—as opposed to "natural time," which governed tribal life. A second factor was the organizational challenges of managing several hundred Indian children twenty-four hours a day. For these reasons, until the more military aspects of the boarding schools were relaxed in the 1930s, the atmospheric earmarks of school life were strict regimentation, surveillance, and obedience.[26] Thus, the first generation of Alamo Navajo children quickly discovered they had entered a world of bugles, bells, marching, and drilling. This was an abrupt change from their earlier upbringing. As one man explains, "At home we have our freedom. We play when we want to, ride our horses when we pleased. There's hardly any work . . . but herd sheep. It seems like we had the authority, not our parents, so we came when we wanted to, go when we pleased. If we heard about a rodeo, we would pack and leave and not get any permission from our parents. When there was a ceremony on, we went without telling our parents where we are going."[27] Now all the power and authority over their movements had shifted to strangers who were the "big bosses." As one veteran of the system described it, "Get up bright and early—five o'clock. Five-thirty we'd be in the field drillin' with rifles before breakfast. About that time they blew a lot of bugles. We'd come in, put up our rifles, wash up, line up, and go to chow line. It was pretty hard." Another remembers, "We don't sit down until they say grace, a few words, and then we all sit down. I can't get over it. This roar—there's too many kids here. I could hear it—this roar—just like bees." After eating, "we line up and then we march to school. We march all the time it seems like. When we not doing nothing we march, I guess to keep us in school."[28]

Curriculum

In the early years, both Albuquerque and Santa Fe offered eight grades of instruction. By 1930 Albuquerque had expanded its curriculum to twelve grades and Santa Fe to ten, with two more to follow shortly. The curriculum was broken into two broad divisions, academic and industrial, although after 1900 vocational subject matter infused much of the academic content.[29] Still, teachers devoted much effort to teaching the three r's—reading, 'riting, and 'rithmetic. Neither policy makers nor teachers ever questioned the assumption that Indian children must learn English if they were to enter into the path of progress and citizenship. Indeed, citizenship training constituted another priority in the educational program. Teachers instructed students in the rights and obligations of citizenship, the fundamentals of the US Constitution, and finally, strove to instill a deep and abiding love of country. As commissioner of Indian affairs Thomas J. Morgan outlined the task two decades before the Alamo Navajos' arrival, Indians "should be taught to look upon America as their home and upon the United States Government as their friend and benefactor. They should be made familiar with the lives of great men and women in American history, and be taught to feel pride in all their accomplishments." The aim of instilling patriotic citizenship spilled over to the drill field, where students routinely honored the flag and participated in the celebration of national holidays. The curriculum also called for instructing students in the rudiments of science and geography.[30] Most likely in the midst of their geography lessons Alamo Navajo students realized Anglo teachers had never heard of the names the *Diné* had given prominent features in the region. How did it come to pass that one of the four sacred mountains, *Tsoodzi*, came to be called Mt. Taylor? The white people had different stories.

The vocational side of the curriculum operated at two levels. On the one hand, it was built on the foundational belief that Indians, to be fully "Americanized," must be converted to the ideal of self-reliant individualism. Only when students embraced the value of work, only when they took to heart the concept of possessive individualism, only when they ached to fill their pockets with dollars, it was believed, would they be fit citizens of the nation. On another level, the vocational education program was designed to provide students the skills needed for their occupational destinies and self-support. Boys spent half the school day in classes devoted to such subjects as farming, stock raising, blacksmithing, furniture making, shoe repair, printing, and carpentry. Girls focused on the various realms of domestic training: cooking, sewing, housekeeping, and child raising. By the 1930s the vocational curriculum was broadened to include subjects such as auto repair for boys and nursing for girls. At both New Mexico schools girls might select a class devoted to a native skill the BIA had come to recognize as an important source of income for many Navajo families—rug weaving.[31]

The vocational curriculum dovetailed with extensive chore assignments. In fact, vocational instruction and chores were often indistinguishable from one another in a system dependent on student labor for the daily operation of the school. Cows had to be milked, livestock fed, manure shoveled, gardens maintained, uniforms cleaned, floors scrubbed, bathrooms sanitized, dresses sewed, bedding washed, cooking pots scoured, and dishes cleaned. This aspect of the boarding school program, combined with the meager quality and quantity of food, was singled out by the Meriam Report in 1929 (a federally commissioned investigation of off-reservation schools) as one of the most egregious features of the system.[32]

A few Alamo Navajo students also participated in the schools' "outing" program, which encouraged older students to live with and work for Anglo middle-class families for a few months. Originally the brainchild of Richard H. Pratt at Carlisle, the original outing concept was to provide students an opportunity to experience firsthand the nuclear family ideal while enhancing their work skills. But as the idea moved west, the potentially exploitative possibilities of the program became ever more manifest; farmers, ranchers, and various agricultural businesses were only too happy to hire cheap labor. At least one Alamo Navajo male student earned a very modest summer wage in a work gang harvesting Colorado sugar beets and presumably never witnessed the wonders of a middle-class household. Girls, on the contrary, hired themselves out as domestic workers and were much more likely to view close up the inner workings of the patricentered nuclear family.[33] Meanwhile, local merchants were only too happy to relieve outing students of their earnings. As an advertisement in one boarding school newspaper proclaimed:

> Early to bed and early to rise,
> Love all the teachers and tell them no lies.
> Study your lessons that you may be wise
> And buy from the men who advertise.[34]

To be sure, life at the Albuquerque and Santa Fe schools was not all about work and deciphering texts. Both schools offered an array of activities designed to brighten the students' days. Some found enjoyment in various school clubs, the school newspaper, learning how to play a musical instrument (perhaps well enough to play in the school band), or participating in competitive sports. Both schools, for instance, fielded football teams, and one Alamo Navajo student remembers years later, "I wasn't too good, just good enough for sideline. It was those husky guys [who got to play]." Playing or not, football was a popular sport throughout the boarding school system, and although neither New Mexico school attained the notoriety of the famous Carlisle Indian team, Albuquerque students between 1927 and 1932 cheered the school team on to a record of thirty wins, nine losses, and four ties. Basketball was also becoming popular and was a sport both boys and girls played. School spirit was especially high at Albuquerque in 1928 when the boy's team won the state championship. Weekly socials, which offered opportunities to mix and dance with the opposite sex, were another activity to which students looked forward, but at the same time these moments could be particularly tricky for Navajo students, who knew that interclan intimacy was strictly forbidden—a reality of which teacher-chaperones, urging students onto the dance floor, were often unaware.[35]

Learning English

Few children entered school knowing more than a few isolated words in English. Gilbert Guerro, for instance, arrived with three words in his vocabulary: "hello," "alright," and "candy." Another claims he left Alamo knowing just one English word—"apple." Such limited vocabulary was of little use in the first few hours amid the swirl of orders. Although interpreters were helpful, new arrivals frequently found themselves in situations without go-betweens. As one woman recalls, "I didn't know what they were talking about because we never talk to an Anglo before." Another recalls the first English words she learned were "yes," "no," "Come here," "Let's go," "eat," and "food." In short, the first words learned were about survival. Navajo aids were a godsend. "We got most of our understanding . . . through another Navajo," one man remembers. "If we were over there, and she say *hágo*, she would translate in English, 'come here.' That way we start out alright."[36]

The challenge was not so much that they were learning a second language, a common necessity among groups living in borderland regions. The particular challenge facing Navajos was the extent and nature of the linguistic gap to be traversed.[37] Every language has its own vocabulary, its own phonology or system of sounds, its own morphology or structure, and finally its own syntax, or way of combining separate units into complete thoughts. Unlike the linguistic challenge facing Hispanics, Navajo children found themselves confronting a foreign tongue entirely outside their morphological and syntactical frame of reference—an entirely different way of thinking. As anthropologists Clyde Kluckhohn and Dorothea Leighton point out, "Every language has an effect upon what the people who use it see, what they feel, how they think, and what they talk about." Never more so than in the case of Navajos.

> Take the example of a commonplace physical event: rain. Whites can and do report their perception of this even in a variety of ways: "It has started to rain," "It is raining," "It has stopped raining." The People can, of course, convey these same ideas—but they cannot convey them without finer specifications. To give a few instances of the sorts of discrimination the Navaho must make before he reports his experience: he uses one verb form if he himself is aware of the actual inception of the rainstorm, another if he has reason to believe that rain has been falling for some time in his locality before the occurrence struck his attention. One form must be employed if rain is generally round about within the range of his vision; another if, though it is raining round about, the storm is plainly on the move. Similarly, the Navaho must invariably distinguish between the ceasing of rainfall (generally) and the stopping of rain in a particular vicinity because the rain clouds have been driven off by the wind. The People take the consistent noticing and reporting of

such differences (which are usually irrelevant from the white point of view) as much for granted as the rising of the sun.[38]

In the beginning, teachers relied mostly on the so-called object method of instruction.[39] As one Alamo Navajo man explained the process, "She show us the object. She repeats the same thing, over and over. We repeat the same thing they say, and they thought we were learnin'." But putting words together in sentences, moving from simple oral exercises to reading them on the printed page, and finally, making sense of them, were all monumental steps in the climb up the linguistic mountain. One Alamo Navajo student says his first reading triumph was making sense of the story "The Little Red Hen." The Navajo aids were helpful, but essentially the program was one of uncompromising immersion. "If we talk Indian in the classroom, we were punished for it." The same went for the playground.[40] Because both Santa Fe and Albuquerque were off-reservation schools, enrolling several tribal groups (mainly Pueblos), enforcing the English-only rule was easier than in reservation schools, where students naturally gravitated to their native tongue at every possible opportunity. Indeed, most of the older Alamo Navajos ascribe much of their progress to this fact. "See, [at] Santa Fe we were all mixed—Acoma, Laguna, Santa Clara, Mescalero [Apache]—we were all mixed. We all have different language. So the only thing we talk is English," one man says. A woman recalls, "I learned how to talk English with goin' around with some Pueblo Indians."[41]

Students developed various strategies to crack the language barrier. Gilbert Guerro, who it may be remembered desperately wanted to learn English before entering school, developed a disturbing stutter when first trying to communicate in this new language. Determined to succeed, he kept telling himself, "Your eye must be always open. Your ear must be always open. Regardless what it is. So I combine this all the time. I didn't waste my time. When I'm learning the word, I had to study what they mean, find the definition of the word, and on and on—especially when I discovered the dictionary."[42] Another man found this strategy helpful: "I would listen to the conversation of these children of all tribes. Sometimes I would repeat what they have said, like if I was teasing them. . . . So I think by doing this kind of thing, you would learn English a lot faster. You say what they said. Like if you don't know what they said, repeat what they say every time. This way I learn a lot faster."[43]

Looking back, many older Alamo Navajos regard their acquisition of English, however imperfect, as the chief benefit of their boarding school experience.[44] Even so, this new language could never replace their deep attachment to their mother tongue, the language that had shaped their consciousness from their first days in a cradleboard. Even though Gilbert Guerro never regretted his determination to learn English, his quest was not without disappointments.

> Let me demonstrate it by this. Suppose I have a nice cake here, decorated so nice, so pretty, all color. Looks so sweet and nice. But suppose you do not have any flavor in the cake. It looks sweet, it looks so nice, it looks so beautiful, but it is tasteless. Today, no matter how much I speak in English . . . it don't mean nothin'. When I go to speak my own language . . . it goes clear into my veins, into my blood, into my body, into my soul. That's the way it is in your own language.[45]

Religion

While new arrivals were dealing with loneliness, adjusting to the regimen of institutional life, and struggling with a new language, they were also encountering the Anglo God in religious services either in town or on campus. For school officials the immediate challenge was sorting out children according to church affiliation. When children were unable to make the choice, an effort was made to contact relatives. Thus, on January 9, 1922, the superintendent at Santa Fe wrote H. C. Medley (a rancher who had helped round up children) requesting information on a particular child's placement. Was the child Catholic or Protestant? In this instance, word came back that the adults in charge of the child "prefer the Catholic religion." By the late 1920s, parents were asked to sign a card indicating their preference.[46] Because the Protestants were latecomers to Alamo country, most of the earliest enrollees no doubt attended Catholic services, but this pattern would change dramatically over the years. Every Sunday morning, students put on their best clothing and, after breakfast, set off for church. One man who entered school as a Catholic recalls that girls were "put in wagons" to convey them to a downtown church. The boys walked. If officially some effort was made to distribute children among the churches by the families' preferences, mistakes were made—perhaps purposely: "See, when we went to school we were Catholic. I don't know how we change it. We went to Presbyterian church."[47]

After they were in church, children struggled to make sense of the meanings and rituals of what was, for many, if not most, a new religious outlook, communicated moreover in a language they were only beginning to understand. "I don't know what they're saying," one man remembers. Another recalls, "They teach us God so loved the world—somethin' like that." Those who entered school with only a traditional background immediately took notice of how different the new religion was.

> Being at home if there was a ceremony held anywhere on the reservation we attended it. When I arrive at school I was asked which church I go to. But traditional teaching doesn't ask which ceremony you attend. In church you are taught to sing, memorize a verse in the Bible. In traditional teaching the medicine man does all the singing, praying, but passes the medicine around to the people. Church was held once a week and was on the same day too, but traditional teaching ceremony is held any day of the week.[48]

The greatest challenge was making sense of the more esoteric strands of church doctrine. Gilbert Guerro, who attended the Catholic church at Santa Fe, endlessly wrestled with the meaning of the phrase "in the name of the Father, Son, and the Holy Ghost." How could the Holy Spirit be in three forms at once? Thinking long and hard on the subject, he found the answer in the metaphor of water, snow, and ice. Were they not also made of the same substance—water? It must be the same with God.[49]

It is difficult to assess the impact of the religious program. Certainly younger children came to school with only the sketchiest knowledge of traditional Navajo religion. Indeed, for policy makers this was one of the chief merits of the off-reservation model of schooling: it removed impressionable children from the paganism of the tribal community. However, compared with children's other concerns, most of which dealt with day-to-day emotional survival, taking the Christian god into their hearts was probably a low priority. For now, Changing Woman and the *Diné*'s Holy People were holding their own. One Alamo Navajo woman says of her boarding school faith, "I didn't know that much about being a born-again Christian."[50] One day she would.

Health and Healing

One of the greatest challenges for the students was staying healthy. Historically, boarding schools were hothouses of contagion where tuberculosis, measles, pneumonia, mumps, and influenza periodically swept through the student body. (Influenza struck both New Mexico institutions with particular force in the years 1919, 1922, 1926, 1928, and 1929. In 1922 Albuquerque alone reported 392 cases.) A number of children arrived at school weakened by poor home nutrition and sanitary conditions, but the concentration of coughing, sneezing, nose-blowing children in crowded dormitories did little to help matters. In a blistering government-commissioned report issued in 1928, Florence Patterson, a Red Cross public health nurse, laid most of the blame for the poor health of students on the institutions themselves—"the strain of bells, bugles, and horns, forming in line five or six times each day, and the mental struggle to combat mental fatigue"—all this on top of undergoing the "terrific shock" of being ripped from their previous existence.[51] The schools' first line of attack against disease and contagion was educational, emphasizing the importance of good health practices: not sharing hand towels, not blowing one's nose "in the air," not sharing band instruments, and of course, overall cleanliness. A reading lesson at one school included:

> In running water I wash my hands,
> In the cool running water.
> I soap them well;
> I watch the soap go away in the running water;
> I think many things as I watch the soap go away;
> I dry my hands on the towel;
> Now my hands are clean.
> I laugh—my hands are clean!
> Once more my hands are sweet and clean.[52]

Although not life-threatening, trachoma, the highly painful and contagious eye disease—dubbed "sore eyes" by students—was particularly discomforting. After it is contracted, trachoma produces granular nodules or bumps on the inner eyelid, which, if not treated, can produce blindness. The disease was rampant in Indian populations, particularly among those living in the Southwest, where the combination of climate and unsanitary living conditions increased the likelihood of infection. Crowded boarding school dormitories only magnified the problem of contagion. Meanwhile, partially blind students found it all the more frustrating to focus on, let alone make sense of, the English words in their classroom readers. (At one point in the 1920s, 48 percent of Santa Fe's students were diagnosed with this debilitating infection.)[53] It followed that scores of children underwent the surgical procedure known as "grattage," which involved scraping the granules off the inner eyelid. Gilbert Guerro recalls the ordeal.

> So I went in hospital. I been treated in the hospital for a long time. Finally, somehow they scrape my eye, both sides. That was itching all the

time, tearing all the time, and finally, they scraped. They used a stick. . . . I don't know what medicine they squirt out, fool around with my eye. And I was in the hospital for a long time for treatment. And then they blind me. I can't see, I can't read, I can't see nothing. So keep from reading. Finally, gradually, it came back and that's how they cure me.[54]

Tonsillectomies were also performed at school, although when the surgery was deemed elective, school officials were required to request permission from the child's parents or guardians. In the case of the Alamo Navajos, the communication flow was slow, with trader Nels Field or a local rancher serving as an intermediary. Thus it was more than a month between the time that the superintendent at Albuquerque wrote Antonio Apachito asking if the doctors could remove his granddaughter's tonsils for reasons of general health and Ida Field's response that "the girl's people would rather that you would not remove her tonsils."[55] Gilbert Guerro, however, underwent the operation and vividly remembers slipping into ether-induced unconsciousness before the doctors went to work.

> They dropped the ether in my nose. And I was expanding, expanding, . . . I remember the nurse, . . . she told me, I will count to ten. When I count to ten, you can get up and you not going to have your tonsil. Okay. And finally, she keep on dropping ether, I can tell, and I just going down, going down, and getting bigger. And she cheat me, I remember, and when she drop to ten, she started over again. It wasn't fair because I was half dead, see. So she started over again and of course I was gone, see. So they take my tonsil out. Well finally they get me out. When I woke up in dormitory and in bed, I look around and I seen some kids were crying in there.

Awake, but still under the spell of the ether, Gilbert was mystified about why the other children were crying. At the moment, it "didn't hurt; don't bother me. That's what I THOUGHT."[56] Shortly, he understood.

Although Albuquerque and Santa Fe recorded few student deaths, as the experiences of two Alamo Navajo brothers, José and John Guerro, illustrate, there was always the possibility of ending up in a graveyard. José arrived at Santa Fe Indian School in the mid-1920s and remembers that only a week later "some kind of sickness" struck the school that sent him to a special dormitory for bedridden children, the hospital being already overcrowded. "I saw a lot of boys who were sick and they just laid in beds. A boy from Alamo died there." When José's condition worsened, the doctor moved him to the hospital. Shortly after, he lost consciousness.

> I don't even know how much of the year I was sick. And then one day I woke up in one little room. I was just laying by myself there. I had a blanket over me, I opened my eyes. I could see the door. I couldn't move my arms or legs. I looked at my bones and there was no meat on it—nothing. I guess they put the people there when they die and then pick them up. I ain't got no meat; just the bone. The door open and it was an Anglo girl. She looked at me with surprise and she said something and the door close. I just heard footsteps. A few minutes later, a man came in with the girl. He was trying to move me around. I was skinny with hardly no meat on me. My body was stiff.[57]

About this time his older sister Dora came to visit him. Dora told him that because the school year was over, he would soon probably be going home for the summer. José was confused by the announcement. "I couldn't remember where home was." In fact, Dora was overly optimistic in her assessment as to her brother's release. José spent the next few weeks recovering, including learning to walk again. Then one day the nurse informed him that he was being transferred to a facility near Laguna Pueblo, closer to home. Even more interesting, he would be joining an old friend there, "but I didn't know who they were talking about." Arriving at his new location, he discovered that this mysterious "friend" was none other than his brother John.

John had come to the hospital by a different route. After being at Santa Fe for a year, he and his cousin Frank decided to run away for the summer and live on their own. Life at school was impossible. "The boys were mean to us. Big boys, they abuse us, they kick us and do a lot of mean things to us." The general plan was to hide out and scavenge for food. Taking blankets from the dormitory, they set up camp under a bridge and proceeded to steal eggs, chickens, and apples from the school farm, bread from the school bakery, and "eat trash where they throw watermelons and stuff."[58]

The two survived in this manner until late August, when John contracted pneumonia and was burning with fever. Late one night Frank decided he must take his sick cousin to the hospital. A day or two later, the school superintendent notified John's father that his son's heart was "badly affected," so if "you hear any startling news concerning him don't be surprised." On September 11, Superintendent John D. DeHuff sent a telegram to local rancher H. C. Medley requesting him to inform John's parents that the boy was now very sick with pleurisy, his lungs filled with fluid, and his heartbeat irregular. "Hoping avoid operation, but if needle-pump operation should appear necessary to save boy's life, may we proceed?" Eight days later, Medley notified the school that the requested permission was granted. A few days later, another telegram: the doctors had held off tapping the boy's lungs, but he was "in a bad way and the chances for his recovery are not all good." A few days later, the news was more optimistic. Deciding on the needle-pump procedure, the doctor had removed eight ounces of "abnormal fluid," after which the patient was soon judged to be on the road to recovery.[59]

Meanwhile, John was living in a half-conscious, hazy world beyond the doctors' knowing. Perhaps it was the medicine. Perhaps it was his way of coping, of walling himself off from the incomprehensible technical language of the doctors and nurses as they discussed his condition and fate. In any event, he slipped into the land of dreams. "I dreamed I was here on the reservation. I was here where they took me, where I used to herd sheep. . . . I could hear the bells. I was satisfied. I could hear the bells. I know the sheep was pretty close. Them days, if you don't hear those bells, you'd better go look for them. So I had the dream all the time. I wasn't scared. I wasn't hurtin' no place. I lay there."[60]

He recovered. Sent to the hospital near Laguna, John slowly regained his strength and joined his brother José, who had undergone his own ordeal. The two had much to talk about, and for that matter, much to be thankful for.

Discipline and Punishment

There were so many ways to get into trouble: speaking "Indian," fighting, destroying school property—"we used to get slingshots and bust the windows"—petty thievery, classroom pranks, bed wetting, running away, and generally disobeying authority. Punishments for these offenses ran the gamut from minor disciplinary measures to more severe ones.[61] Losing weekend privileges, scrubbing bathrooms, picking up rocks, wearing dresses (for the boys), and kneeling on pebbles were all part of the program. For more serious infractions there was the school jail or a good strapping. "In those days we get whipped like nobody's business," one man recalls. "Oh boy, you do something wrong and there was a thick strap or ruler."[62] Because corporal punishment was relatively rare in traditional Navajo society (although a few Alamo Navajos admit to having experienced it at home), this was yet another assault on their cultural identity.[63]

Stiff punishments naturally bred great bitterness—especially when the supposed offenders were victims of misidentification. Such was the case at

Santa Fe when two Alamo Navajo students, Benjamin Apache and Gilbert Guerro, were unfairly and severely whipped for an infraction of which they were completely innocent. As part of their chore assignment, and under the supervision of the school farmer, Benjamin and Gilbert's job was to care for the livestock. One Sunday morning the two boys set about their chores. On this particular morning, the farmer instructed them that after the milking and feeding, they should walk to the rear of the kitchen and haul the "slop can" (sitting on a sled hitched to two burros) out to the hog pen. Completing all their chores, Benjamin and Gilbert returned to the dormitory. Shortly afterward, however, they were notified that they should immediately report to the boys' advisor's office, the office responsible for disciplinary measures.

> So we went over to the office. There were no questions, just a couple of chairs. The chairs were leanin' over. He said, put your pants down. And we say what for? He said, never mind, put your pants down. Well, they kind of force us to put our pants down. And we got a strappin'. The leather was about three layers tacked with copper rivets. And we got a strappin'. And it really hurt. Of course we cried and everything.[64]

It was after the whipping that they learned the reason: they had been observed in the company of some boys parching corn—a strict violation of school rules.

The following day, both angry and sore, the two boys decided not to report for work duty, which prompted the farmer to come looking for them. Unaware of what had occurred the day before, he demanded to know why they had failed to report for work. After listening to the boys' accounts of the previous day, and perhaps inspecting the damage—"our hind seat was black and blue"—the enraged farmer, with the two boys in tow, set out for the advisor's office. Arriving at the office, the boys then looked on in surprise as the farmer, who Benjamin remembers as having "big arms," immediately approached the startled advisor and proceeded to give him a good thrashing: "He just let him have it. He sure slugged him." When asked who had authorized the whipping, the advisor responded that the superintendent had approved it. At this point, the farmer turned to Benjamin and Gilbert and said, "Let's go see him."

The next scene was even more extraordinary. Still blistering mad, the farmer, boys in hand, strode to the superintendent's office, fronted by a stairway, and called for him to step outside. The superintendent did so, only to be greeted by the farmer's instruction to descend the stairs. "I want to talk with you." Surveying the scene below suspiciously and worried for his physical welfare, the superintendent responded with, "I can talk from here." So it went, back and forth, until the farmer bounded up the stairs, and in the midst saying, "If this is the way you want to come down, okay," muscled his "boss" down the stairs. After they reached the ground level, the farmer dished out the same treatment to the superintendent that he had given the advisor just minutes before. "He just let him have it too." After the pummeling, he shouted in the superintendent's face, "You'd better start packin' your things because you're not gonna be here as long as I'm on this campus." Remarkably, it turned out that way. Shortly, both the superintendent and advisor were gone. The farmer remained.

So did Benjamin and Gilbert. As small boys growing up at Alamo, both had heard the hogan winter stories of how the Hero Twins—Born for Water and Monster Slayer—had dispatched the monsters following the *Diné*'s emergence from the three worlds below this one, the Glittering World. Now here was this justice-seeking *biligáana* farmer-warrior. He might not merit the status of the Hero Twins, but surely he deserved to be remembered.

Crownpoint

For two decades the Alamo Navajos attended the off-reservation schools at Santa Fe and Albuquerque. In 1931 they began attending a new school at Crownpoint, New Mexico. Located on the southeastern border of the "Big Navajo" reservation, Crownpoint was technically a reservation boarding school. But the designation made no sense for the Alamo Navajos, who lived for all practical purposes on a different reservation.

The move to Crownpoint was in conjunction with one of the great transitions in federal Indian policy. The groundwork for the change came in 1928 with the release of the previously mentioned Meriam Report, which as part of its condemnation of Indian policy called for "a change in point of view" in how Indians were educated. Foremost among its educational recommendations was that younger children should be educated closer to home—preferably in community day schools—before moving on to higher-level schools. In keeping with the new outlook was the belief that the children's adjustment to "white civilization" should be more gradual and built upon their understanding and appreciation of their own native culture. The shift in outlook was not surprising given the fact that the section of the report on education was written by W. Carson Ryan, a noted progressive educator. In 1931, Ryan was appointed director of education, and two years later, after John Collier's appointment as commissioner of Indian affairs, the new outlook was pursued even more aggressively. For the next twelve years, the new orientation guided federal Indian education policy.[65]

The move to Crownpoint was significant for several reasons. First, reservation boarding schools were generally less intertribal in composition. Other than enrolling a few Hopis, Crownpoint was overwhelmingly Navajo. Second, academic, vocational, and extracurricular branches of the program were less developed than at either Santa Fe or Albuquerque. Third, whereas students at Albuquerque or Santa Fe had some contact with a wider "urban" setting, Crownpoint was for all practical purposes an isolated outpost. Finally, at Crownpoint Alamo Navajo children encountered the new educational philosophy of progressive education.

Since the publication of John Dewey's *School and Society* in 1899, progressive education had evolved into a set of interconnected but loosely defined propositions that challenged long-standing assumptions on pedagogical aims and practices. Four in particular shaped the Crownpoint program. First, progressives believed that the curriculum, rather than ignoring the children's cultural background, should build upon it. Unless or until the children could see connections between the school curriculum and their previous cultural experience, it was reasoned, little real headway could be made in the larger project of acquainting them with the ever-expanding horizons of human knowledge and progress. Second, for learning to be truly genuine—especially for younger children—it must be experienced, a proposition that found expression in the "activity movement," or "learning by doing." The third and fourth pillars of progressive education grew out of the belief that education was in large part a social process. Thus, by the 1920s educators were advocating the "project method," a curricular strategy that called for teachers to engage students in joint problem-solving ventures around subject matter that was both relevant to their lives and a platform for further intellectual and social development. Finally, progressives believed schools should be community centers, spaces where adults were welcomed as cultural resources and where the community came together to deliberate issues of pressing concern. (This last belief was more relevant to the greater emphasis being placed on day schools but was not without implications for reservation boarding schools as well.)[66]

In keeping with the idea that teachers should build upon the children's cultural background, the BIA employed a number of anthropologists to conduct summer school courses and in-service training sessions in selected locations. (Anthropologists also participated in the development of bilingual readers.)[67] At Crownpoint, it fell to Lucella M. King, who attended a summer institute taught by noted anthropologist Ruth Underhill, to translate the new philosophy into pedagogical practice. Speaking to teachers in one session, King emphasized, "The idea is not [to] make the Navajo into a Scotchman, Englishman, nor Dutchman, but rather to leave him alone and help him preserve the worthwhile in his own culture." To be sure, Navajo children must be prepared to live in the larger society. The Navajo people "must change with others year by year. It is inevitable as he comes in contact with other people and civilizations than his own." Meanwhile, teachers should build upon the children's background. As for the method of instruction, King strongly endorsed the importance of experience. "The experience method is to help people to help themselves by actually placing them in the various situations as presented by life's activities."[68]

It was a tall order, and the evidence suggests that teachers, even if convinced of the new approach, struggled to implement it. Probably their most successful effort in this regard was a unit on shelter—the so-called hogan project. In the fall of 1934, one teacher summarized her class's work. "The completion of the north Hogan has been the basis of [the] effort on the part of the children. The plastering of the exterior; the painting of the woodwork; putting another coat of plastering on the floor; cleaning the yard; and aiding with a new chimney; fixing the screens; making a stone walk has all been completed since the first of October by the boys." Meanwhile, the girls were working on making curtains for the interior. Consistent with the progressive idea of "expanding horizons," children also read about how other peoples of the world solved the problem of shelter, compared the differences between mud and stone houses, and considered the benefits of modern heating and lighting. Over the course of the unit, students compiled their findings in a booklet, kept a diary on related interests, and acquired new vocabulary. In an attempt to weave math into the unit, teachers taught hogan builders the importance of knowing how to measure and calculate the cost of building materials.[69]

Crownpoint teachers found other ways to implement the new philosophy. One teacher reported, "For my own experimentation, if I knew the Navajo word for an object or action, I told that to them first and then the English word. It seemed to me that the association helped them to remember some of the words." Another teacher brought a live turtle into class as the basis for a vocabulary and writing exercise. Older students studied the problem of erosion and overgrazing and then wrote paragraphs endorsing the government's soil-conservation and stock-reduction policies on the "Big Navajo" reservation. (This policy was controversial and generally opposed by the *Diné*.) Finally, there were moments when the boundaries between school and community collapsed. "Some of the children have learned kindness to others. A little boy's mother came to see us one day. I was busy serving and did not see her right away, but one of the little boys saw her sitting on the floor beside her son, so he brought her a chair. This same boy went to the cupboard and brought her a cup and spoon. She had lunch with us that day."[70]

In keeping with the idea that experience should be a central strand of children's expanding knowledge of the world, in 1937 Crownpoint's superintendent, Hugh Carroll, arranged for some twenty students—admittedly a small proportion of the student body—to take a whirlwind field trip to Southern California to witness firsthand the wonders of modern civilization. One of the students selected was Wilson Guerro, a young lad from Alamo. Like other sojourners, Wilson was asked to write a report on his experiences upon his return to Crownpoint. Still struggling with English, Wilson could barely express his excitement about riding the "Cyclone Racer," the famed Long Beach roller coaster that swept out over the shoreline of the Pacific Ocean. "We were going slow when we got to the top down we went and everybody were hollering and our eye were about to come out soon we stop and everybody were looked pail." Several of the boys, including Wilson, also went deep-sea fishing, where "we catch some fish and put it in the sack." Other adventures included visiting the zoo (where the animals "say hello" to their Indian visitors), a stopover at the planetarium for a closer view of the heavens, riding a department-store escalator, seeing a movie, and riding a streetcar. Passing through Nevada on the way home, "we came to the Dam we can see the people below as a little ant." One can only wonder how Wilson calculated his cultural self-esteem against the backdrop of one of modern civilization's engineering triumphs. He was a long way from home.[71]

Crownpoint's realization of the progressive promise fell short in three respects. First, it appears that few teachers had any real knowledge of Navajo culture, including language. It is revealing, for instance, that one of the teachers who attended Underhill's summer institute regretted that it was not possible "for each teacher to have reference material bearing directly" on the Navajo. Why not, she asked, provide the teachers opportunities to conduct "research work" in the summer, that is, "collect the material" relevant to their pedagogical aims?[72] Second, some teachers never embraced or understood the new educational outlook. Their confusion was evident in the minutes of a teachers' meeting in late 1934. Although some of the abbreviated comments clearly reflected progressive sentiments ("Build a Hogan and buy sewing machine" or "Get viewpoint of adult Indians"), other comments ("Have stronger discipline" or "Go back and teach phonics") reflected more traditional approaches. The minutes also reflected some confusion over the question of how much emphasis should be placed on bringing the children into the modern world. Thus, when one teacher defined her understanding of the new method as being "to improve life on the reservation" and "to make more profitable [the Navajos'] contact with their environment," King responded that the comment was "almost correct" and required clarification—namely that "the environment can be interpreted as more than a local one. It can be enlarged to include the state and the nation. Then those [Navajos] who are especially adapted to take . . . their places in the larger environment will receive the training which will help them in that [larger] environment."[73] Finally, as much as the new philosophy proclaimed to be a substantive change in orientation, for those Alamo Navajo children in attendance the Crownpoint experience was all too familiar in one important respect. Crownpoint, like the more distant schools, was still engaged in forced child removal, ripping children away from their families and community.

Response

So exactly how did Alamo Navajo children respond to life at boarding school? The subject is immensely complicated, but three broad categories are discernible: resistance, willing cooperation, and adaptive accommodation.[74] In considering these three patterns it is important to keep the following in mind. First, they were not mutually exclusive. Sometimes gradually, sometimes in whipsaw fashion, students could reassess their feelings about boarding school and how they should respond. Second, most Alamo Navajo children, after their acclimation to the regimen and stress of school life, were more than passive actors in the experience, and they frequently displayed remarkable resourcefulness and resiliency in the face of the institutions' efforts (especially in the early years) to achieve a cultural makeover of their Indian subjects. In that respect, it makes little sense to read the response of resistance as the sole definition of student agency, just as it makes little sense to read the response of adaptive accommodation, or even willing cooperation, as synonymous with surrendering to the institutions' objectives. At the same time, borderland regions, particularly when power relations are overwhelmingly one-directional, are thorn-ridden landscapes where the pathways both to identity maintenance and to psychological integrity can be terribly imperiled—especially for children. So it was for the Alamo Navajos.

Resistance manifested itself most dramatically in efforts to physically escape.[75] The decision to run was prompted by a combination of pull-push factors. Foremost among the former was the deep longing for family. There was so much to miss: the sight of a grandmother at her loom, a grandfather skinning a buck, the smell of a cookpot simmering with mutton stew, the winter hogan stories of the Holy People, the anticipation of a piñon-picking expedition—and yes, the daily chore of herding sheep. On the other side of the ledger: the endless regimentation, the stress of learning a new language, and the sting of the disciplinarian's strap. One boy ran away from Santa Fe when it dawned on him that while he was going to bed hungry every night, President Herbert Hoover "was just feeding his face."[76] Also, it appears that Alamo Navajo students, particularly boys, may have had an especially difficult time negotiating their relationship with students from the "Big Navajo" reservation, many of whom questioned their southern cousins' cultural credentials. Some Alamo Navajo students, for instance, remember being called *Tsé deałíí* ("Rock Chewer"), or descendants of the scorned *Diné Anaa'í* ("Enemy Navajo"), or being more Mexican or Apache than Navajo. One man says of the "Rock Eater" label, "I guess we were tougher than they were up there." Another dismisses the "Enemy Navajo" accusation with the comment that the northern students were simply "afraid of us." The Apache connection was, of course, true. One man says, "See we're part Apache. So that's why they didn't like us. So they fight us most of the time."[77] There were so many reasons to run.

Running away from Santa Fe could take four to five days, from Albuquerque three to four, and from Crownpoint two to three, depending on whether runaways were able to hitch a ride or find a place to layover and recoup their strength. As for direction, some headed for the Cañoncito Navajo community, where they might gain assistance. Those heading directly south from Santa Fe or Albuquerque followed the Rio Grande or used Ladron Mountain for orientation. Although both boys and girls ran, mainly boys did so. Indeed, one woman recalls that the truck leaving Alamo for Santa Fe was no more under way before "some boys were planning on running away."[78]

Parents understandably cautioned children against running. In addition to the fact that some elders saw the value of school, there were the dangers of children getting lost, dying of starvation or thirst, or suffering an accident. When news of missing children reached the reservation, family members easily imagined the worst. In January 1927, José Apache, with the assistance of a local rancher, wrote Burton I. Smith, superintendent at Santa Fe, that his daughter at the school had written home that one of his four grandchildren had recently run away. After expressing his concern, Apache went on to say that, as a former policeman, he could be counted upon to immediately return the boy if he showed up. As for the present policeman, Apache added, he was terribly neglectful of his responsibilities, having done nothing to return five runaways at large on the reservation. As for his own son, Charley Apache, "tell him that we expect him to stay there and do the very best and always be obedient to the one in charge." A few days later, Apache received word from Superintendent Smith that the grandchild he had originally inquired about had indeed "deserted from this school some time ago and had not returned." Anything Apache could do to return the boy, or for that matter, the other deserters, would be welcomed. As for his son Charley, he was doing just fine, and his father's message had been passed on to him. Meanwhile, José Apache was left with the knowledge that his grandson was absent from the school and had not yet returned to Alamo. Where might the boy be? Was he alive? Such were the thoughts that troubled parents' and grandparents' minds.[79]

Many of the runaway attempts were aborted either because escapees had second thoughts and turned back or because of capture. Manual Guerro and four other boys, for instance, planned their escape from Albuquerque for two weeks, including hiding food to sustain them for the journey. But on the appointed day, they got only as far as the Rio Grande when Manual began to reconsider the wisdom of the whole enterprise. What stuck in his mind was his father's admonition never to run away: it was too dangerous. So after the other boys crossed the river, Manual announced that he was turning back. The others made it home four days later, although just barely.[80]

A good number of escape attempts were foiled by school officials. One boy almost made it back to Alamo before a horseback Navajo policeman overtook him. In another instance, two runaways were caught on the banks of the Rio Grande. The boys had just reached the bridge crossing the river when they caught sight of a horse and buggy in the distance. Correctly surmising that the driver was "hunting for our tracks," the two hid in some bushes some distance from the road, only to be snatched minutes later. On another occasion a Navajo family foiled a runaway attempt from Crownpoint by seven girls—five from Cañoncito and two from Alamo. On the first night they made it to a "friendly lady's house" where they were given food and a warm place to sleep. The next morning the girls passed by a Navajo couple's hogan. When the husband ascertained that the girls were runaways, he offered to take them by wagon as far as Laguna Pueblo, which would reduce considerably the distance of their journey. Meanwhile, he gave the girls some milk cans and directed them to "get our own breakfast" by milking his goats. Delaying the promised wagon ride, the man managed to notify school authorities of the girls' whereabouts. Shortly, Indian policemen arrived and returned the girls to school.[81]

Others were more successful, although the journey was terribly difficult, especially when the runaways miscalculated the distance to be traversed. One man recalls he was one of four boys who ran away from Albuquerque. His motive for running was common enough: "It was hard for me being far away from my relatives. I use to miss my relatives a lot." Operating under the misconception that they could reach Alamo in a single day, the escapees gave no thought to taking provisions. In addition to having no matches for a fire, "none of us didn't took our jacket with us." At day's end, the surge of hunger and thirst swept over them. Then the temperature plunged sharply, exposing them to the bone-chilling cold of the high New Mexico desert. (This was precisely the kind of nightmarish scenario parents—and for that matter, school officials as well—imagined might befall runaway children.) The details of the rest of the journey are not clear, but miraculously, all four made it to Alamo on the third day.[82]

The most graphic account of a successful runaway comes from Norman Secatero, who ran off from Albuquerque with three other boys sometime in the mid-1940s. These runaways had sense enough to wear jackets but failed to pack any provisions. Making good time, by nightfall on the first day they had reached a canyon on the outskirts of Las Lunas. With the temperature dropping to near freezing, "we dug a little hole in there, maybe 4 by 6 feet. We used our jackets to cover the opening, . . . and that's where we spent the night, in that little hole." Unknown to the group, as they huddled in the pit, radio stations were sending out bulletins across the state: be on the lookout for four Indian boys who had run away from school and might be lost and half-frozen.[83]

The next morning, the four set out again. After the sun took the chill away, they began to think about water and food. Fortunately, they soon happened upon a spring covered by a layer of ice. Breaking through the ice, they discovered the water was too salty to drink, so they settled for sucking on the chunks of ice, which had not absorbed the salt. Now they were walking again but terribly hungry. It was then that they caught sight of a spotted calf, their route having taken them across ranchland. Because the rancher was nowhere in sight, and because they had all observed sheep being butchered, the calf appeared to be the answer to their hunger. But catching the calf was harder than it looked. "We ran that calf all over the place, and that calf just run off from us. Damn, we'd throw rocks and hit him all over the place and he was just still goin'. Never did kill him." Later that day, they saw a rock house, perhaps belonging to the same rancher who had nearly lost a calf. Keeping their distance, they observed the man working cattle in the corral, and then they saw him drive them about a quarter of a mile down a hidden draw. This was their chance. "We just ran into that house. We grabbed anything that we could out of the refrigerator." In a matter of minutes, they pilfered pork, chili, cold biscuits, eggs, a one-gallon coffee can, and some matches. With the makings of a meal in hand, they make a rapid retreat. But rather than risk a cook fire so close to the house, they only ate the cold biscuits before continuing their journey south. By day's end, they climbed a rise from which they recognized the distinctive geographic features of Alamo. But they could go no farther. Exhausted, famished, and afraid of losing their way in the dark, they made camp. Building a fire, they mixed their stolen provisions in the coffee can and proceeded to make a stew that was barely edible. "Without thinking of it, those guys, they just cut up all of the chili in there, and man, that chili was HOT. We didn't have no water or anything. Just ruined it, but we had to eat it." After the fire died down, they bedded down for a second night under a wintery sky. In the morning they found themselves covered with two inches of snow. "I don't know why we didn't freeze."

It took all of the third day to reach the outskirts of Alamo, where they were given a ride by two men who delivered them to Norman's home. The anguish-stricken family had feared the worst: "They put our names over the radio. Everybody was listening." After a joyful reunion, Norman's mother "just chewed us out. She thought we was stupid." So after a couple days home, all four boys were taken back to Albuquerque, where they were reminded why they had run off in the first place. "I guess the reason why we ran away from school was some of the guys from the other reservation were fighting us all the time, picking on us. Just because we were the Alamo people, I guess. They thought we don't belong to . . . the big reservation or to the Navajo tribe."

Punishments for running away were designed to publicly demean the guilty party and to dissuade other students from making escapes. One woman recalls the humiliation she experienced when forced to wear pants for a time. Another woman remembers when she and fellow deserters were forced to stand against a wall all night; every time one of the girls started to slip down from exhaustion, her legs were whipped with a belt. "The next day we just went to class without any sleep." Undeterred by the treatment, two of the girls ran off again and "never came back." In addition to forcing boys to wear skirts for a period, disciplinarians had other measures they could inflict.

> To tell you the truth, they were pretty mean. They take us back over there. There were logs about a foot thick and 4 feet long. And there was a square at Albuquerque Indian School. On Saturday afternoon they line us up over there and they call our names, the ones that run off. And they put them logs right on our shoulders. And we have to carry them around pretty near all day around the school grounds. When the bigger boys ran off, they put a chain around their legs and then they have to walk around pretty near all day.[84]

Escape did not always entail heading for home. Recall the story of the two boys who hid out for weeks scavenging for food until the one contracted pneumonia and ended up in the hospital. Sometimes runaways slipped away only for a few hours at night, usually for the purpose of stealing food. "During the night," one man remembers, "some boys and I would get together and sneak out of the dormitory . . . to pick apples, grapes, and even chili. We are hungry for things like this. We had to go about one to five miles away from the school campus just to have a piece of fruit." As one can imagine, there were some close calls. On one of these forays, one of the raiders had just filled his shirt with apples, when "pretty soon we hear the dog. I guess they sicked the dog on us. I just run through the wire [fence] and it tear my shirt and I lost all the apples." But on other occasions "we steal apples and peaches and we never afraid to get shot at. I guess they would have shot us too. We steal watermelon and everything." Surely the subtlest and safest way of running away was to imagine the act without ever acting on it. For these students, merely *thinking* about escape provided the psychological satisfaction that the institution had not entirely worn down their capacity for resistance and agency. One wonders how many Alamo Navajo students, like two girls at another school, periodically plotted running away, always ending with the decision "to wait a day or so."[85]

Boarding school histories tell us that Indian students resisted the system in ways other than escape, among them arson, mimicking and nicknaming school employees, holding surreptitious nighttime meetings, and speaking their tribal language. Interestingly, there is no mention of these in Alamo Navajo recollections. Nor is there any mention of passive resistance, one of the most difficult resistance strategies to detect in the historical record. One wonders, for instance, how many Alamo Navajo students were thinking what Navajo students in another school were thinking when they composed this group poem.

> If I do not believe you
> The things you say,
> Maybe I will not tell you
> That is my way
>
> Maybe you think I believe you
> That thing you say,
> But always my thoughts stay with me
> My own way.[86]

Some Alamo Navajos adopted a second manner of response: willing cooperation. The fact is, some—albeit a minority—Alamo Navajo children looked upon boarding school as a generally positive development in their lives. "In school we were taken care of," one man says. "Shoes, pants, and shirt were furnished. Also the laundry was done for us. We had baths regularly and were dressed neatly at all times. So, for this reason I enjoyed being at school." Another man claims, "They feed us real good. They take care of us real good." Moreover, "I felt I wanted to learn some things in the white man's way. . . . I was not the only one who felt that way. There were a lot of us." As for the discipline and the occasional spankings, "I'm glad they whip me" because the school was dedicated to "learn us the right way." When he, along with other students, was transferred to Crownpoint, he found the change a great disappointment, partly because the "no speaking Navajo" rule was no longer strict policy. He felt cheated. How else was he going to learn English?[87]

For Gilbert Guerro boarding school was a godsend. In addition to the fact that he had always wanted to go to school, and that it had lifted him out of abject poverty, two aspects of his thinking are notable. First, Gilbert came to the conclusion early on during the experience that cultural identity was an either-or proposition. He seems to have drawn this conclusion from the words of one elder who said to him: "When you go over that hill, over the mountain, that's white man's life. . . . That's white man's territory. When you go over there, you'll never come back. Your mind will be different. You'll be different. . . . The way they live, the way they talk, the way they think, the way they work, the way they do things. That's not yours, that's for the white man." So it appeared. When Gilbert returned to Alamo one summer he felt he "was living two lives." At home he was forced to speak and live in the traditional way; at boarding school he was expected to live in the white man's way. At some point, he decided that he must choose one or the other. What appears to have tipped his decision to choose the *biligáana* path was his hospital experiences—being successfully treated for tonsillitis and trachoma. However traumatic the two surgeries were at the time, the doctors

> made me well when they took my tonsils out. They stopped it. I don't have no sore throat. They was good. Would the medicine man do it? Will my people do it? That's what I'm thinking about. They cure my eyes. If I was living on the reservation, I could have been blind. . . . I compared these things. But would the medicine man make me well, cure my eye disease? No. So I compared these both. Okay, I take this one because the white man is right. He proved to me through the sight that is the right place to go.[88]

Other students did not see the choices so narrowly.

Most Alamo students appear to have adopted a third category of response—adaptive accommodation—which constituted a sort of a middle way or in-betweenness. Three aspects of this response are notable. First, after they got beyond the traumas of removal and institutional induction, many could begin to weigh the positive and negative aspects of the experience. Against the negatives of being cut off from home and community, the regimentation, the chores, and the institution's assault on their identities, there were also the positives: a degree of material and nutritional security; the opportunity to learn something about the wider world, including English; the pleasures of participating in extracurricular activities; and surely, the experience of getting to know other "Indians"—even perhaps those from the "Big Navajo." For these students, then, boarding school was a "mixed bag" of negatives and positives. A second factor contributing to this response was the fact that for some the urge to rebel was often an intermittent one. Over the course of a year, a month, or even a single day, a student might experience any number of conflicting emotions—rage, loneliness, humiliation, frustration, but also feelings of satisfaction, accomplishment, even joy. One woman who ran away from Crownpoint reflects, "I don't know why I decided to run away. Being away from home didn't bother me until one of the matron spanks me with leather or spanks me with a stick on my hands, that's when I get lonely and feel like being home." Otherwise, she says, she enjoyed being at school.[89] Finally, there were practical reasons for accommodation. Even if you wanted to run for home, there were good reasons not to. Aside from the punishments in store, one had to consider the prospect of getting lost. There were other terrors as well. "I never did run away because I thought some wild animal might eat me up," one woman admits. Other children reasoned that if they made it home, their parents would simply return them to the school again. Indeed, they were legally bound to do so. "The matron used to tell us that if we ran away and not return to school, our parents will be put in jail."[90] Better to stick it out.

Home Again

Whatever their disposition toward school, nearly all children looked forward to coming home. As the months rolled by, and May turned to June, Norman Secatero recalls:

> You'd be happy and jumping around all over the place and you'd clean up your room and pack up. . . . You'll have everything packed up and ready to go, just waiting for somebody to say LET'S GO—let's go home. So for about two days you can hardly sleep, just waiting to go home. When we come home, we have a really happy feeling. Just run all over the place, visit people—your grandma, your grandpa, and the relatives. You're running all over the place, riding horseback. Just spend the night there and here. Run around with your friends. That's how it used to be.[91]

José Guerro, having nearly died at school, was especially glad to be going home. He remembers it was in spring, when he could see the corn ripening in the school garden, that "they told us we were going home." He and another boy hitched a ride to Cañoncito, another to the Fields' store, and finally to the area where he remembered his parents living.

> We came to a cornfield. We were walking toward the cornfield when we notice in the distance there was a hogan where a small woman was yelling and motioning her arms at us. I guess people had been stealing her corn, and she thought we were going to steal her corn. As we got closer to the hogan the woman was still standing there. It was my grandmother, my mother's mom. I recognized her. She couldn't recognize us. When we got to her hogan, we told her who we were. She was so happy and cried. She said, "Oh it's you, the ones that left a long time ago." She told us where our father lived. She told us that we can't go there by

ourselves. She said, "Vicente will take you home because the dogs are mean." So we walk home with Vicente.[92]

After years of being away, many returned students were successfully reintegrated into Alamo Navajo community life—a world of arranged marriages, extended kinship networks, herding livestock, fence building, jewelry making, rug weaving, chapter meetings, and summer fiestas. Many returnees also assumed leadership positions and succeeded in "turning the power" of their boarding school education to the furtherance of community interests: expanding the reservation land base, improving roads and transportation, increasing federal aid in the form of programs for health and housing, and finally, securing (under terms of the "self-determination" movement in the 1970s) their own school.[93] Others, however, had a more difficult time of it, their lives eaten up by dire poverty and alcoholism. Whatever the course of returnees' lives, the boarding school experience had a profound impact on them. How could it not? Still, most survived the experience with a keen sense of their Indian identities. They were still Alamo Navajos.

But a few knew almost immediately they could not remain at home. When Benjamin Apache (whose parents, recall, were swept away in the 1918–1919 influenza epidemic) returned to Alamo after several years of schooling, he was stung by some elders' derisive laughter at his efforts to speak Navajo, now a language almost beaten out of him. His uncle wanted him to stay, but after months of Benjamin's begging, the old man finally allowed him to return to school. Gilbert Guerro was another one who knew his life lay elsewhere. The boy who had once dreamed of going away to boarding school was not going back to a life of poverty and sheepherding. Still, he would never shake the memory of where life's journey had begun in 1913.

> Where I was born, that tree still stands. Still living. I went back over there many times where I was born, right here in Alamo country. And I was always afraid that someone might cut the tree or burn it. Something might happen. But one day when I came back from school, I made the trademark on the tree, made the year I was born. Within a few years that tree went back together, growed together, so you can't see now. Every year it grows about this much—finally disappeared.

With his initials and year of his birth swallowed up by the tree, Gilbert painted the same marks on a large rock that he placed next to the tree. "So that's still there." Then he adds plaintively, "I don't know why I done it."[94]

Years later, Gilbert must have wondered whether anyone would remember what the rock signified, or how long the markings could withstand the blasts of sun and wind, just as in an earlier time the tree had stretched its bark over his youthful carvings. Would there be anyone to tell the story?

Day School

In the early 1930s, Alamo parents were already pressing for a day school, and in July 1934 John Collier, commissioner of Indian affairs, endorsed the idea. It would take some time to actually build and furnish the school, he explained, but he saw no reason a teacher could not be sent to Alamo "for taking care of the children in the meantime." Surely, "if the Indians can live down there a teacher could too." Although there is no evidence a teacher did indeed precede construction of the school, the day school was up and running in two years.[95] In 1950, two small dormitories were added, making it a combination day and boarding school, although the latter was a miniature facsimile of the Crownpoint model.[96] Determining the number of children in attendance at the day school, or later the boarding school component, is no easy matter. A 1940 school census, for instance, records some sixty-seven children enrolled, whereas another shows a mere forty-three, the latter probably the more accurate number because it is more consistent with the teacher's quarterly reports. On a given day any number of students might not show up.[97]

Although the school was technically primary through eighth grade, in fact, nearly all were in the lower grades. (Older students continued to attend schools off the reservation.) The daily routine was simple enough. The emphasis was mainly on acclimating children to the concept of school itself, teaching them the importance of cleanliness, and introducing them to the three r's. Younger children spent considerable time playing. "In the classroom small children just played with puzzle or Lincoln logs and clay," one woman remembers. "The teacher never paid much attention to us younger ones. Maybe because there were too many of us." Another woman says that at day school she learned to say "yes" and "no" and to sing "The Morning Bells Are Ringing." In 1940, when progressive practices were at their highest, Dorothy Ryan, the teacher, reported, "A Navajo rug project was started by the girls. Four beautiful rugs were made—two small ones and two large ones. They will be sold to purchase supplies for use in rug weaving, after they are exhibited at the state fair in September." A school garden was also under way.[98]

Dorothy Ryan and mostly parents at Alamo Navajo day school, 1940. (Courtesy of John Guerro.)

One can only wonder if the children ever encountered the *Little Herder* series authored by Ann Clark and illustrated by Navajo artist Hoke Denetsosie, a set of four elementary bilingual texts that offered a touching affirmation of traditional culture. In one of the four readers, *Little Herder in Winter,* for instance, the family attends a "sing," or religious ceremony.

Now is the time
for the singing.
Now is the time
for the songs.
We go,
we go,
on the Holy Trail of Song.
We go,
we go,
to hear the voices of the Gods.

Given the influence of the nearby Baptist mission, it is doubtful that these texts ever saw the light of day at Alamo.[99]

In 1949 an anthropology student from the University of New Mexico observed the day school and found much to criticize. Given the Navajos' traditional avoidance of public embarrassment and shaming, he questioned whether the teacher's practice of employing individual competition was good pedagogy. The practice was to encourage students to shout out English words on teacher-held flash cards. The child who gave the quickest correct response was allowed to hold the next card as a reward. For slower students, he surmised, the method could mean nothing but humiliation. He also wondered about the texts being used. "They are the Dick and Jane series . . . designed for English-speaking students, which most of the students are not. The books deal with things [such] as telephones, streetcars, buses, and a host of other things and customs, which must seem strangely unreal to them, but are nonetheless instructive of this other world, even if somewhat uselessly so." Also problematic was the school's relationship with the nearby Baptist church: "Two years ago, the missionary herself was the teacher, and by one account was a religious zealot. The present teacher, when she first took the job, found large quantities of religious literature in the 'school.' All this prompted the observation that, although the missionaries certainly had a right to propagate the faith, they should remain in their 'own domain.'"[100]

Noteworthy—indeed, ironic—is that many students who attended the Alamo school experienced the same loneliness as those sent off the reservation in an earlier time. Some of this can be explained by the fact that for some the day school, after 1950, also functioned as a quasi–boarding school. Still, both day and boarding students had mostly negative feelings about the experience. The memories are vivid: hating the food, throwing up on lunch trays, and being dragged into the bathroom for washing up; having the matron (a local woman) "poke her index finger in my eye" as a punishment for not sleeping during naptime; and being made to stand in the corner for some indiscretion. One of the few positive comments is from a woman who remembers how her grandmother gave the matron a stern lecture that she was not to cut her granddaughter's long hair but simply braid it, how the *same* grandmother gave the matron another tongue-lashing for unjustly punishing her granddaughter, how the *same* grandmother saved her from a father's whipping when she ran away from school, and finally how the *same* grandmother urged her to bust out of the pickup when she was being returned to school—"So we did. I kick the door handle and broke it." As one listens to these stories, one wonders how common the following sentiment was: "All I wanted to do was go home and herd sheep."[101]

Still, the school afforded children more opportunity than had those at Albuquerque or Santa Fe to see their parents. The trading post—within view of the school—was abuzz with adults coming in to pick up mail and purchase groceries. But there again was an irony. For those boarding, the periodic glimpse of family members at the store seems only to have made the separation even worse. Home was so close, yet so far. One woman says her thoughts at school were constantly on home, her most comforting vision that of riding alongside her grandfather in his wagon, the old man working the reins as he sang a favorite Navajo song. "He sounded happy, and it always made me happy." Another girl was constantly on the watch for her parents making a visit to the trading post. "The minute I see them I would run to the door and cry out real loud." After a brief visit, she was carried back to school crying. Similarly, one man remembers, "The happiest memory of my childhood was when my parents came to see me."[102]

Several factors seem to have undermined the day/boarding school's effectiveness. Again, there was the confusion over mission. During the Collier years the day school was conceived as an educational space where Indian children's introduction to the wider world would be a gentle bicultural journey. But as we have seen in the instance of Crownpoint, translating this progressive vision into pedagogical practice was no easy matter. It must have been all the more challenging for a single teacher at a remote location such as Alamo. Not surprisingly, teacher turnover was high. Second, the rhythms of the Alamo economy inevitably interfered with the school's effectiveness—such as it was. In late February 1943, the teacher reported, "Nearly 75% of the Navajos are working away from here. Many are still in the mountains gathering piñons and will not be back until April. [I] have had to drop fourteen from roll during present quarter." Third, the dispersed settlement patterns worked against steady day school attendance, especially during periods of inclement weather. On the other side, for boarders thinking of escape, the location of the school put home within striking distance. Runaways were common. Finally some parents were still deeply conflicted on how much education their children really needed, especially females. Next to the names of her girl students, the teacher sometimes scribbled the reasons for nonattendance: "Works at home," or "Herds sheep." But it was not just a matter of gender. One man recalls, "Every day lots of Navajo children walk to school but as for me I only herd sheeps, eat, and sleep while other Navajo children are learning Anglo language." Eventually, he was enrolled at the day school and later moved on to Albuquerque. But it was a slow beginning.[103]

By 1959, then, the Alamo Navajos had experienced several models of Indian schooling: the off-reservation boarding school, the reservation boarding school, and the combination day/boarding school. But another model was still in the offing. Indeed, 1959 would constitute a major turning point in the education of the Alamo Navajo children—and for that matter, a major watershed in the education of Anglo and Hispanic children as well.

PART THREE

PASTS AND PROMISES

CHAPTER SEVEN

TOGETHER AND APART

In some respects it was an old story. Six-year-old Peter Ganadonegro was at home with his mother when a "strange orange vehicle" drove up the dirt road to his family's dwelling. He noticed with surprise

> that there were some kids about the same age as I was that were sitting in the bus. Some of them I believe were crying. My mom went out to see what they wanted. Then about ten or fifteen minutes she came back inside and told me to put on some decent clothes, wash my face, and brush my hair. Then I asked her why she wanted me to get ready. She told me that I was going down to school in Magdalena. Then I asked her why but the only answer she gave me was you just have to go cause that's the way it is. By this time I was crying, begging my mom to tell the man who was driving the strange yellow vehicle to go away because I didn't wanna go with them cause I was never away from my parents. But still I had to go. I was screaming and kicking but they finally made me get on the strange vehicle. Some of the kids were laughing at me but some were still crying. The ones that were crying started to cry even harder. . . . When I got on the bus I was crying still but after we left from my house I looked back and gave my house the last look. Because I knew I was gonna be gone for a while. After we drove about 5 miles I went to sleep on the bus cause I got tired of crying.[1]

Peter's story has the familiar heart-wrenching element: the traumatic separation of the child from his parents, then being swept off to an uncertain future. But in this instance the destination is all-important and marks a pointed shift in Bureau of Indian Affairs (BIA) education policy. For Peter is not being taken away to a distant boarding school but just 30 miles away to the pink stucco dormitories built in 1959 on the southwest edge of Magdalena. Ten months of the year he will live in these dormitories and attend the Magdalena schools.

By the mid-1950s the "peripheral town dormitory program" (more commonly called the "bordertown program") was emerging as yet another model for educating Navajos, although by necessity limited to those communities located near Anglo towns such as Magdalena. Under the existing system, the BIA admitted, Navajo children were being inadequately prepared for life beyond the reservation. For most, Standard English remained a "foreign language," hardly a recipe for earning a living in the Anglo world.[2] The new model appealed to Alamo Navajo parents for two reasons. First, it enabled more frequent contact with their children. Second, integrated schools promised greater educational opportunities than they had experienced in all-Indian settings. (By 1959 only one Alamo Navajo had graduated from high school.) It followed that members of the Alamo Navajo community voted overwhelmingly on September 6, 1957, to enroll their children in the border town program. Two years later the dormitory facilities were up and running and by 1960 accommodated 128 children. By the end of the decade, an expansion of facilities brought enrollment up to more than 250. A new chapter in the education of the Alamo Navajos had begun.[3]

Magdalena had its own reasons for welcoming the Alamo Navajos. Probably foremost among these was the infusion of federal dollars into the school system in the form of per capita payments for Indian children. Local merchants also saw the economic advantage of having Indian students in the community, the older ones presumably having some spending money. However, one cannot entirely discount philanthropic motives. In the late 1940s Loraine Reynolds, the younger sister of Ray Morley and Agnes Morley Cleaveland, took up the cause of the Alamo Navajos' plight. Living in Datil, Reynolds pressed the case for increasing the Alamo land base, made periodic deliveries of food and clothing to the reservation, lobbied locals to hire Alamo Navajo workers at a fair wage, and argued for the larger community's moral obligation to lift their Navajo neighbors out of poverty. Although there is no evidence that Reynolds specifically supported the border town program, her strongly held belief that the Alamo Navajo people must be brought into closer association with the outside world—including having more than a crude understanding of English—suggests that she looked favorably on the development.[4]

For the children of all three groups the introduction of the Alamo Navajos into the Magdalena schools was arguably the most important development in their lives in the post–World War II era. To be sure, other forces during this period affected their coming-of-age experience, but the entry of the Indians into a social space that up to 1959 was of Anglo-Hispanic construction was a watershed development. Until 1959 the boundaries of power and hierarchy in the Magdalena schools had been drawn on a largely bicultural plane. Over the years Anglos and Hispanics had gotten to know each other up close, and although relations between the two were still often conflict-ridden, things had improved. Meanwhile, Hispanics had made major strides in the academic sphere. The arriving Navajos, on the other hand, had largely experienced the outside world from afar, either from behind reservation boundaries or in the segregated institutions of Albuquerque, Santa Fe, and Crownpoint. Now, all this was about to change. Magdalena was now a tri-ethno-cultural community, a new world in the making.

Dormitory Life

Though the Magdalena dormitories were only 30 miles from Alamo, for the younger children being torn away from their parents, the experience was still traumatic. One sympathetic dormitory staff member remembers the scene. "We would see kids screaming and holding onto the pickups because they didn't want to go in the door, and the parents would have to pry 'em loose and take 'em in crying." Peter Ganadonegro, after being carried away on the "yellow vehicle," recollects that only two children were crying when the bus pulled up to the dormitory.

> I found the dorm very interesting.... It was nice, clean, and neat. There was a lot of children there but some were half as old as I was. At first this one lady separated all of us and asked us what our names were in Navajo. Then finally it was time to eat, so we all were told to wash our hands and get in a straight line, so we did and went outside to this place where they prepare food for us to eat. At first I was scared but in a few hours I got use to it. We all had to learn new things there like how to get our trays, how to eat, what the silverwares were called, where to go when you needed the restroom, and lots of new things I didn't know.

At the day's end, Peter says, "I guess I was still crying when I went to sleep." He was not the only one. "Everybody was homesick, and we heard crying from the younger children," one Alamo Navajo woman recalls.[5] At day's end, when darkness drew down on the buildings and the children were put to bed, the sobs of the distraught filtered out into the halls and night beyond. Because the dormitories were constructed just below the stone-faced mountain image of St. Mary Magdalene, one can only wonder if she took notice of this new chapter in the town's history. There is no record of it.

Morning brought its own terrors and revelations. Some younger children awoke to urine-soaked sheets. (These students were singled out for a special shower and would have to wash the soiled bedding after school.) So the structure of institutional life unfolded as the dormitory principal and a small staff, including two supervisors—one for the boys and one for the girls—inducted the children into the disciplined order that would govern much of their lives. By strict schedule children were awakened each morning to dress, brush their teeth, comb their hair, and eat breakfast. "The girls were required to wear their hair in braids," one Alamo woman recalls. "We were not allowed to wear it down or else we would have it cut." After the morning routine, "we can walk to school with our friends." At the end of the day, school clothes were discarded for jeans, which were standard issue. The day was rounded out with watching television, playing outside, arts and crafts, study hall (for the older students), an evening meal, night roll call, and showers. By one staff member's account, "Poor little kids, the six-year-olds had never seen running water or a shower. You couldn't get 'em under that water. The little ones, we had to herd 'em in there with a washcloth and soap. . . . We'd grab one and put 'em under and they'd go AAH! AHH!" A female supervisor of the smaller boys recalls, "They wanted to play . . . you'd make 'em strip, and you'd see one jumping from bed to bed with no clothes on." At this point she was grateful to have the help of the older boys, who wrestled them into bed. At 10 o'clock it was lights out.[6]

As with the Santa Fe and Albuquerque Indian Schools, assigned chores were part of institutional life. Weekends were a time for older students to clean the dorms, and throughout the week there were beds to be made, socks to be washed, and other assigned duties to be performed. One housemother (a BIA Indian employee) was reportedly "wicked as a witch. She slaved us around. We just don't have any free time of any kind. . . . Sometimes I wanted to walk out of that dorm. But I didn't know where to go."[7]

In the early years, two of the supervisors were clearly caring and sensitive employees. Alamo-born and long-term BIA employee Frank Apachito certainly falls into this category. So does a local Hispanic woman who, in heartfelt sympathy for the children, admits to periodically breaking out in tears over the scenes she witnessed. But the system also produced its share of abuse. The girls' supervisor—a Pueblo woman identified above as the "witch," who also acquired the nickname "Monkey Lady"—had an array of techniques for forcing children into line. To be sure, establishing order and discipline in an institutional environment was a challenging undertaking, but "Monkey Lady" seems to have gained a perverse satisfaction in forcing disobedient children to sit in the corner with clothespins clamped to their ears, washing their mouths out with soap, or pinching children in their beds at night for failing to fall asleep. "Even in the dining room you had to break your bread in fours. If you didn't the matron would hit you in the head with her knuckles."[8]

Living under the supervision of a "housefather"—described by one former student as "mean like a bull"—was also no picnic. Indeed, one woman recalls how after he caught children running away, "he started spanking us with his belt buckle. We had bruises all over our legs." Although supervisors were officially forbidden from striking students, this same employee later explained to me the frustration he felt having to manage so many children. Listen to his account of what it was like rounding up two busloads of older students at the end of a field trip to the New Mexico State Fair, made all the more difficult because an older Alamo Navajo male not in school, Clifford Guerro, had driven a car to the fair to meet up with his girlfriend, Brenda Herrera (pseudonyms). After dark the two bus drivers began searching for those students who failed to show up at the appointed time. Most were on the buses, he explains,

> but we had other kids that hadn't come back, and I went to gathering 'em. I had 'em all but Brenda. I went to get her, and she was in the car with Clifford. She was about seventeen, so I said, "Get in there, let's go." So I gathered her up, took her back, loaded her in the bus. In the meantime two more had got away from us. I went and got 'em. I come back, and SHE had gone. I went back and got her before she got to the parking lot, brought her back. By that time it must have been 1 o'clock or so. Anyway, then I had to go and look for someone else, come back, and SHE was gone. I didn't catch her, so we left without her. And she never went back to school. She married Clifford.[9]

It was not all misery. After the children adjusted to their surroundings, they found there were pleasures to be had. For smaller children, playtime, television, new friendships, and the occasional movie were all diversions from the pangs of homesickness and the regime of dormitory life. Older students found pleasure in having more freedom to choose their clothing and the opportunity to participate in school activities. After 1962 the nearby Baptist Indian Mission, in addition to offering religious services, sponsored Saturday morning activities such as ping pong, softball, horseshoes, and volleyball. By the 1970s nearly all children had Save the Children sponsors who provided them a few dollars to spend at the dorm canteen and local business establishments. Another welcome development was more opportunities to visit home. In the early years home visits only occurred over the summer months and extended holidays, but the paving of the road to Alamo in 1967 and the growing number of parents who owned pickup trucks made weekend visits more frequent. After her father acquired his first pickup, one woman remembers, the family spent occasional weekends together picking piñon. For these children dorm life was bearable, even enjoyable. "We were anxious to get back to the dorm to bathe and wash our clothes," one woman recalls. "Also the dorm had TV and activities. It was good to be with friends."[10]

But it could be a painful journey getting to this point, and for some it never came. One woman, whose parents were off building fences somewhere in Colorado, remembers breaking out in fits of sobbing when she saw other parents come to pick up their children, knowing full well she would be left behind. She was not alone in this memory. Another says she stayed two years at the dorm without a single home visit. Although sympathetic staff members sometimes volunteered to take children left behind into their homes, such well-intentioned efforts were seldom a substitute for home. Indeed, when the stretches of separation were especially long, the despair could be overwhelming. Clara Monte, for instance, found herself constantly thinking about her grandmother and "how my grandfather use to hold me in his arms and sang a song to make me go asleep." Just as she was beginning to adjust to dormitory life, she was called to the office and told that her beloved grandmother had died. "I started crying. I was thinking to myself, where will I go when school is out. But still, my grandpa's still living." After pulling herself together, she knew what she must now do: inform all her relatives at the dorm of the old woman's passing. By another woman's account, "I always thinking about my family. Sometimes it seem like I'm nothing."[11]

With the reservation only 30 miles away, both boys and girls lit out for Alamo. Plans were both hastily constructed and elaborately planned. Younger children, because of their inability to keep up with older escapees, were generally excluded from runaway plots. One woman remembers that when her older sister ran, "she would tell me to stay behind because I couldn't run fast enough."[12] Timing was important. Some left after breakfast on the way to school. Others planned night escapes, a more promising strategy because it provided a window of several hours before being discovered missing. By morning they would have already scampered up the arroyo, crossed the highway, and been well on their way home. The usual route was to follow a path parallel to the road to Alamo, being careful to stay out of view of the dormitory employees now surely searching for them.

Back at the dormitory, the minute children went missing there was a flurry of activity as searchers made ready to track and overtake the runaways. Unlike days of old, when the path of escape was less predictable, now it was more certain. Moreover, parents could also be notified more easily. Still, so much could go wrong, particularly in winter. There was the time, for instance, that three small girls set out for home on the eve of a snowstorm. The trackers were especially alarmed when they discovered two tennis shoes; one of the girls had literally walked out of her shoes in 6 inches of snow. All three girls made it halfway to Alamo before capture. In fact, most runaways were captured before reaching home. One girl remembers how she and two other girls ran into a gathering of "big cows" with enormous horns. When the cows began moving toward them, they climbed a tree and remained there until after dark, when it appeared to be safe to climb down and continue their journey. By the time they struck Barty Henderson's ranch, just outside the reservation line, the trio was desperately "cold and hungry." Then they saw the headlights of the dormitory truck. Within the hour they were back in their dormitory beds.[13]

Just as members of an earlier generation of parents dreaded the news that their children were missing from boarding school, so Alamo Navajo parents, many of whom had either attempted escape or contemplated it years earlier, now worried over the fate of their own children. When a BIA truck pulled up to the hogan of Peter Ganadonegro's parents, the driver explained how Peter had run away with three other boys. The others had been captured, he explained, but Peter, a fast runner, had managed to outrun the trackers. They should keep an eye out for him. Little did the driver or his parents know that Peter was observing the whole scene from a distant hilltop. When the truck left, he descended from his lookout and spent time with his much-relieved parents—until the truck returned to retrieve him, as he knew it would. In this instance the planning had been especially elaborate. The night before striking out, the four had gone back for "seconds" at dinner, the extra food stashed away as provisions. After midnight Peter stole down the hall to make sure the night monitor was occupied. Observing that she was busy mending clothing, he found the coast clear for climbing out of a window and breaking for the arroyo.[14]

Runaways had a much better chance of making it home than those who took flight from Santa Fe or Albuquerque, but as this man's account illustrates things could still go wrong:

My third time I ran away was winter. It was during lunchtime that we decided to run away. We ran and walk trying to go faster so we can at least go halfway before sunset. We spend the night about 6 miles away from the reservation. We help each other go get wood for the night. We spent the night took turns to watch if the fire was going. Two of us have to sleep for two hours. I was the first. And the other watch the fire and I was last. I went to sleep and the fire went out. By that time I thought it was about 4 or 5 o'clock a.m. It was cold with frost on the ground and on us. I wake up and I was half-frozen to death. I look around. I saw the ground was white. The others on the ground like a ball. They were not even moving and the fire died out. I tried to get up and tried to build a fire. My hands were stiff and I was cold. It took me about one hour to build a fire. I tried to call the boys and tried to move them. They were alive, but not strong to get up to help me. But finally . . . they were warm enough to move around and then we set [out] for home. The next day my parents took me back to school. It seems like I ran away for nothing.[15]

Classroom

As the Navajos were adjusting to dormitory life, Anglo and Hispanic parents, their children, and Magdalena's school personnel all wondered how it would turn out. How would the introduction of the Indians alter the educational landscape? To understand the shock to the Magdalena system, one must begin with the numbers. As noted earlier, between 1959 and 1967 the Navajo enrollment rose from 128 to 250, the latter figure amounting to more than one-third of the system's overall enrollment. By 1979, the last year before the opening of the Alamo Navajo community school, the Navajo enrollment soared to approximately one-half of the total enrollment.[16]

Meanwhile, the Alamo Navajo children looked forward to this new chapter in their lives with a mixture of trepidation and excitement. Just as an earlier generation of Hispanics had been forced to crack the code of language in the Magdalena schools, so now it would be their turn, although it is important to point out that the linguistic properties of the Navajo language made the challenge facing Alamo children significantly greater than that faced by an earlier generation of Spanish speakers. Moreover, because Alamo Navajo parents exposed to English at boarding school tended to only speak it when interacting with Anglos, most of their children entered school with little or no facility in English. Indeed, it might be argued that for all the difficulties their parents had experienced learning English, they had still struggled with learning it in a "protected environment," that is to say, strictly among Indians. Now the embarrassments and humiliations were to be played out on a larger stage. In any event, the chasm of language was an immense one. "When I first came to Magdalena," one woman recalls, "it was very hard to speak in English. Like when I need something, or want to go somewhere, or sometime I leave class without permission because I don't know what to say in English, and sometime I talk to little Anglo or Spanish [kids] in Navajo language. They just look at me saying nothing. I feel mad at them." Then the dread that the teacher might call on them took over. "All we did was shake or nodded our heads," remembers one woman. When asked to read a book aloud, "I was always sent back to my desk. Everyone that enroll in Magdalena had no joy in going to school."[17]

Recollections from the other side of the teacher's desk are a bit different. For many years, the youngest children's first contact with school was the kindergarten class taught by Christina Blackburn (daughter of one of the town's elite Anglo families, John and Bessie Mactavish). As Blackburn explains, there was only so much she could teach in one year, especially given the fact that some children in her class were more than eight years old. But she adds, "If you can get a child to WANT to learn, to WANT to do something, they can do it." She began each year teaching the children how to write their names. One incident, she recalls, was the time a youngster named Otto, after writing the letters out, proudly presented his work for approval. "His eyes were like stars, and he smiled and handed me the paper, and it was 'Toot.'" "So from then on I called him Mr. Toot, and I'm sure he loved me." Teaching them English words and their meanings was a constant challenge. "One Halloween I had some cutouts of witches put up in the window, and one little fella came up and said, 'witch, witch—sandwich.' So we had to get that straightened out."[18]

Besides language, Blackburn filled her class with music (she was an accomplished pianist) and drawing. "One thing I had trouble with was the Crayons. They loved to break 'em up into a hundred little pieces. But I had one youngster who didn't, so I bragged on his box of Crayons—boy he sure knew how to take care of them—and that next time I handed them out, I didn't have any problem at all. They wanted to be just as smart." From strict Presbyterian stock, Blackburn also had the opportunity to offer an instructive lesson in religion. The first week of class, "I got word from the office that there was one of my little boys up in the weeds . . . so I sent someone out to bring him in. So then I told him he must be Moses [because] we found him in the bulrushes. He didn't do that again." All in all, Blackburn feels she was a successful, caring teacher. The only time she felt uncomfortable was when some "little fellas" tried to teach her a few words in Navajo. "Well, I wasn't too sure what they were teaching me, so I just didn't try." Why take the risk learning something "you just as well be without?"[19] The kindergartners learned early on that any border crossings would be in one direction.

No one understood the difficulties faced by the Navajo children more than Ray Smith, who for some thirty-one years (1957–1978) served the Magdalena schools in the various positions of teacher, coach, and for the last eleven years, as superintendent. A Navajo from the "big reservation," Smith was married to a Magdalena Hispanic woman who remembered her own painful memories learning English. Smith, then, could view Navajo children's struggle with English from a special vantage point. "A lot of people just failed to realize that . . . a person has to understand what the word means, make a connection between words being said, and what a person is trying to say." Convinced that most teachers simply did not appreciate the complexities of the language issue, Smith thought up a novel strategy. Speaking to parents at an Alamo Navajo chapter meeting, he suggested that parents, when meeting with teachers, should purposely "mix in" some Navajo words, just enough to create cognitive and linguistic "noise" in the communication. Perhaps then teachers would begin to glimpse the problems their Navajo students had deciphering teachers' "chicken cackling." Smith also diplomatically suggested to teachers that they refrain from disciplining children for speaking Navajo outside the classroom, although he admits he was never able to get agreement on this.[20]

By the late 1960s Magdalena had secured outside funding to advance students' academic progress, including sporadic experimentation with bilingual approaches to learning. But these innovations were neither systematic nor continuous, in part because of the sketchiness of funding, in part a result of the overall assimilationist orientation of the Magdalena schools.[21] Given the causative connection between English mastery and academic progress, it followed that many were drawn to classes in jewelry making and rug weaving, taught by two Alamo artists (Herbert Pino and Pauline Padilla). Magdalena's long-standing vocational courses also made staying in high school easier.[22]

Some students found relief in Diego Montoya's auto shop class. Montoya remembers that when he agreed to offer a class in auto repair in his town garage, many locals told him he was "crazy" for taking in such a diverse collection of students. Montoya's response? "I says, I'm not crazy. I know what I'm doing. I don't care if each boy is from Datil or Magdalena or Alamo—they're OUR boys. And as long as they behave and do what they're supposed to do, I can handle all of them. And I did. . . . Yeah, I didn't have a bad boy. I don't care if there was Indians."[23] From all appearances Montoya's auto shop class was a remarkable educational space, mainly because it was a class about much more than auto mechanics. As one of Montoya's former Anglo students, John Miller, remembers it, most of the Alamo Navajo students were barely literate. "They couldn't read and write. They're like in the ninth, tenth grade, and they couldn't read the simplest books. They [only] knew 'a,' 'and,' and 'the.' And they just fell through the cracks and he knew it. . . . Really, there wasn't a lot that he could do for them, but he'd take them off to one side, and . . . relieved a lot of the peer pressure." Describing himself and some of his classmates as a bunch of "smart asses," Miller says that he and friends were soon coaxed into assisting struggling students. "We were helping them read and everything. And we did that." Clearly Montoya saw his mission as building community. "He'd sit you down, and he'd make you think about what's coming up. . . . How are you going to live? And he was kind of like the father, grandfather figure." As for discipline, "If he put you down, that was enough right there. He didn't have to threaten you or raise a hand or anything like that. Having him mad at you, that hurt enough." Looking back, Miller reflects, "We acted like boys, but he treated us like young men. It actually made us step up a level there." How Montoya managed to create such an atmosphere "is kind of a mystery to this day."

If Montoya's auto mechanics class was a welcoming environment for struggling Alamo Navajo students, it was something of an exception. More often than not, most remember the sting of discrimination. One Navajo aide recalls that "the teachers only focus on the Anglos and Spanish students. And the Navajo children would just sit and never ask questions, and when report cards are out I would see all the Ds and Fs." To be sure, issues of culture and language were at play in this dynamic: the Anglo American orientation of the curriculum, the devaluation of students' native heritage, the traditional Navajo reticence toward individual displays of achievement, and the unwelcoming environment in which students found themselves. But teachers' attitudes and lack of training also figured into the equation—an inability or an all-too-often lack of motivation to penetrate the mask behind which students hid their fears and anxieties.[24]

Meanwhile, Alamo Navajo children were being paddled. It should be noted that they were not alone in this respect, but by virtue of their marginality and oppositional behaviors, they probably received a disproportionate number of blows. One woman is still bitter over "doing my best in class, and my teacher still spanks me for not trying hard." Another claims that after "my mother found out that I was getting paddled all the time, she came over to the school, she talked with the principal, Mr. Smith, and told him to go ahead and do some paddling if I was naughty, so the principal paddled me in front of my mother." In this instance, both the principal and the mother were products of the old boarding school system.[25]

It would be wrong, however, to single out the Alamo Navajo students as the only ones struggling in school. Even some Anglo students, who were at the opposite end of the cultural continuum, found aspects of the curriculum if not incomprehensible, at least suspect. One youngster fresh off a ranch recalls his dismay in first grade when the teacher read the class a story about a rabbit. Rabbits were something the boy regarded himself an expert on. So when the teacher read about a "white" rabbit, he remembers thinking, the teacher was not all that smart. He had seen hundreds of rabbits on the ranch. If he knew anything, it was that *real* rabbits were grey, not white. Didn't everybody know that? What the teacher was describing could "not be a rabbit." Rather, it must be "some freak they keep in a cage." When the teacher proceeded to read that rabbits ate carrots, well, that settled it! None of the rabbits he had ever seen had ever eaten carrots. "From that point on, she lost all credibility, and I figured one of these days she's gonna come around and I'll be able to teach HER somethin'. I just didn't get much out of first grade, I guess." For some Anglo ranch children, even speaking Standard English could pose a problem. Ira McKinley freely admits in his memoir, *My Saddle and I*, that having barely gotten out of eighth grade, "My English wasn't too good," a fact that created problems for his eight-year-old daughter, who was attending school in Datil. The seriousness of the problem surfaced when the teacher made a home visit to diagnose "what made Patti talk that way." Listening to McKinley's manner of expression, the teacher immediately discerned the source of the problem and proceeded to explain to McKinley that his daughter was resisting all efforts to improve her speech. McKinley knew that Patti revered him and that she probably was fully convinced that however her father talked would suit her just fine. Still, he wanted to help. So in the interest of his daughter's education, "I told the teacher that I'd change my way of talking the best I could and try to get Patti not to copy me so much."[26]

Achievement and Status

With the Magdalena schools now a tricultural setting, how did the three groups fare comparatively in the academic and social realms? In the area of academic progress, making a well-grounded assessment is difficult for several reasons: the surprising paucity of school records, the number of students leaving or entering the system, and the growing number of students of mixed Anglo-Hispanic ancestry, making surnames increasingly inexact markers of ethnic status. Through the use of school yearbooks and newspapers, however, one can begin to estimate comparative graduation and dropout rates of the three groups. The 1976 and 1978 graduating classes offer a window on the issue, but even then the base years for tracking the two cohorts (tenth and eighth grades) are different. Keeping in mind these limitations, the dropout/graduation ratios of the three groups for the class of 1976 were Anglo 8/5, Hispanic 15/11, and Navajo 16/5. For the class of 1978 they are Anglo 16/5, Hispanic 27/18, and Navajo 45/12.[27] The small number of Anglo students in the system makes generalizations about this group especially risky. What seems to be a reasonable generalization is that Alamo Navajo children were generally dropping out of school at substantially higher rates than students in the other two groups. Indeed, the establishment of the Alamo Navajo community school in 1979 (a subject to be discussed later) was partly motivated by this fact.

Turning to the question of social status, the search for conclusions is more rewarding. As historical documents, school yearbooks offer revealing snapshots on how students sorted themselves out socially. Such is the case in Magdalena, where yearbooks identified class officers, student council officers, homecoming queens, and depending on the years, class favorites in such categories as "best personality," "most liked," and "best looking." For purposes of comparison, six available yearbooks were broken into three periods (Table 7.1). Based on this evidence several conclusions are warranted. In the 1950s, that is to say before the Navajos arrived, Anglos and Hispanics shared equally in the denotations marking popularity. Moreover, in the first decade after the arrival of the Navajos, being Anglo or Hispanic still correlated closely with popularity. In fact, for all the years examined, although twelve Alamo Navajo students were elected as class officers, none served as class president. Still, by 1965 the Alamo Navajos began gaining footholds on the status ladder. In 1968, for instance, Alamo students captured three of the four spots of "class favorites" in both the seventh and tenth grades. In 1979, the last year before the opening of the Alamo community school, Doreen Apachito was crowned homecoming queen. Indeed, in

Table 7.1 Ethnocultural Social Status by Surnames in Selected Yearbooks

	Anglo	Hispanic	Navajo	Unclear
1953, 1959				
CLASS OFFICER	17	17	–	–
CLUB OFFICER	5	6	–	1
FAVORITE	21	23	–	–
CHEERLEADER	8	2	–	–
HOMECOMING QUEEN AND COURT (NOT INDICATED)	–	–	–	–
1965, 1968				
CLASS OFFICER	41	45	10	12
CLUB OFFICER	21	32	7	1
FAVORITE	29	37	29	7
CHEERLEADER	6	14	–	2
HOMECOMING QUEEN AND COURT	6	14	–	1
1974, 1979				
CLASS OFFICER	6	25	2	3
CLUB OFFICER (NOT INDICATED)	–	–	–	–
FAVORITE	7	20	10	5
CHEERLEADER	6	11	–	1
HOMECOMING QUEEN AND COURT	1	4	1	–

Note: The yearbooks selected were determined by availability and differed from year to year in categories covered.

the two yearbooks from the 1970s, the number of Alamo Navajo students selected as "class favorites" was greater than that of Anglos. A combination of growing Alamo Navajo enrollment numbers, increased Anglo and Hispanic acceptance of their Indian classmates, and greater Alamo Navajo participation in school activities account for these proportional gains. (Not shown here is the rise of Alamo Navajo participation in school club membership and in the high-status activity of school sports—especially basketball.) Also noteworthy, however, is the absence of Alamo Navajo females on the school's cheerleading squad, no doubt attributable to traditional Navajo female modesty.

What the yearbooks do not reveal is how students were negotiating the triangulated social universe, where definitions of the "other" were shifting. Before 1959, perceptions of otherness were shaped partly by class, but mainly along an Anglo-Hispanic divide. Although conflict between the two groups had faded over the years, it still constituted an important element in the school social scene. One former student, for instance, vividly recalls the day in the late 1950s when "all the Spanish were lined up on one side of the old gym and the Anglo cowboys on the other side, and they had a free-for-all." Life for children of mixed Anglo-Hispanic ancestry was especially complicated. Even after the Alamo Navajos arrived, Barbara Julian says, "The only problem we had . . . was that my daddy was white and my mother was Hispanic, and if there was ever a fight—which was normal—between a white guy and a Spanish guy, they'd ask us, 'Who you gonna stick up for?'"[28]

But after 1959 a new social divide—Anglos and Hispanics on one side, Navajos on the other—was emerging. That is, otherness was being defined anew. The Alamo Navajos had barely arrived when they found themselves at the bottom of a social hierarchy in which Anglos and Hispanics—now realizing how much they had in common—mostly held their Navajo classmates at arm's length. In this new configuration of social boundaries, border crossings certainly occurred. But in the 1960s this divide mostly pervaded Magdalena's classrooms, hallways, and playgrounds, especially at the secondary level. "We used to fight," one Alamo Navajo man remembers. "All the Navajo kids were on one side and all the Spanish kids and the *biligáana* kids were on the other side. We used to throw rocks at each other. And after school, there used to be a battle—us and the town kids." Sometimes the terrain between the school and the dormitories turned into a moving battleground, with rocks and slingshots serving as the weapons of choice. Interestingly, one Alamo Navajo woman recalls that most of the conflict was between Navajos and Hispanics. Another concurs: "Mostly it was the Spanish and Navajo that were fighting all the time."[29]

Deeply held stereotypes fueled the conflict. One Hispanic woman says, "I remember in the third grade when the Navajo children first came to school. . . . We were so uncomfortable with each other. I really feared them for a long time. They were very unfriendly with everyone and would not try to be friends with us. They [school staff] used to take them out of class and when they'd come back, they'd have their hair full of white stuff. This was to kill the lice they'd had when they'd come off the reservation." Singling out the Navajo children in this manner easily fed the verbal insults, such as "filthy Indians," hurled at the new arrivals. But the fear and loathing was mutual. As one Alamo Navajo woman explains, "We always fight with Anglo and Spanish girls. They always call us bad names like dirty Indians; that's why we fight back—to protect ourselves. We use to call them names too, like dog eaters. They use to make fun about our language. We did the same thing." One Navajo woman confesses, "I didn't even want to touch their skin because I was thinking, if they ever touch me, I might turn into white person."[30]

The negative stereotypes of the Alamo Navajos were surely reinforced by the fact that they were disproportionately struggling academically. One Alamo Navajo woman says, "Sometimes we would fight them in the classroom if they was smart[er] than us. We would tell them to gave us the answer. If they don't we would go over to their desk and gave them a big punch in the head or the back. We would shoot rubber [bands] at them and make them cry." On the other side, some Anglos and Hispanics felt that the Navajos were getting special treatment under the Johnson-O'Mally program, a federal program aimed at aiding Native American children in public schools. Poor Indians receiving clothing and shoe allotments were one thing, many felt, but the other perks that came with being Indian were downright discriminatory. This feeling was probably particularly common among those Anglo and Hispanic families who themselves were strapped for cash. Superintendent Ray Smith frequently received complaints from parents on the issue. One can readily sense the resentment in this Anglo woman's comment years later:

> Another thing that was difficult for me was the way that the dorm students were differentiated from the other students in the classroom. Whenever we lost a book, or were late returning them, we had to either pay for the book or pay a late fine. The dorm students always took books and kept them. The same was true for marking or losing textbooks. Another incident was that at mealtime, we all had to purchase meals. The dorm students got free meals and usually larger helpings. . . . The items that stood out the most were the ones dealing with parties and field trips. When we went on a field trip, Anglo and Spanish kids had to provide their own spending money. The school allocated dorm students money. Then when a party came up, and we had to provide a treat for the whole class or a present for someone, the Anglo and Spanish students had to bring enough or they could not participate. The dorm never provided party treats. If we drew names for a present and drew a dorm name, we bought them a present. When the dorm student drew a name, the BIA would send a brown bag with nuts and fruit. If we didn't buy them a present, the one that we were supposed to get was given to them.

The narrator says the bitterness faded after she reached high school, perhaps because she was better able to understand the Navajo students' situation. Meanwhile, Alamo Navajo students sensed the resentment. "One time there was a party [and] we decided not to eat anything because we didn't bring nothing for the party. They try to tell us to eat something but we didn't eat."[31]

Another source of conflict—mainly it appears between Alamo Navajo and Hispanic males—was the eagerness of the former to strike up amorous relationships with willing Hispanic females. Given the overall tensions between the groups, this development might appear paradoxical. But the adolescent years bring raging hormones, temporary infatuations, and budding romances. At the same time, it is a period when adolescent males (depending of course on historical context) are sometimes given to ethnic boundary maintenance, especially where competition for females is involved. Indeed, one Alamo Navajo man recalls that whenever a Navajo boy showed more than casual interest in a Hispanic female, a fight was sure to break out. The reason for Alamo Navajo males' interest in the female other partly stemmed from the Navajos' expansive, that is to say, clan-based definition of kinship, combined with the fact that the number of clans at Alamo was much smaller than among the "Big Navajo." In short, the number of relatives severely limited opportunities for in-group romantic couplings. Looking back, one Alamo Navajo explains, "Us boys don't really care about the Navajo girls because almost all of them would be relat[ed] to each other [us]." Similarly, one woman vividly recalls her mother eliminating potential boyfriends because of clan connections, a dilemma that provoked the daughter's response, "Well, I guess I'm not goin' to marry a Navajo." And she did not.[32]

But ever so slowly, increasing numbers of students reached across the gulf of difference. Although sensitive parents and teachers facilitated the process, it ultimately fell to children to bridge the yawning cultural chasms and subvert existing hierarchies. One Alamo Navajo boy who had the advantage of living in Magdalena recalls that his first playmate was an Anglo who helped him learn English. After second grade, his friend moved away, and he quickly befriended a Hispanic boy. Because both were struggling to learn English, "we used to teach each other a lot." After a decade or so the frequent hallway brawls and playground conflicts were becoming less common, just as after-school rock fights were giving way to end-of-the-year ritualistic standoffs. According to one Alamo Navajo student of this period, by the mid-1960s relations were much improved "because Magdalena got used to us." Another Alamo Navajo man agrees: "We got used to each other and our language. All of a sudden we all make friends." Although evidence suggests that these rosy assessments overstate the extent of amity, it is also clear that the Magdalena schools were making genuine progress.³³

As for the crosscurrents of intergroup intimacy, if we are to believe the gossip page of the *Steer* (the student newspaper), most cross-cultural romances were of the Anglo-Hispanic variety. Student gossip columns are, of course, notoriously unreliable measurements of female-male amorous connections. Consider this entry: "Corky G. and Lucy C. seem to be getting along pretty good these days! Is it going to last????" By cross-checking surname initials with yearbook names, it is clear that most of these alleged romantic attachments were within Anglo and Hispanic corridors, but not entirely so. "Rudy L. sure has been occupied with a certain cute freshman. It's Cecil H. of course, huh, Rudy???????" Then there was: "Nadine G. and Brian W. seem to be getting along fine these days. Is it spring fever or the real thing?????" Or, "By the looks of things we thought Frank T. and Marie G. would be the recent steadies. That sure was a short courtship kids."³⁴

But this was 1964. Magdalena was a long way off from being a multicultural utopia. On the one hand, relations between Hispanics and Anglos were much improved. The years of association in town and school, together with the arrival of the Indians, contributed to the growing amicability. If relations between these two groups and the Alamo students were far from ideal—indeed, sometimes deeply fractious—here too the three groups were getting to know one another in new and accommodating ways. In the classroom, but especially in the extracurricular worlds of athletics, band, chorus, and various clubs associations, old notions of the other were slowly giving way. Nowhere were possibilities of community and the rewards of pulling together more on display than on the basketball court.

A Team, a Year, and a Photograph

By any measure 1968 was a monumental moment in the nation's history. Newspapers and television reported one dramatic story after another: assassinations of the Reverend Martin Luther King Jr. and Senator Robert Kennedy, the violent confrontation between protesters and Chicago police at the Democratic National Convention, urban race riots, President Lyndon Johnson's surprise announcement that he would not stand for re-election, and massive protests against the Vietnam War. Like all citizens, those in Magdalena followed these events with a mixture of concern, disbelief, anger, and confusion. But during the winter of 1968 the town's focus was mostly on the Magdalena High School basketball team, the Steers. Playing at the Class B division level, the lowest of the three state categories (determined by school size), the Steers' record in mid-February was twenty-four to zero, after they rolled over schools with names such as Jemez Valley, Quemado, Estancia, Menaul, Fort Grant, and Mountainair. As the victories mounted, townspeople were becoming believers. The team might just go all the way. By the first week of March the team's record was twenty-nine to zero. That is where things stood when families piled into cars for the long drive to Albuquerque for the state tournament, the final games to be played at the University of New Mexico's famed "pit," the court named for its distinctive placement below ground level. Rolling into Albuquerque, the Steers were just three games away from winning it all.

In the pit the dreamlike season of the Magdalena Steers came to an emotional, crushing end. The story of that defeat, and the miraculous season that preceded it, is the stuff of local legend. It has been told and retold, lived and relived, across countless kitchen tables and at the town's local drinking establishment, the Golden Spur. In 1988 the *Magdalena Mountain Mail* asked its readers, "Where were you at the final heart-breaking game? In the stands? on the court? listening to the radio? waiting and worrying?"[35] Now I tell the story again, not simply as a story about a small high school's heroic basketball season but as a story about how the convergence of sport and adolescence helped move a town riven with ethnocultural conflict toward a greater sense of community.

One must begin by looking at the team photograph, a mixture of Hispanics, Anglos, Navajos, and one African American kneeling beside a collection of trophies. Underlining the photo are surnames such as Gutiérriz, Martínez, Grayson, Knoblock, Mexicano, and Apachito. Standing tall in the middle is the team's center, Sam Olney, who at 6 feet 5 inches was the only player with any real height. The two starting guards—Ray Martínez and Ramón Gutiérriz—both measured 5 foot 7. Early in the season, anyone watching the team empty out of the bus would have thought twice about challenging the judgment of a newspaper reporter in Farmington, New Mexico, who wrote: "If you saw the Steers walking down the street, in cowboy boots and big hats, chances are you would be hard pressed to believe that this was a basketball team." Another remembers, "They looked more like rodeo riders."[36] Sam agrees that they did not fit the image of the average basketball team, noting that "we had a pretty spicy group. You got Anglo, Spanish, Indian, one black kid. The one common denominator was that we loved to play." Indeed, watching the team on the court, observers were quickly disabused of their initial skepticism about the team's ability

Magdalena Steers team photo, 1968. Standing (left to right): Coach Sid Black, Dave Tafoya, Ray Martínez, Tommy Gene Knoblock, O. D. Murrell, Sam Olney, Steve Grayson, Ernest Baca, Archie Apachito, Ramón Gutiérriz, Scout Tony Armijo. Kneeling (left to right): David Pino, Conrad Chávez, Buddy Mexicano, Edmund Mexicano. (Courtesy of Magdalena Public Schools.)

and could be overheard saying, "These guys are legitimate." At the state finals, the scrappy team from Magdalena was the crowd favorite. Barbara Julian, one of the school cheerleaders, will never forget the enthusiastic support coming from the stands—the rhythmic clapping, foot stamping, and shouts of "Go Steers." "It just got bigger, the whole pit."[37]

To understand the team's journey is to understand the passion for basketball in rural New Mexico. In 1968 football was a nonexistent sport at Magdalena High School, and baseball had a limited following. Although a

number of youngsters was ardent about rodeo, this sport was mostly limited to ranch families. Basketball was something else. The story begins in elementary school, when recess lasted half an hour and lunch a full hour. At both breaks there was an immediate race for the hoops and the choosing of teams. "Sometimes we wouldn't even go eat, we liked to play so much. . . . And we'd go into the classroom sweating," recalls Ray Martínez. Sam adds, "It was one of those deals where we all grew up together, and we all liked the same thing." After school they continued to play. The problem for players was that outside of school, everything was makeshift. The Olneys had a bare rim tacked to a wooden backboard nailed to a telephone pole, but they were still playing on dirt. "The only guy in town," Sam says, "that had cement was Steve Grayson. He used to live at the old Magdalena Hotel. . . . We used to go to his house and play all the time because we had that tiny little piece of cement."

Who were these players that converged on the slab of cement at the old Magdalena Hotel? The place to begin is with the team's two starting guards—Ramón Gutiérrez and Ray Martínez. Ramón was born in 1950 and raised alongside eleven brothers and sisters. Living near the stockyards, some of his most lasting memories are of shipping season and how the hills changed colors depending on the livestock coming in. One day the hills might be a deep bronze, or even maroon, as the sun shone on the backs of the grazing cattle; on another day the landscape was woolen-white with sheep. At night there were the restless sounds of bawling or bleating and the twinkling of campfires where the herders gathered to eat, drink coffee, and bed down, awaiting the next day's work, loading the livestock on the railcars for shipment. "We spent a lot of time in the stockyards . . . trying to help, but mostly being in the way," Ramón recalls. Family and church were sources of stability, but school was becoming an ever more important part of his life. Summers were a time to earn a few dollars. After the town's brick mercantile building burned down, he earned 1 cent for every brick he scraped clean of cement, the same wage he got for collecting and cashing in discarded wine bottles. But mostly it was about basketball. While playing basketball he heard the newsflash that the president of the United States had been shot in Dallas, Texas. Every day after returning from lunch at home several boys would gather for a quick pickup game at a friend's house conveniently within earshot of the school bell. In the midst of playing, they got word of the horrific news and went into the house to see "what was going on." Back in school, they heard the worst.

Reynaldo Martínez was one year younger than Ramón, born in El Paso, Texas. When he was two his father moved the family to California to work harvesting fruits and vegetables. But his mother, New Mexico born, was not sold on the life of migrant workers, so after two years in the fields, the family moved to Magdalena, where Ray's dad found more promising work in the Kelly mines. Although Ray entered school speaking Spanish, he found that English came easily. He also acquired the shortened name of Ray, the teachers finding Reynaldo too cumbersome. But they "were good teachers. I remember them. They were strict; you had to make the grades to go up." Family (three brothers, three sisters) and church, he says, were central to his life. For several years, he was an altar boy, rising each school day early in the morning and riding his bike to St. Mary Magdalene, where he assisted the priest in the performance of mass. (Ray confesses that he and another altar boy once partook heavily of the half gallon of wine the priest kept at the church. "We got sick in church, and Father Felix got mad at us.") His closest friend was Ramón. "We were like brothers. We grew up together. We did everything together. I used to go to his house, and he'd go to my house." They played in the stockyards together, chipped bricks together, and at a local sawmill greased conveyor belts and stacked lumber together. During every free moment, they played basketball together—like brothers. These years of association would later pay dividends on the court, each one knowing instinctually what move the other was about to make. As another member of the team recalls, "They were almost like one person."

Ray was just a freshman and over at Ramón's house when he took notice of his sister, Alice. "You know what happens when you see the woman you feel you want to be with." Alice was running for homecoming queen, so Ray saw an opening and made a bet with her: "If you win, you owe me a kiss." Alice confesses she never thought she would actually win, so offhandedly agreed. When she *did* win, it was time to deliver on the promise. But raised in a strict Hispanic-Catholic household, this presented a problem. "I never went anywhere," she recalls, and she can still remember the admonishment she got from her parents for walking past the West Bar on the way to the local drugstore for an ice cream cone. Still, she had made the bet. So on the night of the big date, and caught between the conflicting poles of conscience—her bet with Ray and her Catholic upbringing—she struck an honorable compromise. She allowed Ray to kiss her hand. (Four years later, they married.) In the meantime, Ray was living a heady adolescent existence.

Archie Apachito's experience growing up Alamo Navajo was common enough: riding horses, herding sheep, and hauling water and wood by horse and wagon. "Each one of us—all my brothers, we had a horse—get up before the sunrise. We put big bell on the horse [so] we know where it is. We get our horse early in the morning. Other people have vehicle; but my dad didn't get a vehicle until later." When Archie reached his teens, he earned spending money during the summer months by helping his dad build fences for local ranchers.

School was a series of difficult adjustments. After spending a year at the Alamo day school, he was transferred to the Albuquerque boarding school, where he spent three years, mostly missing home. "It was hard. Learning was not really important then." On one occasion Archie joined a late-night raid on a local farmer's apple orchard. Then there was the time an older brother announced on the spur of the moment that the two should run away, making their escape at midnight. "I didn't know anything. I didn't even have a shoe on. We just snuck through the back door, down the stairway. I remember that we crossed the street barefoot. We were about two blocks from the dorm, and then he says: 'Let's just turn back.' And we turned back and went to bed." Being transferred to the Magdalena dorms was a godsend. In addition to seeing his parents more often, Archie's outgoing personality, combined with his love of basketball, won him new friends. "It helped me a lot, playin' with other kids. They even invite me to their house—Ramón, Tommy Knobloch, Sam Olney, and Ray Martínez. They invite me to come over and eat a sandwich or something. That made our team more stronger." Archie's growing circle of friends is revealed in the 1966 yearbook photo that shows him as the eighth-grade male "class favorite." Two years later, he was elected vice president of the sophomore class, one of the first Alamo Navajo students to crack the Hispanic-Anglo monopoly on class offices.

Historian Peter Iverson quotes Navajo educator Monty Roessel as saying, "The five major sports on the Navajo Nation are basketball, basketball, basketball, basketball, and rodeo."[38] So it was with Archie. His first memories of playing are at home, where he and friends configured a primitive court. Stitching pieces of ragged cloth around an ancient bicycle rim, they nailed the hoop to some old boards, then to a cedar tree. To keep the dust down, they sprinkled water on the dirt. When electricity came to the reservation in 1967, he followed the game on television. "That's how I learn my passes: look one way and pass this way." The opportunity to play alongside Ramón, Ray, and the others in the school's athletic program sharpened his game, the long shot and "fancy passes" emerging as his specialty. Although not a starter on the legendary 1968 team, to even make the team as a sophomore was a heady accomplishment. He knew all too well that "playing basketball at Magdalena was a privilege."

The only genuinely painful experience—which stemmed from the school's strained financial resources—occurred when he was a freshman and still on the B team. In the first game of the season Archie went up for a rebound and "my trunks ripped open—like I was wearing a skirt." Embarrassed, he pleaded to sit out the rest of the game. "Coach, every time I go up, you can see my shorts." But because the game was tight, the coach's only response was, "I need you to get the rebounds and control the ball." After the victory, the ripped trunks were passed to the coach's wife, who stitched up the tear. But the thread was so thick, the patched area so stiff, the chafing so irritating, merely getting through a game was an ordeal. But short of quitting, which he never considered, there was little he could do. The next year, the 1968 team was blessed with new uniforms.

In the other area of his life, the dorm, he was more successful at getting his way. The main bone of contention was food. Coming back to the dorm every day after practice, he was famished and found that the supper set aside for him by the staff was terribly insufficient. So there was only one thing to do: steal the key to the commissary. "I know it's stealing, okay, but if you want to survive, sometimes you have to break some rules." After recruiting a couple of conspirators, a nightly scenario unfolded. Members of the raiding party snuck into the kitchen storeroom, filled a laundry bag with the desired items, slipped back to the dormitory, consumed the "take," and then made the short trip to the incinerator, where they disposed of the evidence. Remarkably, the midnight raids were never discovered. Archie's second coup was less dramatic but nonetheless satisfying. It occurred one fall when he returned from summer vacation with long hair and protested the staff's annual policy of giving him the standard boarding school haircut, that is to say, a shearing so close to the skin it almost constituted a scalping. Where did this desire for longer hair originate? Archie thinks it came from a greater appreciation for the old Navajo way but also from seeing on television Native American radicals such as Clyde Bellecourt and Russell Means. Then, too, in the 1960s long hair was in fashion among the young. So he helped negotiate a compromise with dormitory staff. When he emerged from the barber chair, he laughingly remembers, he looked more like one of the Beatles than Russell Means.

One of Sam's most vivid memories involves helping his father, who worked for the US Fish and Wildlife Service, trap wild turkeys in the San Mateo Mountains, the object being to reintroduce the captured birds in the Magdalena Mountains. Because there was no existing contraption to trap the birds, his father invented a special cage for the project, something on the order of a sawed-off coyote trap. After six or seven turkeys worked their way into the corn-baited cage and tripped the gate, the birds were penned. The next step was to extract them from the cage for the tagging and transportation. Given that the cage was no more than 4 feet in height, eleven-year-old Sam's job was to crawl into the trap and extract the now much-irritated birds. Bent over and in close quarters, "I'd go in there and get beat up by these turkeys that were ticked off. They'd get ya—wings flappin' everywhere." (One cannot help but wonder if the experience paid dividends years later when he would be fighting for rebounds under the boards—wings flapping everywhere.)

The Olneys were originally Kansas farmers. When Sam was four or five, and the family appeared to be "sittin' on a good maize crop," a violent storm rode over the land and "hailed it all out." It was then that his father announced, "That's it." He was through with farming. His hiring on with the Fish and Wildlife Service brought the family to northern New Mexico for a few years, and then he transferred to Magdalena, where Sam entered school as a fifth grader. Because his father sometimes served as a guide for hunters, Sam grew up chasing more than wild turkeys. He thinks he was eleven when he shot a deer from his father's pickup, twelve when he shot his first bear. For adventure closer to town, he and friends explored abandoned mines in nearby Kelly. "There isn't a hole in this mountain that I ain't been in." Then there was work. Besides various odd jobs, like helping out at the stockyards, Sam spent three summers loading and unloading hay for local ranchers. It was hard work, but at $7 a day good wages. In eighth grade Sam stood 6 foot 3, a promising height for the sport of basketball, but he only weighed 100 pounds and was still terribly awkward. Sam credits his growing improvement in the game to playing every day with shorter and more skilled players such as Ramón and Ray but also to his junior high coach, D. K. Woodward. Coach Woodward did not know much about basketball, Sam recalls, but he could spot potential. Even though "I was terrible, he played me every game," telling Sam's father, "One of these days he is going to be able to play, and the only reason he's going to learn is I gotta leave him in the game and let him play."

So, day after day, in school and out, the adolescents gathered to play basketball, the bonds growing ever stronger between them—Hispanic, Anglo, and Navajo:

> That's why it was actually nice to grow up here, because we had all colors. We all played together. We didn't care. I remember my senior trip, Raymond Apachito and Kenneth Apachito—big time senior trip—we went to Riodoso, New Mexico. We are all in the back of the pickup under a tarp because it was cold and we left school here early in the morning and a spring storm came in. We're sleeping under a tarp. We all ran together, played together. Growing up, you got to remember, I'm a minority. People talk about Hispanics being a minority. No they're not. When I was growing up, I'm the minority. There weren't too many of us white boys here in town. That's why we were such a good team. There was none of that friction—as far as I know. There could have been some with somebody else, but from my vantage point I never realized any of that stuff. We were all Steers. That's all we cared about.

Table 7.2 Magdalena Steers Basketball Record, November 10, 1967–January 6, 1968

11-10-67	Magdalena (home)	85	Jemez Valley	60
11-11-67	Magdalena (home)	68	Encino	46
11-17-67	Magdalena (home)	114	Carrizozo	26
11-18-67	Magdalena	82	Quemado	44
11-22-67	Magdalena	48	Socorro	33
12-1-67	Magdalena (home)	84	Quemado	44
12-2-67	Magdalena	71	Estancia	59
12-8-67	Magdalena (home)	76	Menaul	44
12-9-67	Magdalena	75	Reserve	41
1-6-68	Magdalena (home)	97	Mountainair	43

Source: Magdalena 1968 yearbook.

There were also powerful role models. By 1968, the players had seen local boys such as Ernest Gutiérriz and "Little Jimmy" Latasa put earlier Magdalena teams on the map. Latasa, Sam remembers, "was a little guard and could go inside, throw it up on the big guys, get it to go in the hole." Now it would be Ramón and Ray's turn. "Ramón and Ray tormented everybody in the state. You turned your back on one of them, he was gonna come and get the ball from behind. And this comes from years as kids playing together. We knew what the other guy was GOING TO DO." A younger player on the B team from that era adds, "I've never seen two guards that could read each other just like a book." According to Sam, although Ted Black, the coach of the 1968 team, was well liked, it was really the years of playing together on the slab of cement in front of the Magdalena Hotel that made the team. Coach Black mainly "just set back and watched us win."

Win they did. By January 6, ten games into the season, it was clear that the Magdalena Steers was a team to be reckoned with. Not a single opposing team had come within ten points, and some of the wins amounted to a complete rout (Table 7.2). Following the victory over Mountainair on January 6, the remaining schedule was a combination of regular games and tournaments. By the end of the month the Steers' record was nineteen to zero, and they had won two tournament trophies.

By February it was clear that the team's major competitor was going to be the Albuquerque Boys Academy. On February 17 the two teams squared off for the first of three games, the first contest played in Magdalena's Works Progress Administration (WPA)–built gym. Sometimes called the "Crackerjack Box" because the bleachers were only three or four rows deep, it offered the home team an immense crowd advantage. Hours before the game the gym was packed with Steers fans, leaving furious academy supporters standing in the street. "They had to stand outside and listen and hope," recalls Sam. As for the players, they had "to fight people just to get into the gym to play our own game." Sam recalls he was remarkably loose for the game, and the credit belonged to a local rancher, Richard Spears. On the morning of the game, Spears came to town and asked Sam's dad if his son could help unload a semi-truck full of hay, a request to which his dad responded, "He'll be right there." When Sam protested that this was the day of the big game, his father shot back, "I don't give a damn what you got. They called and need your help. You go and unload that hay!" As it turned out, the heavy work was good medicine for pregame nerves. "That night I was loose and not nervous about anything because . . . I was loose from loadin' that hay."

Even before the game began, the Magdalena players knew they had their hands full. Ray recalls the team's concerns during the pregame warmups, when they got a good look at the size of the academy team. Three players were well over 6 feet and routinely "dunking it." Meanwhile, Ramón could only imagine what was going through the fans' minds, everybody thinking, "They're gonna lose their first game." Fortunately, the team's scout, Tony Armijo, had done his homework; for Magdalena to win they must control Sam Tabbot. "For two weeks that's all we concentrated on. . . . He was the one that scored thirty or forty points. The other guys were good, but they depended on him to carry them." With a game strategy in hand and the "Crackerjack Box" hometown cheering them on, the Steers went to work. "We were so pumped up, we blew them out of the gym the first half of the game," Sam remembers. The final score was seventy-one to forty-eight.

A week later, the two teams locked horns for a second time in the final game at the Mountainair tournament. This time, with the academy fully cognizant of Magdalena's strength, the contest was much tighter. In the last seconds of the game the Steers were down by one point but had possession of the ball. After calling a timeout, they concocted a play: they would feed Sam the ball so he could get off a good shot and maybe get fouled. But then on the sidelines they had trouble getting the ball in play. As Ray recalls the moment, "I was way on top of the key. They passed it to me because nobody was guarding me. I was looking around and everybody was covered." But then in the flash of a second, Ray was covered by a 6-foot-5 academy player. The crowd shouting, "Shoot! Shoot!" Unable to pass, the clock running out, Ray made his move. With the academy player positioned between him and the goal, Ray faked a break to the basket. "The guy knew I was pretty quick." That was when Ray stepped back, jumped, and took his shot. They beat the academy by one point. The following day, the *Albuquerque Journal* reported, "Magdalena, winning its 25th consecutive game, used a twenty-point performance from Sam Olney and two other double-figure ones from Ray Martínez and Ramón Gutiérriz to win easily."[39] Actually, the victory was not that easy, and the next meeting would be less so.

On March 2 the two teams played for the championship in the Socorro tournament. The first half of the game was a disaster, ending with the Steers down by a daunting twenty points. As Ray remembers it, "We went into the locker room. Everybody was down and just said, 'Let's play like we always played.'" So in the second half, little by little, they began to close the gap. Just as in the previous meeting, it came down to the last seconds of the game—Steers in control of the ball and a timeout. As Ray remembers the moment, "I told Ramón, they're gonna expect Sam or somebody else to get the ball. We need to set screens. Everybody set screens, so we can turn somebody loose. . . . So I took it out and gave it to Ramón. He was dribbling, so I set a screen for him. I rolled out the screen, he passed the ball behind, and I got it." Ball in hand but his back to the basket, he knew the academy player assigned to guard him stood between him and the basket. "I knew if I went straight to the goal, he was gonna block me. He was 6-foot-5. So I went underneath the goal and shot it through the back, because the goal would protect the block." So it did, and the Steers squeaked out a third victory over the academy.

The following week the whole town's mind was on the state tournament. On Thursday, March 7, Coach Black loaded up the bus for the drive north: the varsity team, the B team, the still junior team (the Calves), and the school cheerleaders. For many on the bus the journey to Albuquerque itself was a special occasion. Barbara recalls the ride: "Driving between Magdalena and Albuquerque in those days, if you saw a car now and again, you'd say 'Wow, let's wait. [We might] know somebody. . . . You just very seldom ever saw a car. . . . So we really were from the little bitty town, and here we go to the big city."[40] Meanwhile, Magdalena was emptying out as cars and pickups headed north. On everyone's mind was the question: Can Magdalena defeat the Albuquerque Boys Academy a fourth time? Those left behind turned on their radios.

The Steers' first game was played in the Johnson Gymnasium against Dora, a small community in Roosevelt County on the Texas border. "Dora was huge. They had the biggest kid in the state," Sam recalls. "He was

6 foot 10. We were really worried about Dora." When Sam and Tommy Knoblock got into foul trouble, the rest of the team knew it was going to be a difficult win. But Steve Grayson came through with fourteen points and fourteen rebounds. Meanwhile, Dave Tafoya came off the bench and began hitting shots from outside the key. Then Ramón and Ray "ate their guards alive," contributing to some twenty-four Dora turnovers. According to the *Albuquerque Journal,* Magdalena's "full-court press gave Dora fits."[41] When the game ended, the score was sixty-two to fifty-six. During the game Barbara recalls hearing a fan call out, "Look at those guys play. They're magnificent. Look at the things they're doing." By the end of the game, all but Dora's fans seemed to be cheering for Magdalena. Everyone knew where the tournament was headed: a contest between the Magdalena Steers and the Albuquerque Boys Academy. Only one team stood in the way—the Cloudcroft Bears—a team from the southeastern part of the state. There was good news on that score. Tony Armijo, who had scouted Cloudcroft, reported back, "No problem. You don't even have to worry about Cloudcroft. You guys will beat them by thirty." Now the Steers were headed for the pit, worlds away from Magdalena's "Crackerjack Box" facility where the journey began.

Seventeen-year-old cheerleader Barbara had never seen anything like the pit. "When we walked in, we were, like, in awe." As in the Dora contest, as soon as the game started, it was clear that Magdalena was the crowd favorite. The roar of the fans was ear shattering as they joined the cheerleaders in the shout: "Go Steers go! Go Steers go!" In a matter of minutes, she remembers, "It just got bigger—the WHOLE pit." Of course the Cloudcroft fans were cheering for the home team, but Barbara remembers everyone else yelling his or her support for Magdalena. In any event, the thunderous noise was deafening—the cheering, clapping, stomping. "You couldn't hear anything. It was so loud and packed. I can't imagine—well, I'll never experience that again—the pit screaming and yelling, calling out for the Steers."

The game started well enough. "Cloudcroft was scared of us. I could feel it," Ray remembers. But as the game progressed, it was apparent that it was not going to be as easy as Armijo predicted. Cloudcroft had the height advantage, physical strength under the boards, and two solid guards. Still, early in the second quarter the Steers were leading twenty-four to fourteen and appeared to be headed for an "easy victory." Then, as the *Journal* described the game, "the taller Bears ran off nine straight points and trailed by twenty-four to twenty-three. Magdalena managed four points before the clock ran out to go into the intermission with a five-point lead." In the third quarter the game tightened again when Sam, who was in foul trouble, spent part of the period on the bench, leaving the rebounding advantage to 6-foot-6 Billy Spears and 6-foot-2 Jim Haynes. The final quarter opened with Cloudcroft scoring the first five points, taking a forty-to-thirty-four lead, its biggest in the game. Then Steve Grayson, who was limping from a knee injury in the previous quarter, hit two long shots, followed by another from Tommy Knoblock. Now, as the reporter for the *Journal* described the final minutes, "the nip and tuck battle was on."[42]

With five minutes remaining, Sam fouled out and watched the agonizing last minutes and seconds from the bench. "I was sittin', realizing I can't do nothing about it. I was hurtin'." The last seconds were all drama. With just sixteen seconds left on the clock, Grayson pumped a 17-foot jump shot that put the Steers ahead forty-nine to forty-eight. Now it was defense, and then the moment that would never be forgotten. The clock ticking down the last seconds, Cloudcroft's Johnny May brought the ball down court, and as described by the reporter, "worked his way to the baseline and took a 7-footer. The ball bounced around, and for a second it looked like it might pop out, but it stayed in and ended Magdalena's thirty-game winning streak."[43] Sam remembers the shot coming from much farther out, but nevertheless still replays in his mind, almost in slow motion, the ball's movement when it made contact with the basket—"kind of popped out, in, out again, then boom, back in." But there were still three seconds left, still a slim chance they could pull off a miracle finish. Calling time out, Ray turned to Ramón, saying, "Ramón, I'm gonna get you the ball one way or another—and you take the shot." So, "I passed it to him and he turned around and just hooked it. I saw the ball go in—then out. When I saw it didn't go in, I just collapsed there, and he was coming from the other side."

That is when the photographer snapped the picture: Ray kneeling, his left hand covering his face, surrounded by consoling cheerleaders; Barbara, with her hand over her mouth, is sobbing; Ramón is kneeling a few feet away, his head buried in his left forearm. The reporter for the *Journal* wrote that the whole team "wept unashamedly," and there is no reason to doubt it.[44] Barbara says, "The picture tells everything, I guess. We were all just crying. We didn't know what to do. I mean we cried, and we cried, and we cried."

With the state trophy out of reach, the Magdalena Steers now had to play for third place against Springer, a game they won handily, seventy-eight to forty-nine. All the more painful was that in the final game—the contest

"A Tearful End." (Courtesy of Albuquerque Journal.)

for state championship—Cloudcroft was defeated by Albuquerque Boys Academy, the very team Magdalena had defeated three times. Then, the long ride home. As Barbara tells it, as the bus rolled south there was "total silence" as the dispirited passengers stared blankly out the bus windows at the passing villages, ranches, and cottonwoods. Coach Black did his best to cheer the team up—"You guys did a good job"—but it was a futile gesture. "It was SO quiet. He was the only one talking." Such was the mood on the bus as it turned west out of Socorro for the long climb to the high country to Magdalena. The town was waiting for them, cars lined up and honking, the community paying honor to the team with the miracle season. But the following Monday the sting of defeat was ever present, casting a gloom throughout the entire school—players, cheerleaders, students, and teachers alike all unable to shake off the wrenching disappointment.

Then something remarkable happened. The photograph caught the wires and went global, bringing the team more recognition in defeat than a victory could have ever brought them. The *Sydney* (Australia) *Morning Herald*'s caption suggested that the scene captured "one of those traumatic moments which can grip a teenager's existence." Then the letters began pouring in, often addressed to those in the photo not by their name but by their station or posture in the image—"to the girl that was standing in front with her hand over her mouth." Then this letter came from Albuquerque:

> Dear Ray:
> This wonderful picture which appeared in the paper moved me to write and express my great admiration for you and Ramon Gutierriz and your demonstration of a great human manifestation of emotion at an important event in your lives. I think the picture is wonderful and I think you and Ramon are wonderful. I don't mind saying I can't keep from crying every time I look at the picture or *think* about it—and I'm much older than you.
> I know a lot of people who have expressed admiration for you and Ramon. Thank you for being a fine young man.
> Sincerely,
> A friend[45]

So what is the meaning of the Magdalena Steers' 1968 basketball season? On one level, it was about individuals, adolescents coming of age and experiencing one of the defining chapters in their young lives. The memories of the miracle season are deep. Looking at the photograph, Barbara tears up and says, "I can still feel it." Sam, who later coached high school basketball, recalls how Coach Johnny May—the same Johnny May who made the winning shot for Cloudcroft in the 1968 playoffs—years later took his undefeated Tularosa Wildcats into the state finals, where they suffered their own defeat. "And I shouldn't have done it, but I went up—this was probably an hour or two after it happened—and I said, 'Well Johnny, now you know how it feels.' And he looked at me and said, 'You son-of-a-bitch.' I said, 'That's all I got to say, Johnny. You and I are good friends. That's all I got to say. Now you know how it feels.'" Sam repeats that he and May are good friends, but "I'm still mad at him to this day." He still feels the pain of sitting on the bench and watching May's shot bounce and rattle around the rim, and then slip through the net, and with it, the sunken hopes of winning it all. That moment "still eats at you."

But the story about the Steers is also about community, a community wrestling with its troubled past. It is an oft-repeated truism that sport reflects society. But it is also true that sport has the power if not to eliminate old antagonisms and prejudices, at least to weaken them. True, such communal feelings seldom outlast the all-too-brief euphoric moments of transcendent unity. A basketball season cannot erase history, and it certainly

TOGETHER AND APART : 297

did not do so in 1968. But it can be a step in a community's journey to a better place. "It's one of those deals that happens in little towns—it unifies everybody," Sam observes. Memory, even incorrect memory, can help the process along. One of the 1968 team's most ardent supporters, for instance, says that players in the heat of a game consciously shouted out plays in Navajo to disorient the opposition. But the players dismiss this. Occasionally Spanish or Navajo words might be called out, but more because of the long hours spent growing up and playing together.

So, locals still tell the story. Almost forty years after the 1968 season, the team photo still hung on the wall at the local drugstore. Sam says, "To this day it's a big deal." Indeed, "If I wanted to be an alcoholic, this would be the perfect place for me. Because of that '68 team, they'll still buy me drinks." Sitting in a bar with players and townspeople from that era, "If we drink a little bit too much, it don't matter where we're at, we're gonna go right back to that game." In 2008 (the year of my interview), Sam was the Magdalena High School basketball coach, and the Steers were in the middle of another winning season. "These kids, when they get older, when they're my age or your age, they can look back. You don't have to win it all for it to be important. You can look back, and it's something to tell someone else about, judge your life by. It's your history. Some people don't have a story to tell. I do have one story to tell, and that's the 1968 basketball team."

CHAPTER EIGHT
LEGACIES AND DEPARTURES

In some respects the coming-of-age experience in west-central New Mexico in the post–World War II era had changed little from that of the first half of the twentieth century. An imaginary sky traveler surveying the landscape below in 1945 would have seen mostly Anglo children setting off alone, horseback, in search of a stray cow, watching their father float a loop over a cow's horns, or cutting a calf out of the herd for branding. Alamo Navajo children were still hitching horses to wagons for the purpose of hauling wood or water and turning out sheep at daybreak for the day's grazing. Hispanic seven-year-olds still nervously wondered what to confess on the day of their First Communion. To this sky traveler it was the same familiar landscape of plains, mesas, and mountains still populated by antelope, deer, coyotes, and mountain lions but also by domestic stock to which both ranchers and Navajos looked for sustenance and income. The locomotive out of Socorro still pulled mostly empty stock cars up the 30-mile grade to the Magdalena stockyards and returned with bawling cattle and bleating sheep, though the latter now constituted a smaller portion of the shipment. Finally, in Magdalena's kitchens, cafes, and bars, and across the Alamo Navajo Reservation as well, the discourse of memory still played itself out in the distinctive tongues of Spanish, Navajo, and English. Old-timers still told stories of how it had been once upon a time. Shale-faced St. Mary Magdalene still looked down from the mountain.

But this sky view was somewhat deceptive, not because the scenes described did not exist but because it ignored the ways in which the region was changing. A closer look at the landscape would have revealed that grizzlies and wolves were now long extinct, the grass much degraded by drought and overgrazing, and the forested mountains more securely under the control of the federal government. Finally, the region was beginning to feel modernity's influence in both small and significant ways. One only had to turn to the heavens to see the changes. Where ranchers had once scanned the heavens for rain clouds, where Navajos searched the starry night for the *yikáísdáhí'*, or Milky Way, so now physicists, military strategists, and engineers turned to the skies both to explore the mysteries of the solar system and to invent new weapons of mass destruction. Consider the following scenes.

Scene 1: Datil, 1945. Let us call her Alice Rudman. On the predawn morning of July 16, Alice is asleep in her mountain cabin when she is jolted awake by what she thinks is a clap of thunder. But when looking outside, she recalls, "There wasn't a cloud in the sky," so "I didn't know what to think." Later in the day, ranchers setting out in the still-darkened dawn reported seeing a great flash of light to the southwest. The next day Alice read in the newspaper that a munitions dump had exploded at White Sands, New Mexico. Miraculously, nobody had been killed in the accident. The true story emerged the next month when news of Hiroshima came over the wires. Alice, who had ridden on roundups, helped push cattle across the San Augustine Plains, and camped out with cowboys around a chuck wagon, suddenly understood that the world had changed: "The first atomic bomb what was ever dropped in the world woke me up."[1]

Scene 2: Alamo Navajo Reservation, early 1970s. On a topographical rise at Alamo Springs, one of the settlements on the reservation, a man lights several candles in paper bags anchored with sand and places them in a circle. In the pitch dark of the night the hilltop luminaries give off an eerie, unworldly glow. Several families live in the settlement, so word spreads quickly about the strange phenomenon. Culturally wired to fear evil as an ever-threatening menace and generally leery of the darkness of night as a natural habitat for the same, some in the settlement suspect the worst. Many in the neighborhood also attend the nearby Word of God church, home to weekly emotional meetings, and are therefore primed to discard strictly rational explanations for the hilltop glow of light. At this point, someone suggests that the lights might be connected to the landing of an unidentified flying object, a handy explanation because elsewhere in the state *biligáana* alarmists have reported such sightings. At this point, panic sets in. One man can be seen running around with a bible in one hand and a pistol in the other. "Yeah, they were panicked," Norman Secatero recalls. "Everybody was loading up, you know. They were stuffing their bedrolls, and everybody was ready to take off, leave the reservation—running around with guns and everything." Something had to be done, so Norman volunteered to climb the rocky hill with his son to get to the bottom of the matter. Reaching the top, he hollered to those below, "There's nothing up here, just a bunch of candles," and then w-h-o-o-s-h, tossed one down to assure the anxious crowd. Fears abated, and those gathered drifted back to their homes. But this strange night could not be easily forgotten. Indeed, the hilltop feature now had a new name, one that exists to this day—UFO.[2]

Scene 3: San Augustine Plains, 1980. This great mountain-bordered basin, once home to vast herds of antelope and wild horses, is now home to a monumental science station devoted to the study of the heavens—the so-called Very Large Array (VLA). Formally dedicated in 1980 and operated by the National Radio Astronomy Observatory, the project began with construction in the 1970s, eventually taking on the shape of two gigantic telescopes and twenty-nine enormous movable dish antennas. As one public relations document explains, "Radio astronomy is the study of celestial objects that emit radio waves. With radio astronomy, scientists can study astronomical phenomena that are often invisible in other portions of the electromagnetic spectrum." At the VLA, "using radio astronomy techniques, astronomers can observe the Cosmic Microwave Background Radiation, which is the remnant signal of the birth of our Universe in the Big Bang. They can also probe the 'Dark Ages' before the onset of the first stars or galaxies, and study the earliest generation of galaxies. Radio astronomers analyze and explore the black holes that live at the hearts of most galaxies."[3]

If ever there were forces designed—unintentionally to be sure—to unhinge old identities, to produce the sensation that one was, in the words of one novelist, "Lost in the Cosmos," modernity's invasion of the San Augustine Plains seems particularly suggestive.[4] But for most earthlings in the region, ethnocultural moorings were not so easily uprooted.

Domains and Contexts

The family remained the earliest institutional influence in children's lives. For Anglo ranch children, the nuclear family was preeminent. With the dictates of aridity and drought requiring an ever-larger expanse of grass and a dependable water source, ranch families in the post–World War II era lived even further apart than in years before. (In 1987 the average size of a ranch in Socorro and Catron Counties was respectively 4,961 and 6,425 acres.)[5] For Hispanics, who mostly lived in Magdalena, extensive networks of uncles, aunts, and grandparents, reinforced by the tradition of *compadrazgo* (godparenting), family structure was, if not tighter, at least more broadly defined. Hispanic mothers now exercised greater autonomy than in the traditional patriarchal family, though many men still adhered to the old maxim *Mientas en mi casa estoy, rey soy* ("As long as I am in my house,

I am king"). In keeping with Navajo tradition, Alamo children continued to grow up with a high degree of autonomy. Similarly, traditional definitions of kinship beyond the nuclear model still largely held sway. Although several assimilative forces—off-reservation employment, years at boarding school, missionaries, and media exposure—had served to weaken the matricenteredness of the community, it too remained a discernible feature of Alamo Navajo social organization.

Religion also continued to shape the lives of children, although the nature of the inscription was by no means uniform. The shrinking Anglo population might attend one of the Protestant churches, although the distance of some ranches, even in the age of the pickup truck, discouraged weekly attendance. In 1983, mostly Anglo worshippers congregated at the annual Montosa Camp Meeting, by then a fifty-year-old gathering. But as the *Magdalena Mountain Mail* noted, the hymn singing and preaching mostly held its appeal for adults. "This year there was an increase in the number of young people . . . and their presence caused some minor problems. Next year the camp rules will be posted in obvious places. Parents will be asked to keep an eye on the children, and more activities will be planned for the young ones." On Thursday night, members of the Alamo Baptist Church joined the gathering for some praying and singing. "Their songs were enjoyed by all, but the audience had trouble meeting the challenge of singing Amazing Grace when the leaders were singing in Navajo." As we have already seen, the conversion of the Alamo Navajos to Christianity was decades in the making, but the force and enormity of the change were now being realized.[6] Meanwhile, Catholicism remained an important element in Hispanic identity. If the church's influence was somewhat diminished compared with that of an earlier time, it remained an enculturating force of significance. The Church of St. Mary Magdalene remained the site where children, under the guidance of the priest, learned the teachings of the church, the rituals of worship, and perhaps most significantly, that being Hispanic meant being Catholic.

Children's traditional patterns of work and play were still evident as well. Navajo children still gathered wood and water, picked piñon, performed household tasks, helped raise smaller siblings, and herded sheep. Anglo ranch children still pursued a range of demanding chores associated with the cattle economy, and regardless of gender, generally preferred those activities that put them in touch with animals. In town, various household chores and odd jobs—remember Ray Martínez and Ramón Gutiérriz cleaning bricks—still occupied a segment of children's lives. In the realm of play, younger children still played games involving running and jumping; they now also played with modern toys such as Legos and Cabbage Patch dolls. Although older ones still sought out the adventure of riding horses, exploring, hunting, and camping, the fact was that school athletics was now swallowing up much of their playtime. The great exception to this development was the sport of children's rodeo, where the domains of play and work were fused in dramatic combination. (Extensive treatment of the subject follows.)

In the realm of pleasures—material, sensual, and romantic—the world had changed considerably over the century. Ranch house dances, box suppers, the months of longing for the sight of Magdalena, and the weeks of waiting for the latest order from the Montgomery Ward Catalogue were all things of the past. For mainly Anglo and Hispanic adolescents, greater access to cars and pickups, television and radio, but particularly the increasing influence of "teenage culture," including ever-more-suggestive song lyrics (think Madonna's "Like a virgin / Touched for the very first time / Like a virgin") contributed to a general relaxation in sexual mores. The disciplined steps of the square dance—"meet your lady and turn right back"—had long given way to the intimacy of the last slow dance at a school affair, followed by the short drive up to the ghost town of Kelly, which, in the words of one woman, was everybody's favorite "lovers' lane." For older Hispanics who had grown up under the tradition of strict chaperonage, the transition was especially hard to accept. One woman laments, "I know a lot of the Spanish girls. Now they have babies without getting married. And they don't seem to think anything of it."[7]

As we have already seen, over the course of the century, schools, as agencies for building literacy and citizenship, or more problematically, as instruments of internal colonialism, emerged as an increasingly determinative force in the lives of children. In Magdalena's classrooms, hallways, and playing fields Anglos, Hispanics, and Navajos came to know one another and along the way chose to participate, or not, in intercultural border crossings. The story of the schools in this ongoing intercultural drama, as we shall shortly see, would become even more complicated in the years ahead. But before returning to this subject, developments in two other cultural realms—religion and play—require further consideration.

Religion

In this year of 1989 Candelaria García is worried. For more than fifty years she has been instructing children in the foundations of the Catholic faith. But it has all changed somehow. In her youth it was much stricter, more demanding. For one thing, parents cared much more. There was a time when parents helped instruct their children in the catechism, taught them their prayers, and insisted on their going to church. No longer. More and more, she sees families coming to church only "when they need it"—for baptisms, marriages, and funerals—and do not even know how to conduct themselves properly. Now too many parents do not "even tell them to pray at night. But I can't go to their homes and tell them just do that." Then, too, the after-school Confraternity of Christian Doctrine (CCD) classes only meet once a week. Thirty years ago it was twice, and on occasion, even three times a week. "But there wasn't so much sports then. And now everything is sports, and the people go more for sports than religion."[8]

But it is her calling to carry on. The children's very souls are at risk. So, assisted by three other Hispanic women, some thirty children are sorted out in three age groups for instruction, Candelaria taking the oldest. For those younger children coming from the most devout families this instruction will help prepare them for a central moment in their lives, First Communion. As one scholar explains, "First Communion is a rite of passage in which initiates move from one status to another in their religious community. Joined to the Church through Baptism, the children can now unite with God and the Church through the partaking of Jesus' body and blood in the consecrated bread and wine of the Eucharist." Candelaria's special challenge this year is to prepare two boys for this moment, no easy task because they come to her terribly unprepared. How can she teach them in one year all that is required? What will the priest say when he examines them and finds their knowledge wanting? She will have to explain to the Father that if she does not "put them through" this year, the two will likely not return the following year and will therefore be lost to the church. Certainly the Father will understand the dilemma. Meanwhile, "it all relies on me."[9]

At the heart of the Catholic worldview is that a loving God is the ultimate source of all that is good in the world, so loving that He sacrificed his only Son, Jesus, in order to "save us" from our sins and offer us the promise of everlasting life. The youngest children must be made to understand that their very existence, and the existence of everything they hold dear, is because of God. "What did He give you?" the teacher asks the youngest class. With some prompting, several children name parts of their body—their eyes, ears, and mouths—but then broaden the horizon to include parents and extended family members. The teacher then extends the boundaries of thankfulness even further. "And He made the world and what is good in the world." All that they love is because of God. The teacher, who is barely out of her teens, and whom the children seem to look upon as an older sister, explains: "God wants me to know more about how much He loves me. I will listen and learn more about God. I am learning to love my God. My parents and teachers tell me about God. They tell me about the many ways that God shows His love for me. . . . Because of God's love for me I can say, 'Thank you God. I love you very much.'"

So they begin their spiritual journey into belief. The pedagogy is more than drill and memorization, although there is much of both. Each class begins with reciting the Sign of the Cross, the Lord's Prayer, and Hail Mary. It is painstaking labor and requires much patience. The teacher's manual, for instance, suggests that some of the smaller children will not know their left from their right hand, so in teaching the Sign of the Cross, the teacher should stand behind each child, take his or her right hand and walk them through the prayer.[10] Considerable time is spent reading stories, engaging in role playing, and coloring pictures. All four teachers are gentle and understanding, an extension of the homes to which the children will run after class. Or at least that is the earnest hope: that family and church are working in concert. "Every night when you're going to say your prayers, don't go to sleep. Tell mama, I need to say my prayers." At one point the teacher asks, "Can you tell me how many people are needed to make a family? and then answers, "God is the main one," followed by fathers, mothers, brothers, sisters, aunts, uncles, and grandparents. Just as their family at home loves them, she continues, so it is with the larger family of God. "Jesus is with us ALL the time. He takes care of us. Always remember that God is taking care of us. Even when we're playing on the playground . . . or when we are doing our work at home." Because they are part of one spiritual body, that is to say, one family, "EVERYBODY goes to church as a family."

There is a bewildering mélange of information to convey to their young hearts and minds, and it must be scaled down to what they can comprehend: points of doctrine, the sacraments, the prayers, the meaning behind the array of rituals and symbols, bible stories, the religious calendar, including the days of obligations. Advent and Lent receive special attention. In the former instance the younger children listen as their teacher explains that during the four-week period of Advent they are awaiting the birth of Jesus. So they might better remember the significance of Advent, the younger children are given a handout to color—a ribboned wreath encircling four candles. The teacher instructs them to color the wreath green (everlasting life), the first three candles purple, the fourth pink (signifying the birth of the baby Jesus), and the ribbon red (the blood of Christ). Months later, one of the teachers of the older students announces, "Close your books so I can talk about Lent." She explains about the forty days of Lent, how the priest will put ashes on their foreheads, and then she moves quickly to a discussion of Holy Week, culminating in the crucifixion and resurrection. She concludes by emphasizing that the forty days of Lent are days of obligation—that children, as Catholics, should make some small sacrifice, something on the order of giving up candy. "Ooh, that's a hard one, huh? Or not chewing gum. That's hard, too."

Over the course of the year considerable time is devoted to the Blessed Mother—"Hail Mary, full of Grace." "She's my mother, your mother, and everybody's mother," Candelaria García passionately tells her class. "But She was born WITHOUT sin. We are born WITH sin, but the Blessed Mother wasn't. She was free from sin, and She was selected to be the Holy Mother of God." There is another Mary also, she explains, the one whose face adorns the mountain. This is the Mary for whom the town is named, the same Mary who is the patron saint of the very church in which they will receive First Communion. Unlike the Blessed Mother, this Mary was not of pure origins. Candelaria tells them how Mary Magdalene was a "thief, a cheater, and a liar"—in short, a sinner. The people shunned her and kept her away from their children. Then Jesus called her "to a new way of life." She was sorry for her sins, and Jesus forgave her. "When He was nailed to the cross, she stood there near Him. The Apostles were scared, but not Mary." So at the time of the Resurrection, it was Mary to whom the Lord Jesus Christ appeared. Surely there is a lesson here: "No matter what you've done, as long as you are sincere about wanting to be forgiven, God will forgive you." The stone face on the mountain is an ever-present reminder of this possibility.

The subjects of belonging and protection are also strong themes. The teacher of the youngest children reads, "It is good to be together. We belong to one another. It is good to be together. We belong to God our father. It is good to be together. We belong to Jesus our Brother. It is good to be together." Then she asks; "Is it nice to be all by yourself? Or is it nice to be together?" The class calls out, "To be together." Never more so, the teacher emphasizes, than when they are frightened. Fear is something that the smaller children understand, and the teacher plays on it. "You need to always remember that you're not alone all the time, even when your mom and dad are not with you, or your brothers and sisters, or your friends. . . . You have to remember that Jesus is there." When they are alone and frightened, they should ask Jesus for help. On the subject of spiritual protectors, they also learn about guardian angels. These heavenly spirits, sent by God, are truly wonderful, the teacher explains, because they can protect them from terrible things, like a bad dream. "When you are having a bad dream, the guardian angel is there" watching over them. Indeed, "all the time the guardian angel takes care of us." One way they do this, she explains, is to keep us from sinning. There is a prayer, of course, and the youngest are encouraged to memorize it.

By the age of eight or nine, Catholic children will have experienced three of the church's seven sacraments.[11] The first of these is Baptism, and the teacher goes to great lengths to impress on the children that this was their first initiation into the church's fold, the moment the priest put water on their infant foreheads and recited the words, "I baptize you in the name of the Father and the Son and of the Holy Spirit." This sacrament was now behind them—almost. After showing the youngest class a photograph of a child being baptized, the teacher springs a monumental question on the class. What if there is no priest in the area, and they come across a baby "and he's real sick, and there is nobody to baptize this baby and you don't want this baby to die without being baptized?" Then the teacher's answer: "You can do it. You can baptize the baby." This is new information: most have never heard such a thing. The teacher continues, "Anybody can baptize. That's why I teach you to do this, so that you can LEARN, so that in CASE—it doesn't really happen, but sometimes it does—then you can baptize that baby. . . . Okay? You think you can do it, if ever you needed to? Okay? It's very important for a baby to be baptized. You think you can baptize somebody?" One girl thinks she can do it, so utters a timid "yes."

But these classes are largely focused on the next two sacraments: Reconciliation and the Holy Eucharist. The children learn that the two are closely linked. The first is essentially about healing, purification, and God's forgiveness of past sins. Reconciliation embodies four phases: contrition, the sinner's remorse for wrongdoing and "hurting Jesus"; confession, the sinner's private moment of telling the priest of his or her sins; absolution, the priest's bestowal of God's forgiveness; and penance, the priest's directive of acts to be performed by the remorseful sinner to atone for past mistakes. After the requirements of Reconciliation are fulfilled, the child can participate in the Eucharist, that is, make his or her first Holy Communion. This ritual moment marks a defining moment in the child's spiritual evolution, a rite of passage that permits him or her to partake in the consecrated bread and wine—the body and blood of Christ—symbolizing the child's new connection with God through his Son, who was sacrificed upon the cross. As the teachers' program manual states: "Receiving the Eucharist is the Christian's way of acknowledging, 'Yes, I belong!'"[12]

Much attention is given to the subject of sin. The children learn that there are two categories of sin, venal and mortal, and because they are young, they have only committed the former. But as the teachers make clear, there is a long list of these. Examples include disobeying parents, unnecessary arguing, fighting, cheating at school, telling hateful stories about other children, cruelty toward animals, and lying. On the latter, Candelaria tells the younger children, "Maybe your mama has some good things in the icebox, and she told you not to eat them until she gave them to you, and you go ahead and steal them. And then Mama said, 'Where did my cookies or my pudding . . . disappear to?' And then you say, 'I didn't do it, Mama. I didn't do it.' That's a sin." To the older ones the pitch is decidedly more emphatic. "We must always remember that we are children of God. Remember that. Remember, you are always children of God, no matter what—no matter if you say I'm no good, I'm a sinner. . . . God forgives us all. So we are all children of God. See he loves us, no matter if we sin. If we fall again, get up. But remember, ask God to forgive you. Say, God forgive me, I'm your child."

The two boys on the precipice of making the Act of Contrition for the first time are noticeably nervous and must be carefully prepared for the moment. (One will drop out.) They need to memorize the ritualistic steps. When entering the confessional, they should say, "Bless me, Father, for I have sinned. This is my first confession." Upon finishing their list of sins, they should say, "That is all, Father." At this point the priest will give them their penance. Perhaps they will be instructed to pray the Lord's Prayer, perhaps three Hail Mary's, or they might be directed to perform some good deed. Following the priest's instruction, they must be prepared, if the priest requests it, to pray the Act of Contrition.

> O my God, I am sorry for my sins.
> In choosing to sin and failing to do good,
> I have sinned against You and Your Church.
> I firmly intend, with the help of Your Son,
> to do penance and to sin no more.

When the priest dismisses them, they must not forget to say, "Thank you, Father."

On the day of the child's First Communion a special program usually accompanies the ritual. This year it will be less elaborate than in years past, when more children were undergoing the celebration. When several children are involved, the celebration might include a procession and a painted banner, the children reading a piece of scripture or singing a hymn ("Here I Am Lord" is a favorite), or the priest gathering the children around him for special remarks. One year, for instance, two glasses—one filled with dirt, one with water—were placed on a table, whereupon each child was handed the glass of water, signifying the absolution of sin, a necessary condition for the moment of receiving the body and blood of Christ during Holy Communion. Whatever the ritualistic accoutrements, at the conclusion of the rite the children have now achieved a new spiritual status. The faithful sing "Amen, Amen."

But there is something else going on in these classes. Over the course of learning to be Catholic, the children are also hearing a strong social message about their responsibility to others, including showing compassion for the less fortunate. For the youngest the message is mostly about family members and playmates. For instance, in the context of talking about the meaning of sin and penance, the teacher shows her class a picture of two children, one of them crying, and then she explains: "That little one is crying over here. And that's why she [the other] has to be sorry. She's probably going to have to go and tell her 'I'm sorry.' That's what we have to do when we do something wrong. When we're fighting, and you're sorry that you're fighting with whoever you're fighting with, you have to go say 'I'm sorry because I was mean to you.'" She adds this comment: "You might not like everybody, but you have to try and love everybody."

For the older children the message is broader and deeper. Candelaria reminds her class of Jesus' words to his followers: "For I was hungry and you gave me to eat; I was thirsty and you gave me to drink; I was a stranger and you took me in. Naked, and you covered me; Sick, and you visited me; I was in prison, and you came to me." When His followers professed no memory of this, Jesus responded, "I say to you, as long as you did it to one of these my least brethren, you did it to me." Candelaria then proceeds to explain how all these are "acts of mercy," and how, as Catholics, they must strive to practice them, how when they give food and clothing to the needy and visit those in prison, "You're doing it for God." Once more, "Never be ashamed . . . to bring poor children into your home. Never be ashamed to help someone who has less than you do. . . . Sometimes you can't take someone in your home. But you can pray. That's one thing nobody can take away from you. Pray." She asks the children if they see lines of people on television asking for food. They nod that they have seen this. Some might think, she continues, that the poor are simply lazy. "But we don't know," she offers. "We can't judge; we don't know. If you are faced in a situation like that, the best thing to do is . . . give them something to eat, even if you don't have much yourself." Indeed, Candelaria explains that the message of compassion extends to all of God's creatures. She asks, Do the children kick or hit their pets with sticks? The question meets with a resounding "NO!" She then tells them that some people are "very mean" to animals, for example, mercilessly whipping their horses. Such individuals "don't cherish what God has given them."

For the most part, the children, especially the younger ones, are cooperative. The teachers' friendly and caring manner along with the mix of pedagogical practices make for a positive learning atmosphere. After all, these mother-teachers are devoting these hours to save their little souls. But these same souls are capable of testing the spiritual waters. When the younger children are asked how they can show their love "for all living things," a child responds with, "Take care of them." So far, so good. The teacher presses, "What sort of living things?" At this point, a child responds, "How about bugs?" The teacher can only respond, "What kind of bugs?" This is their opening, and all manner of insects are offered up for protection—spiders, ladybugs, potato bugs. The teacher, realizing she is in dangerous territory, suggests higher forms, that dogs and cats might be better candidates. But one boy will have no part of it and returns to less desirable creatures. Why not rats? The class breaks out in laughter. Realizing this is going nowhere, the teacher returns to an earlier theme of the day: "What can you thank God for?" This moves the discussion to safer ground, from bugs to rainbows. Such is the risk in soliciting children's thinking on such heavy matters. In another class, the teacher asks, "What should we do if we wake up in a bad mood?" and meets with the unexpected response: "Go crazy." "NO," the instructor emphasizes, "We should pray! You can always make your prayers."

As a historian, I ask myself, What is the significance of these classes in the overall coming-of-age experience? The most obvious is that they provided an all-encompassing and coherent worldview that, if taken to heart, offered children spiritual solace and guidance throughout the balance of their lives. But one is also struck by the extent to which the classes reinforced the other institutions in which the child was embedded, namely, school and family.

The church-family connection is self-evident. The church-school connection is less so, but evident in three ways. First, although the classes did not explicitly aim to build academic skills, the amount of time teachers spent helping children read aloud, that is, helping younger learners pronounce and understand the meaning of words, surely enhanced their reading abilities. Second, time and again the teachers made clear their support for the overall importance of education. During a lesson on saints, for instance, the teacher asked, "What do you pray to St. Thomas for? When the child responded, "To help us in school," the teacher added, "We really need to learn. God gave us a mind, but sometimes we need help. It's sort of hard to learn, so we pray to St. Thomas so he can help us learn." In a session devoted to the Fourth Commandment, after the children agreed that they should honor God and their parents above all, Candelaria, who once taught school, emphasized: "And what about your teachers in school? You're supposed to obey and respect [them] when you go to school. The teachers take the place of your parents. Remember that. You say, the teacher doesn't [should not] boss me. Don't say that, because the teacher takes the place of your parents while you're in school." Finally, the message of compassion for others carried over to the schools. Lest her students miss the connection, Candelaria lectured her class:

> Some people do not have the capacity that you have. They can't think as well as you do. So they ask for your help. Don't send them away.... Like in school, maybe some of you can work arithmetic. Maybe your friend can't. So help 'em. Or maybe you learned your English, proper words, your spelling; these are sounds they don't know. Even [if] he or she tries it, they can't get it. That means they're not ignorant: they're slow.... So help them. Don't say they're ignorant.

Meanwhile, the youngest children are learning to recite the lines: "For the times I have not shown love at home, Jesus, I am sorry. For the times I have hurt others at school, Jesus, I am sorry."

One can never know how this carries over to a school where Anglos, Hispanics, and Navajos are still negotiating the boundaries of difference. At the same time, one cannot help but think that CCD classes have played some part in enlarging the circle of mutual acceptance, of bridging the barriers of history and difference. Meanwhile, the stone face on the mountain looks down on the town wondering, one imagines, What will become of the children? What will become of the town? She has seen much and knows there are so many reasons for Acts of Contrition. In the small good works of children, there is hope.

The Alamo Navajos and God

The story of Hispanic Catholicism is largely one of continuity. The Alamo Navajos' march toward Protestantism, on the other hand, was quite the opposite. As we have already observed, the Alamo Navajo community's exposure to Christianity came in waves: Catholic priests, Baptist missionaries, boarding school, and later, the Magdalena Baptist Mission's outreach to children in the town's dormitories. Also, recall that the absence of a fully developed ceremonial system, that is to say, an insufficient number of singers or medicine men to offer the full complement of traditional ceremonies, made the Alamo Navajo community, especially the children, particularly susceptible to these incursions. In these contexts the rapid conversion to Christianity since the 1960s can be understood.

By the mid-1980s, two churches on the reservation, both led by local pastors, were competing for followers. The first was the Baptist church, established in the early 1930s. The second, the Word of God church, was founded in the 1960s and quickly gained in popularity owing to its Pentecostal orientation. Because the Word of God church appealed to a growing number in the community, membership at the Baptist church declined. A third force in the area was evangelical tent meetings both on and off the reservation. Both the Word of God church and the tent meetings were characterized by emotional preaching, singing, praying, shouting, fits of shaking, speaking in tongues, emotional conversions, and miraculous healings.[13] To be sure, the shift to Christianity was not absolute. A few Alamo Navajos still practiced the old ways, with some taking an additive posture toward the two systems of belief. For instance, one man says, "I believe in going to church. I also go to squaw dances. I still believe in the old traditional way because it was made for the Navajo people." But by the end of the 1970s this attitude was not widely held.[14]

To understand the force of the Alamo Navajo community's embrace of evangelical Protestantism one must listen to the dramatic conversion stories of those living on the reservation. While doing so, this writer was immediately struck by the ways in which the "new religion"—strange as it may seem—functioned in important ways like the "old" one. How was this so? First, just as traditional Navajo rituals were often healing ceremonies, so many conversion stories involve the curing of various physical and psychological maladies—including alcohol addiction. Listen to this account by "Sister" Helen Rincon, who with her husband, "Brother" Gabley, conducted summer revival camp meetings at Alamo. In the midst of Gabley's preaching, Rincon says she was approached by members of Larry Monte's family who explained that the elder was deathly ill. Would Sister Helen come and pray over him?

> Brother Larry's leg was full of big running sores, one of which was down to the bone. He was in great pain. They asked me to pray for him. I told them I knew they knew the Lord could heal Larry, and He would do it that night. I took out some anointing oil, all the time praying to God for a miracle so that the unbelievers would see and know God's power. I began at the knee of Larry's leg with the oil, and as I was coming slowly down the leg with it, I felt God's power surging through my body to Larry. Right before the eyes of all, the sores disappeared, the family crying and praising God. [Someone] said, "Dad, look at your leg." He began crying and said the next day he would go out and tell everyone of his healing.[15]

Larry Monte's healing, locals say, was a major factor in the growth of Pentecostalism at Alamo.

Alcoholism has played havoc in many Native American communities, and so it has at Alamo—with dire consequences for children.[16] The Navajo pastor of the Baptist church confesses, "About twenty years I was so bad. Too much drink. That's about all I think about. I live in this house—dirt floor. I have seven girls—children—five boys. And I don't even think about it. Every time I get a little money I want to go to Magdalena and drink. Nobody over here to take care of my children. Finally, we got so bad . . . both of us start to drinkin'—myself and my wife." At this point a relative came by and insisted that he come to a revival meeting.

> I said okay. I don't get my hat. I don't even wash my face, puttin' new clothes or anything like that. I just say okay. I don't even ask my wife. Let's go. I just went, and I guess she follow me. We get over there. We sit way in back row. And there was a lot of singing goin' on in Navajo—hymns. They sing, they testify. So we just sit in the back. Finally, he finished preaching. He said: "Anybody want to accept the Lord as their savior?" So I just got up. I don't even ask my wife. I just got up and went over there. The only thing he said to me: "You gonna trust in Jesus?" I said "yes." He told me, "Talk about what your problem is." I just raise my hand and I said: "Lord, I don't want to drink no more wine. I don't even want to think about it—beer, whisky, cigarette, somethin' that's dirty—I don't want it no more." So he told me: "Kneel down . . . and pray some more." I say the same thing again. That's about all I say. And we come back that night. Next morning I get up fine. I'm still that way. It changed my whole life.[17]

The most dramatic occurrence comes from an older man, Samuel Apache, who recalls what happened one November when he and his wife went into Magdalena to vote. "We went over there, me and my wife. A lot of the guys started drinkin', and I joined them. My wife, she begged me, let's go home. And I still stayed and got drunk." There was an old house nearby where the Indians sometimes congregated to recover from a night of drinking.

> I don't know how I got over there. It was about midnight and all these Navajos were laying around. And they had an old stove. And I was getting pretty cold. I had no coat. I laid beside that stove. And somebody called me and said, "You want more drink? . . . And he give me one of those little jugs of wine. And then I started drinking, and soon I pass out. And then I don't know what I was doin' there . . . and I turned to the stove there. My knee was against the stove. It was [like] red fire. I didn't even know I was getting burned, I don't know how long, see, but somebody pulled me off. And then next day I woke up. I don't know this thing, see. And then my wife, she came there after me, and we came back home. . . . And then . . . I said, "I don't know what's the matter with my knee. It start itching." And then I pull off my pants and there's nothin' but water burstin' out the burn. O-o-h, it starts hurtin'. And then I stay here all day. Overnight it starts hurtin' more and swell up down to the foot. They took me to the hospital.

After a couple of days in the hospital, the scorched leg was still swollen and excruciatingly painful. Unable to do anything for him, the doctors informed Samuel they would have to send him up to a hospital in Albuquerque where they would have to amputate. But his wife would not hear of it and soon appeared with someone to take him home. Back at Alamo, she took him to an all-night prayer meeting held at Larry Monte's. The next day Samuel awoke to find that his leg "didn't seem to hurt no more," and he could take small steps. The praying had done it. "It just heal up."[18]

A second connection between traditional Navajo ceremonialism and the new religion was their shared belief in evil as an ever-present, palpable, and destructive force in their midst. For those growing up with a fear of witchery, the Pentecostal fixation with evil made perfect sense.

References to Satan in Alamo Navajo conversion stories are frequent. Thus, after describing how he was cured of serious back pain, one man says: "The devil will destroy any way it's possible." Another man tells of how he began hearing strange sounds, the condition aggravated, he believes, by heavy drinking. "I began to wonder what caused that sound. Would it be those traditional ways? Am I being witched? As my wife would follow me around outside, we would talk about it all the times.... A man by the name of Tom came and suggested that I should have one of the ceremonies for me. So I had one, and I even got worse. This time I was seeing things. I was seeing some creature." As a last resort he turned to the Pentecostals, who organized several prayer meetings on his behalf. Because of these prayer sessions, he contends, he was cured.[19] Then there is this startling account, again from Sister Helen Rincon:

> Some people from Alamo came to a tent meeting at Socorro. My husband was preaching. A lady told me to come to the pickup—they needed help. I went to the pickup. A girl was in the back. She was tied up. She was devil-possessed and wild. I told her to get down and come in the meeting, we wanted to help her. She said, "No, I don't want it." I went back to the meeting and told my husband, [so] he went to the pickup and jumped in, looked down at the girl, and said, "Get out and come to the meeting so we can help you." She looked up to him. She recognized his authority through God. They untied her, she got down, and we all went back to the tent. There we prayed for and laid hands on her. She was healed and saved that night.[20]

So how did the rapid and dramatic conversion of the Alamo Navajos to fundamentalist Protestantism, especially the Pentecostal variety, affect children's lives? Most immediately, it appears to have improved the quality of their daily physical and emotional existence. When scarce resources were diverted from putting food on the table to buying jugs of wine, children suffered from hunger, neglect, and abuse. One woman recalls she was just ten years old when her parents went to Magdalena to drink, leaving her to babysit the other children. "Whenever they go to town . . . they never come back until late at night." On these occasions, she was nearly petrified by her fear of skinwalkers, about which her parents had told her many stories. All she could do was gather the children around her in bed. It was especially terrifying, she says, when the dogs began howling, and she could hear the children's hearts beating.[21] When parents gave up drinking, children in such families lived in a much more emotionally secure environment. The second consequence of this shift in religious outlook was more problematic: it had important implications for how elders perceived themselves as transmitters of the Navajo cultural heritage—that is to say, how Alamo Navajo children should come to know themselves as cultural beings. The importance of this question would emerge in the years following 1979, when the Alamo Navajo community established its own school.

Children's Rodeo

While the Alamo Navajos were denying their youth a key element of their ancestral tradition, mostly Anglo ranchers were doubling down on the central myth of the West, personified by the region's foremost cultural hero—the cowboy. The sport of rodeo is a public ritualistic performance in which contestants compete for buckles, saddles, and money prizes in various events involving riding and roping.[22] As both the outgrowth and celebration of the ranching life and the "cowboy way," rodeo, as we have already seen, has deep roots in New Mexico history. Because rodeo can be traced back to the Spanish and Mexican eras, and because of the Navajos' long experience with horses and livestock, participants in children's rodeo in the Magdalena region during the 1980s were not exclusively Anglo, but mainly so. This was testimony in large part to the fact that most ranches in the area were owned by Anglos and that considerable expenses are accrued when pursuing the so-called rodeo circuit. Still, myth, memory, and the excitement of "making a good ride" continue to give the sport great appeal across the three groups.[23]

New Mexico youths participate in rodeos in several venues, ranging from the local to the national level. Various associations such as 4-H, the New Mexico Junior Rodeo Association, and the National High School Rodeo Association set the guidelines and rules for the sport, including the determination of contestant qualification, age categories, scoring guidelines, dress, conduct, and the treatment of livestock. Generally speaking, boys and girls compete separately. At the High School National Finals in 1989, for instance, the events strictly open to boys were calf roping, bareback bronc riding, steer wrestling, bull riding, and saddle bronc riding. Girls competed in barrel running, pole bending, breakaway calf roping, goat tying, and the contest for rodeo queen. The "cutting horse" event was open to both boys and girls, but competition was strictly separate. The only event in which both sexes competed together was "dally team roping." For many rodeo youths the opportunity to compete in the national finals, an honor earned by being a top contender at the state level, is an unforgettable experience. Remarkably, in both 1988 and 1989, two young rodeo cowboys from the Magdalena region—Jimmy Don McKinley and Ty Saulsbury—captured the coveted "all-around" title, a distinction achieved by "placing" in two or more events.

What follows is not a comprehensive description of all aspects of the rodeo scene but an exploration of how it shapes participants' identities and social outlook. We begin with the sights and sounds of the rodeo arena. After attending the Socorro County Fair rodeo in September 1990, I wrote in my journal:

> There is something primordial about a man/beast contest in a lighted arena in desert country, something starkly raw and essential about it. Kids are everywhere, hanging on the fences watching cowboys spur saddle broncs, rope and throw steers, and ride bulls, and in the middle of it all, watching them get bucked, thrown, and stomped on. Rodeo critics complain about the exploitation of the stock, but tonight the stock fared better than the cowboys. One rider was rushed to the hospital after the bull pitched him into the air, landing him on his head. By the time the pickup man and paramedics reached him, he was lying on his side, his head violently jerking from side to side. By night's end, the darkening sky gave way to forbidding black storm clouds and streaks of lightning.

Welcome to rodeo.

Rodeo opening ceremonies generally include a grand entry and the presentation of the flags (at Socorro those included the US, state, and state rodeo association's flags), a prayer, and the singing of the national anthem. Sitting in his elevated "box," the announcer makes clear that rodeo is about God, country, and the frontier heritage. "I think tonight when you leave here, if you don't have a chill at your back and a lump in your throat, and thank God for being an American, then something is wrong with ya. Because we're gonna present you tonight the western heritage . . . to bring that chill in your back and that lump in your throat—to be thankful to be an American." These themes are reinforced in the prayer:

> Heavenly Father, as we cross this country . . . and as we see the beauty of the sunset, the grandeur of the mountains, the strength and power of the waterfall, and the helplessness of the newborn calf, we thank You for this opportunity to come together and share in this celebration. And we ask that You watch over us, both man and animal. . . . We ask that You guide us in this arena by honesty and fair play. Protect our leader so that the free enterprise system and the American way of life will endure. We ask these things in the name of Jesus Christ. Amen.[24]

Although God and nation figure prominently in the rodeo narrative, the sport is essentially a paean to the frontier, or more precisely, the cowboy heritage. In children's rodeo this is clearly reflected in the various rulebooks governing participation. The National High School Rodeo Association (NHSRA) rules, for example, stipulate, "Contestants, parents, adults, helpers, and assistants must wear western attire: western hat, long-sleeved shirt (must be wrist-length sleeved shirt, with collar and cuffs)." Shirtsleeves, moreover, "must be rolled down" except for those of bareback and bull riders who, while competing, are permitted to "roll up sleeves two rolls, not exceed the elbow on riding arm only." As for cowboy hats, the rules specify that they must have a 2.5-inch minimum brim and 5-inch minimum crown. The New Mexico Junior Rodeo Association rules also require that "western boots" be part of the attire and that "boys' hair may be no longer than the back, lower edge of the collar and must be well groomed."[25] The only gender-specific rules (aside from gendered event categories) are the NHSRA rules for the queen, which, in addition to recognizable beauty contest scoring categories (modeling, appearance, etc.), include proven skill in horsemanship and the predictable cowgirl attire.[26] In short, the imagery of rodeo performers consciously projects an idealized conception of the ranching and cowboy heritage.

Livestock, of course, plays a central role in rodeo. Indeed, anthropologist Elizabeth Atwood Lawrence asserts that rodeo at its deepest level is a ritualized performance of the culture/nature, man/beast, and tame/wild dichotomies at the heart of the ranching economy. She asks, What was the western ranching story about if not conquering the land, eliminating species (wolves, grizzlies, coyotes) posing a threat to the pastoral economy, and finally, dominating and managing livestock? What was the West without the violence of breaking horses and roping cows for branding? Lawrence also points out that there is a definite livestock hierarchy in rodeo, the horse at the top, followed by the cow, and at the bottom, the lowly goat, a rough approximation of the pyramidal respect ranchers accord their livestock. (Bull riding, she argues, although not a ranch tradition, constitutes the ultimate in the man/beast contest.)[27] Rodeo enthusiasts bristle at the notion of animal cruelty. The *New Mexico 4-H Rodeo Rule Book*, in fact, includes a long list of requirements for minimizing injury to animals, including these: "Riders in the bareback and saddle bronc events cannot wear 'locked rowels' or 'sharpened spurs'; calves cannot be intentionally 'busted' in the roping event; in steer wrestling gouging the animal's eyes or nose with fingers is forbidden; [and] only sheepskin-lined flanking straps shall be

Table 8.1 Kids Rodeo Contestants by Gender, Ethnocultural Status, and Surname in 1985

	Male	Female	Unclear
Anglo	36	26	3
Hispanic	6	6	0
Navajo	2	0	0
Unclear	0	1	0

Note: In three instances Anglo contestants' first names were not a clear guide to gender status.

Source: Magdalena Kids Rodeo Program, 1985.

used on bucking stock."[28] Still, in the bareback saddle bronc and bull-riding events, riders hope for a good "draw," knowing full well that their score will depend in large part on their spurring. Meanwhile, in the events of goat tying and steer wrestling, animals are violently thrown to the ground. In short, although many precautions are taken to protect livestock, rodeo is inextricably rooted in the domination and exploitation of animals, and this is something youth participants take for granted. The myth demands it. It comes with the territory.

The 1984 Magdalena Old-Timers Rodeo, which by tradition scheduled one day for "kids' field events," and especially the 1985 Magdalena Kids Rodeo provide a revealing glimpse into how children are socialized into the sport. The latter event was the sixth year of a stand-alone rodeo for children ranging from ages under five to seventeen. Both boys and girls, depending on age, compete together and separately in the standard events of goat tying, pole bending, flag racing, barrel racing, team roping, and breakaway calf roping. The events of calf roping, steer riding, and bull riding are male-only competitions.[29] Again, the breakdown of the participants reveals that although the sport has wide appeal to both genders, when it comes to levels of ethnocultural participation, it is largely an Anglo affair (see Table 8.1). The last point calls for the following qualifications: the limitations for surnames for distinguishing ethnic ancestry in an era when intermarriage was becoming more prevalent and the fact that Alamo Navajos occasionally held their own rodeo. Still, given the fact that Anglos are a distinct minority in the area, the overrepresentation of this population is a telling reminder of the group's identification with the frontier heritage.

The opening prayer sets the tone for the day's events. At the 1984 rodeo, held on the July Fourth weekend, it was offered by the local Baptist minister,

George Britten. After thanking God for the many daily blessings of life, including that of living in the United States, Reverend Britten prayed for "our community who has come through a hundred years of frontier living . . . and for your blessings upon these young cowboys and cowgirls. We pray that you'll just give them ability even beyond their own today, help them compete like winners, realizing that not everyone will win. Help them, Lord, to sit deep in the saddle and not to throw too wide a loop. . . . Bless these young people now and keep your hand upon them and their mounts. [This] is our prayer in Jesus' name, Amen." Asked later about the meaning of "sitting deep in the saddle" and not throwing "too wide a loop," Reverend Britton explained that it was all very practical. If riders did not sit deep in the saddle, "they might fall off," and if they threw too wide a loop with their rope, "the steer runs through it." But the meaning, I sensed, ran deeper, which prompted him to elaborate that rodeo was also about building character. The young cowboy, he emphasized, "needs to know WHERE HE IS, WHY HE IS, and WHO HE IS. He needs to be able to look himself in the mirror in the morning and like that person he or she sees. He needs to walk with a firm step, or stand firmly wherever he is."[30]

So the rodeo begins. Sitting in the announcer's box, Barbara Foard narrates one event after another, calling out the names of each contestant, announcing the scores, and calling up winners to pick up their prizes: "Brandon, are you anywhere around? Would you like to come up to the announcing shed and get your buckle?" With the rodeo in full swing, one by one the young contestants, atop their favorite ranch horses and decked out in pearl-snap shirts and blouses, western hats and boots, jeans, and a rodeo prize buckle, enter the arena to attack goats, rope calves, or guide their horses around barrels in record time. For those riding bucking stock, spurs and chaps give added weight to the sense that the cowboy myth is alive and well. The sounds of swinging gates, the thud of horses' hooves, the bawling of calves, the clanging of bull bells, and the periodic shouts of encouragement from the grandstands all contribute to the scene.

As the contestants sally forth one sees all manner of youthful courage and skill but also the sheer luck in the participants' scores—that is to say, the quirkiness of the animal being roped or ridden. From her perch in the announcer's box, Foard's running account is both encouraging and sympathetic to the contestant's efforts. Sometimes she injects comments on the animal's supposed thoughts and occasionally is unable to suppress laughter at a particularly humorous moment. During the Five-Under goat tagging event: "Okay, Tawana McPhaul, are you ready? This is what you call a little bitty cowgirl. Look at that. I don't know how she's gonna get off and get back on [her horse] but I bet she can show us how. There she goes. That's the way we get off. Now come here goat. Get back here. There, now let's see her get back on now. Give her just a little help, Tom [Olney]." In the six-to-nine age group of goat tying: "Okay, this is Bradley Harrison. . . . His horse wants to go somewhere else. He don't like that goat. . . . He says, come on, let's do it this way. (Laughs.) The goat says, no! I don't like it that way. (Laughs.) Whoops. Get up and try again, Bradley. (Laughs.) Okay, Bradley, that was good." Then later, "Oh! Bless his heart. That dirt out there is a little deep when you step off your horse." The bad luck of the goat tiers aside, the announcer surmises that the goats themselves might not be all that thrilled with the event. "I've had just about enough of this," she imagines a weary goat thinking. But shortly the good news (for the goat) comes from the box: "We've got to change the goats."

Boys competing in steer riding (ages ten to thirteen) have the challenge of staying atop the jumping animal for eight seconds, and on this day most riders had more than they could handle. "Okay, here comes Michael Gonzales. Come on Michael, hang on there. Okay. . . . Amen. Let's give him a big hand. That's the way it's done." But from there on it was mostly downhill. "Hang on there, Travis. Oh, oh. . . . Well, that's too bad. . . . I think he kinda got the air knocked out of him. . . . It takes a little help to get out of there. Let's give him a big hand anyway." Or this comment while the grandstand waits for the next steer rider to come out of the chute: "Chuck Muncy, he's settin' up there on his steer just lookin' like he's just not concerned about it at all. . . . If I had to sit up there lookin' at those horns, I'd probably get off and run. . . . Chuck Muncy comin' out. . . . Oh, oh." (The rider is bucked off.) Then later, "Hang on there, Ryan. . . . Hang on there. . . . Whoops." So it went.

It is a full day, with parents, arena assistants, and onlookers offering support for winners and losers alike. There are many prizes. Many take home buckles, spurs, and checks. Even the day's "hard-luck" cowboy and cowgirl receive buckles donated by the Magdalena Old-Timers Association. Before dusk settles, the horses and riding gear are loaded up; parents and riders, many of whom will see each other down the rodeo circuit, bid their farewells; and the caravan of pickups and horse trailers head out for home. Now it is time for the contestants to reflect on their performances and take pleasure in any prizes won. Serious contenders look down the road to the next contest and contemplate winning even bigger prizes at more prestigious competitions. At the state 4-H finals, for example, a select few can win boots, breast collars, saddles, horse trailers, and even college scholarships.

Most rodeo youths are remarkably self-possessed before their performance. One young cowgirl who regularly enters barrel racing and goat tying claims that before her ride she is so focused on the work at hand, she closes out the world around her. "I don't hear nothing. You just pay attention to the goat or the barrels. I don't hear nothing. I just go down there and get it done and come back." Still, the pressure can be immense. One rodeo mom tells of how a couple of days before a rodeo her daughter was "throwing up and sick at her stomach, and she'd be like that until we'd come back." Such was the "pressure and tension." At the time of the interview, her son was gearing up for the state finals in calf roping. Although he was ahead in accumulated points for the year, he could still lose the prize buckle if he should have a bad day. "These finals are going to tell it, so he'd better pressure up. He'd better throw some good loops." One father tells how his son, a calf roper, is so "tied up" emotionally, he goes off alone and sits in the horse trailer. "Now if he has a bad rodeo, you miss him and go look for him, he'll be sitting in the stall with the horse. . . . He just goes off by hisself."[31]

As the above accounts suggest, contestants handle this pressure in various ways. When roping calves, Nacona McPhaul, one of the region's leading female performers, sometimes drew on a dream for inspiration, a dream in which she pictured throwing a perfect loop around the neck of the breakaway calf. Some abide by superstitions, such as not wearing the color yellow or wearing a lucky shirt. For those riding in rough stock events, where the same broncs and bulls are rotated around the rodeos, gaining information on the tricks and ticks of a particular animal from previous riders can help force concentration and keep nerves under control. Speaking of preride jitters, one young man says, "You get nervous about it. You shake. You can sit down and talk with somebody. Talk to somebody that's been on the horse, somebody that's been on the bull." That way, you pick up "little secrets."[32]

Still, how does one fully prepare for climbing on a bull whose every desire and sinew is devoted to removing you from his back? In this, the most dangerous rodeo event, it is little wonder that controlling your nerves is a monumental challenge. One rodeo announcer says, "Where I'm at in the announcer's stand, I can walk out and I can watch the bull riders underneath, back behind the chutes. And those kids are just like an adult—especially in the high school shows. I watch the kids a lot. And you'll see the bull riders come down, and they'll kneel and say a prayer. Nearly all of them. . . . They'll be back there doing exercises. There is just all kinds of stuff getting ready. They're not laughing and joking and carrying on;

Waiting his turn. Children's rodeo, Magdalena, New Mexico, ca. 1985. (Photo by author.)

they're concentrating on what they've got to do and what's coming up." From my field notes, there is this moment:

> This morning I stood behind the bucking chutes as the young bull riders climbed aboard their bulls. One rider was thrown off almost immediately. After the ride he was visibly sick, and it took several minutes to collect himself. For five minutes he kneeled next to one of the chutes heaving and coughing, mumbling over and over, "I had to get fuckin' sick." After a while, when the heaving and coughing was over, he sat with his back against the chute digging his spurs in the dirt, still trying to collect himself. When his father approached him, the boy volunteered, "I got fuckin' sick." The father's reply: "I think you were scared." This met with the boy's response: "I wasn't scared. I was just fuckin' sick. I was fuckin' sick." Through all this, other riders kept their distance. All seem to know that at such moments the bull rider requires time for coming down from the fever-pitch intensity of that few seconds on the back of a bucking bull.[33]

It is the second night of the 1990 Socorro County rodeo. Just before the bareback event, the announcer calls out: "Mamas and dads, if you have your children here tonight, get those children away from the fences. Kids, back off the fence line.... We don't want any of you hurt." A few minutes later a rider comes out spurring a bronc, trying to make his eight seconds. When he is barely into the ride, the crowd hears from the announcer's box: "Oh. We need the paramedics, please, on the double! Ladies and gentlemen, please keep your seats. The paramedics are here; they will take care of him." For those who missed what occurred, he explains that when the rider was thrown off, his head struck the fence. Then there was the reassuring news that the cowboy was "moving" and would be checked out at the hospital. Later in the evening there is another call for the paramedics. Now a bull rider is lying in the dirt. "Ladies and gentlemen ... this is one of the things we are always faced with. The cowboy's ... got a little problem with his jaw, probably got a pretty severe break to his jaw. He hit head first." While the paramedics are working over the body, the announcer engages in a humorous question-response routine with "Frosty," the rodeo clown. Because Frosty could not be heard by the crowd, the announcer repeated over the microphone Frosty's response to his questions.

> ANNOUNCER: Frosty, what does it take to be a bull rider?
> FROSTY: Take a hand full of marbles, stick 'em all in your mouth. Every time you make a qualified ride, you spit one marble out.

ANNOUNCER: Then what happens?
FROSTY: When you've lost all your marbles, you're a bull rider.

By now the injured rider was moving and being strapped to a board. From the announcer's box came the news: "Another ambulance is on the way. . . . The cowboy is takin' his journey to hospital land. Give him some support for me." (Crowd applauds.) "We hope you'll be okay, cowboy."[34]

Both parents and children accept the fact that there will be injuries along the way. In this sport of hooves and horns, the possibilities are endless. Riding bulls is especially risky. A 4-H official told me how one stock contractor in the state was known for having particularly rank bulls he termed "chute fighters." "They're fighting bulls, and they'll really hurt you," so badly, in fact, that some parents call ahead to learn the contractor's name, not allowing their children to compete when these bulls are scheduled. Other parents try to steer their sons away from the event altogether. It is bad enough contemplating the prospect of a horse falling while running barrels, or bucking. The last thing a parent, or for that matter, contestants want to hear from the announcer's box—as I heard at one children's rodeo in 1989—was that one of the performers in the program would not be making an appearance that day because a bull had "stomped on his head last night."[35]

Almost any performer, if he or she has contested for any length of time, can rattle off near disasters. One of the region's outstanding rodeo performers recalls one of his first efforts at bull dogging (also known as steer wrestle), which calls for the rider to jump from a running horse, grab the steer by the horns—a moment called "getting down in the hole"—and then wrestle the animal to the ground. "I drew a white steer with a black spot on him." He says he could tell the steer was "real nervous." The ride started well enough, his horse catching up with the steer, perfect for making his jump. But then, "I get to the steer, and I get down in the hole, and my arm hits his back, and the steer jumps off the ground about 4 feet." This was unusual, he explained, because most of them "don't jump like that." The result was, "I went right over his horns, and [it] knocked me out." Actually, he said, he could not remember the entire episode, only landing on the steer's back and then "getting off the ground." Young performers' capacity to block out pain is revealed in a rodeo mom's account of her son's performance at state finals. "He rode his bull, and he completed the ride but as he was gettin' off, he pitched forward and the bull caught him in the head with a horn. He had ninety stitches and came back that night and rode his saddle bronc. These kids are really tough."[36]

A close call. Young April Guin jumps from her horse as it heads for a mud puddle, ca. 1970. (Courtesy of James Guin.)

Even barrel racing has its risks. Witness this remarkable moment at the local Datil rodeo, when a horse nearly rolled over a young female rider named April. Her father, James Guin, walked me through the episode:

> It seems like it always rains when we're in the Datil rodeo. So the horse had been standin' there tied to the fence waitin' for April's turn to go do the barrels. When it rains like that, a horse, when it's hot, they like to get down and roll in the moist dirt. He'd been standin' there pawin' at the ground after it rained, kickin' up that wet dirt. Anyway, when she went to do the barrels, she did the first barrel, and the second barrel, and headed toward the third one, and . . . he got to smellin' that good, nice, wet dirt up there, and he decided that he'd just lie down and roll in it. She just knew that horse was goin' down. So he went down, and she jumped off and took off runnin' back. . . . I knew what was gonna' happen when it started slowin' down and he started to kneel, and I had jumped the fence and had already started that way. . . . She was hollerin' "Mommy, Daddy." It scared her pretty bad too.

But the story does not end there. Guin continues, "After I got out there and got her calmed down, I put her back on the horse, and she went in there and finished her run."[37]

What is the meaning and significance of the children's rodeo in the coming-of-age experience? On one level rodeo, like all sports, functions as a powerful forum for building participants' self-esteem and self-confidence, measured by the accumulation of buckles, spurs, saddles, and prize money. Such awards also have honorific and social value as well, evidenced by one girl's comment that she would rather win a buckle than a pair of spurs because "you can wear a buckle to school." Second, there is the sheer adventure of it all, the excitement of displaying one's horsemanship before a crowd of onlookers—one's skill at perfectly dropping a lasso over the neck of a breakaway calf or the intoxicating rush that comes with staying aboard a bucking bronc. As one rodeo mother told me, it "gets in your blood." The pain, the danger, and the broken bones are somehow worth it. A young bull dogger goes even further. "Crazy," he says. "You ever make one smooth run, it'll last you the rest of your life."[38]

Third, in no other sport are the realms of work and play so intertwined. Historically on the working ranch one saw skilled riders floating lassos over breakaway calves, calves being wrestled to the dirt, riders on a "cutting horse" extracting a single cow from a herd, and young cowboys climbing aboard an unbroken horse. It is the same with rodeo. In children's rodeo the work responsibilities of ranch youths have been merely elevated to the level of serious play, where winners win buckles and spurs as honorific signification of their role as valued workers in the ranching economy. Contestants are still measuring up to that standard of worth to which young cowboys—and cowgirls too—always aspired, namely, being "good enough to take along." Children on the ranching frontier were always creative in finding ways of turning work into play.[39]

Fourth, rodeo teaches children a host of values and character traits. The ones most commonly mentioned by rodeo parents are the virtue of hard work, individual responsibility, perseverance, self-discipline, and the importance of cooperation—the same values children acquire growing up on ranches. As Sharon Cline, mother of Will Cline, a leading performer in the rough stock events of bull and bronc riding, explained to me in 1990, Will grew up learning responsibility at a young age: "Will would be ahorseback, and he could move 300 or 400 head of cattle by himself by the time he was seven years old." On a ranch comprising thirty sections, "You had to know boundaries, you had to know the country, you had to know that you were capable of riding that far and coming back. Will knew all these things." And he also learned the importance of cooperation. Ranching was a family affair. "We were all ahorseback, or we were all in the doctorin' pens, or we were all in the kitchen tryin' to get a meal ready. Everybody helped everyone. We would brand numerous sets of calves in a day. And the work is hard. It's cold . . . leave early in the morning, 4 o'clock in the morning, it's cold and you come in after dark, and it's cold, and there is still chores to do."[40]

Indeed, a fifth theme in rodeo is family. Behind most rodeo contestants are parents and grandparents who have invested countless hours and resources in the young performers' success. "The whole thing is a family deal," one rodeo parent observes. "You travel together, you eat together, and you sleep together. . . . That's the main part of it we like." When I asked Beau Bruton who taught him what he needed to know about roping, he answers easily: "My dad, he spent years with me. . . . About every day I team rope with my dad." (At the time of my interview, Beau and his dad had won the father-son competition at a local rodeo two years in succession.) This leads to the point that most young rodeo performers have deep intergenerational rodeo roots, a circumstance that suggests a high degree of intergenerational continuity in cultural and social outlook. The reason is simple enough: in a postmodern world of hypertechnological and social change, not much has changed in the skills required for roping calves or staying aboard a saddle bronc. Rodeo remains a world in which grandfathers have a valued fund of knowledge to pass on to the "little britches" just thrown off a bucking horse.[41]

Sixth, rodeo is about gender. Although certain rodeo events such as saddle bronc and bull riding are reaffirmations of the idea that "winning the West" was a highly masculine enterprise, other events offer young cowgirls the opportunity to display their own horseback skills and to remind onlookers of the oft-neglected role of women on the ranching frontier. Listen to one mother describe the performance of a ten-year-old Magdalena girl:

> This was two weeks ago. . . . The weather is beautiful. It is just like a picture out of paradise, pine trees, and then this big huge arena right in the middle of it. And then the clouds coming in, and it is just like a painted picture, and all the kids out here competing. And then the rainstorm came, and they had a little hail. And here is this little girl, with a great big powerful $2,500 horse she is riding. And it is just pouring rain. And here is this little girl, sitting for her turn—to goat tie in the rain, mind you. She went out there and performed in that pouring rain. And here she is trying to struggle with that goat, and did quite well too.

In the scene depicted above one sees the gritty determination that informed generations of ranch women who, in addition to managing a household and raising children, braved the elements to make a ranch or homestead a going concern. It also reminds one of an earlier era in rodeo history when women such as Tad Lucas rode bucking horses, Mabel Strickland roped steers, and New Mexico's own Fern Sawyer rode bulls. Despite the fact that females are no longer permitted to perform in rough stock events, rodeo still offers them ample opportunity to demonstrate their vital place in the ranching tradition.[42]

Rodeo is also about livestock. There is little question that children derive immense pleasure participating in a sport built around working with animals—especially horses. Not enough can be said about the ranchers' love of horses—a reverence at times almost mythical in proportions. As noted earlier, nearly all have grown up forming deep bonds with their first or favorite horses. At the same time the ranching economy is based on the management and slaughter of livestock for profit. It follows that rodeo is about taming and management of animals for human purposes. True, rodeo defenders profess a genuine respect for livestock, but a goodly portion of this respect is born of the firsthand knowledge of rough livestock's capacity to do serious injury to the humans who seek to dominate them. As one old rodeo hand told me, "By God, if I'm a bull and you get aboard, I'm gonna try and unload your butt. . . . I got respect for him." The same respect is accorded a bucking bronc, for "he's got an art—the art of stickin' your head in the dirt!"[43] Anthropologist Lawrence has already been cited on the point that the human/nature and wild/tame dichotomies are at the very heart of rodeo. Thus, it is of little surprise that in the animal hierarchy cows and goats merit little "respect." In the midst of talking about calf roping, one parent volunteered, "Three of our roping calves died, and we about roped the others to death." Although there is much truth in rodeo supporters' argument that the humane treatment of stock is rigidly enforced, as the following entry from my field notes indicates, the sport produces its share of abuses:

> Before the rodeo today several girls were practicing their goat tying on three or four goats tied to posts. One after another the goats were hoisted in the air and slammed to the ground, where they were tied. Each goat was thrown to the ground several times, where they lay subdued after the tying. On one occasion the cowgirl stomped a tied goat in the ribs for no apparent reason other than to demonstrate her domination.[44]

This writer could not help but imagine how this lowest of rodeo animals—staked and stomped on—would have rejoiced hearing Foard call out at the Magdalena rodeo, "It's time to change the goats!"

Finally, children's rodeo is about the frontier myth. Indeed, one cannot conceive of the popularity of the sport without the westering experience and its iconic symbol—the cowboy. One cannot think about the West without conjuring up images of cowboys breaking horses, roping cows, and throwing them to the ground for branding. This, the myth says, is how the West was won. Rodeo sanctifies a way of life still lived and honored by the households that speckle the plains and high country of the West, a way of life where the past and present converge in the image of a young roper, his hat tucked down low against the wind, his rope ready, his horse pressing up against the barrier, and then his nod to the chute man to release the calf. Then there is the moment where the cowboy, horse, and cow are caught up in a ritualistic reenactment of their historic roles as scripted in the national memory, roles immortalized in books, film, and song. It is about Willie Nelson singing "My Heroes Have Always Been Cowboys."

A New School for the Alamo Navajos

Having their own school, a full-fledged K–12 school, was a longtime dream of Alamo Navajo elders. One elder recalls that community leaders approached the Bureau of Indian Affairs (BIA) on the matter several times, but they were always met with the same response: "They tell us: too much money. There are a lot of boarding schools to send your children to. We always tell 'em: We want it here at Alamo."[45] The reasons for the request were many. Certainly one was the off-reservation boarding school legacy, the painful memories of child removal and the attendant abuses that accompanied it. The Magdalena dormitory program was an improvement but still bespoke of the old system tradition of separating children from parents. Then there was the issue of the Magdalena schools. On the one hand, Alamo Navajo children were now being educated in an integrated setting; on the other, they suffered from new forms of humiliation. So the dream remained just that—a dream.

Meanwhile, developments in the 1960s and 1970s on the national scene were clearing the path for Indian communities to take control of their children's education. The capstone in the movement was congressional passage of the 1975 Indian Self-Determination and Educational Assistance Act. The twin watchwords of this new era in Native American rights were "community control" and "bicultural education." By the mid-1970s, two promising experimental Navajo models of the new policy were already in place, Rough Rock Demonstration School and Rock Point, both located on the "Big Navajo" reservation. By the end of the decade, some twelve so-called contract schools were in operation. But in the swirl of these developments the Alamo Navajo community was stuck. Its members needed an individual with the knowledge and ability to help them negotiate the complex legal, political, and bureaucratic obstacles standing in the way of having their own school.[46]

That person was John Loehr. In 1978 several Alamo Navajos met Loehr at the University of New Mexico, where he was working in a special program for Navajo teacher training. When Loehr suggested that the Alamo Navajo community establish its own school, community leaders jumped at the idea. Following a community vote of ninety-two to zero in November 1978, Loehr was invited to spearhead the effort, which he quickly agreed to do. Shortly thereafter, a lawyer with extensive experience in Indian law was brought on board, and applications to the BIA and the Navajo Nation for planning monies soon followed. In time, Navajo educator Abe Plummer, along with William Berlin, an Anglo with experience in Indian education, also joined the project. Meanwhile there was so much to be done: the certification of an Alamo school board; meetings in Washington, DC, and Crownpoint (the area BIA office); endless negotiations over contractual specifics; development of a comprehensive educational program; hiring teachers and support staff; purchasing curriculum materials; and arranging for temporary mobile units to accommodate administrative offices, classrooms, and a cafeteria. At one juncture the goal of opening the school in the fall of 1979 seemed all but impossible. The BIA was dragging its bureaucratic feet, congenitally resistant to turning loose of its historic control over Indian schooling. Then there was the problem of the Magdalena school system, at which officials quickly discerned that losing a sizable proportion of enrollment would mean losing a sizable chunk of funding. At a joint meeting of the Alamo and Magdalena school boards in July, worried superintendent Mike Dickson could only ask, "What's going to happen to our district?" But the die was cast. Over the summer of 1979 the BIA finally approved the Alamo contract. The school opened in October.[47]

The first years were a time of struggle. Administrative mismanagement, the Alamo Navajo school board members' unpreparedness for their roles, the lack of a coherent instructional program, and community factionalism all played a part in undermining the school's success. Indeed, the convergence of these factors in the fall of 1980 produced a major crisis that nearly resulted in the school being closed down. Only a major overhaul of the school administration, including the removal of John Loehr, managed to keep the school afloat. Meanwhile, one of the most striking features of these early years was the failure to embrace a bicultural curriculum—but understandable given the community's gravitation toward Christian fundamentalism. Little wonder that many parents objected to students participating in activities that smacked of traditionalism. Thus, when a Native American teacher (not from Alamo) enlisted several girls to perform a native dance as part of the school's celebration of a national day honoring American Indians, two Alamo teachers berated the girls, one asking, "I thought you were a Christian?" The one area in which Navajo culture was evident was language. (By 1982 a skeletal bilingual program was in place.) But anything beyond language was perceived as dangerously flirting with the devil himself. During this early period, one Navajo-speaking Anglo teacher (married to a northern Navajo) was moved to remark, "When I was at the university they used to talk a lot about the culturally deprived child. I never liked the term because I always thought they were REALLY talking about people who were just culturally different. But you know, these people really ARE culturally deprived. . . . They don't know anything about the old Navajo ways. Now, finally, I think I know what the term culturally deprived means." But for the moment most in the community seemed content with the fact that they had wrenched control of their children's education from the BIA. The song that one of the *biligáana* teachers, Daniel Sparks, wrote for a community meeting, "A Place Called Alamo," caught the spirit:

> People there have built a school
> To teach their children Golden Rules
> You know that they ain't got no fools
> Down in Alamo.[48]

Over the next decade, however, there were signs that some in the community wanted more and began asking questions such as: Community control for what purpose? What should it mean to grow up Alamo Navajo? In keeping with these questions, teachers began slowly introducing lessons on such topics as the symbolism of the cradleboard and the heritage of Coyote stories. Another step in the direction of traditional culture was the 1990 school yearbook, which identified graduating seniors' clan affiliations.

But these allusions to traditionalism never reached the depth achieved by the searchlight schools in the north. It was difficult to imagine students at Alamo reading passages such as the following one, which appears in a 1971 Rough Rock Demonstration School text on Navajo history and tells

Children at Alamo Navajo Community School graduation ceremony, 1982. (Photo by author.)

the story of the *Diné*'s journey through successive underworlds before their eventual emergence into this, the Glittering World: "At the beginning there was a place called the Black World, where only spirit people and Holy People lived. It had four corners, and over these four corners appeared four cloud columns, which were white, blue, yellow, and black. The east column was called Folding Dawn; the south column was called Folding Sky Blue; the west one was Folding Twilight; and the north one was Folding Darkness."[49]

Still, the Alamo Navajos had their own school. A signal moment in the school's evolution occurred on September 1, 1986, when 80 people crowded into the school's gymnasium to hear Peterson Zah, president of the Navajo Nation, dedicate a long-anticipated modern school building to replace the original mobile units. Three years later, Alamo celebrated the ten-year anniversary of the school's existence. The festivities included the crowning of grade-level queens and princesses, a parade, a baby beauty contest, student work exhibitions, cross-country races, gunnysack races, chainsaw cutting contests, and finally, a coffee boiling competition (strictly female). Meanwhile, under a large tent several community leaders spoke of the past and future. One community leader observed, "Ten years is a long time. If you planted a cottonwood tree by your house in 1979, it would just be gettin' big enough to shade the house now." In 1979 the Alamo Navajos had "dreams for a better future for our children. . . . We wanted to stop sending our children away for other people to educate them." Just as the ten-year-old cottonwood was now giving protective shade for the house, so the community school gave protection to the children.[50] The boarding school years and the Magdalena dormitory years were over.

Together Still

Anyone living in the greater Magdalena-Alamo region in the early twentieth century would have been stunned by the ethnoracial breakdown in 1990: non-Hispanic white, 572; Hispanic, 628; and Native American (Navajo), 1,307. What had once been a small band of Navajos now constituted more than 50 percent of the region's residents. Perhaps more surprising is that after Navajo parents actually faced the choice of sending their children to the Alamo or Magdalena schools, a sizable number chose the latter. Indeed, of the 300-plus students in Magdalena in 1990, roughly one-third were Navajos, making them the second largest group in the system (Hispanics being the first). In short, the Magdalena schools were still very much a tricultural system.[51]

Why did a significant number of Navajo parents continue to send their children to Magdalena? First, some surely preferred their children to have an integrated school experience. Closely related was the issue of language. Although nearly all Navajo parents had bitter memories of the "no Indian" rule during their own school years, many also felt that mastery of English was an essential prerequisite for educational and economic advancement. In this regard, the community school's bilingual focus might have been perceived as a risky venture. Third, community factionalism and suspicions surrounding the Alamo school's leadership and organization weakened support for the school. Finally, because Magdalena could no longer take its Navajo enrollment for granted—a situation made all the more serious given the town's determination to build a new physical plant—a special effort was made to make Alamo Navajo students feel welcome. For all these reasons, the *Magdalena Mountain Mail* reported in the summer of 1986 that the "Magdalena Schools have arranged for extra bus runs this fall. Four buses will be making the Alamo runs. Arrangements have been made for an Activity bus to make a late run so Alamo students may participate in sports." Meanwhile, Alamo Navajo students were graduating from Magdalena at higher rates.[52]

In 1990 the town of Magdalena and its schools continued to be a complicated social space. Old prejudices against the Alamo Navajos died hard—especially among older residents. One old-timer, for example, proclaimed, "They're a damn bunch of renegades. . . . Basically, they don't want to conform to anything anybody wants." Another, commenting on the dramatic increase in the Alamo Navajo population, said, "Just like rats they breed. . . . It wouldn't surprise [me] if eventually they own this whole town." As for the problem of Indian drinking, "Every year it's getting worse and worse. The damn Indians lay in the stockyards there. And they don't care if it's cold, or warm, or raining, they sleep out there. That's what burns me up about it. They don't get sick. . . . The cold wind blows over them. Next morning they're up wantin' money. Of course there are a few Indians that are good." As for the source of the alcohol problem, the same speaker offers that the Alamo Navajos are "in between the human being and the wild animal, more or less." Another old man offers this bit of prophecy: "When the human race is gone there'll be two things left—Navajos and coyotes."[53]

Given the troubled history of group relations in the area, it is not surprising that old animosities continued to play out in classrooms, hallways, and the cafeteria. According to one elementary teacher, both Anglo and Hispanic children still had a tendency to reduce Alamo Navajo children to their group identity—"that Indian"—when identifying the perpetrator of some hurtful act. When this happened, she said, "I always say THAT kid has a name. He didn't call you a Mexican. He didn't call you a gringo. You tell me WHO hit you or WHO did what." A non-Navajo student from this later period observed:

> In grade school I had a bunch of Navajo friends. That's who I hung out with. You know, I'd take them to the house, and we'd stay there all weekend, and we'd just play around, but you know, as you get into high school, that's when you start separating into their own little groups and fighting. Cursing each other and challenging each other. Trying to say I'm better than you are. My culture is better than yours. . . . They like to see who can knock each other the lowest.

Occasionally, derogatory slurs, both of old and new invention, were traded across groups: "redskin trash," "gringo *salado*," "ten-gallon hats," "horse-shit-eating honky," "flour skin," "dirty Mexicans," "damn Spanish fly." Still, the same speaker also said that her "best friend is half Navajo and half Spanish, and we always stick together."[54] In this there is hope.

But New Mexico is also a land of border crossings, some of the most intimate nature. Consider marriage patterns for the years 1975–1984. Of the 158 marriages recorded in the county during the decade, 34 were of mixed surname ancestry: 19 Anglo/Hispanic, 7 Hispanic/Navajo, 8 Anglo/Navajo. (The surname ancestry of 8 couples was not clear.)[55] The point here is that by the last decades of the twentieth century the number of children of mixed ancestry had grown sufficiently to complicate essentialist ideas about blood and identity. Those who still held tightly to such archaic notions were increasingly likely to discover they now had grandchildren, nieces, and nephews of mixed ancestry. Thus, if Magdalena had not achieved universal harmony by the 1990s, it had made considerable progress. As one Anglo man explained:

> There's still families that . . . hold on to stuff like that [prejudice]. I mean it hasn't all gone away. I guarantee you that. And it probably never will, you know. But the majority of it [has]. Life is what you make out of it, I guess. If you want to be hung up on your own little prejudices, or whatever, you can do that. . . . What I really like about New Mexico is that there are three cultures. If you get tired of one, you can go give up on them for a while, and you can go live with somebody else and do it their way. And [if] you get tired of them, well you can go on to something else

you know. But myself, I'm comfortable in any one of the three. I mean I can just jump right in there and you know I'm accepted.[56]

In this instance the speaker attributed some of this ethnocultural ecumenism to his school experience. It was at Magdalena High School where he took notice of a Navajo girl from Alamo—and eventually married her.

AFTERWORD

West-central New Mexico is a storied land. It is, of course, not unique in this regard. As humans that is what we do: we construct narratives about ourselves, about others, and about how we are connected to the land. William Kittredge is probably right when he says narratives "may well be our fundamental survival strategy."[1] Taken together, stories tell us who we are and where we fit in the scheme of things. They begin with children.

The concept of culture looms large in this enterprise. Some time ago, cultural anthropology taught us the three-part truth that each person is like all other humans, like some other humans, and like no other humans.[2] The early chapters of this study focus mainly on the middle zone, that is to say, how children in west-central New Mexico grew up as cultural beings. Cultures, then, write the scripts that ethnocultural groups consciously or unconsciously draw upon to transmit to succeeding generations a collective identity, a sense of who they are as a people. All cultures have their belief systems, lifeways, languages, kinship and gender systems, and mythic stories. Juan de Oñate was not George Washington, just as Changing Woman was not Mary, Mother of Jesus. In west-central New Mexico only Navajo females celebrated the onset of puberty with a *Kinaaldá,* it was mostly Hispanic children who spent hours preparing for their First Communion, and it was only Anglos who grew up listening to their mothers sing an old Texas love song. To be sure, there were areas of overlap. Anglo cowboys and Spanish-Mexican *vaqueros* shared much in common, just as Catholics and Protestants knew something about Adam and Eve or danced some variation of the polka, but culture mattered.

When ethnocultural groups encounter each other the stage is set for all manner of responses and processes. Moreover, when these encounters are accompanied by differing power equations and presumptions of superiority—as they were in New Mexico—patterns of subordination and marginality are all-too-frequent outcomes. The New Mexico story is somewhat unique in that the region was colonized first by Spain, and after twenty-five years of Mexican independence, colonized again by the United States. Because most nineteenth-century Anglos viewed Mexicans as culturally backward, racially suspect, and of questionable loyalty, it is not surprising that policy makers turned to legal and institutional instruments to incorporate the former citizens of Mexico into the US empire. Schools, we have seen, played a major role in this effort. However, there were limitations—partly by design, partly owing to political realities—as to how far the incorporation project would or could proceed. First, although Anglo leaders were convinced that conquered Mexicans must be converted into English-speaking patriotic citizens, they stopped short of efforts to strip them of all vestiges of their Hispanic past. Second, Hispanic population numbers and their deep cultural attachments made wholesale assimilation impossible. Remember the last lines of the play *Kearney Takes Las Vegas*, how the bride-to-be Dolores responds to Robert Kearney's declaration that the "United States has taken New Mexico." "No," she replies, "New Mexico has taken the United States."

The configuration of Anglo–Alamo Navajo power relations was more one-sided. The dichotomy posed by the "savagism-civilization" gap justified in the minds of policy makers a full-throated assault (at least until 1928) on indigenous cultures—a much more egregiously aggressive program than ever contemplated against Hispanics. Thus, although this assault on the "lost band of the Navajos" came relatively late (1913), it came with stunning force in the form of boarding schools and child removal. Missionaries, mainly of the Protestant variety, helped the process along. In a world of boundaries and border crossings, no group faced a greater challenge of how to negotiate the power-skewed ethnocultural landscape.

Children have not been passive witnesses in this story. Certainly the region has seen its share of victims—childhoods pinched or cramped by circumstances beyond their control. However, feats of agency, both large and small, have also been on display. Think of the Navajo boys being trucked off to boarding school, how they were scarcely across the reservation line before they were planning their escape, and conversely, how Gilbert Guerro, who wanted nothing more than to learn something about this "different kind of people," was eager to climb aboard the truck so he might fulfill this childhood dream. Think of Vicente Tafoya taking umbrage at the school superintendent's slur that a student was just a "Mexican," leading a protest march out of Magdalena High School to a local lawyer's office. Think of little Katherine Field, stricken with polio, waiting to be rigged up in a special saddle so she could join her sister in trapping coyotes. Think of Buddy Major and his sister rolling boulders down a bluff to put an emaciated colt out of its misery. Think of Juan Jaramillo, the altar boy who upon discovering that the barrel for holding holy water was empty, refilled the container and then slipped into the absent priest's vestments to perform the sacred blessing. Then Juan's response to the priest's strong admonishment: "Father, don't get mad. You're the first one kickin' about it. You already baptized five kids, and the people have been using it every day. Nobody has kicked—only YOU."

I end this story of stories with yet another story and with a document of an unusual sort—a scribbled note passed by an Alamo girl to an Anglo boy newly enrolled in Magdalena High School:

Brian,

Hi! How is life these days? For me alright I guess. I want to invite you to homecoming, and I hope you do have a good time. And I want to find out more about you so I am going to ask you some questions. Where do you stay at? How old are you? When is your birthday? Where did you use to live before you came here? How many people do you have in your family? I'll tell you about me with the same questions I ask you. I stay in Alamo with my mom and dad, my 3 sisters, 1 brother, and another baby on the way. My oldest sister is 16, her name is Shirley, my younger sister is 11, going to be 12 in November, her name is Melinda. My little brother is 6, his name is Daniel, but we call him by his middle name Michael, my baby sister is 11 months, going to be 1 year in November. I'm 14. I hope my age don't matter. My birthday is May 18th. I've lived in Magdalena all my life, I've come to school here all my school years. I hope I haven't bored you to death or anything. Sorry I invited you so late, but I was waiting for an answer from someone else, but forget it! Well I'll write more if you write me back soon. Well I'm running out of words to say right now. So I guess I'll go now! I'll just wait to hear from you! So bye for now! Sorry so short an sloppy

Always me,

Brenda Apache[3]

In this land of immense ethnocultural diversity, where emerging identities are variously essentialistic, layered, blended, and braided, Brenda says: this is my story. Who are you? What is your story? I am listening.

ACKNOWLEDGMENTS

I must begin by thanking the innumerable individuals who shared their stories on their experiences growing up in the region, conducted interviews of others for me, and assisted in the transcription and/or translation of those interviews conducted in Spanish or Navajo. For a list of those individuals interviewed or who otherwise contributed material for this study, see the bibliography. I also owe a debt of gratitude to the several individuals who stepped forward to translate and transcribe interviews collected as part of the Alamo Navajo Oral History Project, available at the Center for Southwestern Research, University of New Mexico. Among these are Nora Baca, Rosie Baca, Don Padilla, Jackson Pino, Marie Pino, Lupe Sandoval, and Shorty Secatero.

Over the years I have been the beneficiary of various grants and fellowships vital to the completion of this project. A special thanks to Cleveland State University and the Spencer Foundation, most generous in funding the early stages of this enterprise. The William P. Clements Center for Southwest Studies at Southern Methodist University is a special place, and my yearlong fellowship there was crucial to advancing this project. I will be forever grateful to David J. Weber, director, Sherry L. Smith, John Chávez, and Brian Delay (another fellow) for reading portions of the manuscript and offering advice. Andrea Boardman and Ruth Ann Elmore were also endlessly wonderful in making my stay in Dallas a special experience. Another remarkable place, the Huntington Library, was also invaluable in moving this study to completion. Chasing grants and fellowships requires letters of support, so I am most appreciative of the assistance by Brian Delay, Richard W. Etulain, Peter Iverson, Margaret D. Jacobs, L. G. Moses, and the ever-supportive Sherry Smith.

A special thanks also to Brenda Wilkinson at the Bureau of Land Management, Socorro office; Katherine Ferris at the Center for Southwest Research, Zimmerman Library, University of New Mexico; José Villegas Sr. and Daphne Arnaiz-DeLeón at the New Mexico State Records Center and Archives, Santa Fe, New Mexico; Sara N. Ash Georgi, Alisa M. Monheim, Danielle Rudeen, and Jaeda Snow at the Huntington Library; and Becky Vega, Carmen Gallegos, Audry Armijo, Betty McDaniel, and Falina Lopez at the Socorro County Clerk's Office. I also thank Florence Hawley Ellis for sharing papers with me from the 1949 Alamo Navajo field study and Darlis Miller for sharing material on Agnes Morley Cleaveland.

Several individuals assisted me in searching and gathering high school yearbooks and photographs. Among these are Eliseo Baca, Tom Barrington, Eric Bitner (National Archives, Rocky Mountain Region), John Blackburn, Patricia Grueninger-Beasley, John Guerro, José Guerro, James Guin, Charlotte Henderson, Austin Hoover (New Mexico State University–Las Cruces), Rudy Latasa, Alice Martínez, Sheila Pool (US Department of Agriculture, Forest Service), Clara Winston, and Barbara Zellers. Clara Lucero, Mike Chambers, and Dr. Vannetta Perry at the Magdalena Public Schools were also immensely helpful along the way, as were Yvonne Magener, Lucy Pino, Adrienne Mathewson, and Jessica Carranza at the Magdalena Public Library. A special thanks to Laurie Taylor Gregg for helping out at crucial moments in the project. Lee Scholes and Lucinda White Horse (New Mexico Tech Library) also came to the rescue at crucial times. Two individuals at Cleveland State University deserve special mention: Toni Foster for her assistance in transcribing interviews and Dennis DeCoulo for his incomparable skills at map-making and his photographic assistance during the production phase of the book.

Along the way several individuals read, critiqued, and offered advice on the emerging manuscript. The final product is much stronger for the thoughtful and invaluable comments of Brian Delay and Margaret D. Jacobs, whose recommendations have been taken to heart. Others who have either read portions of the manuscript or assisted me with factual and translation issues include Beth Tatko, Laura Moll, Ann Waters, Robert "Buzz" Davis, and Rick Boyages. A special note of appreciation to my lifelong partner, Vicki, and Nathanial Adams, who poured over large portions of the manuscript, offering invaluable suggestions for improving it.

I cannot say enough about how welcoming the Magdalena and Alamo communities were to me and my family. Charlotte and Bern Henderson, Mary Hart, and Shorty and Nora Secatero made our time spent in the region both memorable and life-changing. Thank you for this. I would also be remiss if I did not call out a special thanks to Fred Woodward at the University Press of Kansas, who believed in this project from the very beginning, and Kim Hogeland, who was incredibly generous with her time and support in moving the manuscript into production. In the final stages of production Jane Raese, production editor, and the remarkable Melanie Stafford, copy editor, were also central to the completion of the manuscript.

Finally, my heartfelt thanks to my family, who in 1981 accompanied me on the road to Magdalena. A special thanks to son Jason, who joined me again in the fall of 1989 when we shared for a second time the wonders of New Mexico chili, breathtaking vistas, and the scent of pine logs on winter nights. For Amanda, Jason, and Nate, attending the Magdalena schools was something on the order of "culture shock," but they emerged, I believe, much wiser and stronger for the experience. As for my dear Vicki—friend and loving wife—her support in this long adventure was central to its completion. There will always be Paris—but there will also be Magdalena.

ABBREVIATIONS

ACSA	Alamo Community School Archives
AJ	author's journal
ANOHP	Alamo Navajo Oral History Project
AUTO	autobiography, author's collection
CCF	Central Classified Files
CSWR	Center for Southwestern Research, Zimmerman Library, University of New Mexico
DF	Decimal File
ENA	Eastern Navajo Agency
FHEAFSP	Florence Hawley Ellis Alamo Field Study Papers
HL	Huntington Library, San Marino, California
INT	interview
MDS	Magdalena *Dichos* Survey
NA	National Archives, Washington, DC
NA-CP	National Archives, College Park, Maryland
NA-PSR	National Archives, Pacific Southwest Region, Riverside, California
NA-RMR	National Archives, Rocky Mountain Region, Denver, Colorado
NMSRCA	New Mexico State Records Center and Archives, Santa Fe, New Mexico
RG 35	Records of the Civilian Conservation Corps
RG 69	Records of the Works Progress Administration
RG 75	Records of the Bureau of Indian Affairs (Office of Indian Affairs)
RG 124	Records of the Surplus Marketing Administration
SAC	Sophie D. Aberle Collection, Center for Southwestern Research, Zimmerman Library, University of New Mexico
WPA	Works Progress Administration

NOTES

PREFACE

1. Jeremy Adelman and Stephen Aron, "From Borderlands to Borders: Empires, Nation-States, and the Peoples in between in North American History," *American Historical Review* 104 (June 1999): 814.

2. The scholarly discussion on the place, merits, and limitations of the term "frontier" in conceptualizing the history of the West is extensive. For an introduction, see Patricia Nelson Limerick, *The Legacy of Conquest: The Unbroken Past of the American West* (New York: Norton, 1987); Limerick, Clyde A. Milner II, and Charles E. Rankin, eds., *Trails: Toward a New Western History* (Lawrence: University Press of Kansas, 1991); Kerwin Lee Klein, "Reclaiming the 'F' Word, or Being and Becoming Postwestern," *Pacific Historical Review* 65 (May 1996): 179–215; Richard W. Etulain, *Re-Imagining the Modern American West: A Century of Fiction, History, and Art* (Tucson: University of Arizona Press, 1996). For two examples of broadening the term, see Andrew R. L. Cayton and Fredrika J. Teute, eds., *Contact Points: American Frontiers from the Mohawk Valley to the Mississippi, 1750–1830* (Chapel Hill: University of North Carolina Press, 1998); Arnoldo De León, *Racial Frontiers: Africans, Chinese, and Mexicans in Western America, 1848–1890* (Albuquerque: University of New Mexico Press, 2002). For the Delay quote see Brian Delay, ed., *North American Borderlands: Rewriting Histories* (New York: Routledge, 2013), 3.

3. This study embraces Steven Mintz's assertion that "childhood is not an unchanging biological stage in life, but is, rather, a social and cultural construct that has changed radically over time." See Mintz, *Huck's Raft: A History of American Childhood* (Cambridge, MA: Harvard University Press, 2004), viii.

4. Elliot West, *Growing Up with the Country: Childhood on the Far Western Frontier* (Albuquerque: University of New Mexico Press, 1989).

5. Kerwin Lee Klein, "On the Emergence of Memory in Historical Discourse," *Representations* 69 (Winter 2000): 129–130.

6. Ibid.; Richard White, *Remembering Ahanagran: Storytelling in a Family's Past* (New York: Hill and Wang, 1998), 292.

7. Limerick, *Legacy of Conflict*, 292.

INTRODUCTION

1. See, for example, *Socorro Chieftain*, December 28, 1929, 4; *Socorro Chieftain*, May 11, 1935, 5; Socorro County: Points of Interest, WPA Files, 1938–1939, Box 24, NMSRCA; Thomas Ewing Dabney, "Kelly—and Our Lady of Magdalena," *New Mexico Magazine* (November 1946): 32; and "Magdalena before 1884," in *Celebrating 100 Years of Frontier Living*, ed. Jacky Barrington (Magdalena, NM: Centennial Committee, 1984), 5–11.

2. For a legend in the region involving a Spanish soldier and a Navajo maiden, see Paige W. Christiansen, "The Legend of Montosa Wells," *Publications in History* 1 (Socorro County Historical Society, February 1965): 27–28.

3. For overviews of Spanish colonization in the Southwest, including New Mexico, see David J. Weber, *The Spanish Frontier in North America* (New Haven, CT: Yale University Press, 1992); John L. Kessell, *Spain in the Southwest: A Narrative History of Colonial New Mexico, Arizona, Texas, and California* (Norman: University of Oklahoma Press, 2002).

4. The best overview of the subject is Marc Simmons, *The Last Conquistador: Juan De Oñate and the Settling of the Far Southwest* (Norman: University of Oklahoma Press, 1991). See also, Kessell, *Spain in the Southwest*, chap. 4.

5. For an overview of Spanish-Pueblo relations, including the southern Piros, see John L. Kessell, *Pueblos, Spaniards, and the Kingdom of New Mexico* (Norman: University of Oklahoma Press, 2008); Albert Schroeder, "Pueblos Abandoned in Historic Times," in *Handbook of North American Indians*, vol. 9, ed. Alfonso Ortiz (Washington, DC: Smithsonian Institution Press, 1979), 236–242; Schroeder, "Shifting for Survival in the Spanish Southwest, " in *New Spain's Far Northern Frontier: Essays on Spain in the American West*, ed. David J. Weber (Albuquerque: University of New Mexico Press, 1979), 246–247; Jack D. Forbes, *Apache, Navajo, and Spaniard* (Norman: University of Oklahoma Press, 1960), 186–187, 235, 243; Michael Bletzer, "'The First Province of That Kingdom': Notes on the Colonial History of the Piro Area," *New Mexico Historical Review* 88 (Fall 2013): 437–459.

6. See Charles Wilson Hackett, ed., and Charmion Clair Shelby, trans., *Revolt of the Mexico and Otermin's Attempted Reconquest, 1680–1682*, 2 vols. (Albuquerque: University of New Mexico Press, 1942); Joe S. Sando, "The Pueblo Revolt," *Handbook of North American Indians*, vol. 9, ed. Alfonso Ortiz (Washington, DC: Smithsonian Institution, 1979), 194–197; Andrew L. Knaut, *The Pueblo Revolt of 1680: Conquest and Resistance in Seventeenth-Century New Mexico* (Norman: University of Oklahoma Press, 1995); David J. Weber, ed., *What Caused the Pueblo Revolt of 1680?* (Boston: Bedford/St. Martins, 1999); and Bletzer, "'First Province of That Kingdom," 452–453.

7. Kessell, *Spain in the Southwest*, 160–163, 171–179; Richard L. Nostrand, *The Hispano Homeland* (Norman: University of Oklahoma Press, 1992), chap. 2; and Oakah L. Jones, *Los Paisanos: Spanish Settlers on the Northern Frontier of New Spain* (Norman: University of Oklahoma Press, 1979), 114–129.

8. Quoted in Bernardo P. Gallegos, *Literacy, Education, and Society in New Mexico, 1693–1821* (Albuquerque: University of New Mexico Press, 1992), 79.

9. Declaration of Fray Miguel de Menchero, May 10, 1744, reprinted in *Historical Documents Relating to New Mexico, Nueva Vizcaya, and Approaches Thereto, to 1773*, ed. Charles Wilson Hackett (Washington, DC: Carnegie Institution of Washington, 1937), 407.

10. Jones, *Paisanos*, 149–162; Paul Horgan, *Great River: The Rio Grande in North American History*, vol. 2 (New York: Rinehart, 1954), 175–176, 368–387.

11. See Weber, *Spanish Frontier in North America*, 326–327; Ramón A. Gutiérrez, *When Jesus Came, the Corn Mothers Went Away: Marriage, Sexuality, and Power in New Mexico, 1500–1846* (Palo Alto, CA: Stanford University Press, 1991), chaps. 5–7 and 328.

12. Gutiérrez, *When Jesus Came*, 179, 226; Weber, *Spanish Frontier in North America*, 326–328.

13. See Gutiérrez, *When Jesus Came*, chaps. 6–7, for a particularly insightful analysis of gender-specific codes of behavior and their implications. For the more flexible gender codes in the lower strata, see Weber, *Spanish Frontier in North America*, 331; Janet Lecompte, "The Independent Women of Hispanic New Mexico, 1821–1846," in *New Mexico Women: Intercultural Perspectives*, ed. Joan M. Jensen and Darlis A. Miller (Albuquerque: University of New Mexico Press, 1986), 71–93. For the general status and roles of women, in addition to Lecompte, see Yolanda Chávez Leyva, "'A Poor Widow Burdened with Children': Widows and Land in Colonial New Mexico," in *Writing the Range: Race, Class, and Culture in the Women's West*, ed. Elizabeth Jameson and Susan Armitage (Norman: University of Oklahoma Press, 1997), 85–96.

14. Weber, *Spanish Frontier in North America*, 328. See also Gutiérrez, *When Jesus Came*, 328.

15. Andrés Reséndez, *Changing National Identities: Texas and New Mexico, 1800–1850* (Cambridge, UK: Cambridge University Press, 2005), 1, 237–253. For the Santa Fe trade and conditions on the eve of the US conquest, see also David J. Weber, *The Mexican Frontier, 1821–1846: The American Southwest under Mexico* (Albuquerque: University of New Mexico Press, 1982), 122–135, 239–241, 242; Thomas D. Hall, *Social Change in the Southwest, 1350–1880* (Lawrence: University Press of Kansas, 1989), 147–156; Howard R. Lamar, *The Far Southwest, 1846–1912: A Territorial History*, rev. ed. (Albuquerque: University of New Mexico Press, 2000), chap. 3.

16. Quoted in Stephen G. Hysop, *Bound for Santa Fe: The Road to New Mexico and the American Conquest, 1806–1848* (Norman: University of Oklahoma Press, 2002), 335.

17. The interconnections between the image of the West and conceptions of democratic opportunity are explored in Fred Somkin, *Unquiet Eagle: Memory and Desire in the Idea of American Freedom, 1815–1869* (Ithaca: Cornell University Press, 1967), chap. 3; Rush Welter, *The Mind of America, 1820–1860* (New York: Columbia University Press, 1975), chap. 12. For manifest destiny and related themes, see Frederick Merk, *Manifest Destiny and Mission in American History* (1963; repr. New York: Vintage Books, 1966); A. K. Weinberg, *Manifest Destiny, A Study of Nationalist Expansionism in American History* (Baltimore: Johns Hopkins Press, 1935); Walter Nugent, *Habits of Empire: A History of American Expansion* (New York: Knopf, 2008).

18. As Carl Kaestle notes, the three pillars were capstone mixtures of ten interlocking propositions: "The sacredness and fragility of the republican polity (including ideas about individualism, liberty, and virtue); the importance of the individual character in fostering social morality; the central role of personal industry in defining rectitude and merit; the delineation of a highly respected but limited domestic role for women; the importance for character building of familial and social environment (within certain racial and ethnic limitations); the sanctity and social virtues of property; the equality and abundance of economic opportunity in the United States; the superiority of American Protestant culture; the grandeur of American destiny; and the necessity of a determined public effort to unify America's polyglot population, chiefly through education." Kaestle, "Ideology and American Educational History," *History of Education Quarterly* 22 (Summer 1982): 127–128.

19. Quoted in Welter, *Mind of America*, 312.

20. See Robert W. Johannsen, *To the Halls of the Montezumas: The Mexican War in the American Imagination* (New York: Oxford University Press, 1985), 168; Reginald Horsman, *Race and Manifest Destiny: The Origins of American Racial Anglo-Saxonism* (Cambridge, MA: Harvard University Press, 1981), 232–233. The *New York Sun* is quoted in Merk, *Manifest Destiny*, 122–123.

21. See Robert E. Bieder, *Science Encounters the Indian, 1820–1880: The Early Years of American Ethnology* (Norman: University of Oklahoma Press, 1986), chap. 3; and Horsman, *Race and Manifest Destiny*, chaps. 7–8, 10.

22. David J. Weber, "'Scare More Than Apes': Historical Roots of Anglo-American Stereotypes of Mexicans," in *New Spain's Far Northern Frontier: Essays on Spain in the American West, 1540–1821*, ed. David J. Weber (Albuquerque: University of New Mexico Press, 1979), 293–307; Laura E. Gómez, *Manifest Destinies: The Making of the Mexican American Race* (New York: New York University Press, 2007); Gómez, "Off-White in an Age of White Supremacy: Mexican Elites and the Rights of Indians and Blacks

in Nineteenth-Century New Mexico," *Chicano-Latino Law Review* 25 (2005): 9–59; Anthony Mora, *Border Dilemmas: Racial and National Uncertainties in New Mexico, 1848–1912* (Durham, NC: Duke University Press, 2011), 43–46.

23. Josiah Gregg, *Commerce of the Prairies*, vol. 1 (1844; repr. Ann Arbor: University of Michigan Microfilms, 1966), 217–223, 236–239, 252–255; W. W. H. Davis, *El Gringo; or, New Mexico and Her People* (1856; repr. Santa Fe, NM: Rydal Press, 1938), 84–85, 97.

24. Kearney is quoted in Frank McNitt, *Navajo Wars: Military Campaigns, Slave Raids, and Reprisals* (Albuquerque: University of New Mexico Press, 1972), 101. Chávez is quoted in Weber, *Mexican Frontier*, 212. For the subject of captive taking and Navajos in the Southwest, see James F. Brooks, *Captives and Cousins: Slavery, Kinship, and Community in the Southwest Borderlands* (Chapel Hill: University of North Carolina Press, 2002); Brian Delay, "Blood Talk: Violence and Belonging in the Navajo New Mexican Borderland," in *Contested Spaces in Early America*, ed. Juliana Barr and Edward Countryman (Philadelphia: University of Pennsylvania Press, 2014), 229–256.

25. Ralph Emerson Twitchell, *The Leading Facts of New Mexican History* (Cedar Rapids, IA: Torch Press, 1917), 4: 284–289; E. W. Northnagel, "Kelly's Ghost," *New Mexico Magazine* (February 1960): 3–7. For a series of articles by Thomas Ewing Dabney, all published under the general title of "Kelly—and Our Lady of Magdalena," see *New Mexico Magazine* 24 (November 1946): 31–32; *New Mexico Magazine* 24 (December 1946): 31–32; *New Mexico Magazine* 25 (January 1947): 31–32; *New Mexico Magazine* 25 (February 1947): 31–32, 43.

26. For a general discussion, see Paul Starrs, *Let the Cowboy Ride: Cattle Ranching in the American West* (Baltimore: Johns Hopkins University Press, 1998), chap. 3; Victor Westphall, *The Public Domain in New Mexico, 1854–1891* (Albuquerque: University of New Mexico Press, 1965), 42–45, 48, 119–120; Gerald Robert Baydo, "Cattle Ranching in Territorial New Mexico" (PhD diss., University of New Mexico, 1970), chap. 7; William W. Dunmire, *New Mexico's Spanish Livestock Heritage: Four Centuries of Animals, Land, and People* (Albuquerque: University of New Mexico Press, 2013), 95. Regarding land acquisition strategies adopted by ranchers in southwestern New Mexico, see the comments of an early rancher in the area, Montague Stevens, available in Pioneer Foundation Oral History Collection, microfilm, reel 5, tape 323, CSWR. The devices—legal and extralegal—used by early cattle ranchers to expand their land holdings during this period are part of the region's folklore.

27. For land polices during this period, see Paul Gates, *History of Public Land Law Development* (Washington, DC: Government Printing Office, 1968), chap. 18; E. Louise Peffer, *The Closing of the Public Domain: Disposal and Reservation Policies, 1900–1950* (Palo Alto, CA: Stanford University Press, 1951), chap. 8; Stanford J. Layton, *To No Privileged Class: The Rationalization of Homesteading and Rural Life in the Early*

Twentieth-Century American West (Salt Lake City, UT: Charles Redd Center for Western Studies, 1988); Karen R. Merrill, *Public Lands and Political Meaning: Ranchers, the Government, and the Property between Them* (Berkeley: University of California Press, 2002), chaps. 1–2. Regarding Pie Town, see Kathryn McKee Roberts, *From the Top of the Mountain: Pie Town, New Mexico, and Neighbors!* (N.p.: Roger Coffin, 1990); Joan Myers, *Pie Town Woman: The Hard Life and Good Times of a New Mexico Homesteader* (Albuquerque: University of New Mexico Press, 2001); Paul Hendrickson, "Savoring Pie Town," *Smithsonian* (February 2005): 72–82.

28. Agnes Morley Cleaveland, *No Life for a Lady* (1941; repr. Lincoln: University of Nebraska Press, 1977), 332–333; Myers, *Pie Town Woman*, 44.

29. F. Stanley, *The Magdalena New Mexico Story* (Nazareth, TX: n.p., 1973), 3–10; Twitchell, *Leading Facts of New Mexican History*, vol. 2, 357–358; David F. Myrick, *New Mexico's Railroads: A Historical Survey* (Albuquerque: University of New Mexico Press, 1970), 15, 32; "Magdalena: The Glory Years," in *Celebrating 100 Years of Frontier Living*, ed. Jacky Barrington (Magdalena, NM: Centennial Committee, 1984), 10–11.

30. Cleaveland, *No Life for a Lady*, 23.

31. The spelling most common for the Hispanic community is Puertecito and in the records of the Bureau of Indian Affairs this spelling was sometimes used for the Navajo community as well.

32. William Quinn, Comprehensive Ethnohistorical Report on the Cañoncito and Alamo Navajo Bands, unpublished report, Washington, DC: Bureau of Indian Affairs, 1984, 29–30; Florence Hawley Ellis, *Navajo Indians*, vol. 1 (New York: Garland, 1974), 483–487; John Maltrotti, "History of the Alamos," Ellis unpublished field study, 1949. (Maltrotti's paper is one of several produced by students during a summer field study conducted at Alamo in 1949 under the direction of anthropologist Florence Hawley Ellis and will be cited in the above manner.) See also INT-47; INT-53; ANOHP (José Guerro).

33. Curiously, Ellis's published account of the field study, *Navajo Indians*, does not reflect some informants' accounts on the pre–Fort Sumner origins of the band. See Maltrotti, "History of the Alamos," 4–8. For further evidence, see Glen S. Condon, *An Archeological Resource Investigation of Historic Navajo, Hispanic, and Prehistoric Pueblo Sites on the Alamo Band Navajo Reservation, Socorro County, New Mexico* (Santa Fe: Museum of New Mexico, 1980), 13; and Nicole Plett, "Alamo Navajo Rediscover Their Heritage," *New Mexico Magazine* (November 1986): 25–28; Robert C. Euler, "Aspects of Political Organization among the Puertocito Navajo," *El Palacio* 68 (Summer 1961): 119; ANOHP (Martíniano Apachito); INT-96.

34. Albert Schroeder, "Navajo and Apache Relationships West of the Rio Grande," *El Palacio* 70 (Autumn 1963): 11; Donald C. Simmons, "The Alamo Navajo Kinship and Sib Systems" (master's thesis, Yale University, 1950), 4; ANOHP (Denny Apachito);

INT-96; "Casamira Baca, " in *Navajo Stories of the Long Walk Period*, ed. Broderick H. Johnson (Tsaile, NM: Navajo Community College Press, 1973), 139.

35. Quoted in William A. Keleher, *Turmoil in New Mexico, 1846–1868* (Albuquerque: University of New Mexico Press, 1952), 313; Quinn, "Comprehensive Ethnohistorical Report," 132.

36. For the Enemy Navajos, see Brooks, *Captives and Cousins*, 110–111, 212–213, 251–254. The association of the Alamos with the Enemy Navajos is made by Clyde Kluckhohn and Dorothea Leighton, *The Navajo* (Cambridge, MA: Harvard University Press, 1946; repr. Garden City, NY: Doubleday, 1962), 36.

37. ANOHP (Martíniano Apachito). John Guerro also denies the connection as quoted in Dorothy Chapin, "A Brief History: The Alamo Navajo," unpublished paper, 1973, author's collection.

38. Simmons, "Alamo Navajo Kinship and Sib Systems," 34; Ellis, *Navajo Indians*, 485–486.

39. Written statement by Manual Cháves, April 17, 1982, author's collection; INT-21; INT-48; INT-49; INT-50; INT-55; INT-110; INT-112; ANOHP (Hattie Apachito); ANOHP (Louise Abeyta); ANOHP (Pauline Padilla); ANOHP (Martíniano Apachito). For a snapshot of Alamo naming practices in transition, see Census of the Puertocito Navajo Band of Navajo Indians, June 30, 1920, Indian Census Rolls, 1885–1940 (Southern Pueblo Agency, 1920–1921), RG 75, NA-RMR.

40. Euler, "Aspects of Political Organization among the Puertocito Navajo," 120.

41. Simmons, "Alamo Navajo Kinship and Sib Systems," 5; Chapin, "Brief History," 4; INT-50; INT-94; ANOHP (Louise Abeyta). See also INT-44; INT-96; INT-107.

42. The secondary literature on the Navajos is extensive. Valuable introductions to the subject include Kluckhohn and Leighton, *Navajo*; James F. Downs, *The Navajo* (New York: Holt, Rinehart, and Winston, 1972); John R. Farella, *The Main Stalk: A Synthesis of Navajo Philosophy* (Tucson: University of Arizona Press, 1984); Jerrold E. Levy, *In the Beginning: The Navajo Genesis* (Berkeley: University of California Press, 1998); Gladys A. Reichard, *Navajo Religion: A Study in Symbolism* (New York: Pantheon Books, 1950); Gary Witherspoon, "Navajo Social Organization," in *Handbook of North American Indians*, vol. 10, ed. Alfonso Ortiz (Washington, DC: Smithsonian Institution Press, 1979), 524–535.

43. Marshall Tome, "The Navajo Nation Today," in *Handbook of North American Indians*, vol. 10, 683. For the concept of *hózhó*, see Leland C. Wyman, "Navajo Ceremonial System," in *Handbook of the North American Indians*," vol. 10, 537.

44. INT-44.

45. Quinn, "Comprehensive Ethnohistorical Report," 32–33; Donn V. Hart, "The Economy of the Alamo Navahos of New Mexico," 24–26, FHEAFSP; INT-41; ANOHP (John Guerro); ANOHP (José Guerro). For the growth of restrictive game laws in the

region and their impact on Indians in the area, see Louis S. Warren, *The Hunter's Game: Poachers and Conservationists in Twentieth-Century America* (New Haven, CT: Yale University Press, 1997), chap. 3.

46. INT-44.

47. Quinn, "Comprehensive Ethnohistorical Report," 32; Susan E. Lee, *These Also Served* (Los Lunas, NM: author, 1960), 39–40, 70; *Socorro Chieftain*, September 13, 1904; Cleaveland, *No Life for a Lady*, 299–300.

48. Quoted in Quinn, "Comprehensive Ethnohistorical Report," 34.

49. Ibid., 34–36, 40; P. T. Lonergan to Reverend Father Anselm Weber, August 29, 1913, ANOHP; S. F. Stacher to Chester Faris, December 19, 1928, ENA, CCF 1926–1939, Box 18, RG-75, NA-PSR. Also see J. W. Ashcroft to S. F. Stacher, November 9, 1932, ENA, CCF 1926–1939, Box 20, RG-75, NA-PSR; S. F. Stacher to J. W. Ashcroft, November 12, 1932, ENA, CCF 1926–1939, Box 20, RG-75, NA-PSR.

50. Statement Regarding Navajo Use and Occupancy of Land in the Alamo Navajo Community, ANOHP, Box 1, CSWR; P. T. Lonergan to Reverend Father Anselm Weber, August 29, 1913, ANOHP, Box 1, CSWR; ANOHP (John Guerro).

51. Albert B. Fall to Office of Indian Affairs (copy), May 6, 1913, Albert B. Fall Papers, Box 53, Folder 4, HL; and C. T. Haute to Albert B. Fall, Albert B. Fall Papers, Box 53, Folder 9, HL.

52. INT-53.

53. Quinn, "Comprehensive Ethnohistorical Report," 36–37, 40–42; Constitution of the Alamo Chapter of the Alamo District of the Navajo Tribe of New Mexico—1943, SAC, Box 5A.

54. Olson Apachito's talk, July 25, 1944, SAC, Box 4. In 1943 the population at Alamo was 288 with a land base of 25,908 acres (20,298 patented trust allotments and 5,610 acres in public-domain grazing permits). See Reservation Program: United Pueblos Agency, March 1944, SAC, Box 5A.

55. The literature on New Mexico statehood is especially rich. See David V. Holtby, *Forty-Seventh Star: New Mexico's Struggle for Statehood* (Norman: University of Oklahoma Press, 2012); Robert W. Larson, *New Mexico's Quest for Statehood, 1846–1912* (Albuquerque: University of New Mexico Press, 1968); Linda C. Noel, *Debating American Identity: Southwestern Statehood and Mexican Immigration* (Tucson: University of Arizona Press, 2014), pt. 1; Noel, "Anglos, Mexicans, *Nativos*, and the Debate over Arizona and New Mexico Statehood," *Pacific Historical Review* 80 (August 2011): 629–666; Gabriel Meléndez, "Nuevo México by Any Other Name: Creating a State from an Ancestral Homeland," in *The Contested Homeland: A Chicano History of New Mexico*, ed. Erlinda Gonzales-Berry and David R. Maciel (Albuquerque: University of New Mexico Press, 2000), chap. 5; Beck, *New Mexico*, chap. 12; Lamar, *Far Southwest*, 161–172.

56. US Bureau of the Census, *Twelfth Census of the United States*, New Mexico,

1900; US Bureau of the Census, *Fourteenth Census of the United States*, New Mexico, 1920; Twitchell, *Leading Facts of New Mexican History*, vol. 4, 282. For territorial and statewide population patterns, see John M. Nieto-Phillips, *Language of Blood: The Making of Spanish-American Identity in New Mexico, 1880s–1930s* (Albuquerque: University of New Mexico Press, 2004), chap. 3. In 1921 the state legislature carved a new county out of the western portion of Socorro County. Extending to the Arizona border, Catron County was named for prominent landowner and politician Thomas B. Catron and encompassed the settlements of Datil, Pie Town, Mangas, and Quemado.

57. The figures are based on the US Bureau of the Census, Fourteenth Census of the United States, New Mexico, 1920.

58. *Magdalena News*, February 3, 1916, 1. For other examples of boosterism, see *Magdalena News*, "Our Big Booster Edition," August 26, 1915; *Magdalena News*, February 17, 1916, 9; *Magdalena News*, August 17, 1918, 2; *Magdalena News*, July 17, 1919, 1; *Magdalena News*, January 20, 1921, 2.

59. By 1940 Magdalena's population was 1,420 and Kelly's was a mere 101. US Bureau of the Census, *Sixteenth Census of the United States: 1940, Population*, vol. 2, pt. 4 (Washington, DC: US Government Printing Office, 1943), 1012.

CHAPTER ONE. FAMILY AND RELIGION

1. INT-75.

2. INT-20.

3. INT-39. For Navajo views and practices involving the dead, see Clyde Kluckhohn and Dorothea Leighton, *The Navajo* (Cambridge, MA: Harvard University Press, 1946; repr. Garden City, NY: Doubleday, 1962), 89, 184–185.

4. *Magdalena News*, September 17, 1936, 1. Until 1929 the state of New Mexico neglected to compile statistics on infant mortality. When compiled, the figures signaled a serious public health problem. With a 140 infants out of 1,000 dying in their first year, the mortality rate was slightly more than double the national figure, which stood at 61 per 1,000. Moreover, the situation worsened in the 1930s before improving by 1940, when the figure fell to 96. For child welfare advocates, who had waged a twenty-year campaign on behalf of children's health, the 1940 figures were both evidence of marked improvement and the work yet before them. Congressional passage in 1921 of the Federal Maternity and Infancy Act, also known as the Sheppard-Towner Act, was a significant turning point in the campaign. The same year brought the creation of the New Mexico Department of Public Welfare and two subsidiary agencies, the Bureau of Child Welfare and the Bureau of Public Health. In the coming years Hispanic and Anglo mothers and children would benefit from a host of services. On a county-by-county

basis, nurses made home visits, distributed pamphlets on infant care, organized baby clinics, conducted prenatal care classes, and trained midwives. In Socorro and Catron Counties, where geographical isolation and poverty were commonplace, these services—not the least of which was improving the quality of midwifery—were essential programs both for improving infancy survival rates and for children's overall health. See Sandra Schackel, *Social Housekeepers: Women Shaping Public Policy in New Mexico, 1920–1940* (Albuquerque: University of New Mexico Press, 1992), chaps. 1–2; *Magdalena News,* July 16, 1931, 1.

5. The distinction between "social childbirth" and "medically managed birth" is made in Mary Melcher, "Times of Crises and Joy: Pregnancy, Childbirth, and Mothering in Rural Arizona, 1910–1940," *Journal of Arizona History* 40 (Summer 1999): 181. For a general treatment of the subject, see Dorothy C. Wertz, *Lying-in: A History of Childbirth in America* (New Haven, CT: Yale University Press, 1977), esp. chap. 2. For the use of midwives in New Mexico, see Schackel, *Social Housekeepers,* 14, 47. Many of Magdalena's Hispanic babies were delivered by Placido Chávez, who received state certification as a midwife in 1940. Over the course of her career Chávez delivered some 167 babies, often charging families a fee as little as $5. See *Magdalena Mountain Mail,* February 1, 1988, 4.

6. *Magdalena Mountain Mail,* February 22, 1986, 2.

7. INT-65.

8. This paragraph is based on Boland's paper (no first name indicated), "Navaho Infants, Toddlers, Children: Alamo Area," 1–3, FHEAFSP; AUTO-11; INT-55.

9. Boland, "Navajo Infants," 3.

10. Many of the proscriptions surrounding cradleboard construction were apparently fading by the mid-twentieth century. Boland says, "Although my informants recognized the first legend of the first cradleboard, they no longer follow the ancient regulations involved in the making of one." Thus, the description above, including the prayer, is based on Dorothea Leighton and Clyde Kluckhohn's discussion of the subject in *Children of the People: The Navajo and His Development* (Cambridge, MA: Harvard University Press, 1947; repr. New York: Octagon Books, 1974), 18–26. However, it should be noted that many Alamo Navajo mothers continued to use cradleboards. In 1981, when I purchased one from an older woman, she related to me the symbolic significance of each part of the item.

11. INT-40.

12. *Magdalena Mountain Mail,* January 31, 1985, 7.

13. Ralph Emerson Twitchell, *The Leading Facts of New Mexican History,* vol. 4 (Cedar Rapids, IA: Torch Press, 1917), 363–364; Susan E. Lee, *These Also Served* (Los Lunas, NM: author, 1960), 30–32.

14. INT-4; INT-76.

15. Agnes Morley Cleaveland, *No Life for a Lady* (1941; repr. Lincoln: University of Nebraska Press, 1977), esp. 5–6, 17, 23, 36–37; Norman Cleaveland, with George Fitzpatrick, *The Morleys: Young Upstarts on the Southwest Frontier* (Albuquerque, NM: Calvin Horn, 1971), 225; Lee, *These Also Served,* 67–68; INT-18. For a biography of Agnes Morley Cleaveland, see Darlis A. Miller, *Open Range: The Life of Agnes Morley Cleaveland* (Norman: University of Oklahoma Press, 2010). Ray Morley was without question one of the two or three most noted persons in southwest New Mexico. After attending a Pennsylvania military academy, he first attended the University of Michigan before moving to Columbia University to play football. After achieving national fame on the gridiron and armed with a college diploma, Morley was soon back in the Datils managing the ranch and running his Navajo Lodge, which served tourists heading west on the Ocean-to-Ocean Highway (for which Morley was a major lobbyist) and game hunters. Over the years Morley served as president of the New Mexico Cattle Growers Association, was a major investor in Magdalena businesses, and was a major stockholder in the First National Bank of Magdalena. Strong-willed, fearless, and a renowned practical joker, he was as much at home in the bucking corral as a fine drawing room. In many ways, he was a fascinating syncretic integration of the two great influences on his life—cowboy ways and a Columbia education. Ada's other children, Agnes Morley Cleaveland and Loraine Reynolds, a lifelong force for civic improvement, also managed to successfully straddle the two worlds so much a part of their upbringing.

16. Norman Cleaveland, *Morleys,* 237; Agnes Morley Cleaveland, *No Life for a Lady,* 35.

17. Twitchell, *Leading Facts of New Mexican History,* vol. 4, 366–368, 369–371, 382–383; *Magdalena News,* August 16, 1915, 22, 28; and *The Magdalena County High School* (Albuquerque: Evening Herald, 1917), 7.

18. For the history of the organization, see Olivia Arrietta, "*La Alianza Hispano-Americana,* 1894–1965: An Analysis of Collective Action and Cultural Adaption," in *Nuevomexicano Cultural Legacy: Forms, Agencies, and Discourse,* ed. Francisco A. Lomelí, Victor A. Sorell, and Genaro M. Padilla, 109–125. Local membership is drawn from Twitchell, *Leading Facts of New Mexican History,* vol. 4. For the Kelly building, see *Magdalena News,* February 28, 1918, 5.

19. INT-11.

20. For comparison, see Donovan Senter, "Acculturation among New Mexican Villagers in Comparison to Adjustment Patterns of Other Spanish-Speaking Americans," *Rural Sociology* 10 (March 1945): 36.

21. Kathryn McKee Roberts, *From the Top of the Mountain: Pie Town, New Mexico, and Neighbors!* (n.p.: Roger Coffin, 1990), 116, 170. Roberts's book includes a compilation of settlers' remembrances of homesteading Pie Town. Giles's and subsequent

recollections will be cited under the Roberts heading. See also Joan Myers, *Pie Town Woman: The Hard Life and Good Times of a New Mexico Homesteader* (Albuquerque: University of New Mexico Press, 2001).

22. Roberts, *From the Top of the Mountain*, 101, 121.

23. INT-53; INT-107; AUTO-13.

24. For a discussion of the various functions of families as social units, see Elliot West, *The Way to the West: Essays on the Central Plains* (Albuquerque: University of New Mexico Press, 1995), chap. 3.

25. Quotation is from Mary Shepardson, "The Gender Status of Navajo Women," in *Women and Power in Native North America*, ed. Laura F. Klein and Lillian A. Ackerman (Norman: University of Oklahoma Press, 1995), 162. For an extensive discussion of Navajo kinship, including the role and status of females, see David F. Aberle, "Navajo," in *Matrilineal Kinship*, ed. David M. Schneider and Kathleen Gough (Berkeley: University of California Press, 1961), 96–201. See also Mary Shepardson, "The Status of Navajo Women," *American Indian Quarterly* 6 (Spring/Summer 1982): 149–169; Charlotte J. Frisbe, "Traditional Navajo Women: Ethnographic and Life History Portrayals," *American Indian Quarterly* 6 (Spring/Summer 1982): 11–33; Marsha Weisiger, *Dreaming of Sheep in Navajo Country* (Seattle: University of Washington Press, 2009), chap. 4; James F. Downs, *The Navajo* (New York: Holt, Rinehart, and Winston, 1972), 22–24, 28–30, 39; Gary Witherspoon, *Navajo Kinship and Marriage* (Chicago: University of Chicago Press, 1975); Dianna Jeanne Shomaker, "Fosterage as a Form of Exchange among the Navajo" (PhD diss., University of New Mexico, 1984).

26. Downs, *Navajo*, 37–41; Kluckhohn and Leighton, *Navajo*, 104–105; and Boland, "Navajo Infants, Toddlers, and Children," 19.

27. Boland, "Navajo Infants, Toddlers, and Children," 19; Donald C. Simmons, "The Alamo Navajo Kinship and Sib Systems" (master's thesis, Yale University, 1950), 34–35.

28. Kluckhohn and Leighton, *Navajo*, 273.

29. ACSA. These stories are taken from an untitled document. The stories were apparently collected in 1987 for a project on Alamo Navajo history under the direction of Henry Walt.

30. Particularly good on Navajo values are Down, *Navajo*, 24–27; and Ethel M. Albert, "The Classification of Values: A Method and Illustration," *American Anthropologist* 58 (April 1956): 221–248. "It's up to him" is taken from Shomaker, "Fosterage as a Form of Exchange among Navajo," 320. McGrath is quoted in Gary Witherspoon, *Language and Art in the Navajo Universe* (Ann Arbor: University of Michigan Press, 1977), xix.

31. Alamo interviews, ACSA; AUTO-14; AUTO-21; INT-44; INT-50; INT-47; INT-109; INT-112; INT-48; INT-54; INT-107.

32. Ramón A. Gutiérriz, "Family and Kinship in the Spanish and Mexican Borderlands: A Cultural Account," in *On the Borders of Love and Power: Families and Kinship in the Intercultural American Southwest*, ed. David Wallace Adams and Crista DeLuzio (Berkeley: University of California Press, 2012), 130. See also Arthur L. Campa, *Hispanic Culture in the Southwest* (Norman: University of Oklahoma Press, 1979), 191; Nancie L. González, *The Spanish-Americans of New Mexico: A Heritage of Pride* (Albuquerque: University of New Mexico Press, 1967), 59–63.

33. Early on in my research I shared with selected community members copies of Charles Aranda's *Dichos: Proverbs and Sayings from the Spanish* (Santa Fe, NM: Sunstone Press, 1977), asking them to identify those *dichos* they heard growing up. *Dichos* identified in this manner will be cited as the Magdalena *Dichos* Survey (MDS). Other *dichos* were collected in the process of conducting interviews and are cited as such. Also see Nasario García, comp. and trans., *Más Antes: Hispanic Folklore of the Río Puerco Valley* (Sante Fe: Museum of New Mexico Press, 1997), 9–21; Rubén Cobos, comp. and trans., *Refranes: Southwestern Spanish Proverbs* (Santa Fe: Museum of New Mexico Press, 1985).

34. These generalizations closely mirror those of Sarah Deutsch's study of Hispanic women in northern New Mexico and southern Colorado, and it is from Deutsch that the phrase "labor and production" is drawn. See Deutsch, "Women and Intercultural Relations: The Case of Hispanic New Mexico and Colorado," *Signs: Journal of Women and Society* 12 (Summer 1987): 721–732; Deutsch, *No Separate Refuge: Culture, Class, and Gender on an Anglo-Hispanic Frontier in the American Southwest, 1880–1940* (New York: Oxford University Press, 1987), chap. 2. Also see Janet Lecompte, "The Independent Woman of Hispanic New Mexico, 1841–1848," in *New Mexico Women: Intercultural Perspectives*, ed. Joan M. Jensen and Darlis A. Miller (Albuquerque: University of New Mexico Press, 1986); Joan M. Jensen, "'I've Worked, I'm Not Afraid of Work': Farm Women in New Mexico, 1920–1940," in *New Mexico Women: Intercultural Perspectives*, ed. Joan M. Jensen and Darlis A. Miller (Albuquerque: University of New Mexico Press, 1986). For the concept of social capital, see Robert D. Putman, *Bowling Alone: The Collapse and Revival of American Community* (New York: Simon and Schuster, 2000).

35. INT-10; INT-45; INT-66. Writing of nineteenth-century New Mexico, Janet Lecompte, previously cited, says: "Bearing children out of wedlock was common among all classes."

36. INT-57.

37. INT-63; INT-64; AUTO-9. See also INT-21.

38. MDS; INT-63.

39. INT-63.

40. INT-61; INT-1; INT-32; INT-57.

41. INT-22; INT-59; AUTO-9.

42. INT-63.

43. INT-45. See also INT-65.

44. MDS; INT-65.

45. INT-20; INT-65.

46. MDS; INT-45; INT-66.

47. INT-45. See also MDS.

48. INT-45. See Paul Kutsche and John R. Van Ness, *Cañones: Values, Crises, and Survival in a Northern New Mexico Village* (Albuquerque: University of New Mexico Press, 1981), 141.

49. INT-14. See also INT-122; INT-98.

50. INT-16.

51. US Bureau of the Census, Fourteenth Census of the United States, New Mexico, 1920.

52. No attempt will be made to cite this literature, which is nothing less than voluminous.

53. The literature on women's western experience is rich. I have found the following especially useful: Glenda Riley, *The Female Frontier: A Comparative View of Women on the Prairie and the Plains* (Lawrence: University Press of Kansas, 1988), 2–4, 195–196, 201; Sandra L. Myers, *Westering Women and the Frontier Experience, 1800–1915* (Albuquerque: University of New Mexico Press, 1982), chaps. 1, 6–7; Elizabeth Jameson, "Women as Workers, Women as Civilizers: True Womanhood in the American West," in *The Women's West*, ed. Susan Armitage and Elizabeth Jameson (Norman: University of Oklahoma Press, 1987), 145–164; Robert L. Griswold, "Anglo Women and Domestic Ideology in the American West in the Nineteenth and Early Twentieth Centuries," in *Western Women: Their Land, Their Lives*, ed. Lillian Schlissel, Vicki Ruiz, and Janice Monk (Albuquerque: University of New Mexico Press, 1988); Vera Norwood, "Woman's Place: Continuity and Change in Response to Western Landscapes," in *Western Women: Their Land, Their Lives*, ed. Lillian Schlissel, Vicki Ruiz, and Janice Monk (Albuquerque: University of New Mexico Press, 1988), 155–181; and Jacqueline S. Reiner, "Concepts of Domesticity on the Southern Plains Agricultural Frontier, 1870–1920," in *At Home on the Range: Essays on the History of Western Social and Domestic Life*, ed. John R. Wunder (Westport, CT: Greenwood, 1985), 57–72.

54. Material for this paragraph is drawn from Mabel Hobson Draper, *Though Long the Trail* (New York: Rinehart, 1946), 271–278.

55. Ibid., 282–286.

56. See in particular Katherine Harris, *Long Vistas: Women and Families on Colorado Homesteads* (Niwot: University of Colorado Press, 1993), 139–143, 155–156; Dee Garceau, *The Important Things of Life: Women, Work, and Family in Sweetwater County,*

Wyoming, 1880–1929 (Lincoln: University of Nebraska Press, 1997), 76, 80–88, 93, 158.

57. Lillian Schlissel, "Rawhide Heroines: The Evolution of the Cowgirl and the Myth of America," in *The American Self: Myth, Ideology, and Popular Culture*, ed. Sam B. Girgus (Albuquerque: University of New Mexico Press, 1981), 170.

58. Cleaveland, *No Life for a Lady*, 27–28. For different generational perceptions see Elliot West, *Way to the West*, 134–135, 153; West, *Growing Up with the Country: Childhood on the Far Western Frontier* (Albuquerque: University of New Mexico Press, 1989), 45; and Garceau, *Important Things of Life*, 106–107, 111, 154.

59. For Anglo frontier value orientations, see Ray Allen Billington, *America's Frontier Heritage* (New York: Holt, Rinehart, and Winston, 1966), 219–235; West, *Growing Up with the Country*, 252–253. West notes that the individualistic frontier attitudes were not really a break with historic tradition but "were splendidly suited to a setting for which they were never intended—the peculiar world of the frontier West." Evon Z. Vogt, in his study of homesteading in Fence Lake, New Mexico, identifies the five major value orientations of its Anglo settlers (mostly from the southern plains of the Texas Panhandle), who moved into the area in the late 1920s and early 1930s: individualism, mastery over nature, living for the future, hard work, and group superiority. See Vogt, *Modern Homesteaders: The Life of a Twentieth-Century Frontier Community* (Cambridge, MA: Harvard University Press, 1955), esp. 191–208. On the question of feelings of group and racial superiority, in addition to Vogt see Jacqueline M. Moore, *Cow Boys and Cattle Men: Class and Masculinities on the Texas Frontier, 1865–1900* (New York: New York University Press, 2010), 135–140.

60. Moore, *Cow Boys and Cattle Men*. See p. 215 for the forging of personas.

61. INT-90.

62. INT-90.

63. Draper, *Though Long the Trail*, 276.

64. "Magdalena: The Glory Years," in *Celebrating 100 Years of Frontier Living*, ed. Jacky Barrington (Magdalena, NM: Centennial Committee, 1984), 11.

65. *Magdalena News*, July 13, 1939, 1; *Magdalena News*, August 21, 1982, 2.

66. INT-76; INT-18; INT-75.

67. INT-24; INT-3. Regarding cowboy preachers, see Janice E. Shuetz, "A Rhetorical Approach to Protestant Evangelism in Twentieth-Century New Mexico," in *Religion in Modern New Mexico*, ed. Ferenc M. Szasz and Richard W. Etulain (Albuquerque: University of New Mexico Press, 1997), 131–135.

68. INT-70. See also INT-83.

69. Joe M. Evans, *Ol' Spot the Lead Steer: Bible Stories Told in Cowboy Language* (El Paso, TX: privately printed, 1964), 19–20; Evans, *The Cow: All I Know I Learned from a Cow* (El Paso, TX: Guynes Printing, 1944), 55.

70. INT-83.

71. Roberts, *From the Top of the Mountain*, 61, 97, 157, 165, 171, 180, 188; INT-34.

72. Roberts, *From the Top of the Mountain*, 195, 118, 117.

73. INT-79.

74. Not to say that there were not schisms among New Mexico Catholics, but these were restricted, it appears, to the northern part of the territory. See E. A. Mares, ed., *Padre Martínez: New Perspectives from Taos* (Taos, NM: Millicent Rogers Museum, 1988); Paul Horgan, *Lamy of Santa Fe* (New York: Farrar, Straus, and Giroux, 1975), esp. 230–251; Angélico Chávez, "A Nineteenth-Century New Mexico Schism," *New Mexico Historical Review* 58 (January 1983): 35–54.

75. *Magdalena News*, June 4, 1931, 1; INT-17; INT-21; INT-52; INT-62; INT-116. See also Rodolfo Rocha, "Early Ranching along the Rio Grande," in *At Home on the Range: Essays on the History of Western Social and Domestic Life*, ed. John R. Wunder (Westport, CT: Greenwood, 1985), 12–13.

76. INT-1; INT-30; INT-58.

77. INT-11; INT-14.

78. See Rev. Thomas L. Kinkead, *An Explanation of the Baltimore Catechism of Christian Doctrine for the Use of Sunday-School Teachers and Advanced Classes* (New York: Benziger Brothers, 1891).

79. INT-64; INT-66; INT-63. See also INT-7; INT-17; INT-98; INT-118.

80. INT-99; INT-10; INT-58.

81. INT-35; INT-61; INT-16; INT-64.

82. INT-14; INT-32; INT-35; INT-63; INT-67.

83. INT-14; INT-116; INT-52.

84. INT-1.

85. INT-11.

86. INT-65; INT-67.

87. INT-61.

88. INT-10. See also AUTO-1. For background on La Llorona, see Campa, *Hispanic Culture in the Southwest*, 200–201.

89. INT-10. See also AUTO-29; INT-31; INT-63; INT-118.

90. On *brujas*, see Campa, *Hispanic Culture in the Southwest*, 198–199.

91. INT-63; AUTO-1; INT-60.

92. For background, see Campa, *Hispanic Culture in the Southwest*, 201. The quotation is from INT-117. For other accounts, see AUTO-1; AUTO-9; INT-60; INT-63.

93. INT-67; AUTO-9.

94. For the lack of a word for religion, see Downs, *Navajo*, 95. The literature on Navajo spirituality is extremely rich. In addition to Downs, *Navajo*, 109–110, this paragraph draws heavily on Kluckhohn and Leighton, *Navajo*, 192–193, 200–202,

240–242; Alexander H. Leighton and Dorothea Leighton, *The Navajo Door: An Introduction to Navajo Life* (Cambridge, MA: Harvard University Press, 1944), 24–26.

95. Kluckhohn and Leighton, *Navajo*, 184–193, 200–206, 304; Downs, *Navajo*, 82. The taboo against cussing the wind is taken from Donn V. Hart, *The Economy of the Alamo Navajos of New Mexico*, 23, FHEAFSP. The quotation is from Leighton and Leighton, *Navajo Door*, 25.

96. Regarding the ceremonial system, see Kluckhohn and Leighton, *Navajo*, 217–221; Sam D. Gill, *Sacred Words: A Study of Navajo Religion and Prayer* (Westport, CT: Greenwood, 1981); Downs, *Navajo*, 101–102; Katherine Spencer, *An Analysis of Navaho Chantway Myths* (Philadelphia: American Folklore Society, 1957).

97. INT-44; INT-49; INT-99; INT-107; INT-112.

98. INT-36; INT-43; INT-49; INT-54.

99. INT-54; INT-55; INT-94; INT-99; INT-106; INT-107.

100. INT-94; AUTO-10. See also INT-43; INT-48.

101. INT-36. This incident took place in 1971. For background on Enemy Way, see Kluchhohn and Leighton, *Navaho*, 222–223; Downs, *Navajo*, 103–107.

102. INT-46; INT-49; Alamo interviews, ACSA.

103. ANOHP (Bessie Baca).

104. Regarding witchcraft, see Downs, *Navajo*, 109–111; Kluckhohn and Leighton, *Navajo*, 187–192; Kluckhohn, *Navajo Witchcraft* (Cambridge, MA: Peabody Museum of American Archaeology and Ethnology, 1944); Margaret K. Brady, *"Some Kind of Power": Navajo Children's Skinwalker Narratives* (Salt Lake City: University of Utah Press, 1984), chap. 1.

105. Kluckhohn, *Navajo Witchcraft*, 84; INT-36.

106. INT-114; INT-105. See also INT-94; INT-96; INT-103. It should be noted that many Alamo Navajos have long dismissed the supposed powers of skinwalkers, whereas others see the stories as a handy disciplinary device for parents. See INT-54; INT-103; INT-105.

CHAPTER TWO. WORK AND PLAY

1. Norman Cleaveland, with George Fitzpatrick, *The Morleys: Young Upstarts on the Southwest Frontier* (Albuquerque, NM: Calvin Horn: 1971), 5–7.

2. INT-58; AUTO-9; Bernadyne Powell Brown, *A Happy Life* (n.p.: privately published, 1993), 4; INT-115.

3. INT-16; INT-11; *Magdalena News*, June 29, 1916, 6; Diego Montoya, "Fun and Games," in *Celebrating 100 Years of Frontier Living*, ed. Jacky Barrington (Magdalena, NM: Centennial Committee, 1984), 111.

4. INT-3.

5. For an insightful examination of the role and nature of play on the Anglo frontier, see Elliot West, *Growing Up with the Country: Childhood on the Far Western Frontier* (Albuquerque: University of New Mexico Press, 1989), chap. 5. Regarding play in other rural areas, see Pamela Riney-Kehrberg, *Childhood on the Farm: Work, Play, and the Coming of Age in the Midwest* (Lawrence: University Press of Kansas, 2005), chap. 5; Marilyn Irvin Holt, *Children of the Western Plains: The Nineteenth-Century Experience* (Chicago: Ivan R. Dee, 2005), chap. 6.

6. INT-57; INT-28.

7. INT-75.

8. Brown, *Happy Life*, 4; INT-38.

9. Don V. Hart, "The Economy of the Alamo Navahos of New Mexico," 34–35, FHEAFSP; AUTO-26; INT-44; INT-55.

10. This aspect of play in rural settings is emphasized in Riney-Kehrberg, *The Nature of Childhood: An Environmental History of Growing Up in America since 1865* (Lawrence: University Press of Kansas, 2014), chap. 1.

11. INT-31; Kathryn McKee Roberts, *From the Top of the Mountain: Pie Town, New Mexico, and Neighbors!* (n.p.: Roger Coffin, 1990), 92.

12. INT-120; INT-74. See also Agnes Morley Cleaveland, *No Life for a Lady* (1941; repr. Lincoln: University of Nebraska Press, 1977), 80–81; INT-2; INT-24; INT-33.

13. INT-29; Cleaveland, *No Life for a Lady*, 67.

14. Quoted in LaVerne Harrell Clark, *They Sang for Horses: The Impact of the Horse on Navajo and Apache Folklore* (Tucson: University of Arizona Press, 1966; repr. Boulder: University of Colorado Press, 2001), 36.

15. INT-49; INT-54; INT-46.

16. *Magdalena Mountain Mail*, October 29, 1983, 3.

17. Joe M. Evans, *The Cow: All I Know I Learned from a Cow* (El Paso, TX: Guynes Printing, 1944), 43.

18. INT-13; Cleaveland, *No Life for a Lady*, 77.

19. INT-74.

20. INT-8; INT-79.

21. INT-3.

22. INT-57.

23. INT-9.

24. INT-57.

25. Brown, *Happy Life*, 16; INT-85.

26. INT-94; AUTO-26; AUTO-27.

27. AUTO-15; INT-114.

28. As Steven Mintz has pointed out, two conceptions of childhood were in con-

tention in the nineteenth century: the first was the concept of a "useful childhood," in which children's work was deemed essential to the family's welfare; the second was "protected childhood," in which children "were sheltered from the stress and demands of the adult world." The first conception was mainly associated with "pioneer families," the latter with the rising urban middle class. See Mintz, *Huck's Raft: A History of American Childhood* (Cambridge, MA: Harvard University Press, 2004), 152–153. The tensions between work, play, and schooling are a dominant theme in David I. Macleod's *The Age of the Child: Children in America, 1890–1920* (New York: Twayne, 1998). Regarding the nature and significance of children's work in the West, see West, *Growing Up with the Country*, chap. 4; Riney-Kehrberg, *Childhood on the Farm*, chap. 2.

29. Regarding the role of sheepherding in Navajo children's enculturation, see James F. Downs, *The Navajo* (New York: Holt, Rinehart, and Winston, 1972), 86–87; Dorothea Leighton and Clyde Kluckhohn, *Children of the People: The Navajo and His Development* (Cambridge, MA: Harvard University Press, 1947; repr. New York: Octagon Books, 1974), 57–58; Gary Witherspoon, "Sheep in Navajo Culture and Social Organization," *American Anthropologist* 75 (October 1973): 1444.

30. "Reservation Program," United Pueblo Agency, March 1944, 10, Sophie D. Aberle Collection, Box 5A, Folder 28, CSWR. Regarding the nature and significance of wage labor for Navajos generally, see Colleen O'Neil, *Working the Navajo Way: Labor and Culture in the Twentieth Century* (Lawrence: University Press of Kansas, 2005), esp. chaps. 2 and 4.

31. INT-48; INT-54. See also AUTO-24.

32. INT-106.

33. INT-33; INT-23.

34. Haven Tobias, "New Mexico Labor Legislation, 1912–1949," in *Labor in New Mexico: Union Strikes and Social History since 1881*, ed. Robert Kern (Albuquerque: University of New Mexico Press, 1983), 285–288. Several informants make references to working in the Kelly mines as children. See INT-5; INT-27; INT-35.

35. INT-52; INT-17. For background, see N. Howard Thorp, "Following the Flocks," *New Mexico Magazine* (November 1936): 9–11, 36–37.

36. INT-12; INT-38; INT-33. The anonymous poem appeared in the *Magdalena Mountain Mail*, October 1, 1988, 1, but appears under a matching 1942 sketch by local artist Katherine Field and therefore was probably written during the same year.

37. Ramon F. Adams, *Cowboy Lingo: A Dictionary of the Slack-Jaw Words and Whangdoodle Ways of the American West* (1936; repr. Boston: Houghton Mifflin, 2000), 119; Philip Ashton Rollins, *The Cowboy: An Unconventional History of Civilization on the Old-Time Cattle Range*, rev. ed. (Scribner's, 1936; repr. Norman: University of Oklahoma Press, 1997), 242–243.

38. INT-120. See also INT-13; INT-38.

39. INT-82.

40. INT-13; INT-38; INT-82.

41. INT-38; INT-18. See also INT-80.

42. INT-80; INT-57; INT-38.

43. INT-75. See also INT-65; INT-69; Langford Ryan Johnston, *Old Magdalena Cow Town* (Magdalena, NM: Bandar Log, 1983), chap. 8.

44. INT-43.

45. Ibid.

46. INT-57.

47. INT-13.

48. INT-12; INT-24; INT-37.

49. For both an extreme and amusing example of the punishing work expectations to which children were sometimes subjected, see Norman Cleaveland's account of his uncle Ray Morley's exacting demands in *Morleys*, 245–249. See also INT-18.

50. INT-38; INT-2. See also INT-17; INT-23; INT-26; INT-57; INT-80.

51. INT-65.

52. INT-2; INT-28.

53. Cleaveland, *No Life for a Lady*, 151. See also INT-26; INT-13; INT-37; INT-59; INT-75.

54. INT-24.

55. INT-38; INT-26. See also INT-57; INT-80.

56. INT-9.

57. INT-13.

58. INT-80.

59. INT-33; INT-23.

60. INT-80. See also INT-75.

61. INT-120.

62. INT-80; INT-38; *Magdalena Mountain Mail*, September 1, 1988, 1.

63. The standard treatment of the New Deal's impact on the West is Richard Lowitt, *The New Deal and the West* (Bloomington: Indiana University Press, 1984). For a splendid examination of the CCC in New Mexico, see Richard Melzer, *Coming of Age in the Great Depression: The Civilian Conservation Corps Experience in New Mexico, 1933–1942* (Las Cruces, NM: Yucca Free Press, 2000). The CCC's educational programs are discussed in David Tyack, Robert Lowe, and Elisabeth Hansot, *Public Schools in Hard Times: The Great Depression and Recent Years* (Cambridge, MA: Harvard University Press, 1984), 116–122. For the history of the Magdalena Stock Driveway, see Recent History of Grazing—Especially Taylor Grazing Act, WPA Files—Grazing and Livestock Industry, 1934–1940, Exp. 10, NMSRCA. Regarding CCC camps and their activities in the Magdalena area, see Camp Report (DG-42-N), October 10, 1935, RG

35, Entry 115, Box 145, NA-CP; Camp Report (DG-42-N), August 3, 1937, RG 35, Entry 115, Box 145, NA-CP; Camp Inspection Report (DG-42-N), November 23, 1938, RG 35, Entry 115, Box 145, NA-CP; Camp Inspection Report (SCS-25-N), February 28, 1940, RG 35, Entry 115, Box 145, NA-CP; *Magdalena News*, March 26, 1936, 1; *Magdalena News*, April 23, 1936, 1; *Magdalena News*, November 30, 1939, 3.

64. For the scope of the program, see Reports and Related Correspondence with State Relief Directors Regarding Cattle, 1934–1938, RG 124, Entry 16, Box 5, Folder—New Mexico, H. L. Kent, NA-CP; Reports and Related Correspondence of Livestock Disposal Program, 1934–1938, RG 124, Entry 11, Box 9, folder—New Mexico, Final Drought Cattle Report, NA-CP; *Magdalena News*, June 28, 1934, 1; *Magdalena News*, August 30, 1934; *Magdalena News*, October 18, 1934, 1; *Magdalena News*, January 5, 1935, 1.

65. INT-23; INT-24; INT-38.

66. INT-75.

67. James W. Ashcroft to S. F. Stacher, November 9, 1932, RG 75, ENA, CCF, 1926–1939, File No. 052.4, Box 20, Station 4, NA-R; S. F. Stacher to James W. Ashcroft, November 12, 1932, RG 75, ENA, CCF, File No. 052.4, Box 20, Station 4, NA-R; William Quinn, "Comprehensive Ethnohistorical Report on the Cañoncito and Alamo Navajo Bands," unpublished report, Washington, DC: Bureau of Indian Affairs, 1984," 40–41. Field's quotation is from the *Magdalena News*, July 30, 1936, 8.

68. INT-11.

69. INT-76; INT-9.

70. INT-43; INT-94; ANOHP (Louise Abeyta); AUTO-11. Also see Mary Shepardson, "The Gender Status of Navajo Women," in *Women and Power in Native North America*, ed. Laura F. Klein and Lillian A. Ackerman (Norman: University of Oklahoma Press, 1995), 165–166; and O'Neil, *Working the Navajo Way*, 11.

71. Quoted in Peter Nabokov and Robert Easton, *Native American Architecture* (New York: Oxford University Press, 1989), 326.

72. INT-55. See also INT-121; ANOHP (Pauline Padilla).

73. The literature on Navajo weaving is rich. Essential texts are Gladys A. Reichard, *Spider Woman: A Story of Navajo Weavers and Chanters* (New York: Macmillan, 1934); Gary Witherspoon, *Language and Art in the Navajo Universe* (Ann Arbor: University of Michigan Press, 1977), chap. 4; Kathy M'Closkey, *Swept under the Rug: A Hidden History of Navajo Weaving* (Albuquerque: University of New Mexico Press, 2002); Erika Marie Bsumek, *Indian-Made: Navajo Culture in the Marketplace, 1868–1940* (Lawrence: University Press of Kansas, 2008); Teresa J. Wilkins, *Patterns of Exchange: Navajo Weavers and Traders* (Norman: University of Oklahoma Press, 2008).

74. INT-43. See also INT-121; ANOHP (Louise Abeyta); ANOHP (Pauline Padilla).

75. *Socorro Chieftain*, September 13, 1902, 4; *Magdalena News*, August 1, 1929, 1.

76. Several Alamo Navajo weavers are singled out for notice in Gregory Schaaf's *American Indian Textiles: 2,000 Artist Biographies* (Santa Fe, NM: CIAC Press, 2001). For a brief but insightful article on the history of Alamo Navajo weaving, see Marian E. Rodee, "Modern Eye Dazzlers: Weaving of the Alamo Navajo," *American Indian Art Magazine* 14 (Summer 1989): 54–61. Rodee points out that in years past male weavers also existed at Alamo.

77. *Magdalena Mountain Mail*, July 1, 1989, 4; INT-122. See also INT-101; INT-116.

78. INT-20; INT-63; INT-65; INT-122.

79. Sarah Deutsch, *No Separate Refuge: Culture, Class, and Gender on an Anglo-Hispanic Frontier in the American Southwest, 1880–1940* (New York: Oxford University Press, 1987), 51–54; Darlis A. Miller, "The Women of Lincoln County, 1860–1900," in *New Mexico Women: Intercultural Perspectives*, ed. Joan M. Jensen and Darlis A. Miller (Albuquerque: University of New Mexico Press, 1986), 177–178.

80. Brown, *Happy Life*; INT-122. See also, INT-65; INT-77; INT-79; Roberts, *From the Top of the Mountain*, 89–91, 126.

81. INT-72; INT-74; Cleaveland, *No Life for a Lady*, 106–107.

82. *Magdalena Mountain Mail*, July 1, 1989, 4.

83. INT-74.

84. INT-63; INT-65; AUTO-9.

85. Cleaveland, *No Life for a Lady*, 110; INT-77; INT-68; INT-72; INT-74.

86. Bessie's story is drawn from INT-3; INT-69.

87. The poem and drawing were originally published in 1939 and were reprinted in the *Magdalena Mail*, April 24, 1982, 1.

88. *Magdalena News*, April 11, 1929, 1. For a brief account of Katherine Field's career, see *Magdalena Mountain Mail*, March 29, 1986, 1, 7. For stories of another Field daughter, Daisy, see Cleaveland, *No Life for a Lady*, 60–64.

89. Mintz, *Huck's Raft*, 112.

90. INT-2.

91. INT-24; INT-71; INT-2.

92. West, *Growing Up with the Country*, 143.

93. *Magdalena News*, August 8, 1929, 8.

CHAPTER THREE. PLEASURES AND TRANSITIONS

1. INT-38; INT-9; INT-79.

2. Bernadyne Powell Brown, *A Happy Life* (n.p.: privately published, 1993), 21; INT-37.

3. INT-38; INT-72.

4. INT-17.

5. Jane Pattie and Tom Kelly, *Cowboy Spur Maker: The Story of Ed Blanchard* (College Station: Texas A&M University Press, 2002), 48.

6. "Rodeo," in *The New Encyclopedia of the American West*, ed. Howard R. Lamar (New Haven, CT: Yale University Press, 1998), 970–974; Mary Lou LeCompte, "The Hispanic Influence on the History of Rodeo, 1823–1922," *Journal of Sport History* 12 (Spring 1985): 21–38; Clifford P. Westermeier, *Man, Beast, Dust: The Story of Rodeo* (1947; repr. Lincoln: University of Nebraska Press, 1987); Michael Allen, *Rodeo Cowboys in the American Imagination* (Reno: University of Nevada Press, 1998), chap. 1; Wayne S. Wooden and Calvin Ehringer, *Rodeo in America: Wranglers, Roughstock, and Paydirt* (Lawrence: University Press of Kansas, 1996), chap. 1.

7. *Magdalena News*, August 7, 1918, 1; "Rodeo," in *Celebrating 100 Years of Frontier Living*, ed. Jacky Barrington (Magdalena, NM: Centennial Committee, 1984), 54–56; Langford Ryan Johnston, *Old Magdalena Cow Town* (Magdalena, NM: Bandar Log, 1983), 106–109. For the history of women in rodeo, see Mary Lou LeCompte, *Cowgirls of the Rodeo: Pioneer Professional Athletes* (Urbana: University of Illinois Press, 1993), chaps. 1–3; Teresa Jordon, *Cowgirls: Women of the American West* (Garden City, NY: Anchor Books, 1984), esp. chap. 8.

8. *Magdalena News*, August 4, 1929, 1; *Magdalena News*, August 31, 1939, 6–7; Victor Batchler, "The Annual Rodeo at Magdalena," Socorro County—History and Pioneers, WPA files, 1938–1939, Box 24, NMSRCA.

9. *Magdalena News*, August 10, 1918, 1; Johnston, *Old Magdalena Cow Town*, 107–109; INT-18.

10. *Magdalena News*, August 10, 1918, 1.

11. Brown, *Happy Life*, 21.

12. Norman Cleaveland with George Fitzpatrick, *The Morleys: Young Upstarts on the Southwest Frontier* (Albuquerque, NM: Calvin Horn, 1971), 1–2.

13. Ibid., 2–3.

14. For this aspect of frontier life, see Elliot West, *The Saloon on the Rocky Mountain Mining Frontier* (1979; repr. Lincoln: University of Nebraska Press, 1996); West, "Heathens and Angels: Childhood in the Rocky Mountain Mining Towns," *Western Historical Quarterly* 14 (April 1982): 149–152; David Dary, *Seeking Pleasure in the Old West* (New York: Knopf, 1991), esp. 127–130, 232–234, 260.

15. INT-42; INT-73; INT-79.

16. INT-79; Johnston, *Old Magdalena Cow Town*, 79, 107; INT-76; INT-23.

17. INT-37.

18. For prostitution in the West, see Anne M. Butler, *Daughters of Joy, Sisters of Misery: Prostitutes in the American West, 1865–1890* (Urbana: University of Illinois Press, 1985); Dary, *Seeking Pleasure in the Old West*, 129–133, 259–266; Max Evans, *Madam*

Millie: Bordellos from Silver City to Ketchikan (Albuquerque: University of New Mexico Press, 2002); Jan MacKell, *Red Light Women of the Rocky Mountains* (Albuquerque: University of New Mexico Press, 2009). Regarding the brothel trade in Magdalena, see INT-2; INT-62; INT-70.

19. *Magdalena News*, May 22, 1918, 1; *Magdalena News*, June 1, 1918, 3.

20. INT-42; INT-58; INT-62; INT-73; INT-10; INT-57.

21. INT-2; INT-58; INT-62.

22. INT-63.

23. INT-67; INT-14.

24. INT-58.

25. INT-13.

26. Ibid.

27. INT-71.

28. INT-79; INT-77; INT-74.

29. INT-64.

30. Paul Kutsch and John R. Van Ness, *Cañones: Values, Crises, and Survival in a Northern New Mexico Village* (Albuquerque: University of New Mexico Press, 1981), 117, 121.

31. MDS; INT-64; INT-63; INT-66.

32. INT-14.

33. Ibid.

34. Mary Shepardson, "The Gender Status of Navajo Women," in *Women and Power in Native North America*, ed. Laura F. Klein and Lillian A. Ackerman (Norman: University of Oklahoma Press, 1995), 164. The following discussion draws heavily from Charlotte Johnson Frisbie's *Kinaaldá: A Study of the Navajo Girl's Puberty Ceremony* (Middletown, CT: Wesleyan University Press, 1967). See also Leland C. Wyman and Flora L. Bailey, "Navajo Girl's Puberty Rite," *New Mexico Anthropologist* 25 (January–March 1943): 3–12.

35. Frisbie, *Kinaaldá*, 347–350.

36. Ibid., 290; INT-43.

37. INT-55; AUTO-19; Alamo interviews (Alta Secatero), ACSA; Frisbie, *Kinaaldá*, 269.

38. INT-43; AUTO-19; Frisbie, *Kinaaldá*, 189, 350, 353–356.

39. INT-108. See also INT-69.

40. Clyde Kluckhohn and Dorothea Leighton, *The Navajo* (Cambridge, MA: Harvard University Press, 1946; repr. Garden City, NY: Doubleday, 1962), 229.

41. INT-94; INT-106; INT-108; INT-121; *Magdalena News*, September 3, 1931, 3; *Magdalena News*, August 29, 1935, 8.

42. *Magdalena News*, July 27, 1916, 1; *Magdalena News*, July 19, 1920, 4. For back-

ground, see Mary Montaño, *Tradiciones Nuevomexicanas: Hispano Arts and Culture of New Mexico* (Albuquerque: University of New Mexico Press, 2001); Arthur L. Campa, *Hispanic Culture in the Southwest* (Norman: University of Oklahoma Press, 1979), 243; Evon Z. Vogt and John M. Roberts, "A Study of Values," *Scientific American* 195 (July 1956): 29–30; Janet Lecompte, "The Independent Women of Hispanic New Mexico," in *New Mexico Women: Intercultural Perspectives*, ed. Joan M. Jensen and Darlis A. Miller (Albuquerque: University of New Mexico Press, 1986), 75–76. For local accounts, see INT-10; INT-62; INT-64; INT-101; AUTO-9.

43. INT-11; INT-35; INT-64; INT-117; INT-118; AUTO-9.

44. INT-63; INT-64; AUTO-9.

45. INT-35; INT-11.

46. INT-22; INT-63; INT-59; INT-64; INT-58; INT-98.

47. INT-35; INT-57.

48. INT-15.

49. Regarding Pie Town social life, see Kathryn McKee Roberts, *From the Top of the Mountain: Pie Town, New Mexico, and Neighbors!* (n.p.: Roger Coffin, 1990), 93, 99–100, 108–109, 195.

50. *Magdalena Mountain Mail*, September 28, 1985, 1. See also INT-8; INT-75; INT-79; and Joan Myers, *Pie Town Woman: The Hard Life and Good Times of a New Mexico Homesteader* (Albuquerque: University of New Mexico Press, 2001), 129–138.

51. INT-6; INT-8; INT-13; INT-24; INT-33; INT-71; INT-72; INT-75; INT-77; INT-78; INT-79; Roberts, *From the Top of the Mountain*, 172; Agnes Morley Cleaveland, *No Life for a Lady* (1941; repr. Lincoln: University of Nebraska Press, 1977), 169–172. The injury at Beaverhead, originally reported in the *Magdalena News*, was reprinted in the *Magdalena Mountain Mail*, January 30, 1982, 1.

52. INT-8; INT-71; INT-75; INT-77; INT-81. The rhyme is from "A Cowboy Ball," Cultural History—Western Songs and Verses, WPA files, 1937–1938, Box 16, NMSRCA.

53. *Magdalena Mountain Mail*, September 28, 1985, 1; INT-75. See also Loraine Morley Reynolds, "We Danced the Fiddler Down," *New Mexico Magazine* (August 1954): 20, 48–49.

54. Blake Allmendinger, *The Cowboy: Representations of Labor in an American Work Culture* (New York: Oxford University Press, 1992), 63.

55. Lloyd Shaw, *Cowboy Dances: A Collection of Western Square Dances* (Caldwell, ID: Caxton Printers, 1941), 156.

56. Ramon F. Adams, *Cowboy Lingo: A Dictionary of the Slack-Jaw Words and Whangdoodle Ways of the American West* (1936; repr. Boston: Houghton Mifflin, 2000), 184; INT-78; Shaw, *Cowboy Dances*, 157.

57. INT-37.

58. Adams, *Cowboy Lingo*, 190; INT-13.

59. INT-79.

60. INT-75; INT-26; Shaw, *Cowboy Dances*, 234.

61. INT-13; INT-75; INT-77; Roberts, *From the Top of the Mountain*, 92.

62. Roberts, *From the Top of the Mountain*, 177.

63. Johnston, *Old Magdalena Cow Town*, 60; Roberts, *From the Top of the Mountain*, 92, 145; INT-81.

64. Dee Garceau, *The Important Things of Life: Women, Work, and Family in Sweetwater County, Wyoming, 1880–1929* (Lincoln: University of Nebraska Press, 1997), 71.

65. INT-71.

66. Camp Report (D-G 42-N), August 3, 1937, RG 35, Entry 115, Box 145, NACP.

67. AUTO-26.

68. US Census, New Mexico (Santa Rita), 1930; Donald C. Simmons, "The Alamo Navajo Kinship and Sib Systems" (master's thesis, Yale University, 1950), 16; ANOHP (Elsie Monte); Alamo interviews (Fred Apache), ACSA.

69. Simmons, "Alamo Navajo Kinship and Sib Systems," 18; Kluckhohn and Leighton, *Navajo*, 112; and James F. Downs, *The Navajo* (New York: Holt, Rinehart, and Winston, 1972), 36.

70. ANOHP (Elsie Monte); ANOHP (Billy Apachito); ANOHP (Jose Guerro); INT-106; Alamo interviews (Fred Apache), ACSA; Simmons, "Alamo Navajo Kinship and Sib Systems," 8. As Simmons points out, although the custom of plural wives existed at Alamo, it was relatively rare (15–16).

71. Simmons, "Alamo Navajo Kinship and Sib Systems," 19–20; INT-106; INT-121; ANOHP (Louise Abeyta); ANOHP (Huskie Monte).

72. ANOHP (Pauline Padilla).

73. Cynthia Culver Prescott argues that the transition from the conditions of frontier living experienced by first-generation settlers in the West (Willamette Valley, Oregon) to the more settled and prosperous conditions of the second generation affected females' approach to matrimony. Whereas first-generation marriages were characterized by patriarchy and reciprocal labor roles, the second were based more on middle-class conceptions of romantic love, companionship, and shared decision making. Although Prescott's thesis is suggestive, it must be remembered that arid west-central New Mexico was not western Oregon, where the frontier period was relatively brief. Still, for those living in the Magdalena region the material conditions of life were gradually improving. See Prescott, "'Why She Didn't Marry Him': Love, Power, and Marital Choice on the Western Frontier," *Western Historical Quarterly* 38 (Spring 2007): 25–45.

74. INT-11.

75. INT-64.

76. Regarding José Aragón, see Jacky Barrington, ed., *Celebrating 100 Years of Frontier Living* (Magdalena, NM: Centennial Committee, 1984), 137; Ralph Emerson

Twitchell, *The Leading Facts of New Mexican History* (Cedar Rapids, IA: Torch Press, 1917), 4, 337–368; *Magdalena News*, August 26, 1915, 22. The story of the marriage proposal comes from INT-62.

77. INT-62.

78. Ibid.

79. The description of the wedding comes from the *Socorro Chieftain*, June 16, 1900, 1. For Abran Abcyta's background, see Twitchell, *Leading Facts of New Mexican History*, 393.

CHAPTER FOUR. POINTS OF CONTACT

1. Agnes Morley Cleaveland, *No Life for a Lady* (1941; repr. Lincoln: University of Nebraska Press, 1974), 44–45.

2. INT-53.

3. For the conceptual basis for "points of contact," see Andrew R. L. Cayton and Fredrika J. Teute, *Contact Points: American Frontiers from the Mohawk Valley to the Mississippi, 1750–1830* (Chapel Hill: University of North Carolina Press, 1998), 1–12. Regarding the Southwest generally and New Mexico specifically as a borderland, see Charles Montgomery, "The Trap of Race and Memory: The Language of Spanish Civility on the Upper Rio Grande," *American Quarterly* 52 (September 2000): 478–513; David J. Weber, "Conflicts and Accommodations: Hispanic and Anglo-American Borders in Historical Perspectives, 1670–1853," *Journal of the Southwest* 39 (Spring 1997): 1–33.

4. INT-112; INT-114.

5. ANOHP (José Guerro).

6. The above story is a composite of several versions told to me. INT-44; INT-46; INT-49; INT-119.

7. ANOHP (Martíniano Apachito); INT-40; ANOHP (Billy Apachito); INT-80.

8. John Donald Robb, *Hispanic Folk Music of New Mexico and the Southwest: A Self-Portrait of a People* (Norman: University of Oklahoma Press, 1980), 604–605.

9. INT-22; INT-101; INT-117. See also INT-115.

10. INT-93; AUTO-29.

11. INT-21; INT-48; INT-50; INT-59; INT-61; INT-103; INT-116. By one account a Hispanic rancher in the Puertecito area made a small fortune by hiring Navajos over several years to pick piñon nuts. The profit came from two sources: in addition to the truckloads of nuts, he reportedly sold wine to the Indians, purchased at 50 cents a quart and sold for $1.50. INT-80.

12. INT- 48; INT-59; INT-106; INT-112.

13. INT-21.

14. INT-59; INT-62.

15. This discussion had benefited greatly from Charles Montgomery, *The Spanish Redemption: Heritage, Power, and Loss on New Mexico's Upper Rio Grande* (Berkeley: University of California Press, 2002); John M. Nieto-Phillips, *The Language of Blood: The Making of Spanish-American Identity in New Mexico, 1880s–1930s* (Albuquerque: University of New Mexico Press, 2004); Nieto-Phillips, "Spanish American Ethnic Identity and New Mexico's Statehood Struggle," in *The Contested Homeland: A Chicano History of New Mexico*, ed. Erlinda Gonzales-Berry and David R. Maciel (Albuquerque: University of New Mexico Press, 2000), 97–142.

16. For the Texas story, see Arnoldo De León, *They Called Them Greasers: Anglo Attitudes toward Mexicans in Texas, 1821–1900* (Austin: University of Texas Press, 1983); David Montejano, *Anglos and Mexicans in the Making of Texas, 1836–1986* (Austin: University of Texas Press, 1987); Neil Foley, *The White Scourge: Mexicans, Blacks, and Poor Whites in Texas Cotton Culture* (Berkeley: University of California Press, 1997).

17. Carolyn Zeleny, *Relations between the Spanish-Americans and Anglo-Americans in New Mexico* (New York: Arno, 1974), 131, 229–230; Juan Gómez-Quiñones, *Roots of Chicano Politics, 1600–1940* (Albuquerque: University of New Mexico Press, 1994), 328–333. For local examples, see *Socorro Chieftain*, November 19, 1904, 4; *Socorro Chieftain*, November 10, 1900, 4; *Magdalena News*, November 4, 1920, 1.

18. *Magdalena News*, April 4, 1918, 1.

19. Marc Simmons, *New Mexico: An Interpretive History* (repr. Albuquerque: University of New Mexico Press, 1988), 182. The idea that New Mexico and the Southwest were lost lands is a theme in John R. Chávez, *The Lost Land: The Chicano Image of the Southwest* (Albuquerque: University of New Mexico Press, 1984); Zeleny, *Relations between the Spanish-Americans and Anglo-Americans*, 293–307; Pablo Mitchell, *Coyote Nation: Sexuality, Race, and Conquest in Modernizing New Mexico* (Chicago: University of Chicago Press, 2005), chap. 7; and Montgomery, *Spanish Redemption*, 39–46.

20. William C. McDonald Papers, special reports, 1914, NMSRCA.

21. *Socorro Chieftain*, October 6, 1900, 4.

22. *Socorro Chieftain*, January 5, 1900, 1. See also INT-24.

23. For accounts of the episode see James B. Gillett, *Six Years with the Texas Rangers, 1875–1881* (New Haven, CT: Yale University Press, 1921), 211–222; Chester D. Potter, "Reminiscences of the Socorro Vigilantes," ed. Paige W. Christiansen, *New Mexico Historical Review* 40 (January 1965): 23–53; Erna Furgusson, *Murder and Mystery in New Mexico* (Albuquerque: Merle Armitage, 1948), 15–32; Herald L. Edwards, "Trouble in Socorro," *True West* (Winter 1990): 42–47.

24. *Socorro Chieftain*, February 9, 1901, 1. It should be noted that several factors mitigated against viewing sheepherder-cattlemen disputes in strictly ethnic terms.

Although the big cattle concerns were overwhelmingly Anglo, Anglos were also represented in the higher echelons of the sheep business. Thus, when woolgrowers met in Magdalena in 1902, two prominent Anglos, Frank Hubbell and Montague Stevens, were elected to the executive committee. Likewise, the Cattle and Horse Protective Association included members from both groups. Finally, both Hispanic and Anglo livestock growers worked together in support of state and federal programs to rid the region of wolves and coyotes. See *Socorro Chieftain*, March 1, 1902, 1; *Socorro Chieftain*, February 22, 1902, 1.

25. *Magdalena News*, August 26, 1915, 22. See Montgomery, "Trap of Race and Memory," 492; and Zeleny, *Relations between the Spanish-Americans and the Anglo-Americans*, 302.

26. Montague Stevens, Pioneer Oral History Collection, microfilm reel 5 (tape 297), CSWR; INT-31; INT-64. For discussions of the patterns of Hispanic self-definition over the years, see Phillip B. Gonzales, "The Political Construction of Latino Nomenclatures in Twentieth-Century New Mexico," *Journal of the Southwest* 35 (1993): 158–185; Joseph Metzgar, "The Ethnic Sensitivity of Spanish New Mexicans: A Survey and Analysis," *New Mexico Historical Review* 49 (January 1974): 49–73.

27. INT-31; INT-63.

28. INT-82. See also INT-42; INT-75.

29. *Socorro Chieftain*, October 20, 1900, 4; *Magdalena News*, September 10, 1904, 1; *Socorro Chieftain*, December 22, 1906, 1; *Magdalena News*, September 16, 1915, 1; *Magdalena News*, October 28, 1915, 1; *Magdalena News*, November 11, 1915, 1; *Magdalena News*, December 30, 1915, 1; *Magdalena News*, March 1, 1917, 1; *Magdalena* News, April 20, 1922, 1; *Magdalena News*, June 1, 1922, 1; *Magdalena News*, August 29, 1935, 1; *Magdalena News*, March 30, 1939, 1.

30. *Magdalena News*, October 28, 1915, 1; M*agdalena News*, December 30, 1915, 1; *Magdalena News*, May 8, 1919, 4.

31. INT-37; INT-6. See also INT-30; INT-56; INT-57; INT-71; Thomas Ewing Dabney, "Kelly—and Our Lady of Magdalena," pt. 3, *New Mexico Magazine* 45, no. 1 (January 1947): 32.

32. INT-37; INT-75.

33. INT-23; INT-75.

34. INT-75.

35. Ibid.; INT-23.

36. INT-1; INT-35.

37. INT-37; INT-64; Bernadyne Powell Brown, *A Happy Life* (n.p.: privately published, 1993), 10.

38. INT-115. There is considerable difference among those who grew up during the

1920s and 1930s about the extent of friendliness between the groups during these years, testimony to the fact individuals either had different experiences or have differently remembered the times. See INT-1; INT-11; INT-118.

39. INT-115; INT-16.

40. INT-65.

41. For studies of ethnoracial mixing in the far West, especially fine studies are Anne F. Hyde, *Empires, Nations, and Families: A History of the North American West, 1800–1860* (Lincoln: University of Nebraska Press, 2011); Hyde, "Hard Choices: Mixed-Race Families and Strategies of Acculturation in the U.S. after 1848," in *On the Borders of Love and Power: Families and Kinship in the Intercultural American Southwest*, ed. David Wallace Adams and Crista DeLuzio (Berkeley: University of California Press, 2012); Albert L. Hurtado, *Sex, Gender, and Culture in Old California* (Albuquerque: University of New Mexico Press, 1999), chap. 2. For the New Mexico story, see Mitchell, *Coyote Nation,* esp. chap. 5; Pablo Mitchell, "'You Just Don't Know Mrs. Baca': Intermarriage, Mixed Heritage, and Identity in New Mexico," *New Mexico Historical Review* 79 (Fall 2004): 437–458; Deena J. González, *Refusing the Favor: The Spanish-Mexican Women of Santa Fe, 1820–1880* (New York: Oxford University Press, 1999); Nancie L. González, *The Spanish-Americans of New Mexico: A Heritage of Pride* (Albuquerque: University of New Mexico Press, 1967), 165–172; Zeleny, *Relations between the Spanish-Americans and Anglo-Americans*, 318–323; Rebecca McDowell Craver, *The Impact of Intimacy: Mexican-Anglo Intermarriages in New Mexico, 1821–1846* (El Paso: Texas Western Press, 1982). Regarding the motivations for intermarriage on both sides, see Darlis A. Miller, "Cross-Cultural Marriages in the Southwest: The New Mexico Experience, 1846–1900," *New Mexico Historical Review* 57 (October 1982): 335, 339–340, 342.

42. On the levels of mixed marriage prior to 1900, see Craver, *Impact of Intimacy*, 4; Miller, "Cross-Cultural Marriages in the Southwest," 341, 351. For the Albuquerque figures, see Mitchell, "'You Just Don't Know Mrs. Baca,'" 440. The data for Bernalillo County come from Zeleny, *Relations between the Spanish-Americans and Anglo-Americans*, 322; González, *Spanish-Americans of New Mexico*, 165–172.

43. Socorro County marriage records. It should be noted that a number of surnames were not identifiably Hispanic or Anglo. Also complicating the picture is that occasionally a spouse's full name suggests mixed-marriage parenthood. (One wonders for example about the ancestry of Guadalupe Patterson, classified as Anglo by surname but probably the child of a mixed marriage.) It should also be noted that in the thirty-three mixed marriages recorded for the two decades, Anglo women in fourteen instances and Hispanic women in nineteen instances married men of the opposite ethnicity.

44. INT-2; INT-37; INT-85; INT-31. See also see INT-56; INT-63.

45. INT-60.

46. *Magdalena News*, November 18, 1915, 1.

47. Pablo Mitchell points out that "the naming process was critical to the creation of identity in New Mexico" and drawing from the 1880 census for Bernalillo County discusses at some length the varying patterns of assigning first names in Anglo, Hispanic, and mixed-marriage families. During this period Spanish-surnamed families assigned traditionally Spanish first names, and Anglo-surnamed families assigned traditional English names. Interestingly, children of mixed marriages might be assigned either English or Spanish names. Speaking of the latter, he observes, "Some of these names so clearly challenge an unclouded allegiance with Anglo America that one can easily imagine a certain glee and mischief in the minds of parents who endowed their children with such glistening names as Quirino, Coulter, Prajedes, Ayres, and Estefina Farr." Mitchell, "'You Just Don't Know Mrs. Baca,'" 446, 456n22. The Magdalena 1920 census and 1930 census show much the same pattern, except for the instances of intermarriages, so few as to make generalizations difficult. Perhaps most significant is the extent to which the 1930 census reveals Hispanic parents continuing to adhere to Spanish first names as markers of Hispanic identity—such as Juanita, Juan, Soledad, Rosario, Candelaria, Sabino, and Clementia. At the same time, one can also see a growing tendency for families to give their children traditional English names such as Frank, Nellie, Joe, and Mabel.

48. *Socorro Chieftain*, October 12, 1907, 1.

49. *Socorro Chieftain*, January 19, 1907, 1; *Socorro Chieftain*, April 7, 1917, 1. For another account of the death of Capitan, see Langford Ryan Johnston, *Old Magdalena Cow Town* (Magdalena, NM: Bandar Log, 1983), 76.

50. INT-23; INT-46; INT-48; INT-44. See also INT-49.

51. INT-70; INT-68.

52. INT-75.

53. INT-33.

54. INT-13.

55. INT-23.

56. Ibid.

57. INT-18; *Magdalena News*, October 25, 1928, 8.

58. INT-75.

59. INT-3.

60. Ibid.

61. ANOHP (Bessie Baca).

62. Ibid.; INT-69; INT-74.

63. Loraine M. Reynolds to Frank M. King, November 29, 1950, Frank M. King Papers, Box 14, Folder 54, H.L.

64. For an overview of the Navajos' contact with Christianity, see Steve Pavlik, "Navajo Christianity: Historical Origins and Modern Trends," *Wicazo Sa Review* 12 (Autumn 1997): 43–58.

65. INT-61; INT-40. See also INT-50; INT-53; INT-110.

66. Delbert G. Fann, "A Look at the Alamo and Magdalena Indian Mission Fields," unpublished manuscript, 1966, Baptist Church Records, Magdalena, New Mexico, 2; INT-21; INT-40; INT-46; INT-48; INT-50; INT-109; INT-112.

67. Cleaveland, unpublished manuscript, Agnes Morley Cleaveland Papers, Rio Grande Historical Collections, Box 15, Folder 10, New Mexico State University Library.

68. *Magdalena News*, July 30, 1936, 8; INT-69; INT-47.

69. INT-48; INT-54; INT-103; INT-114; INT-121; AUTO-6.

70. INT-106. Regarding the problem of understanding despite translators, see INT-50; INT-119; INT-48; INT-21; INT-69.

71. ANOHP (Bessie Baca).

72. INT-112.

73. Regarding Navajo adaptation, see Clyde Kluckhohn and Dorothea Leighton, *The Navajo* (Cambridge, MA: Harvard University Press, 1946; repr. Garden City, NY: Doubleday, 1962), 171; James F. Downs, *The Navajo* (New York: Holt, Rinehart, and Winston, 1972), 130; William Hodge, *The First Americans: Then and Now* (New York: Holt, Rinehart, and Winston, 1981), 224; Peter Iverson, *Diné: A History of the Navajos* (Albuquerque: University of New Mexico Press, 2002), 4. For the additive versus replacement model of acculturation, see Robert L. Bee, *Patterns and Processes: An Introduction to Anthropological Strategies for the Study of Sociocultural Change* (New York: Free Press, 1974), 105; James A. Clifton, "Alternate Identities and Cultural Frontiers," in *Being and Becoming Indian: Biographical Studies of North American Frontiers*, ed. James A. Clifton (Chicago: Dorsey, 1989), 29–30; Malcolm McFee, "The 150% Man, a Product of Blackfeet Acculturation," *American Anthropologist* 70 (December 1968): 1096–1107.

74. INT-50; INT-91. See also INT-119.

75. INT-99.

76. INT-76.

CHAPTER FIVE. ANGLOS AND HISPANICS AT SCHOOL

1. INT-61.

2. W. W. H. Davis, *El Gringo; or, New Mexico and Her People* (1856; repr. Santa Fe, NM: Rydal Press, 1938), 66.

3. Major sources for the history of New Mexico education include Lynne Marie Getz, *Schools of Their Own: The Education of Hispanos in New Mexico, 1850–1940* (Al-

buquerque: University of New Mexico Press, 1997); Getz, "The Romance and Reality of Hispano Identity in New Mexico Schools, 1910–1940," in *The History of Discrimination in U.S. Education: Marginality, Agency, and Power,* ed. Eileen H. Tamura (New York: Palgrave Macmillan, 2008), 117–140; Rosina A. Lozano, "Managing the 'Priceless Gift': Debating Spanish Language Instruction in New Mexico and Puerto Rico, 1930–1950," *Western Historical Quarterly* 44 (Autumn 2013): 271–293; Jon Wallace, "Protestants, Catholics, and the State: The Origins of Public Education in Territorial New Mexico, 1846–1912," *New Mexico Historical Review* 83 (Winter 2008): 57–92; Dianna Everett, "The Public School Debate in New Mexico, 1850–1891," *Arizona and the West* 26 (Summer 1984): 107–134; Gladys A. Wiggin, *Education and Nationalism: An Historical Interpretation of American Education* (New York: McGraw-Hill, 1962), chap. 13; Robert Arthur Moyers, "A History of Education in New Mexico" (PhD diss., George Peabody College for Teachers, 1941). The figures on illiteracy and school enrollment are from Getz, *Schools of Their Own,* 25.

4. On the 1891 school code and the Cháves quotation, see Getz, *Schools of Their Own,* 16, 20. For a list of 1889 Socorro County adoptions, see Mildred Gunn Fitzpatrick, "Textbooks Used in the Elementary Schools of New Mexico, 1846–1964" (EdD diss., University of New Mexico, 1965), 177. For Chase's comments, see the *Socorro Chieftain,* January 31, 1890, 1.

5. Getz, *Schools of Their Own,* 27, 38–39; Erlinda Gonzales-Berry, "Which Language Will Our Children Speak?," in *The Contested Homeland: A Chicano History of New Mexico,* ed. Erlinda Gonzales-Berry and David R. Maciel (Albuquerque: University of New Mexico Press, 2000), 183.

6. Adolfo Chávez is quoted in Gonzales-Berry, "Which Language Will Our Children Speak?," 184, 189. See also the *Socorro Chieftain,* June 28, 1924, 1.

7. INT-26; INT-86.

8. For surveys of the history of US education, see William J. Reese, *America's Public Schools: From the Common School to "No Child Left Behind"* (Baltimore: Johns Hopkins University Press, 2005); Wayne Urban and Jennings Wagoner, *American Education: A History,* 2nd ed. (Boston: McGraw-Hill, 2000). Especially good on the history of schooling in rural and western regions are Jonathan Zimmerman, *Small Wonder: The Little Red Schoolhouse in History and Memory* (New Haven, CT: Yale University Press, 2009); Wayne E. Fuller, *The Old Country School: The Story of Rural Education in the Middle West* (Chicago: University of Chicago Press, 1982); Elliot West, *Growing Up with the Country: Childhood on the Far Western Frontier* (Albuquerque: University of New Mexico Press, 1989), chap. 8; Marilyn Irvin Holt, *Children of the Western Plains: The Nineteenth-Century Experience* (Chicago: Ivan R. Dee, 2005), chap. 4; Pamela Riney-Kehrberg, *Childhood on the Farm: Work, Play, and the Coming of Age in the Midwest* (Lawrence: University Press of Kansas, 2005), chap. 3.

9. INT-10.

10. INT-11.

11. INT-1; INT-16; INT-115. See also INT-58; INT-59.

12. INT-116. See also INT-97; INT-66.

13. INT-64; INT-66.

14. INT-63; INT-32.

15. INT-57; INT-21.

16. MDS.

17. INT-63; INT-65; INT-22.

18. INT-24; Kathryn McKee Roberts, *From the Top of the Mountain: Pie Town, New Mexico, and Neighbors!* (n.p.: Roger Coffin, 1990), 181.

19. INT-37; INT-33; INT-75; INT-79.

20. INT-75; INT-3.

21. INT-37; INT-79.

22. INT-72.

23. For individual portraits of schools in the Pie Town area, including the quotation, see Roberts, *From the Top of the Mountain*, chap. 9. The *Magdalena News* and the *Socorro Chieftain* contain numerous articles on funding efforts. For the role of the federal government, see the correspondence contained in the Federal Emergency Relief Administration, Central Files, 1933–1936, Entry 10, Box 194, RG 69, NA-CP.

24. INT-80; INT-75; Roberts, *From the Top of the Mountain*, 62. See also INT-9; INT-38; INT-71; INT-77; INT-120; Roberts, *From the Top of the Mountain*, 97, 126, 143–144, 177, 186.

25. Minutes of the Meeting of the Board of Education of the Territory of New Mexico, 1891–1911, Department of Education—Territorial Papers, Folder 23, NMRCA; *Territory of New Mexico: Report of the Superintendent of Public Instruction for the Year Ending December 31st, 1892* (Santa Fe: New Mexican Printing, 1892), 63–64; *Nineteenth and Twentieth Annual Reports of the Territorial Superintendent of Public Instruction to the Governor of New Mexico for the Years 1909–1910* (Santa Fe: New Mexican Printing, 1911), 45–46.

26. INT-34; INT-77; INT-81; Roberts, *From the Top of the Mountain*, 97, 126, 134, 178, 193.

27. Agnes Morley Cleaveland, *No Life for a Lady* (1941; repr. Lincoln: University of Nebraska Press, 1977), 121–126; *Magdalena News*, December 15, 1921, 1.

28. Roberts, *From the Top of the Mountain*, 65; INT-26; Helen Tipton, *For the Living* (n.p., 1970), 12–14. The so-called itch was not that uncommon in rural schools. In 1935 this news item was posted from Datil: "Dr. Long from Las Cruces was called out to Catron County to investigate the schools and told our Datil teacher her school was the only one so far that he had visited that did not have the itch." *Magdalena News*, December 5, 1935, 5.

29. Bobbie Mathers was originally from Texas. Her reason for leaving Reserve was her marriage to Sidney Padgett in 1920, a homesteader in the Greens Gap area, whereupon she soon took over the school. Bobbie Mathers Papers (author's copy); INT-77; Roberts, *From the Top of the Mountain*, 65, 132.

30. INT-77; Bobbie Mathers Papers.

31. INT-77.

32. INT-80.

33. Ibid.

34. INT-38; INT-120.

35. INT-13; INT-59.

36. *Magdalena County High School* (Albuquerque: Evening Herald, 1917); *Magdalena Mountain Mail*, October 1, 1987, 1; Suzanne Bramlett, "Education in Magdalena," in *Celebrating 100 Years of Frontier Living*, ed. Jacky Barrington (Magdalena, NM: Centennial Committee, 1984), chap. 8.

37. County School Superintendent Statistical Reports, 1906, Socorro, Department of Education Reports, NMSRCA; Children Attending Public Day Schools, Annual Report County School Superintendents, 1924, Socorro, vol. 5, Department of Education Reports, NMSRCA; George Sánchez, "School Census Distribution in N.M. for 1931," *New Mexico School Review* 11 (January 1932): 18; Georgia L. Lusk, "Eighteenth Biennial Report of the Superintendent of Public Instruction for the Biennium July 1, 1944, to June 30, 1946," 179, NMSRCA; Tom Wiley, "Twenty-First Biennial Report of the Superintendent of Public Instruction for the Biennium July 1, 1950, to June 30, 1952," 229, NMSRCA.

38. *Magdalena News*, March 20, 1919, 1; *Magdalena News*, March 27, 1919, 2; *Magdalena News*, April 3, 1919, 1. See also *Magdalena News*, April 7, 1921, 4.

39. INT-16; *Magdalena News*, May 19, 1921, 1; *Magdalena News*, September 7, 1922, 1; *Magdalena News*, September 6, 1934, 1; *Magdalena News*, May 4, 1939, 1. For the rural school appointments, see *Socorro Chieftain*, June 14, 1935, 1.

40. For broad overviews on how public schools have responded to diversity, see Jonathan Zimmerman, *Whose America? Culture Wars in the Public Schools* (Cambridge, MA: Harvard University Press, 2002); David Tyack, *Seeking Common Ground: Public Schools in a Diverse Society* (Cambridge, MA: Harvard University Press, 2003), pt. 2; Zoë Burkholder, *Color in the Classroom: How American Schools Taught Race, 1900–1954* (New York: Oxford University Press, 2011).

41. *Magdalena News*, November 9, 1916, 7. Regarding Anglo suspicions, see Phillip Gonzales and Ann Massman, "Loyalty Questioned: Nuevomexicanos in the Great War," *Pacific Historical Review* 75 (November 2006): 629–666.

42. *Magdalena News*, August 28, 1919, 1; *Magdalena News*, December 23, 1920, 2; *Magdalena News*, May 10, 1928, 1; *Magdalena News*, September 8, 1932, 3; "Twenty-

Seventh and Twenty-Eighth Annual Reports of the State Superintendent of Public Instruction to the Governor of New Mexico for the Years 1917–1918," 15–16, NMSRCA; *The Magdalena County High School*.

43. Regarding the elementary school, see *Magdalena News*, September 28, 1939, 3; *Magdalena News*, February 29, 1940, 3; *Magdalena News*, March 7, 1940, 3; *Magdalena News*, March 21, 1940, 3; *Magdalena News*, April 25, 1940, 3; *Magdalena News*, May 2, 1949, 3; *Magdalena News*, October 10, 1940, 3. Regarding the high school, see *Magdalena News*, April 9, 1931, 1; *Magdalena News*, February 1, 1934, 1; *Magdalena News*, March 22, 1934, 1; *Magdalena News*, November 30, 1939, 3. The 1939–1942 Magdalena High School yearbooks (author's collection) report on various club activities. For the origins and nature of the nineteenth-century high school, see William J. Reese, *The Origins of the American High School* (New Haven, CT: Yale University Press, 1995). The connection between school reform and twentieth-century state building is emphasized in Tracy L. Steffes, *School, Society, and State: A New Education to Govern Modern America, 1890–1949* (Chicago: University of Chicago Press, 2012). Regarding the rise of vocational education, see Herbert M. Kliebard, *Schooled to Work: Vocationalism and the American Curriculum, 1876–1946* (New York: Teachers College Press, 1999); John L. Rury, *Education and Women's Work: Female Schooling and the Division of Labor in Urban America, 1870–1930* (Albany: State University of New York Press, 1991).

44. Terman is quoted in Leon J. Kamin, *The Science and Politics of I.Q.* (New York: Wiley, 1974), 6. For the cultural deficiency explanation, see Carlos Kevin Blanton, "From Intellectual Deficiency to Cultural Deficiency: Mexican Americans, Testing, and Public School Policy in the American Southwest, 1920–1940," *Pacific Historical Review* 72 (February 2003): 39–62. Regarding George Sánchez, see Carlos Kevin Blanton, *George I. Sánchez: The Long Fight for Mexican American Integration* (New Haven, CT: Yale University Press, 2014); Ruben Flores, *Backroads Pragmatists: Mexico's Melting Pot and Civil Rights in the United States* (Philadelphia: University of Pennsylvania Press, 2014), chap. 4; Getz, *Schools of Their Own*, chap. 3; Michael Welsh, "A Prophet without Honor: George I. Sánchez and Bilingualism in New Mexico," *New Mexico Historical Review* 69 (January 1994): 19–34. As historian Mario T. García points out, Sánchez favored bilingual and bicultural education in the younger grades but also believed that "the eventual mastery of English and acculturation to an English-language culture was not a betrayal of New Mexican culture but rather a way to empower New Mexicans for a new and more complicated and demanding society." See García, foreword to George I. Sánchez, *Forgotten People: A Study of New Mexicans* (1940; repr. Albuquerque: University of New Mexico Press, 1996), 21.

45. INT-14.

46. INT-60; INT-67; AUTO-29.

47. Quoted in INT-11.

48. INT-60; INT-31; AUTO-9; INT-7. See also INT-52.

49. INT-16.

50. INT-17.

51. INT-5. For other accounts of the difficulties in learning English, see INT-7; INT-10; INT-60; INT-116.

52. INT-61; INT-62; INT-11; INT-122. See also INT-31.

53. INT-31; INT-58; INT-11.

54. INT-56; INT-16; INT-21.

55. INT-60.

56. INT-63; INT-67.

57. Overall there is scant evidence that pluralistic and bicultural visions of school reform exerted much influence in the Magdalena region. Nina Otero-Warren (Santa Fe County School Superintendent, 1917–1929) and educator Aurora Lucero, both descendants of elite Hispanic families, were of signal importance in this effort; also Loyd Tireman, professor of education at the University of New Mexico, and author Mary Austin were important in the movement. See John M. Nieto-Phillips, *The Language of Blood: The Making of Spanish-American Identity in New Mexico, 1880s–1930s* (Albuquerque: University of New Mexico Press, 2004), 197–205; Charles Montgomery, *The Spanish Redemption: Heritage, Power, and Loss on New Mexico's Upper Rio Grande* (Berkeley: University of California Press, 2002), 181–184; Flores, *Backroads Pragmatists*, 107–115, 254–267; David L. Bachelor, *Educational Reform in New Mexico: Tireman, San José, and Nambé* (Albuquerque: University of New Mexico Press, 1991), chaps. 1–3; Getz, *Schools of Their Own*, chaps. 3–5; Getz, "Romance and Reality of Hispano Identity."

58. *Magdalena News*, May 15, 1919, 1; *Magdalena News*, November 11, 1915, 1. See also *Magdalena News*, October 28, 1915, 1; *Magdalena News*, October 5, 1916, 1.

59. *The Magdalena County High School*, 14; *Magdalena News*, August 28, 1919, 1; *Magdalena News*, September 8, 1932, 3.

60. *Magdalena News*, April 20, 1922, 1; *Magdalena News*, November 24, 1932, 1. For other Spanish Club activities, see *Magdalena News*, October 28, 1915, 1; *Magdalena News*, October 5, 1922, 1; *Magdalena News*, November 3, 1932, 2; *Magdalena News*, February 1, 1934, 1; *Magdalena News*, March 22, 1934, 1; *Magdalena News*, September 30, 1937, 5; *Magdalena News*, April 25, 1940, 3.

61. For background on the festival, see Coronado Cuarto Centennial, CCC Programs—Folk Festivals, 1939–1940, Box 4, CSWR; Denise Pan, "Commercializing the Spanish Past: The Coronado Cuarto Centennial, 1935–1940," in *Explorations in American History*, ed. Sandra Varney MacMahon (Albuquerque: Center for the American West, Department of History, University of New Mexico, Occasional Papers no. 8, 1995), 81–109.

62. García's research, which she discussed with me in a 1981 interview, eventually became part of Espinosa's *Romancero de Nuevo Mejico* (Madrid: Instituto Miguel de Cervantes, 1953). For background on Espinosa, see Nieto-Phillips, *Language of Blood*, 176–187.

63. Magdalena 1940 high school yearbook; *Magdalena News*, March 28, 1940, 1; *Magdalena News*, April 4, 1940, 1.

64. The announcement of the performance of *Kearney Takes Las Vegas* appeared in the *Magdalena News*, May 2, 1940, 3. The script for the play is available in the WPA New Mexico collection, 1936–1940, CSWR. For background on Lucero-White, see Montgomery, *Spanish Redemption*, 205–208.

65. *Socorro Chieftain*, February 6, 1904, 4.

66. *Socorro Chieftain*, February 13, 1904, 4.

67. Fourteenth Census of the United States, 1920, New Mexico; Fifteenth Census of the United States, 1930, New Mexico.

68. *Magdalena News*, May 24, 1928, 1; *Magdalena News*, May 30, 1929, 1; *Magdalena News*, May 11, 1933, 1; *Magdalena News*, May 23, 1935; *Magdalena News*, May 31, 1934, 1; *Magdalena News*, May 21, 1936, 1; *Magdalena News*, May 20, 1937, 1; *Magdalena News*, May 12, 1938, 1; *Magdalena News*, May 25, 1939, 1; *Magdalena News*, May 9, 1940, 3. For statewide Hispanic school performance, see Sánchez, *Forgotten People*, 30–31.

69. INT-52; INT-113; INT-21. See also INT-15; INT-98; INT-117.

70. INT-98; INT-97; INT-116.

71. Sánchez, *Forgotten People*, 31.

72. INT-8.

73. INT-115.

74. INT-63; INT-65; INT-57.

75. INT-56; INT-58; INT-30. See also INT-31; AUTO-29.

76. INT-63. For other examples of conflict, see INT-13; INT-21; INT-120.

77. INT-2.

78. INT-58.

79. Ibid. Mauricio Miera was an ardent defender of Hispanic pride and identity. In 1933, he played a major role on a state committee investigating allegations that an attitude survey developed by University of New Mexico professors to measure prejudice against Hispanics was in itself derogatory and served to reify existing lines of prejudice. Miera took great exception, for instance, to questions such as: "No matter how much you educate Spanish-speaking people, they are nothing but greasers." For the controversy, see Phillip B. Gonzales, *Forced Sacrifice as Ethnic Protest: The Hispano Cause in New Mexico and the Racial Attitude Confrontation of 1933* (New York: Peter Lang, 2001).

80. INT-58.

81. INT-74.

82. INT-75; INT-11. See also INT-17; INT-45; AUTO-29.

83. For the lower representation of Hispanics in leadership roles, see *Magdalena News*, September 20, 1928, 1; *Magdalena News*, November 7, 1929, 5; *Magdalena News*, October 8, 1931, 1; *Magdalena News*, October 13, 1932, 2; *Magdalena News*, February 16, 1933, 2; *Magdalena News*, November 29, 1934, 3.

84. Magdalena High School 1939 yearbook.

85. INT-122.

86. *Magdalena News*, February 13, 1919, 4.

87. These and other instances of disobedience are reported in INT-23; INT-32; INT-62; INT-71; INT-76; INT-83.

88. INT-75.

89. INT-42; INT-83; INT-115. See also INT-13; INT-22; INT-23; INT-70; INT-122; *Magdalena News*, February 13, 1919, 4.

90. INT-12; INT-13; INT-23; INT-33; INT-75.

91. INT-2; INT-57. See also INT-13; INT-33; INT-59; INT-68; INT-75; INT-86.

92. INT-3; INT-69.

93. *Magdalena News*, May 6, 1937, 4; *Magdalena News*, May 20, 1937, 1.

94. INT-11.

CHAPTER SIX. THE ALAMO NAVAJOS AT SCHOOL

1. INT-53.

2. See Roy Harvey Pearce, *The Savages of America: A Study of the Indian and the Idea of Civilization,* rev. ed. (Baltimore: Johns Hopkins University Press, 1965), 3–4; Bernard W. Sheehan, *Seeds of Extinction: Jeffersonian Philanthropy and the American Indian* (Chapel Hill: University of North Carolina Press, 1973), chaps. 1–2.

3. For the doctrine of historical progress and its implications for Indians, see Fred W. Voget, "Progress, Science, History, and Evolution in Eighteenth- and Nineteenth-Century Anthropology," *Journal of the History of the Behavioral Sciences* 3 (April 1967): 132–155; Brian W. Dippie, *The Vanishing American: White Attitudes and U.S. Indian Policy* (Middletown, CT: Wesleyan University Press, 1982), chap. 7.

4. For broad policy aims, see Frederick E. Hoxie, *A Final Promise: The Campaign to Assimilate the Indians, 1880–1920* (Lincoln: University of Nebraska Press, 1984); Francis Paul Prucha, *The Great Father: The United States and the American Indians,* vol. 2 (Lincoln: University of Nebraska Press, 1984), chaps. 24, 26–27.

5. In recent years the scholarship on Indian boarding schools has blossomed. Notable overviews are David Wallace Adams, *Education for Extinction: American Indians*

and the Boarding School Experience, 1875–1928 (Lawrence: University Press of Kansas, 1995); Michael Coleman, *American Indian Children at School, 1850–1930* (Jackson: University of Mississippi Press, 1993); Jacqueline Fear-Segal, *White Man's Club: Schools, Race, and the Struggle of Indian Acculturation* (Lincoln: University of Nebraska Press, 2007); Margaret D. Jacobs, *White Mother to a Dark Race: Settler Colonialism, Maternalism, and the Removal of Indigenous Children in the American West and Australia, 1880–1940* (Lincoln: University of Nebraska Press, 2009); Clifford E. Trafzer, Jean A. Keller, and Lorene Sisquoc, eds., *Boarding School Blues: Revisiting American Indian Educational Experiences* (Lincoln: University of Nebraska Press, 2006); Cathleen D. Cahill, *Federal Fathers and Mothers: A Social History of the United States Indian Service, 1869–1933* (Chapel Hill: University of North Carolina Press, 2011). Because the Alamo Navajos attended both the Albuquerque and Santa Fe boarding schools, the writer has benefited immensely from John R. Gram, *Education at the Edge of Empire: Negotiating Pueblo Identity in New Mexico's Indian Boarding Schools* (Seattle: University of Washington Press, 2015). For other institutional and cultural case studies, see K. Tsianina Lomawaima, *They Called It Prairie Light: The Story of the Chilocco Indian School* (Lincoln: University of Nebraska Press, 1994); Brenda J. Child, *Boarding School Seasons: American Indian Families, 1900–1940* (Lincoln: University of Nebraska Press, 1998); Robert A. Trennert Jr., *The Phoenix Indian School: Forced Assimilation in Arizona, 1891–1935* (Norman: University of Oklahoma Press, 1988): Adrea Lawrence, *Lessons from an Indian Day School: Negotiating Colonization in Northern New Mexico, 1902–1907* (Lawrence: University Press of Kansas, 2011); Clyde Ellis, *To Change Them Forever: Indian Education at the Rainy Mountain Boarding School, 1893–1920* (Norman: University of Oklahoma Press, 1996); Sally McBeth, *Ethnic Identity and the Boarding School Experience of West-Central Oklahoma American Indians* (Washington, DC: University Press of America, 1983); Sally Hyer, *One House, One Voice, One Heart: Native American Education at the Santa Fe Indian School* (Santa Fe: Museum of New Mexico Press, 1990); Myriam Vučković, *Voices from Haskell: Indian Students between Two Worlds, 1884–1928* (Lawrence: University Press of Kansas, 2008); Matthew Sakiestewa Gilbert, *Education beyond the Mesas: Hopi Students at Sherman Institute, 1902–1929* (Lincoln: University of Nebraska Press, 2010); Clifford E. Trafzer, Matthew Sakiestewa Gilbert, and Lorene Sisquoc, eds., *The Indian School on Magnolia Avenue: Voices and Images of Sherman Institute* (Corvallis: Oregon State University Press, 2012). For a general overview of Native American education, see Jon Reyhner and Jeanne Eder, *American Indian Education: A History* (Norman: University of Oklahoma Press, 2004); K. Tsianina Lomawaima and Teresa L. McCarty, *To Remain an Indian: Lessons in Democracy from a Century of Native American Education* (New York: Teachers College Press, 2006); Adrea Lawrence, KuuNUx TeeRIt Kroupa, Donald Warren, eds., special issue on the history of Native American education, *History of Education Quarterly* 54, no. 3 (August 2014).

6. School Superintendent to Commissioner of Indian Affairs, September 7, 1911, ANOHP, Box 1, CSWR. It is impossible to assess the veracity of the claim that the boy's life was in danger. The claim may have come from local whites who misread the situation or simply out of the desire to improve his prospects. One Alamo Navajo informant (INT-99) whose family lived on the northern edge of the reservation and worked for a rancher claims he went away to boarding school in 1906, but this was an isolated case.

7. Pueblo Indian Agency and Day Schools Annual School Census Report, 1912–1916, 1922, RG 75, NA-RMR; T. P. McCormick to Commissioner of Indian Affairs, August 23, 1926, ANOHP, Box 1, CSWR; James W. Ashcroft, Farmer's Weekly Report, July 15, 1931, July 16, 1931, August 23, 1931, August 24, 1931, Box 20, ENA, CCF 1926–1939, RG 75, NA-PSR; Ashcroft, Farmer's Weekly Report, August 24, 1929, Box 20, ENA, CCF 1926–1939, RG 75, NA-PSR; H. D. Carroll to Nels Field, September 14, 1936, Box 108, ENA—Subject Files Related to Education, RG 75, NA-PSR; *Magdalena News,* September 17, 1936, 8.

8. INT-39; INT-49. See also INT-36; INT-95; INT-114.

9. INT-44; INT-102. See also INT-53. For the use of boarding schools as welfare agencies, see David Wallace Adams, "Beyond Bleakness: The Brighter Side of Boarding Schools, 1870–1940," in *Boarding School Blues: Revisiting American Indian Educational Experiences,* ed. Clifford E. Trafzer, Jean A. Keller, and Lorene Sisquoc (Lincoln: University of Nebraska Press, 2006), 38–40; Child, *Boarding School Seasons,* 15–20; Vučković, *Voices from Haskell,* 242.

10. Memorandum to files, United Pueblo Agency, General Superintendent's File, 1940–1943, Box 4, RG 75, NA-RMR.

11. Reuben Perry to John D. DeHuff, August 31, 1920, Santa Fe Indian School, student folders, 1910–1934, Box 1, RG 75, NA-RMR.

12. INT-39; INT-44; INT-48; INT-49; INT-50.

13. INT-49; INT-96; INT-91.

14. For a general discussion of induction into boarding school, see Adams, *Education for Extinction,* 100–112.

15. INT-49; INT-99; INT-48; INT-55; INT-104; INT-41.

16. INT-40; INT-50; INT-49; INT-99.

17. INT-50; INT-53.

18. INT-114; INT-40; INT-91.

19. INT-39.

20. See Adams, *Education for Extinction,* 108–112; Daniel F. Littlefield Jr. and Lonnie E. Underhill, "Renaming the American Indian, 1890–1913," *American Studies* 12 (Fall 1971): 33–45.

21. INT-50; Albuquerque Indian School, School Census Reports 1912–1915, 1922,

Albuquerque Indian School, Pueblo Indian Agency, Box 1, RG 75, NA-RMR. For other examples of other name changes, see INT-39; INT-49; INT-91.

22. Memorandum, Santa Fe Indian School, student folders, 1910–1934, Box 1, RG 75, NA-RMR; INT-99.

23. INT-44; AUTO-26; B. L. Smith to Mr. Anderson, Mrs. Wilcox, and Miss Cassell, January 14, 1929, Santa Fe Indian School, student folders, 1910–1934, Box 1, RG 75, NA-RMR.

24. INT-40; INT-55; AUTO-26; INT-53. See also INT-49; INT-114; AUTO-23.

25. INT-50; INT-91. See also INT-102; INT-110.

26. Regarding this aspect of boarding, see Adams, *Education for Extinction*, 117–121. Regarding the relaxation of the military aspects of boarding school life, see Margaret Szasz, *Education and the American Indian: The Road to Self-Determination, 1928–1973* (Albuquerque: University of New Mexico Press, 1974), 64.

27. INT-114.

28. INT-40; INT-44. See also INT-50; INT-53; INT-54; INT-96; INT-99; AUTO-6; ANOHP (Bessie Baca).

29. For the curriculum at Albuquerque and Santa Fe, see Gram, *Education at the Edge of Empire*, 114–120; Lillie G. McKinney, "History of the Albuquerque Indian School," pts. 1–3, *New Mexico Historical Review* 20 (1945): 109–138, 207–226, 310–335. For general discussions of the curriculum in off-reservation schools, see Adams, *Education for Extinction*, chap. 5, and the many institutional case studies cited in an earlier note. The vocational curriculum is given particular attention in Alice Littlefield, "Learning to Labor: Native American Education in the United States, 1880–1930," in *The Political Economy of North American Indians*, ed. John H. Moore (Norman: University of Oklahoma Press, 1993; K. Tsianina Lomawaima, "Estelle Reel, Superintendent of Indian Schools, 1898–1910," *Journal of American Indian Education* 35 (Spring 1996): 5–31; Jane E. Simonsen, *Making Home Work: Domesticity and Native American Assimilation in the American West, 1860–1919* (Chapel Hill: University of North Carolina Press, 2006). For Alamo Navajo accounts, see INT-99; INT-110.

30. The discussion on citizenship is drawn from David Wallace Adams, "Land, Law, and Education: The Troubled History of Indian Citizenship, 1871–1924," in *Civic and Moral Learning in America*, ed. Donald Warren and John J. Patrick (New York: Palgrave, 2006), 126–127.

31. Regarding the emphasis on self-reliant individualism, see Adams, *Education for Extinction*, 22–23. For the vocational subjects offered at the two schools, see Gram, *Education at the Edge of Empire*; McKinney, "History of the Albuquerque Indian School." In 1946, when the New Mexico State Fair awarded prizes in the category of Indian handicrafts, nine of the fourteen prize winners in the textile-rug category were Alamo

Navajo weavers, some of whom, *El Palacio* suggested, "had the benefit of training at the Santa Fe and Albuquerque Indian Schools." *El Palacio* 54 (January 1947): 13–14.

32. Institute for Government Research, *The Problem of Indian Administration* (Baltimore: Johns Hopkins University Press, 1928), chap. 3. For discussion and background on the report, see Szasz, *Education and the American Indian*, 16–24; Prucha, *Great Father*, vol. 2, 806–813.

33. For the nature and extent of the outing program at the New Mexico institutions, see Gram, *Education at the Edge of Empire*, 121–126; McKinney, "History of the Albuquerque Indian School," 136–137, 210–211, 212–215. For Alamo Navajo participation, see ANOHP (José Guerro); INT-103; INT-110; INT-111; INT-103. For the role of the outing system in boarding schools generally, see Adams, *Education for Extinction*, 156–163; Robert A. Trennert, "From Carlisle to Phoenix: The Rise and Fall of the Indian Outing System, 1878–1930," *Pacific Historical Review* 52 (August 1983): 267–291. Books on individual boarding school also examine the subject. For a particularly nuanced study, see Kevin Whalen, "Labored Learning: The Outing Program at Sherman Institute, 1902–1930," in *The Indian School on Magnolia Avenue: Voices and Images of Sherman Institute*, ed. Clifford E. Trafzer, Matthew Sakiestewa Gilbert, and Lorene Sisquoc (Corvallis: Oregon State University Press, 2012), 107–136.

34. Quoted in Adams, *Education for Extinction*, 156.

35. INT-79. See also INT-99. For a fuller discussion of this phase of the two schools' activity programs, see Gram, *Education at the Edge of Empire*, 126–128. Two important studies on the changing place of music in Indian education are John W. Troutman, *Indian Blues: American Indians and the Politics of Music, 1879–1934* (Norman: University of Oklahoma Press, 2009); Melissa D. Parkhurst, *To Win the Indian Heart: Music at Chemawa Indian School* (Corvallis: Oregon State University Press, 2014). The story of the Carlisle football team is told in Adams, *Education for Extinction*, 181–190; Adams, "More Than a Game: The Carlisle Indians Take to the Gridiron, 1893–1917," *Western Historical Quarterly* 32 (Spring 2001): 25–53. For the success of one off-reservation school's girls' basketball team, see Linda Peavy and Ursula Smith, *Full-Court Quest: The Girls from Fort Shaw Indian School, Basketball Champions of the World* (Norman: University of Oklahoma Press, 2008).

36. INT-53; INT-110; INT-47; INT-39; AUTO-26; INT-50. See also INT-41; INT-99; ANOHP (Huskie Monte).

37. For the role of boarding school in the creation of "Indian English," see William Leap, *American Indian English* (Salt Lake City: University of Utah Press, 1993), 157–165. Recent scholarship suggests that some students at boarding school found learning to speak, read, and write in English empowering in ways unanticipated by school authorities. See Amelia V. Katanski, *Learning to Write "Indian": The Boarding-School*

Experience and American Indian Literature (Norman: University of Oklahoma Press, 2005); Ruth Spack, *America's Second Tongue: American Indian Education and the Ownership of English, 1860–1900* (Lincoln: University of Nebraska Press, 2002).

38. Clyde Kluckhohn and Dorothea Leighton, *The Navajo* (Cambridge, MA: Harvard University Press, 1946; repr. Garden City, NY: Doubleday, 1962), 271–273.

39. See Adams, *Education for Extinction*, 137; Spack, *America's Second Tongue*, 60–61.

40. INT-39; INT-47; INT-105; INT-114; ANOHP (Huskie Monte); AUTO-23.

41. INT-50; INT-44; AUTO-23; INT-111.

42. INT-53.

43. INT-102.

44. See, for example, INT-91; INT-114.

45. INT-53.

46. John D. DeHuff to H. C. Medley, January 9, 1922, Santa Fe Indian School, student folders, 1910–1934, Box 1, RG 75, NA-RMR; H. C. Medley to John D. DeHuff, January 10, 1922, Santa Fe Indian School, student folders, 1910–1934, Box 1, RG 75, NA-RMR; religious affiliation card, Santa Fe Indian School, student folders, 1910–1934, Box 1, RG 75, NA-RMR.

47. INT-50; INT-53; INT-99; INT-109; INT-49.

48. INT-49; INT-50; INT-114. See also INT-91.

49. INT-53.

50. INT-91. See also INT-50.

51. For an overview of the health issue in boarding schools, including the Patterson report, see Adams, *Education for Extinction*, 124–135. For an excellent discussion of health conditions at both the Santa Fe and Albuquerque schools, see Gram, *Education on the Edge of Empire*, 131–138.

52. *Indians at Work: A News Sheet for Indians and the Indian Service* (Washington, DC: Office of Indian Affairs, October 1, 1935), 23. See also Miss Debay's Diary, 1934–1935, ENA, School Files 1912–1936, Box 108, NA-PSR.

53. Particularly good on Navajo health and government policy are Robert A. Trennert, *White Man's Medicine: Government Doctors and the Navajo, 1863–1955* (Albuquerque: University of New Mexico Press, 1998); Wade Davies, *Healing Ways: Navajo Health Care in the Twentieth Century* (Albuquerque: University of New Mexico Press, 2001). For the trachoma figures at Santa Fe, see Sandra K. Schackel, "'The Tales Those Nurses Told': Public Health Nurses among the Pueblo and Navajo Indians," *New Mexico Historical Review* 65 (April 1990): 228.

54. INT-53.

55. Ida Field to A. B. Smith, November 27, 1928, Santa Fe Indian School, student folders, 1910–1934, Box 10, RG 75, NA-RMR. Needless to say, parents and relatives worried greatly over the state of children's health. See Antonio Apachito to A. B. Smith,

October 21, 1928, Santa Fe Indian School, student folders, 1910–1934, Box 10, RG 75, NA-RMR; Nels Field to A. B. Smith, June 12, 1929; Santa Fe Indian School, student folders, 1910–1934, Box 29, RG 75, NA-RMR; *Magdalena News*, November 29, 1928, 4.

56. INT-53.

57. This account is a compilation of INT-48 and ANOHP (José Guerro).

58. ANOHP (José Guerro); INT-39; INT-44.

59. INT-39; INT-44; John D. DeHuff to José D. Apachito, August 31, 1925, Santa Fe Indian School, student folders, 1910–1934, Box 25, RG 75, NA-RMR; John D. DeHuff to H. C. Medley, September 11, 1925, Santa Fe Indian School, student folders, 1910–1934, Box 25, RG 75, NA-RMR; H. C. Medley to John. D. DeHuff, September 19, 1925, Santa Fe Indian School, student folders, 1910–1934, Box 25, RG 75, NA-RMR; John D. DeHuff to H. C. Medley, September 22, 1925, Santa Fe Indian School, student folders, 1910–1934, Box 25, RG 75, NA-RMR; John D. DeHuff to H. C. Medley, September 29, 1925, Santa Fe Indian School, student folders, 1910–1934, Box 25, RG 75, NA-RMR.

60. INT-44.

61. All the previously cited boarding school case studies include some discussion of disciplinary policy. For an excellent article-length study of one school, see Robert A. Trennert, "Corporal Punishment and the Politics of Indian Reform," *History of Education Quarterly* 29 (Winter 1989): 595–617. Regarding the Albuquerque and Santa Fe schools, see Gram, *Education on the Edge of Empire*, 90–95.

62. INT-40. See also INT-41; INT-44; INT-47; INT-91; INT-96; INT-99; INT-102; ANOHP (John Guerro); AUTO-6.

63. The disjuncture between traditional Navajo disciplinary patterns and those of boarding school is a strong theme in Dorothea Leighton and Clyde Kluckhohn's *Children of the People: The Navajo and His Development* (Cambridge, MA: Harvard University Press, 1947; repr. New York: Octagon Books, 1974). For instances of corporal punishment at Alamo, see INT-44; INT-91.

64. INT-39.

65. For the shift in educational policy see Szasz, *Education and the American Indian*, chap. 3; Reyhner and Eder, *American Indian Education*, chap. 8; Adams, *Education for Extinction*, 328–333. For background on Collier and his policies, see Kenneth R. Philp, *John Collier's Crusade for Indian Reform, 1920–1954* (Tucson: University of Arizona Press, 1977); Lawrence C. Kelly, *The Assault on Assimilation: John Collier and the Origins of Indian Policy Reform* (Albuquerque: University of New Mexico Press, 1983); Prucha, *Great Father*, vol. 2, chaps. 36–39. For the Navajo story, see Donald L. Parman, *The Navajos and the New Deal* (New Haven, CT: Yale University Press, 1976).

66. The scholarly literature on Dewey and other progressive reformers is voluminous. For an introduction, see Martin S. Dworkin, ed., *Dewey on Education* (New York: Teachers College Press, 1959); Lawrence A. Cremin, *The Transformation of the School*

(New York: Columbia University Press, 1962). For the impact of progressive education on Indian policy, see Szasz, *Education and the American Indian*, chaps. 4–8; Reyhner and Eder, *American Indian Education*, chap. 8. Progressive education on the Navajo reservation is examined in Parman, *Navajos and the New Deal*, chap. 8; Katherine Jensen, "Progressive Education for Native Americans: Washington Ideology and Navajo Implementation," *Review Journal of Philosophy and Social Science* 3 (Winter 1978): 231–255; Jensen, "Teachers and Progressives: The Navajo Day School Experiment," *Arizona and the West* 25 (Spring 1983): 49–62; Thomas James, "Rhetoric and Resistance: Social Science and Community Schools for the Navajos in the 1930s," *History of Education Quarterly* 28 (Winter 1988): 599–626.

67. Szasz, *Education and the American Indian*, 55–59.

68. Teachers' meeting minutes, 1932–1935, subject files relating to education, 1909–1942, ENA, Box 120, RG 75, NA-PSR.

69. See Maxine Schrimsher Folder, subject files relating to education, 1909–1942, ENA, Box 120, RG 75, NA-PSR. See also Ina Mae Ance Folder, subject files relating to education, 1909–1942, ENA, Box 108, RG 75, NA-PSR.

70. Ance Folder; ENA, CCF 1926–1939, Box 67, File No. 806, RG 75, NA-PSR.

71. ENA, CCF 1926–1939, Box 67, File No. 806, RG 75, NA-PSR.

72. Schrimsher Folder, subject files relating to education, 1909–1942, ENA, Box 120, RG 75, NA-PSR.

73. Subject files relating to education, 1909–1942, ENA, Box 120, RG 75, NA-PSR.

74. On student response, see Adams, *Education for Extinction*, chaps. 7–8; Adams, "Beyond Bleakness," 35–64; Clyde Ellis, "'We Had a Lot of Fun, but of Course, That Wasn't the School Part,'" in *Boarding School Blues: Revisiting American Indian Educational Experiences* (Lincoln: University of Nebraska Press, 2006), 65–98; Colman, *American Indian Children at School*, chaps. 8–9; Lomawaima, *They Called It Prairie Light*, 115–126; Child, *Boarding School Seasons*, chap. 7; Vučković, *Voices from Haskell*, chap. 7.

75. For the subject of runaways at the Santa Fe and Albuquerque schools, see Gram, *Education at the Edge of Empire*, 95–105.

76. INT-109.

77. INT-125; INT-39; INT-54.

78. INT-44; INT-47; INT-102; INT-103.

79. José Apache to B. L. Smith, January 28, 1927, Santa Fe Indian School, student folders, 1910–1934, Box 25, RG 75, NA-RMR; B. L. Smith to José Apache, January 31, 1927, Santa Fe Indian School, student folders, 1910–1934, Box 25, RG 75, NA-RMR.

80. INT-55. See also AUTO-13.

81. INT-47; INT-49; INT-41; INT-91. See also INT-111; AUTO-26.

82. INT-95.

83. INT-54.

84. INT-91; AUTO-6; AUTO-26; INT-49. See also INT-96.

85. INT-92; INT-47. See also INT-53; INT-55. For the story of the two girls, see Diana Meyers Bahr, *The Students of Sherman Indian School: Education and Native Identity* (Norman: University of Oklahoma Press, 2014), 10.

86. Quoted in Adams, *Education for Extinction*, 231.

87. INT-102; INT-96; INT-50.

88. INT-53.

89. INT-103. See also INT-102; INT-109; INT-111; INT-114; AUTO-13.

90. AUTO-6; INT-114; INT-103.

91. INT-54.

92. ANOHP (José Guerro).

93. The phrase "turning the power" comes from Trafzer, Keller, and Sisquoc, *Boarding School Blues*, 237.

94. INT-39; INT-53.

95. Farmer's Weekly Report, February 18, 1933, ENA, CCF 1926–1939, Box 20, File 052.4, RG 75, NA-PSR; Farmer's Weekly Report, April 29, 1933, ENA, CCF 1926–1939, Box 20, File 052.4, RG 75, NA-PSR; Minutes of the Navajo Tribal Council (copy), July 10–12, 1934, Navajo Agency Files, 1934, ACSA; *United Pueblos Health Quarterly*, October 1939, 4, records of the rehabilitation division, project records, Box 49, United Pueblos, general correspondence, RG 75, NA.

96. *Magdalena Mountain Mail*, September 10, 1989, 1.

97. *United Pueblo Quarterly Bulletin*, October 1939, 35, Sophie D. Aberle Collection, Box 5, Folder 33, CSWR; Indian school population chart, June 28, 1940, United Pueblo Agency, general superintendent's decimal files, 1937–1939, Box 10, RG 75, NA-RMR; school census of Indian children, June 1940, United Pueblo Agency, general superintendent's file, 1937–1939, Box 10, RG 75, NA-RMR. For quarterly day school reports from 1940 to 1943 see United Pueblo Agency, general superintendent's decimal files, 1938–1952, Box 31, RG 75, NA-RMR.

98. AUTO-10; AUTO-16; Quarterly Day School Report, March 31, 1940, Records of the United Pueblo Agency, general correspondence files, 1935–1952, Box 31, RG 75, NA-RMR; Quarterly Day School Report, February 28, 1942, Records of the United Pueblo Agency, general correspondence files, 1935–1952, Box 31, RG 75, NA-RMR.

99. Ann Clark, *Little Herder in Winter* (Washington, DC: Office of Indian Affairs, 1942), 84. For context see Peter Iverson, "Speaking Their Language: Robert W. Young and the Navajos," in *Between Indian and White Worlds: The Culture Broker*, ed. Margaret Connell Szasz (Norman: University of Oklahoma Press, 1994), 255–272. It should be noted that because stock reduction was not an issue at Alamo, the Clark readers may have been viewed as less relevant.

100. Leo Thaler, "The Acculturation of the Alamo Navajo," 17–20, FHEAFSP.

101. AUTO-10; AUTO-15.

102. AUTO-10; AUTO-23; INT-105.

103. Quarterly Day School Report, February 28, 1943, United Pueblo Agency, general correspondence files, 1935–1952, Box 31, RG 75, NA-RMR; INT-104; AUTO-10; school census of Indian children, June 1940, United Pueblo Agency, general superintendent's file, 1937–1939, Box 10, RG 75, NA-RMR; INT-43; AUTO-13; INT-111; INT-95.

CHAPTER SEVEN. TOGETHER AND APART

1. AUTO-25.

2. Robert W. Young, ed., *Navajo Yearbook: A Decade of Progress, 1951–1961*, vol. 8 (Window Rock, AZ: Bureau of Indian Affairs, 1961), 42. By 1977, there were eight border town programs across Arizona and New Mexico. Magdalena, with an enrollment of 277, was the largest. See Robert A. Roessel Jr., *Navajo Education, 1948–1970: Its Progress and Its Problems* (Rough Rock, AZ: Navajo Curriculum Center, Rough Rock Demonstration School, 1979), chap. 4.

3. *Magdalena Mountain Mail*, November 17, 1984, 1; Young, *Navajo Yearbook*, 22; Floyd M. Mansell Jr., "Problems in Program Direction: Considerations in a Sequential Developmental Program for Alamo Navajo Pupils," unpublished report for the Magdalena School Board, 1967–1968, 4, 15, author's collection. For several years the Magdalena dormitories were superintended by Floyd Mansell. See *Magdalena Mountain Mail*, March 1, 1989, 8.

4. For an example of Reynolds's efforts to raise public sympathy for the Alamo Navajo see Letter to the Editor, *Socorro Chieftain*, May 15, 1947, 8. As for the importance on learning English, see Loraine Morley Reynolds to Frank M. King, June 18, 1951, Frank M. King Papers, Box 14, Folder 54, HL.

5. INT-31; AUTO-25; AUTO-15. See also INT-51; AUTO-17; AUTO-19; AUTO-27; AUTO-31.

6. INT-39; INT-31; INT-30; AUTO-16; AUTO-17; INT-92; AUTO-12; AUTO-15. For an upbeat account of life in the Magdalena dormitories, see the New Mexico State Department of Education Division of Indian Education, *Newsletter* (February 1962): 4–10.

7. AUTO-31; AUTO-15. See also INT-55; INT-92; AUTO-10; AUTO-17; AUTO-27.

8. AUTO-16; INT-31; INT-55; AUTO-4.

9. AUTO-31; AUTO-4; INT-30.

10. INT-92; INT-30; INT-31; INT-51; AUTO-7; AUTO-10; AUTO-15; AUTO-18; AUTO-25; AUTO-27; Delbert G. Fann, "A Look at the Alamo and Magdalena Indian

Mission Fields," unpublished manuscript, 1966, Baptist Church records, Magdalena, New Mexico, 3; AUTO-31.

11. AUTO-18; AUTO-19; INT-31; AUTO-4; AUTO-27.

12. AUTO-10.

13. INT-30; AUTO-27.

14. AUTO-25.

15. AUTO-31. Regarding runaways, see also INT-39; INT-51; INT-92; AUTO-4; AUTO-16; AUTO-17.

16. It should be emphasized that these figures are rough calculations based on a combination of Mansell, "Problems in Program Direction" and Magdalena's yearbooks for 1968 and 1979.

17. AUTO-27; AUTO-15. See also AUTO-17.

18. INT-4.

19. Ibid.

20. INT-56; *Magdalena Mountain Mail,* November 1, 1988, 1.

21. At the federal level, in addition to providing public schools funds to compensate them for enrolling Indian students ("federally impacted area"), two other sources were the Johnson-O'Mally program (originally authorized in 1928) and the Elementary and Secondary Education Act (ESEA) in 1965. As the latter was periodically amended, bilingual programs received federal authorization and funding under Titles I, IV, and VII. See Margaret Szasz, *Education and the American Indian: The Road to Self-Determination, 1928–1973* (Albuquerque: University of New Mexico Press, 1974), chap. 14; K. Tsianina Lomawaima and Teresa L. McCarty, *To Remain an Indian: Lessons in Democracy from a Century of Native American Education* (New York: Teachers College Press, 2006), 116.

22. Herbert Pino and Pauline Padilla are pictured in the 1979 Magdalena yearbook.

23. INT-61; INT-87.

24. AUTO-10; INT-39; INT-31.

25. AUTO-15; AUTO-17. See also INT-39.

26. INT-87; Ira McKinley, *My Saddle and I* (n.p.: privately published, 1978), 75.

27. These figures are derived from the school yearbooks for 1974, 1978; *Magdalena Mountain Mail,* May 31, 1986, 1. The latter lists the 1976 graduates.

28. INT-31; INT-127.

29. INT-55; AUTO-31; INT-51. See also AUTO-15; AUTO-17; AUTO-21; AUTO-25.

30. AUTO-22; AUTO-4; AUTO-27.

31. AUTO-25; INT-56; AUTO-30; AUTO-31.

32. AUTO-21; AUTO-25; INT-51.

33. AUTO-21; INT-55; AUTO-25; AUTO-4. See also INT-31; INT-62; AUTO-17; AUTO-18; AUTO-22; AUTO-30.

34. *Steer*, September 25, 1964, 5; *Steer*, May 22, 1964, 6. As for progress in the gradual acceptance of intergroup relationships, including marriage, see INT-51; INT-56; INT-87; AUTO-14; AUTO-17.

35. *Magdalena Mountain Mail*, March 1, 1988, 8.

36. Both quotations are from the *Tucumcari Literary Review* 1 (September/October 1988): 27.

37. Unless otherwise indicated, this section is based on interviews conducted with Ramón Gutiérrez, Antonio Reynaldo Martínez, Alice Martínez, Sam Olney, Archie Apachito, Barbara (Julian) Zellers, and Mike Julian.

38. Peter Iverson, "Our Future Is Burning Bright: American Indian History as Continuing Stories," in *Reflections on American Indian History: Honoring the Past, Building a Future*, ed. Albert Hurtado (Norman: University of Oklahoma Press, 2008), 94.

39. *Albuquerque Journal*, February 24, 1968, A-12.

40. Other cheerleaders for the team were Diana Candelaria (captain), Flora Candelaria, Sarah Baca, and Elsie Madril.

41. *Albuquerque Journal*, March 8, 1968, C-2.

42. *Albuquerque Journal*, March 9, 1968, B-2.

43. Ibid.

44. Ibid.

45. *Tucumcari Literary Review* 4 (March/April 1989): 25; courtesy of Ray Martínez.

CHAPTER EIGHT. LEGACIES AND DEPARTURES

1. INT-72. For an excellent account of the White Sands blast and its aftereffects in the region, see Ferenc Morton Szasz, *The Day the Sun Rose Twice: The Story of the Trinity Site Nuclear Explosion, July 16, 1945* (Albuquerque: University of New Mexico Press, 1984), chaps. 6–7.

2. INT-54. It should be pointed out that supposed UFO sightings were hardly limited to Navajos, and several UFO incidents were reported in New Mexico, including in the Socorro region. See Kevin D. Randel and Donald R. Schmitt, *UFO Crash at Roswell* (New York: Avon Books, 1991); William E. Gibbs, "The Roswell Incident: An Unsolved Mystery or an 'Unsolvable' One?" in *Telling New Mexico: A New History*, ed. Marta Weigle with Frances Levine and Louise Stiver (Santa Fe: Museum of New Mexico Press, 2009), 309–319; "Socorro/Zamora UFO Incident—1964," http://www.cufon.org/contributors/chrisl/socorro.htm.

3. See http//www.nrao.edu/index.php/learn/radioastronomy.

4. Walker Percy, *Lost in the Cosmos* (New York: Farrar, Straus, and Giroux, 1983).

5. Agriculture Census for Socorro County, New Mexico, and Agriculture Census for Catron County, New Mexico. See http://govinfo.kerr.orst.edu/cgi-bin/ag-list?01-003.nmc.

6. *Magdalena Mountain Mail*, August 1983, 6.

7. AUTO-22; INT-10.

8. INT-66.

9. Susan Ridgely Bales, *When I Was a Child: Children's Interpretations of First Communion* (Chapel Hill: University of North Carolina Press, 2005), 5; INT-66. Unless otherwise indicated, the following narrative is based on my observations of selected classes, taped recordings, and extensive interviews with Candelaria García (pseudonym), who graciously allowed me to collect material during the winter of 1989.

10. Because Candelaria had taught these classes for many years, she had a wealth of materials at hand. But the core curriculum documents are Sister Mary Fearon and Sandra J. Hirstein, *Celebrating the Gift of Jesus* and *Celebrating the Gift of Forgiveness* (Dubuque, IA: Wm. C. Brown, 1987). Both texts are accompanied by a program manual and parent guide.

11. The seven sacraments of the Catholic church are Baptism, Confirmation, Reconciliation, the Eucharist, Marriage, Holy Orders, and the Anointing of the Sick.

12. Fearon and Hirstein, *Celebrating the Gift of Jesus*, 23–24.

13. For the origins of Pentecostalism at Alamo, see William H. Hodge, "Navajo Pentecostalism," *Anthropological Quarterly* 37 (1964): 73–93; INT-40. For the Alamo Navajo religious landscape, see William Quinn, "Comprehensive Ethnohistorical Report on the Cañoncito and Alamo Navajo Bands," unpublished report, Washington, DC, Bureau of Indian Affairs, 1984, 48; Dianna Jeanne Shomaker, "Fosterage as a Form of Exchange among the Navajo" (PhD diss., University of New Mexico, 1984), 108; Carol K. Lujan, "American Indians and Imposed Law: The Impact of Social Integration on Legal Perceptions among Two Southwestern Tribes" (PhD diss., University of New Mexico, 1986), 132–134; Delbert G. Fann, "A Look at the Alamo and Magdalena Indian Mission Fields," unpublished manuscript, 1966, Baptist church records, Magdalena, New Mexico.

14. ANOHP (José Guerro).

15. INT-100. See also INT-40; INT-44.

16. The literature on the place of alcohol in Native American history and communities is extensive. For period treatments, see Peter C. Mancall, *Deadly Medicine: Indians and Alcohol in Early America* (Ithaca: Cornell University Press, 1995); William E. Unrau, *White Man's Wicked Water: The Alcohol Trade and Prohibition in Indian Country, 1802–1892* (Lawrence: University Press of Kansas, 1996). For alcoholism among the Navajos, see Stephen Kunitz and Jerrold Levy, *Drinking Careers: A Twenty-Five Year*

Study of Three Navajo Populations (New Haven, CT: Yale University Press, 1994); Levy and Kunitz, *Indian Drinking: Navajo Practices and Anglo-American Theories* (New York: Wiley, 1974); Maureen Trudelle Schwarz, *Navajo Lifeways: Contemporary Issues, Ancient Knowledge* (Norman: University of Oklahoma Press, 2001), chap. 6. In her study of fosterage in three communities, Shomaker wrote that "health care workers in all three areas state there is a pronounced occurrence of babies born with the characteristics of Fetal Alcohol Syndrome." Other children suffer from alcoholic parents, malnourishment, abuse, and abandonment. See Shomaker, "Fosterage as a Form of Exchange among Navajo," 110.

17. INT-50.

18. INT-49. See also INT-47; INT-88; INT-94.

19. INT-44; INT-102.

20. INT-100.

21. AUTO-27.

22. For an introduction to the literature on rodeo, see references cited on the subject in Chapter 4.

23. On the subject of the Indian cowboy tradition, including rodeo, see Peter Iverson, *When Indians Became Cowboys: Native Peoples and Cattle Ranching in the American West* (Norman: University of Oklahoma Press, 1994).

24. AJ.

25. *National High School Rodeo Association: Rules, Constitution, and By-Laws* (NHSRA, 1989), 22, 19; *New Mexico Junior Rodeo Association: Rules and By-Laws*, rev. ed. (New Mexico Junior Rodeo Association, 1986), 5. See also *New Mexico 4-H Rodeo Rule Book* (New Mexico 4-H, n.d.).

26. NHSRA, *Rules, Constitution, and By-Laws*, 92–94.

27. Elizabeth Atwood Lawrence, *Rodeo: An Anthropologist Looks at the Wild and the Tame* (Knoxville: University of Tennessee Press, 1982), 7–8, 63–65, 76, 140, 188–198, 270–271.

28. New Mexico 4-H, *New Mexico 4-H Rodeo Rule Book*, 20–22.

29. Magdalena Kid's Rodeo (program), June 16, 1985. Author's collection.

30. AJ.

31. INT-140; INT-85; INT-89.

32. INT-131; INT-137; INT-132; INT-141.

33. INT-85; AJ.

34. AJ.

35. Ibid.

36. INT-147; INT-139.

37. INT-84.

38. INT-140; INT-139; INT-137.

39. Elliot West, *Growing Up with the Country: Childhood on the Far Western Frontier* (Albuquerque: University of New Mexico Press, 1989), 104–107.

40. INT-139. It should be noted here that rodeo parents make a point of arguing that the value of cooperation is displayed in the rodeo arena as well, evidenced by the willingness of some riders to lend their horse to a competitor, the need for teamwork in the team roping event, and the tradition to share information on the "tricks" of a recognized animal in a rough stock event. For the entire range of values taught in rodeo, see INT-9; INT-28; INT-29; INT-128; INT-135; INT-140.

41. AJ; INT-132.

42. INT-140. For the history of women's rodeo, see Mary Lou LeCompte, *Cowgirls of the Rodeo: Pioneer Professional Athletes* (Urbana: University of Illinois Press, 1993); Teresa Jordan, *Cowgirls: Women of the American West* (Garden City, NY: Doubleday, 1984), chaps. 8–9; Renée M. Laegreid, *Riding Pretty: Rodeo Royalty in the American West* (Lincoln: University of Nebraska Press, 2006).

43. INT-9.

44. AJ.

45. INT-50. See also INT-44; INT-54.

46. For the federal context, see Francis Paul Prucha, *The Great Father: The United States Government and the American Indians,* vol. 2 (Lincoln: University of Nebraska Press, 1984), 1139–1149, 1157–1162; Margaret Szasz, *Education and the American Indian: The Road to Self-Determination, 1928–1973* (Albuquerque: University of New Mexico Press, 1974), 149–155, chap. 13; K. Tsianina Lomawaima and Teresa L. McCarty, *To Remain an Indian: Lessons in Democracy from a Century of Native American Education* (New York: Teachers College Press, 2006), chap. 6. For a fine case study of a community-controlled school, see Teresa L. McCarty, *A Place to Be Navajo: Rough Rock and the Struggle for Self-Determination in Indigenous Schooling* (Mahwah, NJ: Erlbaum, 2002). The possibilities of using self-determination schools as institutions for fostering Navajo-ness is emphasized by Deborah House in *Language Shift among the Navajos: Identity Politics and Cultural Continuity* (Tucson: University of Arizona Press, 2002).

47. Jennifer J. Pruett, "A History of the Alamo Navajo Community Schools," paper prepared for the Alamo Navajo School Board, December 1979, 6–19, ACSA. Dickson is quoted in Pam Livingston, "Alamo Navajos Fighting for Educational Autonomy," *Prime Times* (August 6–20, 1979): 2.

48. AJ.

49. Quoted in McCarty, *A Place to Be Navajo*, 71.

50. *Defensor Chieftain*, September 1, 1986, 3; *Defensor Chieftain*, October 19, 1989, 1; AJ.

51. The enrollment numbers are approximate, based on data from both the National Center for Educational Statistics (NCES), School District Data Book Profiles, http://

govinfo.kerr.orst.edu, and the 1990 Magdalena and Alamo yearbooks. (It should be noted that comparing the NCES data with that drawn from the two schools' yearbooks, it is clear that the former data source often combines the Alamo Navajo community enrollment figures with those of the Alamo Navajo enrollment in Magdalena.)

52. For the progress on Magdalena's new physical plant, see *Magdalena Mountain Mail*, February 23, 1985, 7. Regarding the bus transportation to Alamo, see *Magdalena Mountain Mail*, July 26, 1986, 1. The statement on improved Alamo Navajo graduation rates at Magdalena High School is based on surnames of graduating seniors as indicated in yearbooks and the *Magdalena Mountain Mail*. Over a seven-year span between 1981 and 1990 (three years were not available), the number of graduates by surname were Navajo, seventy-three; Hispanic, sixty-seven; Anglo, thirty-five; and unidentifiable, twenty-one.

53. INT-80; INT-42; AJ.

54. INT-60.

55. Marriage records, County of Socorro.

56. INT-87.

AFTERWORD

1. William Kittredge, *The Nature of Generosity* (New York: Knopf, 2000), 63.

2. Clyde Kluckhohn and Henry A. Murray, "Personality Formation and Determinants," in *Personality in Nature, Society, and Culture,* ed. Kluckhohn and Murray (New York: Knopf, 1949), 35.

3. Author's collection. For obvious reasons I have altered names throughout the document.

SELECTED BIBLIOGRAPHY

ARCHIVAL SOURCES

Center for Southwestern Research, Zimmerman Library, University of New Mexico
    Alamo Navajo Oral History Project
    Pioneer Foundation Oral History Collection
    Sophie D. Aberle Collection
Huntington Library, San Marino, California
    Fall, Albert B., Papers
    King, Frank M., Papers
    Ritch, William G., Papers
National Archives and Records Administration
    RG 69, Records of the Federal Emergency Relief Administration, 1933–1936
        (College Park)
    RG 75, Records of the Bureau of Indian Affairs
        Albuquerque Indian School, 1886–1954 (Denver)
        Eastern Navajo Agency, 1912–1939 (Riverside)
        Santa Fe Indian School, 1910–1934 (Denver)
        Southern Pueblo Agency, 1911–1935 (Denver)
        United Pueblo Agency, 1940–1943 (Denver)
    RG 124, Records of the Surplus Marketing Administration (College Park)
        Federal Emergency Relief Administration, 1933–1936
        Livestock Disposal Program, 1934–1938
New Mexico State Records Center and Archives, Santa Fe, New Mexico
    Annual Reports of the State Superintendent of Public Instruction, 1892–1911
    Minutes of the Meeting of the Board of Education of the Territory of New Mexico,
        1891–1911
    Works Progress Administration Files—Grazing and Livestock Industry,
        1934–1940
Socorro County Courthouse, Socorro, New Mexico
    Marriage Records, 1900–1990

PERIODICALS

Alamo News
Albuquerque Journal
Magdalena Mountain Mail
Magdalena News
New Mexico Magazine
Socorro Chieftain
Tucumcari Literary Review

INTERVIEWS AND AUTOBIOGRAPHICAL ACCOUNTS

Flora Abeyta, Louise Abeyta, Narciso Abeyta, David Apache, Fred Apache, Lucy Apache, Anna Apachito, Archie Apachito, Billy Apachito, Denny Apachito, Frank Apachito, Helen Apachito, Jay Apachito, Lorene Apachito, Lorenzo Apachito, Martíniano Apachito, Patsy Apachito, Paul Apachito, Raymond Apachito, William Apachito, Adela Armijo, Barbara Baca, Benito Baca, Bessie Baca, Elfego Baca, Eliseo Baca, Mary Baca, Christina Blackburn, John Blackburn, Jim Bonds, George Britton, Beau Bruton, Jack Bruton, Jack Bruton Jr., Sissie Bruton, Frances Castillo, Alma Chávez, Anastacia Chávez, Herman Chávez, Manuel Chávez, Norman Cleaveland, Sharon Cline, Lee Coker, Helen Dennis, Elaine Dooley, Philip Dooley, G. W. "Pete" Evans, Olive Forbes, Lilly Ganadonegro, Nora Ganadonegro, Cecelia García, Trinidad García, John Gatlin, Lillian Love Gatlin, Theodore Gatlin, Annie Guerro, Domingo Guerro, Frank Guerro, John Guerro, José Guerro, Juanita Guerro, Manuel Guerro, Mary Guerro, Solomon Guerrero, Tennie Guerro, Tony Guerro, James Guin, Eulalio Gutiérriz, Ramón Gutiérriz, Rebecca Gutiérriz, Jack "Hoot" Hart, Mary Hart, Barty Henderson, Bernold Henderson, Charlotte Henderson, Jo Ellen Henderson, Ray Lee Henderson, Mike Julian, Bessie Kelly, Jim Kelly, Tom Kelly, Ann Key, Cenaida Key, Tom Key, Alice Knoblock, Tommy Knoblock, Lupe Ladd, Sheila Lewis, Brenda Ligon, Pat Ligon, Clara Lucero, Buddy Major, Fred "Boog" Martin, Alice Martínez, Antonio Reynaldo Martínez, Jimmy Don McKinley, Adrian McPhaul, Jerry McPhaul, Marguerite McPhaul, Nacona McPhaul, Nelda McPhaul, Antonia Mendoza, Buddy Mexicano, Ruth Mexicano, Sarah Molina, Huskie Monte, Maggie Monte, Diego Montoya, Adrian Nuanes, Liberato Nuanes, Nellie O'Conner, Sam Olney, Julian Ortega, Aurelia Ortiz, Cecil Owsley, Vera Owsley, Laverne Padilla, Pauline Padilla, LeRue Parker, Cecelia Pino, Herbert Pino, Jackson Pino, Maria Lucianita Pino, Rita Pino, Faith Reed, Helen Rincon, Arch Rinehardt, Kathryn Roberts, Maud Rudder, Tony Sais, Morgan Salome,

Ben Sanchez, Leo Sanchez, Lupe Sandoval, Leburt Saulsberry, Linda Saulsberry, Alta Secatero, Jimmy Secatero, Bernice Shirley, Ella Singer, Ray Smith, Rosela Smith, Ray Sparks, Birdie Spears, Guy Spears, Claudine Storus, Adolpho Tafoya, David Tafoya, Diane Tafoya, Candelario Torres, Edward Torres, Cleo Trujillo, Manuel Trujillo, Margaret Trujillo, Tony Trujillo, Bernice Valenzuela, Regina Valenzuela, Jake Vicente, Juan Vicente, Lee Vicente, Grace Vinyard, Lucy Wallace, Bob Winston, Clara Winston, Benita Zamora, and Barbara Zellers.

UNPUBLISHED MATERIALS

Baydo, Gerald Robert. "Cattle Ranching in Territorial New Mexico." PhD diss., University of New Mexico, 1970.

Fitzpatrick, Mildred Gunn, "Textbooks Used in the Elementary Schools of New Mexico, 1846–1964." EdD diss., University of New Mexico, 1965.

Lujan, Carol K. "American Indians and Imposed Law: The Impact of Social Integration on Legal Perceptions among Two Southwestern Tribes." PhD diss., University of New Mexico, 1986.

Quinn, William. "Comprehensive Ethnohistorical Report on the Cañoncito and Alamo Navajo Bands." Washington, DC, Bureau of Indian Affairs, 1984.

Shomaker, Dianna Jeanne. "Fosterage as a Form of Exchange among the Navajo." PhD diss., University of New Mexico, 1984.

Simmons, Donald C. "The Alamo Navajo Kinship and Sib Systems." Master's thesis, Yale University, 1950.

PUBLISHED SOURCES: PRIMARY

Brown, Bernadyne Powell. *A Happy Life*. N.p.: privately published, 1993.

Cleaveland, Agnes Morley. *No Life for a Lady*. 1941. Reprint edition, Lincoln: University of Nebraska Press, 1977.

Cleaveland, Norman. *The Morleys: Young Upstarts on the Southwest Frontier*. Albuquerque, NM: Calvin Horn, 1971.

Davis, W. W. H. *El Gringo; or, New Mexico and Her People*. 1856. Reprint edition, Santa Fe, NM: Rydal Press, 1938.

Draper, Mabel Hobson. *Though Long the Trail*. New York: Rinehart, 1946.

Evans, Max, and Gene Peach. *Making a Hand: Growing Up Cowboy in New Mexico*. Santa Fe: Museum of New Mexico Press, 2005.

Gregg, Josiah. *Commerce of the Prairies*. 1844. Reprint edition, Ann Arbor: University of Michigan Microfilms, 1966.
Johnston, Langford Ryan. *Old Magdalena Cow Town*. Magdalena, NM: Bandar Log, 1983.
Pattie, Jane, and Tom Kelly. *Cowboy Spur Maker: The Story of Ed Blanchard*. College Station: Texas A&M University Press, 2002.

PUBLISHED SOURCES: SECONDARY

Adams, David Wallace. *Education for Extinction: American Indians and the Boarding School Experience, 1875–1928*. Lawrence: University Press of Kansas, 1995.
———. "Fundamental Considerations: The Deep Meaning of Native American Schooling, 1880–1900." *Harvard Educational Review* 58 (February 1988).
Adams, David Wallace, and Crista DeLuzio, eds. *On the Borders of Love and Power: Families and Kinship in the Intercultural American Southwest*. Berkeley: University of California Press, 2012.
Adelman, Jeremy, and Stephen Aron. "From Borderlands to Borders: Empires, Nation-States, and the Peoples in between in North American History." *American Historical Review* 104 (June 1999).
Allmendinger, Blake. *The Cowboy: Representations of Labor in an American Work Culture*. New York: Oxford University Press, 1992.
Armitage, Susan, and Elizabeth Jameson, eds. *The Women's West*. Norman: University of Oklahoma Press, 1987.
Ashcroft, Bruce. *The Territorial History of Socorro, New Mexico*. El Paso: University of Texas at El Paso, 1988.
Barrington, Jacky, ed. *Celebrating 100 Years of Frontier Living*. Magdalena, NM: Centennial Committee, 1984.
Berkholder, Zoë. *Color in the Classroom: How American Schools Taught Race, 1900–1954*. New York: Oxford University Press, 2011.
Blanton, Carlos Kevin. "From Intellectual Deficiency to Cultural Deficiency: Mexican Americans, Testing, and Public School Policy in the American Southwest, 1920–1940." *Pacific Historical Review* 72 (February 2003).
———. *George I. Sánchez: The Long Fight for Mexican American Integration*. New Haven, CT: Yale University Press, 2014.
Bletzer, Michael. "'The First Province of That Kingdom': Notes on the Colonial History of the Piro Area." *New Mexico Historical Review* 88 (Fall 2013).
Brooks, Connie. *The Last Cowboys*. Albuquerque: University of New Mexico Press, 1993.

Brooks, James F. *Captives and Cousins: Slavery, Kinship, and Community in the Southwest Borderlands.* Chapel Hill: University of North Carolina Press, 2002.

Bsumek, Erika Marie. *Indian-Made: Navajo Culture in the Marketplace, 1868–1940.* Lawrence: University Press of Kansas, 2008.

Butler, Anne M. *Daughters of Joy, Sisters of Misery: Prostitutes in the American West, 1865–1890.* Urbana: University of Illinois Press, 1985.

Cahill, Cathleen D. *Federal Fathers and Mothers: A Social History of the United States Indian Service, 1869–1933.* Chapel Hill: University of North Carolina Press, 2011.

Campa, Arthur L. *Hispanic Culture in the Southwest.* Norman: University of Oklahoma Press, 1979.

Cayton, Andrew R. L., and Fredrika J. Teute, eds. *Contact Points: American Frontiers from the Mohawk Valley to the Mississippi, 1750–1830.* Chapel Hill: University of North Carolina Press, 1998.

Chávez, John R. *The Lost Land: The Chicano Image of the Southwest.* Albuquerque: University of New Mexico Press, 1984.

Child, Brenda J. *Boarding School Seasons: American Indian Families, 1900–1940.* Lincoln: University of Nebraska Press, 1998.

Christiansen, Paige W. "The Legend of Montosa Wells." *Publications in History* 1 (Socorro County Historical Society, February 1965): 27–28.

Coleman, Michael. *American Indian Children at School, 1850–1930.* Jackson: University of Mississippi Press, 1993.

Cordon, Glen S. *An Archeological Resource Investigation of Historic Navajo, Hispanic, and Prehistoric Pueblo Sites on the Alamo Band Navajo Reservation, Socorro County, New Mexico.* Santa Fe: Museum of New Mexico Press, 1980.

Dary, David. *Cowboy Culture: A Saga of Five Centuries.* New York: Knopf, 1981.

———. *Seeking Pleasure in the Old West.* New York: Knopf, 1991.

Davies, Wade. *Healing Ways: Navajo Health Care in the Twentieth Century.* Albuquerque: University of New Mexico Press, 2001.

Delay, Brian. "Blood Talk: Violence and Belonging in the Navajo New Mexican Borderland." In *Contested Spaces in Early America.* Edited by Juliana Barr and Edward Countryman. Philadelphia: University of Pennsylvania Press, 2014.

De León, Arnoldo. *Racial Frontiers: Africans, Chinese, and Mexicans in Western America, 1848–1890.* Albuquerque: University of New Mexico Press, 2002.

———. *They Called Them Greasers: Anglo Attitudes toward Mexicans in Texas, 1821–1900.* Austin: University of Texas Press, 1983.

Deutsch, Sarah. *No Separate Refuge: Culture, Class, and Gender on an Anglo-Hispanic Frontier in the American Southwest, 1880–1940.* New York: Oxford University Press, 1987.

Downs, James F. *The Navajo.* New York: Holt, Rinehart, and Winston, 1972.

Dunmire, William W. *New Mexico's Spanish Livestock Heritage: Four Centuries of Animals, Land, and People.* Albuquerque: University of New Mexico Press, 2013.

Ellis, Clyde. *To Change Them Forever: Indian Education at the Rainy Mountain Boarding School, 1893–1920.* Norman: University of Oklahoma Press, 1996.

Ellis, Florence Hawley. *Navajo Indians.* New York: Garland, 1974.

Etulain, Richard W. *Re-Imagining the Modern American West: A Century of Fiction, History, and Art.* Tucson: University of Arizona Press, 1996.

Fear-Segal, Jacqueline. *White Man's Club: Schools, Race, and the Struggle of Indian Acculturation.* Lincoln: University of Nebraska Press, 2007.

Flores, Ruben. *Backroads Pragmatists: Mexico's Melting Pot and Civil Rights in the United States.* Philadelphia: University of Pennsylvania Press, 2014.

Forbes, Jack D. *Apache, Navajo, and Spaniard.* Norman: University of Oklahoma Press, 1960.

Frisbie, Charlotte Johnson. *Kinaaldá: A Study of the Navaho Girl's Puberty Ceremony.* Middletown, CT: Wesleyan University Press, 1967.

Fuller, Wayne E. *The Old Country School: The Story of Rural Education in the Middle West.* Chicago: University of Chicago Press, 1982.

Getz, Lynne Marie. *Schools of Their Own: The Education of Hispanos in New Mexico, 1850–1940.* Albuquerque: University of New Mexico Press, 1997.

Gilbert, Matthew Sakiestewa. *Education beyond the Mesas: Hopi Students at Sherman Institute, 1902–1929.* Lincoln: University of Nebraska Press, 2010.

Gómez, Laura E. *Manifest Destinies: The Making of the Mexican American Race.* New York: New York University Press, 2007.

Gonzales, Phillip B. "The Political Construction of Latino Nomenclature in Twentieth-Century New Mexico." *Journal of the Southwest* 35 (1993).

Gonzales-Berry, Erlinda, and David R. Maciel, eds. *The Contested Homeland: A Chicano History of New Mexico.* Albuquerque: University of New Mexico Press, 2000.

González, Deena J. *Refusing the Favor: The Spanish-Mexican Women of Santa Fe, 1820–1880.* New York: Oxford University Press, 1999.

Gram, John R. *Education at the Edge of Empire: Negotiating Pueblo Identity in New Mexico's Indian Boarding Schools.* Seattle: University of Washington Press, 2015.

Gutiérrez, Ramón A. *When Jesus Came, the Corn Mothers Went Away: Marriage, Sexuality, and Power in New Mexico, 1500–1846.* Palo Alto, CA: Stanford University Press, 1991.

Holt, Marilyn Irvin. *Children of the Western Plains: The Nineteenth-Century Experience.* Chicago: Ivan R. Dee, 2005.

Holtby, David V. *Forty-Seventh Star: New Mexico's Struggle for Statehood.* Norman: University of Oklahoma Press, 2012.

Horsman, Reginald. *Race and Manifest Destiny: The Origins of American Racial Anglo-Saxonism.* Cambridge, MA: Harvard University Press, 1981.

Hyde, Anne F. *Empires, Nations, and Families: A History of the North American West, 1800–1860.* Lincoln: University of Nebraska Press, 2011.

Hyer, Sally. *One House, One Voice, One Heart: Native American Education at the Santa Fe Indian School.* Santa Fe: Museum of New Mexico Press, 1990.

Hysop, Stephen G. *Bound for Santa Fe: The Road to New Mexico and the American Conquest, 1806–1848.* Norman: University of Oklahoma Press, 2002.

Iverson, Peter. *Diné: A History of the Navajos.* Albuquerque: University of New Mexico Press, 2002.

———. *When Indians Became Cowboys: Native Peoples and Cattle Ranching in the American West.* Norman: University of Oklahoma Press, 1994.

Jacobs, Margaret D. *White Mother to a Dark Race: Settler Colonialism, Maternalism, and the Removal of Indigenous Children in the American West and Australia, 1880–1940.* Lincoln: University of Nebraska Press, 2009.

Jameson, Elizabeth, and Susan Armitage, eds. *Writing the Range: Race, Class, and Culture in the Women's West.* Norman: University of Oklahoma Press, 1997.

Jensen, Joan M., and Darlis A. Miller, eds. *New Mexico Women: Intercultural Perspectives.* Albuquerque: University of New Mexico Press, 1986.

John, Elizabeth A. H. *Storms Brewed in Other Men's Worlds: The Confrontation of Indians, Spanish, and French in the Southwest, 1540–1795.* College Station: Texas A&M University Press, 1975.

Jones, Oakah L. *Los Paisanos: Spanish Settlers on the Northern Frontier of New Spain.* Norman: University of Oklahoma Press, 1979.

Kaestle, Carl. "Ideology and American Educational History." *History of Education Quarterly* 22 (Summer 1982).

Katanski, Amelia V. *Learning to Write "Indian": The Boarding School Experience and American Indian Literature.* Norman: University of Oklahoma Press, 2005.

Keleher, William A. *Turmoil in New Mexico, 1846–1868.* Albuquerque: University of New Mexico Press, 1952.

Kessell, John L. *Pueblos, Spaniards, and the Kingdom of New Mexico.* Norman: University of Oklahoma Press, 2008.

———. *Spain in the Southwest: A Narrative History of Colonial New Mexico, Arizona, Texas, and California.* Norman: University of Oklahoma Press, 2002.

Kittredge, William. *The Nature of Generosity.* New York: Knopf, 2000.

Klein, Kerwin Lee. "On the Emergence of Memory in Historical Discourse." *Representations* 69 (Winter 2000).

———. "Reclaiming the 'F' Word, or Being and Becoming Postwestern." *Pacific Historical Review* 65 (May 1996).

Kliebard, Herbert M. *Schooled to Work: Vocationalism and the American Curriculum, 1876–1946*. New York: Teachers College Press, 1999.

Kluckhohn, Clyde. *Navajo Witchcraft*. Cambridge, MA: Peabody Museum of American Archeology and Ethnology, 1944.

Kluckhohn, Clyde, and Dorothea Leighton. *The Navajo*. Cambridge, MA: Harvard University Press, 1946. Revised edition, Garden City, NJ: Doubleday, 1962.

Kunitz, Stephen, and Jerrold Levy. *Drinking Careers: A Twenty-Five-Year Study of Three Navajo Populations*. New Haven, CT: Yale University Press, 1994.

Lamar, Howard R. *The Far Southwest, 1846–1912: A Territorial History*. 1966. Revised edition, Albuquerque: University of New Mexico Press, 2000.

———, ed. *The New Encyclopedia of the American West*. New Haven, CT: Yale University Press, 1998.

Larson, Robert W. *New Mexico's Quest for Statehood, 1846–1912*. Albuquerque: University of New Mexico Press, 1968.

Lawrence, Adrea. *Lessons from an Indian Day School: Negotiating Colonization in Northern New Mexico, 1902–1907*. Lawrence: University Press of Kansas, 2011.

Lawrence, Adrea, KuuNUx TeeRIt Kroupa, and Donald Warren, eds. Special issue on the history of Native American education, *History of Education Quarterly* 54, no. 3 (August 2014).

Layton, Stanford J. *To No Privileged Class: The Rationalization of Homesteading and Rural Life in the Early Twentieth-Century American West*. Salt Lake City, UT: Charles Redd Center for Western Studies, 1988.

LeCompte, Mary Lou. *Cowgirls of the Rodeo: Pioneer Professional Athletes*. Urbana: University of Illinois Press, 1993.

Lee, Susan E. *These Also Served*. Los Lunas, NM: Author, 1960.

Leighton, Dorothea, and Clyde Kluckhohn. *Children of the People: The Navajo and His Development*. Cambridge, MA: Harvard University Press, 1947. Reprint edition, New York: Octagon Books, 1974.

Levy, Jerrold E. *In the Beginning: The Navajo Genesis*. Berkeley: University of California Press, 1998.

Limerick, Patricia Nelson. *The Legacy of Conquest: The Unbroken Past of the American West*. New York: Norton, 1987.

Limerick, Patricia Nelson, Clyde A. Milner II, and Charles E. Rankin, eds. *Trails: Toward a New Western History*. Lawrence: University Press of Kansas, 1991.

Lomawaima, K. Tsianina. *They Called It Prairie Light: The Story of the Chilocco Indian School*. Lincoln: University of Nebraska Press, 1994.

Lomawaima, K. Tsianina, and Teresa L. McCarty. *To Remain an Indian: Lessons in Democracy from a Century of Native American Education*. New York: Teachers College Press, 2006.

Lozano, Rosina A. "Managing the 'Priceless Gift': Debating Spanish Language Instruction in New Mexico and Puerto Rico, 1930–1950." *Western Historical Quarterly* 44 (Autumn 2013).

McBeth, Sally. *Ethnic Identity and the Boarding School Experience of West-Central Oklahoma American Indians*. Washington, DC: University Press of America, 1983.

McCarty, Teresa L. *A Place to Be Navajo: Rough Rock and the Struggle for Self-Determination in Indigenous Schooling*. Mawah, NJ: Erlbaum, 2002.

M'Closkey, Kathy. *Swept under the Rug: A Hidden History of Navajo Weaving*. Albuquerque: University of New Mexico Press, 2002.

McNitt, Frank. *Navajo Wars: Military Campaigns, Slave Raids, and Reprisals*. Albuquerque: University of New Mexico Press, 1972.

Miller, Darlis A. "Cross-Cultural Marriages in the Southwest: The New Mexico Experience, 1846–1900." *New Mexico Historical Review* 57 (October 1982).

———. *Open Range: The Life of Agnes Morley Cleaveland*. Norman: University of Oklahoma Press, 2010.

Mintz, Steven. *Huck's Raft: A History of American Childhood*. Cambridge, MA: Harvard University Press, 2004.

Mitchell, Pablo. *Coyote Nation: Sexuality, Race, and Conquest in Modernizing New Mexico*. Chicago: University of Chicago Press, 2005.

———. "'You Just Don't Know Mrs. Baca': Intermarriage, Mixed Heritage, and Identity in New Mexico." *New Mexico Historical Review* 79 (Fall 2004).

Montaño, Mary. *Tradiciones Nuevomexicanas: Hispano Arts and Culture of New Mexico*. Albuquerque: University of New Mexico Press, 2001.

Montgomery, Charles. *The Spanish Redemption: Heritage, Power, and Loss on New Mexico's Upper Rio Grande*. Berkeley: University of California Press, 2002.

———. "The Trap of Race and Memory: The Language of Spanish Civility on the Upper Rio Grande." *American Quarterly* 52 (September 2000).

Moore, Jacqueline M. *Cow Boys and Cattle Men: Class and Masculinities on the Texas Frontier, 1865–1900*. New York: New York University Press, 2010.

Mora, Anthony. *Border Dilemmas: Racial and National Uncertainties in New Mexico, 1848–1912*. Durham, NC: Duke University Press, 2011.

Myers, Joan. *Pie Town Woman: The Hard Life and Good Times of a New Mexico Homesteader*. Albuquerque: University of New Mexico Press, 2001.

Myers, Sandra. *Westering Women and the Frontier Experience, 1800–1915*. Albuquerque: University of New Mexico Press, 1982.

Nieto-Phillips, John M. *The Language of Blood: The Making of Spanish-American Identity in New Mexico, 1880s–1930s*. Albuquerque: University of New Mexico Press, 2004.

Noel, Linda C. "Anglos, Mexicans, *Nativos,* and the Debate over Arizona and New Mexico Statehood." *Pacific Historical Review* 80 (August 2011).

———. *Debating American Identity: Southwestern Statehood and Mexican Immigration.* Tucson: University of Arizona Press, 2014.

Nostrand, Richard L. *The Hispano Homeland.* Norman: University of Oklahoma Press, 1992.

O'Neil, Colleen. *Working the Navajo Way: Labor and Culture in the Twentieth Century.* Lawrence: University Press of Kansas, 2005.

Ortiz, Alfonso, ed. *The Southwest.* Vols. 9–10, *Handbook of North American Indians.* Edited by William C. Sturtevant. Washington, DC: Smithsonian Institution Press, 1979, 1983.

Parman, Donald L. *The Navajos and the New Deal.* New Haven, CT: Yale University Press, 1976.

Philp, Kenneth R. *John Collier's Crusade for Indian Reform, 1920–1954.* Tucson: University of Arizona Press, 1977.

Reese, William J. *America's Public Schools: From the Common School to "No Child Left Behind."* Baltimore: Johns Hopkins University Press, 2005.

———. *The Origins of the American High School.* New Haven, CT: Yale University Press, 1995.

Reichard, Gladys A. *Navajo Religion: A Study in Symbolism.* New York: Pantheon Books, 1950.

Reséndez, Andrés. *Changing National Identities: Texas and New Mexico, 1800–1850.* Cambridge, UK: Cambridge University Press, 2005.

Reyhner, Jon, and Jeanne Eder. *American Indian Education: A History.* Norman: University of Oklahoma Press, 2004.

Riney-Kehrberg, Pamela. *Childhood on the Farm: Work, Play, and the Coming of Age in the Midwest.* Lawrence: University Press of Kansas, 2005.

Robb, John Donald. *Hispanic Folk Music of New Mexico and the Southwest: A Self-Portrait of a People.* Norman: University of Oklahoma Press, 1980.

Roberts, Kathryn McKee. *From the Top of the Mountain: Pie Town, New Mexico, and Neighbors!* N.p.: Roger Coffin, 1990.

Sánchez, George I. *Forgotten People: A Study of New Mexicans.* 1940. Reprint edition, Albuquerque: University of New Mexico Press, 1996.

Sánchez, Joseph P., Robert L. Spude, and Art Gómez. *New Mexico: A History.* Norman: University of Oklahoma Press, 2013.

Schaaf, Gregory. *American Indian Textiles: 2,000 Artist Biographies.* Santa Fe, NM: CIAC Press, 2001.

Schackel, Sandra. *Social Housekeepers: Women Shaping Public Policy in New Mexico, 1920–1940.* Albuquerque: University of New Mexico Press, 1992.

Schlissel, Lillian, Vicki Ruiz, and Janice Monk, eds. *Western Women: Their Land, Their Lives*. Albuquerque: University of New Mexico Press, 1988.

Schroeder, Albert. "Navajo and Apache Relationships West of the Rio Grande." *El Palacio* 70 (Autumn 1963).

Schwarz, Maureen Trudelle. *Navajo Lifeways: Contemporary Issues, Ancient Knowledge*. Norman: University of Oklahoma Press, 2001.

Shaw, Lloyd. *Cowboy Dances: A Collection of Western Square Dances*. Caldwell, ID: Caxton Printers, 1941.

Shepardson, Mary. "The Gender Status of Navajo Women." In *Women and Power in Native North America*. Edited by Laura F. Klein and Lillian A. Ackerman. Norman: University of Oklahoma Press, 1995.

Simmons, Marc. *New Mexico: An Interpretive History*. Reprint edition, Albuquerque: University of New Mexico Press, 1988.

Simonsen, Jane E. *Making Home Work: Domesticity and Native American Assimilation in the American West, 1860–1919*. Chapel Hill: University of North Carolina Press, 2006.

Spack, Ruth. *America's Second Tongue: American Indian Education and the Ownership of English, 1860–1900*. Lincoln: University of Nebraska Press, 2002.

Spicer, Edward H. *Cycles of Conquest: The Impact of Spain, Mexico, and the United States on the Indians of the Southwest, 1533–1960*. Tucson: University of Arizona Press, 1962.

Steffes, Tracy L. *School, Society, and State: A New Education to Govern Modern America, 1890–1949*. Chicago: University of Chicago Press, 2012.

Szasz, Ferenc M., and Richard W. Etulain, eds. *Religion in Modern New Mexico*. Albuquerque: University of New Mexico Press, 1997.

Szasz, Margaret. *Education and the American Indian: The Road to Self-Determination, 1928–1973*. Albuquerque: University of New Mexico Press, 1974.

Trafzer, Clifford E., Jean A. Keller, and Lorene Sisquoc, eds. *Boarding School Blues: Revisiting American Indian Educational Experiences*. Lincoln: University of Nebraska Press, 2006.

Trennert, Robert A. *The Phoenix Indian School: Forced Assimilation in Arizona, 1891–1935*. Norman: University of Oklahoma Press, 1988.

———. *White Man's Medicine: Government Doctors and the Navajo, 1863–1955*. Albuquerque: University of New Mexico Press, 1998.

Twitchell, Ralph Emerson. *The Leading Facts of New Mexican History*. Cedar Rapids, IA: Torch Press, 1917.

Tyack, David. *Seeking Common Ground: Public Schools in a Diverse Society*. Cambridge, MA: Harvard University Press, 2003.

Vogt, Evon E. *Modern Homesteaders: The Life of a Twentieth-Century Frontier Community.* Cambridge, MA: Harvard University Press, 1955.

Vučković, Myriam. *Voices from Haskell: Indian Students between Two Worlds, 1884–1928.* Lawrence: University Press of Kansas, 2008.

Wallace, Jon. "Protestants, Catholics, and the State: The Origins of Public Education in Territorial New Mexico, 1846–1912." *New Mexico Historical Review* 83 (Winter 2008).

Warren, Louis S. *The Hunter's Game: Poachers and Conservationists in Twentieth-Century America.* New Haven, CT: Yale University Press, 1997.

Weber, David J. "Conflicts and Accommodations: Hispanic and Anglo-American Borders in Historical Perspectives, 1670–1853." *Journal of the Southwest* 39 (Spring 1997).

———. *The Mexican Frontier, 1821–1846: The American Southwest under Mexico.* Albuquerque: University of New Mexico Press, 1982.

———, ed. *New Spain's Far Northern Frontier: Essays on Spain in the American West.* Albuquerque: University of New Mexico Press, 1979.

———. *The Spanish Frontier in North America.* New Haven, CT: Yale University Press, 1992.

Weigle, Marta, ed., with Frances Levine and Louise Stiver. *Telling New Mexico: A New History.* Santa Fe: Museum of New Mexico Press, 2009.

Weisiger, Marsha. *Dreaming of Sheep in Navajo Country.* Seattle: University of Washington Press, 2009.

West, Elliot. *Growing Up with the Country: Childhood and the Far Western Frontier.* Albuquerque: University of New Mexico Press, 1989.

———. "Heathens and Angels: Childhood in the Rocky Mountain Mining Towns." *Western Historical Quarterly* 14 (April 1982).

———. *The Saloon on the Rocky Mountain Mining Frontier.* 1979. Reprint edition, Lincoln: University of Nebraska Press, 1996.

Westphall, Victor. *The Public Domain in New Mexico, 1854–1891.* Albuquerque: University of New Mexico Press, 1965.

White, Richard. *Remembering Ahanagran: Storytelling in a Family's Past.* New York: Hill and Wang, 1998.

Wilkins, Teresa J. *Patterns of Exchange: Navajo Weavers and Traders.* Norman: University of Oklahoma Press, 2008.

Witherspoon, Gary. *Language and Art in the Navajo Universe.* Ann Arbor: University of Michigan Press, 1977.

———. *Navajo Kinship and Marriage.* Chicago: University of Chicago Press, 1975.

Wooden, Wayne S., and Calvin Ehringer. *Rodeo in America: Wranglers, Roughstock, and Paydirt*. Lawrence: University Press of Kansas, 1996.

Zimmerman, Jonathan. *Small Wonder: The Little Red Schoolhouse in History and Memory*. New Haven, CT: Yale University Press, 2009.

———. *Whose America? Culture Wars in the Public Schools*. Cambridge, MA: Harvard University Press, 2002.

INDEX

Aberle, Sophie, 17
Abeyta, Abran, 141, 142
Abeyta, Encarnación, 141
Accommodation, 149, 158, 194–195, 199, 206, 256
  adaptive, 248, 255
  political, 152
Acculturation, 173, 227, 378n73, 382n44
  adaptive, 150
  forced, 195
Achievement, 275
  disparity in, 194
  status and, 277–282
Acoma, 236
"Adam and Eve" (dance), 129, 338
Adams, Ramon, 79, 130–131
Adelman, Jeremy, x
Agriculture, hunting and gathering versus, 223
Ah Shit Mountain, 16
Akers, Melvin, 80, 85, 86, 105, 212, 219
  on prostitutes, 114–115
Alamo, Dora, 229
Alamo, Marie, 229
Alamo Baptist Church, 302
Alamo Navajo, 11–17, 34, 58, 59, 70, 95, 120–121
  acclimation by, 248
  advocating for, 167
  allotments for, 16
  Anglos and, 147, 150, 162–174, 280
  Apaches and, 13, 27
  Big Navajo and, 13, 16, 249
  ceremonial system of, 173
  chapter house, 170, 274
  community, 168, 173, 257, 312, 316, 331

cultural makeup of, 13–14
economic relationships with, 15
geographical displacement of, 107
growing up, 35–36
Hispanics and, 146–151, 162, 279–280, 281
image of, 162, 227
per capita income for, 76
population of, 59, 164, 335
resources of, 92–93
Alamo Navajo Community School, children at, 333 (photo)
Alamo Navajo Indian Reservation, 275, 299, 300–301
  arrival at, ix
  distinctive features of, 252
  population of, 354n54
Alamo Navajo school board, 331
Alamo Springs, 300
Albuquerque, 110, 183, 221, 226, 230, 236, 238, 240, 293, 314
  boarding schools in, 386n5
  mixed marriages in, 160
Albuquerque Boys Academy, basketball and, 291, 293, 294, 296
Albuquerque Indian School, 134, 224, 226, 245, 260, 287
  chores at, 268
  curriculum at, 232
  health issues at, 240
  life at, 234
  runaways from, 249, 251, 252, 253, 271
  school spirit at, 234
  segregation and, 267
  students of, 228 (photo), 229
Albuquerque Journal, on Magdalena Steers, 293, 294–295

Alcoholism
  Navajo and, 163–164, 313–315, 335, 397n16
  poverty and, 257
Alhambra Mine, 8
Alianza Hispano-Americano, 155
"Amazing Grace" (song), 302
Anasazi ruins, 59
Ancestry
  Anglo-Hispanic, 277, 279–280
  ethnocultural, 22
  mixed, 336
  Spanish, 154
Anglos, x, 6–11, 303
  arrival of, 8, 158
  contacts with, 199–200
  education and, 183–184, 209, 262
  empire and, 6
  growing up of, 44, 61
  Hispanics and, 151–162, 175, 208, 211–212, 216, 267, 278–279
  Navajo and, 147, 150, 162–174, 280
  play of, 65
  population of, 17
  working for, 76–77
  work of, 75, 77, 78
"Annual Round-up" (1924), 110
Anthony (Navajo child), adoption of, 168
Anti-child-labor law, 77–78
Apache, Benjamin, 22, 257
  punishment and, 243–244
Apache, Bernice, 226
Apache, Brenda, letter from, 340
Apache, Charlie, 250
Apache, Fred, marriage and, 135
Apache, José María, 16, 250
Apache, Marie, 229
Apache, Samuel, 314
Apache clan, 13, 35, 229
Apaches, 4, 165, 249
  Alamo Navajo and, 13, 27
  escapee settlement of, 11
  fear of, 27
  raids by, 1, 3, 12, 63
  stories about, 149
  subjugation of, 8
  thievery by, 6
Apachito, Antonio, 240
Apachito, Archie, 284–285 (photo), 287, 288, 289, 396n37
Apachito, Bish-Ha-Dispah, 230
Apachito, Casamira, 150
Apachito, Doreen, Alamo community and, 277–278
Apachito, Frank, 268
Apachito, Kenneth, 290
Apachito, Martiniano, 13, 16, 33
Apachito, Olson, 230
Apachito, Raymond, 290
Aragón, José Y., 30, 139–140, 175, 177
  described, 154
Aragóns (baseball team), 155
Argall, P. H., 192
Armijo, Don Feliciano, 202, 204, 206, 220
Armijo, Manuel, 183–184, 209
Armijo, Mary, 203 (photo)
Armijo, Tony, 284–285 (photo)
  basketball and, 292, 294
Aron, Stephen, x
Assimilation, 8, 152, 302
  criticism of, 230
  education and, 210
Astronomy, radio, 301
Athletics, 215, 282, 288, 303
  religion and, 304
  See also Extracurricular activities
Austin, Mary, 383n57
Austin, Tex, rodeos and, 110–111
"Ave Maria" (song), 52
Ayshia (Navajo boy), 169

Baca, Bessie, 59
Baca, Casmira, 12

416 : INDEX

Baca, Ernest, 284–285 (photo)
Baile, 123, 124, 204
Baptism, 171, 304, 306, 307, 340
   Navajo ways and, 172–173
Baptist church, 260, 312, 313
Baptist Indian Mission, 269
Baptists, 46, 47, 48, 137, 170, 171, 174,
   259, 319
Barrel racing, 319, 322, 326
Barreras, Rosa, 176, 177, 193, 198–199,
   201
Barrowdale Hall, 123
Barrowdale Opera House, 162
Bartlett Hotel, 111
Baseball, Spanish American, 155
Basketball, Navajo and, 282–285, 287,
   288, 290, 293–294
Beagle, Ben, 177
Becker-Blackwell store, 29
Becker-Mactavish store, 29, 65
Bellecourt, Clyde, 289
Benavides, Fray Alonso de, 2
Berlin, William, 331
Bernalillo County, 160, 377n47
BIA. *See* Bureau of Indian Affairs
Big Bucket clan, 35
Big Navajo, 12–13, 244, 247, 255, 281,
   331
   Alamo Navajo and, 13, 16, 249
   boarding school and, 224
Biligáana, xii, 244, 255, 279, 300, 332
Billings, Agnes, 72, 130, 131
Billings, Fred, 21, 67, 81, 156, 165
   cattle drives and, 92
   Hispanics and, 157
   horses and, 82
   pranks and, 218
   ranch environment and, 185
   school days of, 187, 218, 219
Billings, Maureen, 21
Billy the Kid, 186
"Billy the Kid" (song), 190

Bingham, Caleb, painting by, 42
"Bird in the Cage" (dance), 129
Black, Ted, 284–285 (photo), 291, 293,
   296
Blackburn, Christina, teaching by,
   273–274
Blackburn, John, depression and, 93
Black World, 334
Blanton, Jack, 132
Blessingway, 173
"Blind Man Fell Off," mesa, 35
Blue Boy, 13
Blue Dog, 24
Boarding schools
   advertisement for, 23
   Alamo Navajo and, 224, 225, 248,
      254–255, 334, 386n5
   attending, 339, 386n5
   BIA and, 226
   case studies on, 391n61
   discipline at, 391n63
   effectiveness of, 261
   health issues at, 239, 390n51
   life at, 226–227, 229–232, 248–249,
      254–256, 257, 388n26
   off-reservation, 223, 233, 261, 330
   quasi-, 260
   reservation, 223, 245, 261–262
   running away from, 249–254,
      269–272
   See also Schools
Bonner, Ray, 73, 74, 88–89, 93
Border crossings, x, 206, 274, 336
"Bordertown program," 266
Born for Water clan, 244
"Bow and Kneel to That Lady" (dance),
   129
Boy Scouts, 65
Bradford, M., 192
Branding, 66, 68, 69 (photo), 79–80,
   80–81, 82, 87, 98, 100, 220, 330
   playing at, 67

Britten, George, 320
Bronc riding, 66, 316, 318, 319, 327, 328, 329
Brothels, 38, 107, 115, 217, 370n18
   saloons and, 113–114
   visiting, 113–114, 116
Bull dogging, 325, 327
Bull riding, 316, 318, 319, 322, 324–325, 329
Bureau of Child Welfare, 355n4
Bureau of Indian Affairs (BIA), 12, 15–16, 17, 162, 223, 227, 233, 245, 268, 280, 332
   assimilation policies and, 230
   children and, 224, 266
   education policy of, 265
   Indian schools and, 224
   juvenile delinquency and, 225–226
   schools and, 330, 331
Bureau of Public Health, 355n4
Burnett, Brother, 170
Burreros (burro boys), 78
Burros, 70, 156, 157
Bushnell, Horace, on war with Mexico, 6
Bustamante, Alfredo, 52, 53, 158
Butchering, 68, 252

California Argonauts, 42
Calvert Course, 184
Calves, 92, 117, 181–182, 320, 327, 328
   branding, 80–81, 82, 98, 220
   busting, 104
   cattle and, 89
Cañoncito, 58, 174, 256
Cañoncito Navajo, 13, 249, 250
Capitalism, 6, 7
Carlisle Indian School, 223, 224, 234
Carlton, Thomas, 12
Carroll, Hugh, 247
Casa Grande (brothel), 114
Castrating, 98, 99

Catechism, 50, 184, 304
Catholicism, 7, 155, 158, 175, 237, 238
   Hispanics and, 302, 312
   impact of, 52
   instruction in, 303, 304, 305–307, 308, 309, 310, 311
   nonsectarian education and, 178
   teaching of, 52
   worldview of, 304–305
Catholics, 4, 46, 49, 170, 175, 237, 338
   Hispanic, 23
   Mexican, 46
   schisms among, 362n74
Catron, Thomas B., 355n56
Catron County, 55, 73, 355n56, 356n4, 380n28
   ranches in, 301
   schoolhouses in, 187
Cattle, 85, 86, 89, 90, 92, 99, 181–182, 185
   eye disease and, 83–84
   personalities of, 79–80
   rounding up, 220
   stampeding, 91
   stealing, 82, 127
   wild, 88
Cattle and Horse Protective Association, 375n24
Cattle drives, 90–91, 92, 100
Cattle economy, 79–82, 89, 91
   education in, 79–80
   rodeos and, 110
Cattlemen, 62, 79, 82, 86, 221
   cowboys and, 44
   Hispanic/Anglo, 152, 184
   race war and, 153
   sheepherders and, 152, 153, 374–375n24
   working for, 78
CCC. *See* Civilian Conservation Corps
CCD. *See* Confraternity of Christian Doctrine

Ceremonies, 60, 173, 317
    Navajo, 58, 314
Changing Woman, 14, 26, 36, 58, 119, 120, 238, 338
Chantways, 107
Chase, James P., 178–179
Cháves, Amado, 178
Chávez, Adelita, 41
Chávez, Adolfo, 179
Chávez, Conrad, 284–285 (photo)
Chávez, José, 16
Chávez, Miguel, 216
Chávez, Placido, deliveries by, 356n5
"Cheat and Swing" (dance), 129
Cherokees, 214
Childbirth, 119
    medically managed, 23, 356n5
    Navajo, 23, 24–25, 26
    social, 23, 356n5
Childhood
    associations, 159
    borderland history and, x–xi
    protected, 365n28
    as social/cultural construct, 347n3
    stories of, 21–22
Chisholm Trail, 99
Chores, 41, 75, 84, 243, 268, 302
    assigning, 233–234
    boys and, 94
    girls and, 94, 96, 104
Christianity, 3, 4, 6, 61, 173, 238
    Navajo and, 170, 171, 172, 174–175, 302, 312, 378n64
    paganism versus, 223
Church of Nazarene, 48
Church of St. Mary Magdalene, 49, 302
Citizenship, 206, 232, 303, 388n30
Civilian Conservation Corps (CCC), 16, 91, 133, 366n63
Civilization, 6, 42, 126, 244
    savagism and, 7, 223, 339
Claghorn, Shorty, 81

Clans, 13, 14, 229, 244
    Navajo, 34–35, 135
Clark, Ann, 259, 393n99
Classrooms, 272–276, 280
Cleaveland, Agnes Morley, ix, 9, 30, 100, 167, 171, 266, 357n15
    Alamo Navajo and, 145
    on branding, 98
    on dances, 127
    discovery of the other and, 146
    horses and, 70, 87
    on Magdalena, 11
    ranch and, 44
    Stoffel and, 170
    teaching by, 188
    toys and, 66
    translators and, 172
Cleaveland, Norman, 366n49
    guns and, 63–64
    horse riding and, 63
    Magdalena trip of, 112
    religious instruction and, 46
    work/play and, 64
Cline, Sharon, 327
Cline, Will, 327
Clothing, 96–97, 123, 147
    makeshift/poor, 227
    Navajo, 280
    school, 268, 269, 271
Cloudcroft Bears, 294–295, 296, 297
Club/class officers, by surname, 216 (table)
Club memberships, 278, 282
Coker, Lee, 84, 89, 166, 191
Collier, John, 16, 93, 245, 258, 261
Colonialism, 1, 3–4, 6, 195, 202
    internal, 303
    savagism and, 223
Comanches, 4
Coming-of-age experiences, 22, 299, 310
Commerce of the Prairies (Gregg), 7

INDEX : 419

Community, 31, 37, 39, 168, 173, 257, 312, 316, 331
  control, 332
  gatherings, 122, 257
  Hispanic, 4, 154, 160
  institutions, 44
  religious/secular, 40
  schools and, 191, 247
  tribal, 231, 238
Compadrazgo, obligations of, 36–37
Confraternity of Christian Doctrine (CCD), 304, 311
Conquistadors, 151, 162
Contact, 199–200
  points of, 146, 162, 164, 373n3
  separateness and, 174–175
Context
  culture and, 194–201
  domains and, 301–303
Contreras, Herman, 53–54
"Corazon Santo" (song), 52
Cordova, Julian, 125
Coronado, Francisco Vázquez de, 1, 2, 202
Coronado Cuarto Centennial, 202, 206, 221
  dance/queen of, 203 (photo)
Cosmic Microwave Background Radiation, 301
"Cowboy Ode" (song), 220
Cowboys, 10 (photo), 17, 38, 87, 89, 93, 104, 105, 110, 156, 174, 220, 317, 320, 327
  Anglo, 126, 221, 338
  cattlemen and, 44
  fantasy of, 67–68
  hiring, 80, 86
  Hispanics and, 155
  homesteaders and, 131
  images of, 330
  Navajo, 169
  pleasures for, 107, 113, 114
  pranks by, 132
  rodeo, 110, 316–317
Cowgirls, 320, 322, 327
"Cowman's Grievance, The" (*Socorro Chieftain*), 152
Cowman's Prayer, text of, 48
Cow pens, 10 (photo)
"Cow Thieves' Ball," 127
Coyote, 14, 36, 174
  heritage of, 332
  stories of, 57
Coyotes, 335, 375n24
  trapping, 101–102, 101 (photo), 339
Cradleboards, 26, 28, 168, 237, 356n10
  medicine bundles and, 27
  symbolism of, 332
Crawford, Betsy, 117, 133, 218
Crownpoint, 249, 250, 255, 261, 331
  boarding school at, 224, 225, 226, 244–248, 254, 258
  segregation and, 267
Cuadrilla, 123, 204
Cultural beings, 33, 61, 315, 338
Cultural borderlands, 149, 173, 311
Cultural issues, 43–44, 161, 162
Culture, 119, 121, 227, 275, 338
  building, 41–42
  consumer, 152
  context and, 194–201
  as destiny, 61–62
  dominant, 195
  Hispanic, 3, 105, 217
  honoring, 201
  language and, 152
  marriage and, 134
  mixed, 161
  Navajo, 35, 105, 135, 150, 173, 247, 332
  play and, 66–67, 303
  politics of, 177–179
  religion and, 303, 311
  teenage, 303
Cumberland Gap, 42

Curanderas, 23
Curly Hair, 13
Curriculum, 193, 221, 232–234, 245
    academic/industrial, 232
    bicultural, 332
    vocational, 233–234, 388n29
Cutting horse event, 316, 327
Cyclone Racer, 247

Daddy's Boots (Field) (sketch), 102 (fig.)
"Daddy's Boots" (Field and Kiskaddon), text of, 102
"Dance of the Saddle," 124
Dances, 122–133, 159, 160
    Alamo Navajo and, 122
    broom, 132
    children and, 124–125, 128, 129 (photo)
    described, 127–128, 131
    "gents' choice," 132
    "ladies' choice," 132
    Leap Year, 132
    Mexican, 155–156
    night, 124, 150
    ranch house, 122, 123, 130, 133, 185, 303
    school, 133, 191, 213, 220
    square, 108, 127, 128, 129–130
    squaw, 312
Dante's *Inferno*, religious instruction and, 46
Datil, 9, 23, 55, 77, 99, 131, 132, 140, 154, 158, 165, 167, 180, 188, 266, 275, 276, 300
Datil Canyon, 44, 86
Datil Mountains, 11, 70
Datil Post Office, 63
Datil ranch, 30, 159, 164
Davis, William Watts Hart, 7, 178
Day schools, 244
    Alamo Navajo, 258, 259 (photo), 260
    reservation, 223, 258–262

"Day When Dreams Come True, The" (Calamity), 18
De Dios Maes, Don Juan, 202, 204–205, 206
DeHuff, John D., 242
DeLay, Brian, x
Dempsey, Jack, 31
Denetsosie, Hoke, 259
Deutsch, Sarah, Hispanic women and, 359n34
Dewey, John, 245, 391n66
Dichos, 37, 40, 118, 125, 159, 359n33
Dickson, Mike, 331
Diné, 11, 14, 57, 58, 92, 117, 173, 174, 229, 233, 235–236, 238, 244, 247
    emergence of, 36
    journey of, 334
Diné Anaa'í, 12–13, 249
Dirty Water clan, 35
Discipline, 30, 44–45, 67, 73, 81, 84, 98, 117, 134, 176, 182, 198, 211, 248, 253, 254, 260, 276
    motivations for, 39
    punishment and, 242–244
    school policy and, 219, 391n63
Discrimination, 41, 215, 235, 275
Divide School, 181
Division of labor, Navajo, 94
Diyin Din'é, 173
Doig, Ivan, quotation of, ix
Domains, contexts and, 301–303
Domesticity, 106, 209–210, 350n18
    ideology of, 42
    women and, 43
Domestic workers, 233, 234
Don Quixote (Cervantes), 31, 181
"Don't Touch Her" (dance), 129
Dormitories, 265, 266, 289, 330
    cleaning, 268
    health issues at, 239
    life in, 231, 267–272, 279, 280, 288, 334

Douglas, Jay, 48
Douglas, Mildred, 110
Dramatic Club, performance by, 202
Drinkhouse, Elena, 161–162
Drinking, 113, 147, 313, 314–315
Dropout rates, 137, 277
Drought, 3, 18, 46, 91–93, 221, 299, 301
Duena, 203, 204

Eagle's eggs, story about, 68
Eastern Navajo Agency, 15, 93
Economic growth, 151
　English language and, 335
Economic issues, 15, 37, 41
Economic status
　education and, 183
　ethnicity and, 28–29
　Hispanics and, 209
　marriage and, 141
Education, 41, 43–44, 119, 176, 200, 221, 225
　Alamo Navajo and, 223, 231–232, 244, 261–262, 272–278, 330–337
　Anglos and, 183–184, 209, 262
　assimilation and, 210
　attaining, 182, 183
　attitudes toward, 179–184, 308
　bilingual, 179, 201
　boarding school, 257
　in cattle business, 79–80
　ethnicity and, 208, 213–214
　Hispanics and, 183–184, 194, 208, 209, 262
　history of, 219
　importance of, 177, 182, 184, 197, 217, 311
　models of, 223, 261–262
　nonsectarian, 178
　philosophy, 245
　policy/federal, 245
　progressive, 245, 392n66
　ranch house, 184–186

　religious, 303, 304, 305, 306, 308, 309, 310, 311
　segregated, 267
　sex, 116
　vocational, 91, 233
　women and, 182–183, 193
Elementary and Secondary Education Act (ESEA) (1965), 395n21
El Gringo (Davis), 7
Ellis, Florence Hawley, 352nn32–33
El Palacio, on boarding schools, 389n31
El Pupito de Diablo (play), 202
Enemy Navajo, 12–13, 249, 353n36
Enemy Way, 58, 59, 122
English language, 178, 276, 299, 335
　Alamo Navajo and, 236–237, 266
　learning, 179, 197–198, 199, 200, 201, 210, 225, 234–237, 239, 260, 261, 266, 272–273, 274, 281, 311
　speaking, 196, 237, 266, 273, 339
Enlarged Homestead Act (1909), 9
Espinosa, Aurelio Macedonio, 202
Ethnic divide, 212, 213–214, 215, 281
Ethnicity, 28–29, 32 (table), 142, 153, 159, 277
　education and, 208, 213–214
Ethnic slurs, 211, 212, 213
Ethnocultural groups, 104, 107, 174–175, 177, 319, 337, 338, 340
Ethnoracial groups, 194, 200, 376n38, 376n41
Evans, Beulah, 47
Evans, Dub, 47
Evans, Joe, 47–48, 71
Evans, Pete, 85, 87, 92
Evil Way, 58
Extracurricular activities, 215, 216 (table), 217, 255, 282
Eye disease, cattle and, 83–84

Fairs, 122–133, 150, 163, 269, 317
Fall, Albert B., 16

Families
  Anglo/makeup of, 42
  church and, 310–311
  Hispanic, 42
  matricentered, 302, 223
  Navajo, 33–45, 233
  patriarchal, 301, 223
  ranching and, 327–328
  school and, 310
  as social units, 33, 358n24
Federal Emergency Relief
    Administration (FERA), 187
Federal Maternity and Infancy Act
    (1921), 355n4
Federal Surplus Relief Corporation,
    91
Felix, Father, 287
Fence Lake, homesteading in, 361n59
Field, Bessie, 60, 99, 101 (photo), 102,
    168, 220
  Christmas and, 66
  dangerous play and, 72–73
  marriage of, 169, 174
  Moody and, 47
  on school days, 185
  on Stumph, 172
  work of, 100–101, 106
Field, Daisy, 72
Field, Ida, 15, 16, 60, 104, 168, 240
  children of, 99
Field, Katherine (Katie), 100, 101
    (photo), 103 (photo), 168, 339,
    365n36, 368n88
  marriage of, 170
  poetry of, 102, 104
Field, Nels, 15, 60, 92, 95, 102, 104, 145,
    168, 220, 224–225, 240
  on alcoholism/Navajo, 163–164
  children of, 99
  language and, 222
  Navajo and, 169–170
  on Stumph, 171

Fields' ranch, 83, 99
Fields' store, 83, 95, 164, 166, 222, 224,
    256
Fiestas, 110, 122, 124 (photo), 217, 257
  Alamo Navajo, 123, 166, 170
  Hispanic, 123–124
"First Brandings" (Schmidt), 220
First Communion, 51 (photo), 299, 304,
    306, 307, 308–309, 338
  described, 50–52
First Man, 14
First National Bank of Magdalena, 29,
    30, 357n15
First Woman, 14
Foard, Barbara, 320, 329
Folding Blue Sky, 334
Folding Darkness, 334
Folding Dawn, 334
Folk beliefs, 55–56, 351n26
Foote, Jack, story of, 44–45
Fort Craig, 12
Fort Sumner, 11, 12, 186
Fort Wingate, 58
4-H, 191, 193, 316, 318, 321, 325
Fourth of July, 127, 319
Freedom, 6, 43, 105, 133
Frontier, 11, 23, 43–44, 320, 327,
    347n2
  racial, 62
  rodeos and, 330
Frosty (rodeo clown), 324

Gabley, Brother, 312
Gallegos, Tomasita, 118–119
Gambling, 77, 112, 113, 147
Games, 127, 128
Ganadonegro, Peter, school days of,
    265, 267, 271
Gangs, Anglo/Hispanic, 157
García, Adelia, 24–25
García, Alberto, 138, 139
García, Benjamin, 24, 25

INDEX : 423

García, Candelaria, xiii, 21–22, 39–40, 98, 117, 158, 182, 397nn9–10
  brothels and, 115
  education for, 184
  on epithets, 212
  First Communion and, 51–52
  marriage and, 138
  religious instruction by, 303–311
  research by, 384n62
  school days of, 200
  superstitions and, 56–57
García, Eduardo, 182
García, Estella, 25
García, Josefita, 138, 139
García, Juan, 141
García, Juan A., Jr., 141, 153, 192
García, Lorenzo, 141, 142
García, Margarita, 24–25, 65, 98
  language and, 196
  on Mactavish, 53–54
García, Mario T., 382n44
García, Mr., 181
García, Mrs., 159, 160
García, Trinidad, celebration and, 202
Gardening, 76 (photo), 97, 137
Gatlin, Carl, 70, 71
Gender, 94–102, 104, 209, 209 (table), 230, 338
  behavior and, 349n13
  boundaries, 97, 104
  rodeos and, 319 (table), 328–329
  roles, 61, 106
  work and, 96, 99, 302
"Get Along Little Dogies" (Stinnett), 220
Giles, Alma, 32, 357–358n21
"Girl's Dance," 122
Glittering World, 244, 334
Goat tying, 319, 322, 329
God, 304–305, 310, 311, 318
  Alamo Navajo and, 312–316
  encountering, 237, 238
  Jesus and, 307–308

Golden Spur, 283
Gomez, Ed, sheepherding and, 157
Gómez-Quiñones, Juan, on Hispanics/state offices, 152
Gonzales, Jerry, 192
Gonzales, Michael, rodeo and, 321
Gorman, Al/Hal, 13
Goze, George, 193
Grade School Echo, 193
Graduation rates, 193, 277, 400n52
Graphic Mine, 8
"Grattage," described, 239–240
Grayson, Steve, 284–285 (photo)
  basketball and, 286, 294, 295
Great Depression, 18, 32, 53, 91–94, 125
Great Pueblo Rebellion (1680), 3
Green House, 114
Greens Gap School, 181, 188–189, 190, 191, 381n29
  students at, 189 (photo)
Gregg, Josiah, Santa Fe trade and, 7
Gringo *salados*, 154, 211, 212
Growing Up with the Country: Childhood on the Far Western Frontier (West), x
Guerrero, Dora, 229, 230
Guerro, Clifford, 269
Guerro, Gilbert, 222–223, 236, 258, 339
  boarding school and, 254–255, 257
  Catholic church and, 238
  childhood of, 33
  discovery of the other and, 146
  English language and, 234–235, 237
  on "grattage," 239–240
  language and, 222
  punishment and, 243–244
  on whites, 145–146
Guerro, John, 16, 353n37
Guerro, José, 256
Guerro, Juan, 148
Guerro, Manuel, 250
Guerro, Tennie, 68, 95

Guerro, Wilson, 247
Guin, April, 326, 326 (photo)
Guin, James, 326
Gutiérrez, Ramón A., 4
   on *compadrazgo*, 36–37
Gutiérriz, Alice, 287
Gutiérriz, Ernest, 291
Gutiérriz, Ramón, 284–285 (photo), 297, 396n37
   basketball and, 283, 286, 287, 288, 290, 291, 292, 293, 294, 295
   chores for, 302

Halsey, Burt, 67, 68, 81, 91
   cattle and, 88, 92
Harrison, Bradley, 321
Hawley, Jeanie, 192
Haynes, Jim, basketball and, 295
"Headin' for the Last Roundup" (Armijo), 220, 221
Health
   boarding school, 239, 390n51
   children's, 390n55
   healing and, 238–242
   Navajo, 240, 390n53
Henderson, Barty, 271
"Here I Am Lord" (song), 309
Heritage, 332
   colonial, 202
   cowboy, 318
   cultural, 201, 202, 315
   ethnic, 161–162
   frontier, 327
   racial, 7
Hero Twins, 14, 26, 36, 70, 244
Herrera, Brenda, 269
Hickle, Ralph, 90
Hierarchy
   academic, 206–210, 267
   cultural, 206, 281
   livestock, 318
   social, 4, 142, 206, 279

Higgins, Grace, 71, 97, 98, 213, 214
Higgins, Johnny, 112
Hispanics, x, xiii, 1–6, 53, 105, 109, 177, 193, 303, 339
   accommodation with, 152
   Alamo Navajo and, 146–151, 162, 279–280, 281
   Anglos and, 151–162, 175, 208, 211–212, 216, 267, 278–279
   arrival of, 8
   cowboys and, 155
   depression and, 93
   education and, 183–184, 194, 208, 209, 262
   election of, 152
   growing up of, 61
   integration of, 201
   play of, 65
   political power of, 178
   population of, 17–18, 208
   public identity for, 151
   racial status of, 177
   self-definition of, 375n26
   Spanish ancestry of, 154
   work of, 75, 77, 78
Hobson, Louisa, 43
Hobson, Mary Quinn, 42–43
Hogans, 34, 61, 135, 137, 145, 222, 229
   as woman's dominion, 94, 106
"Holy, Holy, Holy" (song), 171
Holy Catholic Church, 3–4
Holy Communion, 299, 304, 306, 307, 308–309, 338
Holy People, 57, 121, 173, 174, 238, 249, 334
"Home on the Range" (song), 220
Homestead Act (1862), 9
Homesteaders, 8–9, 10, 17, 154
   Anglo, 159, 212
   arrival of, 192
   children and, 107
   cowboys and, 131

Homesteaders, *continued*
    Magdalena visits by, 108
    Protestant, 61
Hondo Valley, 180
Hoover, Herbert, 249
Hopis, 245
Horsemanship, 70, 110, 327–328
Horses, 73, 84, 85, 88–89, 97–98, 100, 172, 179–180, 183, 185
    breaking, 81, 82, 98, 106, 219, 330
    bucking, 71, 219
    capturing, 21, 82, 86
    castration of, 99
    fears about, 87
    outlaw, 110–111
    play and, 70–71
    riding, 63, 64, 69–70, 71–72, 74, 303
    wild, 83, 301
Howard, Mr., 73, 74
Howell, Anabel, 23–24, 127, 128, 191
Hózhó, 14, 57
Hubbell, Frank, 78, 142, 375n24
Huck's Raft: A History of American Childhood (Mintz), x
Hughes, Angelo, 111
Hutchason, J. S., mines of, 8

Identity, x, 18, 37, 177, 210, 317
    assault on, 255
    bicultural, 201
    blood and, 336
    collective, 338
    construction, 195
    cultural, 142
    ethnic, 142, 161
    Hispanic, 151, 152, 208, 384n79
    maintenance, 249
    Mexican, 193
    Navajo, 242, 257
    school and, 177
    Spanish, 229

Ideology, 42, 45–46
    patriarchal, 4, 301
Ilfield, Charles, 65, 66
Illnesses, 56–57, 59, 222, 225, 238, 255, 257
Indian New Deal, 16, 93
Indian Self-Determination and Educational Assistance Act (1975), 330
Individualism, 6, 41, 44, 105, 350n18, 361n59
    self-reliant, 233, 388n31
    tribalism and, 223
Infant mortality, 23, 355–356n4
Influenza, 59, 222, 225, 238, 257
Inman, Deming, 87, 88
Institutional life, 62, 231, 255, 267–268
Interethnic relations, 212
    at schools, 214–217
Intermarriage, 319, 376n41, 377n47
Isolation, 106, 126, 133, 156, 356n4
Iverson, Peter, 288

Jaramillo, Carla, 139, 140
Jaramillo, Eduardo, 41
Jaramillo, Juan, 139–140, 170, 195, 198, 199
    on Alamo Navajo girls, 150–151
    as altar boy, 54–55, 339–340
    marriage of, 140, 141
    school and, 176
Jaramillo, Maria, 140, 141
Jaramillo, Victoria, 176, 177
Jefferson, Thomas, 6
Jesus, 1, 4, 171, 174, 304, 305–306, 309, 311, 317, 320
    God and, 307–308
Johnson Gymnasium, 293
Johnson-O'Mally program, 280, 395n21
Johnston, Langford, 70, 113, 132
    Done Gone and, 111
    on Gatlin, 71

José (Navajo man), 168–169, 242
    illness for, 240–241
Juanita Mine, 8
Julian, Barbara, 279, 284
    basketball and, 293, 294, 295, 296, 297
Julian, Mike, 396n37
Juvenile delinquency, 225–226

Kaestle, Carl, on three pillars, 350n17
Kearney, Delores, 339
Kearney, Robert, 204, 205, 206, 339
Kearney, Stephen Watts, 5, 8, 202, 204, 205, 206
Kearney Takes Las Vegas (play), 202, 204–206, 339, 384n64
Kelly, 10, 31, 49, 52, 77, 93, 156–157, 197, 201, 290, 303
    dances in, 123, 125, 155
    mining and, 8
    mixed marriages in, 161
    population of, 17, 355n59
    settlement of, ix
Kelly, Tom, beer-drinking bear and, 109
Kelly Mine, 8
Kelly Miners' Band, 123, 155
Kelly mines, 8, 217, 221, 286
Kelso, Shorty, 110
Kennedy, Robert, 282
Kinaaldá, 58, 119–120, 120 (photo), 121, 338
King, Lucella M., 246, 248
King, Martin Luther, Jr., 282
Kinship, 33, 61, 257, 338
    Navajo, 134–135, 225, 302, 358n25
Kiskaddon, Bruce, 102
Kittredge, William, 338
Klein, Kerwin Lee, on memory/history, xi
Kluckhohn, Clyde, 60, 122, 235, 356n10
Knoblock, Jennie, 192

Knoblock, Tommy Gene, 284–285 (photo)
    basketball and, 288, 294, 295

La Alianza Hispano-Americana, 31
Ladron Mountain, 249
Laguna Pueblo, 226, 236, 241, 242, 251
La Llorna, 55
Lamar, Howard, 5
Lambing crew, 78 (photo)
Landavaso, Jesus, 193
Landscapes, x, xi, 44, 49, 105
    ethnocultural, 62, 301, 339
    social, 142, 210
Language, 179, 222, 275, 338
    culture and, 152
    importance of, 184
    issue of, 273, 335
    learning, 21, 197–198, 199, 200, 201, 210, 225, 234–237, 239
La Plancha de la Marquesa (play), 202
Las Cruces, working in, 93–94
La Sierra de María Magdalena, 1
"Last Longhorn, The" (song), 190
Latasa, "Little Jimmy," 291
Lawrence, Elizabeth Atwood, 318
"Leap Year's dance," 132
Lee, Alice, 28
Lee, Jesse, 28
Lee, Susan, 27–28
Leighton, Dorothea, 122, 235, 356n10
Leyba, Josefia, 97
Light-Skinned Woman, 13
"Like a Virgin" (song), 303
Limerick, Patricia Nelson, xiii
Literary Society, 126
Little Herder (Clark), 259
"Little Joe the Wrangler" (song), 190
"Little Red Hen, The," 236
Livestock, 8–9, 318
    breeding, 117
    economy, 10–11, 93

INDEX : 427

Livestock, *continued*
  rodeos and, 329
  stealing, 130
Locke, Tom, 87, 88, 179–181
Loehr, John, 331–332
Lois, Sister, 220
Lonergan, P. T., 15
Long Walk, 11, 12
Loretto Academy, 220
Lost Band of the Navajo, 15
Lucas, Tad, bronc riding and, 329
Lucero, Maestro, 184
Lucero-White, Aurora, 202, 206, 383n57
Ludlow, O. E., 214
Luna, Solomon, burro boys and, 78
Luz, Doña, 24–25

Mactavish, Bessie Cameron, 273
Mactavish, John S., 6, 29, 53–54, 175, 273
  depression and, 93
Mactavish's store, 107
Madonna, 303
Madril, Carlotta, First Communion and, 50–51
Magdalena
  adjusting to, 211
  arrival in, ix, x
  decline of, 18
  economic status in, 28–29
  growth for, 192
  map of, xiv
  naming of, 148–149
  occupational status/ethnicity in, 32 (table)
  optimism in, 192–194
  population of, 17, 107, 355n59
  shipping through, 10–11, 100
  visiting, 108–111
Magdalena Baptist Mission, 312
Magdalena Boy Scouts, 74
Magdalena Burro Wars, 156
Magdalena Calves, 293

Magdalena *Dichos* Survey (MDS), 359n33
Magdalena High School, 201, 217–218, 282, 284–285, 337, 339, 340
  extracurricular activities at, 193
  graduation from, 193, 400n52
  gym for, 291–292
  improvement at, 215–216
  opening of, 192
Magdalena Hotel, 159, 286, 291
Magdalena Kids Rodeo, 319
Magdalena Mountain Mail, 283, 302, 335, 400n52
Magdalena Mountains, 8, 289
Magdalena News, 18, 31, 92, 110, 162, 193, 201, 217, 225, 380n23
  booster edition of, 154
  on child mortality, 23
  on dances, 123, 127–128
  on Field, 106
  on Stumph, 171
Magdalena Old-Timers Association, 321
Magdalena Old-Timers Rodeo, 319
Magdalena Presbyterian Church, 29
Magdalena School Board, 31, 331
Magdalena schools, 195, 265, 266, 272, 274, 282, 330, 331, 334–335
  academic and social realm of, 277
  academic hierarchy at, 206
  busing and, 335
  curriculum of, 193
  enrollment at, 192
  Hispanic students at, 207
  power/hierarchy in, 267
  records and, 208–209
Magdalena Steer, 194, 282
Magdalena Steers, 216, 284–285 (photo), 296 (photo)
  dream season of, 282–284, 290–298
  record of, 291 (table)
Magdalena Stock Driveway, 91
Maiz, Ruben, 30
Major, Buddy, 82, 83, 165, 339

428 : INDEX

Mangas, 9, 355n56
   population of, 17
Mangas Fiesta, 124 (photo)
Marcelina (ballad), text of, 148–149
Marriage, 4, 37, 49, 118, 122, 125,
      133–140, 257, 303, 304, 337
   age for, 134, 135, 137
   Anglo-Hispanic, 160, 161
   culture and, 134
   economic status and, 141
   mixed, 160–161, 203, 205, 376nn42–
      43, 377n47
   Navajo, 133–135
   patterns of/Hispanic, 137–138, 139–140
   preparation for, 120
   records, 160–161
   women and, 94, 372n73
Martin, Dave, 210
Martin, Fred, Jr., 69 (photo)
Martin, W. E., Montoya on, 163
Martínez, Alice, 396n37
Martínez, Herman, school days of, 197, 198
Martínez, Ray, 284–285 (photo)
   basketball and, 283, 285, 286, 287,
      288, 290, 291, 292–293, 294, 295,
      396n37
   chores for, 302
   letter to, 297
Martínez, Victoria, 126, 195
Mary, Mother of Jesus, 52, 338
Mary, Sister, 220
Mary Magdalene, 306
   on mountain, 2 (photo)
Mathers, Bobbie, 189–190, 189 (photo), 381n29
Matricentered families, 302
   patri-/nuclear-centered families versus, 223
Maxwell Land Grant, 30
May, Johnny, 295, 297
May Day celebration, 215 (photo)

Mayes, Caroline, 192
Mayo, E. A., 193
McCoy, Bob, 21
McGrath, Jim, 36
McGuffy Readers, 187
McKee, Kathryn, memories of, 68–69
McKinley, Ira, 276
McKinley, Jimmy Don, 316–317
McPhaul, Nacona, 322
McPhaul, Tawana, 320–321
Means, Russell, 289
Measurement of Intelligence, The (Terman), 194
Medicine men, 59, 68, 312
Medley, Bud, 113
Medley, H. C., 237, 241, 242
Medley, L. V., 153
Memory, 16
   history and, xi
   inaccurate, xii, 298
Menchero, Fray Miguel de, 3
Meriam Report, 233, 244
Mescalero Apaches, 11, 13, 236
Mestizos, 4, 5, 7
Methodist Church, 46, 48, 192
Mexicano, Buddy, 284–285 (photo)
Mexicano, Edmund, 284–285 (photo)
Mexicano, Rita, 96 (photo)
Mexicans, 7, 151, 154, 157, 283, 336
   assimilation of, 8
   epithets against, 211, 212, 213
Mexican War, 6, 7
Miera, Mauricio, 30, 213, 384n79
Miller, John, 275
Mining economy, 8, 10–11, 79
Mi Novio Español (play), 202
Mintz, Steven, x, 347n3, 364–365n28
Missionaries, 174, 259, 260, 302
   Baptist, 137
   beliefs of, 172–173
   Protestant, 339
   religious instruction and, 171

INDEX : 429

Mitchell, Pablo, on naming process, 377n47
Modernity, influence of, 299–300
Monkey Lady, punishment by, 268–269
Monster Slayer, 244
Monte, Clara, 270
Monte, Larry, 226, 312, 313, 314
Montgomery, Charles, 151
Montgomery Ward Catalogue, 63, 65, 108, 189, 200, 303
Montosa Camp Meeting, 302
Montoya, Diego, 65, 274–275
Montoya, Dolores, 161–162
Montoya, José, on Martin, 163
Moody, Reverend, visit by, 47
Moore, Jacqueline M., on cattlemen/cowboys, 44
Moore, Paul B., 193
Morality, 37–38, 113, 114, 116, 133
 community, 31, 39, 40
 individual, 31, 46, 115
Morgan, Thomas J., 232
Morley, Ada, 29–30, 46, 357n15
 children of, 30
 guns and, 63–64
 Native Americans and, 167
 saloons/gambling and, 112
Morley, Ray, 9, 29–30, 64, 77, 90, 167, 266, 357n15, 366n49
 cow punching for, 78
 dance by, 127
 Navajo Lodge of, 164, 166
 sheepherders and, 15, 164
 tourism and, 95
 toys and, 66
Morley, William Raymond, death of, 30
"Morning Bells Are Ringing, The" (song), 258
Mountainair High School, 283, 291, 292
Mountain View School, 181

Mt. Taylor, 233
Muncy, Chuck, rodeo and, 321
Murders, stories of, 147–148
Murrell, O. D., 284–285 (photo)
Music, 52, 171, 190, 220, 258, 302, 303, 309, 330, 332
 classical, 186
 Navajo, 261
 western, 186
"My Heroes Have Always Been Cowboys" (song), 330
My Saddle (McKinley), 276

Naming process, 228–230
National High School Rodeo Association (NHSRA), 316, 318
National Radio Astronomy Observatory, 301
Native Americans, 7, 145, 223
 day honoring, 332
 Hispanicized, 3
 life/deficiencies in, 231
 renaming, 229
Navajo, x, xii, 4, 11–17, 59, 65, 105, 245, 246, 252
 adaptation by, 248, 378n73
 Anglos and, 147, 150, 162–174, 280
 bands of, 334
 cruelties toward, 2
 discrimination against, 235
 growing up of, 61
 hiring, 169, 373n11
 Hispanics and, 146–151, 162, 279–280, 281
 natural world and, 57
 Spanish language and, 149–150
 subjugation of, 8
 sustenance/income for, 299
 thievery by, 6
 work of, 75, 365n30
 worldviews of, 57

Navajo camps, 26
Navajo children, adoption of, 167, 168
"Navajo Did Not Sabe [Know]" (*Socorro Chieftain*), 163
Navajo Indians (Ellis), 352n33
Navajo language, 35, 57, 173, 254, 298, 299
   learning, 274
   speaking, 146, 257, 273, 274, 332
Navajo Lodge, 164, 166, 357n15
Navajo Nation, 331, 334
Navajo Tribal Council, 16
Navajo ways, 289, 302, 332
   baptism and, 172–173
Navajo Witchcraft (Kluckhohn), 60
Nelson, Willie, 330
New Deal, 16, 91, 93, 105
New Mexico Cattle Growers Association, 357n15
New Mexico Constitution (1910), education and, 179
New Mexico Department of Public Welfare, 355n4
New Mexico 4-H Rodeo Rule Book, 318
New Mexico Institute for the Blind, 224
New Mexico Junior Rodeo Association, 316, 318
New Mexico Relief Administration, 91
New Mexico State Fair, field trip to, 269
New York Sun, on Mexicans, 7
NHSRA. *See* National High School Rodeo Association
No Life for a Lady (Cleaveland), ix
Nuevomexicanos, 5, 6, 151, 184, 193, 206, 208

Ocean-to-Ocean Highway, 15, 357n15
"Ocean Wave" (dance), 129
Office of Indian Affairs, 15, 16
Old Chisholm Trail, 67
"Old Faithful" (song), 220

Olney, Sam, 284–285 (photo), 298, 396n37
   basketball and, 285–286, 288, 291, 292, 293, 294, 295, 297, 298
   memories of, 289–290
Olney, Tom, 321
Oñate, Juan de, 2, 338
"One More Good Indian" (Field), 164
Oregon Trail, 42
Ortega, José, 78, 109, 197, 211
Ortega, Lorenzo, 38, 81
   cattle/eye disease and, 83–84
   on childhood, 66
   on First Communion, 50
   pranks by, 73, 74
Otero-Warren, Nina, 383n57
Outing programs, 233, 389n33
Overgrazing, 246, 299

Padgett, Sidney, 381n29
Padilla, Pauline, 274
Paganism, 171, 223
Paris Tavern, 77
Parker, Tex, 111
Parvis, Dr., 164
Patriarchal ideology, 4, 301
Patri-/nuclear-centered families, matricentered families versus, 223
Patter, Grandma, 24
Patterson, Florence, on student health, 239
Patterson, Guadalupe, 376n43
Pentecostalism, 313, 314, 315, 397n13
Peppers, Dr., 60
Peralta, Esther, 31, 125, 137–138, 181, 199, 215, 221
   on grandfather/confession, 53
   play of, 65
   on store, 93
Perry, Reuben, 224, 226
Pie suppers, 132, 191

INDEX : 431

Pie Town, 32, 62, 68, 73, 93, 129, 131, 355n56, 380n23
   children in, 33
   described, 9
   homesteading in, 357–358n21
   religious influences in, 48
   settlement of, 10
   social life in, 126–127
   work in, 78–79
Pie Town Farm Bureau, 126
Pie Town School, 191
Pino, David, 284–285 (photo)
Pino, Herbert, 274
Pino, Lucy, 51 (photo), 199, 216, 217
   adobe bricks and, 97
   on laundry, 96
Piros, 2, 3
"Place Called Alamo, A" (Sparks), lyrics of, 332
Plains School, 191
Play, 105, 190
   animals and, 69, 70–71
   characteristics of, 70–71, 72–74
   culture and, 66–67, 303
   dangerous sources of, 72–73
   Hispanic, 68
   ranching and, 66–67
   work and, 64, 65, 66, 69, 74–75, 104–106, 327
Plummer, Abe, 331
Points of contact, 146, 162, 164, 373n3
Poisonings, stories of, 147–148
Polkas, 127, 128, 338
Poverty, 23, 33, 40, 104, 257, 356n4
Powell, Bernadyne, 67, 97, 108, 111, 158
Power relations, 18, 62, 339
Pranks, 66, 73–74, 131, 190–191, 197, 218
Pratt, Richard Henry, 233
Prejudice, 335, 336
   Anglo, 158–159, 194
   Spanish, 158–159, 384n79

Presbyterians, 46, 175, 192, 237, 273
Prescott, Cynthia Culver, 372n73
Preservation, enclaves of, 201–202, 204–206
Prostitutes, respect for, 114–115
Protestantism, 6, 7, 46, 47, 48, 49, 61, 155, 170, 175, 237, 302, 338, 339
   Alamo Navajo and, 213, 312, 315
   work ethic, 44
Puberty, 116–122, 338
Pueblos, 2, 3, 236, 268, 348n5
Puertocito, 11, 76, 148, 352n31
Punishment, 219, 256, 260, 276
   bitterness for, 242–243
   corporal, 242–243
   discipline and, 242–244
   for runaways, 252–253, 269
Putney Mesa, 83

Quemado, 9, 53, 355n56
Quinn, William, 12

Race, 3, 5, 194, 213–214, 282
Radio astronomy, 301
Railroad, arrival of, 10, 151, 192
Railston, Cole, 85
Ramah, 58, 59, 174
Ranchers, 81
   Anglo, 147, 184
   drinking/gambling and, 113
   education and, 184
   Hispanic, 123, 147, 150, 184
   land acquisition by, 351n26
   Magdalena visits by, 108, 109
   religion and, 47
Ranching, 301
   Anglos and, 221
   children and, 89, 107, 302
   families and, 327–328
   play and, 66–67
   rodeos and, 318
Ranchos, 123, 204, 221

Religion, 3, 50–52, 57, 237–238, 260, 302, 303–311
   culture and, 303, 311
   functions of, 45, 49
   instruction in, 46–47, 171–172, 273–274
   Navajo and, 26, 173–174, 238, 312–316
   ranchers and, 47
   social distance and, 175
   sports and, 304
Republicanism, 6, 7
Reséndez, Andrés, 5
Reynolds, Loraine Morley, 30, 167, 266, 357n15, 394n4
Rigg, Edwin, 12
Rincon, Helen, 312, 313, 315
Rio Arriba County, Hispanics and, 178
Rio Grande, ix, 1, 2, 3, 11, 12, 147, 180, 249, 250
Rio Salado, 11, 12, 14, 21, 68, 70, 81, 105, 170
Rites of passage, 116–122, 141, 155, 304
Rituals, 53, 57, 122
   Navajo, 58, 59, 312
   public performance of, 316
   religious, 50, 237
   social, 217
"Rock-Chewer," 13, 249
Rock Point, 330–331
Rodeos, 107, 232, 285, 288, 323 (photo), 326 (photo), 399n40
   attending, 111
   children and, 303, 316–322, 324–330
   contestants at/by gender/ethnocultural status, 319 (table)
   cultural outlook and, 328
   Fourth of July, 319
   frontier myth and, 330
   gender and, 328–329
   history of, 110
   injuries from, 324–325
   narrative of, 318
   performers, 318, 325, 327, 328
   prayer for, 317, 320
   ranching and, 318
   stand-alone, 319
   values/traits and, 327
   women and, 369n7
Roessel, Monty, 288
Romero, J. Frank, 193
Roosevelt County, 293
Roosevelt Elementary school, May Day celebration at, 215 (photo)
Roping, 66, 70–71, 99, 110, 318, 320, 328, 330
   calf, 98, 319, 322, 329
   playing at, 67
   sheep, 167
   team, 316, 319, 399n40
Rough Rock Demonstration School, 330, 332, 334
Round Dance, 123
Rudman, Alice, 300
Run-Around Shoe, 13
Runaways, 249–250, 256, 261, 270–272
   punishment for, 252–253, 269
   successful, 251–252
Running Horse, Gilbert, 229
Russell, Jack, 89, 90, 187, 191
Ryan, Dorothy, 258, 259 (photo)
Ryan, W. Carson, appointment of, 244–245

Sally's Pine School, 181
Saloons, 109–110, 112, 155, 217
   brothels and, 113–114
Salt clan, 35
San Augustine Plains, 9, 11, 75, 90, 97, 131, 180, 300, 301
   horses on, 70, 81
Sánchez, Ernest, 214
Sánchez, George I., 194, 210
Sánchez, José María, 191
Sánchez school, 191, 192

San Mateo Mountains, 289
San Miguel Band, 141
Santa Ana County, Hispanics and, 178
Santa Fe, 7, 53, 110, 151, 169, 221, 226, 230, 236, 239, 241
Santa Fe Indian School, 169, 224, 226, 229, 230, 245, 260
   chores at, 268
   curriculum at, 232
   discipline at, 243
   health issues at, 239, 240
   life at, 234, 241
   runaways from, 249, 250, 271
   segregation and, 267
Santa Fe Railroad, 10, 151
Santa Fe Trail, 5, 42
Santa Rita, 17, 52, 156
Saulsbury, Ty, 316–317
Savagism, 148, 149, 162, 227
   civilization and, 7, 223, 339
Save the Children, 269
Sawyer, Fern, bull riding and, 329
Schmidt, Edith, retrospective by, 220
School and Society (Dewey), 245
School attendance, 192, 224
   Anglo/Hispanic compared/by gender, 209 (table)
Schooling. *See* Education
Schools
   Alamo Navajo and, 330–337
   community connections with, 191, 247, 399n46
   establishing, 181, 331
   ethnocultural groups and, 177
   growth of, 178
   influence of, 177
   interethnic relations at, 214–217
   Native American, 168
   off-reservation, 236, 238, 244, 388n29
   one-room, 187–192
   primary, 179
   public, 177, 178
   reservation, 236
   rural, 193, 380n28
   as social/academic settings, 210
   See also Boarding schools
Schroeder, Albert, 11–12
Sears and Roebuck Catalogue, 108
Secatero, Alta, 136 (photo), 229
Secatero, Margaret, on sing, 58–59
Secatero, Norman, 251–252, 256, 300
Sedillo, C. B., 30
Segregation, 134, 267
Self-esteem, 89, 247, 327
Self-reliance, 44, 45, 64, 105
Separateness, contact and, 174–175
Sex education, girls and, 116
Sexual conduct, 4, 116, 117, 118
Sexual mores, 132, 303
Sheepherders, 17, 93, 107, 148, 183, 211
   brothels and, 114
   burro boys and, 78
   cattlemen and, 152, 153, 374–375n24
   drinking/gambling and, 113
   encountering, 147
   Navajo, 15, 162
Sheepherding, 34, 78, 95, 137, 150, 157, 172, 183, 222, 232, 242, 249, 257, 260, 261, 299
   children and, 75, 76, 146–147, 365n29
   girls and, 104, 106
Sheppard-Towner Act, 355n4
Shetland pony, story about, 73–74
Silver Bell bar, 30, 159
Simmons, Marc, 152, 372n70
Sings, 26, 58–59, 312
Skinny Lady, 13
Skinwalkers, 60, 315
Smith, A. T., 217
Smith, Burton I., 249
Smith, Joy, 127–128
Smith, Ray, 274, 276, 280

"Smith, Walkin'," 185, 186, 186 (photo)
Social boundaries, 155, 215, 279
Social change, rodeos and, 328
Social Darwinism, 105
Social development, 213, 245
Social distance, 159, 175
Social gatherings, 47, 120, 122, 175
   interethnic, 155–156
Social life, 107–116, 172
   children and, 126–127
Social outlook, 105, 328
Social relations, 14, 18, 31–32, 214
   Anglo, 158, 266–267
   Hispanic, 158, 266–267
   mixed couplings and, 160
Social status, 3, 4, 5
   Alamo Navajo, 277
   ethnocultural/by surname, 278 (table)
   women's, 37–38
Socorro, ix, 2, 3, 8, 10, 12, 85, 94, 141, 149, 160, 170, 182, 220
   tent meeting at, 315
   tournament, 293
Socorro Chieftain, 95, 141, 142, 152–153, 163–164, 380n23
Socorro County, 9, 30, 55, 355n56, 356n4
   census of, 192
   childbirth in, 23
   education in, 182
   Hispanics and, 178
   marriage records for, 376n43
   population of, 17, 152
   ranches in, 301
   schoolhouses in, 187
Socorro County Board of Education, 179, 193
Socorro County Fair, 163, 317
Socorro County rodeo, 324
Socorro Health Department, 22
Socorro Sun, 153
Sore eyes. *See* Trachoma
Southern Pueblo Agency, 15

Spaniards, 1, 3
   colonization by, 348n3
   legacy of, 6
   Pueblo and, 348n5
   revenge of, 7
Spanish Club, 202
Spanish language, 178, 200, 298, 299
   learning, 179, 197, 198, 201, 217
   Navajo and, 149–150
   speaking, 195, 196, 201, 211, 217, 272, 273
Sparks, Daniel, song by, 332
Spears, Billy, basketball and, 295
Spears, Birdie, 74
Spears, Guy, 74, 81
Spears, Richard, 292
Spelling bees, 217, 219
Spirituality, 305, 307, 309, 310
   Navajo, 57, 58, 362–363n94
Springer High School, game against, 295–296
Square dances, 108, 127, 128
   patter of, 129–130, 131
   titles of, 129
Squaw Dance, 59
Standing House clan, 35
Stapleton, Amelia, 142
Steer riding, 319, 321
Stereotypes, 162–163, 279, 280
Stevens, Montague, 154, 351n26, 375n24
Stillbirths, Navajo, 25–26
Stinnett, Superintendent, 220
St. James of Spain, 1
St. Mary Magdalene, 1, 148, 195, 267, 286, 299
Stock Raising Homestead Act (1916), 9
Stock reduction, 246, 393n99
Stoddard, Jane, 210
Stoffel, Father, 54–55, 65, 170, 172
Stokes, Eunice, 132
Strickland, Hugh, 110
Strickland, Mabel, 110, 329

INDEX : 435

Stroud, Leonard, 110
St. Thomas, 311
Students
    Anglo, 189 (photo), 211, 216, 217, 220, 280
    health of, 239
    Hispanic, 207, 211, 215, 216, 217, 220, 280
    Navajo, 228 (photo), 229, 232–233, 234, 236, 243, 253, 254–255, 275, 277, 278, 279, 280, 281, 288, 335
Stumph, C. W., 170, 171, 172, 174
Sun, Hero Twins and, 14
Supernatural, children and, 45–62
Superstitions, 52, 55, 56–57, 322
Sweetwater County, 133
Sydney (Australia) *Morning Herald*, 296

Tabbot, Sam, 292
Taboos, 14, 26, 36, 57, 121, 135, 158, 363n95
Tafoya, Dave, 284–285 (photo), 294
Tafoya, Vicente, 199, 212–213, 339
Taggert, Alvira, 186
Taggert, Cecil, 108, 113, 155, 158, 186
    honor/respect and, 156
    horses and, 85
    on Smith, 185
"Take a Little Peck" (dance), 129
Taos County, Hispanics and, 178
Teacherage, described, 188–189
Teachers, 213, 214, 234, 247–248, 305, 310, 311
    Anglo, 332
    challenges for, 187–190
    discipline problems and, 190
    housing for, 188–189
    Native American, 332
    Navajo-speaking, 332
    pranks and, 218
    ranch environment and, 185
Teaching, 238, 273–274, 274–275

Terman, Lewis, 194
Thin Man, 13
Thomas, Ann, 142
Tipton, Helen, teaching by, 189
Tireman, Loyd, 383n57
Toledo, Herman, language and, 196, 197
Tonsillectomies/tonsillitis, 240, 255
Torres, A. C., 207, 208
Torres, Adolfo, 31
Toys, 65, 66, 303
Trachoma, 239, 255
Trading post, day school, 260–261
Trapping, 101–102, 101 (photo)
Tribalism, individualism and, 223
Trujillo, Herman, 184
Tuberculosis, 238
Tularosa Wildcats, 297
Turner, Frederick Jackson, x
Two Come after the Water clan, 35

UFOs, 301, 396, 396n2
Underhill, Ruth, 246, 247
United Pueblo Agency, 17, 93, 226
University of New Mexico, 259, 283, 331
US Army, 168
US Fish and Wildlife Service, 289, 290

Valentine's Day, dances on, 127
V+T ranch, 85

Vaqueros, 221
    rodeos and, 110
    Spanish-Mexican, 338
Vargas, Diego de, 3
Very Large Array (VLA), 301
Vicente, 13, 229, 257
Victorio, 165
Virginity, 37–38, 118, 126
Virgin Mary, 4, 306
Vogt, Evon Z., 361n59

Walt, Henry, 358n29

Warren, Johnny, 72
Washington, George, 188, 338
Watson, Mother, 114–115, 116
Weaving, 70, 137, 257, 258
   income from, 95
   Navajo, 104, 106, 367n73, 368n76, 389n31
Weber, David, 5
Wedding, special, 141–142
West, Elliot, x, 104, 361n59
West Bar, 159, 287
West Hotel, 114
"What a Friend We Have in Jesus" (song), 171
Wheeler, Jerry, saloon of, 112
Whippings, 30, 39, 44–45, 67, 73, 81, 84, 98, 117, 134, 176, 182, 198, 211, 219, 242, 243, 248, 253, 254, 260, 276, 310
White, Richard, xi
White Sands, 300
Wild West shows, 45, 110
Wilson, George, 170
Witches, 55–56, 57, 60, 61, 273
Womanhood, 117–118
   transition to, 119, 120, 121
Woman's Temperance Union, Morley and, 112
Women
   domesticity and, 43, 350n18
   education and, 193
   frontier, 43–44
   rodeo and, 369n7
   work and, 96
Women's rights, 167
Woodward, D. K., 290
Word of God church, 300, 312
Work
   children and, 75–91, 94, 366n49
   gender and, 96, 99, 302
   play and, 64, 65, 66, 69, 74–75, 104–106, 327
   work ethic, Navajo, 75
Works Progress Administration (WPA), 91, 187, 291–292
Wright, Ed, Done Gone and, 111

Yellow Man, 13

Zah, Peterson, 334
Zeller, Barbara, 396n37
Zunis, 13